MW00353267

Stravinsky and Balanchine

Stravinsky &
Balanchine

A JOURNEY OF INVENTION

Charles M. Joseph

YALE UNIVERSITY PRESS   NEW HAVEN AND LONDON

Copyright © 2002 by Yale University. All rights reserved. This book may not be reproduced, in whole or in part, including illustrations, in any form (beyond that copying permitted by Sections 107 and 108 of the U.S. Copyright Law and except by reviewers for the public press), without written permission from the publishers.

Set in Adobe Garamond and Stone Sans types by
The Composing Room of Michigan, Inc.

Printed in the United States of America by Edwards Brothers.

Library of Congress Cataloging-in-Publication Data
Joseph, Charles M.
    Stravinsky and Balanchine : a journey of invention / Charles M. Joseph.
        p.   cm.
Includes bibliographical references (p.   ) and index.
    ISBN 0-300-08712-8 (alk. paper)
    1. Stravinsky, Igor, 1882–1971. Ballets.   2. Balanchine, George.
3. Ballet.   4. Choreography.   I. Title.
ML410.S932 J665   2002
781.5′56′092—dc21

                                                2001007130

A catalogue record for this book is available from the British Library.

The paper in this book meets the guidelines for permanence and durability of the Committee on Production Guidelines for Book Longevity of the Council on Library Resources.

10 9 8 7 6 5 4 3

For Jennifer and Amy

Contents

Preface

My youthful introduction to the music of Igor Stravinsky came by way of *The Firebird.* The music's memorable melodies and colorful orchestration shimmered. Curiosity quickly led me to *Petrushka,* with its seemingly aberrant rhythms and even more bizarre harmonies. Finally, a friend (with a knowing smirk on his face) suggested that I listen to *The Rite of Spring.* Initially it seemed a blur, an unbridled, alluring jumble of dissonance gone over the edge; consequently, it immediately fascinated me. Each score drew me in more deeply, although my reaction was entirely visceral. Although I couldn't yet articulate what I was experiencing musically, let alone intellectually, I knew that I was hopelessly hooked. As for all three pieces being ballets . . . I hardly gave that a moment's thought. I'd never seen any of them staged and knew next to nothing about dance. Besides, Stravinsky's music seemed to speak forcefully enough on its own merits, so why muddy the waters with some supplemental—and surely extraneous—visual embellishment?

Eventually, of course, I did see all three landmark ballets danced. Although I wasn't quite sure what to expect, I remember that as thrilling as these productions were, they left me a little disconcerted. The combined choreography and music struck me as a "mismatch," to use T. S. Eliot's description of *The Rite*'s 1921 revival. As a musician, I didn't sense a musical-choreographic parity, let alone the artistic synthesis I had expected. I realize now that my view was both narrow and uninformed. For one thing, it was historically decontextualized. In the world of 1910–13, when all three ballets premiered, it was neither necessary nor even particularly desirable to think primarily in terms of synthesis; nor was the concept of a genuine, coherent artistic synthesis universally defined. Most relevant, dance and music were not always considered equal partners. Later, in the hands of Stravinsky and George Balanchine, they became so.

As a ballet composer who understood the language of dance better than any other musician of the twentieth century, Stravinsky needed to find an artist—a very sympathetic artist—capable of complementing his own clearly envisaged ideas. Visualizing music in terms of correlative physical movement that would, above all else, serve the composer's score was the crucial issue. And although this was hardly the only way to conceive choreography, for Stravinsky it was an unconditional, nonnegotiable assumption. Balanchine, given his own background and beliefs, perhaps more than any choreographer before or since had no qualms in accepting this sine qua non. This mutual understanding formed the crux of their partnership.

Some have argued that Balanchine's submissive acceptance amounted to acquiescence. But in fact, the Stravinsky-Balanchine partnership was much more elastic, much more contrapuntal than might first appear. As a choreographer, Balanchine was primarily in the business of relating the movement of human bodies to one another. He was interested in the inherently fundamental tensions of theater and drama. He wanted to explore all types of counterpoints: male and female, spatial, rhythmic, and most broadly, aural-visual symmetries. Similarly, Stravinsky looked upon the art of composition as nothing more than relating one note to the next, although typically, his tersely phrased pronouncement, calculated to come across as provocative, belies a deeper complexity. How the sequence of those notes would be ordered—harmonically, linearly, texturally, structurally, rhythmically—this is what constituted the compositional interplay of musical elements. It was all a matter of selecting the one right relation, the right order, and most important, the right balance. Balance was everything.

Simply put, no one balanced Stravinsky better than Balanchine. From the start, he was the ideal partner—"the perfect collaborator," as Stravinsky referred to him. The ballets they forged together stand as one of the most extraordinary collaborative triumphs of the twentieth century.

But why Balanchine and Stravinsky? What was it about the choreographer that enabled him to illuminate the composer's music so vibrantly and, by Stravinsky's own admission, so instructively? Just as I can recall first hearing *The Firebird*, so I can remember my first viewing of *Apollo*, which left an even more indelible impression. And just as I could not at first verbalize why the music of *Petrushka* had so mesmerized me, neither could I initially explain why Balanchine's choreography for an already dynamic score like *Agon* widened my understanding all the more.

Intuitively I understood that Balanchine's sense of movement counterbalanced the music in a way that was neither superficially nor superfluously imitative. His control of motion visually concretized musical relations otherwise likely to have been missed. His choreography didn't offer banal derivatives or garnish the music by adding another layer, nor did he allow the music to function as a subsidiary platform for the dance. In my viewing of *Apollo* and all the subsequent Stravinsky-Balanchine ballets, it seemed to me that the musically astute choreographer possessed the uncanny gift of clarifying what my ears heard through what my eyes saw. Musicians may argue that I am giving Balanchine too much credit. They might contend (even as Stravinsky himself sometimes did) that the composer's music did just fine on its own. Even Balanchine quipped that if you didn't like the dancing, you could close your eyes and listen to the music, since it was more important anyway. On the other hand, dancers may feel I've unfairly minimized the choreography's importance. After all, who's onstage and who's in the pit? For myself, I must confess that as compelling as the music is, I now actually need the choreography for *Apollo* and *Agon*. Physical movement and sound complete each other in a fulfilling equilibrium, an artistic sum that in this case is more expressive than its two separate parts.

Violette Verdy, one of Balanchine's most musical ballerinas, remembers that the choreographer thought of dance as music's younger sister. By his own insistence, when it came to Stravinsky's music Balanchine's only goal was to illumine the score, not to decorate—and certainly not to subsume—it. How he managed to attain that goal is what magnetized me when I first saw *Apollo, Orpheus, Movements,* and *Stravinsky Violin Concerto.* I wanted to know how he went about making his choreographic decisions: how he determined that a particular gesture or combination was appropriate at exactly that moment. I admired his willingness—his audacity, even—in allowing the dance to recede occasionally and unobtrusively into an auxiliary role when the music warranted time and room to breathe freely without visual competition. These were the achievements of an integrally linked musical-choreographic dialogue. These were the fruits of balance.

In compiling this study, I have attempted to strike another kind of balance. Ballet is by nature interdisciplinary. In hoping to create a broad enough context to enfold both dancers and musicians, I must at times beg the reader's indulgence. Often I rehearse what one discipline or the other will take as familiar or assumed facts. Moreover, although my bias as a musician has no doubt already surfaced, I have endeavored to approach the Stravinsky-Balanchine collaborations from several perspectives. Sometimes I lean toward historical reconstruction, especially when certain archival documents help clarify issues or offer alternative interpretations. Elsewhere I have stepped gently into several disciplines beyond music and dance, particularly poetry, literature, semiotics, philosophy, psychology, mythology, and frequently architecture. I do so only because both the composer and choreographer did so. Sometimes their allusions were metaphoric, but frequently they heavily and directly relied upon the fundamental cross-disciplinary precepts of these related fields.

The book's organization is straightforward. In my introductory chapter I range widely over the foundational similarities and differences that connected Stravinsky and Balanchine. There I introduce several recurring thematic motives that will prove increasingly overarching as one witnesses the maturation of the two men's partnership. I next take up Serge Diaghilev's pivotal role in bringing the composer and choreographer together. Thereafter, the chapters proceed chronologically, covering Stravinsky and Balanchine's jointly conceived ballets, events that influenced the direction of their work both as independent artists and as collaborators, and finally, works that Balanchine choreographed during the twelve years following Stravinsky's death. Where I focus on a major work like *Apollo, Agon,* or *Stravinsky Violin Concerto,* I have divided the study into discrete discussions underlying the historical framework of the ballet, musical-choreographic analyses, sketch studies, and interdisciplinary influences and connections.

Such a diversity of explorations raises several red flags: How familiar must the musician be with ballet's vocabulary to grasp what Balanchine was doing? Perhaps even more problematic, mustn't the dancer be able to deal with music notation if any substantive analytic discussion is to be included? This looms particularly relevant since Balanchine often carefully dissected Stravinsky's scores, regularly using such analyses in informing his choreographic judgments. To understand Balanchine's Stravinsky ballets fully, we must understand the music fully: there is simply no way around it. There is also the considerable obstacle of discussing physical movement with only words and a few photographs—a difficult but remediless task. Mindful of these considerations, I have had to make certain decisions, only a few of which, I hope, will appear exclusionary. For the most part, I have avoided the standard French terms for classical dance positions and combinations. Likewise I have tried to dodge the musician's technical jargon as much as possible. Still, there are a few selective musical examples where I finally determined that skirting an expository discussion of certain passages would prove more confusing than confronting them directly. When I felt that some of my analytic meandering might have turned a tad too abstruse, I banished it to a note.

In dealing with the discussion of music, it would be handy to have a piano, the score, and audio recordings available, but this is by no means necessary for the general reader. A video player, however, would be useful. Especially in discussing three particular ballets, *Apollo, Agon,* and *Stravinsky Violin Concerto,* I devote a fair amount of time to analyzing pertinent passages in musical and choreographic detail. I have chosen these three ballets because they are cornerstone works in the repertory, and as such they are the ones the public is most likely to see performed regularly. They are programmed almost annually, for example, in New York and Saratoga Springs. Moreover, these three are the most accessible works, given their ready availability on commercially released videotapes (although I should quickly add that numerous film clips from all the ballets are available for those with the desire and energy to visit such repositories as the Jerome Robbins Dance Division of the New York Public Library for the Performing Arts).

Achieving musical unity is in itself difficult enough. But when one intermingles the mysterious act of composing with that of choreographing—perhaps an even more elusive creative process—the waters become murkier. Collaborations of any kind constitute a precariously fragile business. In the end, a successful artistic partnership may be as much alchemy as carefully planned strategy. But whatever the mix, certain questions surface. Are the collaborators conversant with the interdisciplinary considerations involved? Does each understand the fundamental grammar of the other's discipline? Do they share common goals in working toward a homogeneously articulated artistic message? Is there flexibility, a sense of compromise, a dialogue of opinion? And finally, is the process built upon the grounds of a far-reaching, mutual sense of purpose and balance? Stravinsky and Balanchine may not have seen eye to eye on every measure of music or every choreographic gesture, but their many collaborations mark a shared and joyous journey of invention. Retracing that journey has absorbed me in collecting the thoughts that follow.

Acknowledgments

A book that crosses disciplinary lines presents an unusually broad range of issues and problems with which to deal. In addressing some of these, I have called upon the help of many wonderful friends and colleagues from the worlds of both dance and music. In every case their support, patience, and cooperation have been nothing short of magnanimous.

Several institutes, grant agencies, and repositories have greatly advanced my research. The Paul Sacher Stiftung of Basel, Switzerland, generously provided a fellowship in 1991–92, allowing my study of Stravinsky's archival materials throughout that academic year. A special word of thanks to the Stiftung's Ingrid Westen and Ulrich Mosch, both of whom know the Stravinsky collection inside out, thereby facilitating my work and saving me precious research time. During the 1999–2000 academic year, I was also fortunate enough to be appointed the Howard D. Rothschild Visiting Fellow in Dance at Harvard University—an award made possible under the aegis of the Houghton Library. As a consequence I was able to work through the many treasures of the George Balanchine Archive in the Harvard Theatre Collection. My thanks to the Theatre Collection's curator, Fredric W. Wilson, and to its research and reference librarian, Annette Fern, for their unwavering support during my residency in Cambridge. In between these bookend fellowships, travel grants from both the National Endowment for the Humanities and Skidmore College also sustained my work throughout the eight years of research leading to this study. I wish also to express my thanks to the William R. Kenan Jr. Charitable Trust for appointing me to an endowed chair at Skidmore, providing me with the additional funding and time required to complete this project.

Filmmaker Tony Palmer graciously met with me in Zurich to discuss his Stravinsky documentary, several segments of which are referenced throughout this book. Film composer David Raksin also spoke with me several times regarding his relationship with Stravinsky, and in particular about his contribution to one Stravinsky and Balanchine ballet detailed in Chapter 7. Translations for passages from several documents originally in French and Russian were kindly provided by Lynne Gelber, Dorothy Manning, and Elizabeth C. Sander. Michael Arnush of Skidmore's Classics Department and Terrence Diggory of the Department of English also contributed to my work on the ballet *Agon.* Another of my close colleagues at Skidmore, Isabel Brown, with whom I have had the pleasure of team-teaching a Stravinsky and Balanchine course for more than a decade, served as both my own personal ballet teacher and good friend while the book took shape. I would also like to thank Andrew Lefkowitz of Skidmore for his preparation of the music examples. David Porter, president of Skidmore while this book evolved, was particularly supportive of my work with his always encouraging remarks. Several of my music colleagues outside Saratoga have also offered advice, guidance, and permitted me to rely upon their work. These include Maureen Carr, Joan Evans, Richard Parks, Mark Richardson, and Lynne Rogers.

The dancers and dance historians who unhesitatingly spoke with me in person, over the telephone, and through correspondence to offer so many useful suggestions to the text are numerous. Listing their names is small tribute indeed. Thanks to Todd Bolender, Lynn Garafola, the late Tanaquil Le Clercq, Kay Mazzo, the late Jerome Robbins, Robert Tracy, Karin von Aroldingen, Violette Verdy, and Vera Zorina. Barbara Horgan, Stephanie Jordan, and Nancy Reynolds read the first draft of what you now see, offering corrections and other invaluable revisions.

In addition to the Sacher Stiftung and the Harvard Theatre Collection, I also had the privilege of working frequently in the Jerome Robbins Dance Division of the New York Public Library for the Performing Arts, where its curator Madeline Nichols was of great assistance. During the early stages of my bibliographic work at the Jerome Robbins Dance Division, Kara Gardner worked with me under the sponsorship of a Skidmore collaborative research grant. Research for portions of one of the *Apollo* chapters was conducted at the Library of Congress, where Gillian Anderson and Wayne Shirley were most helpful. A word of thanks to Linda Golding, president of Boosey and Hawkes, for permission to reprint passages from several of Stravinsky's scores. And I especially wish to recognize the cooperation of Paul Epstein, president of the George Balanchine Foundation; Leslie Hansen Kopp, general administrator; and once again both Barbara Horgan, general director, trustee, and chairman of the George Balanchine Trust, and Nancy Reynolds, research director for the Balanchine Foundation.

Yale University Press has stood by my work over many years, and I owe a tremendous debt of gratitude to my editor Harry Haskell, who saw the manuscript through to completion. I cannot think of a more helpful, well-informed person with whom I might have collaborated. Susan Laity, with whom I have had the pleasure of working before on another dance project, provided the kind of guidance and wisdom one always hopes for in a manuscript editor. Her contribution to this book deserves special recognition.

Finally, a word of appreciation to my wife, Lucy, and daughters, Amy and Jennifer, who have endured this project over the better part of a decade. My daughter Jennifer, especially, had a greater hand in this study than she may have known. Her love of ballet, and the discipline she gained from its study over most of her young life, proved a guiding light as my interest in the Stravinsky-Balanchine partnership evolved.

Stravinsky and Balanchine

Chapter 1 Commonalities and Contrasts: A Meeting of Minds

Choreography, as I conceive it, must realize its own form, one independent of the musical form though measured to the musical unit. Its construction will be based on whatever correspondence the choreographer may invent, but it must not seek to duplicate the line and beat of the music. I do not see how one can be a choreographer unless, like Balanchine, one is a musician first.

—*Igor Stravinsky*

When I choreograph Stravinsky's music, I am very careful not to hide the music. You see, usually choreography interferes with the music too much. When too much goes on on stage, you don't hear the music. Somehow the messy stuff obscures the music. I always do the reverse. I sort of subdue my dances. They're always less than the music. As in modern architecture, you rather should do less than more.

—*George Balanchine*

In reviewing the 1972 Stravinsky Festival of the New York City Ballet, Andrew Porter wrote in the *New Yorker* that ballets like *Stravinsky Violin Concerto, Orpheus,* and *Agon* seemed "almost to flow from a single mind; an entity called Stravinsky-Balanchine." No conjoining of two artists' names was ever more appropriate. Beginning with their initial meeting in 1926, a binding covenant quickly developed, a union that would connect them personally and professionally for the rest of their lives. In Balanchine's eyes, Stravinsky was a colossus, the "Orpheus of the twentieth century." Along with Mozart and Tchaikovsky, no composer inspired him more. Even as a young ballet student at the Imperial Theater School in Petersburg, Georgi Balanchivadze was immediately drawn to Stravinsky's vibrant music. By the time of his death in 1983, he had choreographed many of the composer's most important works. The powerful pulse of Stravinsky's music flowed relentlessly forward, begging to be placed into physical motion, to be visualized, to be danced. Even through those electrically charged Stravinskyan moments of silence that so powerfully jolt the music's continuity, "life goes on," Balanchine remarked. No matter what the piece, the genre, the instrumentation, the choreographer declared that "every measure Eagerfeodorovitch ever wrote is good for dancing."[1]

What was it about Balanchine and Stravinsky that jibed? In the eyes of both artists, music and dance were simple, elegant expressions of the manipulation of time and space. And as drearily antiseptic as such an unemotional depiction may at first appear, theirs was a passionately shared conviction in the timeless order of beauty. For both men, the ancient Pythagorean notion of beauty as "the reduction of many to one" provided a beacon. Moreover, order furnished a sanctuary, a controlled environment within which reason prevailed. Stravinsky found that the process of ordering musical elements was perfectly natural for him—a periodic and habitual practice in which he happily engaged. Nor was Balanchine about to "sit and wait for the Muse." Both men were makers, craftsmen—manual laborers, as they thought of themselves—who needed to put things together. The act of assembling a composition or ballet ("God creates, I assemble," to invoke a famous Balanchinian aphorism) was exhilarating, and certainly more gratifying than the final product. Or, to put it the other way around, the work that resulted was closer to a byproduct, a residue of the process itself. "I care less about my works than about composing," the composer declared. Similarly, finished ballets for Balanchine seemed largely irrelevant. His attitude is reminiscent of many creative artists: "I truly do not care about a book once it is finished," offered John Steinbeck. "The line of books on the shelf are to me like very well embalmed corpses." For both Stravinsky and Balanchine, it was the thrill of the chase that mattered most.[2]

Both men also recognized the elemental force of musical and physical motion. It was this sense of propulsion that drove their preoccupation with the boundaries of time, or "temporality," as they referred to it. "Music is a *chrono-logic* art [which] presupposes before all else a certain organization of time, a chrononomy—if you will permit me to use a neologism," the composer re-marked. Balanchine's analogy was even more cosmological: "We are represent-ing [the] art of dancing, [the] art of body movement, in time, in space. It is the music, it is really time more than the melody, and our body must be subordi-nated to time—because without time, dance doesn't exist. It must be order—it's like a planet. Nobody criticizes the sun or moon or the earth because it is very precise, and that's why it has life. If it's not precise, it falls to pieces."[3]

Boundaries were liberating, not constrictive. They provided a primary cata-lyst, first to jump-start one's thinking, then as a shaping influence in sculpting a work's final version. Freedom born of boundaries is hardly a new notion. "No sooner do I form a conception of a material or corporeal substance," Galileo observed in 1623, "than I feel the need of conceiving that it has boundaries and shape." Likewise, throughout his life Stravinsky emphatically claimed that his powers of imagination were unshackled by imposed confinements. Balan-chine, too, dealt with whatever set of impediments he faced. "A dog is going to remain a dog, even if you want to have a cat; you're not going to have a cat, so you better take care of the dog because that's what you're going to have." As Vi-olette Verdy recalled, Balanchine did not try to transform or force a situation. "He accepted what he had to deal with . . . and gladly dealt with the conditions offered to him."[4]

Order, precision, boundaries, time and space, the inerrancy of motion—all these abstractions were channeled through both men's razor-sharp visual acuity. For the composer, visual impressions were often indelibly recorded, as he once remarked, "on the retina of my eye." From his earliest childhood memories of a red-shirted country peasant making the most earthy kind of music to his 1947 viewing of a Hogarth exhibit he happened upon in Chicago (which inspired his 1951 opera *The Rake's Progress*), the composer was deeply touched by painting, sculpture, and especially architecture. These visual arts came alive for Stravin-sky as each unfolded in its own rhythmic motion. The bridge to ballet was a short one. As the composer's biographer Mikhail Druskin suggests, "Is not this the reason for Stravinsky's long affection for the ballet, with its 'graphic' purity of movement, and especially for classical ballet?—for his interest in rhythmic accentuation, which translates the gestures of mime, becoming thereby a 'speaking gesture'?"[5]

Likewise, Balanchine was capable of conjuring up eye-appealing geometric patterns with the deftness of a skilled draftsman. He not only saw things clearly, but his visual horizon was unusually wide. He possessed both the eye and the ear to discern far-reaching musical-choreographic relations others could easily miss. Moreover, this visual sharpness encompassed a keen sense of temporal perception. He understood the visual rhythms of a structure, in the same way an architect does, and he matched them convincingly with underlying aural patterns. His sense of space, and of how space should be apportioned in sonic and visual terms, was unparalleled.

Both men were in some ways uncomplicated, in others elusive. Their stubborn refusal to be pegged neatly as a certain kind of artist surely strengthened their personal bond. It would be terribly misleading simply to categorize the composer and choreographer as formalists (as so many analysts wrongly do) if by that term we mean an excessive adherence to the belief that only design matters. Both were more than conceptualists, formalists, abstractionists, or constructionists—all tidy pigeonholes they considered nothing more than rigmarole. Both needed to roll up their sleeves and root up ideas with their bare hands (like a pig snorting truffles, to paraphrase one of the composer's descriptive images from his *Poetics*). Although Stravinsky, in particular, was prone to a kind of cerebral, circumlocutory doublespeak, he, like Balanchine, proudly considered himself a blue-collar artisan (fig. 1.1). The composer's portraiture of the hunt for new ideas captures his and Balanchine's approach: "A composer improvises aimlessly the way an animal grubs about. Both of them go grubbing about because they yield to a compulsion to seek things out. . . . So we grub about in expectation of our pleasure, guided by our scent, and suddenly we stumble against an unknown object. It gives us a jolt, a shock, and this shock fecundates our creative power."[6]

Above all else, both men were theater artists; and both were themselves full of theatricality. While Balanchine could create some of the most exquisite, breathtaking choreographic images ever staged, he could also be downright funny, even silly—an entertainer or "circus man," as he once unapologetically described himself. Stravinsky, who could sermonize with the best of them in defending his often-embattled works, also had an impish, vaudevillian side. The theater was deeply etched in his heritage, and he skillfully utilized the stage as a forum in a way few musicians ever achieved. For Balanchine, the elasticity of dance was broad enough to embrace a spectrum of brilliant colors—colors that few other choreographers were capable of envisioning.

Their unique success as collaborators appears all the more extraordinary given that Stravinsky routinely voiced harsh dissatisfaction with the librettists, costumers, set designers, painters, and producers with whom he worked. When

1.1 Stravinsky and Balanchine (photo by Fred Plaut; courtesy the Fred and Rose Plaut Archives, Yale University Music Library)

it came to getting what he wanted, he could be inflexible, intimidating. Choreographers, like conductors, constantly came under fire. Fokine, Nijinsky, Nijinska, Massine, and Bolm—at one time or another all close Russian colleagues—fell from his grace. Almost every joint venture the composer undertook resulted in an uneasy alliance, owing not only to the complex and frangible nature of collaboration itself but also to the composer's rigorously imposed standards and hidebound attitudes. Yet his compositional productivity was wrapped tightly around the necessity of collaboration, and consequently there was a constant search for partners who were equally inventive and sympathetic yet willing, ultimately, to accede to his carefully thought-out vision. As a young, untested composer, his earliest ballet collaborators had forced him to make too many concessions, and he resented it. He was not about to make the same mistake.

In reviewing the 1913 premiere of *The Rite of Spring*, Jean Cocteau commented that the ballet failed primarily because the music and movement were parallel; they lacked internal "play." Consequently, the ballet missed the interchange of dance and music that such an overwhelming, groundbreaking artistic work demanded. For Cocteau (and Stravinsky, too), the parallelisms of *The Rite* were, rightly or wrongly, perceived as no more than redundancies. Balanchine was the first of the composer's collaborators gutsy enough to sidestep the hazards of simple choreographic imitation. He refused to accept this mimicry as the equivalent of genuine musical-choreographic unity. Such ersatz correlations provided too superficial a solution to Stravinsky's music—dynamic music demanding an equally creative counterpart.

Often in vain, Stravinsky persistently argued that music and dance were more disconnected than connected. Indeed, it was from the unexploited potential of such disconnectedness that ballet would draw significant strength in becoming an expressive, independent art form. Efforts to synthesize a ballet's score and choreography through undisguised imitation created no true synthesis at all, both men contended. Such tautology only created an illusory reassurance, leading audiences to believe that in immediately seeing how closely the music and movement were coordinated, they had succeeded in perceiving the work's oneness. But nothing could be further from the truth. Using dance to "interpret" the music was a slippery slope, especially for Stravinsky, whose public views on performers were notoriously chary.

Any form of interpretation constituted a bugaboo. The composer's position was most explicitly expressed in the last of his six lectures, "The Performance of Music," originally given at Harvard University during the 1939–40 academic year and later incorporated into his *Poetics of Music*. A summary of this last lecture (entitled "Of the Art of Execution" in the printed synopsis distributed to the Harvard audience) holds that there are "two kinds of executants: the mere executant and the interpreter. The former is held only by the obligation to play his part, the latter not only subordinates himself to the necessity of his duty, which is to transmit the music, but must also convey the intentions of the creator. He is the representative of the author; he must be both interpreter and executant; but not vice versa." The duties of a performer were clear to Stravinsky: the "infallibility of the execution [and] the submission to the spirit of the work performed which presupposes a technical mastery, a sense of tradition, a perfection of culture."[7]

Tempo was a favorite target. As his younger son, Soulima (who often performed with his father in duo-piano works), recalled, "correct rhythm and tempo relationship" were imperative. Soulima remembered further that his father was "absolutely merciless" when it came to such matters. Above everything, "the pulse should be right. . . . Function normally and keep the steady pulse—that was his advice."[8] No wonder, as the choreographer's dancers report, Balanchine always came to rehearsal armed with a metronome. He would constantly run to the piano, checking Stravinsky's carefully set tempi. The composer's music was not to be interpreted; it was to be executed. Excessive interpretation—always a concern of the composer's when placing his scores in the hands of others—would lead audiences astray. After all, Stravinsky implied, it was his music, his thoughts, and should be honored as such. Balanchine understood this, and his fears of overinterpreting a gesture, a role, a ballet were similar to Stravinsky's. He wanted dancers to "transmit" the ballets, as he put it—simply to "dance the steps," in his well-known laconic understatement.

Moreover, the coordination of dance and music at the surface is quite a different matter from a work's substructural coherence. As Balanchine recognized, too effortless a comprehension of what one sees and hears could prove enfeebling: "When you're *immediately* together," he offered, the stamina of the statement being made is likely to "evaporate." Rather than aiming for an explicit matching of sound and dance, Stravinsky preferred to speak of the push and pull between choreography and music—a jousting that would eventually produce a more compelling artistic statement. As he commented in a 1935 article for the Parisian journal *Candide,* "What are the connections that unite and separate music and dance? In my opinion the one does not serve the other. There must be a harmonious accord, a synthesis of ideas. Let us speak, on the contrary of the struggle between music and choreography." Balanchine agreed, believing that any struggle should, ideally, ultimately lead to "being together," as he put it.[9]

Far more than any other choreographer with whom the composer collaborated, Balanchine employed choreography as a conduit through which to emphasize the message of Stravinsky's music. In some ways it was a jeopardous position. For many, it proved a heretical reversal of tradition, turning the pyramid precariously upside down. But Balanchine remained undaunted. He heeded the composer's belief that stimulation of the eye and the ear demanded careful apportioning; otherwise it was impossible to process meaningfully the mix of aural and visual data the senses were being asked to absorb. Balanchine intuitively understood the psychology of information theory. Thus he was capable of adroitly balancing what could easily become the overwhelming visual stimuli of physical movement.

Our eyes are simply more experienced, more agile receptors than our ears. Then too, we must remember that Stravinsky's scores were unlike any other music Balanchine set. Consequently, the choreographer immediately understood that the genius of the music would need to be set differently. The composer did not provide accompanimental music for the ballet. (Nor, for that matter, did most of the composers Balanchine favored.) So rather than glossing over the music's prominence, Balanchine addressed its force head-on, realizing that traditional choreographic solutions would fall short. How unusual an attitude this is compared to, for example, that of the eminent dancer-choreographer Serge Lifar, who believed that the weakness of Stravinsky's ballet music—its "fatal mistake" as he put it—was inherent in its subjugating rather than "enriching" dance.[10] For Balanchine it was an issue of neither subjugation nor enrichment; rather, it was a question of fashioning an effective, unified gestalt (a label the choreographer would undoubtedly have detested).

Balanchine spoke of striking a temporal and spatial equipoise wherein all components would be carefully fused. "Music is something that occupies architecturally a certain portion of time," he told an interviewer for the *Herald Tribune*. "In the dance, unless your body fills time, occupies time, as music does, then it means nothing. Gesture itself is meaningless." His often quoted maxim of "seeing the music" explicitly challenged audiences to grasp the multiple musical layers of Stravinsky's scores—scores that bustled with activity. One must listen intently to a Stravinsky score to discern its many internal dialogues. Balanchine's choreography was primarily intended to magnify the music's architecture, to clarify such internal dialogues in three-dimensional space. He liked to compare the making of his ballets to the construction of a building. And although he referred to Stravinsky as "the architect of time," he himself was no less aware of music's temporal architectonics. He possessed his own internal gyroscope, which allowed him to keep every element spinning in perfect structural balance. He thought the way composers and architects think. For him, there was no disparity between function and beauty.[11]

Balanchine explained his approach to choreography with a breezy kind of make-what-you-will-of-it demeanor. He enjoyed confounding pedants who hung on his every word. He compared himself to a cook, a carpenter, all the while insisting that the craft of choreography was not so very complicated. Yet he profoundly understood that technique and discipline formed the cornerstone of any focused activity, be it in the kitchen, the shop, or the dance studio. Whatever his self-effacing description, Balanchine was an assembler of parts, a master builder. Moreover, he knew that the parts themselves were not nearly as important as the actual assembly, the seamless joining of one section to the next. As physicist and cosmologist A. S. Eddington wrote in his celebrated 1928 treatise *The Nature of the Physical World,* "We often think that when we have completed our study of *one* we know all about *two*, because 'two' is 'one and one.' We forget that we have still to make a study of 'and.'" For both Balanchine and Stravinsky, *and* was the litmus test of how well music and dance were linked. In the same way, as Stravinsky's compositional sketches reveal, as well as the memories of Balanchine's dancers, it was this *and* with which both men seemed to labor the most in finding the right solution. "For Balanchine," Suzanne Farrell recalled, "dancing did not reside in the pose but within the transitions themselves; the act of getting from one step to another, and one place to another, *is* the dancing."[12]

Their many similar views on such lofty and often inexplicable issues as time, motion, and space provided the footings for a singular artistic vision, a way of communicating through a mutually understood language. But the underlying bond that united them most ardently began and ended with a shared and fiercely retained ethnicity. To say merely that Stravinsky and Balanchine were Russian too easily masks how deeply rooted this ineffaceable heritage was. To begin with, there was the primitive power of both religious and folkloristic rituals—timeless and ancient rites that both men imbibed from the days of their childhood. The lessons left an imprint that would forever be part of their artistic souls. Most notably, the fundamental seeds of theater resided within the often dramatically acted-out rites they soaked in. Such traditions produced a consanguinity that stretched across the composer and choreographer's age difference.

Stravinsky's reliance on this power is absolutely central to an understanding of his early attraction to dance as the most visible, demonstrative artistic form of expression. If we are to believe his earliest memoirs, dance was even more meaningful to him than music. Druskin goes so far as to contend that for Stravinsky, "the origin of every ritual lay, as he believed, in the dance." He was fascinated with physical movement; nor is it any coincidence that many of the dance rituals of preliterate Russian folklore with which he was familiar sparked his imagination in visualizing musical ideas. His inextricable connection to the memory of both a cosmopolitan, westernized Petersburg and the Ukrainian countryside is evidenced in virtually every piece he wrote—even those which at first seem removed from these enduring impressions. In later years he still recalled "the singing of the women of the neighboring village [as] they sang in unison on their way home after the day's work": "To this day I clearly remember the tune, and the way they sang it." So cogent are the ethnic underpinnings and ritualistic origins of his evolving compositional style that they can never be dismissed, even in works ostensibly quite different, written long after he had left his homeland. Toward the end of his life, Stravinsky remarked, "St. Petersburg is so much a part of my life that I am almost afraid to look further into myself, least [*sic*] I discover how much of me is still joined to it. . . . It is dearer to my heart than any other city in the world."[13]

The impressionable young Balanchine was equally touched by the grandeur of rites and religious rituals—sensorial ceremonies that included the smell of incense, the sight of brightly emblazoned ecclesiastical vestments, and the solemn, magisterial processions of high priests. For Stravinsky and Balanchine, both of whom shunned blasphemy at all costs, religion was essentially a performance art. Elaborately designed sacred services were, by Balanchine's own admission, enthralling "productions." His uncle became the archbishop of Tbilisi, and the young boy often participated (or "acted," as he put it) in liturgical ceremonies. As Francis Mason reported, Balanchine remembered how fond he was of "playing church on his own, of blessing objects, of making the sign of the cross in his own private church theatricals."[14]

Like Stravinsky, Balanchine not only assimilated the classical traditions of music and dance to which he was exposed in a culturally vibrant Petersburg, but he also eagerly digested the peasant traditions of song and dance. His childhood memories are astonishingly close to Stravinsky's in both tone and substance. They are sensorial memories, recalling sounds, sights, and smells. Both recall the rhythmic clacking of droshkies rolling down the street, the pealing of cathedral bells, and the aromas of appetizing foods seeping from corner stores. There is a tribalism to both men's memories, atavistic and visceral, rather than intellectual in spirit. Such retrospection attests to the strong ancestral ties Stravinsky and Balanchine shared. Moreover, this inextricably ingrained cultural bond eased the younger Balanchine's entry into Stravinsky's world when they later met. They found an immediate, communal past. From their first meeting until their later years, they conversed in Russian during their collaborations both privately and often publicly in the rehearsal studio. They celebrated the customs and traditions of their heritage, everything from feasting on elaborately prepared dinners to reliving their inextirpable memories of Petersburg. Regardless of whatever series of metamorphoses they supposedly traveled through, whatever musical and choreographic changes emerged at the surface level of their artistic collaborations, the powerful residue of those formative impressions was ubiquitous, cutting to the bedrock of their creativity.

As far back as his childhood memories reached, Stravinsky was fascinated with how the human body moved. He retained a vivid remembrance of summers in the country, of dance contests for the local peasantry. In St. Petersburg, the young boy was dazzled by the spectacle of the Imperial Theater, in which his father, Fyodor Ignatyevich Stravinsky, one of the preeminent opera singers of his day, performed in productions that often featured dancing as a divertissement. He saw the wonderfully opulent Tchaikovsky ballets of the 1890s, remembering particularly *The Sleeping Beauty*—the dawn of his musical consciousness, as he recalled in his autobiography. Dance was part of the culture for most Russian children, and the young Stravinsky became familiar with the classical vocabulary of ballet early on. Not only did he know all the fundamental academic positions, he apparently was easily cajoled into demonstrating them. His earliest letters record his interest in drawing, painting, amateur theatricals, and, especially, his enthrallment with dance. Music often received no more than a passing mention.

In *Memories and Commentaries,* the composer provided a quick history of his acquaintance with dance. He confirms how important and familiar ballet was to his childhood. He recalls knowing the stories of the great ballets. He remembers that his father was a friend of the distinguished and influential choreographer Marius Petipa, and even recalls seeing him. Indeed, in the *Candide* article, the composer referred to Petipa as "the greatest artist of all, the founder of the choreographic canon." Stravinsky was familiar with the ballets danced by Anna Pavlova, and Tamara Karsavina lived in the flat just above them. Moreover, he learned the essentials of dance technique from the legendary dance instructor Enrico Cecchetti, who would later work with Diaghilev. Thus his youthful exposure to dance was unusually rich, and because of this background, even Diaghilev himself would have to admit that Stravinsky, more than any other composer he employed, understood choreographic movement.

Among the leading composers of Stravinsky's formative years, dance, as an art form, was considered somewhere between suspicious and disreputable (or "slumming," as Richard Taruskin calls it). Ludwig Minkus and Cesare Pugni were regarded as little more than perfunctory composers, manufacturing workaday music as needed. Among musicians, any association with them was thought to be unsavory, an abasement. Even Stravinsky's teacher, the highly respected Nikolai Rimsky-Korsakov, cast a disapproving eye at the dancing of the Maryinsky corps de ballet, as well as at its instructors, not excepting Cecchetti.[15] But by the time Stravinsky entered the emerging world of the Ballets Russes, the prominence of dance and dancers was beginning to make itself felt. Still, musicians, both performers and composers, were not held in high esteem, and Stravinsky, especially with his rather broadly based knowledge of dance, took note, and maybe even umbrage.

Whatever his feeling, it did nothing to dim his enthusiasm for ballet. On the contrary, he defended ballet's artistic legitimacy at a time when it was under attack. His rhapsodic 1911 letter to Rimsky-Korsakov's son Vladimir is particularly insightful. It is, as Taruskin rightly labels it, the composer's "declaration of independence," and as such deserves reprinting: "I love ballet and am more interested in it than in anything else. And this is not just an idle enthusiasm, but a serious and profound enjoyment of scenic spectacle—of the art of animated form [*zhivaya plastika*]. And I am simply bewildered that you, who so loved the plastic arts . . . pay so little attention to choreography . . . and consider ballet to be a lower form than opera. If a Michelangelo were alive today, I thought, looking at the frescoes in the Sistine Chapel, the only thing his genius would recognize and accept would be the choreography that is being reborn today. Everything else that takes place on the stage he would doubtless call a miserable farce. For the only form of scenic art that sets itself, as its cornerstone, the *tasks of beauty,* and *nothing else,* is ballet. And the only goal Michelangelo pursued was visible beauty."[16]

Years later, in *The Message of Igor Stravinsky,* the composer's son Theodore wrote that his father was drawn to ballet specifically because of its "aristocratic severity." It provided a forum for discipline, structure, clarity; a battlefield where rules would triumph over arbitrariness—a familiar Stravinskyan shibboleth reiterated throughout the composer's life. Theodore wrote specifically of rhythm as the element that wed music and dance, declaring that every rhythm evoked a "kinesthetic reaction, and though this reaction is not yet 'dance,' it is the first element of it." Moreover the composer did not content himself with such armchair cerebration. As Theodore also observed, theater was deep in his father's blood, and the composer needed to express this physically.[17]

A 1918 letter from C. F. Ramuz, Stravinsky's collaborator in *L'Histoire du Soldat,* confirms that the composer actually considered dancing the prodigious part of the devil in the production's Swiss premiere. Indeed, throughout his career there are frequent reports detailing Stravinsky's willingness—or as some would observe, his compulsion—to become directly involved in ballet rehearsals by demonstrating with animated gesticulations the choreography he envisioned. Nor were his contributions limited to the choreography itself. Only two weeks before the premiere of *L'Histoire,* he searched for the exact style of ballet slippers that he insisted be worn. He busied himself with everything because he simply could not sit still. (Similarly, Balanchine has been likened to Dr. Coppélius, reigning over his workshop of dolls. He too became involved in every aspect of a production, even tasks as basic as sewing costumes, checking on tights, and choosing shoes.)[18] Stravinsky knew what he wanted, he felt what he wanted, and he saw no reason not to show or tell others precisely what that was. Psychologically, like many great artists, he was compelled to permit virtually nothing to pass beyond his immediate control. It was simply too risky.

Surely the origin of the composer's need to move physically was fundamental. Stravinsky was the least sedentary creature imaginable. He was a vortex of activity both mentally and physically. His curiosity knew no boundaries; but it was not the kind of contemplative curiosity that finds outlet in unhurried, dispassionate reflection. He once declared that his metabolism allowed him to wait patiently for creative ideas to arrive, "like an insect waits," conjuring up the vision of a spider motionlessly stalking a prey; but his analogy, while charming, could not have been further off the mark. The notion of a Stravinskyan web lying in wait for an idea to sashay in approaches absurdity. Indeed, can there be any doubt that the hyperactive tautness of his being, ready to uncoil at any moment, was largely responsible for the tension, and often intolerance, that characterized his mercurial actions and personal relationships? Not only did the composer abhor complacency, but even the most fleeting sense of contentment, let alone achievement, was utterly foreign to his fidgety spirit. Yet despite history's obvious recognition of Stravinsky's lifelong devotion to ballet as the most explicit manifestation of his attachment to physical movement, we might still be underestimating his instinctive need for such movement.[19]

Motion was the core of his uncurbed energy. "Stravinsky composed with his whole body. Not just with his enormous ears and his sharp eyes," wrote Roger Shattuck. "I think it's essential to understand that Stravinsky's music emanates from a whole dancing body, his own."[20] He was perpetually restless; there was no room for inertia. The composer walked in a sprightly manner, spoke with animation, prepared for performances with a rigorous routine of calisthenics, and personally, physically, demonstrated his balletic ideas to dancers during rehearsals.

In a similar way, Balanchine needed to work in a rehearsal hall, with his dancers' malleable bodies present and ready to be molded. He would manipulate their positions during rehearsals as one manipulates clay, experimenting, improvising, adjusting, and shaping gestures until he hit upon something suitable. Balanchine could not conceive of abstractly "planning steps ahead of time." He once remarked that from the beginning of their relationship, he saw that Stravinsky was lithe, quick, and needed to move. As he told an interviewer for *Newsweek* in 1972, "Stravinsky could walk on his hands like an acrobat and he liked social dancing." And as Shattuck reports, musicians witnessing Stravinsky's conducting of rehearsals offer one shared description: "They all use exactly the same verb for him: *dance*."[21]

If a dancer's heart beat within Stravinsky, that of a musician invigorated Balanchine. He was, as the distinguished Russian designer Pavel Tchelitchev (also spelled Tchelitchew) remarked, a musician first. Simply stated, music completely shaped Balanchine's approach to dance. Indeed, as critics complained, Balanchine was too musical for his own good. Compared to other choreographers, Balanchine used a different yardstick. Consequently, critics often offered little more than bunkum in attempting to understand the musical impetus driving his work. Music was a prism through which Balanchine had viewed dance from his earliest days. Just as Stravinsky was initially more attracted to dance than to music, the young Balanchine embraced music long before his serious study of dance; for music was as much a part of the Balanchivadze household as it was of the Stravinsky.

Like Stravinsky's mother, Anna, Maria Nikolayevna Vassilyeva Balanchivadze was a competent and sensitive pianist; and just as Stravinsky remembered sitting at the keyboard with his mother sight-reading music, Balanchine recalled hours at the keyboard with Maria. She became the five-year-old Georgi's first piano teacher. Soon thereafter he began piano lessons with a series of doctrinaire piano instructors who left him uninspired—just as did Stravinsky's early piano teachers. Also similarly, Balanchine's father, like Stravinsky's, was a highly respected musician in St. Petersburg circles. Meliton Antonovich Balanchivadze resembled Stravinsky's father in other ways as well. He was often off on one venture or another, and Balanchine remembers him the same way Stravinsky does his own father: as an intolerant and often standoffish paterfamilias. Meliton played virtually no role in Balanchine's early musical education. And while Stravinsky's father at least permitted his son access to his music library and the Maryinsky rehearsals, it is clear from Igor's bitter memories that his father never encouraged him as a musician. Balanchine's father sought a military career for his son. "For a while," Balanchine recalled, "it was thought that I would become one of the Tsar's cadets."[22] Stravinsky's father insisted that his son become a lawyer, and in fact he did matriculate and eventually graduate as an attorney, studying music on the side.

Beginning in 1891, Meliton Balanchivadze actually studied composition for a few years with Rimsky-Korsakov, and his interest in promoting the goals of Russian nationalism led him in 1907 to finance the publication of Mikhail Glinka's private correspondence. A respected ethnographer and a collector of Georgian folk songs, Meliton became known as "the Georgian Glinka." But he also wrote several operas, including *The Perfidious Tamara,* an important enough opus to be performed in St. Petersburg in 1897. As early as 1913, his son George heard Rimsky's opera *Tsar Saltan*. The young Balanchine too, of course, came to know Petipa's *The Sleeping Beauty*, actually participating in a 1915 production while he was studying at the Imperial Theater Ballet School. As late as the summer of 1982 (his last summer, as it would turn out to be) Balanchine still remembered that "everyone was well dressed in blue on a beautiful stage and I liked participating. And it became a kind of drug."[23]

These are the kinds of ineradicable impressions that shape a young artist's future. Adding to his parents' love of music, Balanchine's sister played the violin. But in more practical day-to-day terms, it was his younger brother Andrei who sparked his love of actually making music. Yuri Slonimsky remembers that "Andrei and George played nocturnes and marches which they had composed themselves, preferring these genres above all others. They performed the four-hand piano pieces of Haydn, Mozart, and Schubert."[24] Perhaps more important, George and Andrei often improvised together at the keyboard. In fact, like Stravinsky, tinkering with new ideas at the keyboard seemed to interest Balanchine far more than the mechanical drilling of required études; from all accounts among his contemporaries at the conservatory, Balanchine became quite a facile improviser. The piano became a functional tool for both Balanchine and Stravinsky, allowing them close contact with the actual making of music, as well as the ability to earn a little income.

In their teens, Balanchine and Stravinsky both worked as pianists in silent movie theaters, in houses of ill repute, and as accompanists for other performers. Balanchine also earned money as a ballet studio pianist, working several hours daily. He also played in cabarets, where he sometimes accompanied the singer-dancer Tamara Geva, who became his first wife.[25] Geva recalls that the piano was always the focal point of their apartment: "He only cared about the piano and the kitchen," she told Francis Mason, adding that he would sometimes sit at the piano with Stravinsky as they studied scores together. Violette Verdy told me that in his later years in New York, when he hardly needed to add the role of rehearsal pianist to his many other duties, Balanchine still enjoyed playing during rehearsals, often remaining afterward to play a little more. She remembers that he was often the last to leave, making sure that the pianos were properly cared for, cleaning them, polishing them, and closing their lids. "Pianos are people," she recalls him saying.[26]

Balanchine attended concerts whenever he could, familiarizing himself with the standard classical repertoire. His own pianism developed quickly, as evidenced by recital appearances that included works of Bach, Beethoven, and Chopin, all standard fare for any aspiring young performer. In the summer of

1.2 Manuscript of "Love Is a Simple Thing," by George Balanchine (The Harvard Theatre Collection, the Houghton Library; © The George Balanchine Trust)

1919, he was admitted to the Petrograd Conservatory as a piano student (although he did not actually matriculate as a full-time student until 1921), but his interest in composition remained high (fig. 1.2). In his summary of Balanchine's musical schooling, Slonimsky reprints a revealing 1922 document in which the young man's skills receive a written evaluation. He has a "good ear, rhythm, good arm, good fingers," noted the evaluator. The commentator spoke of his dedication under the most difficult circumstances, practicing "in the winter in the unheated theater hall, sometimes even with gloves." Moreover, he seems to have had a taste for improvising, just as Stravinsky did, preferring to explore his own ideas at the keyboard rather than concentrate on finger-building études. And apparently he could not walk by an unoccupied musical instrument without picking it up and discovering how it worked.[27]

Slonimsky further recalled that Balanchine also studied French horn, trumpet, and the violin (later buying his own instrument) so as to familiarize himself with their capabilities. As a result, not only did he gain a physical appreciation of the mechanics and techniques of these instruments, but he also learned to read orchestral scores with a fluency that few choreographers ever achieve. Moreover, as Igor Youskevitch recalled, "Balanchine could be inspired by looking at the score, by the intricacy of the composition. That's what excited him, rather than the actual sound."[28] Score reading was a skill that served him especially well in dealing with Stravinsky's imaginative orchestration. He often took into consideration the separate choirs of the orchestra as he plotted his choreography. Frequently the partitioning of a corps de ballet or a group of soloists can be understood purely along the lines of Stravinsky's instrumentation, as we shall see in such works as *Agon* and *Stravinsky Violin Concerto*.

In later years, the conductor-violist Leon Barzin, who played an important role in bringing some of the Stravinsky-Balanchine repertoire alive, spoke of regular Friday evening musical gatherings in Balanchine's New York apartment. The Russian violinist Nathan Milstein and others would join Balanchine to play the chamber music of Mozart and Tchaikovsky (some of which Balanchine later used for his ballets). Even as late as 1949, Stravinsky invited Balanchine himself to perform the composer's 1937 piano arrangement of a jazz band piece entitled *Preludium* as part of an upcoming concert of Stravinsky's works. Although there is much speculation about the proficiency level of Balanchine's pianism and the possibility that he might have opted for a concert career, it is doubtful that his skills were so highly developed. As Milstein recalls, "Of course, George was no virtuoso—he couldn't have given recitals—and I doubt that he ever could have been a professional accompanist. When he sat down at the piano, he didn't play so much as 'noodle,' blurring over the hard parts. But, really, that didn't matter."[29]

Indeed it didn't, and a distinction must be made here, for whether Balanchine might have become a professional concert pianist is of no consequence. It was his abilities—and rather remarkable abilities at that—as a pianist that would stamp his musicianship upon every score he choreographed. Let me be clear: it was not Balanchine's knowledge of the standard classical repertoire that enabled him to identify with Stravinsky's musical invention, with the composer's expansion of and sometimes breaking free from whatever musical paradigm he was exploring; rather, it was his facility as a deftly skilled, astute, all-around musician who just happened to be a pianist. For Balanchine the piano was never viewed principally as a vehicle for concertizing, for interpreting the repertoire he learned as a student in Petersburg. It was an expedient and personal means of getting to know the interior configuration of the music by literally touching it, manipulating the notes with his two hands. In this sense, his approach to the keyboard was not so different from that of Stravinsky, who always considered the instrument an indispensable part of the compositional process. The physical, artisan side of both men again becomes apparent. They placed their trust in the value of touch as well as instinct as an unerring guide in searching out the expression of ideas.

Balanchine was at home at the keyboard. It provided him with a certain security, a tactile means of keeping "in touch" with the sound, just as he had to keep in touch with the dancers with whom he worked. Feeling the sound physically with one's fingers is a very personal experience, completely different from listening to a recording or entrusting the performance of the music to a rehearsal pianist—and as a dancer and musician himself, Balanchine knew that better than anyone. There was an intimacy with the keyboard that was manifested in several ways. His dancers not only remember Balanchine playing the piano, they remember him "noodling," as Milstein put it, that is, letting his fingers roam freely over whatever thoughts came to mind. In the process, the sounds seemed to inspire choreographic settings of the lines or chords he hit upon.[30]

I remember Stravinsky's son Soulima telling me that his father often did the same thing. He remembers hearing him at the piano for hours, intently testing one chord after another, sometimes altering the spacing of a chord slightly. The composer often referred to these explorations as a search for "fingerprints" that would eventually provide the raw materials of a composition. At that point the real composing would begin, wherein any number of compositional ideas would be linked together cohesively. Just so, Paul Mejia remembers that in teaching seminars Balanchine would take the basic permutation of a triadic chord—major, minor, diminished, augmented—and using three dancers visualize the sonic quality of each chord differently. "Here is a major chord," Mejia recalls Balanchine beginning. "Now, how are you going to go from a major to a minor, let's say? We know that the one note goes down half a step, but that doesn't mean the dancers are going to do that. How can you visualize it?"[31] It was these subtleties that Balanchine understood, and understood not only instinctively but from the standpoint of a musician conversant with the fundamental principles of voice-leading, that is, the way each component of a musical progression flows from one chord to the next.

Balanchine was a serious student of music theory and composition for most of his life. Even in Petersburg, he would compose dances for his friends or arrange the music of others so that it suited the choreographic production he had in mind. His teachers recall that he divided his time among dance, piano, and composition, taking as many harmony and counterpoint classes as he could. When he arrived in New York in the early 1930s he immediately resumed his study of music theory with Nicolas Nabokov, his friend from the Diaghilev days.

The Balanchine archives of the Harvard Theatre Collection provide an amazingly complete picture of how thorough and ongoing his commitment was. Literally hundreds of pages recording Balanchine's written-out music theory exercises are preserved (fig. 1.3). Virtually every aspect of fundamental theory training is included, from countless intervallic exercises to part-writing, attentive analytic labeling of nonharmonic tones, exercises in which dissonances are carefully resolved, cadential progressions notated in several keys, four-part harmonizations, methodically completed exercises in modulation, orchestration studies, and even some species counterpoint (in fact, Balanchine writes the word *species* in English, whereas all of his other notations are in Russian). He dutifully works out all quality of chords and their inversions, includes analysis of chordal passages, and carefully notates the instrumental ranges of most of the orchestral instruments, even including some of the so-called special effects, such as string harmonics and certain bowing techniques. These telltale documents reveal a compendium of techniques familiar to the professional musician. Quite simply, Balanchine understood music theory inside out.

Even more remarkably, Balanchine's pianistic and musical skills enabled him to prepare piano reductions of orchestral scores as thorny as Alban Berg's complexly orchestrated opera *Lulu*. In Saratoga Springs, for example, where he first started to think about repertoire for the 1972 Stravinsky Festival, he prepared a reduction of Stravinsky's youthful Symphony in E-Flat. But the Balanchine archives in the Harvard Theatre Collection demonstrate that the choreographer had been making such reductions all his life. Barbara Horgan remembers that he would complete these almost as one does a Sunday crossword puzzle. It

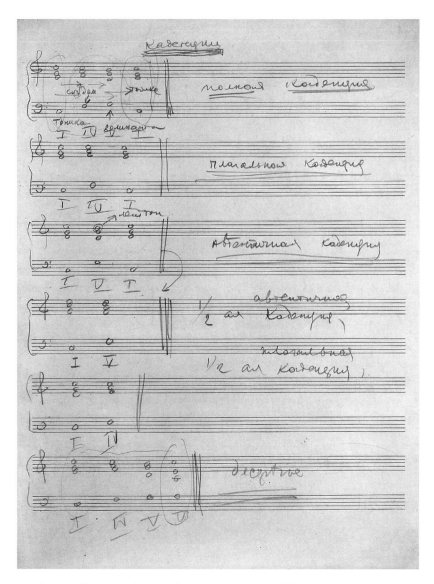

1.3 A sample of Balanchine's music theory exercises. Here he labels various cadences in Russian: full cadence, plagal, authentic, half, deceptive. (The Harvard Theatre Collection, the Houghton Library; © The George Balanchine Trust)

became a leisurely but productive occupation of his time away from the rehearsal studio and a means of familiarizing himself with the music by transcribing it note by note. For example, as detailed in Chapter 14, Balanchine spent considerable time studying and choreographing the music for the first

Aria of *Stravinsky Violin Concerto*. He prepared his own reduction of the movement rather than relying upon Stravinsky's preexisting arrangement for piano and violin. Indeed, it is clear from a study of Balanchine's score that he made his reduction directly from Stravinsky's orchestral score, demonstrating how conversant he was with both matters of orchestration (transposition, changing clefs, and so on) and the conversion of instrumental lines to the keyboard.[32]

This expertise cannot be overestimated, especially in terms of the choreographer's relationship with Stravinsky. In fact, the Balanchine archives hold other piano reductions of Stravinsky scores that the choreographer decided against or never got around to preparing as ballets. There is an exquisitely notated piano reduction of the first movement of Stravinsky's early *Three Pieces for String Quartet* (fig. 1.4).[33] The skillful Balanchine meticulously arranged the four string lines to fit the pianist's hand in a reduction as deftly constructed as any I have ever seen. The composer would often discuss short scores (abbreviated compilations of a full score that is not yet entirely orchestrated) with Balanchine. Sometimes Stravinsky would send the music to Balanchine a few pages at a time so that the choreographer-pianist could study the work immediately. As musicians will attest, reading short scores is no easy task; frequently these are not finished piano reductions that fit the hands comfortably. But Balanchine was able to deal with them in a way that many pianists cannot.

It would be a mistake to believe that the two men's similarities ended with their musical bond, or that sharp dissimilarities did not exist. Here one must be careful not to apply a too broad, and thus useless, brush. For a fuller portrait of their professional relationship to be drawn, the private lives of both the composer and choreographer—their habits, joys, fears, priorities, foibles, and interactions with others—must be considered as well. The frequent intersections of their personal and professional lives, as well as their individual responsibilities and pursuits, make up an important reality.

Stravinsky had a sense of his own importance, his legacy. He needed to know what others thought of him. When asked what his eventual position in history would be, he replied that history would decide, not him. But his unpublished papers divulge his readiness to help history along by projecting a certain urbane image. The composer constantly monitored his press, bitterly snapping at his detractors. Often he covertly employed friends as sentinels who would attend performances and gather reviews and published articles that he then scrutinized warily, parsing words, correcting inaccuracies, and grousing over perceived injustices. The marginalia of his private papers spill over with concealed feelings of self-doubt—the last thing one might expect of a composer whose

1.4 Balanchine's piano transcription of the first movement of Stravinsky's *Three Pieces for String Quartet* (1914) (The Harvard Theatre Collection, the Houghton Library; © The George Balanchine Trust)

music brims with confidence. His carefully cultivated image, as filtered, for example, through his editorially scrubbed correspondence (much of which has been suppressed or expunged), does not really allow a complete and impartial profile.

In contrast Balanchine generally conveyed an appearance of indifference about his eventual role in history. His history would be part of the future, and the future didn't particularly interest him. When Bernard Taper's biography of the choreographer first appeared, Balanchine told his friend and co-author Francis Mason that Mason might want to read it, but he himself was not interested.[34] Stravinsky, conversely, read much of what was written about him. He collected biographical surveys, for instance, checking to see whether he was included. Balanchine saved few press clippings, keepsakes, or chronicles of his accomplishments. He displayed a certain ennui, and seemed disarmingly unconcerned about his image and the impermanence of his ballets. Museums were no more than monuments to mummification, he scoffed. Why be concerned with the dead? Better that we should live in the present.

For the most part, he chose to remain above the fray of the sometimes shrill public invective that dogged him. When he did respond, there is a mixture of confidence, obstinacy, even arrogance. As he told *Time* magazine in 1964, "It's like the Pope represents Christ. I represent Terpsichore, goddess of the dance." One never knows how far Balanchine's tongue-in-cheek sardonicism extended. When subscribers to his ballet seasons voiced displeasure about a particular ballet or the casting of a dancer (and complain they did, as hundreds of letters in the Harvard Theatre Collection attest), Barbara Horgan, his ever-tactful assistant, always responded with thoughtful and often judiciously detailed replies.

Unlike Stravinsky, the choreographer often summarily ignored criticism rather than waste time answering it. He had little interest in explaining his work. His pithy rejoinders were renowned: analyses of his ballets were "too fancy"; roses should not be explained; ballets were butterflies destined to fly away. There is a litany of sententious Balanchinian one-liners: to the question, "What is your ballet about?" came his jaunty response, "About twenty-eight minutes." He never engaged in the kind of bravado the composer sometimes mounted. When Balanchine did respond, he often did so glibly, echoing Stravinsky's indictment of a philistine public: "To find a wine too dry is merely to express a personal limitation," he once defended the composer.[35] In contrast, Stravinsky often sent lengthy, perorational letters to established scholars and students alike, preachily explaining his position on the most harmless point of inquiry.

Largely, one suspects, because of the early mistreatment of his works and the remuneration he was denied, Stravinsky engaged often in self-advocacy. He mostly steered clear of potential entanglements, such as lobbying for the visibility of the arts as a national value. Unlike contemporaries Pablo Picasso and

Frank Lloyd Wright, he chose not to politicize himself or his views, preferring instead to maintain a neutrality that could not be misconstrued as an endorsement of this or that cause. As an independent composer, he had to be primarily concerned with obtaining commissions that would underwrite the projects he wished to pursue. And of course, he was offered commissions constantly: for symphonic and choral works, for concertos, and quite often for ballets. In each case the composer was able to weigh the advantages and disadvantages of accepting whatever would suit his artistic and financial needs best.

Not so with Balanchine, charged with the responsibility of a complex and very public enterprise—an enterprise that, like Diaghilev's, would rise or fall largely upon the box-office merits of its productions. Musicians, at least, seem to forget that Balanchine had to develop a balance-sheet acumen upon which an entire company, not only himself, depended. Like Stravinsky, Balanchine spent considerable time contemplating projects that in the end he simply could not do. As the Harvard archives reveal, composers constantly approached him, hoping he would consider choreographing their scores. In 1981 Yehudi Menuhin attempted to interest him in staging Bartók's Concerto for orchestra for the composer's centennial. Krzystof Penderecki was interested in composing a new score for a ballet or having Balanchine use one of his existing scores. Ravi Shankar suggested a ballet to his Concerto for sitar and orchestra. Even Stravinsky's son Soulima asked Balanchine to do a ballet to a set of his own compositions. But Balanchine's business affairs were time-consuming almost beyond belief, making one marvel all the more at his prolificacy as a choreographer. Moreover, other unpublished archival material confirms that Balanchine regularly waived personal fees, choosing instead to request donations to his company. He often lobbied for his dancers, never for himself.

Balanchine actively involved himself as a public spokesperson of the arts, assertively using his status as a platform. He saw himself as a denizen of New York City and the state of New York, befriending mayors John Lindsay and Ed Koch, as well as governors Nelson Rockefeller and Hugh Carey. In 1961 he urged Rockefeller to use his leadership position to support the arts by making a television speech which "would be good because people could see your face and believe in your feeling for art. And everyone could listen. A speech at a dinner or meeting would be reported in the newspapers . . . but on television everyone would hear it."[36] But Balanchine's political efforts extended beyond state lines. His dancers participated in the inauguration festivities for President Eisenhower; they appeared at the "Camelot" White House; they danced in the Carter White House in 1978 for a NATO summit meeting.

In return, Balanchine gained the ear of those with federal power, or those who sought it. In a 1952 letter to Dwight D. Eisenhower, Balanchine wrote, "Dear General, . . . This letter is written in the hope that the suggestion it humbly submits may bring more votes to our future President." He advises Eisenhower that the artists of America will exercise "a vital influence on public opinion" and can be used as "an instrument of the 'propaganda of truth.'" He concludes by requesting that the candidate "recognize the American artists in one of your speeches and to appeal to them and you will get a million votes," even hinting that government subsidy of the country's artists would be welcome.[37]

Finally, the amicable relationship Balanchine enjoyed with Jacqueline Kennedy provided a promising opportunity to lobby a First Lady whose appreciation of the arts was a matter of national record. His extraordinary letter to her of 1 August 1961 says a great deal about his attitudes, especially as they relate not only to Kennedy herself but to his views about "woman" generally, and about women and ballet:

> You have already made yourself very important in this country, in Europe, in fact in the whole world. . . . You are expected to be almost a "spiritual saviour" of America. I don't mean in the religious sense, but I mean to distinguish between material things and things of the spirit—art, beauty. No one else can take care of these things. You alone can—if you will. Your husband is necessarily busy with serious international problems and cannot be expected to worry too much about the nation's art and culture. But woman is always the inspiration. Man takes care of the material things and woman takes care of the soul. Woman is the world and man lives in it. Woman makes the earth into a home for man.
>
> Even in art, it is woman who inspires man. God creates, woman inspires and man assembles. I firmly believe that woman is appointed by destiny to inspire and bring beauty to our existence. Woman herself is the reason for life to be beautiful, and man should be busy serving her. . . . I don't mean this abstractly. I am saying it because you, personally, must be not only the First Lady but the First Woman. . . . My hope is that your lasting fame . . . will be that you united the soul of the United States. People are waiting for you to do this. It needs to be done.[38]

Balanchine knew where power rested. And he could quickly switch his many hats, changing from lobbyist to musician to choreographer. On the one hand he genuinely wanted his audiences to be uplifted, but if they were not, he simply moved on. As for the work itself, it was imperative for him to understand precisely what Stravinsky was doing, and his considerable musical skills enabled him to deal with the hidden, cohesive links of the composer's often convoluted scores. Yet he didn't care a whit whether the audience was aware of the music's substructure. The proof was in the pudding, and if the ballet did not work for Balanchine, if the audience did not see what he saw, he would shrug it off. Such a laissez-faire attitude stood in notable contrast to that of the composer. If Balanchine's work was attacked, especially in later years, he displayed indifference, real or feigned: "What difference does it make as long as people pay to come and to see it, and they applaud."[39]

Stravinsky, conversely, was more insistent that his efforts be understood; if they were not, he reflexively deflected blame to others. In an unreleased film clip from the 1966 CBS television documentary *Portrait of Stravinsky,* for example, at eighty-three years of age, he still grumbled about the reaction to the premiere of *The Rite.* It was not the music that had incited the riot, "but what the audience saw on stage. They came for *Scheherazade,* they came to see beautiful girls, and they saw *Le Sacre du printemps,* and they were shocked. They were very naïve and very stupid people." Resignation came less easily to him than to Balanchine.

Stravinsky wanted his scores to be accurately preserved. He is often viewed, unfairly, as an intractable composer unwilling to change his mind once his ideas were committed to paper. His unpublished scores and sketches, however, reveal that to the contrary, he was perfectly amenable to altering a passage if the music was better served thereby. Indeed, the annotations entered into the scores from which he conducted establish that he would frequently modify the music at the last moment. Here the similarity with Balanchine is notable. He too would often walk into a dress rehearsal and at the last moment modify a passage to accommodate a dancer, and thus the dance. And while such on-the-spot adjustments are not unusual for choreographers, Balanchine's endless imagination allowed him to do so with seeming effortlessness.

Both the composer and the choreographer were devoted to their respective crafts. They could produce powerful moments of great solemnity, but they could also be droll, sharing a rather ribald sense of humor. Violette Verdy told me that when they were together they jokingly sparred like Laurel and Hardy. They were caricatures of themselves, she recalled; and their quick-witted banter revealed a genuine fondness of being with one another. Stravinsky enjoyed visiting zoos, playing cards, attending movies. Balanchine had his interludes too, watching television (once declaring that the best thing in America, artistically, was the Western), doing laundry, puttering around the apartment, and composing little pop songs for relaxation. His friends report his mellowness during the more leisurely summers in Saratoga Springs. There is a wistfulness

1.5 "Ashfield's Nights," by George Balanchine, with a dedication to Lincoln Kirstein (The Harvard Theatre Collection, the Houghton Library; © The George Balanchine Trust)

to many of the pieces he wrote there, as with a charming and well-crafted little waltz (undated) dedicated to Lincoln Kirstein entitled "Ashfield's Nights, Remembrance of the Things Past" (fig. 1.5).

Still, as relaxed as Balanchine often appeared, like Stravinsky he was not averse to using his muscle when needed. Stravinsky's saber rattling often surfaced in contract negotiations and misunderstood commissions. Having been deprived of royalties from his early blockbuster ballets, he pored over every contractual clause carefully, making demands that indemnified his own interests. Balanchine once threatened to pull his company from its projected Lincoln Center residency unless the State Theater's orchestra pit, then under construction, were expanded to accommodate the size of ensemble needed to support certain ballets. And just as an easily riled Stravinsky could toss aside old friends, Balanchine was capable of vindictiveness, especially when it came to the always-sensitive issue of casting roles. For both men, the borders of their tolerance could be easily tested. Yet they always exercised patience and flexibility with each other, compliantly making changes without any external sign, at least, of objection.

Their notoriety brought constant invitations for honorary degrees and other public tributes; but neither sought trophies. Lifar offered Stravinsky and Balanchine the Prix de Serge Diaghilev in 1959 as part of a fiftieth anniversary commemoration of the Ballets Russes. But having parted company with Lifar long before, Stravinsky didn't even reply, even though Balanchine was asked to share the award for his work as director of the New York City Ballet. Harvard University, on separate occasions, offered honorary doctorates to both. Kirstein thought it appropriate for Balanchine to accept the honor from his own alma mater, but the choreographer declined. He simply did not have the time.[40] Neither did Stravinsky.

Both the composer and choreographer became household names across America, appearing on the covers of weekly newsmagazines like *Time* and having dinner at the White House with the Kennedy family. Stravinsky seemed to revel in it, counting among his Hollywood friends everyone from Harpo Marx to Orson Welles. He was invited to the Playboy mansion, and frequently attended social affairs. The composer's name pops up on almost every millennial survey of the twentieth-century's hundred most influential people. Portions of *The Rite of Spring* are included in a time capsule aboard the *Voyager* spacecraft launched in 1977. He was the subject of several film documentaries. Balanchine, conversely, though almost equally famous, displayed little interest in the notion of posterity. The Harvard archives are overflowing with requests from filmmakers wanting to do a documentary on him, from publishers willing to supply a ghostwriter for an autobiography, and with hundreds of interview requests for magazines, pledge week cameos, television quiz shows, and children's shows. Like Stravinsky, he had become a contemporary icon. Their views were newsworthy and therefore solicited on virtually every subject.

Whereas Stravinsky seemed at ease living among the glitterati of Hollywood, the choreographer's stay there ended as soon as he was able to return to New York. The composer refused to teach, proclaiming that it sapped his creative energies. Balanchine remained a teacher, even if sporadically, for most of his life. From his student days in Petersburg, where he helped his friends to arrange dance programs, to his establishment of an important school in New York immediately following his immigration, he understood the value of consistent, disciplined training, and continued offering classes through his later years.

Stravinsky and Balanchine's similarities and differences were many—far too many to explore here further; yet in profiling their historic relationship, it will be useful to keep in mind their personality contrasts—contrasts as important to their collaborative success as their similarities. In the end, however, the fertility of their collaborations is rooted in certain deeply shared and permeating artistic beliefs: a mutually embraced ethnicity and a binding aesthetic; a methodical approach to creativity; a blending of pragmatism and idealism; a veneration of classical order and structure; a thoroughgoing knowledge of and affinity for the other's art. Taken collectively, these were the immutable elements that provided the common ground for their abiding friendship and artistic union. It was a union like no other in the annals of ballet; a singularly productive alliance first traceable to the intercession of Serge Diaghilev, the powerful and enormously influential sphinx of the Ballets Russes. It is with him that their epic journey began.

Chapter 2 At the Crossroads:
The Intercession of Diaghilev

The figure of Diaghilev fixed itself deeper and deeper in the realm of ambiguity. He seemed to me an impenetrable being, whose fame . . . contained elements of princely splendor, the onus of sexual irregularities, and rumors of terrible irascibility and haughtiness. . . . How difficult it was for me to understand how a man who did not compose, did not play, sing, paint or write, should become so famous. . . . I often asked myself, "What is his *real* relation to music, to painting, to the theater?" It took some fifteen years to understand, in part, the uniqueness and complexity of Diaghilev's genius.
—*Nicolas Nabokov,* Old Friends and New Music

Like the central panel of an ancient Russian triptych, Serge Pavlovich Diaghilev stands at the intersection of the Stravinsky-Balanchine union. In retracing the origins of the composer and choreographer's collaborations, the knotted relationship of the two men with the baronial director of the Ballets Russes must be considered. The contradictions so evident in the tangled web of Diaghilev's bigger-than-life image have provided the grist for numerous important biographical studies.[1] Little wonder, for his elusive personality as well as his heated interchanges with contemporaries, especially Stravinsky, reads like a romantic novel. Beyond the ambiguity and impenetrability to which Nabokov refers, an undercurrent of untrustworthiness was noted by many—Stravinsky and Balanchine included. Who was this messianic figure whose audacious young company jarred the international art world during the first quarter of the twentieth century? The broad reach of his influence quickly became manifest, first in the museums, concert halls, and theaters of Paris, then in Brussels, Berlin, London, and New York. More than any visionary of his day, Diaghilev widened the purview of artistic taste, opening new avenues of creative expression at a time when such exploration was anything but safe.

It was he who initially propelled the successes of Stravinsky and Balanchine, first individually, then as collaborators. Without his intercession, the path leading to their legendary accomplishments might never have been cut. Yet both men were reluctant to acknowledge his genius unconditionally—at least until after his death. Even then their testimony was often tepid. What was Diaghilev's role in helping to galvanize the partnership of Stravinsky and Balanchine during the brief but critical period from 1925 to 1928, when the three worked together? What circumstances led to the tensely conflicting interpersonal dynamics that frequently ensnarled their triangular relationship? How did the animosity both men increasingly felt toward Diaghilev partially alienate them from the man to whom they owed so much? And more consequentially, how did their ambivalent feelings about him drive them toward each other?

Diaghilev and Stravinsky maintained an extraordinarily productive, albeit abrasion-riddled, relationship long before Balanchine joined the Ballets Russes. Both were notoriously bullheaded. Each seemed eager to confront the other in a machismo tug of authority. Theirs was the classic attraction-avoidance relationship. Piercing the dementia marking almost every page of the diary of Diaghilev dancer Vaslav Nijinsky is Nijinsky's insight that Diaghilev "cannot live without Stravinsky, and Stravinsky cannot live without Diaghilev. They understand each other. Stravinsky is clever in the way he fights with Diaghilev. I know all their tricks, both Stravinsky's and Diaghilev's."[2] The composer's friendship with the "ringmaster," to use Stravinsky's epithet, constantly teetered on the edge of dissolution, and in the end, sadly, crumbled. Perhaps they were simply too much alike.

Diaghilev was a muddle of odious personal traits and eccentricities—"the wickedest man in Europe," as Lincoln Kirstein's autobiographical character Roger later characterized him in his first novel, *Flesh Is Heir*.[3] He could be unforgiving without cause, often lashing out vindictively. Like Stravinsky, he demanded deference. The maledictions each hurled at the other and the constant haggling over financial matters strained the glue of their alliance. In fact, Stravinsky often went uncompensated for his work with the Ballets Russes. Financial misunderstandings frequently ignited an intense squabbling, often measured in years of pouting. In numerous letters to his most trusted friends, Stravinsky complained sharply of Diaghilev's parsimony.[4] The impresario's correspondence was equally incriminating, lecturing Ballets Russes conductor Ernest Ansermet that Stravinsky was vilely preoccupied with money. Diaghilev was especially unnerved by Stravinsky's covert efforts to secure commissions outside the company. Such mutinous acts were unforgivable.

After Diaghilev's death, the composer's memories grew more benevolent. Even so, his tributes often had the ring of a rehearsed script, peppered with repeated anecdotes ranging from hearsay to fiction to nothing more informative than entertaining pre-curtain program notes. In countless newspaper and journal interviews, and in the later well-known series of conversation books with Robert Craft, it is never quite clear how much is gloss. In a November 1953 article for the *Atlantic Monthly* entitled "The Diaghilev I Knew," an uncharacteristically panegyric composer eulogized the grand Russian *barin* generously. Diaghilev wanted nothing for himself, Stravinsky declares, adding in a curious reversal that any hint of "commercialism was entirely foreign to his nature."[5]

With the release of Stravinsky's long inaccessible source materials, history's perception of the composer's partnership with Diaghilev and his company will change. For instance, if one watches several important interviews cut from Tony Palmer's epic 1982 documentary for London Television, *Aspects of Stravinsky,* one can better realize Stravinsky's pivotal place in Diaghilev's enterprise.[6] For beyond his personal skirmishes with Diaghilev, he moved freely throughout the Ballets Russes world, working closely with many of the troupe's principals. With remarkable élan, Stravinsky made his presence felt in Diaghilev's oligarchy (fig. 2.1).

The twenty-six-year-old, virtually untested composer first became affiliated with Diaghilev's upstart company at the moment of its 1909 inception. An even more inexperienced twenty-year-old Balanchine entered the company in late 1924, five years before Diaghilev's death. Stravinsky was ten years younger than Diaghilev; Balanchine thirty years his junior. The composer arrived at the bright sunrise of a promising, courageously collaborative experiment. Balanchine came on board when the potency of the once mighty juggernaut was beginning to fail, as Diaghilev's efforts to keep his troupe before the public's fickle

2.1 (Left to right) Ernest Ansermet, Serge Diaghilev, Igor Stravinsky, Sergey Prokofiev, Madrid, 1921 (The Harvard Theater Collection, the Houghton Library)

eye faltered. Diaghilev's insistence on staging productions judged "trendy" was a survival reflex triggered by the Parisian public's insatiable appetite for novelty. After all, he had a business to run. In the estimate of both Balanchine and Stravinsky, however, Diaghilev was corruptible. They feared that his artistic priorities were being increasingly misplaced, sacrificing content for titillation.

Their misgivings notwithstanding, Diaghilev and his company transfigured the careers of both men. The cosmopolite glitter of the Ballets Russes enjoyed considerable compass—a transoceanic range that quickly credentialed both the composer and choreographer. The company's annals chronicle the young century's need to stretch its artistic wings. Diaghilev assembled a brilliant constellation of dancers, composers, designers, and painters—an astonishing array of artists eager to risk all in catching the electricity of the moment. The exhilaration was palpable, the cause common, and for both Stravinsky and the much younger Balanchine, Monte Carlo and Paris provided the launching pad from which to test their ideas, despite endless internal schisms and cabals within the company.

Diaghilev shrewdly implemented one political gambit after another in keeping the company au courant. His behavior could be buoyant, listless, penurious, bellicose, quixotic, doctrinaire, meddlesome, invidious, even maniacal. One senses that his erratic actions were premeditated, as if being viewed as both tyrant and conundrum would augment his power. His ruthlessness was feared; his control was unbridled; and his strategy transpicuous in advancing his own vested interests—interests that were often carnally motivated. As the troupe's helmsman, Diaghilev claimed the right of intervention in both private and professional affairs. As Ballet Russes composer Vittorio Rieti recalled in an unreleased film clip from Palmer's 1982 documentary, "Diaghilev had everything in his hands, from every bar of the music to every aspect of the costumes to the choreography in which every step was under his control. He was absolutely the soul of the show." Such sweeping power helped ensure that productions unfolded as originally envisioned. But given Stravinsky and Balanchine's equally resolute desire to control the artistic message of their creations, Diaghilev's monolithic rule chaffed. Considering the confidence, if not obstinacy, of their constitutions, it is inevitable that clashes took place between the three men. Yet by the same token, their eagerness to confront convention provided a common ground. In essence, this was the homogenizing spirit animating the Ballets Russes.

The genesis of such a crusade is traceable to the end of the nineteenth century and an epoch-changing transformation of ballet and opera in Russia. Grand ballet as an independent art form, free from its historical appurtenance to opera, held little interest for the most innovative minds of the day. Other than Tchaikovsky, the roster of hired-hand composers who provided little more than humdrum accompaniments for the Russian ballet is musically forgettable. Moreover, an aging Marius Petipa, who with Tchaikovsky created such scintillating masterworks as *The Sleeping Beauty, The Nutcracker,* and *Swan Lake* during the 1890s at the Maryinsky, now found himself a relic in a rapidly waning era.

The Imperial Ballet was in a state of decline, but a decline whose ashes created the opportunity for rebirth. Diaghilev, along with other members of the *Mir iskusstva* circle ("World of Art," the title of his influential journal disseminating the group's innovative ideas), seized the moment. They stood at the gateway to a new era, defiantly challenging the Imperial Theater's decadent canon. The young Diaghilev glimpsed the future, and knew how to market it. He also knew that the seeds of revolution were there. As Richard Taruskin adjudges, the Russian ballet had become "a kind of *belle au bois dormant. . . .* It was *Mir iskusstva* that planted the awakening kiss."[7]

A proprietary sense of Neonationalism, as it came to be called, was in the air. The staples of the Ballets Russes repertory lay anchored in the scores of late nineteenth- and early twentieth-century Russian composers: Arensky, Balakirev, Borodin, Glazunov, Glinka, Larinov, Liadov, Rimsky-Korsakov, Tcherepnine, and others. The exotica of these works not only delighted Parisian theatergoers; they would soon bewitch American audiences as well, as the reviews of Diaghilev's earliest tour of the United States confirm. Diaghilev's company was, in the words of Olin Downes, who reviewed a February 1916 performance in Boston, "the last word in all that is gorgeous and intoxicating in Oriental art," although the convenient tag of "orientalism" was often sloppily applied.

The historic trilogy of Russian ballets that Stravinsky composed and Diaghilev produced—not in Petersburg but in Paris—guaranteed the company's eminence. Although not particularly expansive in its musical horizons, *The Firebird,* which premiered on 25 June 1910 at the Théâtre National de l'Opéra with choreography by Michel Fokine, immediately established Stravinsky's facility (especially his "witchery of modern orchestration," as André Levinson described it) in matching Fokine and Diaghilev's sense of orientalism. *Petrushka,* first staged a year later, on 13 June 1911, at the Théâtre du Châtelet, with Nijinsky's legendary performance and Fokine's choreography, represented a new plateau in the composer's musical and theatrical growth. The score was an emancipation, releasing Stravinsky from the baldly nationalistic constraints his contemporaries had neither the talent nor the cheekiness to transcend. And finally, the cataclysmic *Rite of Spring,* which premiered on 29 May 1913 at the Théâtre des Champs-Elysées with Nijinsky's choreography, marked a genuine sea change—the "birth certificate of modernism," as Pierre Boulez anointed the work.

Stravinsky involved himself directly in shaping all these ballets, especially in rehearsals. With *Firebird,* Tamara Karsavina recalls, he worked with the dancers individually, exercising extraordinary patience: "Often times he came early to the theatre before a rehearsal began in order to play for me over and over again some specially difficult passage. . . . There was no impatience in him with my slow understanding." She remembers too that Stravinsky's whole body vibrated while playing the piano; he punctuated accents with his head as "the rhythm lived in, and at times took possession of[,] his body."[8] He could also become agitated, behaving like a "madman" as others remember. Entrusted with *The Rite*'s premiere, conductor Pierre Monteux remembered Stravinsky rehearsing the work at the piano for Diaghilev and him for the first time: "Before he got very far I was convinced he was raving mad. . . . The very walls resounded as Stravinsky pounded away, occasionally stamping his feet and jumping up and down to accentuate the force of the music." Even during rehearsals, and again at the keyboard, he would tear through the music at breakneck speed, breaking the strings of four pianos in a single week's rehearsal.[9]

With both *Petrushka* and *The Rite,* one was compelled to rethink deep-seated, ossified attitudes not only about music but also about how music and dance might be coupled. But the chronicles of these three seismically disruptive works rest beyond the scope of this book. With the exception of Balanchine's 1949 restaging of *The Firebird,* they have little to do with the Stravinsky-Balanchine nexus. The seeds that eventually blossomed into the full flower of these works, however, are relevant, for they allow a window on Stravinsky's early contact with Diaghilev.[10]

The "awakening kiss" of Russian ballet led to a synthesis of collaborative artistic expression that combined music, dance, painting—virtually all the elements of theater—into a publicly graspable, if not always coherently unified, form. Diaghilev's highly acclaimed 1906 exhibit of Russian art in Paris, including examples of Mir iskusstva's work, marked a turning point. The die was cast. Thereafter Diaghilev returned to Paris annually, especially commanding attention for his lavish opera productions. The fantasy and ostentation of opera appealed to the French. Except for the prohibitive financial cost (especially the high price tags of such enormously popular singers as Feodor Chaliapin), Diaghilev might well have continued staging such successful productions exclusively. But box-office revenues were insufficient to sustain future seasons of opera alone. Largely as a consequence of financial exigency, Diaghilev was forced to mount ballets as a cost-effective way of remaining before the Parisian public. He first turned to Michel Fokine, whose *Le Pavillon d'Armide* (to the music of Nicholas Tcherepnine, with sets and costumes by Alexandre Benois, and a cast that included Nijinsky) premiered in Paris on 18 May 1909.

Officially instituted that same year, the Ballets Russes never performed in its homeland. Diaghilev's experiments and publicly flamboyant lifestyle soon precipitated his dismissal from the Maryinsky Theater in St. Petersburg. The interdiction was necessary, the administration claimed. Diaghilev had undermined the inviolable traditions of the academy long associated with the Imperial Theaters. His course was thus clear: he would assemble a coterie of artists, including aspiring young composers such as Stravinsky, who were willing to stage the kind of ballet capable of seducing Paris. The young composer's orchestral piece *Fireworks* furnished the passport allowing his entry into this dazzling world. Both Diaghilev and Fokine had attended the premiere in mid-1909, conducted by Alexander Siloti at one of his prestigious St. Petersburg concerts. (Diaghilev had heard Stravinsky play the piano reduction earlier as an audition.) The brilliant score immediately struck Fokine with its orchestral vigor—just the kind of panache that would complement his forthcoming ballet, *The Firebird.*

Upon hearing *Fireworks,* Diaghilev invited Stravinsky to orchestrate two Chopin piano works (the Nocturne in A-flat, op. 32, no. 2, and the Grand Valse Brillante, op. 18), serving as the opening and closing sections, respectively, of Fokine's 1909 *Les Sylphides.*[11] Diaghilev next asked the obviously facile and eager composer to complete a few quick turnaround pieces, including an arrangement of a short Edvard Grieg piano piece entitled *Kobold,* with which Diaghilev wished to showcase Nijinsky.[12] Such commissions allowed Stravinsky to work with Nijinsky, Léon Bakst, Karsavina, Benois, and other luminaries in Diaghilev's circle. But it was primarily his association with Fokine that proves instructive here.

Stravinsky's later, harsh reproof of the choreographer as an uncooperative and churlish collaborator notwithstanding, the composer initially believed that Fokine had completely changed the face of ballet. Even though they had worked together on a few of the earlier, less well-known works mentioned above, *Firebird* marked their first significant collaboration. How much of a true collaboration it was, however, is arguable. It was more in keeping with the Petipa-Tchaikovsky association, whereby Petipa typically specified a certain number of composed-to-order passages. Stravinsky likewise served at Fokine's mercy. Still, such strictures proved a useful lesson for the young composer. For one thing, he quickly learned to deal with artistic boundaries that surely constrained his imagination. Indeed, self-imposed restrictions, especially regarding the temporal dimension of ballet, later became a hallmark of his approach to dance. Although it is true, as we shall see, that Stravinsky and Balanchine pre-compositionally mapped out separate sections of their ballets with great temporal precision, still, their working method hardly paralleled the composer's with Fokine. By the time Stravinsky began working with Balanchine, he was no longer willing to be held hostage by a storyline whose narrative constricted his own inventiveness—as he later complained *Firebird* had done—nor would Balanchine have been interested in such mimed storytelling. But what really irked Stravinsky was Fokine's dismissive view of him as a neophyte. The young composer's music was viewed as but a subsidiary accompaniment to the experienced Fokine's choreographic conceptions (at least so Stravinsky later carped).

Although Fokine's concept of the scenario may have been clear, Stravinsky recalls that Diaghilev's "artistic committee" pieced together the action. As Karsavina also remembered, "Around the table sat wise men . . . drinking weak tea and hatching daring ideas. . . . [Diaghilev] kept a vigilant eye on his collaborators."[13] Included in this group were Bakst, Benois, the composer and writer Walter Nouvel, Alexander Golovin (who prepared the sets and most of the costumes), and other trusted Diaghilev contributors. Stravinsky's charge was simple: compose and deliver the music to Fokine, section by section. The choreographer then immediately worked out the stage action for each page of the score. As Fokine remarked in his *Memoirs,* his collaboration with Stravinsky was close, and he set about choreographing each section of the ballet as it was composed: "Stravinsky visited me with his first sketches and basic ideas, he played them for me, I demonstrated the scenes to him. At my request he broke up his national themes into short phrases corresponding to the separate moments of a scene, separate gestures and poses."[14]

According to Karsavina, when Stravinsky's music did not match Fokine's often on-the-spot inspiration, the composer was enjoined to rewrite the passage. Even though Stravinsky participated fully in rehearsals, still, at that early juncture he was hardly in a position to protest too vehemently any *pas d'action* that to his way of thinking wandered aimlessly. But in fact the confident (and by his own honest assessment, "arrogant") young composer did protest, and Fokine, sometimes against his better judgment, not only listened but incorporated Stravinsky's suggestions. In the ballet's memorable final scene, for example, Fokine originally planned to close the ballet with a dance, but Stravinsky objected, and thus the stilted, coronation-like wedding of Ivan and Princess Unearthly Beauty concludes the work (using costumes from Diaghilev's earlier staging of *Boris Godunov*). "Perhaps [Stravinsky] wished to concentrate on the ending a specific musical effect," Fokine mused. "This was the only place in the ballet on which we disagreed."[15]

Here Fokine's memory fails him. An informative compositional draft of the ballet (probably the rehearsal manuscript from which Stravinsky played; there are abundant piano fingerings and annotations in his own hand) demonstrates that in the end, Stravinsky made concession after concession at Fokine's behest.[16] Extensive sections are excised, shortened, expanded, repositioned. Compositionally, Stravinsky's first conceptions make good musical sense. It appears, therefore, that the alterations were frequently made solely to oblige the choreographer's wishes. Often passages seem no more than filler—the kind of profligate marking of time that ran completely counter to the composer's musically unwavering focus. Especially instructive is Stravinsky's reworking of the Infernal Dance of Kastchei, which choreographically, Fokine remembers, had "great difficulties." Consequently, it demanded considerable reworking on the composer's part, though ultimately Stravinsky found Fokine's staging ineffectual.

As Stravinsky swiftly rose in the company's hierarchy, he increasingly voiced his resentment at Diaghilev's and Fokine's attempts to reformulate his musical ideas. His letters speak of Fokine as an artist who had lost his way. As *Petrushka* evolved, the composer feared that Diaghilev would also ask Fokine to choreograph *The Rite of Spring,* the earth-shattering ballet that was eventually assigned to Nijinsky.[17] As though the ferocity of *The Rite* was not enough to deal with, Nijinsky felt himself under siege, especially given his servility to Diaghilev, the omnipotent pharaoh who was jealous of anybody close to his "show pony," as Nabokov cruelly described Nijinsky. Even as *The Rite* began to take shape in his mind in early 1913, the sexually conflicted Nijinsky met and eventually married (that same autumn) Romola de Pulszky. A storm was brewing, for Diaghilev was not about to concede the marriage without a fight. Still, as rehearsals for the new ballet went forward that spring, Diaghilev turned his gaze to *The Rite;* for it seems he was more interested in provoking a pressworthy scandal with the unprecedented ballet than in anything else.

As political unrest escalated in his homeland, Stravinsky basked in his newfound Parisian notoriety. After the brilliant theater successes of 1910–13, the adversities of war took their toll on both men. Rather than return to St. Petersburg, Stravinsky retreated to the Alpine towns of neutral Switzerland (where so many Russians, including Tchaikovsky, summered) in self-imposed exile. Diaghilev scurried to keep his company afloat, seeking whatever jobs could be found. As his finances dwindled, Stravinsky pressed Diaghilev, accusing him of withholding the composer's rightful royalties. And as the war intensified, Stravinsky and Diaghilev's fragile partnership grew more frictional. But lured by several incentives, including the chance to reenter the Parisian limelight, the composer rejoined the company in 1920. He was especially attracted by the prospect of working with Picasso (whom he had known since 1917) on a new ballet that Diaghilev had in mind. The painter was equally eager to work with Stravinsky, and their collaboration resulted in *Pulcinella,* the farcical commedia dell'arte ballet that premiered in Paris during the spring of 1920.

Although their views often differed, Stravinsky remembered that collaborating with a painter whose work struck a sympathetic chord with him was especially tantalizing. *Pulcinella* developed amid Diaghilev's constant remonstrations. The impresario's initial rejection of Picasso's designs was "very brusque," as the composer recalled, but an indignant Stravinsky felt even more mistreated by Diaghilev's reproaches concerning the score. Having achieved a significant measure of international renown by this point, Stravinsky knew his own marquee value.

The program booklets of the Ballets Russes demonstrate how prominently Stravinsky was promoted over the years. Photographs through the 1920s continue to bill him as the company's star composer. He is marketed as "the amazing Stravinsky," and "the bold innovator of Harmonies." Yet given what he interpreted as shabby treatment by Diaghilev, the composer was now more than ever disinclined to limit himself to the orbit of Diaghilev's Paris. He covertly resorted to enlisting the help of Ernest Ansermet in deluding Diaghilev about commissions being arranged quietly outside the company. As correspondence in the Sacher Stiftung at Basel proves, for example, Stravinsky entreated the conductor—perhaps out of a combined sense of guilt and mistrust—to suppress the details of a possible tour of America with Leopold Stokowski's Philharmonic Orchestra of New York.

Stravinsky's unedited correspondence rails against Diaghilev's frequent diatribes. His letters turn steadily more contemptuous, initially expressing questions about Diaghilev's morals, his integrity, and the soundness of his artistic judgment, later accusing him of outright duplicity. Eventually, Stravinsky discounts Diaghilev as no more than a subordinate figure in his life—a distortion if ever there was one. Not only did Diaghilev commission the composer's earliest works, but he also staunchly supported them at an early point in Stravinsky's career when he was not in a political position to raise his own defense. Diaghilev passionately supported Stravinsky as one does a family member, in the face of stern opposition. Likewise, and even late in his life, Stravinsky, off the record, would defend Diaghilev. As letters in the Sacher Stiftung show, when the composer's biographer Eric Walter White included slightly derogatory remarks about the impresario in a draft sent to Stravinsky, the composer became enraged. Criticizing Diaghilev remained his privilege alone.

By the time of Diaghilev's death in Venice on 19 August 1929, the two were no longer speaking. In his *Autobiography,* Stravinsky remarks that the last time he saw Diaghilev was in Paris, when they boarded the same train at the Gare du Nord to take their separate ways to London. Diaghilev was in the company of his protégé, the sixteen-year-old Igor Markevitch. The young man was to be the last shooting star in Diaghilev's pantheon—"the new Igor," as he was grandly christened by *Le Monde Musical* (or the "half-Igor," as Prokofiev spoofed)—an epithet that angered Stravinsky all the more.[18] A pianist, a composer, and eventually a conductor, Markevitch remembered that Diaghilev spoke "with great bitterness" when Stravinsky defected to Ida Rubinstein's company in 1928 to write *Le Baiser de la Fée,* which premiered that November, only six months after the Ballets Russes production of Balanchine's *Apollon Musagète.*

The collapse of his friendship with Diaghilev haunted the composer for the remainder of his life. Despite their constant bickering, an abiding affection had persevered and even ripened during that unequalled period of artistic foment. Early attempts at reconciliation had no lasting effect. Letters exchanged in 1926, for instance, are astonishingly conciliatory as each begs the other's forgiveness. But whatever temporary rapprochement was reached soon vanished. In Palmer's trimmed interview with Soulima Stravinsky, the composer's son confirms that "Diaghilev's death was hard on my father. It was as if it was a brother or more, even more."[19] Soulima remembers too that it was Diaghilev's kaleidoscopic world of pomp and splendor that not only charmed him but also continued to enthrall his father, regardless of his personal scuffles with the impresario. Always a man of ritual and of the theater, the nomadic Stravinsky found a haven in the Ballets Russes—just as he would eventually consider the New York City Ballet his home.

Long after Diaghilev's death, Stravinsky's friend the writer Christopher Isherwood records in a diary entry of 1958 that Igor and his wife Vera still included Diaghilev as a recurring part of their dinner conversation. Stravinsky "used to tell Vera all about [Diaghilev's] boyfriends. . . . Igor said that Diaghilev surrounded himself with people who were inventive. 'And inventions,' Igor added, 'are the only things worth stealing.'"[20] Thirteen years later, Stravinsky died. The composer's burial site, only a few headstones away from Diaghilev's on the beautiful isle of San Michele off the coast of Venice, symbolizes a final, bittersweet reunion.

2.2 George Balanchine, around 1925 (The Tang Teaching
Museum and Art Gallery Collection, Skidmore College)

In an examination of Balanchine's relationship with Diaghilev, their age difference becomes pertinent. The fifty-two-year-old worldly wise impresario saw
the twenty-year-old unproven dancer as a potentially gifted but naive, untu-
tored apprentice (fig. 2.2). From the start Diaghilev expected submissiveness
from the young man. Yet the already cocksure Balanchine immediately contested his prescribed role. The two first met in the autumn of 1924. Balanchine
had just fled Russia, where socialist realism was stamping its imprimatur on the
commodious proven ballet classics; he recalls needing to test his own dancing
and choreographic abilities. Balanchine was instinctively drawn to unortho-
doxy. As a young man he had enrolled in the Imperial Ballet Academy in Petrograd and was soon being admonished by his instructors for a hard-edged "ambition" that was considered entirely improper. "I was in trouble," he wrote,
"because I made a pas de deux in which I lay on the floor and the girl leaned

over in an arabesque and touched me with her lips. That was thought indecent and at age 15, I was nearly thrown out."[21] His detractors instantly charged him with a dangerously libidinous inclination to eroticize dance, one of many tarnishing contrarieties that were symptomatic of the evils of modernism.

By his own description, Balanchine was a "hippie," questioning the sanctity of tradition and seeking alternatives. He was among a group of student petitioners who in 1919 drafted a "Program of Activity and Objectives of the Student Committee" of the Imperial Ballet Academy, demanding a broader exposure to the arts, not just to ballet. Yuri Slonimsky remembers that Balanchine took an interest in the poetry of Lermontov, Mayakovsky, and Pushkin, all of whom were proscribed by the faculty before the Revolution. He participated in experimental theater productions that took their literary cues from such writers as Traubeg and Yutkevich. He read heterodox publications calculated to inflame, including Kryzhitsky's 1922 *Eccentrism.* There was also a distinctly American flavor to several of the plays Balanchine attended in Petrograd in 1923. Many adopted jazz idioms and comedic characters based on Charlie Chaplin. Balanchine organized his own Young Ballet troupe, in which novelty, no matter how outrageous, was permitted. He consequently caught the attention of the press, as a 1923 review in the *Krasnaya Gazeta* establishes:

> From the old classic adagio to modernism (a foxtrot), [Balanchine's] style for the moment involves a skillful combination of extremes. . . . Balanchine is bold and insolent, but in his insolence one can see genuine creativity and beauty. Balanchine's character dancers are much less successful than the classical and abstract ones. They lack vividness and color, strong temperamental movements. Although in the classical work he does misuse poses, he combines them in such an interesting way and creates such beautiful if unexpected transitions that one can grudgingly excuse this defect. . . . From the stage has come a burst of fresh air—the Young Ballet has proven its "viability."[22]

At the same time, Balanchine claimed that the walls of the ballet world in which he felt imprisoned were closing in. Lenin's Committee on Education and the Arts was just beginning to ban all artistic "deviations"—anything that did not conform to Communist precepts of what propagandistic art should communicate. By 1922 mass deportations had begun. The Soviet Union offered a bleak future for creative thinkers who felt that expressing independent ideas would probably meet with considerable resistance from the Bolshevik government.[23]

Still, throughout 1922–24, despite the evident risks, Balanchine sided with avant-garde preconstructionists like Bruni, Puni, Klyun, Malevich, Rodchenko,

Tatlin, and Tairov. And he especially identified with the physicality of the Moscow Theater's Vsevolod Meyerhold.[24] (Already at age nine, for example, Balanchine had taken part in a Meyerhold production of Gluck's *Orfeo ed Euridice* that incorporated the director's theories of "planes in action.")[25] Such innovative artists touched an inherently rebellious strain in the young dancer. They envisioned a new world order of dispassionate precision and clarity, rejecting the mawkishly narrative representations that surfeited nineteenth-century dance. Their works explored the realm of abstraction, particularly in terms of the cubist influences of around 1909–13. Theirs was a lesson well-learned, prompting Balanchine to think about fundamental geometric issues, including the pulling and pushing of symmetries with asymmetries, the kind of thing that is so apparent in the Stravinsky scores he eventually choreographed.

Branded extremists, some of these renegade artists eventually surrendered to the utilitarian ideology of the Lenin regime in the early 1920s. With each capitulation, the free-spirited Balanchine knew he would be forced to choose between working within what he considered the politics of repression or going elsewhere to try out his burgeoning ideas. Actually there was no choice; artistically he was compelled to leave. But although he never forgot his Russian roots, he did not depart with the same nostalgic feelings that Stravinsky had manifested in his settings of Afanasiev's deeply Russian folkloristic fables, composed during his homesick exile in Switzerland during World War I. Stravinsky's works mused longingly of a motherland lost. But the Russia in which Balanchine spent his earliest years was strikingly different from Stravinsky's (and Diaghilev's). The political rumblings in their homeland greatly disturbed Stravinsky and Diaghilev, but it disturbed them from a safe distance; their physical well-being was never in question. Their pre-Revolutionary lives in tsarist Petersburg were, for the most part, quite comfortable.

Balanchine's artistic schooling, however, took place in a stygian world of famine and terror under the martial law of a scorching civil war. The scars were indelible. In the years following the bloodbath of the 1917 October Revolution, the thirteen-year-old Balanchine feared for his life, particularly during the harsh winter of 1919–20. Eventually the withering toll of that period cost him his health, including a lung. To survive he was forced to steal food from the Bolshevik troops—troops that eventually closed and occupied the Imperial Ballet Academy in which he was training. Balanchine vividly remembered standing in the crowd below the palace balcony of prima ballerina assoluta Mathilda Kchessinska as Lenin addressed the public: "I remember hearing him that night. I had gone with a group of my fellow students from the school. . . . All of us thought the man on the balcony must be a lunatic. Then we were young; we did not understand the Revolution." These were frightening, enduring impressions that left the young man first perplexed, then embittered. But the hard times brought about by the October Revolution produced at least one applicable benefit: as late as 1961, Balanchine remembered that "poverty taught me to be very skillful, economical and resourceful in my art."[26]

Given the different environments in which they lived their childhoods, it is understandable that he and Stravinsky reconstructed their past through different sides of a prism. Nowhere was that more apparent than in the outspoken, contrasting remarks each made during their brokered revisit to the Soviet Union in 1962, at the height of the Cold War. When his plane touched down that September, Stravinsky immediately reaffirmed his roots, declaring that he was still Russian to the bone. But Balanchine, upon landing in Moscow a month later (in the middle of the Cuban Missile Crisis), snapped sharply to someone who welcomed him back to his homeland that he was American, not Russian.[27] The composer and choreographer may have agreed about artistic conceptions once they began collaborating under Diaghilev's aegis, but they arrived at them by routes that could not have been more different.

It was thirty-eight years before that visit, in July 1924, that Georgi Balanchivadze, Alexandra Danilova, Nicolas Efimov, and Tamara Gevergeva, billed as the Principal Dancers of the Russian State Ballet, left the Soviet Union, thanks to the efforts of their manager Vladimir Dimitriev, who managed to secure permission for a summer tour. The itinerant troupe performed throughout Germany, where a large colony of White Russians helped fill the house. The dancers performed wherever they could: in dance halls, beer gardens, even an asylum, doing whatever they had to to make ends meet. Just as their fortunes were waning, they were contracted for a month's engagement at the Empire Music Hall in London. Reviews were mixed, but Balanchine, who was choreographing some of the programmed ballets, was gaining notice. Fatefully, the Ballets Russes's Boris Kochno and Anton Dolin attended one of the performances and immediately contacted Diaghilev. Shortly thereafter, in Paris, Balanchine and his small traveling troupe auditioned for the Ballets Russes director and a few company principals.[28]

Serge Lifar was present at the audition. In an unreleased film clip from Palmer's Stravinsky biopic, Lifar recorded his impressions of what proved a most auspicious encounter:

> So I was taken to Madame [Misia] Sert's by Diaghilev to see the Soviet dancers who
> had chosen freedom. They did not invite the directress, who was Nijinska. . . . I went
> to Madame Sert's, and in the large salon I saw the young dancers. There were four of
> them. I looked at them and saw that they were dancers of my generation, and I said
> to Diaghilev—knowing nothing about their qualities—I said to Diaghilev, "We
> must take these youngsters," and Diaghilev agreed. And when Nijinska learned that
> I had helped to recruit members to the troupe, she immediately left the com-
> pany. . . . It is because of what I said that Balanchine was in the troupe . . . and Dia-
> ghilev entrusted the creative side to himself.[29]

When Palmer asked Lifar for more about Nijinska's departure, Lifar claimed
credit: "I had wreaked havoc in that extraordinary . . . warrior-like family."

As a Maryinsky soloist, Danilova, who performed an excerpt from *The Firebird,* resented auditioning for what she considered an unknown and inferior
company. But Balanchine, seizing the opportunity, danced a pas de deux with
Geva to the music of Scriabin that he had choreographed shortly before leaving
Russia. Diaghilev took note. By 1924 his troupe was fighting to survive, and talented Russian dancers were scarce. Geva recalled in her interview for Palmer
that in the 1920s "Diaghilev's corps was awful . . . just absolutely terrible. . . .
What the kids dance now could never have been even attempted by the dancers
in the Diaghilev company." On her former husband's relationship with Diaghilev, Geva told Palmer,

> George at that time certainly had a dream that he never lost. And he was sure of him-
> self. I don't think he ever had a moment's doubt about his talent. They got along all
> right because in a way Diaghilev [had] met his match. Diaghilev considered himself
> a great musician, and then he met George who is a better musician. That took a bit
> of wind out of Diaghilev's sails. See, Diaghilev always mixed his emotionalism, his
> personal life, with the person he promoted. Outside of George there was no man
> that was not emotionally connected with Diaghilev. And here was a man that was his
> own boss, and his own man, and who was a wonderful musician with talent.

Soon after the Paris audition, Diaghilev and Balanchine met again in London, where, evidently without notice, the expatriate dancer was summoned to
choreograph a short work for several Ballets Russes dancers. Ninette de Valois
recalls, "Of all things [Balanchine] arranged a little number for the five or six of
us to the *Funeral March* of Chopin. . . . Diaghilev came in about two hours
later and looked at it with Kochno and Grigoriev. That was the start."[30] While
it marked the start for Balanchine, it also hastened the end of Bronislova Nijinska's association with the company. What many considered Diaghilev's impul-

sive appointment of a very young, virtually untested choreographer sent an unmistakable signal: Nijinska would be locked out of Diaghilev's male conclave. By the time Balanchine officially joined the company in Monte Carlo (12 January 1925), Nijinska had announced her imminent departure.

The impresario's abrupt shift in allegiance among his various in-house choreographers was not unusual. Constantly in search of new ideas, he displayed no compunction in offending his veteran dancers, painters, composers, and especially choreographers. During the winter of 1924–25, Diaghilev not only desperately needed fresh dancers, he needed a new choreographer—and he needed one immediately. Balanchine's situation was even more dire: he needed a steady job. The urgency of their circumstances led to a hastily arranged pact in late 1924. The young dancer instantly found himself choreographing for a world-class company that was still closely watched and judged by the influential Parisian art world.

His first assignment was in Monte Carlo. The Ballets Russes enjoyed the patronage of the Monte Carlo Opera Company, and opera productions meant regularly injected ballet scenes. Choreography had to be manufactured quickly. Nijinska alone had created more than a dozen production ballets, which had earned her the tightfisted admiration of Stravinsky, both as a choreographer and dancer. But despite Nijinska's successes, Balanchine was not about to let his opportunity slip away. His confidence was buoyed by his own youthful performances in opera while still in Russia, including appearances in *Prince Igor, The Magic Flute, Tannhäuser,* and importantly, as will become evident, Gluck's *Orfeo ed Euridice*. In the fall of 1923, while still in Russia, Balanchine prepared the choreography for a production of Rimsky-Korsakov's opera *Le Coq d'Or*.[31]

Given these experiences, Balanchine made known his readiness to fill Nijinska's anticipated vacancy. During his first year with the company, he produced a dozen ballets for opera productions, including Ravel's *L'Enfant et les Sortilèges* (with Ravel at the piano for some of the rehearsals). Again it is Valois who recalls that while Balanchine danced "somewhat indifferently" in the company, he excelled in his preparation of the opera choreography from the first: "The quality he could put into an opera ballet was absolutely extraordinary. But he was always very funny. He took it all as a huge joke, took all the opera ballets as a huge joke; he wasn't the least bit pompous, but he obviously was going to be the coming one when Nijinska left. We knew he was going to take over."[32]

It was a heavy gauntlet that Diaghilev threw down before Balanchine. But meeting one deadline after another proved invaluable. To the end of his life Balanchine was known as a remarkably adept and flexible choreographer, capable of working with astonishing speed under almost any conditions. He accepted every challenge and, as with Stravinsky, the tighter the box, the more fertile his imagination. Moreover, he, like Stravinsky, gained a special appreciation for the operas of Verdi, staging *La Traviata, Un Bal Masqué,* and *Rigoletto* in 1927, 1928, and 1929, respectively. "From Verdi's way of dealing with the chorus," Balanchine recalled, "I learned how to handle the corps de ballet, the ensemble, the soloists—how to make the soloists stand out against the corps de ballet and when to give them a rest."[33]

At the outset, however, the critics were by no means universally enamored of Balanchine's work. Cyril Beaumont thought Diaghilev too hasty in choosing him; Lifar contended that at times Balanchine's choreography profoundly disappointed Diaghilev. The tautly strung, highly competitive community into which Balanchine was dropped was at first skeptical of his abilities. Hostility was evident. The triumphant years of the troupe were for the most part over, and nerves became increasingly frayed. A young Lincoln Kirstein, seeing the company perform in London and recording his impressions in a diary entry of June 1926, expressed dismay at the tenuous situation into which Diaghilev had descended: "Diaghilev is bankrupt; Lord Rothermere will put up no more money; he must play in a vaudeville theater; Stravinsky had deserted to Ida Rubinstein. . . . I expected more. Not much dancing; not enough dancers."[34] Diaghilev's appointment tested Balanchine's mettle, and the young man responded with an unflappable self-assurance that rapidly earned his colleagues' respect. In fact, the confident choreographer may have won the company's affection a little too quickly, for Diaghilev soon grew fearful of losing control. Moreover, Balanchine's imprudently announced suspicions about his employer's artistic deficiencies engendered an uncomfortable standoff, each man growing increasingly wary of the other.

From the start, Balanchine espoused strong personal beliefs about dance. Those closest to Diaghilev foresaw an inevitable collision. Would Balanchine be able to subjugate himself to Diaghilev while throttling his own choreographic vision? Although he could sense Balanchine's raw talent, Diaghilev also judged him culturally crude. From his angle, Balanchine resented Diaghilev's patronization, and with considerable esprit flaunted his coarseness and ignorance. He goaded Diaghilev, taking pleasure in mocking the pretensions of the effete society in which the aristocratic impresario moved. Balanchine was proud of his Georgian rather than Slavic descent, he made very clear. Culturally, he identified himself with Mediterraneans, not Russians.

Cultural anthropologists argue that the world into which we are born is more embedded in us than those in which we later reside. Both Stravinsky and Balanchine were creatures of their past. But Diaghilev was intent on forcing his young choreographer to assimilate a new environment, even at the cost of forswearing his old. Diaghilev had not rejected his own past; on the contrary, Serge Grigoriev's accounts of Diaghilev speak of his sincerely felt love for Russia. But business was business, and those in his employ would become westernized. Diaghilev immediately took it upon himself to enact a transformation of his newest child. He changed the young dancer's name from Balanchivadze to the anglicized Balanchine. He attempted to transfuse his own worldly savoirfaire. He introduced the young man to the treasures of Europe, particularly in Italy, where museum visits became an important part of Balanchine's practicum. And as the young man's horizons widened, so did his impertinence in repulsing Diaghilev's attempts to remake him:

> We were in Florence together. Diaghilev led me to the Uffizi Gallery, sat me in front of Botticelli's *La Primavera,* and said, "Look at it." Then he went off with Lifar and Kochno to have lunch. It wasn't very nice on his part. When Diaghilev returned . . . [he] asked me, "Well do you understand anything?" Of course I had seen that *La Primavera* was a wonderful painting, but I was angry with Diaghilev. Lifar and Kochno were his favorites, he dressed them well and fed them well. And, of course, they played at being great connoisseurs of art. To spite Diaghilev, I said that I didn't understand a thing: well, a painting like any other, so what? Nothing special.[35]

In deliberately prodding Diaghilev, Balanchine was no less belligerent than Stravinsky in contesting the entrepreneur's assumptions. Quite happy with his rough edges, Balanchine resented Diaghilev's efforts at enculturation, as well as his sciolism and blatant political posturing. One can only imagine how differently the well-heeled Riviera society struck Balanchine. As Kirstein later observed, Balanchine must have been baffled: "At the age of twenty-one he found himself entrusted with great artistic responsibility. The technical competence . . . was unperturbed even by the united opposition and virtual revolt of Diaghileff's troupe." Kirstein further implies that Balanchine must have felt "ridiculous" given Diaghilev's insistence on staging the "preposterous" productions he knew would prove marketable. "It was not easy for an inexperienced youth from early Soviet Russia to understand the depths of cynicism, such heights of disinterestedness based on so much human experience and cultivation and breeding."[36]

In the middle of this jarring adjustment, Balanchine cussedly refused Diaghilev the respect he demanded. Conversely, his devotion to Stravinsky approached piety—undeservedly so, in Diaghilev's estimate. Feeling snubbed, the impresario denounced Balanchine's fondness for the composer as an act of idolatry, as well as an intentional display of insolence. Simultaneously, Stravinsky and Balanchine grew more simpatico. It was disconcerting for the paternalistic Diaghilev to witness the bonding of his old colleague Stravinsky with the young, resistant Balanchine. So vexatious was the choreographer's intractability that in the fall of 1928, only months after the premiere of *Apollon Musagète,* Diaghilev considered dismissing him. The two quarreled over certain passages that Diaghilev wished to cut from the ballet. His decision to cut the Terpsichore variation, for example, is well documented. As Tamara Geva recalls in an unreleased film clip, the decision was, not surprisingly, politically motivated:

> Apparently one of the variations in *Apollo* was not to Diaghilev's taste. He thought it too long, too repetitious . . . and he told George that the variation was no good, and that he didn't like the music. George said, "It is your dancer that isn't any good," and it was Nikita [Alice Nikitina]. . . . George wouldn't change the variation so Diaghilev took it out. And one day, in Covent Garden, just before the performance of *Apollo,* Diaghilev rushed in looking for George absolutely in such a state of fear that George said he was trembling. . . . "Put the variation in quickly . . . Stravinsky is in the audience." So George had to grab the lady who was dancing Terpsichore and quickly rehearse her just before she went onstage. That shows you very much the relationship between Diaghilev and Balanchine, and who was the boss.

Geva's recollection also goes some distance in explaining the antagonism that marked the Balanchine-Diaghilev relationship. Shortly after their clash over *Apollo,* Grigoriev recalled that when he asked Diaghilev whether he had remembered to renew Balanchine's contract, the entrepreneur immediately retaliated by threatening to dismiss the choreographer, though the altercation was eventually resolved. Still, for all their wrangling, Diaghilev helped transform the young man's aesthetics, and Balanchine knew it. Twenty years after Diaghilev's death, in a 1949 issue of *Dance News,* he paid rare homage to Diaghilev's ingenuity, there referring to him as a patron of the arts and a man of high culture.

But there was never a sense of personal gratitude nor a hint of closeness. As with Stravinsky, Balanchine's relationship with Diaghilev reveals a deeply rooted ambivalence. Balanchine realized that he owed the launching of his star to Diaghilev's intercession. But Diaghilev's ignominious behavior—at least as Balanchine saw it—was nettlesome. He had tried to rob Balanchine of his self-sovereignty. He saw Balanchine's youth as a license to shape the choreographer's thinking. To Diaghilev's disillusion, Balanchine turned to Stravinsky, not him, for both professional advice and personal understanding. And ironically, it was

Diaghilev who unwittingly became the catalyst in helping to forge what became a strong and enduring personal alliance between the composer and choreographer.

In assessing the dynamics of how each of the three men viewed the others, the issue of sexuality must be raised, for it is tied to almost every decision Diaghilev made. His homosexuality was primarily responsible for forcing the Ballets Russes from St. Petersburg. Stravinsky charged that Diaghilev deliberately plotted the scandal of Nijinsky's *Faune* in Paris, claiming that Nijinsky, in undertaking the provocative performance, was doing so out of fear. Fokine did not mince words in describing the infamous closing moments of the ballet ("I could not believe my eyes"), charging that Diaghilev used Nijinsky as nothing more than a tool to shock his audience. He hinted that scandal was Diaghilev's goal, for salaciousness would attract an audience. "Had not the Russian Ballet got along without any pornographic filth during the four years of its triumphant European tours?" he asked.[37]

Maybe so, but the Left Bank progressivism of Paris exuded a voracity for the kind of prurient "sexual deviation" (as Fokine scolded) that Diaghilev was more than willing to serve up. Ironically, the societal penalties of Diaghilev's lifestyle in Russia—which forced the company's exodus to the theaters of Paris—enabled Stravinsky, Balanchine, and others to find personal voices that doubtless would have been silenced at the Maryinsky. Unlike Tchaikovsky, constrained to conceal his homosexuality and made to feel penitent about it as well, Diaghilev was not about to make apologies for his sexual orientation. Many cheered his emboldened embrace of this "illicit conduct" as an act of empowerment. His troupe often performed across the Channel, where the Bloomsbury crowd hailed Diaghilev and Nijinsky as heroic bohemians daring enough to express freely their individual sexual choices. Nijinsky's insinuative performances in *Faune* and later in *Le Spectre de la Rose* signaled just the kind of libertine battle cry that challenged the bounds of acceptable public behavior.

Stravinsky and Balanchine saw things differently. By the time their collaborations intersected with Diaghilev's troupe in the mid-1920s, the company's "homosexual mafia," as Nicolas Nabokov and others snottily referred to it, had become a predominant theme in public reviews, frequently overshadowing the musical and choreographic merits of the production itself. Stravinsky, Balanchine, and Nabokov held Diaghilev culpable for tilting the emphasis away from the artistic intent of their work. Shortly after the Parisian premiere of *Apollon Musagète,* for example, an article in *Vogue* snippily reported that Diaghilev's company was now "distinguished by the beautiful burgeoning boys who seem to recline on art like Madame Récamier on her couch and to regard the dancers and the *décor* as a kind of personal adornment. Indeed they might also be said to wear the Russian Ballet like a carnation in their button-holes."[38] In a Palmer trim, Virgil Thomson, living in Paris in the late 1920s, sanguinely describes the popularity of Diaghilev's company with the rich: "They were fashionable, and art was fashionable among the rich. The rich liked to invite the ballet dancers [to their houses]. It was always some group that the rich slept with; before the war it was opera singers, after World War I it was ballet dancers."

Diaghilev insisted that associating with women was artistically enfeebling, even admonishing Stravinsky with a warning that such derelict pursuits would corrupt his artistry. But though Stravinsky frowned on Diaghilev's mores, the composer was older than Balanchine, and publicly, at least, voiced his aversion judiciously. Balanchine was openly indiscreet, and his candor came at a price. During his 1925–29 tenure, Diaghilev frequently snubbed him, inviting choreographers from outside the company to prepare major ballets. Dancers too were the recipients of favors; if uncooperative, they soon became casualties of Diaghilev's rage. Lifar paints the impresario's portrait as an obsessive autocrat who demanded both professional and personal fidelity. Diaghilev chided Lifar for any contact with the women in his company, threatening to kick all the offending parties out. Other company members, including Léonide Massine, also tasted Diaghilev's wrath when their heterosexual escapades crossed whatever arbitrary line he chose to draw.

Balanchine's less than enthusiastic endorsement of Diaghilev's artistic vision may have been clouded by his feelings about the older man's sexual persuasion. Almost fifty years after Diaghilev's death, Robert Craft asked Balanchine about rehearsals for the Parisian premiere of *Apollon Musagète,* to which the choreographer bawdily replied, "Nobody will believe me of course, but Diaghilev did not know anything about dancing. His real interest in ballet was sexual. He could not bear the sight of Danilova and would say to me, 'Her tits make me want to vomit.' Once when I was standing next to him at a rehearsal for *Apollo,* he said 'How beautiful.' I agreed, thinking that he was referring to the music, but he quickly corrected me: 'No, no. I mean Lifar's ass; it is like a rose.'"[39]

Lifar also questioned Diaghilev's knowledge of dance, considering him a more reliable judge of painting and music. But whatever Diaghilev's powers as an arbiter, his judgments were, unquestionably, sexually linked. As for Diaghilev's opinion of Balanchine's own not-so-secret sexual conquests, his criticism was no less denigrating, going so far as public deprecation of his choreographer's "morbid interest in women."

Given these mutual suspicions, it did not take long for the irreconcilable distrust between Diaghilev and Balanchine to congeal. Stravinsky, too, grew more skeptical, especially about Diaghilev's ability to make artistic decisions unlinked to a personal agenda, and although even then he harbored similar feelings about Diaghilev's sexual politics, he only aired them in his later writings, when retaliation was no longer a threat. Regarding his mistreatment of Nijinska, for example (Diaghilev often commented that she would have been a wonderful choreographer if only she had been a man), Stravinsky remembered that after Nijinsky married, Diaghilev became overwrought and turned his rancor toward Nijinsky's sister, partially because her physical appearance painfully reminded him of her brother.

Diaghilev's loyalists tried to shelter him from his own peccadilloes. Why wouldn't they? For many of the troupe's members, he was the caretaker of their financial and artistic livelihood. Nabokov privately referred to Diaghilev as the director of a "musical zoo," wherein complete disarray reigned. But publicly he argued that Diaghilev's menagerie was, if not oblivious, at least willing to turn its gaze away from the public scandals and character idiosyncrasies that dogged him. Nabokov claimed that even though Diaghilev asserted his homosexuality publicly, only a handful of people were troubled by this private conduct. "Men like Stravinsky, Debussy, Falla, Prokofiev, Picasso, Balanchine and many others," Nabokov remarked, "regarded all this as none of their concern." He was a great man, they contended, and because of this, was to be forgiven "his temper, his haughtiness, his intolerance to men and ideas."[40]

But Nabokov could not have been more wrong, nor did he really believe this. Late in his life, he volunteered that Diaghilev flaunted the "mystique" of his homosexuality as one more tool to call attention to himself and to his enterprise.[41] In turn, a sense of heterosexual fraternity bonded Bakst, Benois, Nabokov, Stravinsky, and Balanchine; and if they were not guilty of homophobia, they were at a minimum, judgmental—as Stravinsky's writings demonstrate. Moreover, as corroborated by their private papers and remembrances, it was precisely such issues that perturbed Stravinsky and Balanchine. Indeed, it was not only, or perhaps even primarily, their questioning of Diaghilev's artistic vision that brought Stravinsky and Balanchine closer together; it was largely their shared commiseration for having to endure him as best they could.

Their feelings for Diaghilev pulled in opposite directions. Nabokov's simplism notwithstanding, we must not underestimate the effects of Balanchine and Stravinsky's forced adaptation in sometimes succumbing to Diaghilev's crushing personality. Like it or not, they had to cope with his whims and ploys.

They were compelled to adjust because in a real sense they were the victims of their own emotional blackmail. They couldn't extricate themselves from a stream of equivocal feelings—feelings of gratitude, injustice, indebtedness, antipathy, admiration, anger, guilt, hostility, and frustration—indeed, an emotionally exhausting gamut of conflicting feelings and hobgoblins more elemental in their impact than music and dance history often allow. Such baggage heaped up gradually as each man watched and studied the other, all the while developing a personal rapport that would sustain them for the rest of their lives. Their first meaningful contact occurred in early 1925, soon after Balanchine joined Diaghilev's company. It marked the beginning of a friendship that would last almost half a century, as well as a partnership that would change some of the fundamental ways we think about music and ballet as a collaborative art form.

Chapter 3 An Early Encounter

Le Chant du Rossignol

I reached the conclusion—very regretfully, since I was the author of many works for the theatre—that a perfect rendering can be achieved only in the concert hall, because the stage presents a combination of several elements upon which the music has often to depend, so that it cannot rely upon the exclusive consideration which it receives at a concert. I was confirmed in this view when two months later, under the direction of . . . Ansermet, *Le Chant du Rossignol* was given as a ballet by Diaghileff at the Paris Opera.

—*Igor Stravinsky,* An Autobiography

The checkered history of the 1925 *Chant du Rossignol* provides an early landmark. It was the first Stravinsky opus Balanchine prepared for the Ballets Russes as well as the first ballet Diaghilev entrusted to him. Its genesis, however, occurred sixteen years earlier, long before the choreographer began his formal study of dance. The composer himself was still a student when, in 1908, while still under Rimsky-Korsakov's tutelage, he began composing his first opera in Ustilug, his family's summer home. Rimsky seems to have heard the preliminary sketches for the work, and according to Stravinsky at least, signaled his approval.

The notion of writing an opera at so tender and still compositionally inexperienced an age was quite a leap. Nonetheless, Stravinsky was determined to write "a musical fairy tale" to a well-known story by Hans Christian Andersen. The work would be entitled *Le Rossignol,* or *The Nightingale,* with the libretto scripted by the composer's friend Stepan Mitusov. Stravinsky worked for the better part of a year on the first of what would eventually be three acts. (The piece is often considered a one-act opera in three scenes because of its brief, forty-five-minute duration.) But the second and third acts were not written until 1913–14, a delay precipitated by Diaghilev's sudden, not-to-be-denied interest in snatching the young man away from his current writing projects and convincing him to write for the Ballets Russes in 1909.

Stravinsky finally returned to his unfinished opera in 1913, a few months after the premiere of *The Rite* and just as his meteoric star was rising dramatically with Diaghilev's company. But after his Parisian triumphs, he resumed work on the opera with only a modicum of enthusiasm. He was commissioned to complete the composition for the Théâtre Libre of Moscow, though he initially rejected the offer. But he had a change of heart and, with certain conditions settled, agreed. When the Théâtre failed financially, Diaghilev (none too happy with the prospect of Stravinsky working under the sponsorship of another) stepped in and secured the first performance for the upcoming Ballets Russes seasons in France and England.

Diaghilev was already familiar with the score since Stravinsky had played it for him even before its completion. (The composer often previewed unfinished works for Diaghilev.) Alexandre Benois, who became familiar with Stravinsky's initial plans for the opera as early as 1911, was engaged for the stage direction, sets, and costumes. Boris Romanov prepared the choreography; indeed, the dancing was an integral part of the staging, rather than the typical ancillary divertissement often associated with operatic productions.[1] The premiere took place on 26 May 1914 in Paris, with Pierre Monteux conducting. In attempting to capture the "oriental" flavor of the story, the composer fashioned a particularly opulent instrumentation, including a large complement of brass, a celesta, a piano, two harps, and optional parts for guitar and mandolin. The percussion battery was also augmented, including cymbals, antique cymbals, triangle, several drums, campanelli, tambourine, and tam-tam.

The composer was skittish about finishing the work. Given the rapid development of his musical language during the 1909–13 period, he feared that adding a second and third act to preexisting music would present problems of coherence. Moreover, he was particularly uneasy about writing an opera, now that his reputation was firmly established as a highly visible and successful ballet composer. Previously, he had issued a rather puzzling, even antagonistic statement to the London *Daily Mail* (13 February 1913), proclaiming his aversion to opera: "Music can be married to gesture or to words—not to both without bigamy. That is why the artistic basis of opera is wrong and why Wagner sounds at his best in the concert-room. In any case opera is in a backwater." With such misgivings, Stravinsky welcomed the opportunity Diaghilev offered toward the end of 1916: he suggested that the opera could be reworked into a ballet, by means of numerous but strategic cuts, which Diaghilev was quick to specify.[2] Stravinsky proposed an alternative. He would prepare a concert piece based upon the music of the second and third acts, thus circumventing the problem of enfolding the earlier and by now stylistically dissimilar music composed for the first act. If Diaghilev chose, he could use the symphonic version as he wished, and Stravinsky would provide an appropriate scenario (although it is quite likely that Stravinsky conceived of his "tone poem" as a ballet from the time Diaghilev first presented the idea). It was agreed, and the composer finished the twenty-minute work in Morges during the spring of 1917. Toward the end of 1919, with Ernest Ansermet conducting, the Orchestre de la Suisse Romande in Geneva presented *Le Chant du Rossignol* in its symphonic version. But the newly arranged composition, whose Schoenbergian dissonance caught many off-guard, met with harsh criticism not only at its premiere but in several subsequent performances as well.

Stravinsky retained the essentials of the original opera scenario as a basis for Diaghilev's 1920 ballet production, staged in early February, a few months after the premiere of the symphonic version. The story of the nightingale that sang for the Chinese emperor, and the enchanting bird's rescue of the ruler from the grasp of death, was just the kind of mandarin exotica Diaghilev knew would appeal. The ballet consisted of four main divisions. The opening Fête in the Emperor of China's Palace finds the Nightingale singing sweetly, with bells ringing and flowers adorning the room. "The Nightingale is placed on a golden perch; and a Chinese March signals the entrance of the Emperor." The second scene, The Two Nightingales, finds the emperor of Japan bringing the gift of a mechanical nightingale that sings so beautifully that no one notices that the real Nightingale "had flown away out of the open window." In Illness and Recovery of the Emperor of China, the Emperor confronts Death, who has stolen his crown, sword, and other treasures. At the moment that all seems lost, the real Nightingale is heard singing outside the window; he convinces Death to give up the Emperor's possessions and spare him. Finally, in the closing Funeral

March, "The courtiers came in to look at their dead Emperor, and—yes, there they stood astounded, and the Emperor said 'Good morning!' Meanwhile, the friendly Nightingale has flown back to the fisherman[,] who is heard singing his song once more."[3]

The futurist painter Fortunato Depero was commissioned to prepare the scenery and costumes for an ultimately unrealized performance in 1917. The dancers would be masked, and the costumes, as Lynn Garafola remarks, were to consist of "geometrized space suits that concealed not only the body, but the hands and face, while geometric protuberances indicated whiskers, eyes, and mouths" (fig. 3.1).[4]

3.1 Fortunato Depero's 1917 model for the unrealized production of *Le Chant du Rossignol* (Jerome Robbins Dance Division, The New York Public Library for the Performing Arts, Astor, Lenox and Tilden Foundations)

Diaghilev had invited Massine, who was "dreaming about presenting the ballet," to choreograph the work; but the production fell through, perhaps, as Garafola suggests, because the Ballets Russes's recently completed tour of America did not generate sufficient revenue. The Ballets Russes premiere took place on 2 February 1920 at the Théâtre National de l'Opéra in Paris. The dancers included Tamara Karsavina as the real Nightingale and Stanislas Idzikowski as the Mechanical Nightingale, as well as Lydia Sokolova and Serge Grigoriev (who both also participated in the 1925 revival). Stravinsky was not convinced that the adaptation of operatically inspired music to symphonic suite, then to ballet, would work: "I had destined *Le Chant du Rossignol* for the concert platform," he wrote in his autobiographical account, "and a choreographic rendering seemed to me to be quite unnecessary. Its subtle and meticulous writing and its somewhat static character would not have lent themselves to stage action and the movements of dancing." His fears may have been well placed. The reviews were mixed at best; some praised the ballet as a new watershed in Stravinsky's oeuvre, while Charles Tenroc, writing for the *Courier musical,* denounced the music as "arthritic." Thus when the prospect of resurrecting the ballet in 1925 was raised, the composer was skeptical. He sensed that Diaghilev was trying to "entice me—the lost sheep, so to speak—back into the fold."[5]

One must remember that by the time Stravinsky first met Balanchine, the music of *Le Chant* was as different from the composer's then-current neoclassic writing as could be imagined. Compositions such as *L'Histoire du Soldat* (1918), *Ragtime* (1918), *Piano-Rag-Music* (1919), *Symphonies of Winds* (1920), and especially the Octet for winds (1923), as well as the Concerto for piano and winds (1924) set a new sail, in which a more formalist, abstract style prevailed. The Octet was no more nor less than a "musical object," Stravinsky proclaimed in a January 1924 article in *The Arts,* and that object "has a form and that form is influenced by the musical matter with which it is composed"—as cut and dried as that. *Le Chant* was part of the past, and Balanchine, who heard Stravinsky's music as often as he could (and procured as many scores as possible to play and study at his ever-present piano), would have understood this. Nonetheless, Stravinsky was not about to turn his back on a new production. The chance to be heard again in the theaters of Paris was too appealing. Whatever Diaghilev's motive, and whatever Stravinsky's qualms about the opera–symphonic poem–ballet evolution, the production was well received, and numerous performances followed during the balance of the season.[6]

According to the dancer Felia Doubrovska, Diaghilev purportedly told Balanchine shortly after he joined the company that he, Diaghilev, just happened to have the score for *Rossignol* in his cellar. Would Balanchine like to try chore-ographing it? The ambitious young man consented without blinking, respond-ing that it was "no big deal." Balanchine knew, and for the most part greatly ad-mired, Stravinsky's music at least ten years before Diaghilev assigned him *Le Chant*. He had danced in a few productions of *The Firebird* and played the walk-on role of a street vendor in a 1916 production of *Petrushka* at the Maryin-sky. While still in the newly renamed Leningrad, he remembered choreograph-ing the composer's *Ragtime,* though no record of the production survives.

A piano reduction of *Pulcinella* made its way to the Soviet Union as well, and Balanchine's Young Ballet began preparing the 1920 work in early 1924. As Slonimsky remembers, "*Pulcinella* attracted Balanchine with its embodiment in dance of the masked-comedy of stage characterization. Meyerhold had long been drawn to acting of this kind, so reminiscent of popular street shows."[7] Initially, Vladimir Dimitriev championed the production, and as Balanchine himself remembers, even Fyodor Lopukhov (Balanchine's "boss") enthusiasti-cally contributed ideas. But Balanchine's young troupe had already alienated many, and the wherewithal needed to mount the ballet was not forthcoming. Dancers choosing to appear in a work choreographed by Balanchine ran the risk of being ostracized. He abandoned the project shortly before heading for the West, though in fact Dimitriev and Lopukhov did stage the work at the Maryinsky soon after Balanchine's departure, as the choreographer remem-bered disdainfully in later life.

Balanchine not only knew Stravinsky's 1914 original operatic version of *Le Rossignol,* but he recalled playing a small role in a 1918 production staged by Meyerhold in Petrograd: "In the *Nightingale* the soloists sang from scores, sit-ting on a bench [with] a lively pantomime unfolding around them. No one no-ticed Meyerhold's innovations . . . because by then no one had time for the the-ater; it was right after the Bolshevik uprising, there was nothing to eat. But I learned the music well, and so later, when Diaghilev asked me to stage Stravin-sky's ballet *Le Chant du Rossignol,* I was able to do it quickly."[8]

Slonimsky further recalled that Balanchine "had not always approved of Stra-vinsky," and regarded the music of *Le Rossignol* "almost as cacophony." With Diaghilev's revival of the opera as a ballet, Balanchine not only choreographed the work but also participated in the stage action, as the Mechanical Nightin-gale. Pavel Tchelitchev remembers that Balanchine once substituted for Alicia Markova as the Nightingale (Markova was ill, but Diaghilev refused to cancel since royalty was expected to attend the performance), though Tchelitchev was not aware of the last-minute replacement: "My God what happened to Alicia? She looks like a big fat rabbit." Tamara Geva told Francis Mason that when Balanchine, in white tights, emerged from the cage: "He burst into some light fantastic dance, trying to remember his own choreography. Of course he couldn't dance on pointe, so it was quite different. He didn't imitate a bird . . . but he laughed himself sick. So did the audience."[9]

For better or worse, Balanchine inherited the original 1920 Massine production, along with the albatross of its history. He had to find a fresh tack in dealing imaginatively with a preexisting ballet staged by Massine, one of Stravinsky's preferred choreographers. And he had to do it knowing that the composer himself had only reluctantly endorsed the venture. This was the period in which Stravinsky, having signed a contract with Pleyel, was recording a great deal of his music on piano roll, so as to ensure a lasting testament of how his music should be played. As usual, he made quite a fuss over the need for performers to "execute" his scores with absolute allegiance—something that must have been more than a small concern for the young Balanchine as well. *Le Rossignol* was, after all, placing the untested choreographer squarely on trial. Not only would he be closely watched; inevitably he would be harshly judged. That, plus the added weight of setting the music of a composer with whom he was already enraptured, created precisely the kind of double-edged challenge the fearless young man welcomed.

The remembrances of several Ballets Russes principals are instructive in setting the scene into which Balanchine was suddenly thrust. They also provide a perspective on the choreographer's early interactions with both Diaghilev and Stravinsky. None are more important than those of Markova, who reprised Karsavina's 1920 role. Her eyewitness recollections provide a touchstone for framing the early Stravinsky-Balanchine relationship as each man came to know the other personally for the first time.

Markova had already watched Balanchine dance with his own company, the Russian State Ballet, before joining the Ballets Russes. She remembers her first meeting with him. In 1925 Diaghilev instructed Balanchine to audition her for the Stravinsky ballet. He asked her to perform several unusual extensions and positions, especially "acrobatic things," including (as she told Millicent Hodson in a 1995 taped interview) "landing on her tummy" after being flung through the air. Moreover, Markova remembers that the dancing was not so much classical as rooted in modern dance. While musicians, at least, are most likely to associate Balanchine with the classicism of the later *Apollon Musagète,* during the early 1920s Balanchine was essentially a modernist, in sympathy with such progressive choreographers as Kasyan Goleizovsky, whom he admired above all others.

Boris Kochno states that Diaghilev would have preferred retaining Goleizovsky at the time Balanchine auditioned for the company. As Grigoriev reports, since Balanchine had just arrived from Russia, Diaghilev eagerly quizzed the young dancer about balletic developments in Leningrad, and especially about Goleizovsky's productions, "whose main aim was the achievement of sculptural effects, for which he was wont to denude his dancers of all clothing."[10] Only when Diaghilev failed to attract Goleizovsky did grooming Balanchine as a choreographer surface as an option. Balanchine himself was so taken with Goleizovsky's ideas that in 1923 he taught a class in choreographic improvisation in the Goleizovsky style. During the 1923–24 season of the Maly Opera Theater in Russia, Balanchine even briefly served as a ballet master; not surprisingly, his choreography reflected Goleizovsky's modernistic conceptions. Thus it would have been perfectly natural to enfold some of Goleizovsky's new-fashioned ideas into his own first efforts. Though André Levinson found in Balanchine's production of *Le Chant* "a warmth, a breath of life, nuances of naïve grace and a sound instinct for the picturesque," he also criticized the ballet for its "low music-hall acrobatics," of the kind for which Goleizovsky was most often attacked.[11]

Diaghilev actively promoted such bespangled productions. In the 1920s he turned increasingly to younger dancers and faddish theatrics as a means of rejuvenating a company now in decline. Beyond her obvious talents, with the young Markova in the principal role (at age fourteen, she was Balanchine's first "baby ballerina") Diaghilev would ignite the buzz he desired. When an approving Diaghilev turned to Balanchine after Markova's audition to ask for the choreographer's opinion, one wonders whether Balanchine had any choice but to agree. Like Stravinsky fifteen years earlier, Balanchine completely understood in whose hands his future rested.

Markova recalls Balanchine exercising considerable patience in working tirelessly with her, as this child, really, prepared for the unusual and prodigious role. He proceeded methodically and calmly, devoting countless extra rehearsals to making her comfortable with the score and his to some extent unprecedented choreography. He explained that she had to appear as "small" as possible in the birdcage carried by the four men. She also recalls Stravinsky's advice in learning the score: "You can't count, you must know the sound of every instrument," but she adds that she had to watch the conductor intently to catch the basic beat of each measure. The pulse served as a lifeline in negotiating some of the complex and purposely free rhythmic patterns.[12]

Kochno remembers that Balanchine would arrive at a rehearsal as though he had nothing preconceived in mind. He gave the distinct impression that he would simply improvise as he went along. Balanchine demonstrated the many "inventions" he was to incorporate into *Le Chant*—inventions Markova claims later choreographers stole from him (fig. 3.2). Alexandra Danilova added to this list châiné turns, which Balanchine introduced: they had never been seen in any previous ballet.

Describing the young choreographer's relationship with Diaghilev and his company, Markova remembers Balanchine as a "loner," while Kochno portrays him as both "colorless" and capable of rising above whatever current imbroglio consumed the company. At parties, Markova recalls that Balanchine "would sit alone or look immediately for the piano." He would just sit and play, apparently oblivious to the revelry that surrounded him. Markova adds, "For George, it was music always. Since I was the baby and didn't dance at parties, I often used to sit on the piano bench next to him." Kochno, who was probably as close to Balanchine as any other company member, remembers that Balanchine "sought no intimacy with Diaghilev, no closeness. . . . [He] was not a member of Diaghilev's family. He was more of a *naïf,* surprisingly blessed, but a guest."[13]

Balanchine's inclination to distance himself from the vicissitudes of Diaghilev's world, at least as much as he could, served him well. His aloofness was perhaps attributable to a certain imperturbable bent by nature, but more likely it was due to a growing sense of independence, maybe even distrust. His social detachment from the supercilious affectations of Diaghilev's Riviera milieu was evident. Stravinsky, whose sensitivity to such matters was always keen, would have observed Balanchine's composure and empathized. Typically, if the composer was personally unable to control the conditions of a situation himself, he resorted to separating himself by writing off such interactions as beneath him. In the beginning of their work together, both Stravinsky and Balanchine surely took notice of the demeanor in which each handled personal and professional circumstances within the politically volatile and often pernicious arena of Diaghilev's empire. In learning about each other, they became further united in fundamental interpersonal ways that would have resonated.

Palmer interviewed Markova about her relationship with Stravinsky. Her comments, restored from a trim, provide an unusual insight into Stravinsky's participation in the company's rehearsals. Her affectionate memory is of kind-

3.2 Dame Alicia Markova coaching Iohna Loots, Royal Ballet School graduate, in the Nightingale Variation from George Balanchine's *Le Chant du Rossignol,* January–February 1995 (The George Balanchine Foundation Archive of Lost Choreography; Photograph by Brian Rushton)

ness and patience, but she remembers that many of the Ballets Russes dancers were terrified of the composer. Knowing his exacting demands, the thought of his conducting a performance of one of his own ballets often elicited a palpable sense of panic and anxiety among the dancers. Moreover, Markova perceived that Stravinsky enjoyed the sense of intimidation he stirred up, although once the imposing barrier attached to his reputation was breached, he was extremely kind to all involved:

> My first meeting with the great man was when I was fourteen in Monte Carlo, and I hate to tell you, I think the very first time I was in a flood of tears because Balanchine was choreographing for me, and suddenly I was thrown into Stravinsky and I really panicked. It was something I felt I was never going to be able to cope with, and Stravinsky walked into the rehearsal after dinner that evening and he found me in tears. He said, "What's the matter?" and I said, "I'm very sorry, but I know I've lost the chance of a lifetime, I'm never going to be able to dance this." And he inquired why. And so Stravinsky took me by the hand and took me over to the piano and he said, "Now come with me, little one," as he always used to call me, and he sat down and he started to demonstrate a little bit, and then the most important thing he said was, "Now you have to learn everything by ear," and from that moment on, if you can imagine, at age fourteen, I learned all his scores by ear—instrumentation, everything—and after that I was always so grateful to him, thankful because I had no fears with any music, and of course with the time I was in the Diaghilev company I think I almost danced in all the Stravinsky ballets. I can recall . . . he would come to rehearsals, yes, he'd drop in, and often in the early days in Monte Carlo for the first rehearsals of *Rossignol* we couldn't have a pianist, it was all on pianola. We had to use pianola. And then I think when we revived, and there were other Stravinsky ballets, by that time we had a wonderful pianist . . . Rika Fox, who we called Foxy. And so she could always deal with the music and Stravinsky used to work with her a lot. . . . Often if she was playing, he'd get up and go over and add the other two hands, making it four hands.

Markova's reference to the pianola is enlightening. Even though cost prohibited the regular employment of a live pianist, Stravinsky may just as well have preferred the mechanical instrument. In his estimate, using any rehearsal pianist (other than himself, of course) was chancy, particularly given the precision of his tempi. Lifar also recalls Stravinsky sitting at the keyboard rehearsing the dancers, as the animated pianist "thumped the keys, panted, made up for missing chords by kicks on the pedal . . . or to keep up the tempo he would bring his elbows crashing down on the piano." When he was not around, Lifar continued, Stravinsky "had a barrel-organ sent down from Paris and on its rolls was inscribed the music of the ballet. We then had the extraordinary spectacle of an accompanist transformed into a mechanic and turning the handle."[14]

Stravinsky's future wife Vera Sudeikina also played an integral but often overlooked role in *Le Chant*'s history. She had previously appeared in the 1921 Ballets Russes production of *The Sleeping Beauty*. (Balanchine danced in the ballet several times; see figure 3.3.) Stravinsky too participated in the Tchaikovsky revival, reorchestrating several passages cut by the Russian Imperial Theater from the original score.[15] Sudeikina frequently worked for Diaghilev, preparing costumes not only for *Le Chant* but also for *The Firebird*, Nijinska's *Les Biches* (1924), and Balanchine's *Prodigal Son* (1929). It was, in fact, Diaghilev who introduced Stravinsky to Sudeikina. But no sooner did he play matchmaker than he became critical of the couple's intimacy. Sudeikina remembers that once her relationship with Stravinsky blossomed, a jealous Diaghilev would sulk whenever he saw her in the composer's company.

In correspondence with Stravinsky, Henri Matisse discusses how Markova should appear in the ballet, suggesting that Marie Muelle prepare the costume. But it was Sudeikina who should be credited, a few years later, with the Nightingale's famous look. Massine recalls in detail how Matisse identified with the original 1920 scenario and how involved he became:

> He had hundreds of exotic birds . . . and even carried about an official document testifying to the vocal range of his favourite nightingale. He was naturally delighted at the idea of doing the décor for *Le Chant du Rossignol*. . . . He was also very interested in the problem of dressing the real and the mechanical nightingales. I remember when he came to Paris, we went to the Cluny Museum[,] where he stood for a long time in front of a statue of a Chinese warrior. I watched him as he sketched it from various angles, and was not surprised to see the costume of this warrior reproduced in the costumes of the Emperor's bodyguard. . . . The backdrop was white, and there were three overhanging friezes with black painted scalloped edges. When the dying Emperor . . . came back to life at the end of the ballet, he stood up and loosened his black mantle, which flowed down, and covered about sixty square feet of the stage with its magnificent vermilion lining.[16]

In comparison, Markova's comments, again restored from the Palmer trims, reveal the extent to which Matisse and other Ballets Russes principals jointly overhauled the original design for the 1925 revival:

> After the rehearsals in Monte Carlo, the premiere was arranged for Paris in June, and so we arrived in Paris, and Matisse was designing my costume. He had designed the production originally, so they were using [that] production, but it was decided that

3.3 George Balanchine and Vera Nemchinova in *The Sleeping Beauty,* 1923 (The Tang Teaching Museum and Art Gallery Collection, Skidmore College)

he would redesign the Nightingale's costume design because I was only fourteen, this very thin little bird. . . . So we were in Paris rehearsing, and about two weeks before the premiere, I was given instructions from Grigoriev to see Vera Sudeikina for my costume. For the fitting for the Nightingale. . . . Diaghilev was there, and Matisse,

Balanchine, and Stravinsky, and so there was a conference. I remember standing in what I was to wear, and it was decided that I would wear white silk tights, which had been made for me, and then they decided I would have these large diamond rhinestone bracelets on my ankles and one on the arm, the other on the wrist, and a little diamond necklace. And then Matisse decided that no hair should be showing at all, [there would be] a tiny little white chiffon bonnet with my hair out of the way and studded with rhinestones. So there was this discussion that was decided, and then Madame Sudeikina produced a piece of white osprey . . . and she suggested that it should be put over my bonnet just around my face as there was no hair to soften it. Diaghilev and Matisse agreed and then Boris Kochno . . . said the budget couldn't handle the osprey, but Stravinsky and Matisse said they would pay for the osprey between them, and that was how my original costume came into being. It was Madame Stravinsky, Vera, who did my costume and then of course the opening performance Stravinsky conducted me himself. So maybe that's why I've always felt secure with him.

Diaghilev was delighted to have Matisse play such an important role in conceiving the original 1920 production. The painter had made his mark earlier in the century as a leading exponent of the fauve style, and his work gained notoriety in Russia about the same time Diaghilev entered the scene. According to art historian Alfred Barr, Diaghilev and Stravinsky visited the painter in 1919, hoping to entice him into preparing the sets and costumes for either *Schéhérazade* or *Le Chant du Rossignol*. Apparently Diaghilev thought that Matisse would prefer *Schéhérazade*, but "after listening to Stravinsky play music from both scores on the piano, Matisse decided in favor of *Le Chant du Rossignol*." Stravinsky seems to have encouraged the painter to take on the project, though Matisse himself was unsure of his abilities to design for ballet.[17]

Just as Stravinsky would have learned by observing Balanchine actually choreograph in the studio, so too Balanchine noted Stravinsky's physically demonstrative, kinesthetic approach to working with dancers. He was not a composer to stand to the side or remain uninvolved, and surely Balanchine, who likewise participated in every facet of a production, must have appreciated this. It was at this time too that Stravinsky was performing publicly more and more, playing his Piano Concerto all across Europe and the United States as he attempted to supplement his income as a conductor and concert pianist. He was in touch with the instrument, literally, just as Balanchine had to be physically in touch with his dancers. The closeness and directness of actually making music at the keyboard would have impressed Balanchine in a way that Diaghilev's sometimes puffed-up homiletics about art did not.

In fact, Stravinsky had departed for his first concert tour of the United States in the same month that Balanchine auditioned for Diaghilev, December 1924. While Balanchine was exposed to the embroiling politics of the Ballets Russes, the composer spent the winter months of 1925 touring America, then returning for further concertizing in Europe that spring. Balanchine's new version of *Le Chant* premiered in early June, and it is likely that Stravinsky visited Monte Carlo in May as final preparations for the production were taking place. He records his remembrance of the remounted ballet in his autobiography, although, oddly, he describes seeing the new Massine production and doesn't even mention Balanchine's name. But this is surely only one of many Stravinskyan memory holes. Not only did he rehearse and conduct the new version of the ballet, but as usual, he exercised considerable guidance in the restaging (he also played the piano at several rehearsals). His exchanges with Balanchine were frequent. The composer was living in Nice, just a short distance from Monte Carlo, and as both Markova and Nabokov confirm, Stravinsky regularly visited the rehearsal studio to watch Balanchine work.

One such encounter was captured in Palmer's film. Here Balanchine, in one of his last interviews, recounts the first time he and Stravinsky met, during rehearsals of *Le Chant*. The composer had come to the studio to check on the ballet's tempi. As a dutiful young apprentice, Balanchine was following Diaghilev's directions. But Stravinsky found the tempi too slow and insisted on a faster pace. Complying with his wishes, Balanchine made the adjustment, as did the dancers. At a subsequent rehearsal, and in Stravinsky's absence, Diaghilev countermanded the composer's directive, forcing the choreographer to reinstate the tempi the impresario favored. Balanchine was caught in the middle.

This was one of many jurisdictional disputes, and neither Stravinsky nor Diaghilev was willing to budge. Vladimir Dukelsky (later, Vernon Duke), whose ballet *Zéphire et Flore* was being rehearsed around the same time with Massine's choreography to a libretto by Kochno, remembers being taken aback by the intensity of Stravinsky's rancorous comments concerning Diaghilev and his company. He complained about the "'execrable' orchestral performances, the cynicism with which his music was mutilated, the disgracefully inadequate rehearsals"—all caused by Diaghilev's bankrupt leadership.[18]

Stravinsky was especially displeased with Diaghilev's intrusive intervention into musical matters. As Nicolas Nabokov relates, Diaghilev particularly relished cutting and rearranging various compositional passages. To Stravinsky's mind this was the ultimate trespass, yet one more opportunity for Diaghilev to impose his strong-armed will. It became almost a "delightful ritual," Nabokov recalls. Diaghilev would casually suggest that a certain section of a ballet was too long, leaving little margin for argument: "And before you could say yes or no, one of his helpers would hand him the score and he would point to the spot he wanted cut, saying 'I looked at it carefully yesterday and I think the cuts should be made here and here . . . don't you agree?'"[19]

Though Diaghilev continued to incense him, the composer publicly feigned his fondness, at least obliquely, for Diaghilev's *Le Chant.* He praised Diaghilev as a man of vision and courage in staging the production. But privately (and in his later writings) Stravinsky expressed his dissatisfaction. As his correspondence reveals he was just as distressed and displeased as Balanchine over Diaghilev's waning artistic integrity. Moreover, critics were poised to measure the success of the ballet by the achievement of Diaghilev's newest in-house choreographer. André Levinson, familiar with Balanchine's dancing as far back as his student days, was especially eager to see what had become of the young man. His review of the 1925 *Le Chant* was mixed. In addition to the praise quoted above for its " warmth, a breath of life, nuances of naïve grace and a sound instinct for the picturesque," Levinson criticized the choreographer for relying too heavily upon some of the less successful qualities associated with Massine. Balanchine himself had little to say about the work, although Stravinsky's score, more than the ballet's somewhat stilted staging, must have intrigued him, especially within the context of the newer neoclassic works the composer was then writing.[20]

Stravinsky saw his old colleague resorting to shallow trickery in desperately trying to satisfy the fickle desires of the Parisian public. Productions bespoke an artistic fraudulence employing too many vulgar clichés. To Stravinsky and Balanchine, Diaghilev had been reduced to a caricature of the man who had so captured the affections of Paris with his bold artistic statements in earlier years. To be sure, the company's popularity still held sway with much of the general public. As they entered the final, 1929 season, a Parisian newspaper proclaimed: "To conquer Paris is difficult. To hold its subjection for twenty years is a feat." But even if Diaghilev had lived to continue managing the company, it must have been apparent to both Balanchine and Stravinsky that they would soon need to move on.

Thus their initial exchanges during *Le Chant du Rossignol* must be viewed within the context of their own failing relationship with Diaghilev. The anxieties produced by that deterioration may have facilitated the collegial refuge Stravinsky and Balanchine found in each other, both personally and artistically. It would be a mistake, however, to assume that Balanchine and Stravinsky befriended each other principally on the strength of their similarities. On the contrary, they were in many ways quite unalike, and accordingly, reacted to Diaghilev differently. Diaghilev provided the first focal point by which both artists came to see and understand their differentness—in the most subtle ways—but still as a critical identification of their individualism. In the years ahead the Stravinsky-Balanchine partnership flourished both personally and professionally not because of their samenesses but largely because they complemented each other.[21]

Two years after the choreographer's first encounter with the composer, at the premiere of *Oedipus Rex* (30 May 1927) Stravinsky also conducted a performance of *The Firebird* in which Balanchine played the ogre Kastchei, one of his favorite roles. Vera Stravinsky later remembered that in the weeks preceding the performance, her husband attended rehearsals along with Balanchine, and it seems safe to assume that their friendship deepened. By all accounts, Balanchine's presence onstage, even though the role demands little dancing, was captivating, and Stravinsky took note. Nor would it be unreasonable to assume that Stravinsky shared his evolving thoughts about the frozen, statuesque qualities of Greek drama as exhibited in *Oedipus* and the possibilities of a future "Apollonian" ballet in a similar vein. So, struck with Balanchine's equanimity, his understanding of music, his appreciation of artistic balance, and his refreshing, atypical thinking about movement, Stravinsky's interest in dance was rekindled. He reengaged with the world of ballet—the world that only a few years earlier he had repudiated out of religious convictions.[22]

Classicism was in the air, especially among some of the Ballets Russes designers Stravinsky and Balanchine came to know in the mid-1920s. The presence of André Derain, to name only one among Diaghilev's cohorts, surely exerted some influence in Stravinsky and Balanchine's classical approach to dance at that time. Derain, as Roger Fry once commented, was an exponent of the "purest French classicism." His work with Diaghilev included sets and designs for such productions as *La Boutique Fantasque* (1919) and *Jack-in-the-Box* (1926). Guillaume Apollinaire anticipated the essence of what Stravinsky and Balanchine would soon accomplish with *Apollon Musagète* in his description of Derain's achievement: "With unequaled daring, [Derain] went beyond the most audacious forms of contemporary art and the discipline which stem from such an exercise."[23] One can hardly mistake this as the bedrock upon which Stravinsky launched his own passionately embraced rediscovery of classicism.

Still, there was no direct creative interaction between Stravinsky and Balanchine immediately following *Le Chant,* perhaps because Diaghilev feared that pairing the two would fortify their antipathy to his authority. Over the next few seasons the composer and choreographer did not collaborate on a single project, although Stravinsky did continue to observe Balanchine dance, just as he certainly saw some of the choreographic creations unfold in the studios of Monte Carlo and the theaters of Paris.[24] It was not until 1928 that *Apollon Musagète* provided a fitting vehicle to arouse Stravinsky's interest in the expressive possibilities of ballet. By then, Diaghilev's Ballets Russes, for all of its flaws, had performed an enormous service for Balanchine: he discovered there a lifelong confidant. In Stravinsky, Balanchine found the artistic mentor Diaghilev originally set out to be. The remarkable collaborations that were to follow demonstrate how thoroughly Balanchine instinctively grasped, respected, and choreographically matched the musical aesthetic Stravinsky was about to proclaim with his next ballet.

Chapter 4 From Delos to Paris:

The Voyage of *Apollo*

Such is the holy gift of the Muses given to humanity. So it is from the
Muses, and from Apollo of the far cast, that there are men on earth who
are poets, and players of the lyre.
—*Hesiod,* Theogony

Apollon Musagète embodies the essence of classicism. At one level, the
ballet is an achievement of sheer visual beauty, asking little beyond
what our senses instantly tell us. At another, the work's lyrical music
and classically steeped dancing represent the purest of Stravinsky and
Balanchine's neoclassic masterpieces. Free of ethnicity, preexisting
tunes, or an explicit narrative, the composer deemed *Apollo* (the title
he came to prefer) the least "contaminated" of his compositions up to
that point. He admitted to seeking a melodic style that would not be-
tray his folkloristic past—a crucial about-face from his earlier Russian
ballets. Moreover, he applied himself to writing melodies that were
beautiful at a time when he felt that melody had nearly been abandoned as a compositional element. Beyond its suffusive gracefulness,
this 1928 collaboration signals a memorable juncture, a historic
merger of mind and spirit marking the first genuine partnership of

the composer and choreographer. Yet even though *Apollo* now stands as one of ballet's most venerated cultural symbols, a certain lore distorts the origins and subsequent development of the work. To understand the ballet's long voyage, several fictions must be swept away.[1]

"Ballet began when Terpsichore touched Apollo's finger, as on the Sistine ceiling God touches Adam's and inspired a pas de deux that holds implicit all dance, past, present and future." Although Andrew Porter thus eloquently depicted one of the work's most telling images, Stravinsky and Balanchine probably would have scoffed at such effusion.[2] The notion of excess in music and dance—to say nothing of portraying their respective arts so melodramatically—was intrinsically alien to their deepest aesthetic convictions. Composing and choreographing were no more than daily praxes, and the ongoing task of "making" a work was not to be sentimentalized. Why then did both men so uncharacteristically single out this particular opus as an epiphany?

Balanchine's grand pronouncement that *Apollo* was "the crucial turning point in my artistic life" (words he later suggested were put in his mouth) arose from his effort to match Stravinsky's disciplined, restrained score. Almost suddenly, Balanchine claimed, he understood that in choreography, as in music, he could "eliminate . . . limit . . . clarify . . . reduce." He described nothing less than a revelation: "It was in studying *Apollon* that I came first to understand how gestures, like tones in music and shades in painting, have certain family relationships. As groups they impose their own laws. The more conscious an artist is, the more he comes to understand these laws, and to respond to them. Since this work, I have developed my choreography inside the framework such relations suggest."[3]

The somber expressiveness of *Apollo* appeared at the height of "the frathouse insouciance of Jazz Age spontaneity." Almost defiantly, the ballet boldly confronted the currently fashionable notion of novelty. It is difficult to imagine what Parisians must have made of it, especially given the expectation of titillation they had come to assume whenever Diaghilev mounted a new work. Yet *Apollo* is emblematic of classicism's melding of malleability and constancy— and the durability of such constancy was just then very much on Stravinsky's mind. Designating the score his own "U-turn," the composer was as prophetic as Balanchine in assaying the work's momentousness. *Apollo* represents a profound redirection. In a film clip from a 1957 NBC television documentary, first aired on the eve of *Agon*'s premiere, Stravinsky declared that *Apollo* was "far more important than people realize. I think of *Apollo* as something entirely new in my music."[4]

This newness was rooted in something very old, for the ancient power of classicism as an overarching artistic principle now provided Stravinsky with a beacon. We know that as a young man he was drawn to the writings of the Mir iskusstva community, as well as to the artistic sentiments expressed in the slightly later 1909 journal *Apollon*. The ascetic spirit of a Greek-inspired classicism was essential—a resurrected classicism epitomized most regally during the monarchy of Louis XIV and revived more than two centuries later by Stravinsky's much-admired contemporary Alexandre Benois.[5] In the aftermath of a horrific world war that left many early twentieth-century artists spiritually scarred—although Stravinsky escaped relatively unscathed, he was forever exiled—a rededication to the classical ideals of Versailles would, it was believed, restore order and sanity, even purposefulness. The real newness of *Apollo,* then, came in the challenge of writing a ballet wherein austerity and homogeneity were valued above all else. "I had specially in my thoughts," the composer remembered, "what is known as the 'white ballet,' in which to my mind the very essence of this art reveals itself in all its purity."[6] He sought a complete expunction of all "superfluities," to use his expression. Balanchine later remembered the composer seated at the piano, insisting upon the unhurried, pristine temperament of the new work, all the while clarifying his conception of the *blanc en blanc* ballet.

The mystical tranquillity of the music is owing directly to a pivotal transfiguration in the composer's life. The score belies an introspective turnabout. In the mid-1920s, just about the time Stravinsky first met Balanchine, the often querulous composer reexamined many personal issues. Order in his music was always a manifestation of the need for orderliness in his life. But now the composer sought more: he needed to find a sense of quietude, a spiritual deliverance through repentance. From 1926 through 1929 he again became a church communicant, begging absolution from none other than Diaghilev himself. Richard Buckle is not far from the mark in referring to *Apollo* as "holy music." Stravinsky's son Soulima, raised in a household darkened by his father's thinly disguised extramarital affair with Vera Sudeikina, remembers his father suffering an intensifying guilt stemming from his double life. The tender music of *Apollo*'s pas de deux, stirred by the composer's ardent love for Sudeikina, is unconcealed. But the equally sublime music of the composer's slightly earlier *Serenade en la* (1925)—music plainly akin to *Apollo* in its suppleness—was written for his wife Catherine. The fact is, the emotional turmoil in Stravinsky's private life was attributable to a divided love for both women—a deeply felt friction that makes the serene poise of *Apollo* all the more extraordinary.

Stravinsky's need to bring a measure of repose to his life is evident in almost every bar of the score. While the composer, with his sudden turn to neoclassicism's prickly and dry formalism (as it was categorized), was attacked during the 1920s for its jejuneness, there is an ineffable earnestness to *Apollo*'s music. Writing in *The Dial,* Boris de Schloezer felt that the ballet demonstrated "Stravinsky's thirst for renunciation, his need for purity and serenity." Nor is Stravinsky's change of heart and mind unlike Apollo's own transmogrification. In the *Homeric Hymn to Hermes,* Apollo is portrayed as a callous slayer, constantly engaged in theomachy and intent on gaining spoils at any cost: "Oh father, you, who scoff at me for being the only one who is fond of booty." Only later does Apollo put aside his whip and arrows for the oracular lyre (the central symbol of the Stravinsky-Balanchine ballet): "The far-shooting lord Apollo . . . took the lyre in his left hand and tried it by striking successive notes. It sounded in startling fashion at his touch and the god sang a beautiful song in accompaniment."[7]

The composer's self-scrutiny is also traceable to his ruminative study of Jacques Maritain's theological monographs. Born the same year as Stravinsky, Maritain was proclaimed by T. S. Eliot to be the "most important influence in contemporary French philosophy." Deeply concerned with existence, being, rationality, and, as Joseph Chiari summarizes, "the importance of Time as informed with God's presence," Maritain's writings had an immediate appeal for Stravinsky. Rooted in Aristotelian thought and the teachings of Thomas Aquinas, Maritain's neo-Thomism prized the efficacy of clarity, order, and proportion as eternal verities. In "Concerning Poetic Knowledge," the philosopher-theologian wrote of a lifelong underlying process in which humans become "progressively conscious" of themselves. "The distinctive property of spirit is to be able, the ancients said, to return entirely upon itself, to accomplish a perfect reflexion." His sense of reflexivity as a means of penetrating the innermost self immediately appealed to the now older, more contemplative Stravinsky. Moreover, the composer clearly grasped the fundamental link between myth, religion, and ritual. The spiritual impetus for Stravinsky's "Greek" works is surely traceable to Maritain's influence. Moreover, Soulima Stravinsky remembers Diaghilev inviting his older brother, Theodore, and him to lunch, then complaining bitterly about their father's unhealthy interest in religion, particularly his deep devotion to Maritain's writings.[8]

Unlike his opera-oratorio *Oedipus Rex* (written just before *Apollo* and presented by Diaghilev in 1927), wherein the dramatic text explicitly provided the voice for Stravinsky's personal identification with tragedy, the wordless *Apollo* now offered a different, perhaps more weighty challenge. Here was the perfect subject matter. Apollo, Greek mythology's most paradoxical figure, stood as the archetype of the gods' anthropomorphic dilemma, revealed in their binary mix of human confusion and godly omnipotence.

Lincoln Kirstein once commented that Stravinsky "never drugged himself with identity-crises. He'd always known who and for what, he was."[9] But is that really so? The composer's limitless vigor in exploring new horizons may have been due precisely to neither knowing nor being content with his "identity." Stravinsky, like Apollo, was ineluctably waged in a tortuous struggle to find himself. Mark Morford and Robert Lenardon ascribe the complex nature of Apollo, "the most Greek of Greek gods," to the "many contradictions in the tragic dilemma of human existence." Characterized by polarities ranging from gentle to vehement, compassionate to ruthless, guilty to guiltless, his emotions have a boundless intensity. Yet he also personifies antiquity's classical restraint, the need to look inwardly for truth, and the perils of excess. "From a sea of blood and guilt, Apollo brings enlightenment, atonement, and purification."[10]

Surely *Apollo*'s solemnity reflects the composer's own need to step back and weigh the course of his future. Through the imperishable power of myth, as Jungians would argue, Stravinsky forced himself to face up to his behavior, even to redress his sins as part of a primitive "collective unconscious." These primordial images sprang forth from Jung's "all-controlling deposit of ancestral experience"—an experience most effectively released (or, to use Jung's language, "brought to the surface") through the poetic expression of the inexorable images rooted in "mythological motifs."

Whatever the psychology, it is clear that Stravinsky was drifting. Composing *Apollo* would serve as a purging act of self-consciousness. The plasticity of classical dance offered the ideal vehicle for such purifying reflection, he contended, for it combined beauty with discipline. Lucidly structured ideas would inevitably win out over ambiguity, he argued; and above all else, the dominion of order would always triumph. It was a battle of Apollonian and Dionysian principles, as he himself wrote in his *Autobiography;* and the dance, more than any other art form, provided the "theater" for such a confrontation.

Incontestably, Stravinsky's music inspired the young Balanchine; but there was more to it than that. Part of the ambitious choreographer's own artistic growth stemmed from a mounting need to stake his identity in Diaghilev's highly competitive company. Having joined the Ballets Russes only three years earlier, Balanchine felt constrained under the crippling weight of what Kirstein called the impresario's *faux pompier* productions. *Apollo* was an appreciable cut above the shallow plots and musical vapidity of Georges Auric's *La Pastorale,* Lord Berners's *The Triumph of Neptune,* and Henri Sauguet's *La Chatte,* all of which Diaghilev assigned to Balanchine in 1926–27. Even this early in his career, his sharp musical instincts winced at the obvious banalities of such negligible scores.[11] The vitiating dead-end experimentation during the waning years of Diaghilev's company quickly disillusioned the enterprising Balanchine. Still, he was in no position to argue. Stravinsky's new ballet provided a way out. Its classicism afforded the ideal crucible for Balanchine to test his ideas. He eagerly seized the chance to fashion a counterpart to the composer's elegiac score.

For both choreographer and composer, *Apollo* was a revocation. As Balanchine broke free of Diaghilev's manneristic conventions, so too Stravinsky shifted course, shunning the decadent conventions of fluffy nineteenth-century ballet scores. One must also remember that in 1927, at age twenty-three, Balanchine was on the rise of an arc. His thoughts were not nearly as tortuously convoluted as Stravinsky's. Twenty years younger than the composer, he viewed this crossroad not as a crisis of conscience but as a propitious opportunity to accelerate rather than stop and ponder. When Stravinsky was Balanchine's age, he was virtually unknown. Now the internationally acclaimed composer looked back from a midlife plateau that the young Balanchine could not yet know. How different their perspectives were. The real anomaly of *Apollo* is that such a confluence of shared artistic sympathies could have merged out of such dissimilar tributaries. For the self-confident young Balanchine, poised on the threshold of greatness, the ballet stemmed from an eagerness to show what he could do; for the pensive and perpetually flagellant Stravinsky, it represented a reflection on what he had already done.

The ballet's scenario consists of two scenes. The first, marked in Stravinsky's compositional sketchbook as "La Naissance d'Apollon," is adapted from *The Homeric Hymn to the Delian Apollo.* The composer describes the arrival of the mortal Leto on the isle of Delos in the Aegean Sea. With arms wrapped around a palm tree, she gives birth to Apollo. Two handmaidens blanket the child in swaddling clothes bound with a golden girdle. As the first tableau closes, the Muses bring the young god his magical lyre. The second tableau begins with a "boyish and angular" Apollo (to use another Kirstein expression), lyre in hand. The journey of the god's maturation unfolds, leading to his final ascension to Parnassus, where he joins his father, Zeus, among the pantheon of the gods. Three of the nine Muses, as Balanchine stated, "were selected [to be part of the ballet] for their appropriateness to the choreographic art." Stravinsky described the trio in his *Autobiography:* "Calliope, receiving the stylus and tablets from Apollo, personified poetry and its rhythm; Polyhymnia, finger on lips, represents mime. . . . Finally, Terpsichore, combining in herself both the rhythm and eloquence of gesture, reveals dancing to the world and thus among the Muses takes the place of honor beside Apollo." Following the parturition (which the composer intended to be staged as literally as possible), the second scene begins with Apollo's first solo variation. Nearly six times the length of the Prologue, this second tableau consists of traditional solo and ensemble variations, a pas de deux, and an apotheosis.[12]

In a 1988 interview for PBS, Mikhail Baryshnikov described *Apollo* as a ballet about learning, about a young god's education. Stravinsky and Balanchine, however, depicted the Muses more as objectified servants, chiefly intended to gratify or "a-muse" the awkward and immature youth. The composer's inclusion of the word *Musagète* in the original title signified Apollo's leadership as a *conducteur* of the Muses. Balanchine explained that they were "goddesses . . . who derived inspiration from Apollo's teaching. . . . The Muses accept [Apollo's] gifts with delight and respect, form a line, and hop like pleased children to the side of the stage." But this is hardly a fair appraisal of the prominent place occupied by the Muses. Most mythologies have it the other way around. In Hesiod's *Theogony,* for example, the nine daughters of Zeus were empowered "with particular emphasis upon their ability to inspire the infallible revelation of the poet."[13]

Our traditional linkage of *Apollon Musagète* with Diaghilev's Ballets Russes is only a second chapter in its history. While it is true, as Andrew Porter stated, that the ballet "was first shaped in mortal history on the stage of the Sarah Bernhardt Theatre in Paris," the actual premiere took place at the Library of Congress in Washington, D.C., on 27 April 1928. Though this first performance is virtually forgotten, it marks, in fact, the embarkation of *Apollo's* long voyage.

The ballet constituted a benchmark for America. *Apollo* represented, as Olin Downes wrote in the *New York Times* (6 May 1928) review of the American premiere, "the first time in history a major ballet work had its world premiere in America" (by which he meant a major ballet written by a renowned European composer). The score was commissioned by Elizabeth Sprague Coolidge, the American arts patron who established the Coolidge Foundation at the Library of Congress in 1925. The American connection is crucial for defining the boundaries of the ballet's scenario. It is also critical in establishing the ballet's musical and choreographic dimensions—dimensions that not only Stravinsky was obligated to follow in composing the ballet but Balanchine inherited and implemented in Paris.[14]

The opening Friday night program of the library's April 1928 festival promised "a program of dances under the direction of Adolph Bolm [that] will include the first performance of *Apollon Musagètes* [*sic*], a ballet written by Igor Strawinsky for the Library of Congress." Given Stravinsky's eminence, tickets for the 511-seat auditorium were at a premium. The list of musicians attending included Amy Beach, Aaron Copland, Howard Hanson, Fritz Reiner, Wallingford Riegger, and Edgar Varèse. Coolidge had invited her friend Bolm to prepare the production as well as to choreograph the lead piece.[15] In fact from the start, Coolidge intended the library's festival to revolve around the well-respected Bolm, who danced the role of Apollo at the premiere.

Bolm's name is first mentioned in an unpublished letter of 18 November 1926 to Carl Engel, director of the library's music division, from Coolidge. Engel had initially raised the possibility of planning an evening of ballet for the 1928 Coolidge festival: "For the next Festival at the Library, which will take place about the end of April 1928, we should very much like to plan a program of dancing or pantomime, and if possible, have your services on that occasion. . . . We have written to de Falla asking him if he would accept a commission to write something for us, in the form of a pantomime for not more than three characters that would have its first performance in Washington."[16]

The festival director stipulated that the new work was to be a ballet for three characters (eventually a fourth was allowed). Manuel de Falla was first offered the commission; when he declined, Ottorino Respighi, another friend of Coolidge's, was approached. He too declined. Finally, in June 1927, the third choice, Stravinsky, agreed to terms. Frederic Jacobi, who reviewed the premiere for the May–June 1928 issue of *Modern Music,* reported that "Stravinsky inquired for specific details: the exact dimensions of the stage and those of the orchestra pit." But it was Engel who was constantly placed in the unenviable position of dogging Stravinsky, in letter after letter, about the space limitations the commission imposed. In his written reply to Stravinsky's first queries, Engel enclosed a description of both the stage and the "sunken pit," as well as a photograph—all graphic cues intended to impress upon the composer the spatial perimeter within which he must design the work. All was agreeable, and the composer began sketching the music five days later, on 16 July.

A description of the scenario did not arrive until February 1928, seven months later. Because of its difficulty, Bolm was forced to program *Apollo* first, while the dancers were fresh, though Elise Reiman, who danced Calliope at the Washington premiere and Terpsichore in a subsequent 1937 Balanchine production in New York, remembered that the most difficult choreography amounted to "an attitude promenade with one arm around Bolm's neck."[17] Stravinsky himself articulated his choreographic vision, sending specific directions to Bolm. Moreover, by this time the composer had, doubtless, already discussed at least part of the stage action with Diaghilev and Balanchine in Nice and Monte Carlo.

Engel's skepticism grew, for despite repeated pleas about the need for a modestly sized chamber work, it became obvious that the composer's scenario could not be properly realized on a small stage. Confirming Engel's worst fears, Bolm wrote to Engel on 8 February: "My reaction to the scenario of Stravinsky's ballet is not so very stimulating. I think it makes it obvious that your stage is too small for more than three Muses," inviting speculation that more than three may have been initially considered.[18]

Hans Kindler, conductor of the National Symphony Orchestra, found Stravinsky's piano reduction "very ugly." He also derogated the string writing as unidiomatic. Kindler was so bewildered by the score's abrasive dissonances, Charles Rosen remarks, that he considered them "mistakes of the copyist, and replaced them with blander harmonies" when he conducted the premiere.[19]

The composer also dictated costuming details. In a 16 March letter, Stravinsky's agent Gavril Païchadze relayed Stravinsky's wishes regarding the Muses' appearance: "I would like to call your attention on this occasion to a little omission Mr. Stravinsky made in communicating to you the description of the costumes. In that description he wrote that the muses wore the traditional tutu and should hide it under light tunics during the prologue. It is clear that one can hide the tutu with difficulty under the tunic. Stravinsky forgot to add that the dancers should have on over the tunics, the leotard and the breast plate, and put on the tutus after having taken off their tunics, which only takes a few seconds."

The production proved nightmarish for Engel. Bickering almost consumed the dancers, choreographer, conductor, and musicians. A few days before the performance, a complete collapse seemed likely. "If we ever get through this," Engel quipped, "I shall do a dance of my own." The premiere's reception was, to say the least, less than a triumph. In several unpublished letters, Engel and Coolidge lament the blandness of the music, whose unadorned chasteness caught them unprepared. The only kind words Olin Downes could find were for Bolm's choreography. A very young John Martin, having only recently as-

sumed his post at the *New York Times,* also praised Bolm's work. "It is doubtful," Martin wrote, "if [Bolm] or any other choreographer has ever been faced
with a ballet score offering any more difficulties." Martin immediately saw that
Apollo fell far short of the "gala" showpiece the festival had anticipated. It was
the exotic Russian, not the phlegmatic Greek, Stravinsky the Americans had
come to hear. Martin's review wryly observed that in 1928, fifteen years after the
once-scandalous *Rite,* the American audience was abuzz with hopes that a virgin would be sacrificed; nothing less would do.

In his *Autobiography,* Stravinsky hastily downplayed the American reception,
admitting that he was far more interested in the Parisian premiere. Given this
wholesale dismissal, the ballet's American history might be tucked away in a
footnote were it not that the Coolidge commission formatively shaped the
piece's underlying structural dimensions. Kirstein once applauded Stravinsky
and Balanchine's brilliant decision to forsake the traditional "large *corps de ballets* as a background for [the] soloists," thus creating one of "the most surprising
novelties."[20] But given the library's limitations, a large corps was never an option. If there is any brilliance here, it is in the fact that Balanchine altered nothing once he began choreographing in Monte Carlo, though he had few spatial
or personnel constraints.

As for Stravinsky's musical decisions, the *Apollo* sketchbook in Basel leaves a
reconstructible trail. Each sketch is meticulously dated, enabling an unusually
reliable retracing of the compositional process. For example, Kindler's derision
of the poor string scoring notwithstanding, the mellifluous sextet writing of
Apollo clearly contributes to the rich, diaphanous "whiteness" of the ballet.[21]
But the Basel sketches reveal that Stravinsky originally had a different instrumentation in mind: one that included both piano and harp. Given the central-
ity of the lyre in the Apollonian myth, the use of the harp makes sense enough.
The extant sketches for piano are also unsurprising, especially since the keyboard was employed prominently in many Stravinsky works of the period, including *Oedipus Rex.*

The sketchbook further discloses that among the first instrumental drafts,
Stravinsky planned a complement of eighteen strings and allowed space for the
piano and harp, thus totaling the twenty instruments Engel had specified. But
the appropriateness of sound and symbol aside, these two bulkiest instruments
of the orchestra proved impractical for the auditorium's small, sunken pit.
Once Stravinsky conceded that the piano and harp were simply too unwieldy,
his sketchbook, almost to the exact day, shows him undertaking a reorchestra-
tion of the strings. For the first time, sketches for strings written *divisi* (wherein

one string section, such as the violins, is divided into several individual parts) are employed as a functional solution, compensating texturally for the now forsaken harp and piano. As for Apollo's lyre, a solo violin would have to do.

Had the Washington orchestra pit been larger, the scoring might well have been quite different. The specified length of the ballet was decided primarily in keeping with what would be a divertissement for Washington's glitterati, and Stravinsky complied. Most relevant, the dimensions of the choreographic design were delimited by the constrictive size of the stage—a very specific compositional problem. And in finding that solution, Stravinsky demonstrated his masterful ability to deal with whatever limitations were imposed upon him, just as Balanchine would do when faced with similar restrictions.

Apollon Musagète was performed only once during the festival. In the months that followed the Washington staging, Serge Koussevitzky frequently conducted the score as an orchestral suite. In an unpublished letter (4 December 1928) held in the Sacher Stiftung, he wrote to the composer, "Everyone is delighted with Stravinsky, whom it is just as pleasant to hear as Handel. As far as the critics are concerned, as you well know, among them there are always asses." But no matter, for Stravinsky remained indifferent toward any American performance, on- or offstage. The truth is the composer's eyes were trained squarely on Paris from the start. After a single staged performance, to the near effacement of any memory of the Washington premiere, Coolidge's *Apollo* became Diaghilev's *Apollo* forevermore.

On 21 January 1928 Stravinsky telegraphed Diaghilev, inviting him to his home in Nice the next day. He also asked that Balanchine come along. It was then, the young choreographer recalled, that Stravinsky played the ballet at the piano, stressing correct tempi. He repeated them several times so that there would be no mistaking his intent. Choreographing from the composer's recently completed piano score, Balanchine soon put the piece in rehearsal, working first with Alexandra Danilova. There is no question that he and Stravinsky had rehearsed sections of the ballet long before Bolm received the score in Washington. On 15 December 1927, a month before Stravinsky's cable to Diaghilev, Stravinsky had written to Ansermet, detailing his "*Musagète*" and his ongoing discussions with Diaghilev. Two months earlier still, an informative article by Michel Georges-Michel had appeared in the 27 October issue of *Excelsior,* entitled "A New Work by a Great Musician of Today: *Apollon Musagète,* by Igor Stravinsky, and the Unpublished Concepts of the Composer." The author's comments are instructive in previewing details of the in-progress composition as related by Diaghilev. Moreover, the article unabashedly ballyhoos the ballet nearly eight months in advance of the Parisian premiere.[22]

Georges-Michel begins by summarizing his opinion of Diaghilev's contributions:

> Yesterday I had lunch with Serge de Diaghilev, the creator-producer of those astonishing Russian ballets, which for the past twenty years have been the mirror-harbinger of international art. For that magnificent organization, dance is but a magical decoy. And Diaghilev's merit is surely to have revealed painters and musicians more than dancers. Didn't he create this paradox by bringing the fauves and cubists to the stage of our National Music and Dance Academy itself? Picasso, Derain, Matisse. . . . This time he announces to me the "return" of Igor Stravinsky.

He then alludes to Stravinsky's "quasi-religious crisis," suggesting that when Diaghilev asked him in 1926 to do a new ballet, the composer had refused, declaring that ballet was akin to sacrilege. Stravinsky's repatriation with Diaghilev and the Ballets Russes is heralded, as is the important role that Serge Lifar will play in the new ballet—a ballet which will be free of Stravinsky's "own scholasticism." The composer's conception of a simpler music as an antidote to the Teutonic excess of Wagner is stressed. Stravinsky "no longer liked anything except Latin and Slavic music when it was allied with Italian art, and he avoided the colossal and the detested pathos," the author added. Scarlatti, Verdi, Tchaikovsky, Gounod—these were models worthy of emulation, Stravinsky purportedly declared; these were the composers, added Georges-Michel, "toward whom young musicians were attracted, just as young cubists were drawn to Ingres." Next Diaghilev provides a foretaste of the ballet:

> I had the wonderful surprise of hearing Stravinsky say to me, "I wrote simple music so that the choreographer Lifar could make flourishes. *Apollon* is written solely for string orchestra." And Stravinsky has created a new melody in it. It is Bellini. But instead of giving us a melody in feeling, he will give it to us in thematic material. He took scissors and cut the material up into zinc, for heaven's sake. He made a melody as if the movement of a watch could be a melody.
>
> *Apollon* will be something different. A striking example. In *Apollon* there is a dance adagio in four voices. The first voice sings the adagio in a cadence that is twice as fast in two voices, three times faster in three voices, and quadrupled in four voices. In this way the same melody takes on four different manners with a mechanical, fatalistic regularity.
>
> *Apollon* is swarming with these new concepts. And why that title? . . . Shouldn't we see Apollo differently from the way preceding centuries did? Or, if the symbol of

Beauty doesn't evolve as Beauty evolves, or if its appearance in the period doesn't, it is no longer Beauty. Was Apollo thought of under the reign of Louis XV the way Carpaccio painted him? Mustn't Stravinsky and 1927 bring out a masterpiece as a mechanical piece from the viewpoint of their era or that of tomorrow, rather than that of the past?

Vera Stravinsky recalled that Diaghilev, Balanchine, and her future husband regularly discussed *Apollo,* although she added that both the scenario and the actual staging were exclusively Stravinsky's. Almost fifty years after the ballet's premiere, Balanchine remembered Stravinsky seated at the piano articulating what he originally envisioned. Once the composer made clear his intent, Balanchine was then invited to spell out what he had in mind. In a film clip cut from Palmer's television biopic, Soulima Stravinsky reported that because their home in Nice was so close to Monte Carlo, where the Ballets Russes wintered, his father often saw Diaghilev, who "would come very frequently and have meals with us and discuss business. I remember when father was composing *Apollo,* he played for Diaghilev as he was composing what he had already achieved, and he asked me to help him play; he couldn't grasp all the notes on the score, so I played for Diaghilev. I did that for him, for my father."

Diaghilev felt betrayed by what he took to be the composer's treasonous acceptance of the Coolidge commission, and Stravinsky, in turn, complained about Diaghilev's nitpicking. But neither the composer nor the impresario had call to be annoyed. Almost from the moment Coolidge commissioned the ballet, Stravinsky joined with the principals of the Ballets Russes (Balanchine, Diaghilev, Kochno, and Lifar) to mount the Parisian production. In effect, *Apollo* fell into Diaghilev's lap courtesy of Coolidge.

Nicolas Nabokov, who daily witnessed Balanchine's creation of the ballet in Monte Carlo, remembers Diaghilev remarking, "What he is doing is magnificent. It is pure classicism, such as we have not seen since Petipa's."[23] Privately, however, Diaghilev was of a mixed mind. Stravinsky intimated that secretly Diaghilev disliked the music; but perhaps Diaghilev's real misgivings centered on Balanchine's innovative concept of the dance. According to Kochno, Diaghilev was not so much concerned about Stravinsky as he was wary of his impious young choreographer's growing emancipation.

If Lifar and Diaghilev are to be believed, Stravinsky planned the role of Apollo, and indeed the entire ballet, around the premier danseur. In his autobiography, *Ma Vie,* Lifar reports that after he first danced *La Chatte,* Diaghilev told him, "My congratulations, Serge. Stravinsky has said to me some remarkable things about you. He is so enthusiastic about your dancing that although he has a commission from America he wants to write a ballet specially for you."[24] Moreover, Diaghilev's reference to Lifar as the choreographer of *Apollo* in the *Excelsior* article is curious. Perhaps at that early point, Stravinsky did have Lifar in mind. How much say Lifar had in the choreography is difficult to determine, but clearly he was influential, making his wishes known especially with regard to his two solo variations.

Curiously, the original typescript of one of Stravinsky and Craft's conversation books, *Memories and Commentaries* (the typescript with Stravinsky's markings is preserved in the Sacher Stiftung), clearly shows that *Apollo* was jointly choreographed by Lifar and Balanchine; but when Stravinsky proofed the typescript, he deleted Lifar's name. Perhaps the composer dropped the reference because by the late 1950s, when the book was compiled, he was no longer on speaking terms with Lifar. Thirty years earlier, however, when *Apollo* was composed, Stravinsky was genuinely struck by Lifar's unique, athletic dancing, even mentioning in his *Autobiography* that Lifar was "conscientious, natural, spontaneous, and full of serious enthusiasm for his art."[25]

In a 30 September letter to Lifar, Diaghilev describes a visit to Stravinsky in Nice:

> After lunch he played for me the first half of the new ballet. It is, of course, an amazing work, extraordinarily calm, and with greater clarity than anything he has so far done; and filigree counterpoint round transparent, clear-cut themes, all in the major key; somehow music not of this world, but from somewhere above. It seems strange that, though the tempo of all this part is slow, yet at the same time it is perfectly adapted to dancing. There is a short, fast movement in your first variation—there are to be two for you, and the opening is to be danced to an unaccompanied violin solo. . . . The Adagio (pas d'action) has a broad theme very germane to us today; it runs concurrently in four different tempos, and yet, generally speaking, the harmony is most satisfactory. I embraced him and he said: "It is for you to produce it properly for me: I want Lifar to have all sorts of flourishes."[26]

In Diaghilev's eyes, Lifar was Nijinsky's rightful heir. In yet another expurgated film clip from the Palmer interview, Lifar brashly claims that the violin cadenza opening the first Variation d'Apollon was "the highest achievement in ballet, but unfortunately it was discontinued by Balanchine so that dancers nowadays, such as Nureyev and Baryshnikov, no longer do it. I danced that improvisation with all the technique and grace of an Apollo." In the same 1981 clip, Lifar further recounts his memories of *Apollo* and his relationship with both Diaghilev and Stravinsky: "Through Diaghilev I was personally able to get acquainted with Stravinsky, who wrote the ballet *Apollon Musagète* for me in 1928, and he was my conductor. And I must admit that it wasn't Stravinsky's best, from the view of conducting. Also, you cannot imagine what I went through when he decided to give the downbeat as I did my variation. I was doing pliés, I tried to keep up with him, then all of a sudden he gave the downbeat. But all the same he was like a god to me at the time."

Eager to establish his independence, Balanchine was nonetheless Diaghilev's employee. How then would the vulnerable choreographer walk a politically precarious tightrope, especially one confounded by Diaghilev's current intimacy with Lifar? Although it seems implausible that Diaghilev could actually have compelled Stravinsky to compose a score entirely around the dancer, it is likely that the authoritarian impresario cajoled Balanchine into featuring Lifar's strengths. Having choreographed four earlier ballets for Lifar, Balanchine was thoroughly familiar with the dancer's attributes as well as his shortcomings.

As a later Apollo, Jacques d'Amboise, related to Francis Mason, Balanchine worked with Lifar for almost a year before the premiere (a further indication of the intent, long before the score was sent to America, to stage the work in Paris). D'Amboise remembered that Balanchine said that he cursed the premiere "because Lifar had had a big success in *Apollo* and Balanchine did not."[27] Just as Stravinsky had to deal with the severe spatial strictures in Washington, so Balanchine had to accommodate *Apollo's* choreography to Lifar. Kirstein's description of Lifar's dancing, and how it shaped the entire ballet, is informative, particularly in partially explicating the work's prototypic gestures, especially the female variations, "which were organized and designed to be consistent with the unique masculine role."[28]

Balanchine's breach of traditional balletic concepts in *Apollo* rankled its critics. The rudiments of the Petipa tradition—the discrete positionings of the body, the use of the arms, the treatment of the ensemble in itself as well as in its relationship to the soloist—all were frequently altered, even skewed. Something simply wasn't right. The turned-in legs, torso distortions, inverted gestures, unusually wide poses, jutting hips and shoulders—what did these unacademic contortions have to do with classicism? Danilova, who danced the role of Terpsichore, told Mason that the Parisian audience was stunned: "[Balanchine] had us flex our feet, shortening them in our toe shoes . . . and we used angular hands instead of rounded classical hands. Without any ceremony Apollo lifts Terpsichore onto his back! It was free movement . . . a completely new vocabulary." Other Balanchine dancers have agreed, including Maria Tallchief, who spoke of *Apollo's* "turned-in legs, walking on the heels, and contractions of the torso."[29]

During the 1960s in New York, Edward Villella learned the role of Apollo from Balanchine himself. The same kind of refurbishing of fundamental positions was instantly apparent to Villella:

> What followed was extraordinary. Sixty years old at the time . . . he danced this big variation from *Apollo* for me. It was astonishing. . . . He began by showing me that the very first gesture of Apollo's variation with the arms up and hands horizontal is really fifth position high. In this one simple gesture of Apollo's, Balanchine just took fifth position and extended it! Neoclassicism is exemplified by that *single* move. The next gesture in the variation, when Apollo flattens his hands and forearms on his head, is fifth position reduced and flattened. . . . He went on, talking about the second-position step in which Apollo kicks left and right with his working leg.[30]

The elevation of the three Muses as Apollo lifted them, and the support of all three by a single male dancer, were viewed as unprecedented actions. The employment of such a small ensemble of dancers, each taking an important role in a group pas, also seemed peculiar but dynamic. Such "modernization," as it was decried in the 1920s, was viewed as a profanation of classicism itself. Balanchine's inspiration, as noted earlier, is largely attributable to Kasyan Yaroslavich Goleizovsky, the man he so admired in Petrograd. Elizabeth Souritz observes that Goleizovsky "inherited, on the one hand, a profound knowledge of classical dance and respect for it as the professional basis of the art of ballet, and on the other hand, a mistrust for the immutability of academic canons." Goleizovsky's notoriety was such that as early as 1925 his innovative ideas turned up in the pages of the *New York Times Magazine*. He aimed toward "a return to pure dancing art and the creation of forms adequate to it, insisting upon the independence of dance as an art form subject only to its own constructive laws." And further, "The sole material with which choreography works is motion of the human body, taken not in its submissive aspect for the expression of this or that thought and frame of mind, but for itself." Balanchine endorsed such constructivist notions, but rather than renouncing classicism he embraced it with a sense of renewal, just as Stravinsky did. Both chose to recast classicism's fundamental tenets rather than abandon them altogether. Thus *Apollo's* neoclassicism emanates from, but never pedantically follows, the canon of the classical tradition in which Balanchine was schooled.[31]

Given the sharpening criticism Diaghilev's troupe was suffering, a successful mounting of the more soberly conceived and probably less immediately appealing *Apollo* was imperative. Diaghilev himself took charge of preparing the 18 June premiere, leaving the staging of other works in progress, such as Nabokov's *Ode,* to Kochno and Massine. But as with Bolm's American production only six weeks earlier, Diaghilev's staging proved a hodgepodge. Stylistic incongruities clashed in conflating the simplicity of the music and the excessive ornament of the scenery. Moreover, the road between Nice and Monte Carlo ran both ways: while Diaghilev and Balanchine frequently traveled to Stravinsky's home, the composer often visited the Ballets Russes's studios, making his own wishes unmistakably clear.

In matters of costume and especially décor, an outspoken Stravinsky was frequently at odds with Diaghilev. Sensibility suggested that a classicist such as André Derain should design the ballet; or as Stravinsky himself proposed, Giorgio De Chirico, whose designs were known for their classical architecture. Especially given the composer's marmoreal image of *Apollo* as a *ballet blanc,* De Chirico's affinity for whiteness as a unifying foundation seemed an appropriate match. But Stravinsky's preference notwithstanding, André Bauchant was Diaghilev's choice. Touted by fashionable Parisian art dealers as a bright new star, Bauchant was little more than an eccentric gardener who had taken up painting around 1920. Fifty years after the ballet's premiere, Balanchine told Nancy Reynolds that Diaghilev had been passing by Bauchant's farm one day and noticed a few paintings that he found attractive. Since Apollo was to be portrayed as a young boy—"a *primitive* Apollo," as Balanchine characterized him— Bauchant's "primitive" paintings struck Diaghilev as suitable. Bauchant completed a canvas in 1925 entitled *Apollon apparaissant aux bergers,* complete with chariot and Muses ascending the heavens (fig. 4.1).[32] Moreover, in the years immediately preceding *Apollo,* Bauchant's frequent exhibitions were riding a wave of widespread popularity in France. Undoubtedly the always shrewd Diaghilev wished to capitalize upon Bauchant's current notoriety. But in the end Bauchant's aesthetic was utterly unlike the classicism of Derain or De Chirico, and the original sets proved a distraction.

Stravinsky later stated that he had not seen "eye to eye" with Diaghilev. He had hoped for "short white ballet skirts in a severely conventionalized theatrical landscape devoid of all fantastic embellishment." The composer was unhappy with the choice of Bauchant: "What he produced was interesting, but as I had expected, it in no way suited my ideas."[33] In a letter to Carl Engel a month before the American premiere, Stravinsky outlined his already clearly envisioned ideas about costuming. The length of the tutus—a hotly contested topic of the

4.1 André Bauchant, pencil drawing of an early sketch for *Apollon Musagète* (Jerome Robbins Dance Division, The New York Public Library for the Performing Arts, Astor, Lenox and Tilden Foundations)

1920s ballet world—was specified; he wanted short tutus. Yet at the Parisian premiere, Kochno remembers that the Muses wore long white skirts. The costumes proved so unsatisfactory that Coco Chanel was commissioned to design new ones the next year. Here again, Balanchine's memory is informative. Diaghilev made "lousy costumes," Balanchine told Reynolds. "The tutus were all grayish and dirty looking. One girl had it cut long in back and [short] in front. The other one had it cut [short] in back and long in front. And the third one

4.2 Serge Lifar and the three Muses in the original production of *Apollon Musagète,* Paris, 1928 (Jerome Robbins Dance Division, The New York Public Library for the Performing Arts, Astor, Lenox and Tilden Foundations)

[was] cut [short] in front and back. Idiotic, awful, the idea. Lifar's [costume] was red and gold, and very badly made" (fig. 4.2).[34]

Stravinsky conducted the premiere on the same program as his popular *Pulcinella* and *Firebird.* (Balanchine danced the evil Kastchei in the latter.) The inclusion of these chestnuts surely was calculated to garner a favorable response. Lubov Tchernicheva danced Calliope, and Alice Nikitina and Danilova alternated as Terpsichore. Felia Doubrovska danced Polyhymnia. Many years later, in an interview, Doubrovska said that "Diaghilev generally didn't like too much emotion from a woman onstage, and if Diaghilev decided something, there was no discussion. One day, Boris [Kochno] called me to Diaghilev who said to me 'Where do you dance . . . Do we agree this is not a music-hall? Why do you do so much with your face, your eyes? You have to have more dignity.'"[35]

Although Stravinsky expressed indifference about the Washington production and the criticisms that followed, Paris was a different matter. With typical revisionism, the composer avowed that the "French" *Apollo* had succeeded marvelously. Lifar, Grigoriev, and Diaghilev later bolstered what was little more than wishful thinking, for most reviews were harsh. Guido Pannain caustically pronounced the ballet impotent, atavistic, and guilty of "fake classicism." Arthur Lourié, considered both a champion of Stravinsky's music and the composer's confidant, charged Stravinsky with deserting the classical principles that had guided his music for the past decade: "For my part I see in it a decline of the neoclassic current and an attempt to make room for the romantic tendency."[36] And as might have been anticipated, the Soviet press, which by now had disowned Stravinsky and his bourgeois brand of Western classicism, was even more vitriolic. Prokofiev found *Apollo* uninteresting and creatively feeble.

The most gratuitous assault was launched by Boris Asaf'yev (himself a ballet composer) in his once-banned *Kniga o Stravinskom,* first released in Leningrad in 1929: "Almost all of the music of *Apollon* bears witness to the annoying attempt to make new cloth out of old thread: the ear is continually drawn to patches of cheap, old material that spot the fabric of the sound. . . . [The] result is a hyper-refinement of texture and a simplification that is itself an utter failure." Given Asaf'yev's ideological allegiance to socialist realism, his mourning of Stravinsky's repulse of his Russian folktale heritage seems predictable. The composer's adoption of the storyless ballet in *Apollo* was also tossed off as folly: "By refusing to have a coherent extra-musical theme for *Apollon,* Stravinsky breaks with those who expect the musical theater to be a force of aesthetic value."[37]

Balanchine fared no better. His choreography employed gestures and movements deemed "horrifying." The choreographer was reproached for everything from pontifical solemnity to "refrigerated classicism," as André Levinson later accused.[38] Although it was inevitable that Balanchine's *Apollo* would be assailed as a corruption of classical dance, just as Stravinsky's score would be maligned as a dismal gallimaufry, what went unmentioned was the artistic cohesion the composer and choreographer had forged. It was a fusion all the more impressive given the stipulations of the American commission and Diaghilev's personal agenda. Balanchine had crafted an astonishingly compatible complement to Stravinsky's classicism, a synergistic vision glimpsed through the same side of the neoclassic prism that Stravinsky had originally imagined.

For the composer, this imagination was chiefly stirred by a resurgence of interest in the ancient, enduring beauty of classicism. Everything "Greek" captivated him, from medieval iconography and its embrace of the mysterious power of numbers and symmetry to the Pythagorean view of beauty as the reduction of many to one. But more than anything it was Stravinsky's study and adoption of classical literary models in creating *Apollo* that looms most meaningful. Typically, Stravinsky's studies proceeded with an air of erudition. Balanchine—no less a disciple of classicism's tenets—approached matters more instinctually. With his musical gifts as a reliable guide, his keen eye easily tracked the compositional path Stravinsky paved. But just how did Stravinsky find that path; what specifically were his models; and what might his compositional sketchbook tell us about the ballet's genesis and development?

Chapter 5 The Evolution of
Apollo: Poetry, Musical
Architecture, and
Choreographic Equilibrium

Architectural design is neither competitive nor curative nor delusionary. I
say that the architectural scheme must be made apparent to the observer
because all conveyance of meaning of whatever sort must ultimately be in
the revelation of structure, order, and relationships. . . . How much of
structure needs to be revealed to free it of the charge of being concealed?
The "how" of it is of little interest to the observer, nor should it be shown
in its entirety even if we wanted to. It is enough if the structural scheme is
made understandable.
—*Eugene Raskin,* Architecturally Speaking

More than a hundred pages of compositional sketches provide a window on the evolution of *Apollo's* musical structure. Also retained in
the Basel archives is Stravinsky's instructive 1927 piano reduction,
which is useful for outlining the ballet's initial staging specifications.
For example, the composer changed his mind, perhaps in consulta-
tion with Balanchine and Diaghilev, about the opening curtain
(*rideau*). Originally it was to have risen at an earlier juncture of the
Prologue's opening music. The keyboard score is also filled with
Stravinsky's own piano fingerings—not at all unusual inasmuch as the

tactilely oriented composer-pianist frequently drafted ideas arising from figurations fitting his hand. The fact that he took the time to enter the fingerings so carefully suggests that he practiced the keyboard score seriously, probably in preparation for playing the score himself during at least some of the rehearsals.[1]

"The last thing one discovers in composing a work is what to put first," Pascal observed. Just so, beginnings of works often proved problematic for Stravinsky. A composition's critical embarkation point had to be earned, and that could only occur after either the middle or the ending of the piece was worked out first. Consider the evolution of Stravinsky's earliest sketches for the Prologue. Figure 5.1 summarizes the compositional chronology of the opening thirty-two measures. Preliminary ideas were initially cast in eleven separate blocks—separate in that each is isolated from the other in the layout of the actual sketch pages. The composer carefully dated each block. The material ultimately used as mm. 15–16 of the Prologue, for example, was actually drafted during Stravinsky's first composing session on 16 July 1927, shortly after he accepted the American commission.

The music that eventually served as the ballet's all-important first two measures was not written until several days later, on 20 July. Stravinsky first notes the distribution of the orchestra's twenty instruments on the same day: four first violins; four second violins; four violas; two first cellos; two second cellos; two contrabasses, plus the originally planned piano and harp, for which several sketches were completed. As the first day's sketching ended, Stravinsky notated

Block	Measures	Date
1	15–16	16 July 1927
2	12–14	16 July
3	11–14	16 July
4	15–18	16 July
5	Pas de deux	16 July
6	19–22	18 July
7	3–5	18 July
8	6–10	19 July
9	1–2	20 July
10	30–32	20 July
11	23–29	20 July

5.1 Sketch summary of individual compositional blocks in the Prologue of *Apollon Musagète*

his initial thought for the Pas de deux (just the rough thematic material of what would become the first few measures). As becomes evident, the Pas de deux was on the composer's mind throughout *Apollo*'s drafting.

The next day, 17 July, Stravinsky drafted the opening of the Prologue. Who knows how much prenotational exploration went on at the keyboard? Soulima Stravinsky reported that his father constantly tried new combinations of chords and figurations before writing out those he favored. Whatever the extent of this process, Stravinsky typically composed short, two- or three-measure segments. Only later did he assemble the final sequence that would appear in the ballet. Here, and at later moments in the sketchbook, the composer writes in Russian, "insert," revealing that certain measures were added between already composed segments. Remarkably this seemingly desultory approach does nothing to undermine the organically seamless nature of the ballet. On the contrary, it provides the cradle for many of the ballet's fundamental figures.

The first measures notated in the sketchbook on 16 July (mm. 15–16) mark the music Stravinsky initially intended to accompany the opening rideau, where Leto gives birth to Apollo. Throughout the sketches a similar pattern emerges. The composer begins by articulating a pivotally important musical idea, then composes toward that moment. Finally, on the reverse side of virtually every sketch page, Stravinsky tabulates the duration of each individual compositional unit. Specific notations such as "Durée 1′35" are frequently recorded, evincing the composer's constant temporal awareness generally, and more specifically the imposed time strictures of the Coolidge commission. Nor is it unimaginable that Balanchine, Diaghilev, and Lifar may have at least advised the composer in temporal matters since Stravinsky regularly played sketches for them as the work evolved. We also know from the later collaborations in *Jeu de Cartes, Orpheus,* and *Agon* that Stravinsky often asked Balanchine precisely how much time was needed to accommodate his choreographic conceptions.

Consider the Pas d'action, where for the first time Apollo is joined by all three Muses. Balanchine was particularly fond of this music's unusually serene melodic flow. Some have speculated that the beautiful line must have gushed out in one paroxysmal moment, so mellifluous is the melody. But not so, for in composing it Stravinsky sewed together several short, separately conceived ideas. The music begins at what is marked as Rehearsal 24 in the score. (It is assigned the letter *A* in figure 5.2.) Rehearsal 25 in the score (occurring six measures later) is designated here by the letter *B*. Rehearsal 26 is *C,* and so on. Each rehearsal number in the score represents a separate compositional block, that is, something originally conceived of as a unit. The chart provides a timeline sum-

Time line of sketches by block as they were composed	F	I	G	L	*B-C-D*	A	E	M	*J–K*	H	*N–O*
Rehearsal Nos. in published score	29				25–27	24			33–34		37–38
Measure Nos. in published score	38				6	1			78		108

5.2 Sketch chronology and final compositional order of the Pas d'action of *Apollon Musagète*

mary with which to compare the sequence in which Stravinsky composed the music with its ultimate overall order. The first music that Stravinsky composed, designated in the chart by *F* (Rehearsal 29) was not used until the score's thirty-eighth measure. The music that Stravinsky did finally employ as the opening of the Pas d'action, letter *A* (Rehearsal 24), was not written until about midway through the compositional process. With three exceptions, marked by the italicized *B-C-D* (Rehearsals 25, 26, and 27), *J-K* (Rehearsals 33 and 34), and the ending, *N-O* (Rehearsals 37 and 38), each reflecting passages that were composed contiguously, every unit was drafted independently and then repositioned as the piece's architecture unfolded.

Figure 5.3 summarizes similar internal reconfigurations of separately composed modules in four more of the individual dances. In each, the material eventually serving as the beginning of the pas (each letter again designating a rehearsal number, with *A* representing the music ultimately used as the opening of each movement) was not composed first. The one exception appears in the Apothéose, wherein *X* represents music Stravinsky, uncharacteristically, discarded. Consistently, Stravinsky creates musical ideas as they strike him, then later forges a series of musical transitions that ensure the music's overall coherence.

Movement	Compositional Order
Variation de Calliope	C, B, *A*, F, E
Variation de Polyhymnia	D, F, I, E, *A*, B, C, G, H
Variation d'Apollon (the second of two)	E, B, C, D, *A*, F
Apothéose	*X*, *A*, E, C, D, E, F, B

5.3 Summary of the compositional order in the four dances from *Apollon Musagète*

Beyond such internal reordering, what was the nature and extent of Stravinsky's reliance upon preexisting—and, specifically, nonmusical—models? The composer himself points the way. *Apollo* was occupied with iambics, he once remarked. It is the rhythmic figure of a short-long stress (♪♩), or the figure reversed (♩♪), which is unmistakably reminiscent of discernible patterns in Renaissance music and dance. But it was more than that, as Stravinsky explained in *Dialogues*. The ballet was about versification, about prosody, and "the idea of the Alexandrines." He pointed to the rhythm of Calliope's variation (at Rehearsal 41), wherein "the pizzicato accompaniment is a Russian Alexandrine suggested to me by a couplet from Pushkin." Not only was this his first compositional idea, but the entire variation, he added, was "a musical exposition of the Boileau text that I took as my motto."[2]

Why versification as an agent of musical cohesion? The psychologist Julian Jaynes reminds us that there is a god-side to our ancient mentality, and that the first poets were gods speaking and teaching in verse: "Poetry was divine knowledge . . . the sound and tenor of authorization."[3] Stravinsky believed in this timeless, universal divinity, just as in his opera-oratorio *Oedipus Rex* he knew his invocation of Latin, the "deadest of languages," would provide an ageless continuity to his message. If *Apollo's* prosody emanates from various literary models, what were they, and how were they musically transfigured? The answers are traceable to the composer's life-long interest in etymology and poetry. The musical syntax of *Apollo* is inseparably tied to the Greek view of prosody as a basic grammatical device. As with Ezra Pound's "Great Bass," described by R. Murray Schafer as "existing like the keel of a ship, exercising centripetal pull over everything above it," so too *Apollo's* path is guided by its prosodic reliance and underlying rhythmic patterns. Its concept of "absolute rhythm" (in itself fundamentally Greek in origin) speaks directly to Stravinsky's use of versification as its cornerstone.[4]

The composer was always drawn to matters of textual nuance. The meter of verse, the pure sound of the words themselves, served as grist as he plumbed the natural rhythmic flow of syllabication. His sketchbooks consistently exhibit a manipulation of motivic ideas rooted in his affinity for the sounds and rhythms of language. Whether the source was traceable to Russian folk song or Greek prosody, Stravinsky's idiosyncratic style of instrumental writing cannot be dissociated from the patterns of speech accent and dialect he found endlessly fascinating. This critical connection helps explain the fundamental linguistic roots that underlay the distinctive string ensemble figurations of *Apollo*. Moreover, given the dramaturgy of *Oedipus Rex,* a work marked by a motionless, statuesque classicism, the composer's projections of versification onto the ballet's musical and visual structure seem not only reasonable but almost predictable. *Apollo* was the logical next step.[5]

The composer's familiarity with the writings of contemporary French poets and intellectuals—Apollinaire, Cocteau, Lourié, and Valéry—is crucial to an understanding of the classical grammar of *Apollo*'s artistic message. Valéry and Apollinaire in particular advocated a return to the clarity of classicism that is so evident in the ballet. As a perusal of the composer's extant library and correspondence reveals, these literati collectively bent Stravinsky's thinking in far more fundamental ways than are found in the often mentioned but essentially superficial resemblance to the music of Bellini, Delibes, and Tchaikovsky. If the real spiritual and structural fiber of *Apollo* is to be penetrated, a long corridor of poets leading from Horace to the modern classicists of Parisian verse deserve exploration.[6]

Likewise, the underlying bond uniting poetic meter and dance has deep roots. With the establishment of the sixteenth-century *Ballet Comique,* measured verse stood as the guiding principle of dance. Reaching back further to the antiquity of Horace, versification provided the sturdy scaffolding of later Renaissance choreographic structure. As music for the ballet required absolute compliance to the metrical regulations of poetry, so too did dance. At every structural level, the linkage of specific dance steps with specific temporal durations was axiomatic. Nowhere is such interfacing more evident than in Balanchine's setting of *Apollo.* Undoubtedly, the dotted rhythms permeating *Apollo,* from the French overture–like Prologue ♪♫ ♪♫ to the concluding Apothéose, were intended as explicit references to the court of Louis XIV—a court in which the fourteen-year-old *roi soleil* danced the role of Apollo in *Le Ballet de la Nuit* (1653). It was through dance that Louis heralded the splendor of his monarchy most visibly. Moreover, beginning in 1661, Jean-Baptiste Lully, who joined the Versailles court also at age fourteen and later stood next to Louis in performances of *Le Ballet de la Nuit,* was charged with instituting the first true ballet company.[7]

Stravinsky valued civility and protocol. He would have immediately identified with the dignity and clearly defined hierarchy of Versailles. He admired Lully's stature as a composer who was privileged enough to collaborate with Molière and Corneille in several acclaimed ballets. Dancing was serious business at court, practiced every day and designed to teach, not merely to divert. As the most important musical influence for *Apollo,* Lully should not be underestimated. His ballets were exemplars of good taste. As Kirstein noted, Lully's music "provided a sonorous base and background for danced statements of pyramidal political order with, at a choreographic peak, the prince. His music—clear-cut, logical, deliberate, authoritative—suited the firm symmetry of Versailles."[8]

Stravinsky's emphasis on iambic figures and his explicit reference to alexandrines warrant a closer look. The alexandrine (the term derived from the twelfth century, with reference to Alexander the Great) is a measured twelve-syllable verse, marked midway by a pause, or caesura. The form experienced a revival in sixteenth-century France, though its pinnacle is more commonly associated with the eighteenth-century classical tragedies of Corneille and Racine. At the time of *Apollo,* Stravinsky was reading Nicolas Boileau (1636–1711). Revered for his staunch advocacy of artistic discipline and restraint, Boileau was the author of the alexandrine-structured 1674 treatise *L'Art poétique,* the acknowledged magnum opus of classical principles. Given Boileau's fondness for polemics, it is little wonder that Stravinsky was attracted to the witty French contrarian. A friend of La Fontaine, Molière, and Racine, Boileau lampooned his contemporaries (as exhibited in his *Satires* and *Le Lutrin*), taking dead aim at the tendentious and often sermonic squabbling dividing the ancients and moderns.

In his memoir *Mes amis et moi,* Francis Poulenc remembered how Stravinsky would throw himself into a new composition by studying models as a means of steeping his works in authenticity. Just so, the composer was working on the early stages of *Apollo* when Poulenc visited in 1927. Stravinsky excitedly informed Poulenc that he had discovered "le poète Boileau!"—a most marvelous poet, he exclaimed. Perhaps not a Racine, but still a marvelous poet. "I have found a verse in the *Art poétique* that is precisely what I needed to set an exergue for a variation of one of my muses," Stravinsky remarked. Poulenc added that while the didactic verse was unquotable, it served Stravinsky's purpose, and that was all that mattered.[9]

While history is quick to remember that Lully was Louis's in-house composer, we should also be reminded that Boileau was the king's "royal historiographer." Boileau's popular alexandrines carried the status of proverbs, extolling the inviolable sanctity of classicism. His *L'Art poétique* flowed straight from Horace's own *Ars poetica.* As a self-proclaimed *ancien,* Boileau insisted that artistic inspiration could never provide justification for relinquishing the dispassionate temperance of classical reasoning. How remarkably similar in spirit was Stravinsky's own embrace of "divine detachment," as Valéry once described it. Dubbed by his contemporaries "the lawgiver of the French Parnassus," Boileau proclaimed his apologia in the grand manner of Descartes that would have surely warmed Stravinsky's Cartesian core. Given the composer's knowledge of the treatise, it is likely that Boileau's creed, as reflected in a few representative excerpts, provided a model for *Apollo*'s scenario:

> Hear all the world; consider every thought;
> A fool by chance may stumble on a fault.
> Yet when Apollo does your muse inspire,
> Be not impatient to expose your fire.
>
> And by a priest possessed with rage divine,
> Apollo spoke from his prophetic shrine.
> Soon after, Homer the old heroes praised,
> And noble minds by great examples raised.
> The Muses thus their reputation raised,
> And, with gratitude, in Greece were praised;
> With pleasure mortals did their wonders see,
> And sacrificed to their divinity.

Stravinsky adopted much more than the broad spirit of Boileau's message. The musical language of *Apollo* correlates frequently and directly to the poetic feet of Boileau's tightly measured verse. As the composer remarked to Poulenc, one particular alexandrine so interested him that he included the verse in the published score as an exordium prefacing Calliope's variation:

> Que toujours dans vos vers le sens coupant les mots,
> Suspende l'hémistiche, en marque le repos

The couplet is drawn from an especially pertinent section of Canto I of *L'Art poétique*. Inasmuch as it reflects the serenity that imbues *Apollo*, a few stanzas warrant reprinting (the italicized lines provide a translation of the couplet Stravinsky used):

> Offer nothing to the reader
> Except that which pleases him.
> Have a severe ear for cadence.
> *May the intent of your verse always*
>   *Syncopate the words,*
> *Suspend the pause, enhance its repose*
> Be sure that a vowel which runs too quickly
>   Be not from a vowel which bumped
>   into it on its way.
> This is a happy choice of harmonious
>   words,

> Flee the hateful contest of bad sounds.
> The fullest verse, the noblest thought,
> Cannot please the spirit
>   when the ear is wounded.[10]

Stravinsky singled out Calliope's variation as one of his favorite moments. His inscription of the Boileau couplet introducing the Variation de Calliope is the obvious place to begin retracing the conversion of poetic feet into musical-balletic terms. The rhythm of the opening twelve-note melodic figure replicates the duodecimal syllabication of the alexandrine. The composer is so rigorous in his musical transliteration that the "suspende l'hémistiche" directive, literally referring to a marking of the medial caesura, is fortified by Stravinsky's interruptive silence. Even the caesura's duration, occupying three silent pauses, contributes to an evenly paced tripartite symmetry of sound-silence-sound (see fig. 5.4).

Following this three-measure introduction, the iambic hexameter pattern (♪♩♪♩) ensues, continuing throughout with only occasional and subtle changes. So regular is its use that the entire initial section of the dance, consisting of 180 pulses (twenty-three measures in total) is symmetrically divided into fifteen iterations of twelve beats each. Modifications always occur internally, that is, within each alexandrine grouping, but never disrupt the larger flow of the design. Stravinsky's conformity to the paradigm is faithful. Not only does the sketchbook exhibit the regular revision of initial thoughts toward compliance with the poetic meter, but the sketches also reveal attempts to stress the sixth pulse of each alexandrine by placing it at the highest point in the melodic contour, thereby emphasizing the medial point.

On those few occasions when Stravinsky deviated from the classical alexandrine template, he did so with precaution. Wherever an internal reapportionment of the iambic figure occurs, the composer's sketches disclose his careful weighing of how the prosody could be modified without compromising the piece's overall architectural unity. He penciled in precompositional scansion marks at moments where he considered altering the underlying regularity of

Que	tou-jours	dans	vos	vers		///	le	sans	cou-pant	les	mots
1	2	3	4	5	6		7	8	9	10	11	12
♪	♪	♪	♪	♪	♪	ꞌ ꞌ ꞌ	♪	♪	♪	♪	♪	♪
Sus -	pen - de	l'hém -	is -	tiche			et	mar - que	le	re - pose

5.4 Measures 1–4 of the Variation de Calliope, *Apollon Musagète*

Measures	6	7							8			
Scansion marks in sketch	⌣	|	/	⌣	|	/	⌣	⌣	⌣	⌣ |	/	⌣ / ⌣
Alexandrine pattern	1	2	3	4	5	6	7	8	9	10	11	12
Final rhythm of passage	♪	♩	♪	♩	♪	♪	♪	♪	♩	♪	♩	♪

5.5 Measures 6–8 of the Variation de Calliope, *Apollon Musagète*

the pattern. These telltale notations served as on-the-spot references, guiding him in the crafting of the rhythmic permutations. Moreover, these cryptic jottings were configured in abstract rhythmic terms, before any thought was given to specific pitch assignment. Figure 5.5, for example, illustrates a subtle deviation from the iambic norm that is still within the recurring twelve-syllable alexandrine style. In his sketchbook, Stravinsky even draws divisional bar lines between his scansion marks to ensure that the phrase's overall metric regularity will remain undisturbed. The composer's notations, as reprinted above, correspond to the twelve-note melody of mm. 6–8.

Here again, *Apollo* was not "spun out" in some uninterrupted linear procedure. The compositional process generally followed three distinct phases: the composer first made a central point, such as a particular melodic or rhythmic idea that would serve as the principal idea for a section; next he developed the materials, often times by subtle variations; then he composed "around" the passage, writing additional music that functions in either a preparatory or a compensatory fashion. Each layer of this tripartite gesture is composed and timed separately. Sometimes the composer is quite tentative in determining the overall sequence of musical events. At times he will circle two or three measures to be transferred, or add the Russian word for *insert,* with arrows pointing the way, or remark in the sketches that he has found "the solution," further demonstrating his efforts to determine the best order for the passage.

"Rhythm is the first formal esthetic relation of any part to part in any esthetic whole," James Joyce observed. Indeed, the multiple levels of the Calliope variation's architectural rhythms reach far beyond the easily audible iambs and alexandrines of the surface. The introductory material (mm. 1–9) in toto covers a temporal span of sixty eighth-note pulses, including the important rests that serve as caesuras for each hemistich. Within that time span, the melody consists of thirty-six pitches divided evenly: 6 + 6 + 12 + 12. The apex of the melodic line is attained near the "golden mean" (.6178) of the overall thirty-six-pitch melodic gesture. Finally, only after the climax is achieved does the rhythmic modification of the iambic figuration discussed in figure 5.5 commence. The internal divisions of the overall temporal framework of sixty pulses are therefore consistently articulated at symmetrical points (6, 12, 24, 36) along the time line.

Stravinsky's sense of temporal pacing parallels the architectonics of his classical versification models, with their metaphorical, implicit layers of meaning. Apropos of mythology itself, structuralists like Claude Lévi-Strauss argue that it is the intersection of the composite relations of narrative perceived at various levels that bestow upon myth its deepest beauty—a beauty only revealed ultimately in its total unified design. So it is that Stravinsky's Variation de Calliope produces a similar musical design—an indivisible whole, as Joyce sees it—completely consonant with the fundamental principles of classicism.[11]

Balanchine's own conception of the Variation de Calliope is no less sophisticated in its classical proportions, although one could never guess this from his program-book description:

> Calliope comes forward with her tablet. She holds it out before her, then clutches it to her heart. Placing the tablet on the ground, she dances. The melody she moves to is based in form on the Alexandrine, the classic heroic measure of French poetry. Her dance is emotional, yet not weakly so; as she circles the stage before Apollo, her leg boldly sweeps the air before her. She is scribbling hastily on the palm of her hand when her dance nears its end, wondering if she has done well. She becomes a little sad, the music seems to cry out softly with her, and she goes to show Apollo what she has written. He does not approve.[12]

The choreographer's own conception of the alexandrine pattern visually overlays the opening bars of the variation. With each hemistich, Balanchine's Calliope haltingly approaches a seated Apollo. Just as the medial caesura is reached in the music, Calliope both literally and figuratively "suspends" her croisé en avant gesture mid-motion before continuing with the second hemistich. An important distinction is to be made here: rather than terminating her movement in any stationary balletic sense, Balanchine's Muse unexpectedly disrupts what we are visually deceived into thinking is an implied, continuous motion—just as Stravinsky's three-pulse silence also provides an abrupt intervention. Thus the image of suspending the motion (as Boileau's verse advised and Stravinsky heeded), rather than statically dividing it without any sense of propulsion, is wonderfully achieved.

Balanchine understood what architects refer to as a work's edges. Both the initiation and closure of an intact musical gesture—as small as a phrase or as large as an entire pas—were nearly always paralleled in the clarity of the choreographic complement. In the variation's introductory music, Calliope carries her tablet over the sixty pulses of music, placing it on the ground precisely at the moment the introductory music cadences. There is no question as to where ideas begin and end choreographically. However, the simple synchronization of entrances and exits that is immediately obvious to the observer is not what is unusual; rather, it is the manner in which Balanchine internally sculpts the visual space over the sixty pulses.

The choreography shapes the interior of a musical gesture through what linguists have called the conduit metaphor.[13] Once the gateway of the gesture has been established, Balanchine leads us inside the music in such a way that the dance, while retaining its own autonomy, enables us to see more clearly the musical structure. Dance and music unfold in parallel but independent planes throughout the central portion of the gesture or phrase until the point where both visual and aural components coalesce at the music's cadence. It is Balanchine's ability to deal with multiple dimensions of a single, unified artistic expression that brilliantly illuminates the music. His sense of musical texture and musical "space," whereby lines appear and fade in the overall fabric, is ingeniously matched by his apportionment of the stage space.

Rather than merely replicating Stravinsky's musical segmentations, Balanchine's Calliope dances with her own sense of visually classic symmetry, which shuns redundancy. Where Stravinsky sometimes chooses to partition the twelve-pulse alexandrine into two equal halves, Balanchine might slice the visual field into three parts. The passage's appeal does not spring from a musical-choreographic concordance; rather, it is the dissimilarity, the counterpoint, and even the purposeful conflicting of elements that command our attention. Specifically, Calliope performs a series of three piqués en arabesque in contrast to Stravinsky's bifurcated musical divisions. Moreover, Calliope's piqués end just as the melodic apex in measure six is reached, whereupon she immediately initiates a concluding compensatory gesture that ends as she lays down her tablet. Both sonic and visual spaces share common, terminal points, demarcated by clear compositional and choreographic gestures (the cessation of the musical phrase, the placing of the prop on the ground). Balanchine casts off the temptation merely to mimic the music.

Stravinsky's sketchbook reveals that having completed the introduction, he next composed the principal theme, again as a strict alexandrine. As Balanchine describes the action, Calliope circles Apollo in a series of chassés. The sketches suggest that only after the melody was drafted did Stravinsky forge a transition between the introductory passage and this principal melodic theme. Generally, in fact, Stravinsky composed the transitions for each pas last. Here the structural link is a single, arresting, one-pulse sforzando D-minor chord. Its punctuating brittleness is meant to catch the attention (a true epitasis, or plot-thickening moment). And for good reason too, since Stravinsky thereafter employs the chord to herald the iteration of each successive alexandrine. So musically emphatic is the sonority's sudden jolt that Balanchine could neither ignore nor disguise it. Choreographically, it had to be dealt with explicitly . . . but how? Because of its exposed isolation and brevity, how could Calliope truly dance this fleeting, disjunctive chord?

Balanchine's solution has Calliope clenching her arms violently to her body while bending her knees each time the chord is struck. Her entire action is inwardly directed. The gesture's contorted, and very unclassical, motion is every bit as jarring as Stravinsky's wrenching chord. Then, just as the alexandrine melody begins, Calliope rises on pointe, and, quickly extending her arm and hand fully, suddenly opens her mouth, as if attempting to cross over the boundary of dance and actually speak. Calliope—"she of the beautiful voice," as her name literally translates.[14] It is one of the ballet's most stunning images.

Such Stravinskyan moments of compositional disjunction, whereby without warning the musical message is forcibly wrested in an entirely different direction, were part of the composer's compositional identity. But Balanchine's boldness—and some critics objected to this modernistic brazenness—in confronting Stravinsky's startling sonority head-on with this convulsive gesture, was just the kind of audacious stroke needed to match the impact of the dramatic moment.

Although we would expect each of the three contiguous divisions of the variation's *A-B-A* design to be clearly delineated both aurally and visually, it is the transitions between each that prove most informative. Having now seen how the transition was forged between the variation's introduction and the principal melodic theme of the initial *A* section, let us next consider how Stravinsky and Balanchine fuse the link from there to the central *B* section. This crucial transition must not only unify but also distinguish its *A* material from the contrasting *B* section to follow. Whereas Stravinsky strictly complies with the variation's steady iambic hexameter pattern, marking only a slight rallentando at the cadence, Balanchine handles the passage differently.

Using a series of port de bras, Balanchine presents Calliope's repeated arm movements not as a perfunctory duplication of Stravinsky's alexandrine but with a gradually evaporating pace that is visually at variance with the music's iambic figure. In its gentle, fading movement, it is quite a different proposition from the transition discussed above. There the spatial partition was built around slicing the temporal element of the passage in two distinct ways: Stravinsky used halves, Balanchine thirds within a constant tempo. Here, it is the actual tempo of the cadential approach that is divided, proceeding at two contrasting rates. The transition from this variation's *A* to *B* section is unified by Stravinsky's unaltered alexandrine rhythm, while Balanchine's gestural distinction, by virtue of its gradually dissipating arm movement, subtly calls attention to the retention of the music's underlying rhythm. Put simply, the musical gesture provides uniformity while the choreographic gesture provides distinction. Consequently, a remarkable symbiosis of the separate visual and aural spheres is achieved—a dovetailing that because of its unconventional temporal interplay merges all the more magically at its ultimate cadential resolution. No doubt this is what Balanchine had in mind when he observed that "it is generally believed that counterpoint is based on contrasts. Actually, counterpoint is an accompaniment to a main theme which it serves to enhance, but from whose unity it must not detract."[15]

According to Stravinsky, the ensuing *B* section originated in yet another alexandrine, this one by Alexander Pushkin, here assigned as a cello solo. In fact, the *B* section is entirely built around the cello melody. Stravinsky's scoring, consisting solely of a pizzicato string accompaniment, assures the cello's prominence. From a more traditional nineteenth-century balletic perspective, the cello's soaring melody would undoubtedly have been choreographed with an equally eye-catching dance. But once again Balanchine brushes off the obvious. Such a dance would have distracted from the cello's primacy—a primacy Stravinsky took pains to emphasize by scoring the accompaniment so delicately.

Here (and in notable contrast to his handling of the earlier transition) Balanchine opts for a different tack: rather than partnering the cello's melody, Calliope, dancing en pointe, mimics the short-short-long pizzicato background accompaniment note for note. Moreover, just as the composer divides each occurrence of the three-beat rhythmic motive with a pause, so too does Calliope momentarily hesitate on the third pulse of each anapest as a means of punctuation. "Informationally," as cognitive psychology would argue, by melding the visual gesture into the musical accompaniment, only two pieces of "data" are provided: a solo and accompaniment working together as a codified unit. Each component's role is perfectly stable and informationally accessible in its coexistence.

This fragile balance of visual and aural information was always uppermost in Balanchine's mind. It developed during a period when everyone from Maurits Escher to Pablo Picasso to Pavel Tchelitchev was rethinking the visual concepts of "ground" and "figure." As Guy Davenport suggests, the relation between figure and ground is interpenetrative in modernism. "We can explain cubism by noting that Picasso and Braque developed Cézanne so that figure is subsumed by ground. In a pun, figure and ground can change place with each other, as in the pointillist charts for determining color blindness. Like Arcimboldo, Tchelitchew, and Freud's da Vinci, Joyce habitually reworks his ground and renders it figure."[16]

The notion of "equivalence" as Escher addressed it in his famous woodcuts and lithographs (most notably *Eight Heads,* carved in the early 1920s) held that our eyes quickly fix on an object and in the process reduce everything surrounding that object to background. Balanchine instinctively understood such basic tenets of information theory and, consciously or otherwise, applied them throughout *Apollo.* Valéry observed that our senses cannot process every signal received. Most of the impressions we take in are useless because we are overwhelmed by a bombardment of stimuli. Had Balanchine added yet a third source of attention beyond Stravinsky's cello solo—say, a visual solo to this section of the variation—it is likely that the cello's message would have been lost. Seldom can a musical image, distinct though it may be, compete on even terms with a visual focus. There would have been too much information to process. Consequently, it is likely that the musical theme would have been compromised, crossing over into the accompanimental realm as mere background for the dance.

"Flowers are easy to paint. The leaves difficult," runs a haiku quoted by Aldous Huxley in *The Doors of Perception* (1954). Though accompanimental patterns are by definition subsidiary, neither Stravinsky nor Balanchine ever underestimated the indispensable function of these structural joists. They understood the essential role accompaniments serve in reinforcing the architectural substratum of a pas. Musicians and balletomanes alike naturally focus upon thematic materials—prominent melodies or a particular stage action that is spotlighted. But Stravinsky's sketchbook demonstrates that he frequently drafted background patterns even before composing the thematic ideas themselves. His attentiveness in establishing clear-cut pulse and metric patterns early in the compositional process could only have assisted Balanchine in both planning and underscoring each variation's choreographic events. Such figures also provided, right from the start in the sketching process, a sense of stability and recurrence, whence the composer could then feel free to allow an occasional deviation.

While Stravinsky's overlaying of the alexandrine is most perceptible in Calliope's variation, the composer's reliance upon versification as the primary structural agent in terms of both pitch and rhythm is evident throughout the ballet. Figure 5.6 summarizes the relation of the alexandrine to several familiar passages in *Apollo*'s individual dances. Particularly significant is the composer's division of the twelve fundamental "pulses" of the alexandrine into various groupings (for example two divisions of six or three groups of four).[17]

Despite the seemingly awkward starts and stops created by the alexandrines Stravinsky employed, Balanchine maintained a sense of forward drive throughout *Apollo*. These hesitations ("huge sustained attitudes," as Kirstein once described them) help to visualize the alexandrine pauses that Stravinsky constantly writes into the music. Notes of longer durations, or even written-in fermatas for further emphasis, accentuate each pause. Not only do these halting motions appear at the beginning of the Variation de Calliope but, as illustrated in figure 5.6, the Variation de Terpsichore evinces a similar suspension. Given Balanchine's well-known comparison of dancers to thoroughbreds, we can see Terpsichore's familiar pawing of the ground in the first and third measures followed by her twisting on the emphasized notes of measures two and four helping to define visually the alexandrine architecture as the composer segments its two halves. The reversible iamb initially appears in the first of Apollo's solo variations, again illustrated in figure 5.6. This is surely symbolic of the young god's awkwardness—an awkwardness that Balanchine captures choreographically. The figure returns in the opening measures of the Variation de Terpsichore, perhaps as a way of choreographically coupling Apollo's preferred Muse to himself.

In drafting the Pas de deux, Stravinsky worked out the accompaniment for the beautiful cello solo (Rehearsal 68) before composing the solo itself. The accompaniment's pulse and metric scheme are again based upon poetic scansion notations inserted in the sketchbook. Stravinsky first drafted an iambic pattern notated within bar lines to establish the meter, then added the musical equivalent in terms of pitches and rests immediately above the scansion marks. These nonpitch sketchbook scrawlings further evince the composer's reliance upon versification in providing coherence even at the most subsidiary layers including the accompaniment itself.[18]

Pas	Rehearsal Number	Rhythmic Units	Internal Division
Birth of Apollo/ Prologue	First 3 mm.	𝄴 ♩. 𝅘𝅥𝅮𝅘𝅥𝅮 ♩ | ♩. 𝅘𝅥𝅮𝅘𝅥𝅮 𝅘𝅥𝅮𝅘𝅥𝅮 𝅘𝅥𝅮𝅘𝅥𝅮 | ♩ ♪ ♪ ♩ 4 + 8	Twelve beats and pitches divided 4 + 8
Prologue	4 and 15	𝄴 ♩. 𝅘𝅥𝅮𝅘𝅥𝅮 ♩ ♩ 𝅘𝅥𝅮𝅘𝅥𝅮 ♩ 𝅘𝅥𝅮𝅘𝅥𝅮 ♩ (1) (2) (3)	Three units of four beats/ pitches. Rehearsal 15 marks Apollo's fundamental motive and the point where many performances now begin.
Variation d'Apollon	21	𝄽 𝅘𝅥𝅮𝅘𝅥𝅮𝅘𝅥𝅮 | 𝅘𝅥𝅮𝅘𝅥𝅮𝅘𝅥𝅮 | 𝅘𝅥𝅮𝅘𝅥𝅮𝅘𝅥𝅮 | ♩ (1) (2) (3)	Three units of four beats/ pitches. An example of the "reversible iamb" (long-short), thus totaling thirteen beats.
Pas d'action	24–25	𝄽 ♩♩ | ♩♩ | ♩♩ | ♩♩ | 𝄽 ♩♩♩ | ♩ (1) (2) (3)(4) (5) (6)	Twelve beats/pitches divided into six units. Similar pattern closes the pas, as Apollo presents the three symbols to the Muses.
Variation de Polyhymnia	44	𝄼 ♩. ♪ | ♩. ♪ | ♩♩ | (1) (2) (3)	Six pitches grouped into three rhythmic units of two beats.
Variation de Terpsichore	52	𝄽 𝅘𝅥𝅮𝅘𝅥𝅮𝅘𝅥𝅮𝅘𝅥𝅮 ♩. ♪𝄾 ♪ 𝅘𝅥𝅮𝅘𝅥𝅮𝅘𝅥𝅮 | ♩. (1) (2)	Reversible iamb totaling thirteen pitches over four measures, but divided into two large phrases.
Variation de Terpsichore	53	𝄽 ♪ | 𝅘𝅥𝅮𝅘𝅥𝅮𝅘𝅥𝅮𝅘𝅥𝅮 | 𝅘𝅥𝅮𝅘𝅥𝅮𝅘𝅥𝅮 (1) — (2)	Twelve beats/pitches divided into two units with melodic apex (underlined in example) articulated at midpoint of the theme.
Coda	75	𝄽 ♩♪ 𝅘𝅥𝅮𝅘𝅥𝅮 | ♩♪ ♩♪ | ♩♪ ♪ ♩ (1) (2) (3)	Twelve-note main theme over three measure grouping.

5.6 Versification-related transference in eight selected passages from *Apollon Musagète*

Just as Stravinsky designed an unobtrusive aural accompaniment for the ballet's luminous melodies, so too Balanchine often employed the Muses as a visual accompaniment for Apollo's dancing. The three women function as a cohesive unit without sacrificing their individual identity. When Balanchine directs their combined movement as an ensemble, there is often a subtle internal distinction to each dancer's motion, sometimes barely perceptible but enough to integrate the accompaniment into the whole. His choreographic accompaniments are no different from the imaginatively written musical accompaniments. Both are backgrounds, though never uninterestingly so. Seldom does Balanchine allow the ensemble's collective motion to begin or end in unison. Each Muse usually enters or exits an ensemble passage separately, thus averting a rote duplication of the music. There is almost always some interlocking of gestures, as in a beautifully imbricated visual design.

For example, in the Pas d'action immediately following the first Variation d'Apollon, the Muses enter with Apollo at the center. Balanchine comments, "Apollo circles the stage in broad, free leaps as the girls move their arms in rhythm to the music."[19] His synopsis underplays the ingenuity with which the Muses animate their own background figure. While Apollo's turns command our attention, the Muses are intricately involved at a secondary visual level— the same supportive level as Stravinsky's accompaniment. We are conscious of their presence, but almost subliminally. The Muses provide a "neutral presence," as Edwin Denby described this aspect of Balanchine's classicism. Their importance stems from understatement. Balanchine vivifies his visual accompaniment by having the Muses, posed one behind the other, remain in a stationary position while executing port de bras movements. The Muses perform their arm gestures successively, thereby creating a continual, fanlike movement; yet only their arms move while the lower halves of their bodies remain stationary. Balanchine's adoption of épaulement emphasizes the head and arms while splitting the torso as a way of emphasizing Stravinsky's division of accompaniment and theme. The resulting visual geometry is pure Balanchine in its collimating design. Finally, the ensemble's accompanimental action is not assigned to the side or back of the stage but rather positioned at the center, like the hub of a wheel, while Apollo circles the three with his heroic jumps. Thus Balanchine locates the accompaniment where we can see it as a supportive but nonetheless integral component of the larger visual impact.

For the most part, Stravinsky concentrated on the composition of one pas at a time. The Pas de deux provides the lone exception. Judging from the frequent interruptions evident throughout the sketchbook, its design was constantly on the composer's mind. The embryonic motive of what eventually becomes the principal thematic material appears as early as 18 July, just a few days after the composer began the ballet. But the pas was not completed until the end of December. During that period Stravinsky returned to the duet infrequently, and then only briefly, jotting down nothing more than rudimentary ideas. It was not until mid-December that he took up the movement in earnest. Then, as the sketches between 16 and 28 December reveal, he proceeded in his customary "retrograde" manner of composing.

For example, what ultimately serves as mm. 28–29 was composed before what became mm. 1–11; this passage in turn was followed by mm. 38–39 (the last two measures of the piece), but then Stravinsky composed what would be used as mm. 12–16, and so on. As usual, the internal ordering of materials consumed most of his energy. Still, the real curiosity here is Stravinsky's atypically picking the composition up and setting it aside over a protracted period of five months. Nothing in the sketchbook indicates that he actually struggled with his thoughts during this prolonged development. He merely stockpiled ideas before returning to whatever section of the ballet he was currently working out. Apparently, the ideation of the Pas de deux needed to germinate in unhurried reflection. It is the crux of the ballet, wherein, as Balanchine remarks, "an awakening of Olympian power" emerges and sets the direction of the god's fate. Stravinsky was aware of the balletic significance of this section, and from *Apollo*'s inception in July, he aimed for this moment.

This pivotal awakening occurs at a temporally significant juncture. Just as the crux of many of the individual dances of *Apollo* is articulated at or near the golden mean, so too the Pas de deux marks a similar structural crossroads in the ballet's overall pacing.[20] In choreographing the union of Apollo and Terpsichore, Balanchine too grasped the moment's drama in terms of temporal pacing. As the duet begins, the melody that Stravinsky had been working on since he began composing steadily rises in a linear ascent until the structurally important peak is reached at the third measure of Rehearsal 65. Balanchine choreographically matches the attainment of this arrival point. Just at the juncture where the music has been lifted, Terpsichore likewise is lifted from the ground. She is, literally, swept off her feet by a god who has matured—a god now clearly in charge.

Balanchine's Pas de deux exhibits fluidity in every component of every gesture. As was Stravinsky, the choreographer was particularly concerned to devise transitions that would avoid any sense of visual disjunction—especially in the

Pas de deux, where the partnering demanded absolute unification. The initial transition into the pas (and into the opening melody just discussed) is one of the ballet's most poignant moments. This is Balanchine's undisguised homage to Michaelangelo's evocation of God and Humanity on the Sistine ceiling. Similarly, Apollo and Terpsichore's earthly-celestial union is consummated by the fragile touch of a single finger. It is, as Stravinsky reminds us, Terpsichore who "reveals dancing to the world."[21]

More specifically, it is Balanchine's precise placement of this god-Muse conjunction that is enlightening; for rather than marking the beginning of the pas with this image, Terpsichore quietly enters the stage action during the final measures of the previous variation before taking her rightful place next to Apollo. While Stravinsky's music cadences without attempting to forge an aural elision to the forthcoming Pas de deux, Balanchine masterfully covers the seam by annexing a striking visual bridge. Psychologically, so staggering is the image of Apollo and Terpsichore's touch as an unmistakable reference to God's touching of Adam that the impression stays with us even after the music of the variation ends and before the Pas de deux begins. A visual resonance lingers across the musical silence. As Balanchine knew, "A pause, an interruption, is never an empty space between indicated sounds. It is not just nothing. It acts as a carrying agent from the last sound to the next one."[22]

Certainly the most visually gripping moment occurs when Terpsichore, leaving her feet and supported on the back of a kneeling Apollo, assumes a prone position, as if suspended in midair. It is a swimming lesson, Balanchine tells us, "a reward for her beautiful dancing." *Apollo* is set on the isle of Delos in the Aegean Sea, an important consideration in understanding the nature of this dance.[23] He transports his chosen Muse, enabling her to become part of the air. For just a moment she shares with him the freedom of escape. In the same way the enchantment of ballet is occupied with the fantasy of flight, of being godlike. Paul Valéry speaks to the issue eloquently: "The body seems to have broken free from its usual states of balance. It seems to be trying to outwit its own weight, at every moment evading its pull. . . . It seems to be concerned only with itself and one other object, a very important one, from which it breaks free, to which it returns, but only to gather the wherewithal for another flight. . . . That object is earth, the ground, the solid place, the plane on which everyday life plods along, the plane of walking, the prose of human movement."[24]

Terpsichore's swimming lesson is mesmerizing. As ever, Balanchine was mindful when balancing musical and choreographic events. The accompanying music is based upon yet another alexandrine. It is a straightforward melody-and-accompaniment proposition without contrapuntal complexity. And by dispensing its uncomplicated musical information at a leisurely pace, it allows Balanchine to step forward and present his hypnotic stage action without compromising Stravinsky's gossamer music.

While Stravinsky's sketchbook allows us to retrace the evolution of *Apollo*'s musical structure, no such record documents Balanchine's assembly of the choreography. But if his work with dancers on subsequent ballets is a fair guide, it is likely that *Apollo* was choreographed the same way the music was written, that is, from the inside out, and not from beginning to end. We know that Balanchine often played with ideas arising from sources other than those commonly associated with traditional dance vocabulary. Sometimes his first thoughts—like Stravinsky's—were lifted from the most unlikely places.

In the second Variation d'Apollon, for example, consider Balanchine's self-confessed inspiration, as Richard Buckle describes it.

> In Apollo's second variation, Balanchine hit on a startling image to convey that the god is conscious of his divinity. Twice Apollo stands in fourth position, forward left leg bent, left arm behind his back with clenched fist visible to his right, and with the right arm extended upward, the fingers of the right hand splayed like rays of light. Then, as the right fist clenches, the fingers of the left splay out. On—off—on—off; on—off; on—off. Balanchine said this idea came to him from watching an electric sign in Piccadilly Circus.[25]

That such a dramatic point of action owes its inception to such a wholly mechanical origin captures the essence of Balanchine's ability and courage to transfigure whatever natural, even mundane images, caught his eye.

Still, the nature of the bond between Balanchine and Stravinsky does not hinge on the raw materials themselves, but from the way both men manipulated these materials—especially how they apportioned their ideas through time and space. Ezra Pound's attraction to Stravinsky's music emanated from their shared realization that artists deal with two kinds of time: one which runs with the clock, and one which runs counter to it. The essence of the Stravinsky-Balanchine collaborations is their mutual understanding of the ontological and psychological dimensions of time—something both men referred to often. Moreover, Balanchine's choreography often visualizes what cannot be easily understood musically. Constant Lambert once claimed that music was the "most clumsy" of the arts in its inability to provide definition, while choreography was incapable of doing anything obliquely—given its visual and physical nature it had no choice but to define for the audience what things meant. Certainly this goes to the core of Balanchine's setting of Stravinsky's music.[26]

Consider the canonic passage in the Pas d'action in which Apollo and the three Muses participate—the same passage Diaghilev described in his *Excelsior* interview. Stravinsky's sketches disclose that the theme was first imagined in an entirely different context, then put aside.[27] By the end of August he had reworked the theme. He manipulates the idea contrapuntally in augmentation and diminution, with each voice overlapping the other (Rehearsal 35). Stravinsky was pleased with this overlapping, or stretto, passage, referring to it as one of his favorite moments. Such an intricate contrapuntal web understandably goes undetected by most casual listeners and observers. Yet what is perceived, however vaguely, is the unfolding of a musical idea in different layers of time, an idea that had already appeared several times earlier in the dance but as an unadorned single-voiced theme. Subsequently, when the composer contrapuntalizes the theme, the dimension of real time almost ceases in our perception. Now the temporal pace of the music progresses in suspended animation, though in fact the fundamental pulse and meter continue unchanged. Already planted in our memory, the theme moves slower and faster simultaneously because of the layered techniques of augmentation and diminution.

It is not necessary to hear the compositional details of this plexus; rather it is, as Eugene Raskin tells us, the broader, architectural message of such a complex canonic unfolding that is significant. Augmentation and diminution are natural life processes, just as growth and decay are. Everything begins, peaks, and dies. "All or part of this sequence can be used as a rhythm, or the whole may be utilized as a *unit* which is repeated," Raskin adds.[28]

How does Balanchine visualize the ebb and flow of this intricate cycle? Musically, Stravinsky assigns each thematic statement to one of five individual orchestral lines, while Balanchine similarly uses each of the four dancers to portray separate contrapuntal strands. In itself this is not so remarkable. What is enlightening, however, is Balanchine's astute judgment in allowing the temporality of the music to unwind visually. Or stated the other way around, it is the actual evolution of the balletic movement across the musical canon that is vital.

As the canon begins, "Apollo, arms outstretched, supports [the Muses] as they hold hands and form a circular tableau," Balanchine stated. The quartet of dancers stand motionless and with linked hands gaze in four different directions (effacé derrière for the two Muses on the sides). They then begin a series of arabesques penchées, and in effect the visual space begins to mobilize, as does the theme texturally. As the canonic theme now stretches out at different temporal rates in the individual voices, so too does Balanchine animate each dancer individually, turning and crossing under another's arms without ever breaking the continuous bond between them. In an even greater geometrical inspiration, the circle of dancers is now transformed into a row of dancers, each Muse in front of another, with Apollo at the back. The unbroken linkage of the Muses with the young god continues, but seen now from a starkly opposite visual perspective. Each Muse engages—not in unison but in succession—in a series of port de bras, while slightly bending at the hips. They alternate their swaying, ramiform motion to the left or right, so that Apollo, still posed at the back, can be momentarily glimpsed at each rotation. Just as compositionally the canonic theme allows a diversity of views, so too do we now see the changing image of Apollo from different balletic angles.

Rather than crush the canon's intricacy with an equally concatenate dance, Balanchine's choreography remains simple, reserved. It clarifies the music's complex architectonics. We know that Balanchine always saw his mission as helping the audience to see the music. In this instance, the canon is presented in the most basic geometric configurations imaginable—squares, lines, circles. Our familiarity with these recognizable visual shapes allows us to see the concept evolving onstage, though we may be completely unaware of Stravinsky's musical unfolding in the orchestral pit below. As Jaynes would describe the relationship, Stravinsky's canon is the *metaphrand,* or that which is not easily perceptible, and Balanchine's dance is the *metaphier,* the agent of clarification: "In trying to understand a thing we are trying to find a metaphor for that thing. Not just any metaphor, but one with something more familiar and easy to our attention. Understanding a thing is to arrive at a metaphor for that thing by substituting something more familiar to us. And the feeling of familiarity is the feeling of understanding."[29]

The Apothéose provides a fitting summation to illustrate how these choreo-musical complexities are aligned in the service of clarity. The motto iambic motive first announced in the Prologue now returns as an obvious cyclic means of creating closure. Apollo, followed by the Muses, ascends to Parnassus, and it is in these last moments of the ballet, as given in figure 5.7, that Balanchine's instinctive equilibrium of aural and visual materials is again evident.

Once more Stravinsky weaves elaborate rhythmic layers arising from the same fundamental principles of versification that integrate the entire ballet. His motivic manipulation again derives from partitioning the twelve pulses into various slices. The contrabass line, the second cello, the divisi violas and second violins—all these orchestral lines display duodecimal divisions in pat-

5.7 Measures 15–24 of the "Apothéose" from *Apollon Musagète* (Courtesy of Boosey and Hawkes)

terns of two, three, and four note clusters. An augmentation of note values is also evident as the passage continues, thus creating a ritard, or, in terms of psychological time, a gradual braking of the motion without actually changing the tempo.

In fact, the composer refrains from marking any specific retardation of the tempo in the score since it is built into the music. Because the pitch materials employed are limited, often oscillating between two or three notes, the motion seems all the more static, providing a resignation to the music. There is a circular feeling of timelessness to it all, as the music moves in a loop, creating a beguiling sense of stasis. Most important, these concisely formed musical materials, constantly hovering within their confined boundaries, appear just at the critical moment when the balletic action depicts Apollo's departure from his earthly existence, as Zeus summons his son home.

Yet for all these interior structural intricacies, the instrumental parts collectively accrue to no more than an accompaniment, supplying a kind of stability above which the opening iambic motive returns in the first violins and first cellos. Stravinsky repeats the violin and cello's four-note motive six times over the final music of measures 19–24.[30] Each iteration of the by now familiar motive occurs at a different and aurally unpredictable point in the passage's overall pacing. It is this unpredictability, this waiting to hear when the motive might reoccur, that holds our attention by heightening our expectation, thereby creating a sense of drive.

What were Balanchine's options in choreographing these compositional convolutions and the shifting placement of the principal melodic-rhythmic iambic motive? Rather than appending the dance to the musical accompaniment, as was done in the Variation de Calliope; or metaphorically explaining the music, as occurred in the canon of the Pas d'action; or moving to the foreground, as was evident in the Pas de deux—rather than adopting any of these approaches, Balanchine enriches Stravinsky's structural scheme by getting entirely out of the way of the musical action. The cornerstone of the passage is Balanchine's awareness of a fundamental pulse that fortifies the foundation for this vibrantly rhythmic music. At the moment that the music of the Apothéose begins (fig. 5.7), the surge of musical information is complemented by a retreat in the choreographic action. As the music begins, all choreographic movement ceases, except for the most elegantly elementary movement of all: Apollo and the three Muses successively join in a grand promenade, walking slowly and rhythmically across the stage toward Apollo's final ascent.[31]

In later productions, Balanchine eliminated the staircase to Mount Parnassus. Consequently, he also adjusted the choreography. In place of dancers climbing the steps as they looked toward the heavens, as if experiencing a theophany, Balanchine used the now famous "sunburst" figure, in which the Muses stand in arabesque as they lean against Apollo. Originally this aurorean pose was employed at an earlier point in the Apothéose. Balanchine thus did not create something entirely new as he refashioned the ballet's ending, but rather reordered preexisting materials, just as Stravinsky often did compositionally. With all extraneous balletic movement stripped away, the dignity of this regal cortège provides the conjunction tying together music, drama, poetry, and choreography in one empyreal singularity of expression. Not only did Balanchine know when a choreographic foreground would aid the music best, but just as important, he knew when an act of withdrawal, even of submission, was the wisest path to follow.

No sooner had the first curtain fallen in Paris in 1928 than *Apollon Musagète* began to change. In a forgotten clip from *A Stravinsky Portrait,* a documentary shot by Hamburg's Norddeutscher Rundfunk Television in the 1960s, Balanchine is filmed rehearsing some of his New York City Ballet dancers for an upcoming performance of *Apollo.* The camera catches Balanchine and Stravinsky in a casual conversation as the choreographer suggests that *Apollo* moved too slowly for Diaghilev; there was simply not enough action for him. But now the work has become so familiar, Balanchine contends, that "people whistle it in the street." Stravinsky retorts, "Not always in the street, maybe in the bathroom." He then offers Balanchine more to drink, saying, "Let's be drunk. . . . You are not dancing, and I am not dancing."

In another segment filmed during Stravinsky's absence, Balanchine listens to the audiotape of the ballet just recorded by the composer and the Hamburg orchestra. He stands at a piano with his dancers gathered around, telling them that the tempo of this new recording is much faster than when he first choreographed the work nearly four decades earlier. It is so fast that he must adjust some of the choreographic patterns. He complains about the speed of Stravinsky's new interpretation, recalling how in 1928 the composer insisted on very precise and deliberately paced tempi. In a 1982 interview, Balanchine recalled that when he first heard Stravinsky play the ballet in the 1920s, the composer "took the music quite slowly, more slowly than conductors do today. Stravinsky wanted it to sound sustained, endless. Most conductors take it too fast. It should give you the impression of an organ point. . . . It's like the ocean, continuous."[32]

The Hamburg film, directed by Richard Leacock and Rolf Liebermann, also records some irreplaceable sequences of Balanchine working with Suzanne Farrell, who by then had taken her place as the choreographer's most important muse. During the Polyhymnia variation, Balanchine turns the *Apollo* recording off, stands center stage, and sings the whole variation himself while coaching a dancer. He dances the parts of all three Muses, always bestowing special favor on the young Farrell, who is dancing Terpsichore. When today's audiences think of Farrell, we remember the mature ballerina at the pinnacle of her stunning success. But here, as a teenager, Farrell appears diffident (understandably) in the presence of the patriarchal choreographer.

The camera often cuts from Farrell dancing to Balanchine observing. He follows her every move with a "blind infatuation" that Farrell remembers made her feel uncomfortable.[33] She rehearses the Terpsichore variation, timidly covering her face when stumbling over certain steps. She listens to Balanchine's suggestions intently but demurely. A fixated Balanchine seems hopelessly smitten. While the other dancers are rehearsing onstage, Balanchine escorts Farrell off to the side and works with her privately as she quickly assimilates his suggestions.

As mentioned earlier, Diaghilev had originally ordered the Variation de Terpsichore cut, supposedly because it was "too long," though at a minute and a half, it is the ballet's second-shortest pas. (Why delete the dance that showcases the most important Muse?) Diaghilev had removed the pas in several early performances before Stravinsky discovered the omission. When the composer became aware of Diaghilev's directive, he was outraged, threatening to break his contract and pull the ballet from the Ballets Russes repertoire. Diaghilev may have instituted the cut as a petty act of revenge. As Kirstein remembers, Lord Rothermere (who often financed Diaghilev's efforts) "had demanded his protégée, Alicia Nikitina, be given a leading role, which was done." But when Rothermere later withdrew his funding, "Diaghilev vented his fury on the dancer, eliminating her exquisite solo."[34]

Over the years, Stravinsky closely monitored the ballet's fortunes, either conducting it himself or entrusting it to colleagues such as Ansermet and Koussevitzky. Upon settling in America, he continued conducting both the ballet and orchestral versions frequently. When Balanchine first brought *Apollo* to New York, Stravinsky advised the choreographer to observe the score's precise metronomic markings. He also exhorted Balanchine to retain the orchestra's carefully balanced proportions: "L'equilibre de mon ensemble est strictement calculé. C'est un SEXTOUR."[35]

5.8 Lew Christensen in the first American production of *Apollo* (1937) (Jerome Robbins Dance Division, The New York Public Library for the Performing Arts, Astor, Lenox and Tilden Foundations)

Balanchine first staged *Apollo* in New York in March 1937, as part of a Stravinsky festival at the Metropolitan Opera. Kirstein remembers the composer attending a rehearsal and noting how the mien of the ballet was evolving: "Stravinsky particularly liked the scenery for *Apollon: 'ça fait riche; très Poussinesque.'* Lew Christensen [Balanchine's first American Apollo] was everything one could wish. Balanchine threw away his wig. His hair is long enough to be curled tight. Tchelitchew cut away half his gilt leather armor. Improved his makeup; little to do with a head like that but let it shine. At the end of rehearsal, Stravinsky thanked Lew" (fig. 5.8).[36]

Writing in the *New York Evening Post,* Samuel Chotzinoff, who actually attended the original Bolm production, now reviewed the 1937 performance: "*Apollon Musagète* did not sound any better than when I heard it in Washington. Illustrating a dull scenario . . . it shows the celebrated composer in one of his numerous transition periods." Composer Elliott Carter, who attended the original Diaghilev production in Paris, disagreed. In a 1937 issue of *Modern*

Music, Carter wrote of the choreographic differences, finding the new production "less static," and more fluid in its "beautiful plasticity."[37]

Stravinsky always remained actively involved in rehearsing both the music and the dancers. He attended several rehearsals in New York for a 1943 production, proclaiming the performance successful, although not everyone saw it that way. Reviews remained mixed. John Martin was even less kind in 1943 than he had been in 1928, criticizing the dated ballet as bloodless and "moderne" in the worst Diaghilev tradition.

Several male dancers in the early 1960s, including Edward Villella and Erik Bruhn, remember their astonishment as Balanchine demonstrated every step. "Balanchine was inside the music. He danced every part too," Bruhn recalls. "And he showed me how to dance the Apollo part. I danced the *pas de deux* with him—and he was all the Muses."[38] *Apollo* would change, unsurprisingly, as each new dancer came into Balanchine's company. For Balanchine was never above tailoring movements to emphasize strengths or minimize weaknesses.

Apollo's evolution continued even after Stravinsky's death. Balanchine chipped away at what he considered extraneous layers of visual and narrative elements. Today's *Apollo* is a different work from the one last seen by the composer. The costumes and scenery were gone by the late 1950s. Apollo's Greek garb and the tutus of the Muses have given way as well. Productions are now staged against a plain cerulean backdrop. Once-essential props like the chariot and Mount Olympus have vanished. Unvarnished by the excessive ornament first draping the ballet, the music and dance are experienced more directly. Each cutback led to the austerity of a purer classicism Stravinsky would surely have cheered. With each reduction, the music grew in importance.

Still, the composer would never have endorsed Balanchine's extraction, during the late 1970s, of the entire Prologue. It would have been unthinkable while Stravinsky was alive for the loyal choreographer to "decapitate" Apollo, as Robert Garis aptly put it. Did Balanchine really come to feel (as he told John Gruen): "It is my ballet and I can do what I want with it"? In the face of sharp criticism, Balanchine defended his dissevering of the birthing scene, maintaining that Stravinsky originally included it only to make the ballet longer and increase the profit.[39] But profit had nothing to do with it. Much of the ballet's music flows from important compositional motives seeded in the Prologue, and musically, at least, the extraction is a calamitous loss.

The return of the ballet's opening iambic-melodic motive at the close of the Apothéose constitutes no return at all if the opening scene has been cut. Without the Prologue, Stravinsky's recapitulation of this material carries no sense of balance, let alone closure. William Weslow told Francis Mason that Balanchine removed the initial tableau "because he didn't want Baryshnikov to do the wild pirouettes at the beginning and create a sensation. . . . He wanted it cut so that Baryshnikov wouldn't be the great star dancer in the New York City Ballet."[40] Many shared Weslow's view. Balanchine's "no star" policy was well known. Just as he and Stravinsky had accused Diaghilev of unfairly sublimating music and dance in the interests of favored personnel, Balanchine may have felt that the charisma of star dancers might distract from the ballet's message. Peter Martins's staging of the ballet in the 1990s provides at least a partial reincarnation of the ballet's former look. The Prologue has returned (at least in some productions) and the staircase leading to Parnassus at the ballet's end also furnishes a welcome restoration of earlier versions.

Both Stravinsky and Balanchine understood that classicism must not be mummified as some sacrosanct relic. Balanchine, particularly, never saw his "butterflies" as embalmed museum pieces. A ballet was a work in progress. For both men, to deny change was to invite stagnation. In the forty years that followed *Apollo*'s premiere, Stravinsky and Balanchine were to collaborate often. Yet of all their shared achievements, this 1928 ballet, while in some ways it has changed the most, still remains quintessentially the same. Even for a Greek myth, the journey of *Apollon Musagète* has been a curious odyssey indeed. Stravinsky and Balanchine's unswerving devotion to the abiding principles of reason, balance, austerity, and order continues to resonate. Like the myth itself, *Apollo* engenders a transcendental beauty that touches the core of our spirit in ways that are at once personal and universal.

Chapter 6 A New Beginning:

Kirstein, America, and

Jeu de Cartes

It seems a pity that the ballet hangs upon so slender a thread. Why should there be but one creative and imaginative troupe capable of producing the greater stage works? . . . We wait with interest the day that an American Diaghilev shall open the doors to a theatre of modern ballet.
—*Richard Hammond, "The Ballets Russes, 1928"*

With Diaghilev's death in Venice on 19 August 1929, everything changed. For all of the internal squabbling and political posturing dividing their house, the Ballets Russes had been home. Its now devastated members knew that Diaghilev had built careers and forged otherwise unexplored pathways. His demise struck a fatal blow to the company's bold, risk-taking imagination. As Lincoln Kirstein wrote in his novel *Flesh Is Heir,* "It was the end indeed, the end of youth for a distinguished company of human beings, the end of power and endeavor, the end perhaps, of the first quarter of the twentieth century." The already declining company soon disbanded, touching off a balkanizing scramble for several would-be successors, each attempting to assume Diaghilev's mantle and salvage the remnants of the troupe's once enviable reputation.[1]

Diaghilev's passing shook Stravinsky more personally than it did Balanchine. Although the composer's always on-the-brink relationship with the impresario had once again deteriorated after *Apollo,* still, their mutual affection ran deeply enough for Stravinsky to confide to his closest friends that his heart was pained by Diaghilev's death. Balanchine learned of Diaghilev's passing while filming a dance sequence in England for Sinclair Lewis's new talking movie, *Dark Red Roses.* Doubtless he was disturbed by the news, but his always tightlipped reactions were more guarded than Stravinsky's. One never quite knew what this "depthless enigma," as Christian Bérard once described Balanchine, was thinking.

Still, by 1929 Stravinsky no longer relied upon the Ballets Russes as a forum for his new works. Indeed, long before *Apollo*'s premiere, in early December 1927, Ida Rubinstein (just then beginning her own ballet troupe in Paris) had asked Stravinsky's agent whether she might prepare her own production of the forthcoming *Apollo.* Diaghilev was not about to comply. In lieu of *Apollo,* therefore, Rubinstein sought an alternative. Correspondence between Rubinstein, Benois, and Stravinsky ensued, and by mid-January 1928, Stravinsky had accepted Rubinstein's commission of $6,000 (six times the fee Coolidge paid the composer) for a new ballet.[2]

Based on Hans Christian Andersen's "The Ice Maiden," Stravinsky entitled the new work *Le Baiser de la Fée.* Rubinstein and Benois suggested a ballet that would be "inspired" by the music of Tchaikovsky, and, given his long-held fondness for the elder composer, Stravinsky now accepted the commission as a "compatriotic homage." He even affixed a formal dedication to the score: "I dedicate this ballet to the memory of Peter Chaikovsky by relating the Fairy to his Muse, and in this way the ballet becomes an allegory, the Muse having similarly branded Chaikovsky with her fatal kiss, whose mysterious imprint made itself felt in all this great artist's work." Unlike the modestly scored *Apollo,* the forty-five minute *Baiser* utilized a full orchestra of strings (including the harp originally planned for *Apollo*), winds, brass, and percussion. The scenario seemed a far cry from the composer's recent Greek works; but Stravinsky heralded his new ballet as thoroughly classical: "Although I gave full liberty to painter and choreographer in the staging of my composition, my innermost desire was that it should be presented in classical form, after the manner of *Apollo.* I pictured all the fantastic roles as danced in white ballet skirts."[3]

The ballet's compositional sketches as well as the piano reduction are replete with specific directives. Stravinsky asserts his desire for Alpine costumes—specifically, "from around 1850." He identifies Interlaken as the location of the lake. Throughout the final piano score (undoubtedly used in rehearsal) the composer details his wishes, crossing out preliminary ideas and entering his revisions. Although Fokine was initially proposed as the choreographer, Nijinska ultimately prepared the work. And though Stravinsky much preferred the choice, still his usual suspicions surfaced, heightened now by his recent and felicitous association with Balanchine.

In an October letter written only a month or so before the premiere, Stravinsky instructed his agent Gavril Païchadze to withhold the piano score of the ballet from both Rubinstein and Nijinska. He insisted that he himself must play the music for them since neither dancer really understood musical matters, especially the setting of correct tempi. Three days later, Stravinsky eased up a bit, now informing Païchadze that since the production would probably fall through unless rehearsals went forward without him, the rehearsal pianist could have the score. But he quickly added that all the tempi were clearly marked and must be followed without exception.[4] Stravinsky conducted the 27 November premiere at the Paris Opéra, as well as a few other performances soon thereafter. But he was never satisfied with Nijinska's staging, and almost a decade later Balanchine restaged the work in New York, earning Stravinsky's approval.

In the late 1920s through much of the 1930s, largely out of necessity, the composer devoted increasing time to conducting his own works. His career as a pianist now included several joint appearances with his son Soulima, just then launching his own professional career. Also in his role as an accompanist (though the piano parts are far more than accompanimental), Stravinsky frequently collaborated with the American violinist Samuel Dushkin. The composer dedicated more and more time to writing pragmatic works suitable for his international concertizing schedule.

Along with new concerti and chamber works for piano and violin, however, came powerful religious and dramatic works, notably the 1930 *Symphony of Psalms* and the 1934 *Perséphone,* first performed by Ida Rubinstein's company in Paris. The latter was yet another Greek-inspired work, set to a text by André Gide. Originally intended by Rubinstein as a ballet, it was ultimately cast as a melodrama for tenor, narrator, mixed chorus, children's choir, and full orchestra.

Stravinsky continued to reside in France, finally becoming a citizen in 1934. But his peregrinations, as he liked to call them, increasingly took him, Soulima, and Dushkin all over Europe as well as to South America. Most significant, in late December 1934, Stravinsky and Dushkin boarded the S.S. *Rex* bound for

New York, where the composer-conductor-pianist began his second U.S. tour.

Nineteen thirty-five was in its own way a pivotal year for Balanchine, marking the first important public performance in New York of what would become his signature work, *Serenade,* to the music of Tchaikovsky. Balanchine remembered, "I knew and loved Tchaikovsky's *Serenade* ever since I was a child. I always wanted to stage it. And it turned out to be my first ballet in America. I hadn't planned it, it just happened that way. I just wanted to do the *Serenade,* and so I did."[5] But the road that led Balanchine and *Serenade* to New York was a circuitous one.

Following *Apollo,* the choreographer had prepared an array of dances for several Opéra de Monte-Carlo productions, including Gounod's *Roméo et Juliette* and Verdi's *Rigoletto,* both staged in early 1929. He had also choreographed three new ballets for the Ballets Russes: *The Gods Go a-Begging* (July 1928), a musical muddle that was as flawed as *Apollo* was sublime; *Le Bal* (May 1929), in which Balanchine himself danced, to the music of Vittorio Rieti with scenery and costumes by De Chirico; and *Le Fils Prodigue* (*Prodigal Son;* May 1929), to a brilliant Prokofiev score with costumes prepared by Vera Sudeikina.

In 1929 Jacques Rouché, director of the Paris Opéra, invited Balanchine to arrange a ballet to Beethoven's *Les Créatures de Prométhée.* The choreographer began work in October, but almost immediately fell victim to what would become a chronic and at that moment debilitating tubercular condition, thus precluding any consideration of remaining in Paris as the Opéra's permanent ballet master. Lifar, already engaged as the principal dancer for the new ballet, completed the choreography and was subsequently appointed to the post. Shortly thereafter Balanchine found himself again churning out choreographic interludes for opera productions in Monte Carlo, especially between 1932 and 1933. From the Venusberg Ballet of Wagner's *Tannhäuser* to the Bacchanale of Saint-Saëns's *Samson et Dalila*—name an opera and Balanchine set the accompanying choreography (about twenty-five in all). His journeyman abilities also took him elsewhere, including Copenhagen, where he served as a guest ballet master for the Royal Danish Ballet and mounted *Apollo* with Leif Ørnberg as the young god. (Ørnberg was the uncle of Peter Martins.)

Balanchine staged ensemble dances for vaudevillian music and dance skits, including Charles B. Cochran's 1930 Revue in England. Productions included such oddities as "Luna Park," in which Nikitina danced "The One-Legged Woman" and Lifar "The Six-Armed Man." Balanchine became known as a master of such crowd-pleasing folderol—"The Diaghilev of the light-musical stage," as Vladimir Dukelsky (later Vernon Duke) tagged him. He considered joining Anna Pavlova's company on a 1931 American tour but chose to remain in London, choreographing for Sir Oswald Stoll's variety shows at the London Coliseum. His troupe was often billed as "George Balanchine's Sixteen Delightful Dancers," or "Balanchine's Girls," and the versatile choreographer mounted lavish production numbers with the sheen of Busby Berkeley's Gold Diggers films of a few years later in Hollywood—where, in fact, he would soon find himself.

He produced a few full-scale ballets as well, staged specifically for the thirteen-year-old Tamara Toumanova and other "baby ballerinas" (as the American press dubbed them). Toumanova first appeared in Balanchine's *La Concurrence* with music by Les Six composer Georges Auric in 1932.[6] She and the equally young Irina Baronova and Tatiana Riabouchinska were spotlighted in Colonel W. de Basil's Ballets Russes de Monte Carlo, founded in 1932. The successful touring group was one of the companies hoping to fill the gap created by Diaghilev's death. De Basil, a clever entrepreneur whose acumen seems to have compensated for his lack of artistic discrimination, gathered together many of Diaghilev's former dancers and choreographers. The company thrived, for a while anyway, especially under the venturesome management of Sol Hurok, who virtually controlled ballet in America.

Balanchine, still not thirty years old, and Boris Kochno formed their own company in 1933. Funded by Coco Chanel, Cole Porter, and other friends, Kochno and Balanchine's Les Ballets 1933 took up residence at Diaghilev's once triumphant Parisian throne, the Théâtre des Champs-Elysées. Experimentation was the byword, enticing several adventuresome artists to come on board. The company toured London and Paris, programming innovative new works such as Balanchine's *Mozartiana,* set to the music of Tchaikovsky. Such forward thinking was not in line with Parisian taste, but although the company survived only a single season, its appearance at the Savoy in London could not have been more serendipitous.

Stravinsky's and Balanchine's paths did not intersect much after *Apollo.* It was probably the most itinerant time of their lives as both scraped to make ends meet. Balanchine did manage to hear many of Stravinsky's new scores as they made their way quickly through Europe. What must he have thought about Stravinsky's most recent works—such as the gripping *Symphony of Psalms,* which surely made Balanchine thirst for some future collaboration? The choreographer's compositional knowledge enabled him to hear much of the music then being written in France for what it was: clever, witty, at times saccharine, but never terribly meaningful. Meanwhile, Stravinsky's attachment to France rapidly waned during the same period Balanchine was drifting, but for very different, more personal reasons. The composer had become embittered over the country's refusal to recognize his international notoriety. He felt slighted and unappreciated, and he made his discontent known, often offending people in the process.

Jacques Rouché, the domineering director of the Opéra, often locked horns with the composer. In a film clip cut from Palmer's documentary, a voluble Lifar speaks of his attempts to help Stravinsky secure performances of his theatrical works in Paris. He arranged for a Stravinsky-Rouché summit, but the composer's brusqueness wrecked any hope of a détente, let alone the prospect of future productions. "All of a sudden," Lifar recounts, "Stravinsky lost his temper and insulted France, the Opéra, and the administrator. He said that 'unless you include three works, I refuse.' And without as much as a good-bye, he left the office."[7]

While he was touring, the composer's correspondence with Vera Sudeikina divulges a mounting apprehension over Germany's military resurgence and, more personally, its potentially devastating impact on him. Then came the Anschluss and Hitler's invasion of Czechoslovakia in the summer of 1938, and Poland in 1939. Soon Norway, Belgium, Holland, and Denmark would fall. And France? Stravinsky lived in fear of yet another forced exile. The offer to be the 1939 Charles Eliot Norton Professor at Harvard proved a godsend, providing a respectable, face-saving egress from France. Two weeks before departing for Boston, Stravinsky arrived at Nadia Boulanger's country home "with a gas mask in one hand, and a suitcase in another," having been convinced by Sudeikina to flee Paris for fear of the city being bombed.[8]

Balanchine too felt no overriding reason to remain in Europe. As Les Ballets 1933 folded, the choreographer remained rootless, growing despondent. Beyond patching together dances here and there, what was his future? Fortunately for the dispirited Balanchine, an even younger (twenty-six years old) American, bursting with both optimism and means, knew where that future should be. Richard Hammond's "American Diaghilev" arrived in the person of the affluently privileged, Harvard-educated Lincoln Kirstein.[9] The young balletomane dreamed of creating a classical ballet company in the United States, smack-dab in the middle of the bottomed-out economy of the Great Depression. It seemed a Pollyannaish fantasy: Was Kirstein really qualified to don the mantle of a Diaghilev? "Assiduously I researched dance documents in the libraries of the Grand Opéra, the Arsenal, and the new Archives de la Danse in Passy," Kirstein later recalled.

I met historians and critics, survivors and scholars of a golden age. Their clinical attitude about present and future, their presupposed professionalism, added to my conviction that there was a valid body of work, past any trivial gossip, supporting the seriousness of theatrical-dancing. I knew I could not myself be a dancer, but there was a possibility as a scholar, perhaps even as some sort of participant. I did not yet dare think of myself as anything so unlikely as an impresario. But . . . maybe, perhaps . . . in time?[10]

Beginning in 1922 the young Kirstein's leisurely summers in Bloomsbury had infused the impressionable young man with a cultish view of its flagrantly progressive bohemian residents, such as Maynard Keynes, Aldous Huxley, and E. M. Forster. Moreover, he had sensed that the time was right for a new American heritage of dance. Italy and France were in the grips of a smothering fascism; Paris had deteriorated into a haven for "left-overs, intrigue, and dregs from the Diaghilev days," and even England was ineradicably and monolithically a "Diaghilev province."[11] Attending a performance of the Ballets Russes in June 1926, Kirstein had witnessed Diaghilev's sagging fortunes, as well as his admiration for a young dancer appearing in *Firebird*, whose name he did not yet know. "When I asked about him," wrote Kirstein in his diary, "I was told that he was an excellent dancer with bad lungs," who somehow had managed to distance himself from "Diaghilev's intimate court." And further:

> Diaghilev is bankrupt. . . . He must play in a vaudeville theater; Stravinsky has deserted to Ida Rubinstein. . . . I expected more. Not much dancing; not enough dancers. But one exciting moment. In *Firebird*, the magician Kastchei was made up as Genghis Khan; Mongolian, with long fingernails like gilded claws, a frightful vulture. In a fantastically evil way he manipulated the others. Afterward, to a restaurant; there he was, among other dancers. I wanted to ask him for a drink, but didn't dare.[12]

Kirstein soon became familiar with the young man portraying the ogreish Kastchei. He attended a performance of *Apollo* and several Les Ballets 1933 productions while residing in Paris. Balanchine and Kirstein first met in London that summer at a reception following a performance of *Mozartiana*. There the choreographer spoke openly of his restlessness with the declining state of dance in Europe. He complained about the sluggish instruction offered by second-rate, retired, obstinate dancers. He expressed his ennui over relegating himself to staging *Apollo* and *Prodigal Son*. Ballet had to change "like the shifting waistlines of women's dresses," Kirstein recalled Balanchine saying. Yet he vigorously expostulated on the virtues of classical dance, which must be "reconstructed for service in our twentieth century, speeded up, its tempo accelerated."[13]

Kirstein further recalled that Balanchine dropped "hints" that he wanted to emigrate. The young American set his mind on formulating a strategy that would concretize what then seemed no more than a farfetched notion.[14] Balanchine invited Kirstein to lunch, now speaking unreservedly of an escape from the unsettled future that he, like Stravinsky, faced in Europe. On 16 July 1933, a passionately stirred Kirstein wrote to A. Everett Austin, Jr., a friend and potential financial supporter: "This will be the most important letter I will ever write. . . . My pen burns my hand as I write: words will not flow into the ink fast enough. We have a real chance to have an American ballet within three years time. . . . Do you know Georges Balanchine . . . ?" The new troupe would locate in Hartford, Connecticut, secluded from "society and the professional Broadway Theatre." Kirstein further explained to Austin the exact racial mix of students Balanchine envisioned: "For the first he would take 4 white girls and four white boys, about sixteen yrs. old and 8 of the same, *negros* [*sic*]. They would be firmly taught in the classical idiom, not only from *exercises* but he would start company ballets at once so they could actually *learn* by doing. As time went on he would get younger children from 8 yrs. on. He thinks the negro part of it would be amazingly supple, the combination of suppleness and sense of time superb. Imagine them, masked, for example. They have so much abandon—and disciplined they would be *nonpareil.*"[15]

Over the next few months Kirstein arranged transatlantic passage, and on 6 September 1933 cabled $3,000 to Lloyds & National Provincial Foreign Bank in Balanchine's name. Two days later Kirstein contacted Balanchine in Paris suggesting that the choreographer bring as many "costumes and material for your work as you think necessary" while leaving the scenery for such ballets as *Mozartiana* to be transported later. He impressed upon Balanchine the importance of bringing publicity photographs of himself and his ballets as a way of making the prospect more vivid. Perhaps this would encourage his American backers to move forward quickly. In further September cables, Kirstein suggested to Balanchine that he bring along Toumanova because she would "arouse interest[,] showing clearly what can be done."[16] Shortly thereafter Balanchine arrived in New York—just about the time Stravinsky was completing *Perséphone.*

In January 1934 the School of American Ballet, formally founded a few months earlier in Hartford, relocated to New York. Toward the end of that same year, Stravinsky moved his family from Voreppe to Paris, where he could concentrate on *Perséphone,* and began recording the memoirs that became his autobiography.[17] In March 1935, while Stravinsky was concertizing in California and Colorado with Samuel Dushkin, Balanchine's young American Ballet presented the New York premiere of *Serenade*.[18]

Vernon Duke, who as Vladimir Dukelsky had immigrated years earlier and quickly ingratiated himself into the American popular scene, remembered Balanchine's early days in his newly adopted homeland: "It was wonderful to see George again—he was a little thinner, a bit paler, but still unruffled, unspoiled, supremely unconcerned with worldly success, merely intent on doing a good job." Balanchine described to Duke his new compatriots, Kirstein and Edward Warburg, as "enthusiastic, intelligent, and rich—an unbeatable combination."[19]

Kirstein assumed a huge fiduciary risk in subsidizing the Russian émigré, as he was derisively labeled. Was the still very young choreographer capable of establishing a new American company? "What Pope Julius II did for Michelangelo is nothing compared to Kirstein's commitment to Balanchine," declared the choreographer's friend and co-writer Francis Mason. Just so, for if the pope's appointment of Michelangelo can be credited with antagonizing Martin Luther enough to spark the Reformation, then Kirstein's pledge to Balanchine and his young American Ballet did no less to rouse a holy war among American dance critics.[20] Stravinsky retained in his files a program copy that Balanchine sent to him of the company's 1 March 1935 inaugural performance. In the program's prefatory remarks, a shrewd Kirstein raised a rampart against the calumny he knew would follow:

> Can Americans make good ballet dancers? This is a question which is an equivalent to asking whether or not Americans make good violinists, good painters, good poets. Physically speaking, Americans make the best dancers in the world with the possible exception of the Russians. What has the ballet to offer Americans? Is the form of ballet natural to Americans? Ballet has offered the rest of the world the most compact, intense form of lyric theatre[,] with its collaborating arts of painting and music, that exists. America, with its national amalgams[,] can bring more to this highly developed form than ever before. The form is capable of being assimilated by everyone. America is not an exception. Just as the civic symphonic orchestras of America are among the most brilliant in the world, so does America offer the world the possibility of a great ballet.

Just as Kirstein anticipated, John Martin's *New York Times* articles during the spring of 1935 attacked Balanchine's enterprise. The prominent critic fired a burst of abjectly jingoistic rounds, suggesting that Balanchine and his chic, outré "Riviera esthetics" retreat to Paris, where they belonged. Proposing that the company be renamed Les Ballets Americaines, Martin added, "With all due respect to George Balanchine, the great need of the company is American direction." And in one particularly repugnant display of flag-waving, Martin dismissed the choreographer altogether, concluding that the American Ballet should "get rid of Balanchine, with his international notions, and hire a good American dance man."[21]

While Balanchine and Stravinsky did not work together during the early 1930s, they kept track of each other. The composer passed through New York again in January 1935, and once more in the spring of 1936, when he and Balanchine dined together. As Stravinsky and Dushkin concertized throughout the United States, the composer monitored the hostility that the "foreigner" Balanchine endured. Having sustained the wounds of such diatribes himself—even in France—Stravinsky surely commiserated, as he read the critics' attacks against his friend.

A stalwart Kirstein acted as Balanchine's Praetorian Guard, parrying each charge through eloquently written, albeit barefacedly retaliatory, newspaper replies. He repelled Martin's "aggressive nationalism" as xenophobia, castigating the critic for presuming that American dance should have no higher aspirations than to rise above tap-dancing and the Virginia Reel. Kirstein's rebuttals culminated in the brazenly censorious 1937–38 pamphlet "Blast at Ballet." The essay's subtitle, "A Corrective for the American Audience," left no doubt of where Kirstein's counterstrike was aimed. He reproached theater managers, dance critics, journalists, and in particular Martin as collusive demagogues, mounting what he described as "the Great Conspiracy." But Kirstein's public epistle was much more than a fulmination meant to undercut Martin and others for their philistinism. "Blast" had the air of an encyclical. In it Kirstein grandly and cogently laid out his conception of classical dance in America. It was a vision that championed the tenets of Balanchine's classicism.

In spite of Balanchine's phenomenal American success in the popular genre of musical-comedy [by this time Balanchine had choreographed for several hit Broadway musicals] he has tended to remain in the minds of the serious dance public as at best a choreographer's choreographer, and at worst as a perverse and mysterious talent. That is, in his serious work he has been found not to be interested in producing ballets which have any interest other than that inherent in music, or in the dancing as it stems from this music. He has always avoided crass pageantry, showy stage pictures of living models, pictorial build-ups, and parades in which there is no *dancing* as such. . . . He has . . . an extraordinary instinctive gift for finding the quality of coherent gesture to fit the exact shade of quality in the chosen music. His movement is a continual homage to music; the better the music the more effective the choreography. . . . If he is deeply moved by his music Balanchine visualizes amazing cross-currents and short-circuits of representational emotion. These representational fragments are not literal, and hence, have to be watched more closely than the ordinary corroborative mimicry which is easily familiar to superficial audiences. . . . Nor are his gestures "symbolic"; they do not *symbolize* anything; they are themselves deeply and completely lyrical. . . . My admiration for his inventive genius or taste has never for a second faltered. . . . I think he has more to teach a young choreographer about formal gesture in the developed classic tradition than anyone now working in this field.[22]

With Kirstein's support, Balanchine weathered Martin's firestorm. He did so, as he seems always to have done, by swallowing hard and working even harder whenever and wherever he could. A job was a job for Balanchine; services were exchanged, and one moved on. By late 1935 Balanchine's American Ballet had entered into what the choreographer and Kirstein hoped would be a promising affiliation with the Metropolitan Opera Company. The residency was billed as the American Ballet Ensemble; but the partnership, lasting only three seasons, quickly deteriorated. Still, for a brief period it provided Balanchine with visibility and at least some sense of permanency.[23]

During his strained residency with the Met, and like it or not, Balanchine once again staged dancing diversions for *Carmen, Die Meistersinger von Nüremberg,* and other Metropolitan war-horses. John Martin, whose ripostes by then were predictable, complained that "once again American artists have been passed by for a high artistic post for which at least half a dozen of them are eminently fitted. . . . Apparently the old tradition has not yet been eradicated that we are a crude pioneer people and must import our culture from the European fountainhead." But in the same 18 August 1935 *New York Times* article, Martin seemed not to object so much to Balanchine himself ("a gifted artist beyond the shadow of a doubt") as he did to the apprentice quality of the youthful company. He feared that the inexperienced dancers would not muster the talent needed to perform in "the world's leading lyric theatre." Martin had a point: the dancers were, in fact, treated as apprentices. Nora Kaye remembers that they "served as a sort of moving scenery whose principal function was to give the audience something to look at while the singers rested their voices."[24]

Still, Balanchine continued pouring his energies into developing the troupe —sometimes, to management's chagrin, with dancing that eclipsed other on-stage action. As he impertinently told a reporter: "Generally I instructed my dancers to dance all over the place. I advised them to kick the chorus if they got in the way." In "Blast at Ballet," Kirstein confessed that he and Balanchine believed that their youthful company would be able to mount new works, to take chances. They proceeded with a "zeal that exceeded a crusader's." But soon the opera found itself unable to fund the American Ballet Company's own ballets, and the troupe took on a largely utilitarian role as pleasant filler between operatic scenes.

Meanwhile, the versatile choreographer became more and more involved with New York's theater life (the very life he had earlier told Kirstein he "hated"), thanks to the intercession of Vernon Duke. The facile Balanchine adjusted to the populist enterprise without a hitch. He would sit at the piano and improvise the style of music he wanted Duke to prepare for a certain passage. His businesslike approach to production and his ability to work swiftly appealed to commercially minded financiers watching the clock. The 1936 edition of the Ziegfeld Follies (that red-blooded "National Institution Glorifying the American Girl," as it was pitched) found Balanchine a few blocks away from the Met in the Winter Garden, designing opulently staged ballets to the scenery and costumes of Vincente Minnelli, the music of Duke, and the lyrics of Ira Gershwin. The cast included the sensational Josephine Baker, who had returned from France to star in a production that included Fanny Brice and Bob Hope. For the Follies, he prepared several choreographic scenes highlighting Baker's talents. In "5 A.M." Baker danced a short dream sequence amid an assortment of African gods; and in "West Indies," the scantily clad Parisian femme fatale danced a raffish conga. (This was the kind of Ziegfeld typecasting that sent the unhappy and unappreciated Baker back to Paris.)[25]

In a 1949 interview, Balanchine hinted that his collaboration with Baker had heightened his sensitivity to the parochial and sometimes bigoted attitudes of the Broadway public. "They didn't like [Baker] because she was American. If she had been French, they would have gone wild; but an American Negro from Harlem—people said, 'Who the hell is she, who does she think she is?'"[26] Stravinsky too was familiar with Baker (as was Picasso, who painted her, and Hemingway, who befriended her). Indeed, the composer was moved by the music of African American performers, who were the rage in Paris in the 1920s. His enthusiastic embrace of jazz caught many off-guard ("I like jazz when it is the simple expression of *la musique nègre*," he wrote in his *Autobiography*). Indeed the "jazziness" of both Stravinsky's and Balanchine's work (extending even into the 1957 *Agon*) is traceable to this period, or even before.[27]

Balanchine contributed to other Broadway musicals, including Richard Rodgers and Lorenz Hart's 1936 *On Your Toes*. He demanded that producers engage him as a choreographer, not just a dance arranger. He insisted that both dance and dancers be more fully enfolded into the drama. Ray Bolger, billed as the "jazz Nijinsky," who danced in the innovative "Slaughter on Tenth Avenue" ballet from the musical, told Francis Mason that "it was really the first show ever to integrate dance and action, even before Agnes de Mille. I don't think Aggie would have done any show if it hadn't been for *On Your Toes.*" Indeed, Miles Cruger, former president of the Institute of the American Musical, commented that the ballet at the end of the second act was "the most important ballet in the history of the Broadway musical."[28] De Mille's "Americana" works, both for the Ballet Russe de Monte Carlo (such as the 1942 *Rodeo*) and also for Broadway (notably *Oklahoma!* in 1943), unquestionably are beholden to Balanchine's imaginative conceptions of the late 1930s.

On Your Toes was followed by the equally successful *Babes in Arms,* again breaking new ground. The second act ballet, "Peter's Journey," was a spectacular dream fantasy that anticipated by years Gene Kelly and Leslie Caron's final dream ballet in the 1951 film *An American in Paris.* Premiering on 14 April at the Shubert Theatre, the 1937 *Babes in Arms* opened less than two weeks before the Stravinsky-Balanchine partnership suddenly and publicly reemerged. For while Balanchine was darting between the Metropolitan Opera House and Broadway, he was also arranging and rehearsing the first ever American festival of Stravinsky ballets. It was now nearly a decade since the composer and choreographer had collaborated on *Apollo.*

While Balanchine was acclimating himself to New York during the mid-1930s, dividing his time between Broadway and the Met, Stravinsky had remained in Europe. He toured extensively as a conductor and pianist; he prophesied the fate of modern music in countless interviews; along with Nadia Boulanger, he taught (but only occasionally) at the Ecole Normale de Musique in Paris; and he worked on his memoirs. It was a disruptive period, leaving little time for composition, though the works he did manage to complete were significant. Still, there were no new ballets among his most recent oeuvre.

Almost at the same moment that Balanchine began envisioning his preliminary ideas for *Serenade,* Stravinsky spoke out in an interview for the *Manchester Guardian* (22 February 1934). He explained why yet again he had distanced himself from ballet over the past several years. With an eye toward future possibilities, he also shared his personal vision of classical dance—a vision presaging much of what Kirstein's "Blast" would argue a few years later. As to the function of ballet music, the composer's response to the interviewer left little doubt as to his position:

Question: You have composed much music for the ballet. Do you think that there is still a future for ballet in this highly mechanized world, that the dance can be brought up to date as an expression of life in the twentieth century, or must it live on its past glories?

Stravinsky: Assuredly I believe that ballet will live and grow. The dance is as old as man and as young as man. It did not die with the Russian ballet. It is an essential, a dramatic part of the life of the theatre. But there is not a great deal of good ballet music. Either it is sunk in the dance or it is irrelevant to it as a rule. Music and dance should be a true marriage of separate arts, a partnership, not a dictatorship of the one over the other. Ballet music should have an independent existence. Too often it is tied to the theatrical spectacle.[29]

Unsurprisingly, John Martin, who once described music as mere "aural scenery," ensconced himself at the opposite end of the spectrum: "The music is the temporal setting, and nothing more. . . . It is not the dancer's business to exhibit the music, but the musician's to exhibit the dancer. . . . There can be no equality."[30] Whatever Martin's edict, Stravinsky, Balanchine, and now Kirstein, remained steadfast in their shared belief about the mission of classical dance. Having already survived a barrage of criticism, Balanchine's young American Ballet edged farther out on a limb by presenting on 27–28 April 1937 an unprecedented festival dedicated to Stravinsky's ballets. Still in the United States touring with Dushkin, the composer agreed to conduct both New York performances before returning to Europe.

Just as Kirstein had entrusted Balanchine with his fragile dream, Balanchine now placed the precarious fate of his company in the hands of a composer whose more recent, neoclassic works were hardly winning the same acclaim as his earlier, "Russian" works. In fact throughout the 1920s and 1930s, the new Stravinsky works frequently met with disapproval. The pieces were considered too dry, too formalistic. Balanchine's sponsorship of Stravinsky was risky. Perhaps a mixture of loyalty and courage drove him. But whatever the motivation, the choreographer was the first to invite the composer to bring his leaner neoclassic ballets to New York, rather than the more popular, "Once upon a time," Russian ballets, as they were often called.

Ironically, while John Martin and other like-minded critics battered Balanchine for being too Russian, Stravinsky's music was continually assailed in New York for not being Russian enough. Balanchine was forcing an eclectic, Russian-Europeanized classicism on American audiences, while a compositionally depleted Stravinsky—so the ridiculous charges went—had sadly lost his way the moment he turned his back on his motherland. Of Stravinsky's Concerto in D for violin and orchestra, Downes charged that "the concerto joins the lengthening list of the stillborn compositions of the later Stravinsky."[31] As early as 1934 he had alleged that Stravinsky's unpalatable music would not have been programmed at all in New York were it not for a few obsequious acolytes who believed "Stravinsky the prophet can do no wrong." It is true that Stravinsky's loyalists, particularly Virgil Thomson and Elliott Carter, were lobbying mightily in *Modern Music,* hoping to quiet the shrill voices of the composer's detractors. Such blind partisanship, as Downes insinuated, would now put Balanchine on the spot.

Held at the Metropolitan Opera House, the Stravinsky Festival presented three of the composer's ballets, including the first American performance of Balanchine's *Apollo,* nine years to the day after Bolm's already forgotten staging in Washington. Lew Christensen danced the young god, much to Stravinsky's liking. In an interview with Richard Buckle, Christensen spoke of working on the prodigious role with Balanchine, and of his own interpretation compared to Lifar's: Balanchine "went through each detail with me, *over* and *over* and *over* again. . . . Lifar didn't dance like I did. He danced more—easy. I danced hard, fast, sharp, quick. That's what Balanchine liked about it. . . . There were some very fast pirouettes in it—which I'm sure Lifar didn't do. . . . That was the hardest damn thing. I practiced that by the hour."[32] Balanchine also prepared a newly choreographed *Le Baiser de la Fée.* Of the three ballets programmed for the festival, *Baiser* was, in the estimate of John Martin himself, the highlight of the program.

Most significant, the company introduced *Jeu de Cartes,* funded by Kirstein's Harvard classmate and financial partner Edward Warburg. The new work was expressly commissioned to showcase the vitality of the American Ballet's young dancers (twenty-six of them, to be exact). Warburg knew that Balanchine's admiration for Stravinsky was "bordering on filial idolatry," as Kirstein wrote in "Blast at Ballet," and there was an unspoken apprehension that Stravinsky's music might not have been the best choice. After all, box-office receipts could not be ignored, and given the composer's recent string of unprepossessing works, there were fears that his music, no matter how brilliantly staged by the young dancers, might prove a liability. By his own admission Kirstein too was opposed "from the very first" to such an "ambitious scheme." As Anatole Chujoy later read Kirstein's concerns, Stravinsky was a "great dance-musician, [who] had received his due from all Europe, and [who] would never lack a chance to produce his own ballets." Chujoy also felt that Kirstein found all three ballets chancy since they were "each in a different way, retardative."[33]

At the time of the festival, whatever anxieties existed were suppressed; once the decision was made to move forward, Kirstein and Warburg acted unselfishly in backing the event. They had met with Stravinsky in New York during the composer's 1935 tour with Dushkin, broaching the idea of commissioning a ballet for Balanchine's new company. At that time they encouraged him not only to conduct the performances but also to take an active role in promoting the event; and indeed, the composer did so, speaking about the work, agreeing to interviews, and posing for publicity photographs.

Entitled *The Card Game,* or *Poker Game* when it was staged by the Ballet Russe de Monte Carlo a few years later, the ballet is traceable to the composer's life-long enjoyment of card games. In drafting the synopsis and scenario, Stravinsky was assisted by Nikita Malaieff, a friend of his two sons. Earlier, the composer had corresponded with Cocteau, suggesting that he might be involved in developing the story line. As late as July 1936, by which time a good share of the music had already been composed, Stravinsky still hoped to enlist Cocteau, but nothing came of this. The composer eventually arranged his own synopsis for the ballet, based upon a few verses of La Fontaine's apologue "Les Loups et les Brebis" (The Wolves and the Sheep). It was La Fontaine's moralistic poetry, in essence, that provided Stravinsky with the "argument" for *Jeu de Cartes.*[34] Against his publisher Willy Strecker's advice, Stravinsky insisted that a synopsis be printed in the published score, providing what he considered an indispensable introduction to the action. The final verse of the La Fontaine fable was included, wherein the ballet's Joker is portrayed as a constant threat, a wicked enemy to be feared:

Compound not with the wicked—there's my moral.
With such, the wise man has a truceless quarrel.
Peace in itself is a good thing, I know,
But not with a perfidious foe.[35]

The characters proposed for *Jeu de Cartes* were cards in a poker game, led by the duplicitous Joker, who works his chicanery throughout three separate Deals. The composer hinted that initially *Jeu de Cartes* was written without a particular venue in mind, and certainly not intended as a ballet. As his compositional sketches demonstrate, much of the work had been completed before Kirstein and Warburg offered him the commission. Initial sketches dating from December 1935 do suggest that Stravinsky began the work without a clear balletic concept, although perhaps he had at least a basic story line in mind. Writing to Balanchine six months into the composing process, Stravinsky expressed hesitancy about shaping his score for dance, not only because of his qualms about ballet as an art form, but because he had not developed a scenario. Consequently, how could he plan the music's architecture?[36]

The orchestral sparkle of the new work suggested that the score might find separate audiences in the theater and the concert hall. Even before the composer traveled to America for his tour, he had already arranged for several concert performances in London, as an unpublished letter from the secretary of the Cortauld-Sargent Concerts reveals. Stravinsky often began a commissioned work before signing a contract. In this case particularly, it is little wonder that *Jeu de Cartes* was nearly completed before an agreement was finalized in October 1936. By then it was well over a year since Stravinsky had begun, and only a few months before Balanchine put the work in rehearsal.

Beginning around August 1935, a series of letters between Stravinsky, Balanchine, Nabokov, and Dushkin all make allusions to the ballet but without much resolution on matters of finance, story, or staging. Balanchine was not particularly forthcoming in expressing what he wanted, perhaps because he felt that being so would amount to overstepping his position—a position he considered subservient to the composer's. But Stravinsky detested imprecision and let Balanchine know, in no uncertain terms, that he needed a clearly delineated outline. As ever, Stravinsky was also concerned about the contractual conditions, pledging that if legalities could be resolved, the ballet would be ready by fall 1936.

Catherine Stravinsky's correspondence of 17 January 1936 shows that her husband had played part of the work for her around then, though it could only have been preliminary sketches. Still, the contract was not yet in hand, and Stravinsky was anxious. Samuel Dushkin told the composer that Balanchine so wanted the ballet that he was raising the money himself by working for the Ziegfeld Follies. In June, finally, Balanchine wrote to Stravinsky that while he was not expecting a particularly profound ballet, still he wanted something that would not be too lightweight because he had been doing such pieces for a few years and "everyone has begun to copy me."[37]

Years later, Balanchine offered a subtext to the scenario: "Stravinsky and I attempted to show that the highest cards—the kings, queens and jacks—in reality have nothing on the other side. They were big people, but they easily can be beaten by small cards. Seemingly powerful figures, they are actually mere silhouettes."[38] But originally the choreographer had suggested Hans Christian Andersen's "The Flowered Ball" as a basis for the scenario. Stravinsky promptly rejected the idea, thinking it inappropriate if the ballet were to be more than

light fare. At the end of June 1936, no doubt perturbed by what he saw as Warburg's nonfeasance and Balanchine's indecision, Stravinsky drafted his own scenario. He took it upon himself to determine the length of the ballet, the stage
design, the size of orchestra, even the number of dancers. Moreover, the composer wanted his son Theodore to design the costumes, although ultimately the
local New York union would not allow it. Irene Sharaff designed the original costumes, which Stravinsky disliked, considering them too period specific (fig. 6.1).

The Basel archives retain both the original French synopsis of the ballet as
prepared by Malaieff and the scenario Stravinsky drafted. This is quite detailed,
with many choreographic directions already determined. The document offers
a glimpse of the composer's initial thinking. A measure of the specificity of the
action planned is apparent in his summary of the Third Deal:

> The fifteen characters enter and group themselves as follows:
> Right: Joker, Ten, Nine, Eight and Seven of Spades.
> Centre: Ace, King, Queen, Knave and Ten of Hearts.
> Left: Nine, Eight, Seven, Six and Five of Hearts.
>
> The characters of group L. discard their (blue) masks and dominoes one after the
> other and begin calmly to dance a waltz. In this dance they are joined by the charac-
> ters of the two other groups, who, however, remain in disguise. This dance finished,
> they take up their original positions.
>
> At this moment the characters of group R., discarding their masks and dominoes,
> immediately attack group L., who after a desperate struggle realize themselves de-
> feated and fly. The conquerors, chasing their foe, disappear with them off the stage.
>
> Returning at the head of his group, to celebrate his triumph, the Joker is suddenly
> confronted by the five characters of the Royal Flush (central group), who have by
> this time thrown off their masks and dominoes.
>
> Crunched by his defeat, the Joker collapses at the feet of the characters of the
> Royal Flush, who celebrate their victory by a dance of triumph, while four footmen
> in powdered wigs and livery carry off their perfidious enemy.
>
> While the King and Queen of Hearts are crowned by the Ace, the defeated group
> of Hearts returns to the stage and joins in the dance with the central group.

Some of the compositional sketches already include notations positioning
the dancers. Other directions may have been added once the ballet was completed and after rehearsal numbers were assigned. For example, Stravinsky instructs that "as soon as the Joker appears, the characters of the central group admit their defeat, and move off one after the other during the six measures of
REH 20. From REH 21 to 33 bursts of challenge and helpless rage from the Joker
against group L. During the five measures of REH 33 he leaves the stage."

Ariel Lang

Annabelle Lyon and William Dollar

Annabelle Lyon, Hortense Kahrklin, William Dollar, Ariel Lang, Leyda Anchutina

6.1 Three photographs from the 1937 American Ballet Company production of *Jeu de Cartes* (Jerome Robbins Dance Division, The New York Public Library for the Performing Arts, Astor, Lenox and Tilden Foundations)

The brassy fanfare theme that heralds the opening of all three Deals was not composed first. Its notation is literally shoved between several lines of an already worked-out passage. Nor is that already completed passage used at an early point in the final version of the ballet. Rather, much of the material on Stravinsky's first sketch page is withheld, surfacing nearly two hundred measures into the piece. The Basel sketchbook also confirms that Stravinsky often jotted down ideas for all three Deals on the same day. Thus the compositional process was far more scattershot than in *Apollo*. There too, each section of the pas was carefully calibrated, as Stravinsky's constant notation of temporal markings illustrated. With that ballet, obviously, the composer was cognizant of the pacing at every moment of a passage's compositional evolution. After all, from its inception, *Apollo* was designed as a ballet. Not only did he know the music would be danced, but he had a fair notion of *how* it would be danced given the input from Diaghilev, Balanchine, and Lifar.

Yet as he drafted *Jeu de Cartes,* much remained unsettled. Consequently, the sketches reveal quite a different evolution. Here Stravinsky often worked on isolated passages of several measures; then, almost randomly, it seems, he proceeded to sketch entirely unrelated music that was ultimately located in a completely different part of the ballet. For example, on the second day of composing, Stravinsky sketched material that eventually appeared about fifty-eight pages into the final score.

The signature trumpet fanfare introducing each of the three Deals was, as the Basel sketches attest, originally reiterated much more frequently at various internal points in each of the three large movements. In the beginning, for instance, Stravinsky used the fanfare as a bridge leading to a dramatic key change at Rehearsal 16. Further, music that is eventually used at Rehearsals 92, 109, 34, and 6 was initially drafted in that nonsequential succession. The sketches also reveal that Stravinsky often changed his mind about the key in which the music would be situated. And he constantly adjusted the meter, searching for the clearest way of notating his thoughts—something he often did even years after a score was first printed.

No work from the 1930s is more buoyant, evocative, even frolicsome. And nowhere is Stravinsky's wonderful sense of buffoonery more carefully designed than in the ballet's closing pages. He admitted borrowing familiar tunes— Strauss, Ravel, and others—but even if he hadn't confessed, they would be hard to miss. Most familiar is the composer's thematic parody of *The Barber of Seville* overture. Indeed, the Rossini tune was one of the first passages that caught Balanchine's eye when he received the piano reduction in December 1936. This undisguised pastiche was a clever way of quickly winning over listeners. But some found the peppering of blatant quotations not so much witty as slapstick. "Just why the musical setting of a poker game should quote from every musician from Rossini to Ravel is not readily apparent," groused John Martin in his review.

Here again the Basel sketchbook is instructive. The ballet's closing section was finished on 19 October 1936. In November, Stravinsky composed the music leading to the work's final cadence. While the Rossini quotation appears most recognizably at Rehearsal 153 in a transparent reference, Stravinsky next composed backward, just as he did with *Apollo.* The first hint of the forthcoming Rossini quote appeared at Rehearsal 150–52 as developed from a sketch wherein Stravinsky experimented with a rhythmic and metric disruption of the Rossini material. Next, as the carefully dated sketches confirm, the composer abruptly abandoned the Rossini materials and shaped the final cadence of Rehearsal 202. That accomplished, he returned to the Rossini parody, retreating even farther back into the piece. He developed what would eventually become Rehearsal 143, clearly related in its fragmented and imitative motivic derivation to the Rossini tune—a tune which at that point remained unstated. In effect, motivic derivations anticipate their actual source until finally the source manifests itself. It is one of the composer's favorite ploys. Almost subliminally, the fundamental seeds of the Rossini quote are planted in our minds. When we finally recognize Stravinsky's gambit retrospectively, and the tune is stated forthrightly, the joke is all the more farcical. The entire passage was written in reverse and carefully assembled not one measure *after* the next but one measure *before* the next.

Balanchine also was inclined to chart choreographic patterns in the rehearsal studio in reverse sequence. As the choreographer often remarked, he was in the business of assembling steps creatively. The identification of structurally important arrival points was as important to Balanchine as it was to Stravinsky. Edward Villela recalled that Balanchine would firmly determine the beginnings, endings, and focal points of a piece, but everything else was often negotiable, as long as the dancers didn't "distort the choreography beyond the boundaries he controlled."[39]

Other Balanchine dancers too remember how he sculpted a dance's architecture by working in retrograde. In a 1980s filmed interview, Rudolph Nureyev recalls how "Mr B" would ask the pianist to play the main climax of a section, then devise steps leading toward its articulation. Next he would ask the pianist to play the second most important musical high point; then similarly he would work with Nureyev toward marking that structural peak ("Himalayan peaks," Nureyev comments in the film).[40]

So it would continue, always working in reverse, so that the beginning of the pas was often the last section choreographed. Violette Verdy recalls that Balanchine was occupied mainly with the temporal pacing that led to a climax and less with the specific steps that filled the span leading there. Once the climax was defined, he would work backward, often entrusting Verdy "to make up a little something to fill the time."[41] Suzanne Farrell also recalled how Balanchine constructed the 1965 *Don Quixote* for her by beginning with the third act climax: "Knowing where it would end told him where it might begin, and where it had to go."[42] Indeed, Balanchine himself referred to his compositional process as one that had a "reverse-time sense."

Two memories of *Jeu de Cartes*'s premiere, recorded by Francis Mason in interviews, are worth reprinting. Annabelle Lyon, one of the principal dancers in the original production, described how Balanchine worked, and how different he was from another celebrated choreographer. Lyon recalls that one of the first dances Balanchine choreographed was her Queen of Hearts Variation, which was very different "from the usual lyrical *bourrées* that I constantly did." She also remembered that working with Balanchine was unlike working with Fokine, who settled the choreography before the dancers arrived. "You had to do exactly what *he* wanted, while Balanchine choreographed for *you,* for the dancer he was working with. It was tailor made."[43]

Warburg's remembrance of the festival, which opened with a performance of *Apollo,* captures Stravinsky's sometimes-prickly personality:

> Opening night, the New York Philharmonic was in the orchestra pit. [The Philharmonic was hired in place of the Metropolitan's orchestra—an action which did nothing to endear either Stravinsky or Balanchine to the management.] Stravinsky was to conduct. . . . It was my job to tell the maestro we were ready. I went to Stravinsky and said, "Maestro, please." Stravinsky said, "I cannot . . . have you seen the program for this evening's performance? . . . It says in the program, *Apollon,* music by Igor Stravinsky. I will not conduct. . . . [The] program should read *Apollon* by Igor Stravinsky." As if it were [a] new Apollo Belvedere, *sans* Balanchine. He was offended that anyone else should be acknowledged. The choreographer and designer meant nothing to him. The assistant conductor was standing by. I turned to him as calmly as I could and said, "Will you please take the podium?" The words were not out of my mouth before Igor rushed past him into the orchestra pit. The rest was Stravinsky-Balanchine history.[44]

The assistant conductor to whom Warburg refers was Leo Smit, who also served as the rehearsal pianist. Smit later provided one of the more reliable eyewitness accounts of Stravinsky and Balanchine's rehearsal interchanges. The composer's piano reduction arrived in December 1936; but before giving it to Smit to prepare, Balanchine took the score home, as was his habit, and learned the music in what could only have been a day or two. Just as the Basel sketchbook provides clues in tracking the work's compositional development, so too Smit's presence in the studio records the composer's initial impression of Balanchine's choreography, as well as his energetic pianism:

> Stravinsky quickly took a place on the long bench. . . . Beating time with hand, foot, and grunt, he set and controlled the tempos, unfolding the music with a strength and subtlety it did not have before. The choreography pleased him immensely and he only suggested simplifying a few complicated patterns, which concluded the first deal.
>
> [Stravinsky] offered to play the whole of *The Card Game* for me. . . . In some un-

accountable way, without technique[,] he sometimes glissandoed what should have been fingered scales, without beauty of tone (he poked the keys with his large bony fingers muting, muting the dynamics with the left pedal while tapping rhythmically on the right pedal), and keeping time by vigorous gasping counting, he succeeded in conveying the meaning of his musical thought with extraordinary clarity. . . . The silences of rests took on a fierce intensity . . . so unlike the passive waiting or the common injudicious trimming of the supposed non-music rests. . . . By the time he finished playing, I felt I had been initiated into the most secret of Mysteries.[45]

Kirstein was also present, recounting in his celebrated 1937 essay "Working with Stravinsky" memories that, although a bit embellished, still provide a rare eyewitness analysis of the rehearsal process.[46] He contended that *Jeu de Cartes* was "a complete collaboration," though it was hardly that. Stravinsky declared that he was relatively unconcerned with detailing the action too specifically, although his sketches demonstrate that he did so. Certainly, the geographic separation of composer and choreographer alone precluded the kind of regular table talk that Balanchine, Stravinsky, and others had indulged in a decade earlier in Nice. With *Jeu de Cartes,* Stravinsky remembered that as he composed in France and Balanchine worked in New York there was virtually no discussion about the choreography, although it is known that they discussed tempi, at least, when Stravinsky passed through New York on tour with Dushkin.

Both Smit and Kirstein recalled that Balanchine plotted a sizable portion of the choreography before Stravinsky's arrival. Once the composer entered the rehearsal studio in March, however, everything changed. Kirstein claimed that Stravinsky had complete confidence in his partnership with Balanchine. Yet he was quick to add, in a curiously worded statement, that Stravinsky "treated Balanchine like a junior assistant, although on an absolutely equal footing as an expert, since there was a presupposed agreement that the spectacle would be governed by music rather than by any overall concept of stylized movement." Under no circumstances could the kinetic composer ever sit passively in a dance studio while his music was being interpreted. Quite the contrary: Stravinsky participated irrepressibly in rehearsing *Jeu de Cartes,* sometimes, as Kirstein recalled, six hours at a time before "hauling the rehearsal pianist off to his hotel for more work." Whatever choreographic plan Stravinsky had envisioned while composing the work in Europe, there can be no doubt that it was modified once he saw what Balanchine wanted his dancers to do. Still, Kirstein considered that the ballet adhered too restrictively to the "regulations of Stravinsky's very rigidly indicated libretto."[47]

The composer was weariless in physically demonstrating his instructions to the dancers. He would slap his knee, Kirstein described, keeping strict count and "gesticulating rapidly to emphasize his points, [or] suggest a change."[48] Stravinsky apparently refashioned the choreography, sometimes with sharp criticism, as witnesses reported. At the end of the first of the three Deals, for example, alterations were made for the sake of simplicity. One has to wonder what Balanchine privately thought about the composer's reworking of the two Deals he had already designed. Did he interpret Stravinsky's remonstrations as improvements or interventions? And just how much of a "junior assistant" was Balanchine willing to be?

In *Following Balanchine,* longtime ballet observer Robert Garis suggests that the choreographer may have found Stravinsky's untrammeled criticisms and impromptu alterations irksome and excessive. He suggests, quite reasonably, that probably "Balanchine simply gave in" whether he liked it or not, whenever Stravinsky decided what was best. Garis further contends that Balanchine never liked the ballet, choosing not to revive it in later years, most notably excluding it from the Stravinsky Festival in 1972. "By the time the score arrived," Garis adds, "it was fully formed theatrically, in a mode that may not have been congenial to Balanchine's instincts."[49]

Everything that we know about Stravinsky's devouring personality confirms Garis's hunch. Of course Balanchine gave in, despite whatever undertow existed. In the presence of a composer who often ruled by fiat, who wouldn't? Add to that the indissoluble Russian bond that linked the two men, as well as Balanchine's adulation of Stravinsky as his "guru," and one wonders what choice Balanchine had. Moreover, throughout his life, Balanchine relied heavily upon Stravinsky as a source of inspiration musically, artistically, even spiritually. Indeed, to a large extent, Balanchine's almost unconditional submission to Stravinsky is precisely why their collaborations before, during, and after *Jeu de Cartes* flourished. Stravinsky expected those in his presence to abnegate all rights in deference to his wishes. "That's always what he did, ever since I first worked with him on *The Song of the Nightingale* in '24 or '25," Balanchine told Jonathan Cott.[50]

Still, the coin has two sides. Violette Verdy more recently recalled that she was struck by Balanchine's own description of his relationship with the composer, one in which he spoke most comfortably of Stravinsky as the "driver" and himself as the amenable "accomplice."[51] He did not consider his compliance kowtowing. That Balanchine silently internalized at least some modicum of resentment for the composer over the course of a forty-year association seems unsurprising. But without such tolerance, without the forbearance to "accept," could anyone have enjoyed a successful artistic partnership with the willful composer? Balanchine seemed willing to acquiesce. Surely he must have winced at some of Stravinsky's suggestions, but from a technical viewpoint at least, he would have had no trouble making balletic alterations quickly. It was the speed with which he choreographed and adjusted that many of his dancers remember most. Nor did he feel the need to fuss over every measure, every gesture, often entrusting his dancers to "make up a little something to fill the time"—an approach as antithetical to Stravinsky's as one could fathom. It was precisely the foil needed to match an always-punctilious composer, who fretted over every detail of every passage.

Whatever preconceptions the composer may have had about the staging of *Jeu de Cartes,* he was uncharacteristically flexible when Balanchine requested additional time for the choreography to unfold. More than one witness remembers Stravinsky adding music on the spot. The Basel archives retain Stravinsky's sketch score—the score Stravinsky had finished in early December before shipping the piano reduction to New York. This primary source in particular provides insight into whatever collaborative decisions were made. The score is a treasure trove, indicating revisions completed in France as well as what transpired in Balanchine's New York rehearsal studio. Tempo markings are often changed from those Stravinsky originally planned, sometimes drastically. Several instrumental indications are added or rethought, dispelling the fiction that Stravinsky had the precise sound of the piece in his mind from the start. Metric alterations often lead to the rebarring of music in duple meter rather than the originally conceived triple meter.

The first choreographic indications in the score appear at Rehearsal 4 and, perhaps most revealing, at Rehearsal 6, where the composer wanted the opening curtain cue. Stravinsky brackets a single measure, which is immediately repeated in the published score. This, no doubt, is an instance where some music was added "on the spot," perhaps to stretch or in some way accommodate a choreographic action as the curtain was raised. Indeed, the score is copiously marked with arrows, inserts, and directions to repeat measures, sometimes at distant junctures in the score. Many of these revisions could only have been made in the New York studio and point to the composer's willingness to reposition ideas as the ballet was visualized in Balanchine's eyes.

Large sections of music are deleted or shifted to later parts of the score, doubtless to serve better the choreographic action. Figure 6.2 shows the opening of the Valse de la IIIième donne, in which the original opening is deleted and the composer, at the bottom of the page, refers to later pages in the manu-

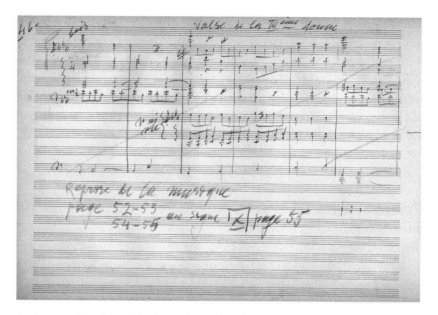

6.2 A compositional sketch by Stravinsky for the Valse de la IIIième donne, from *Jeu de Cartes* (Igor Stravinsky Collection, Paul Sacher Foundation, Basel)

script. It is the music of those pages that is ultimately transferred to the beginning of this waltz.

Illuminating too is the Basel manuscript copy of the piano reduction, prepared by Erich Itor Kahn in the fall of 1937 and sent to Balanchine and Smit in early December. Stravinsky himself entered some improvements. This manuscript also includes important tempo changes that were undoubtedly recorded in the rehearsal studio as choreographic adjustments were made to the music. For instance, the piano reduction displays several junctures at which music was added or relocated. The opening tempo is slowed. Rehearsal numbers are added and adjusted. As a specific example of Stravinsky's modification of the pacing, the composer pencils in a directive to insert, by repeating, the already composed first five measures of variation 5, between Rehearsal 81 and 82, suggesting that Balanchine needed more time for his dancers. Clearly, this was a late adjustment, for once the insertion was made, Stravinsky changed all subsequent rehearsal numbers for the duration of the ballet. Taken together, the sketch score and annotated piano reduction illustrate just how fluid the process of composing and choreographing was, even during the final weeks before the premiere.

Virgil Thomson and Elliott Carter attended the premiere. In an unapologetic defense of Balanchine's company, still being blistered by Martin and other critics, the always acerbic Thomson described the dancers as a "first-class ballet troupe, far superior to any of their local toe-dancing rivals in grace and discipline, and broader in their range of human expression than all of the esthetico-expressionistic groups of the feet-flat-on-the-ground-and-stomach-sticking-out school."[52]

Like Thomson, Carter had known Balanchine's work as early as 1932 in Monte Carlo, as well as in Paris, where the composer had studied with Boulanger. Perhaps more than those of most contemporary observers, his discerning, unbiased comments about Balanchine from a musician's vantage are a reliable guide. Upon watching Balanchine work in the studio, Carter warned that one might erroneously conclude that the choreographer was "inventing things moment by moment, as if there was no plan for anything, as if he was improvising, rather than having one general big picture." Yet when the work appeared onstage, Carter continued, one was aware of the "continuity, the way each moment is being led up to and away from."[53]

Carter's original 1937 *Modern Music* review of the Stravinsky Festival addressed all three ballets, although the author mainly focused on Balanchine's choreography. Having seen the Parisian premiere, he contrasted Nijinska's *Baiser de la Fée* with Balanchine's new conception. Whereas he remembered Nijinska's solo variations as "boring, dull, and badly planned," he found Balanchine's "formal numbers between Gisella Caccialanza and William Dollar remarkable for their tenderness, brilliance, compactness and variety . . . strictly within the classic tradition." As for Stravinsky's Tchaikovskyan score, Carter also found that "Balanchine's worked-out steps were frequently more interesting than the music though he always followed it closely and sensitively." In reviewing *Jeu de Cartes,* Carter once more praised Balanchine's inventive choreography (and Dollar's dancing) while noting "a rather untheatrical libretto, for a pack of cards is a pack of cards and gives little chance for contrast." More than fifty years later, in his interview with Mason, Carter recalled that the ballet "was not such a good idea as a ballet in itself, but the music was wonderful. I thought Balanchine was stuck with just the cards. It would have been better if he'd made the Joker more devilish."[54]

Regardless of whether Balanchine's ballet was successful as a stage work, Stravinsky's orchestral score glittered. The brilliancy of the colorful writing, with an instrumentation that vividly animates every bar, may explain why Balanchine never particularly warmed to the score. As Kirstein astutely observed, the scoring of the ballet "is almost too exquisite, rhythmic irregularities too finely delineated, subtle, sophisticated to ensure a crass success with choreographers . . . or with a public spoiled by successions of larger, harsher, or louder sounds."[55] *Jeu de Cartes* immediately took on its own symphonic life as a remarkably accessible concert piece.

As part of a 1938 French radio broadcast, Stravinsky responded to questions posed by Georges Auric. When asked about *Jeu de Cartes,* its composer used the opportunity as a platform to "spin" the work not as a ballet but as a concert piece.

> Whatever may be the destination of a piece of music—whether intended for the theater, concert hall, or cinema—it is essential it should have its proper intrinsic value, its own existence, its *raison d'être*. . . . That's why, when I am writing for the theater, my first anxiety is to make certain my music has an independent existence and to guard it from the danger of subjecting itself to the demands of the other theatrical elements involved. . . . My later scores are conceived and constructed as separate musical entities, independent of their scenic purpose; and because of that I attach as much importance to their concert performance as to their stage presentation.[56]

Infused with some of Stravinsky's most scintillating writing, the score stands in stark contrast to the darkly contrapuntal black-and-whiteness of Concerto for two solo pianos, written a little earlier. He first conducted the ballet as an orchestral work in Venice the autumn following the New York premiere. Performances followed in London, Amsterdam, Naples, and Paris. Even in Germany, where Stravinsky's music had long been reviled as "unhealthy," with all the racial connotations such an epithet carried, the tuneful *Jeu de Cartes* received numerous performances. It was first presented at the Dresden Staatsoper (only six months after the ballet was first performed in New York), then subsequently in Berlin, Hamburg, and elsewhere. All these engagements suddenly sprang up after a three-year, strictly enforced banishment of Stravinsky's music by the Third Reich. The work was even recorded by the Berlin Philharmonic for Telefunken in February 1938.

Stravinsky's dubious relation with Nazi Germany during this period is frequently swept under the carpet. In truth the composer may have intended the work to appease the Reich's political gods as much as to fulfill Balanchine's request. Stravinsky had taken considerable pains to dispel the notion that he was Jewish—an assumption prevalent in Germany during the late 1920s and early 1930s as the Nazi Party grew in numbers and strength. Whatever his agenda, *Jeu de Cartes* was hailed as a "rehabilitation." Indeed, the first German performance at the October 1937 arts festival in Dresden was underwritten by the

Nazi Party. The music was more melodic, more rhythmically accessible than a work like the thorny Concerto for two solo pianos, which Stravinsky and Soulima performed, to harsh criticism, a few years earlier in Baden-Baden.[57]

The congeniality of this cheerful, uncluttered music reinstated Stravinsky in Joseph Goebbels's good graces, at least partially. But still, Julius Strecker, acting as friend, publisher, and politico, advised Stravinsky to proceed cautiously in his dealings with German authorities. The famous exhibition of *Entartete Musik* (Degenerate Music) opened on 24 May 1938, and, much to the composer's vehement protest, it included his music. But the National Socialists determined that *Jeu de Cartes* was cleansed of Stravinsky's earlier "jazzy" music. ("Jewish jazz," as it was called, had been banned from German radio as early as 1935. Blacks and Jews were viewed as dangerous allies attempting to destroy the treasures of the Bach-Beethoven-Brahms lineage.) Ethically, a complicit Stravinsky approached a dangerous precipice in continuing to perform concerts in Germany during the incendiary days of the late 1930s.

Just how important Stravinsky considered the orchestral score of *Jeu de Cartes* is reflected in his infamous dispute with Ernest Ansermet, who unwisely saw fit to make cuts. The composer complained directly to Ansermet, instructing him not to play the score at all if he felt that cuts were needed. The animosity resulting from the incident proved divisive, perpetuating a bitter feud that lasted for several decades before a reconciliation of sorts was reached toward the end of Ansermet's life.

The original published score, signed and dated by the composer, which Stravinsky used to conduct many concert performances of *Jeu de Cartes,* is retained in Basel. Page after page is marked in red with carefully notated conducting patterns that Stravinsky used as cues. Tempo indications are added, and once again, the revised tempi are still slower than the earlier changes he made in the sketches and piano reduction. Various instrumental lines are highlighted in red for emphasis. The Sacher Stiftung also holds the printed piano reduction, which includes reprints of the original sets and costumes designed by his son Theodore. Here again the keyboard score was used in rehearsals; this is clear from the instrumental indications added in pencil, no doubt as a way of preparing both dancers and conductors for the fuller—and at that point unfamiliar—sound of the orchestra.

While Stravinsky promoted *Jeu de Cartes* as a concert piece, he nonetheless welcomed further theatrical performances in Europe, but now only under Balanchine's direction. He entreated his friend to join him in staging the work abroad. But beyond whatever reservations Balanchine may have harbored about the ballet, he was already committed to several personal engagements, as well as those of his young company (though in fact he and his American Ballet were soon dismissed from the Met). The Paris Opéra wished to mount the work in 1938, but only under Lifar, in whom Stravinsky by then had lost confidence.

Balanchine did remount the work a few years later, in 1940, with the Ballet Russe de Monte Carlo (and in fact a few precious film clips of a rehearsal are retained by the Jerome Robbins Dance Division of the New York Public Library for the Performing Arts). On that occasion, Edwin Denby wrote that the ballet "creeps into your heart as unpretentiously as a kitten," adding that while it was not a major work, it should still be considered a "minor masterpiece." Denby's comments not only addressed the ballet specifically but provided a broader assessment of Balanchine's approach to dance—an assessment that countered the criticisms of Martin and others:

> Balanchine has a profounder choreographic gift. His steps, no matter where derived, are steps that a ballet dancer specifically can do and do best, steps a ballet dancer can be brilliant in. His rhythms, however complex, are grateful to ballet dancers. He seems never to violate the real nature of a dancer's body, the part-native, part-trained relation of trunk and arms and head and feet; so that no matter how odd the movement required, the dancer still remains himself and does not congeal to an impersonal instrument. It is a fact that Balanchine has been able to make the same dancers seem real and true in his ballets who have seemed conventional or stupid in others. All these qualities, being the best qualities of choreography there are, make a good Balanchine ballet as good a ballet as you can get.[58]

Balanchine also remounted the work a decade later for the New York City Ballet, though the reasons for the revival were motivated more by financial exigency than artistic desire, Kirstein confided in a 1950 letter to Stravinsky. The ballet was presented on 15 February 1951. The work virtually lay dormant for the next forty years. In May 1992, Peter Martins choreographed a completely new production with costumes by Barbara Matera and Holly Hynes.

Whatever its success, either staged or as a concert piece, the historical significance of *Jeu de Cartes* is crucial in marking yet another milestone in the Stravinsky-Balanchine partnership. Its production at the Met brought about at least a temporary reunification of composer and choreographer, a rejoining in America, where, with the support of Lincoln Kirstein, all three would collaborate on and off for the next thirty years. Immediately following *Jeu de Cartes,* however, Stravinsky and Balanchine were forced to work wherever they could, sometimes together, but often on their own. Kirstein's account of the Stravinsky Festival in "Blast" reveals the mixed feelings he experienced. By his own admission the event was at best a succès d'estime. Stravinsky was pleased, but he did not have the same personal investment in the event as Balanchine and Kirstein. A week after the festival, Stravinsky sailed back to France, where he continued to work on several compositions, including the Symphony in C, for the fiftieth anniversary of the Chicago Symphony Orchestra.

For Balanchine and Kirstein, the festival led nowhere. Over the summer Balanchine took his dancers to Hollywood for appearances in several movies. Although the American Ballet returned to the Met the next fall, the company soon disbanded. Whatever Kirstein's emotions, the momentum that was gathering toward the realization of the plans he had written about to his friend Everett Austin in 1933 now stalled. What of Kirstein's prophecy? Would Balanchine have the company that had been promised to him by the time he was forty? Just as the better part of a decade separated *Apollo* and *Jeu de Cartes,* so too another ten years would pass before the composer and choreographer's landmark collaboration on the 1948 *Orpheus* came to fruition. On the journey that both men undertook during the eventful interim their paths would only occasionally intersect, and then in the oddest of ways.

Chapter 7 The War Years

Through the spring and summer of 1946, Balanchine and I planned strategy. . . . The famine of the war years had made us hungry and now we were greedy. Our proposals were often reckless or, I suppose, "pretentious." That is, we would pretend to an impact which would be unprecedented in scope and quality. One thing we never considered was "success." There would be no compromise with good taste or establishment standards. . . . Balanchine and I knew that what had been done in the past had no place in a present or future.
—*Lincoln Kirstein,* Thirty Years: Lincoln Kirstein's The New York City Ballet

America's postwar euphoria touched everyone. Upon his military discharge in late 1945, Kirstein rekindled his wide-eyed 1933 dream with resurgent optimism. With an unswayable, noblesse-oblige mission of bringing classical ballet to the people, Kirstein proposed to capitalize upon the lessons learned from the troubled American Ballet affiliation with the Metropolitan Opera. Yet whatever Kirstein's "reckless" aspirations for the future, his recent past had nothing to do with what Balanchine had been experiencing back in the United States. Kirstein had clung to his dream while serving the war effort in Europe; but the vicissitudes of Balanchine's artistic endeavors in New York had led the choreographer to a hard-edged sense of commercial realism, as well as to new personal relationships that were reshaping his thinking.

Examining the path the choreographer traveled during the early 1940s, both with and without Stravinsky, helps us to clarify the interactions of all three men. In repledging his vow to establish a classical ballet tradition in America, Kirstein took stock of Balanchine and Stravinsky's mutually deepening respect. The balletic connection between the composer and the choreographer, now increasingly linked to Pavel Tchelitchev and Eugene Berman, comprised a formidable janissary. The members of this White Russian "inner circle," as Nicolas Nabokov characterized their alliance, confided in and relied upon one another. Kirstein understood that projecting a future with Balanchine probably meant projecting a future with Stravinsky and his coterie.

We must also consider how the strident chauvinism of the late 1930s New York dance world evolved during the war years; and how its tendentiously whipped-up invective might have influenced Kirstein as he embarked anew on his crusade. The years immediately preceding the spring of 1946 provide a critical context for understanding this; they include the composer's transplantation to America, the choreographer's "lingering in the fleshpots of Broadway" (as one critic remarked), and several distinctly different, often historically misjudged, Stravinsky-Balanchine collaborations. The road leading to the fulfillment of Kirstein and Balanchine's dream, as finally and dramatically realized in the creation of the 1948 *Orpheus,* took many odd and unforeseen turns.

Following *Jeu de Cartes,* Balanchine continued working on Broadway. *I Married an Angel,* with music and lyrics by Rodgers and Hart, opened at the Shubert Theatre in May 1938, a year after the Metropolitan Opera festival of Stravinsky's ballets. It featured Vera Zorina, for whom the choreographer arranged dances intended to showcase her talents and beauty. Balanchine was enchanted with Zorina from the beginning, and on Christmas Eve 1938 she became his wife. *The Boys from Syracuse* and *Great Lady* were also produced toward the end of 1938. Balanchine was more in demand than ever, producing several Broadway shows with Vernon Duke, including the pioneering 1940 *Cabin in the Sky,* set to Lynn Root's book and featuring Ethel Waters, Katherine Dunham's dancers, and an all-black cast. Duke remembers that Martin Beck was "alarmed by the sinuous, sex-laden writhing of the Dunham troupe and by Balanchine's novel approach to the Negro dancing." Beck ordered Balanchine to incorporate more "hoofing and tapping" and redo the "silly dances," but the choreographer resisted the stereotype still associated with African American dancers.[1]

Having returned to the United States in the fall of 1939, Stravinsky joined Balanchine for a performance on 9 December. Dunham recalled that when the three met afterward, Balanchine asked the composer to write a piece for her, and "he did persuade Stravinsky to give me a tango. . . . It's autographed to me by Stravinsky." Here Dunham refers to the composer's *Tango,* written a few months earlier in Hollywood by an "Americanized" Stravinsky eager to take advantage of the current ballroom dance craze. Although Dunham never choreographed the work, Balanchine did in 1982, on the opening night of the composer's Centennial Celebration by the New York City Ballet. It was one of the last Stravinsky works Balanchine choreographed.[2]

Balanchine was enamored of American theater and film dancers. He pedestaled Ginger Rogers as the ideal dancer—the perfect example of "the American woman." As for her famous film-star partner, he admired Fred Astaire above all others—the one dancer he liked to watch most, he once remarked. By the late 1930s, Balanchine's name was synonymous with a genial style of sophisticated Broadway dancing. Producers realized that such cosmopolitan charm would add a commercially suave touch of class to their shows. Hollywood agreed. Samuel Goldwyn attended several of the choreographer's New York shows during the 1938 season, after which Balanchine accepted Goldwyn's offer to move to the West Coast and work for United Artists, on condition that his American Ballet dancers accompany him.

His first American film, *The Goldwyn Follies* (1939), with much of the music written by a seriously ill George Gershwin, was a box-office smash. Balanchine's young troupe served as the corps de ballet for the film's two big production dance sequences. The "Romeo and Juliet Ballet" featured feuding tap dancers and ballerinas competing in what is an obvious harbinger of the Jets-Sharks territorial turf wars of *West Side Story.* The more famous "Water Nymph Ballet," with Vera Zorina and William Dollar, was lavishly staged to the music of Duke (who at Balanchine's request completed the film score for the recently deceased Gershwin).[3] The sumptuously orchestrated music is redolent of Ravel's *La Valse.* The ballet itself had virtually nothing to do with the already thin story line. It was a compromise, substituted by Balanchine when Goldwyn shut down production on the choreographer's setting of Gershwin's *An American in Paris,* the ballet that Balanchine really wanted to do.[4]

The opulently staged water ballet features Zorina beguilingly rising and returning into a mirrored pool with a gigantic white horse (in the style of De Chirico, according to Balanchine) in the background upon which the dancer is eventually perched. It may have served as the model for the Dance of the Hours from Ponchielli's *La Giocanda* (in which hippos and ostriches are made to dance), which Walt Disney used in the 1940 *Fantasia.* Nor can the similarities be missed between Zorina's ascension from the pool and Busby Berkeley's "human fountain," in which fifty lavishly costumed showgirls rise above a reflecting pool in the "By a Waterfall" number in *Footlight Parade* (1933).

Goldwyn was not the only film titan to engage Balanchine, now the hottest choreographer in the industry. Hal Wallis of Warner Brothers produced *On Your Toes* in 1939. This West Coast hit was soon followed by the East Coast premiere of the musical revue *Keep off the Grass,* to the music of Duke with staging by Fred de Cordova. The cast included Jimmy Durante, José Limón, and Ray Bolger. Duke recalls that Balanchine pulled the choreography together in a few days, "dancing out whole chunks of it, humming to himself, throwing himself on the floor and saying . . . 'Here I want about a minute of music for the guests . . . tra-ta-ta . . . tra-la-la-lee. . . . That's where Bolger comes in, like this . . . a hop and a couple of turns—'about twelve bars.'"[5]

Balanchine became a U.S. citizen in 1940, the year Darryl F. Zanuck released *I Was an Adventuress* for Twentieth-Century Fox. Not only did the choreographer provide several innovative dance sequences for the movie that capitalized upon camera angles, he also actually played the role of maestro Fortunio Bonanova, conducting sections of Tchaikovsky's score to *Swan Lake.* In 1942 Paramount Pictures's *Star Spangled Rhythm* also incorporated choreography by Balanchine, along with box-office stars Bing Crosby, Dorothy Lamour, Bob Hope, Mary Martin, Ray Milland, Veronica Lake, and others, with Zorina dancing "That Old Black Magic."[6] Ever the perfectionist, Balanchine took his work seriously: "It is absurd to regard movies as only a relaxation and pastime. . . . I also think that the responsibility of anyone working in motion pictures is greater than in the theater because he is addressing not a selected group of people . . . but large masses of people all over the world. This is why I think a serious, artistic, creative, imaginative approach to film is an absolute necessity."[7]

While Balanchine worked the major studio lots of Hollywood, Stravinsky left France to relocate permanently in America. Having endured a harsh New England winter during his 1939–40 Norton professorship at Harvard, Stravinsky settled happily in the warmer climes of Los Angeles. He quickly attempted to Americanize himself while residing among a colony of brilliant émigrés displaced from their various homelands by the war. Aldous Huxley, Thomas Mann, as well as other writers and a host of Hollywood film stars became part of his circle. In addition to his most important orchestral work of the period, the *Symphony in Three Movements* (completed in 1945 and choreographed by

Balanchine for the 1972 Stravinsky Festival of the New York City Ballet), the first half of the decade evinces several compositional attempts cast in the diverse musical styles then popular in America. *Tango* (1940) was followed by *Four Norwegian Moods* (1942), *Ode* (1943), *Scherzo à la Russe* (1944; also later choreographed by Balanchine), *Sonata for Two Pianos* (1944), and the jazz oriented *Ebony Concerto* (1945), dedicated to Woody Herman. In 1944 Stravinsky also produced the short, unaccompanied viola solo *Elégie,* which was choreographed several times by Balanchine. Many of these compositions began as film scores that were later rearranged when studio negotiations were aborted.

Years before his immigration, Stravinsky had discerned the potential of the film industry, both financially and artistically. In a 22 February 1934 interview with the *Manchester Guardian* he declared, "I believe that music has a most important part to play in the art of the cinema. . . . As drama plus music makes opera, so film plus music will make—what? I do not know, but I feel sure it will be something vital to us, something new." Moreover, he was familiar with the rich Russian tradition of filmmaking. In fact, Vera Sudeikina had appeared in several Moscow films as early as 1914, long before the two met. During his Swiss exile, several French film producers hoping to use the music of some of his popular Russian ballets approached the composer; but Stravinsky insisted that he be given considerable say in the final product. His intractability eventually resulted in his alienation from equally unyielding Hollywood studio bosses who demanded total control.

In 1932 Adolph Bolm, who had left Chicago to choreograph for films, wrote to Stravinsky, apprising the composer of the spoils of Hollywood and the possibilities to be realized in working for the industry. Between 1935 and 1938 Stravinsky considered collaborating with Charlie Chaplin on a film (he had known the actor's movies from his St. Petersburg days). But Chaplin's scenario offended Stravinsky, who found the subject blasphemous, and the project, as with so many that Stravinsky considered, was abandoned.[8] Rumors that Stravinsky was undertaking a film score again surfaced in 1937. His American agent Richard Copley exchanged frequent correspondence with Paramount. Copley even attempted to reschedule Stravinsky's concerts in 1938 to allow "two or three weeks [in California] to keep in touch with the picture people." By the time Stravinsky settled in Hollywood in 1940, he was actively seeking an affiliation with the lords of the cinema. Balanchine, who by his own admission was making more money than he knew how to spend, was enjoying quite a success, so why not Stravinsky?

In spite of his failure as a film composer, those sunny Hollywood years allowed Stravinsky much-needed recuperation time. He had to put behind him his final wearisome years in Europe—bleak years both politically and personally. In 1938–39 he had suffered in succession the deaths of his daughter, his wife Catherine, and his mother. Now in America, free to begin again, he and Vera Sudeikina finally married and settled comfortably into a new life. It was a casual time, a time for leisurely dinners, neighborhood walks, and hours of conversations about music. Balanchine saw the composer almost daily, and Stravinsky showed a genuine interest in Balanchine's movies, sometimes attending rehearsals, and even joining the choreographer for a preview of *Star Spangled Rhythm* a few months before the official release. Balanchine, likewise, accompanied Stravinsky to the prerelease screening of *Fantasia* in 1939 (as did the composer's friend Aldous Huxley). Although Stravinsky did not seem to voice any objections to Disney's liberties with the score at the time, he and Disney eventually engaged in a protracted feud over the composer's rights versus the producer's license. Balanchine, while a man of strong convictions, was more willing than Stravinsky to adapt to the often-rigid strictures of the film industry, although eventually he too realized that he was little more than Hollywood chattel and returned to New York.

Lincoln Kirstein sensed the possibilities of film as well, even helping to establish a 1939 journal to promote the notion that cinema, like dance and music, was a legitimate and promising medium. But by 1944, Pfc. Kirstein was in Europe, serving as Gen. George Patton's chauffeur, among his other duties. Balanchine now found himself without the financial sponsorship, and perhaps more important the guidance, that he had enjoyed a few years earlier. While Hollywood provided Balanchine with a well-compensated living, his artistic opportunities to stretch beyond the frippery of production numbers were limited. And given Stravinsky's now notoriously chilly relationship with the moguls of cinema, there was no prospect for the composer and choreographer to collaborate in film. Balanchine turned his attention to diverse venues during the first half of the decade, producing forty-three works during a five-year period— works that included films, musical comedies, and revues, several original and stunning ballets for the American Ballet Caravan (a merger of Kirstein and Balanchine's American Ballet and their later Ballet Caravan), and choreography for still more operas and operettas.

During this period, on three occasions Balanchine and Stravinsky created opportunities to work together. They first collaborated on *Balustrade,* produced in New York in early 1941 with Col. de Basil's now renamed Original Ballet Russe (the company was brought to America by Sol Hurok for the season).

The dance was set to Stravinsky's Concerto in D for violin and orchestra, written ten years earlier for Samuel Dushkin. For the premiere, Dushkin reprised his role as soloist and Stravinsky conducted from the pit of the Fifty-first Street Theater in New York. In her *De Basil's Ballets Russes,* Kathrine Sorley Walker suggests that Tamara Toumanova's presence in New York inspired Balanchine to create a new work for his one-time love interest. The former baby ballerina, who had danced for Balanchine eight years earlier in *Mozartiana,* remembered,

> Balanchine did *Balustrade* for me with Stravinsky and Tchelitchew. . . . We began to rehearse the ballet. Balanchine bought the recording of the Samuel Dushkin performance. . . . He said one day, "Stravinsky is dying to come to rehearsals. He wants to put his nose in, but I will not let him until it's done." Stravinsky was absolutely enchanted. He said, "George, I think this is the epitome of what I thought." When Balanchine and Stravinsky were together, they were like two incredible teachers. Balanchine would stand next to Stravinsky, and they would walk together, Balanchine always saying, "*Da, da, da.*" He never said "No." I think that he became a little boy in Stravinsky's presence.[9]

Stravinsky recalled Balanchine choreographing while listening to Dushkin's recording, carefully mapping out certain coordinated musical-choreographic gestures. The composer also recalled how fond he was of Tchelitchev's sets, which the composer deemed among "the most visually satisfying of all my ballets" (see figs. 7.1 and 7.2).[10] But despite his satisfaction with the staging, it is inconceivable to think that Stravinsky could have abstained from making his ideas known during the many dinners he and Balanchine shared in November and December 1940 in Balanchine's New York apartment. Often de Basil and Tchelitchev joined them. In addition, Stravinsky rehearsed with Dushkin and the dancers several times just before the 22 January 1941 premiere.

It was Balanchine who invited Tchelitchev to do the staging, and the ballet's title stems from his bizarre set design, featuring a low-formed rail and posts, as in a balustrade, stretching across the stage.[11] Historically notable, *Balustrade* presaged the plotless ballet genre with which Balanchine would soon become forevermore associated. There was no superimposed story to prop up the dance movement; rather, the piece was an audacious abstraction eschewing any hint of the fairy-tale morals typical of de Basil's traditional Russian productions. There were only three performances and the choreography was never revived.

Balustrade is an implicative, psychologically loaded ballet replete with surrealistic, intertwined, and sexual connotations (including an especially erotic trio). Toumanova, Paul Petroff, and Roman Jasinsky performed the suggestive trio, which presaged the sexuality of *Agon*'s equally provocative pas de deux. Prec-

7.1 Watercolor by Pavel Tchelitchev for *Balustrade,* 1941,
inscribed, "To Fidelma and Lincoln, a souvenir of pink in a
gray time" (Gift of Lincoln Kirstein, Jerome Robbins Dance
Division, The New York Public Library for the Performing
Arts, Astor, Lenox and Tilden Foundations)

edents to *Balustrade*'s abstraction are traceable to Balanchine's pre-Diaghilev
years and in the influence of Fyodor Lopukhov, especially his innovative 1923
Dance Symphony, produced in Petrograd. Yuri Slonimsky remembers that Lopukhov's ideas "left a permanent imprint on Balanchine's creative consciousness [and] as for Balanchine personally, one could consider *Dance Symphony* his
beginning in the sense that he had found in Lopukhov's production the force of
a positive example." Coincidentally, in the year *Balustrade* came out Gertrude
Lawrence starred in Moss Hart's *Lady in the Dark,* a Broadway show that, as
Donald Dale Jackson wrote, attempted "to mate musical comedy with psycho-
analysis—at [that] time, a theme thought wildly avant-garde."[12]

Writing in the *New York Herald Tribune,* Walter Terry provided the most
complete and memorable picture of the now lost choreography, as well as of the

7.2 Sketch of a costume design by Pavel Tchelitchev for male
dancer in *Balustrade*, 1941 (Jerome Robbins Dance Division,
The New York Public Library for the Performing Arts, Astor,
Lenox and Tilden Foundations)

importance of the ballet's lack of story. His 23 January 1941 review, entitled
"The Balanchine Touch," is worth remembering:

> Last night's performance by the Original Ballet Russe at the Fifty-first Street Theater
> found Mr. Balanchine still taking delightful liberties with the traditional ballet.
> There are the familiar pirouettes, turns in air, arabesques and balletic sequences, but
> they are ever so slightly tinged with a touch of honky-tonk, and a good classic line is
> certain to dissolve into a surrealist design.
>
> Perhaps a good description of some of the movements will give an idea of what
> transpired in *Balustrade*. At one point Tamara Toumanova and Paul Petroff are about
> to cast off into a romantic adagio, but Roman Jasinsky evidently decides that this
> moonlit garden idyll had better be nipped in the bud and, hoisting himself over Mr.
> Petroff's head, he slithers down between the Toumanova-Petroff anatomies, thus
> breaking up the embrace [fig. 7.3]. Balanchine is obviously interested in the move-
> ments of the human leg, and throughout the duo, trio, and ensemble sequences of

7.3 Roman Jasinsky, Tamara Toumanova, and Paul Petroff in *Balustrade,* 1941 (Jerome Robbins Dance Division, The New York Public Library for the Performing Arts, Astor, Lenox and Tilden Foundations)

Balustrade the dancers are called upon to weave their limbs into one fantastic design after another. But Balanchine is a real craftsman and never once does he lose clarity of pattern or misrepresent the rhythm and quality of the Stravinsky music.

There is no story to *Balustrade;* it is only a scene pervaded by moods. Perhaps it is a dream, a fantastic dream that is peopled with unpredictable figures which move as they will move through moods of passion, acquiescence, gayety and low humor. From the point of view of dance construction, *Balustrade* boasts ingenious movements welded together without a hitch. Perhaps you will find that it weaves a spell of fantasy, or perhaps you will find that its odd movements are just plain zany, but however you look at it, *Balustrade* is first-rate entertainment.

Such plaudits reflect only one side of the discord developing among fustigating New York critics, who quickly aligned themselves with or against Balanchine's work. Irving Kolodin's perception offered an alternate view, suggesting that the "costumes look vaguely like what a bat might wear if dressed by Hattie Carnegie." Nor did Tchelitchev's scenery escape Kolodin's caviling. The scenario's "trees were illuminated in one movement and thereafter suggested nerve ganglia. The only rational conclusion is to blame it all on Freud." Not only did Stravinsky retain Kolodin's review, but he also clipped and bracketed the comments of another, unidentified reviewer, who scoffed at Stravinsky and his collaborators, dubbing them "perpetrators" joined in foisting a "total loss" in which "diaphanous, winged ballerinas frolic around in something that cannot even with the greatest generosity be called dancing." As late as 1983, B. H. Haggin maintained that Stravinsky's score "was to my ears . . . and still is extremely unattractive and inexpressive." But at the same time, Haggin added, it demonstrated that Balanchine could perform choreographic miracles with such meager music.[13]

John Martin's point-blank views abetted the widening schism. He summarily dismissed the composer and his friends as a Russian clique: "Nobody involved can have been serious about it, so there seems little reason for anybody else to be. The only thought that gives one pause is that while gifted American artists are starving in the effort to bring their work before the public, there is money available for the production of European importations of this caliber." Martin's harangue seemed scripted. Many reviewers recognized the procrustean provincialism of his crusade against Balanchine. Burns Mantle remembered that the applause for *Balustrade* was great, and there followed a demonstration of high approval evinced by twelve curtain calls. "In my theatre such a demonstration would indubitably spell success. Whether it does in John Martin's theatre or not, I wouldn't know."[14]

Newspaper reviews offered commentary that went far beyond mere partisanship: they bordered on evangelism. As Terry observed, it was almost impossible for American critics and audiences to place stock in any company not carrying the *nihil obstat* of *Russe* in its title.[15] Now that the original choreography of *Balustrade* is virtually forgotten, it is difficult to unscramble the heated oratory in adjudging the historical significance of the work itself. Adding to the significance is that unlike what he did with *Apollo* and *Jeu de Cartes,* Balanchine set the ballet to a Stravinsky score that was originally conceived not for dance but for an instrumental soloist and orchestral ensemble. The choreographer later created a completely new production for the 1972 New York City Ballet Stravinsky Festival. Renamed *Violin Concerto* (and soon thereafter *Stravinsky Violin Concerto*), it is now danced in the famous "practice clothes" look of Balanchine's later pieces. Yet the amazing success of Balanchine's revised choreography should not overshadow *Balustrade* both as an important new mark in the Stravinsky and Balanchine history and as a barometer of the progressively more polarized politics of the time.

* * *

If *Balustrade* seemed capricious to the self-appointed avatars of American culture, what would they make of a ballet composed and choreographed for the elephants of the Ringling Brothers and Barnum & Bailey circus? Among his unpublished papers, Stravinsky sketched a caricature of a little elephant on the cover of a file marked "Miss Modoc." Included was a piece of hotel stationery (upon which Vera Stravinsky and her husband were scoring a card game they were playing in a San Francisco hotel) that listed several questions, including "How many minutes?" and "When must I deliver the score?" The questions were in response to a 12 January 1942 telephone exchange with Balanchine. A month earlier, the "Greatest Show on Earth" had approached Balanchine about preparing a pachydermal extravaganza for its New York spring tour. Balanchine accepted, but with the proviso, supposedly, that Stravinsky write the music. Richard Buckle speculates that Balanchine's conditional agreement stemmed from the choreographer's personal concern for Stravinsky, who "probably . . . needed money." In fact, even before Stravinsky arrived in the United States in the fall of 1939, Balanchine was making inquiries in the composer's interest. In January of that same year, Balanchine wrote to Serge Koussevitzky, encouraging the conductor to perform two Stravinsky works (unidentified but with a suggestion that Tchelitchev stage them) in a Boston Symphony Orchestra program. Moreover the choreographer offered his services free of charge.[16]

Balanchine's benevolence aside, Kirstein reported in a conversation with Samuel Dushkin that the Ringling Brothers Circus specifically wanted the Stravinsky-Balanchine team from the start. Although it is true that Stravinsky's early American years were far leaner than those of the commercially successful and popular Balanchine, the composer nonetheless occupied himself with several projects. Once the circus commission arose, however, he immediately notified Balanchine that he would consider writing the piece, although it would have to be short and the compensation large. Business was business, and the composer required written assurances. In an unpublished January 1942 letter to Balanchine's manager—the dentist turned entrepreneur Milton "Doc" Bender—Stravinsky warned, "A verbal [*sic*] conversation with Mr. Balanchine is not a contract, as the whole business must be transacted by me not with Mr. Balanchine but with Mr. [John Ringling] North" (the circus's owner).[17] By then the *Circus Polka,* as it later came to be called, was already all but fully composed. As the sketches in Basel reveal, the composer worked quickly and effortlessly, although there is still some shuffling of sections, and the stentorian introductory measures, for example, are sketched last, as was the composer's habit.

Stravinsky made it clear that the ballet's scenario was entirely Balanchine's. The choreographer wanted Miss Modoc, the ballet's *premier éléphant,* to carry his screen-star wife, Brigitta (Vera) Zorina. When first staged, the spectacle included not only fifty elephants but also fifty ballerinas, "all in fluffy pink," as one reviewer reported. The short piece culminates with a raucously trumpeted quotation of Schubert's *Marche Militaire.* Stravinsky claimed that the tune came to him naturally, but one wonders. Alicia Markova's remembrance of the piece implies that Balanchine probably requested that Stravinsky include the Schubert quotation as the frothy ballet's punchline. For even before Kirstein brought Balanchine to America, the young choreographer had employed an identical scenario in a ballet scene for a now almost entirely forgotten opera gala—fluffy pink ballerinas and all. As for the inclusion of the famous Schubert tune, Markova recalled:

> At one big gala it was decided that the Schubert *Marche Militaire* would be danced by thirty-two girls, like the chorus girls on Broadway. George adored chorus girls, even though he'd never been to the States. . . . He had us all on pointe, with chiffon skirts, pale pink shoes and tights, and with shields over the chiffon and swords and helmets. He had us marching on pointe. We started out and he gave us a little pat, and we entered like chorus girls, one after the other. . . . There was one performance only.[18]

The memory rings true. Shortly after Balanchine joined the Ballets Russes, Diaghilev had directed the young choreographer to arrange several trifles for private parties given by the princesse héréditaire in Monte Carlo. Markova danced at several of these soirées. The scenario she describes is virtually identical to the version currently danced by the New York City Ballet (with School of American Ballet students now standing in for the elephants in Jerome Robbins's colorful 1972 production). Balanchine himself rearranged the ballet in 1945 (this time *sans* elephants) for a Carnegie Hall program arranged by Kirstein. The ballet was occasionally given as part of several charitable performances for the benefit of the U.S. Armed Forces. No less than Charles de Gaulle heard the *Circus Polka* on one of these programs during a visit to New York in the summer of 1944.[19]

Like Stravinsky, Balanchine was not one to waste ideas. Under its original 1942 title, *The Ballet of the Elephants,* the choreographer apparently recycled the Monte Carlo opera-ballet scenario of years earlier. The first performance, given on 9 April 1942 in Madison Square Garden, was billed as "Fifty Elephants and Fifty Beautiful Girls in an Original Choreographic Tour de Force." It was a crowd-pleaser, of course, eventually being performed more than four hundred times. Only the most dour critics complained that the "modern music hurt the ears of the elephants [and] made them misbehave." Stravinsky's friend David Diamond attended the New York premiere and, writing from the Yaddo artist colony in Saratoga Springs, reported to the composer in California that the elephants handled the music just fine and that Zorina was quite a success.[20]

For all its good-humored frivolity, the farcical ballet can hardly be considered a musical-choreographic collaboration of any consequence. Stravinsky had quickly manufactured mail-order music, then simply handed the score to Balanchine, who appended at least a partially prefabricated balletic plan. The illuminati could make of the *Circus Polka* whatever they liked: "I'm an entertainer, a circus man," Balanchine once commented, caring little about the elitist preconceptions that were often snootily attached to the image of a classical ballet master. His commercial works were often dismissed as applause machines meant to humor society's rabble; but Balanchine knew exactly what he was doing. As he once quipped, vulgarity could be useful when calculated.

Kirstein's observation that the only thing consistent about Balanchine was his inconsistency pertained equally to Stravinsky. The elusiveness of their public personas and the supposed dereliction of their artistic responsibilities surely amused them both. They resisted pigeonholing at any cost. Both were often perceived as rudderless apostates willing to trade on whatever principles served their individual cause best. John Martin and Olin Downes led a swarm of moralizing critics who were pedantically grasping for a thread that would tie together, in a rigidly linear way, the composer and choreographer's natural evolution. If such a progression could not be identified, they sermonized, then where could one turn to find the artistic coherence necessarily underwriting all meaningful creative expression?

Addressing the public perception of the composer in his 1949 essay "Incongruity and Faith," Lawrence Morton had it right when he spoke of Stravinsky's "cultivation of incongruity." Morton understood that critics hell-bent on unearthing some all-encompassing coherence, some grand plan, would despair of making sense out of a composer who dedicated his *Symphony of Psalms* to the glory of God, then turned around and wrote for a three ring-circus. Morton was amused that the intelligentsia would have to "go a-slumming to Madison Square Garden" to hear the latest Stravinsky opus. "There is a dream-like quality about the whole business," he noted. "Values seemed to be turned upside down."[21]

Still, Stravinsky, as was his wont, made more of the little circus piece than it probably deserved. In a 1945 interview in Montreal over Radio-Canada, an interviewer asked the composer, "Did you not follow there the tradition of the great French painters such as Toulouse-Lautrec in his *scene de cirque?*" "Precisely," answered Stravinsky, "it is a musical equivalent of a painting by Toulouse-Lautrec, a satire on a familiar subject. Just as Toulouse-Lautrec depicted a Montmartre scene in terms of visual objects, so this *Circus Polka* suggests a typical circus scene in terms of sound." As commendable as the response was, Stravinsky's unpublished papers reveal that he had no such model in mind. The *Circus Polka* was a gig, an easy commission to be tossed off effortlessly, and Stravinsky's clever on-the-spot rationalizing on Radio-Canada was typical posturing, intended to lend a gloss of credibility to everything he did. He was constantly under attack during the 1940s for writing trifling works, and he sometimes felt called upon to defend every measure he wrote.

While the composer, privately at least, remained troubled about critical opinion, he was more concerned with turning whatever commissions came along to his best advantage. In 1941, even before undertaking Balanchine's *Circus Polka,* about half the music for a new, unspecified work was already finished. Eventually entitled *Danses Concertantes,* the piece had been commissioned by Werner Janssen, who wanted a chamber orchestra piece for his Los Angeles ensemble. In addition to assembling and conducting what Stravinsky himself considered a first-class chamber group, Janssen was a well-known Hollywood composer, writing scores for such films as *The General Died at Dawn.*

Although the light-hearted work was just another commission, Stravinsky, through his close friend Sol Babitz (a knowledgeable violinist who played in Janssen's orchestra), felt obliged to defend the work's compositional style. He did so in a roundabout discourse.

Acting as the composer's apologist, Babitz wrote in the program notes of the retrogressive era in which we lived and the "pressure of a world-wide death struggle in which 'normal' development has no place. Frantic efforts to discover 'progress' in the arts reveal only widespread mediocrity . . . [and] the best of them have begun to wander afield in order to survive." In the most peculiar circumlocution, Babitz spoke not of what Stravinsky said but of how he said it, and of how, "having been influenced by [other] composers, Stravinsky begins to influence the composer with his own composing." More to the point, Babitz added that *Danses Concertantes* revisited the ballet music of the nineteenth century, "noting all its charm and all its fatuity as well." The fact that such oddly meandering thoughts appeared in the program notes suggests that they met with the composer's approval. Stravinsky himself told Alfred Frankenstein (critic for the *San Francisco Chronicle*), "The attention span of today's audience is limited and the problem of the present-day composer is one of condensation"; hence the brevity of the twenty-minute work. He also spoke of the challenge of writing a composition for a small orchestra in a "fairly light vein, but employing big periodic forms and not mere contrasts in tempo."[22]

Was there an ulterior plan behind what some historians assume originated as the pure orchestral work Janssen requested? It is true that *Danses Concertantes* was premiered as such in Los Angeles on 8 February 1942, with Stravinsky conducting. Yet given the ballet notations evident in the earliest sketches (mixed among ideas for the *Circus Polka*), it is likely that choreography was envisioned from the first. Stravinsky probably discussed the music with Balanchine in early 1942, if not earlier, during their companionable, leisurely Hollywood days. Why then did the composer publicly disavow the work's choreographic connection?

We must first remember that many such ironclad Stravinsky denials, recorded years later in his often-unreliable conversation books, are little more than purposeful distortions that quickly crumble in the light of archival examination. That is not to say that *Danses Concertantes,* like *Jeu de Cartes,* might not have been intended as a concert piece; the two possibilities are not incongruous. If Stravinsky had no thoughts of a possible ballet, how do we reconcile Balanchine's reply to an interviewer who asked whether the choreographer ever requested Stravinsky specifically to write ballet music for his use: "If he had free time, I would ask him to write something. Once he said 'Yes, I have time. What would you like?' I said 'just start with something—a variation—anything . . .' so he wrote *Danses Concertantes.*"[23]

As with Elizabeth Sprague Coolidge's commission of the Paris-bound *Apollo,* Janssen's underwriting conveniently provided Stravinsky with an opportunity to write for Balanchine a work which by its very nature seemed tailor-made for a balletic life. Moreover, in another of the composer's unpublished files, marked "Serenades: Concerts at the New York Museum of Modern Art" (one concert included the first New York performance of the as-yet unchoreographed orchestral score), Stravinsky inserted an unpublished 15 February 1942 telegram to Balanchine, care of the School of American Ballet: "My new composition . . . about [which] we spoke, just performed here. . . . Denham [and] myself wish it be included in Ballet Monte Carlo's repertory in your choreography. Please contact Denham upon return to NY about February 25. Miss Modoc dance composed."[24] And since the "Miss Modoc dance" had just been composed (the *Circus Polka* was completed on 6 February), it appears that

Stravinsky was hatching plans for a ballet with Balanchine (who was soon to be named Denham's new ballet master) before Janssen's orchestral work even premiered. Moreover, Stravinsky had lunch and dinner with Denham and Danilova two days before the telegram to Balanchine. By August, Balanchine, Berman, and Denham had all visited Stravinsky's California home to discuss the forthcoming production of *Danses Concertantes.*

Businessman that he was, Stravinsky did not let his admiration of Balanchine dissuade him from exploring other ballet commissions and performances. Ballet was again very much on Stravinsky's mind, and he discussed several production possibilities with Denham. The day before the composer telegrammed Balanchine, he met with his old friend Léonide Massine (now working for Denham's company) to discuss their collaboration on a projected Donizetti ballet, of which several sketches survive in the Sacher Stiftung. Indeed, the envisioned ballet progressed far beyond the preliminary talking stage. Because the composer had purchased the score of Donizetti's *Lucia di Lammermoor,* it is sometimes assumed that this most familiar opera served as source material for Stravinsky's newly planned ballet. But as the Sacher archives demonstrate, it was not *Lucia* but Donizetti's 1842 opera *Linda di Chamounix* that served as Stravinsky's model. The composer chose fifteen excerpts, each carefully marked in the score. For those interested in tracing the roots of the soon-to-be written 1944 *Scènes de Ballet,* an examination of this lesser-known Donizetti opera is the place to begin.

As with *Balustrade, Danses Concertantes* immediately appealed to Balanchine. He found its rhythms innately danceable and its plotless music in line with his own developing balletic notions. In 1944 Balanchine choreographed the work for the Ballet Russe de Monte Carlo at New York's City Center of Music and Drama, with scenery and costumes by Eugene Berman. This was the first work Balanchine created for the company with which he was associated during the 1944–45 season (he replaced Nijinska, just as he had done almost twenty years earlier in Diaghilev's Ballets Russes).

The composer and choreographer met often in April 1943, sometimes rehearsing the ballet at Balanchine's apartment. Stravinsky coached Vladimir Golschmann, who would actually conduct the premiere. In the spring and summer months preceding the September opening of the ballet, Stravinsky met regularly not only with Balanchine but also with Denham and Berman. In fact, the composer and choreographer met more frequently during the preparation of *Danses Concertantes* than for any previous collaboration. Stravinsky also attended many performances of the work when it was programmed in Los Angeles over the next few years. He and Balanchine continued their coast-to-coast meetings, discussing music in Los Angeles whenever Balanchine was in town, as well as in New York, where Stravinsky would often practice piano (since he was still performing in public concerts) at Balanchine's apartment.

Berman showed his set design sketches to Stravinsky in July, but the composer expressed dismay. Within a week (with Vera Stravinsky acting as a diplomatic envoy to appease Berman) the sets were redesigned to the composer's satisfaction. The dancers included both principals from the old Diaghilev days like Alexandra Danilova and some of Balanchine's young School of American Ballet–trained ballerinas, among them Mary Ellen Moylan and Balanchine's future wife Maria Tallchief. At every opportunity Balanchine actively undertook productions that would highlight the burgeoning reputation of students whose development was imbued with his own ideas about technique and style. Tallchief remembers that while Danilova and Frederic Franklin were featured in the central pas de deux, she, Moylan, and Nicholas Magallanes danced a pas de trois "set to jazzy music with a distinct, throbbing underbeat." Nonetheless, Tallchief recalls, "the choreography was based on steps from the classical school, which gave them their form and impact. They were what I learned from Nijinska, but George was presenting them in a new way."[25]

The high-spirited music exuded "the Italian spirit of the *commedia dell'arte,*" about which Balanchine remarked in his famous essay "The Dance Element in Stravinsky's Music." He spoke of his affinity to Stravinsky's dance music, and Stravinsky reciprocated with his own approbation, commenting that Balanchine approached *Danses Concertantes* "architecturally and not descriptively." The composer added that Balanchine "went to the roots of the musical form, of the *jeu musical,* and recreated it in forms of movements." And Stravinsky contended importantly that his music needed to "live side by side with the visual movement, happily married to it, as one individual to another."[26]

Despite this unusually high tribute to his friend, Stravinsky was still wary of those who saw the dance as anything more than a concomitant to his music. In an early review of a recording of *Danses Concertantes,* B. H. Haggin confessed that he was attracted to Stravinsky's music primarily because of Balanchine's choreography, "which was like the additional line of counterpoint that completes a musical texture and gives it the *significance it lacked without such completion.*" Stravinsky questioned such a "completion," underlining this portion of the sentence in his copy of the review and placing a "?" next to the statement. Haggin, like every dance critic in the composer's estimate, had gone a step too far. The music was—thank you—quite sufficient by itself.[27]

Stravinsky was in Los Angeles when the ballet premiered on 10 September 1944 in New York. Balanchine and Berman sent telegrams extolling the work's unqualified success. But whereas Balanchine found the music wonderfully danceable, John Martin did not. His brutal *New York Times* review (which eventually made its way into the composer's file, like most of Martin's reviews) upbraided both the music and the ballet's "abstract" character: "Stravinsky's music is gravely *demodé* [*sic*], belonging to that avant-gardisme of about 1925 which is now as quaint as grandmother's antimacassar. . . . It is also as completely antagonistic to movement as any score within memory, lacking the sustained dynamics which are the very basis of dance. Mr. Balanchine has done a clever, somewhat mathematical, job of choreography, almost totally devoid of dancing. It is extremely difficult . . . and most ungrateful to dance."[28]

But what precisely was "the very basis of dance" to which Martin alluded? How could the work's "sustained dynamics" be so utterly lacking for him, while for Edwin Denby (writing in the *Herald Tribune*) the same ballet was "miraculously logical" within its "single long phrase"? *Danses Concertantes,* like the earlier *Balustrade* and *Circus Polka,* proved bewildering for critics rushing to uncover continuity among these relatively short, and for most sophisticates negligible, works of the early 1940s.

The year 1944 also marked Stravinsky's only Broadway venture, his newly composed *Scènes de Ballet* (completed on the day of the liberation of Paris, as Stravinsky marked in his manuscript). It was written for the Billy Rose production of *The Seven Lively Arts,* although Rose used only a few fragments of the fifteen-minute, $5,000 work. Described by Lawrence Morton as "a solemnization of Broadway, a halo for a chorus girl, a portrait of Mr. Rose as Diaghilev," the Stravinsky ballet premiered on 7 December at the Ziegfeld Theatre.[29] The classically conceived work included eleven dances for a corps de ballet (four men and twelve women) and two soloists. Stravinsky conducted the premiere of the full score the following year with the New York Philharmonic. The dancers included Markova, who first suggested Stravinsky to Rose when the producer asked for the name of the greatest living composer; and Anton Dolin, who prepared the choreography (though Stravinsky would later assert that the choreographic conception was his own, not Dolin's). The composer worked closely with Dolin in August 1944, and Balanchine attended rehearsals. It appears that Stravinsky and Balanchine drafted the final scenario for *Danses Concertantes* on the same day the composer worked out the *Giselle*-like *Scènes de Ballet.*

Despite the less than successful abridged version of his ballet in Rose's show,

Stravinsky pictured a more important balletic future for his score. Almost immediately after the Broadway production (in which he felt his music was mutilated) he openly declared his hope to see it staged again but with more consideration given his original conception.[30] In June 1946 the composer met with Berman and Balanchine to discuss staging the work. Earlier that spring, in fact, negotiations had gone forth with Oliver Smith (Lucia Chase's partner in Ballet Theatre) in California about mounting a production during the next season. But because of Balanchine's unmet demands—demands that included the employment of his own dancers, as well as certain financial considerations—the project went unrealized.

None of these 1940s ballets survive as major repertory; but historically they speak to the wildly divergent and often appallingly snippy opinions that muddled the New York dance scene in the early 1940s. The political fallout of the war manifested itself in its artistic impact upon America, where emigré artists cast a net from Hollywood to New York. Stravinsky sat nervously through West Coast blackouts and air raids while mass hysteria reported Japanese warplanes attacking Los Angeles. Like many Americans tracking the Allied Forces in Europe, he placed pins on a map to mark their advances. The anxious composer thought he might contribute to the war effort by rearranging the "Star-Spangled Banner," although tampering with the anthem was actually illegal, and consequently he was arrested in Boston following a performance. He registered for defense work, participated in gas rationing, and joined in broadcasts for the U.S. War Department—all acts of a "patriot," as he liked to think of himself.

On the East Coast, ballet companies competed intensely with one another. Hurok and Denham's arch-conservative Ballet Russe staged Agnes de Mille and Aaron Copland's popular *Rodeo* in 1942 and 1943 (with seventy-nine performances of this "truly American ballet," as John Martin praised the work) only because, as de Mille herself put it, "it was wartime and they wanted an American ballet on an American theme by an American."[31] A young Maria Tallchief appeared in the square-dance section of the Metropolitan Opera House production. Ballet Theatre hitched its wagon to the young Jerome Robbins and Leonard Bernstein, who produced the jazzy, stylishly quintessentially American 1944 ballet *Fancy Free*—a perfect wartime scenario about three rollicking sailors on shore leave in New York. Ruth St. Denis, Doris Humphrey, Martha Graham, and others (including Lincoln Kirstein) also attempted to Americanize dance. Other successful companies perpetuated the salad days of the great *Coppélia* tradition. Predictably, not everyone was comfortable with attempts to break free of crystallized preconceptions. To do so was to question the basic securities of what one could depend on—securities not to be meddled with in those globally shaky times. Americanizing the dance was fine; so too was the retention of the inviolable classics. But certainly it was not a propitious time to rock the boat too roughly.

Nonetheless, beginning with *Jeu de Cartes* and extending through much of the 1940s, the Stravinsky-Balanchine partnership floated farther down the river that Martin and Downes so vehemently condemned. With the addition of nonconformist designers like Tchelitchev and Berman on top of Balanchine's ostensibly misguided ventures with the plotless ballet, and Stravinsky's *démodé* music to boot, the critics bristled even more. Stravinsky, Balanchine—the entire Russian bloc in fact—were collaborating all right, but at whose expense? For some, collusion was in the air. How else could Stravinsky and Balanchine so willingly participate in a mélange of Broadway shows, Hollywood films, and even the sawdust world of the circus, then be so cheeky as to think they could mount serious ballets for the urbane New York audience?

The composer's friend W. H. Auden tried to explain: "Luckily, we artists in America are still in the position where our chief temptations are the old ones—Hollywood, Broadway, the book clubs, and so on; to these, if we succumb, we at least know it is for the sake of cash and not to satisfy an uneasy conscience. In this, as I say, I think we are fortunate; for it is morally less confusing for the poor Muse to be goosed by a traveling salesman than by a bishop."[32] Still, many felt that such impudence smacked of contempt. What were Stravinsky and Balanchine's fundamental artistic values? Where was the underlying, imperative consistency Lawrence Morton knew the public needed for reassurance? Finally, what had become of Lincoln Kirstein's patrician dream so grandiloquently exhorted only a few years earlier in the pamphleteering "Blast at Ballet"?

During the summer of 1941, through the vision of the young Nelson Rockefeller (appointed by President Roosevelt as the U.S. Coordinator of Inter-American Affairs), Kirstein and Balanchine led a group of dancers known as the American Ballet Caravan on a six-month South American tour. Only partially successful—largely, Kirstein remembered, because there were no stars, and worse yet the ballets were only "remotely Russian"—the trip did allow the choreographer to develop further the plotless style created only a few months earlier in *Balustrade*. Balanchine's balance of sound and movement, largely shunning the artifice of scenery and costume, and fused wholly on the architectural strength of the music, ripened in works like the dazzling *Concerto Barocco* (based upon J. S. Bach's Concerto for two violins).[33]

But American Ballet Caravan proved to be an interlude. Balanchine returned to New York and Hollywood, and in 1943 Kirstein joined the army. Without Kirstein's ministry, and without a company to visualize the principles of their shared devotion to classicism, Stravinsky and Balanchine could not advance their belief in a musical-balletic equilibrium. "Real" ballet had other ideas—mainstream ideas that worked for management, for company artists, for the audience, and most meaningfully, for the powerful New York critics. If Kirstein and Balanchine were to realize their dream, they would have to tackle the competition head-on. And as they waged what quickly spread into an intercity war, Stravinsky became the most sought-after prize.

Chapter 8 Passage to *Orpheus*

Since these pathetic words were sung to music
Even the blood-drained ghosts of Hell fell weeping. . . .
Then, as the story goes, the raging Furies
Grew sobbing-wet with tears. Neither the queen
Nor her great lord of Darkness could resist
The charms of Orpheus and his matchless lyre. . . .
They gave him back his wife
With this proviso: that as he led her up
From where Avernus sank into a valley,
He must not turn his head to look behind him.
—*Ovid,* The Metamorphoses, *Book 10*

As Lincoln Kirstein pleaded his case for contemporary classical dance
in the competitive ballet world of New York, he too looked over his
shoulder. A well-backed competitor was approaching. Using the press
as a bully pulpit, John Martin and his disciples were vocally proclaiming that Lucia Chase's new company, Ballet Theatre, *was* New York
ballet. Debuting on 11 January 1940, Chase's new troupe (performing
Les Sylphides, with Chase herself dancing) virtually overnight became
"the finest company as [has] yet been seen in America," wrote Martin.

"The Ballet Theatre," he continued with a well-aimed barb, "whether by accident or design, has hit on the answer to the question of what constitutes an American ballet. . . . It is a fine thing to have one's novelties and experiments designed to please one's own self instead of being created with the approval of Paris and the Riviera in mind." Within a few years, Martin had added that Ballet Theatre possessed "the most brilliant aggregation of ballerinas to be found in any single company."[1]

In his history of the company (*American Ballet Theatre,* the troupe's eventual name), Charles Payne made no secret of the fact that Chase intended to eliminate "the despotic control of a principal choreographer." He portrayed Balanchine ("a defector") and Kirstein ("a dilettante publisher") as Chase's sworn adversaries. His allegations stemmed from several earlier, fruitless efforts to enfold both men into Ballet Theatre's original plans.[2] Although some have argued that Balanchine was locked out of the enterprise from the start, the choreographer was courted as early as September 1939. With his dancers' welfare foremost in mind, he unsuccessfully insisted on using his own company members as well as his wife Zorina in principal roles. Kirstein was approached too, but made demands that were thought to be furtive. He described his "skittish conversations" with the company as an "aimless flirtation"; before anything meaningful could develop, Kirstein was off to the army.[3] He later proposed an amalgamation of his and Chase's companies on the condition that he serve as general director. The lines were thus drawn, leaving Chase and Kirstein genteel but determined competitors.

Chase is mainly remembered as a woman of unusual savvy and vision. Although Walter Terry faulted her dancing during the 1930s, by 1968 he was praising her accomplishments in a *Saturday Review* testimonial: "Whatever she does or doesn't know, she has guided the American Ballet Theatre to a peak as high as any ever reached in the ancient annals of dance."[4] Realizing that her company would need "the essentiality of stars," Chase aggressively courted first-rate composers and, of course, choreographers. Among Ballet Theatre's earliest guest artists were Ruth Page, Anthony Tudor, Agnes de Mille; a little later came Bolm, Dolin, and Nijinska. Fokine was the first to sign on.

Aggravating Kirstein, no doubt, was the fact that Stravinsky and Balanchine frequently worked for Chase in the 1940s. Unpublished correspondence in Basel reveals that from the beginning Ballet Theatre had approached Stravinsky, hoping he would write for the fledgling company. In 1941 he was offered $500 to arrange the Bluebird Pas-de-deux from *The Sleeping Beauty.* The composer, in fact, completed the arrangement, although it was not published until

1953. Several unpublished telegrams from 1943 mark a trail of negotiations between Hurok and Stravinsky in which the composer considered conducting *Petrushka* for Ballet Theatre at the Hollywood Bowl (with Lucia Chase as the Ballerina). Two years later, Hurok learned that his principal competitor, the Ballet Russe de Monte Carlo, was about to employ George Balanchine and Eugene Berman for a new version of *The Firebird.* Consequently, Ballet Theatre and Hurok hastily arranged funding for Adolph Bolm to rechoreograph the work. Marc Chagall, engaged at Hurok's behest, created the spectacular décor.[5] An unpublished 1945 letter divulges that while Stravinsky found "Marc Shagal's [*sic*] scenery . . . quite successful, Bolm's choreography was '*très quelconque*'"; the composer adds, "I have come to see the opinion that Balanchine had of Lucia Chase and the Ballet Theatre's production."

In a 26 December 1947 letter to Stravinsky, Kirstein's irritation leaks out, as he begrudgingly mentions Balanchine's huge success with Ballet Theatre in a recent production of *Theme and Variations,* commenting that despite its weaknesses the piece does have public appeal. His letter arrived while Balanchine and Maria Tallchief (whom he married in 1946) were spending Christmas with the Stravinskys in California.[6] Despite Chase's rejection of his original demands, Balanchine did work for Ballet Theatre on and off, beginning in 1944 with *Waltz Academy.*

Chase was eager to underwrite any Balanchine-Stravinsky collaboration, including *Scènes de Ballet.* Balanchine seriously considered the proposition, insisting that some of his dancers, perhaps Toumanova, Moylan, or Diana Adams, be engaged. Funds were solicited from Kirstein to assist in the production. As Payne proposed: "Lucia and Oliver [Smith] would of course be happy to entrust to you the complete supervision . . . so that it would be a Kirstein production artistically as well as financially." But having now turned his financial and artistic attention to what would become his own enterprise, he politely declined, explaining that "all the spare cash I have" would go into sponsoring a series of school programs for young students. "I asked George if he would prefer to sacrifice part of the program and do *Scènes de ballet* and after consideration, he decided not." A few weeks later, Kirstein announced the formation of Ballet Society.[7]

Wise enough to treat Stravinsky with the deference he expected, Chase remembered every birthday, every important event, while stroking him with supererogatory attention. Stravinsky seems genuinely to have liked her, even writing a little twelve-tone crab canon to commemorate the twenty-fifth anniversary of her company in 1965. But as an unpublished letter dated a week before the gala reveals, it was Leonard Bernstein who prompted Stravinsky to send Chase a note of gratitude: "Her efforts have been indefatigable in the face of the gravest obstacles."[8]

During the 1940s Kirstein and Chase campaigned vigorously for an exclusive affiliation with Stravinsky. The shrewd composer attempted to strike a balance and retain the favor of each. In an unpublished letter of June 1945 to Stravinsky, Chase writes of her hope to stage *Apollo:* "It seems that there have been several unsuccessful attempts to persuade Balanchine to rehearse someone in Zorina's place. We are most anxious to include this in next season's repertoire if [Balanchine] can be prevailed upon to show somebody the role. Maybe you could help us."[9] Balanchine, however, was not eager to cooperate.

Earlier, in April 1943, the choreographer had, in fact, staged *Apollo* for Chase's company. He met daily with Stravinsky, who attended several rehearsals, offering his usual counsel on everything from staging to tempi. Writing in the *Herald Tribune,* Robert Lawrence called the performance "a cause for the greatest rejoicing," although John Martin's *New York Times* review, true to form, condemned the production as one that only Stravinsky and Balanchine's fawners could admire. But Balanchine did not seem willing to collaborate with Chase a few years later, understandably, given his efforts by this point to advance his own new company with Kirstein. In January 1950, Chase, in an unpublished letter retained by Stravinsky, asked the composer to suggest a ballet to go along with *Petrushka* and *Apollo* for a forthcoming Stravinsky ballet evening. Since Balanchine was unwilling to make suggestions, she wondered whether Stravinsky would. Further, she assured the composer that she was continuing to seek funds for a Stravinsky commission.

In 1945 Chase invited the composer to join Ballet Theatre's Board of Trustees (along with Agnes de Mille, Moss Hart, and others). He agreed, but with the take-it-or-leave-it caveat that while his name could be used, he would provide neither financial nor artistic assistance. Chase was happy to have Stravinsky on board, even if only in a titular role. Moreover, as had been the case when Balanchine made his South American tour, American ballet continued to be used as a political gambit. The composer retained an important 1954 Cold War memo from one of Chase's trustees' meetings in which it is announced that Ballet Theatre wants to tour overseas under the sponsorship of the State Department as a cultural weapon "to mitigate the creeping red influence of Communist propaganda." Chase seemed particularly intent on roping Stravinsky into such machinations, even copying the memo to him in advance of its public press release. She also informed the composer of the Soviet response that followed a few days later: "The Soviet audience is accustomed to seeing the ballet performance as a whole, the existing . . . USA custom of staging only fragments of various ballet [*sic*] will appear to the Soviet spectators as rather unjust and unusual."[10]

Kirstein knew precisely what was going on. He remained wary of what he saw as Chase's wheedling overtures to enfold Stravinsky into her inner circle. Naturally, he feared the composer's identification with any competitor. Nowhere are Kirstein's efforts to dissociate Stravinsky from Chase more transparent—some might say conspiratorial—than in his private correspondence with the composer, especially the letters dating from the mid-1940s. These are rife with inferences that often, regrettably, demean Chase as an interloper and her company as a pleasant but ho-hum enterprise. Kirstein's magnanimous contributions to the advancement of ballet in American society need no defense. But the truth is, his relationship with Stravinsky was nearly as mercurial as the composer's had been with Diaghilev. Already evident in those portions of several revealing but ellipses-riddled letters that Robert Craft published in his first volume of Stravinsky's selected correspondence, Kirstein's gamesmanship is even more explicit in the numerous passages Craft expurgated.

Much of Kirstein's correspondence with Stravinsky (all of which the composer retained and marked in his private archives) discloses the author's sidling. He speaks of his and Balanchine's dream to build a company that will highlight Stravinsky's works. But he quickly adds that their wish will remain only a dream until other groups dissolve of their own accord. He tells Stravinsky of how hopeless it is to cooperate with Chase given her stubbornness, her capriciousness, and her ignorance of musical and artistic matters. What purpose did Kirstein hope to accomplish by whispering to Stravinsky such impolitic opinions? Why would the composer need, or even want to know, such details? Nor are such complaints (many of which are too repellent to repeat) exceptional. Kirstein regularly inveigled, sometimes with undisguised misogyny, Stravinsky by indiscreetly inculpating Chase as an amateur. Often he banked on what he felt was the composer's exclusionary bond with Balanchine as a way to convert the composer to his cause.

Chase's letters to Stravinsky, which the composer also retained, display no hint of contrivance (though Payne's history of Chase's company is fraught with innuendo and malice that easily match Kirstein's guile). She wanted Stravinsky on her side, and she made no pretense about it. Who more than the deftly manipulative Stravinsky would see through Kirstein's blandishments and less-than-subtle scheming? Indeed, in the composer's own unpublished letters to his agents and attorneys, he privately chides Kirstein's "odd behavior" and disingenuous tactics. Yet whatever his ploy, Kirstein's purpose in 1946 was focused. With vision and tenacity, he moved boldly toward building a company that would provide the foundation for all future Stravinsky and Balanchine collaborations. But how?

Kirstein decided to create a membership-supported company that would stand beyond the reach of critics. The press would have to buy tickets to performances like everyone else, Kirstein let it be known. Critics were both curious and suspicious about this peculiar (some thought surreptitious) venture—"Ballet Underground"—as *Time* magazine dubbed it. This new company, entitled Ballet Society, promised to present unfamiliar works to the American public, to commission important new theater and ballet productions, to educate its membership through publications and discussions, and to award fellowships to talented young artists. It was, as Kirstein admitted, an unprecedented foray, full of "pretension." The initial November 1946 program, held in a high school auditorium under the worst possible conditions, included Balanchine's *The Spellbound Child (L'Enfant et les Sortilèges),* to the music of Ravel, and *The Four Temperaments,* set to Paul Hindemith's music for strings and piano—a work Balanchine described as "a kind of stereoscopic choreography for Hindemith's strong score; my dances form a negative to his positive plate."[11] The critical reviews were mostly generous. An important impression was made, and a healthy curiosity about Kirstein's brainchild took hold.

Stravinsky retained a copy of Kirstein's initial announcement of the formation of Ballet Society. The original brochure inviting membership announced: "The Ballet Society will present a completely new repertory, consisting of ballets, ballet-opera and other lyric forms. Each will have the planned collaboration of independent easel-painters, progressive choreographers and musicians, and employing the full use of advanced-guard ideas, methods and materials." The brochure also previewed commissions for the next season (1947–48), including *Orpheus,* with "Book and Music by Igor Stravinsky." As early as the summer of 1945 (while the choreographer was courting Maria Tallchief, whose parents lived not far from Stravinsky), Balanchine was occupied with plans for the new enterprise. Surely he shared his enthusiasm with Stravinsky during their many dinners and visits. He and Stravinsky also met often in early 1946, as plans for Ballet Society went forward with a mixture of excitement and urgency. In February 1946, Stravinsky attended several rehearsals of Balanchine's *Le Baiser de la Fée,* performed by his students from the School of American Ballet.

8.1 Todd Bolender coaching Christopher Barksdale of the Kansas City Ballet in *Renard,* May 2000 (The George Balanchine Foundation Archive of Lost Choreography. Photograph by Brian Rushton.)

Ballet Society's second program, on 13 January 1947 at Hunter College, included Balanchine's new setting of Stravinsky's Swiss demi-caractère burlesque, the 1916 *Renard* (fig. 8.1), conducted by Leon Barzin and based on several Afanasiev tales translated into English by Harvey Officer. The work was first produced by Diaghilev in 1922 with Nijinska's choreography (and later, in 1929, by Lifar). Esteban Francés designed the scenery and costumes. Nearly a year before the rehearsals (in which, typically, Stravinsky played an active role, actually demonstrating for the dancers what he had in mind and instructing the musicians how to interpret passages), Kirstein and Balanchine approached Stravinsky about an idea for a new work.[12]

Even as the choreographer and entrepreneur formulated their initial plans in the spring of 1946, it was clear that if the young company were to make a mark they would need Stravinsky's notoriety. Controversy continued swirling around his music, but his name still commanded the ballet world's attention. Despite Chase's efforts to oblige the composer in any way she could, Kirstein was not going to permit her more-publicly visible company to steal him away. Besides, there had been little doubt in Balanchine's mind, from a purely artistic view-point, that Stravinsky was the musician with whom he most wanted to collaborate, and it had now been too long since they worked together on a new project. First performed in April 1948, Stravinsky and Balanchine's new ballet, *Orpheus,* was two years in the making. Not only did it mark one of the composer and choreographer's closest collaborations, it proved pivotal in the creation of an important new ballet company.

For many years, Kirstein had envisaged an epic ballet trilogy based upon the Greek myths. On the opening night of the Stravinsky Festival at the Metropolitan Opera in 1937, he recalled that he and Balanchine "begged a sequel" to *Apollo* from Stravinsky. "The composer confirmed," Kirstein further reported, that "this must inevitably involve Orpheus, Apollo's Thracian son, whose dam was eloquent Calliope [and] a decade later, after another world war, Stravinsky gave us his 'second act.'"[13] While *Apollo* was Stravinsky's idea alone, the composer confirmed that the 1948 *Orpheus* was every inch a "Balanchine-Kirstein inspiration." Twelve years earlier, Kirstein and Balanchine had staged an *Orpheus and Eurydice* at the Metropolitan Opera during the American Ballet's residence. Tchelitchev prepared both the costumes and the imaginative, if controversial, scenery. According to Kirstein, it was "completely Tchelitchew's show." The music of the 1936 production was based upon Gluck's 1762 opera *Orfeo ed Euridice,* and the work was presented without intermission. Kirstein recaptured their treatment of the legend in the Met production:

> After considerable study and discussion of the legend of Orpheus and Eurydice, we decided to present what was most living for our epoch in the Orphic myth. We saw it as an eternal domestic tragedy of an artist and his wife, with Love himself a male angelic embodiment, with real feather wings and real muscles for flying, not a girl androgyne, which was the tradition of the Paris Opéra. . . .
>
> We saw Hell as a concentration-camp with flying military slave-drivers lashing forced labor; the Elysian Fields as an ether dream, a desiccated bone-dry limbo of suspended animation, and Paradise as the eternity we know from a Planetarium arrayed on the astronomical patterns of contemporary celestial science. The movement was danced and mimed in some of Balanchine's most accomplished erotic patterns, touching and electric encounters, and noble plastic groups. Attic vase drawings, themselves, and not polite dancing-school scarf dances, in his love-knots and amorous garlands had really come to life.[14]

Balanchine had staged Offenbach's *Orpheus in the Underworld* in a 1931 Parisian production. He had even choreographed and staged the famous can-

can in the London Coliseum for one of Sir Oswald Stoll's variety shows. The Orphic myth itself held special meaning for him. As Otis Stuart suggests, "In Orpheus, Balanchine had found an effectively porous hero. The twisting history of the Orpheus legend is an endless process of osmosis and shifting shapes." As a student, Balanchine had danced at the Maryinsky Theater in Meyerhold's production of Gluck's *Orfeo* (with choreography by Fokine). Balanchine remembers, "The idea [of *Orpheus in the Underworld*] was for the audience not to be able to tell where, onstage, the corps de ballet was and where the opera chorus was; one was supposed to blend into the other."[15] The Metropolitan production received but two performances, stirring considerable dissent.

Writing in "Blast at Ballet," Kirstein put it bluntly: "It was a complete failure: a failure echoing with dog-howls of triumph from an opposition that was already vocative." Balanchine positioned the singers in the orchestra pit, not in the wings, as Gluck had done. The choreographer's barefoot dancers only confused and angered many who thought there should be an unbridgeable gulf between classical and modern dance. All these sins constituted an unforgivable blunder to the staid Met audience. Moreover, the dancing was unacceptably erotic. Scandalized audiences, led by Olin Downes, decreed the production "absurd . . . impudent . . . ugly."[16]

The unsuccessful production was not only a setback to the American Ballet's future, but a source of personal pain for Kirstein and Balanchine. Nonetheless, Kirstein realized that Stravinsky, philologically inclined as he was, would find the myth's universal classicism attractive. The composer knew Ovid's *Metamorphoses,* in which the Orpheus and Eurydice legend is related. Moreover, when Guillaume Apollinaire labeled a movement in painting around 1912 Orphism, he was drawing on the Symbolists' earlier use of the term Orphic Art to depict "pure poetry and color." The composer was familiar with both movements. And Stravinsky knew Jean Cocteau's drama and motion picture *Orphée*. With Stravinsky in attendance, Cocteau read his play in Nice in 1925. The composer was impressed enough to invite Cocteau to collaborate immediately on yet another classical project, the 1927 *Oedipus Rex.*[17] In addition, the Orphic eschatology, with its pursuit of morals, judgment, perdition, and the afterlife, thematically parallels Stravinsky and Balanchine's earlier depiction of Apollo's odyssey from birth to Parnassus. And most obviously, Orpheus's command of the lyre—said to be so powerful that it saved Jason's Argonauts from the spell of the Sirens' seductive strains, and even potent enough to move inanimate objects—provided a ready-made coherence for Kirstein's "second act" to the Apollo myth.

Kirstein officially commissioned *Orpheus* in the fall of 1946, although the ballet's scenario and the details of the offer were decided the previous spring. On 7 May 1946, Kirstein wrote to Stravinsky in California, enclosing $2,500, half the commission, for a ballet to be designed for the School of American Ballet. Kirstein was fearful that Stravinsky might offer the work to other companies. As he cautiously stipulated in the same letter, he hoped that Balanchine would be given "*exclusive choreographic rights for five years*" (Stravinsky underlined the passage, placing a "?" in the margin). Of course, Stravinsky would never accede to such a constraint. Moreover, a letter of 31 May from his attorney to Kirstein claims that Stravinsky understood from Balanchine himself that the ballet was projected solely for a "school enterprise." The composer had not realized, so he contended, that the work would be produced commercially by a professional company. Stravinsky was therefore anxious when Kirstein expressed his hope to retain all production rights.

Did Stravinsky really assume that *Orpheus* was only intended for an informal, private school program? Correspondence was regularly exchanged during the next year. Kirstein responded to Stravinsky's lawyer, apologizing for his hurried letter—hurried since Balanchine insisted that a commitment for *Orpheus* be tendered immediately. He did not deny that he was leery of financing ballets that might be exploited by rival companies. He knew that Stravinsky, naturally, wanted as much exposure as possible for any new composition. There would be only two performances, Kirstein assured the composer, adding that since the performances were for Ballet Society members only, the production was not really "*public*" (the word is underlined, with some skepticism no doubt, in Stravinsky's copy of the letter).

Kirstein's apprehension discloses his worry that the opportunistic Stravinsky might offer Chase the ballet, and his fear that the composer might feel that it would generate a real profit. The plain truth is that Stravinsky, who constantly feared being bilked, even by his closest friends, never completely trusted Kirstein. Balanchine's dancers and confidants also suggest that Balanchine himself was frequently dismissive of Kirstein's ideas and wary of his tactics. As Edward Villella observed, Kirstein clearly saw himself as "a latter-day Diaghilev" and acted masterfully in crafting one stratagem after another. Balanchine and Kirstein were different "temperamentally," adds Villella. "They were not really pals. . . . They held opposing opinions on many subjects. Their values and their points of view were often opposite as well, and most of the time they acted as very separate entities." Kirstein himself admitted as much after Balanchine's death: "We were barely friends. . . . I hardly ever saw him except at the theatre. We hardly ever talked."[18]

Only a month before *Orpheus*'s premiere, Chase invited Stravinsky to conduct *Petrushka* and *Apollo* on 27 April, the day before the new ballet's first performance. Ever the quick-witted negotiator, Stravinsky responded to Chase on 10 March, accepting the offer "provided you agree with Lincoln about orchestra rehearsals because I will need a special one for *Apollo* which must not coincide with that one of *Orpheus*. My reduced fee for Lincoln will be the same for you."[19] A week before *Orpheus* premiered Stravinsky attended a Ballet Theatre performance in which Balanchine conducted the pit orchestra, then joined Chase and the choreographer-conductor for dinner—surely to Kirstein's rising blood pressure.

Both Stravinsky and Balanchine continued seeking performances beyond Ballet Society. Curiously, the composer became Kirstein's sounding board. He corresponded frequently with Stravinsky throughout 1946–48, often openly sharing his exasperation about the company and Balanchine himself. He chafed at Balanchine's departure for Paris in late February 1947, shortly before the third program of Ballet Society's inaugural season. The choreographer had accepted a six-month residency as guest ballet master at the Paris Opéra. In July, Balanchine presented *Le Palais de Cristal* (later renamed *Symphony in C,* and still one of the choreographer's most performed works) to a score by Bizet which Stravinsky had recommended. (The composer often suggested danceable music to Balanchine.) During his exasperating stay at the politically labyrinthine Opéra, Balanchine staged Stravinsky's *Apollo* and *Le Baiser de la Fée,* as well as *Serenade.*[20] In a letter of 15 July 1947, Kirstein confesses his edginess, which he attributes to Balanchine's absence; in particular, he does not have the "musical authority" to alter Balanchine's choreography. He further intimates that without Balanchine's guidance, performances have been growing tattered. Balanchine, on the other hand, might well have remained in Paris had he been offered Lifar's post on a permanent basis.

The notion of splitting his time between companies in Paris and New York initially appealed to the choreographer. His wife Maria Tallchief, with him in Paris that summer, recently recalled that the idea of "having a state-supported company with more than a hundred dancers at his disposal was a big inducement. . . . But in the end, he understood it was a dream—not really workable. After six months of Opera politics, and of Lifar's cohorts, I think he'd had enough."[21] In a 20 August 1947 letter to his son Theodore, Stravinsky reports that Balanchine had just returned from France and was immediately flying to Hollywood to resume work on *Orpheus*. He tells his son that Balanchine did not enjoy his stay there because of "cette petite canaille de Lifar."

Even after Balanchine's return for Ballet Society's second season, Kirstein's frequent letters to Stravinsky are marked by jumpiness. He begs the composer's patience in receiving the financial balance of the commission. He also confides to Stravinsky that contributions to Ballet Society have been insufficient because everyone has assumed that his wealth will allow him to finance the venture on his own—adding that this is hardly the case. Finally, in a December 1947 letter, a dispirited Kirstein sighs to Stravinsky that nobody but he, Balanchine, and Leon Barzin [Ballet Society's regular conductor] cares whether Ballet Society survives but that he intends to "struggle along."

Whatever commiseration Kirstein expected, Stravinsky was not about to "struggle along" in promoting his new work. More than for any previous ballet, the publicizing of *Orpheus* became big business for the composer, who was becoming increasingly adept at American marketing. By the late 1940s commercial recordings had provided him with extensive exposure and revenue. Even before the ballet's premiere, Stravinsky conducted excerpts for a broadcast on James Fassett's popular CBS radio program, *Your Invitation to Music*. As always, Stravinsky made his rehearsal demands clear to the network: "One rehearsal of three hours with your excellent musicians (hope no surprise substitutes) will be sufficient, providing concertmaster will prepare his solos at home so as not to lose time at rehearsal."[22]

Radio interviews were also part of the standard marketing package. On 10 April 1948, a few weeks before the premiere, Abraham Chasins interviewed Stravinsky, Balanchine, Kirstein, and the composer's new assistant, Robert Craft, on WQXR. Ten months later, in February 1949, the composer recorded *Orpheus* in New York. The next month Balanchine telegrammed Stravinsky in California that *Orpheus* had been voted the "best Ballet last year by WNYC Radio audiences." Balanchine agreed to accept the award on the air, and wanted "to play excerpts from Victor recording [since it] would be good publicity as I would mention recording soon to be released." Stravinsky informed RCA in early April that broadcasting "a partial use of some fragments" would be acceptable, but was concerned about how much Balanchine's participation would cost. In his response to Richard Mohr of RCA the composer worried, "Of course it is up to you. But I wonder if we can fairly get a favor from Balanchine without letting him have another favor from us." Mohr then informed Balan-

chine that RCA was "unable to give him test pressings of *Orpheus* for the
WNYC radio program." Balanchine agreed to the interview anyway and mentioned that the recording would be available in the fall of 1949.

Toward the further promotion of his score, Stravinsky even answered questions posed by RCA's Allan Kayes, who thought it would be useful for Stravinsky to plug the recording over the radio. Kayes's six questions, submitted
in October 1949, are retained in the Sacher Stiftung along with Stravinsky's
written-in responses. The composer was asked when he first began to think
about doing the ballet and in which musical form he originally imagined it.
(Stravinsky responded in the margin, "polyphonic chant.") He was then asked
to address his collaboration with Balanchine. Further, would he compare *Orpheus* to earlier ballets, specifically *The Rite* and *Petrushka?* Finally came two
questions dealing with the new recording itself: did the composer think in
terms of a recording from the start, and would he comment generally on the
artistic and technical success of his works for RCA?

Stravinsky's unedited, lengthy reply is instructive. He states, for example, "I
did not use the whole story of Orpheus in my ballet. When Balanchin[e] spent
the summer of 1946 in Hollywood we settled the main lines of the legend. We
decided also the exact length of the music or rather the exact duration of each
movement." And a little further into his response, "A thing much more important in a ballet than in any other dramatic form. Precision of timing and the
physical capabilities of the dancers are primary factors which I have always considered in constructing the proportions of my ballets." That conviction alone
clarifies the many carefully timed durations found throughout the sketches for
the composer's ballets. A final section of Stravinsky's script replies most directly
to many of Kayes's questions:

> I visualized the character of this music as a long, sustained, slow chant, composed in-
> dependently of any folkloristic elements, concerning which we know almost noth-
> ing. But even if I knew ancient Greek music, it would be of no use to me. The so-
> phisticated painters of the Rennaissance [*sic*] painted the stories of ancient Greece or
> the Bible in the European landscape and costumes of their own time without at-
> tempting to reconstruct the scenes of Greece or Palestine with historical accuracy. I
> have also avoided all unessential ethnographic details for the sake of a higher sym-
> phonic reality. I should like to add that I have just had the pleasure to hear my new
> R.C.A. VICTOR recording of *Orpheus* which I believe will serve as a document for
> study and to establish the tradition for future performances of this work. I was also
> very happy to have had the opportunity to work with the fine engineering staff and
> musicians of the R.C.A. VICTOR Co.[23]

Both composer and choreographer insisted that their concept of *Orpheus* was not simply a re-creation of a Greek myth but rather the setting of a universal story. As for the work's visualization, Kirstein would exercise considerable control. In an unpublished October 1947 letter, he reveals to the composer his growing consternation about the set designer. Tchelitchev was actively sought, but he balked at the scenario. He also refused to participate if Nicholas Magallanes danced the principal role.[24] Eugene Berman seemed a logical choice, especially given his friendship with Stravinsky during the California years. But both Balanchine and Kirstein objected. Salvador Dalí, with whom Balanchine worked in 1944, was next considered, but eliminated. Esteban Francés, who had prepared *Renard* to Stravinsky's satisfaction, was unavailable, as were several other designers Kirstein approached. Finally, Isamu Noguchi was named. For Ballet Society's first season, Noguchi had created the scenery and costumes for Merce Cunningham and John Cage's contemporary ballet *The Seasons.*

Born the same year as Balanchine, Noguchi was no stranger to the dance world, having collaborated with Martha Graham as early as 1935.[25] Twenty years before *Orpheus,* in fact, Kirstein had been largely responsible for sponsoring the twenty-three-year-old Noguchi's first one-man show at Harvard. He had worked with Brancusi in Paris, was greatly moved by Picasso, knew Alberto Giacometti. Certainly, Noguchi's concept of the interaction of organic abstract sculpture and ritual was much to Stravinsky's liking: "There is joy in seeing sculpture come to life on the stage in its own world of timeless time," Noguchi remarked. He remembers reading "a good deal on Oriental mythology of Joseph Campbell," and in *A Sculptor's World,* he described his work on *Orpheus:*

> Never was I more personally involved in creation than with this piece which is the story of the artist. I interpreted *Orpheus* as the story of the artist blinded by his vision (the mask). Even inanimate objects move at his touch—as do rocks at the pluck of his lyre. To find his bride, or to seek his dream or to fulfill his mission, he is drawn by the spirit of darkness to the netherworld. He descends in gloom as glowing rocks, like astral bodies, levitate: and as he enters Hades, from behind a wildly floating silk curtain the spirits of the dead emerge. Here, too, entranced by his art, all obey him; and even Pluto's rock turns to reveal Eurydice in his embrace (she has been married to Death, as in the Japanese myth of Izanagi-No-Mikoto and Izanami-No-Mikoto).[26]

Noguchi was attuned to the myth's universality, as well as to the concept of time and timelessness. In an interview with Tobi Tobias, he remarked, "*Or-*

pheus is a very good example of . . . where you have a sense of a passage of time, of going into the nether world . . . and coming out again, and this whole transformation that takes place in consciousness involved with time." Moreover, in discussing the transformation that unfolds in the ballet, Noguchi displays his own spiritual connection to Stravinsky and Balanchine's emphasis on ritual: "Eurydice follows Orpheus because he is the artist entranced with his own vision. He doesn't care about reality very much—he doesn't see it because he's blinded by his imagination. . . . So it's an ever-recurring story which, I think, we are all subconsciously aware of. . . . It's the ritual of recurring spring and the immortality of art. It's a kind of ritual dance."[27] A kind of ritual dance."[27]

Kirstein reported that in December 1947 the composer and his wife visited Noguchi's studio to see the "beautiful scale models of *Orpheus*' décor, which they both loved." Noguchi crafted a "handsome lyre for Orpheus, carved in balsa wood. Costumes—embroidered wool, timeless, suggestive of ritual tattoos. Stravinsky thanked him for forgetting about Greece."[28] A few weeks before the premiere the Stravinskys revisited the sculptor's atelier, again praising his conception. This second visit was reported in the Ballet Society *Bulletin* (21 April 1948), a copy of which the composer kept in his file: "Stravinsky was pleased with the simple but personal vision and clear color of the elemental forces involved, which Noguchi created." Yet only a few days before the first performance, Stravinsky attended a dress rehearsal, where he expressed his discomfort with the scenery and costumes.

The chronology of the ballet's two-year evolution is often misdated. Although it is true that Balanchine worked with the composer during June 1946—the date commonly taken as the ballet's inception—the preliminary draft of the scenario was completed in May, over a month before the commission was offered. In fact, it was in early April that the composer met with Balanchine and his longtime rehearsal pianist Nicolas Kopeikine for several concentrated sessions over two days in Los Angeles. There the entire scenario of *Orpheus* was drafted.

Much has been said about Balanchine and Stravinsky's unprecedented collaboration on the ballet. Kirstein pronounced it one of the closest partnerships "since Petipa dictated to Tchaikovsky the precise duration of each section of *The Sleeping Beauty*," although the analogy is not a particularly good one. Petipa's instructions to Tchaikovsky could not have been more firm: "No. 1. At the rise of the curtain a salon march for the entrance of the lords and ladies. No. 2. For Catalabutte's little recitative, the march becomes somewhat more serious. No. 3 Fanfares—broad grandiose music . . ." and so the directives to the composer continue throughout the ballet. But such subordination hardly constitutes the kind of collaborative partnership Stravinsky and Balanchine enjoyed—at least by this point.[29] The most colorful memory of the working process attending the creation of *Orpheus* is still Balanchine's:

> I would visit [Stravinsky's] home in California and we'd talk. "What do you want to do?" he'd ask, and I'd say, "Supposing we do *Orpheus*." "How do you think *Orpheus* should be done?" "Well," I'd say, "a little bit like an opera. . . ." And Stravinsky said, "I'll write the end first; I sometimes have an appetite to write the end first." And that's what he did, with the two horns—it's a beautiful thing, sad, hair flowing. We couldn't have a river on stage, but it suggests something like that. Then he asked, "Now, how to begin?" And I said, "Eurydice is in the ground, she's already buried, Orpheus is sad and cries—friends come to visit him, and then he sings and plays." "Well," Stravinsky asked, "how long does he play?" And I started to count, (Balanchine snaps his fingers), the curtain goes up. "How long would you like him to stand without dancing, without moving? A sad person stands for a while, you know." "Well," I said, "maybe at least a minute." So he wrote down "minute." "And then," I said, "his friends come in and bring something and leave." "How long?" asked Stravinsky. I calculated it by walking. "That will take about two minutes." He wrote it down. And it went on like that.[30]

Balanchine particularly remembered the genesis of the scenario and the durational precision of the ballet's musical-choreographic planning. Both components were drafted simultaneously during those two days in April 1946, as we see in figure 8.2, which shows the choreographer and composer's earliest working notes for the ballet.

These telling notations, all in Russian except for the French titles of the ballet's individual sections, are in Stravinsky's hand. The composer sketched his preliminary ordonnance on both sides of two separate sheets of paper (each about the size of a large index card) and taped them together. Referring to these work sheets, Stravinsky later recalled that he and Balanchine had jointly set the action in three scenes covering twelve separate episodes with the help of "Ovid and a classical dictionary." The ballet begins with Orpheus at the grave of Eurydice. The Angel of Death masks the minstrel and leads him to the underworld. In the second tableau's opening Pas des Furies, set in Hades, the thaumaturgical Orpheus magically quells the Furies' "agitation and their threats" (Stravinsky writes in the published score) as he plays his lyre. So moved by Orpheus's Air de danse are the Furies that Pluto allows a blindfolded Orpheus to lead Eurydice back to earth (fig. 8.3).

To this point at least, the composer and choreographer follow book 10 of the

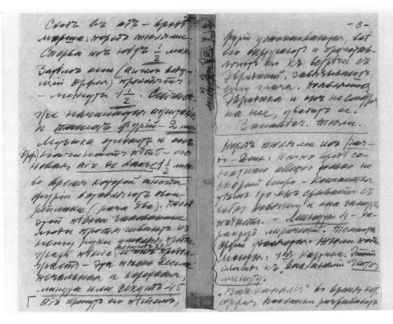

8.2 Working notes for *Orpheus* (The Igor Stravinsky Collection, Paul Sacher Foundation, Basel)

8.3 Maria Tallchief as Eurydice, Nicholas Magallanes as Orpheus, and Francisco Moncion as the Dark Angel, who leads them from Hades (Choreography by George Balanchine © The New York City Ballet. Jerome Robbins Dance Division, The New York Public Library for the Performing Arts, Astor, Lenox and Tilden Foundations.)

Metamorphoses faithfully. As the Pas d'action of the second tableau ends, Orpheus breaks his vow, or as given in Ovid:

> And as they neared the surface of the Earth,
> The poet, fearful that she'd lost her way,
> Glanced backward with a look that spoke his love—
> Then saw her gliding into deeper darkness,
> As he reached out to her, she was gone;
> He has embraced a world of emptiness.

In book 11, Ovid writes of the death of Orpheus, slashed by the Bacchantes, "tearing his body with blood-streaming hands." Or as Stravinsky and Balanchine's scenario states at the beginning of the turbulent Pas d'action, "The Bacchantes attack Orpheus, seize him and tear him to pieces." But in the third scenario of the ballet, Orpheus's Apotheosis, the composer and choreographer seem either to have concocted a suitable ending or to have relied upon other, non-Ovidian interpretations of the Orphic myth. Apollo now appears at the graveside of Orpheus, grieving for his son. With Apollo's command, Orpheus's lyre miraculously rises from the grave "entwined in a long garland of flowers. The lyre rises higher and higher, carrying with it for the ages the tenderness and power of his song."[31]

According to Ovid, Phoebus Apollo did indeed mourn the death of Orpheus, and he reunited his son eternally with Eurydice. But the ascent of the lyre in the ballet's closing moments is closer in spirit to alternative readings. Some interpretations suggest that Apollo originally presented Orpheus with the lyre. Even Ovid speaks of Orpheus being decapitated by the Maenads; his head (still singing) and the lyre itself float safely to the island of Lesbos, the home of the poet Sappho and all lyrical music. Aeschylus claims that the Muses collected Orpheus's limbs and laid them at the foot of Mount Olympus. And in Lucian (and others), Apollo, with the help of the Muses, commands the lyre to ascend to the heavens, where it becomes the constellation Lyra.[32]

The choreography is an imaginative mixture of two-dimensional pantomime and abstract movement that retains only a trace (but an important trace) of the fundamentals of classical technique. *Orpheus* is a work about musical and choreographic space and time—dimensions that unfold in almost suspended movement. Nancy Reynolds suggests that the "ballet's intimacy may have derived from the stage specifications," that is, the stage was long and narrow, producing a friezelike effect.[33] As with the American *Apollo* in Washington twenty years earlier, such limitations may have contributed to, and even shaped, the conception of the dance. Noguchi told Tobi Tobias that he had to redo *Orpheus* completely for a 1972 performance at the New York State Theater: "I redid the whole set to change the scale because of the different size of the theatre. Mainly it had to do with the rocks. . . . In the case of *Orpheus* it mattered because the sets themselves act as a kind of framework, a frame for things: things that come from the side, things that come from above, which were tied to the frame of the proscenium on the stage."[34]

The opening curtain rises on Orpheus standing with his back to the audience, his lyre resting on the back of his right leg. Here is a mournful man, whose physical attitude—static, motionless, crestfallen—defines the empty space around him. And the ballet ends similarly. Ellen Graff's description of the deliberately unfolding action addresses the final scene, and the ancient quality of the ballet: "The stage empties and Apollo enters bearing Orpheus' mask, now huge. For the first time we have the sense of space opening up; he holds the mask aloft, the focus is up and down. . . . The stage space expands into eternity."[35]

Yet the dramatic action cannot be separated from the musical setting. The eerie remoteness of the music, its quiet composure, is reminiscent of the closing moments of *Apollo,* where time has detached itself from the characters. The earliest compositional sketches of *Orpheus* reveal the same ♫ ♩ unifying motive pervading *Apollo.* Only at a later sketching stage did Stravinsky choose to smoothen the more punctual dotted rhythm. In fact, the entire "mournful" (to use Balanchine's description) rhythmic fabric of *Orpheus*'s opening scene completely eschews dotted rhythms in favor of the hypnotic, processional flow of the descending scales.

The Basel sketches further disclose that it was not the haunting modal descent of the harp (which was, in fact, added in red, after these opening measures were first sketched) that was first conceived but rather the interruptive wind music at Rehearsal 2, where the curtain rises and, as written in the score, "some friends pass bringing presents and offering sympathy." As we have seen so often before, once this crucial dramatic juncture was settled, Stravinsky composed toward that moment. The deliberateness of the music is matched by the similarly even unfolding promenade of the dancers, who enter unhurriedly as they pass unnoticed—and, it appears, without any notion of time—by Eurydice's grave. There is a resignation to the music and to the trio of friends who wish to console Orpheus, as they acknowledge his grief, gently touching him before exiting.

Allusions to *Apollo* are also apparent throughout *Orpheus*'s Air de danse, beginning at Rehearsal 4. Just as Apollo picks up and begins to pluck his lyre, so too does Orpheus, while a duet of bassoons signals a call to action with rising scales. The similarity is evident. Orpheus displays the ballet's central symbol in sweeping gestures while the orchestra accompanies him with a pizzicato similar to that of the first Variation d'Apollon. Orpheus's body opens and closes, sometimes pulled in as he bends toward the earth, then arching outward as the music opens as well—all focused on his attention to the oracular lyre, which he cradles gently. He even plucks it gently from his prone position, as the music and action slow just before Rehearsal 13. It is there that the music takes on a brighter hue in D-major (as opposed to the darker, more bereaved music to this point), where "a satyr and four wood sprites leap out from behind rocks in the background in an attempt to distract Orpheus."[36]

Finally, because the music is clearly divided into an *A-B-A* form, Balanchine too makes a similarly clean division. Orpheus rises, recapitulating his opening movements as the music returns to its initial motive at Rehearsal 21. Because the theater of it all is so dramatic, and because the musical design is so clear, Balanchine, judiciously it seems, does not cut choreographically against the score here but reinforces the music's architecture by remaining exactly with it.

The first tableau of *Orpheus* closes with the "L'ange de la mort et sa danse" (Rehearsal 28). The Angel of Death emerges from the shadows accompanied by four French horns, whose muted sound lends to the vaporous atmosphere of the scene. Orpheus is masked and led to Hades while a solo trumpet, again muted, sounds at Rehearsal 38. Whereas *Apollo* relied exclusively on strings, here Stravinsky employs woodwinds and brass in an extraordinarily evocative way. Many sketches demonstrate that he initially doubled French horns with trombones but ultimately thinned some of the lines by cutting doublings and assigning melodies to solo instruments. Thus the scoring is less thick and consequently more in keeping with the entire ballet's fragility. The volume seldom rises to forte. In addition, the music has a spacious quality to it; it is broadly conceived and now includes some of the dotted rhythms that so defined the character of *Apollo*. Here Balanchine's Angel of Death moves with equally broad, sometimes even static gestures. Arms and legs are stretched laterally and upwardly, sometimes in contortions that call attention to the music as it too stretches in all directions. Finally, at Rehearsal 38, a solo trumpet (with all the connotations of divine messengers that the trumpet carries) signals the moment where Orpheus begins his journey to Hades. And it is with this dramatic gesture that Balanchine's Angel places the golden mask over Orpheus's eyes.

The first Interlude follows, depicting the descent of Orpheus and the Angel of Death in front of the billowy curtain used to separate earthly existence from the underworld. The acquisition of this all-important curtain marks another familiar anecdote. Kirstein apparently had no funds to purchase the essential prop. Then Balanchine mysteriously appeared one day with a thousand dollars in cash, but he was unwilling to disclose his financier. "Don't worry. I didn't rob a bank," was all the laconic choreographer would divulge. Noguchi also remembers that the idea of the curtain as an agent of transformation was the choreographer's: "I had the rocks going up all right, but as far as the curtain coming down in quite that way, that was Balanchine's doing." Moreover, the sculptor remembers his conception and preparation of the transition from the upper world to the netherworld: "There was no record of *Orpheus* by Stravinsky, so I got a hold of Arnold Schoenberg's *Verklärte Nacht* and I played that while doing it, and its [*sic*] not too different."[37]

Orpheus and the Angel of Death reappear "in the gloom of Tartarus" (Rehearsal 43) as the curtain is lifted on a darkened stage to reveal the second tableau. The Pas des Furies is unexpected in its thoroughly jazzy rhythms, portraying the Furies' "agitation and threats." The staccato markings and syncopated rhythms of the violins (especially at Rehearsal 63) provide a stark contrast to the empyreal, understated music to this point. The Air de danse of Orpheus that follows at Rehearsal 77 now prominently employs the harp. The Angel of Death constantly cajoles Orpheus to bring forth the sweet sounds of his music as the emblematic lyre literally, physically, joins them. The music, like the action onstage, is thoroughly intertwined. The composer's sketch sheets reveal that he particularly struggled with this dance, constantly reworking and even discarding several versions of individual passages.

Following the Interlude at Rehearsal 89, wherein "the tortured souls in Tartarus stretch out their fettered arms towards Orpheus, and implore him to continue his song of consolation" (as marked in the score), Stravinsky obliges with a resumption of the Air de danse for another ten measures. Then follows the Pas d'action—one of the most beautiful moments in the ballet—beginning at Rehearsal 92.

An eight-measure introduction serves as a transition to Eurydice's solo. But as is typical of Stravinsky, it is much more than an introduction in its presentation of important musical figures supporting the structural basis for the dance itself. A reversed dotted rhythm ($\eighthnote\dottedquarter$), somewhat reminiscent of Apollo's iambic motive, appears in the first two measures (in both the violin and viola). It is hardly audible, so subtle is its iteration, but it will become Eurydice's signature motive once she begins her dance at Rehearsal 94. During these eight measures, the stage space expands, perceptually, in preparation for Eurydice's all-important entrance. The Furies clear the stage while the Angel of Death ushers Orpheus to the side. Balanchine and Mason describe the ensuing action: "In the dark recesses of the stage a strange shape begins to turn toward [Orpheus]. It is Pluto, God of the Underworld. Standing before him, her hands resting on his shoulders, is Eurydice."[38]

Orpheus's disconsolate wife now emerges from the shadows, slowly moving forward, pied à terre (quite purposely), head bowed, during four darkly scored measures of viola and cello music spanning Rehearsal 94 to 95. Musically, Stravinsky now temporarily abandons the $\eighthnote\dottedquarter$ rhythm, employing an evenly paced accompanimental background. Eurydice, literally downhearted, advances with her head hung, arms to the side. Suddenly the dotted rhythm reappears at Rehearsal 95 (as the string accompaniment continues, to maintain musical continuity), but now enchantingly scored for muted trumpets—one of the most delicate and enthralling orchestral moments in Stravinsky's music. The unexpected, soft but bright trumpet entrance matches the beginning of

Eurydice's suppliant dance as she now springs to life. She raises her head and opens her body, hands and legs splayed. She thrusts herself outward and upward to meet the music, then collapses inward (not unlike Orpheus's gesture at the beginning of the ballet) with each repetition of the signature motive. The music rises and falls, and so too does Eurydice.

As with so many moments in *Apollo,* Balanchine understood the drama of the music and matched its subtlety with a choreographic complement that is alternately outward and inward, dynamic and understated. It is a dance of balance in every sense: balance between the choirs of the orchestra, between sound and sight, between Eurydice's dancing publicly for the audience and dancing beseechingly for Pluto as she turns toward him, her back to the audience, in the hope of release. Even the beautiful balance of Eurydice's wonderfully poised pointe work throughout the solo speaks to the variation's overall equipoise. Her dance lasts only a minute, but it is exquisite, particularly in Balanchine's employment of marvelously expressive arms and hands, which sculpt the lines of the music, anticipating similar movements ten years later in portions of *Agon.*

In a richly informative 1996 video of Maria Tallchief dancing and coaching Eurydice's solo, Tallchief speaks of Balanchine's emphasis on hands, elbows, and the presentation of the body. Hands helped to visualize the music, to express the nuances of Stravinsky's score, she remarks, adding, "It was all Stravinsky's music" for Balanchine, always. She also stresses the jazzy nature of the body as it syncopates with Stravinsky's dotted rhythms and pauses. Tallchief comments that the beautiful poses that Eurydice strikes each time Stravinsky's music hesitates on longer note values owes a debt to the elegant poses of Fred Astaire. And for anybody who has watched an Astaire film, the similarity is both striking and obvious.[39]

Toward the end of this Pas d'action, Orpheus, the Angel of Death, and Eurydice join hands, again tied literally and symbolically by the lyre. But as usual, Stravinsky and Balanchine manage to build a bridge for this transitional moment of the story. The three dancers merge in a conjunction that gradually unfolds during four measures of music beginning at Rehearsal 100, written for flutes and clarinets (in opposition to the predominant string music and trumpet solo that preceded this moment). The soft, one might even say minimalist, music that keeps turning back onto itself in a loop ends on a bright D-major chord. It is a crucial moment, reminiscent in both sound and dramatic power of the second Variation d'Apollon, where Terpsichore finally joins Apollo with an equally symbolic touch of their fingers.

Now in front of the curtain, the Angel of Death leads Eurydice and Orpheus back to earth as the Pas de deux opens (Rehearsal 101).[40] Stravinsky scores the radiant F-major music entirely for strings. Moreover, *Orpheus*'s Pas de deux begins almost precisely at the same durational juncture as did *Apollo*'s culminating pas. Orpheus and Eurydice begin their dance nineteen minutes into the thirty-minute ballet, or at .63 of the overall temporal pacing. Eurydice urges Orpheus to remove his blindfold during the central section of the three musically distinct portions. Here again the compositional sketches reveal numerous insertions, repetitions, and adjustments that were, no doubt, a consequence of what unfolded in the rehearsal studio. The five concluding measures (beginning at Rehearsal 121) were actually composed before the ominously silent measure just before, where "Orpheus tears the bandage from his eyes [and] Eurydice falls dead." Typical of his working method, Stravinsky composed toward that climactic moment (fig. 8.4).

8.4 Maria Tallchief and Nicholas Magallanes in the Pas de deux from *Orpheus* (Choreography by George Balanchine © The New York City Ballet. Jerome Robbins Dance Division, The New York Public Library for the Performing Arts, Astor, Lenox and Tilden Foundations.)

8.5 Maria Tallchief in the 1948 Ballet Society Production of *Orpheus* (Choreography by George Balanchine © The New York City Ballet. Jerome Robbins Dance Division, The New York Public Library for the Performing Arts, Astor, Lenox and Tilden Foundations.)

Balanchine persuaded Stravinsky—as no other choreographer ever could—to extend certain passages, including the concluding section of the famous Pas de deux. The extension occurs just at the moment Eurydice dies, as Tallchief remembered (fig. 8.5). The sketches for Rehearsal 118–22 reveal that Stravinsky labored to reapportion the passage according to Balanchine's durational demands for this closing, dramatically pivotal music. There are at least ten separate drafts illustrating that rhythms were altered, meters rethought, melodic motives modified. Moreover, the sketches reveal that the extension was fashioned in both directions. Stravinsky reworked the entire architectural structure of the passage by revising the music not only after the four-beat measure of silence marking Eurydice's death, as Balanchine requested, but also before the fateful event, thus expressing a broader concern for the music's overall structural balance.

Following the next Interlude, in which a "veiled curtain, behind which the décor of the first scene is placed," a second Pas d'action begins at Rehearsal 125. Stravinsky wrote some of the most propulsive, theatrical music of the ballet for this moment, as the Bacchantes rip Orpheus to pieces. The composer had considered including the harp at this point but apparently thought better of it, given the dramatic energy (and sheer overpowering volume) of the action. The high point is articulated at Rehearsal 137 (at *fff* it is the loudest music in the ballet), where the full orchestra virtually shrieks Orpheus's impending death.[41]

The final tableau ensues, with the harp again intoning the plaintive music heard in the ballet's opening. As with the Apothéose that concludes *Apollo, Orpheus* ends as musically, and coherently, as it began. It is perhaps Noguchi who best encapsulates the ballet's final two episodes: "The Furies are like time, they come and destroy everything; but even if time destroys, something else survives. Time and decomposition of things are, in a sense, contested by another factor which is not affected by time at all. A musical composition does not die."[42]

Stravinsky stressed the temporal precision with which he worked out the individual sections of the ballet, which would total a half-hour, he claimed, if the score were executed accurately. In a set of questions posed by Craft in 1964 for Columbia Records (for program-note purposes), Stravinsky provided some direct responses.[43] When Craft asked, "Is the ordering of the plot jointly yours and Balanchine's?" Stravinsky replied, "Together." "Whose revision of the myth did you follow?" to which the composer answered, "I used Ovid and the dictionaries [with] French titles." "Did Balanchine offer any precisions as to the lengths of the individual dances?" The composer replied, "More or less, but we decided together." Finally, Craft asked, "What music by other composers most attracted you at the time and were there any 'influences'?" Stravinsky stated that "nobody's" music especially attracted or influenced the composition.

The original timing was worked out before the commission in the same way an engineer might diagram a blueprint for a project before moving to the next conceptual phase. If we refer again to the Arabic numerals in figure 8.2 (notated in pencil following each part of the scenario on the original note cards), it becomes evident that Stravinsky and Balanchine plotted the temporal architecture of the individual episodes right along with the story. For example, they originally planned a half-minute for the music of Orpheus's lyre to invoke the ballet's haunting opening, then another one and a half minutes to complete the scene—a total of two minutes, as indicated by the bracket in the right margin. Also, as the figure illustrates, throughout the draft these numerals (on the original cards themselves) are underlined in red and blue pencil, though the markings were added at a later point in the composer's ongoing discussions with Balanchine—discussions which were held, naturally, mostly in Russian.

Two years later, in a January 1948 Los Angeles newspaper interview, Balanchine stated that he and Stravinsky were currently "working out the timing" only a few months before the April premiere. But since the durations are present from the start, what did he mean? The explanation rests in Stravinsky's habit of regularly returning to original drafts of scenarios or manuscripts and making additions, typically marked in red and blue pencil. In fact, the durations marked in the figure (again in red and blue in the originals), and slightly different from the earlier conceived plain-pencil markings inserted within the text of the scenario itself, reflect revisions made after the actual writing of the piece began in October 1946. The revisions of the work's temporal architecture (in red and blue) are summarized at the bottom of the fourth page of the original notes. There, rehearsal numbers (also marked in colored pencil) confirm just how late Stravinsky relied on this original document since such rehearsal cues obviously were not assigned until a complete version of the composition was at least drafted. Thus for the Pas de deux, Stravinsky marks "2′ 09″" for Rehearsal 101–9, and "2′ 50″" for Rehearsal 109–22. Rehearsal 47–63, taken from the beginning of the second tableau's Pas des Furies, is timed precisely at 1′ 30″.

Stravinsky and Balanchine's preliminary 1946 estimates of the ballet's temporal design varied little over the subsequent two-year period. Throughout their frequent meetings in 1946 and in 1947, even after the choreography began to come together in the rehearsal studio in 1948, they deviated only slightly from their initial temporal ideas.[44] More accurately stated, such adjustments occurred within the fixed boundaries of each episode's overall time frame. Stravinsky also worked on the scenario himself between the early April meeting with Balanchine and the redrafting of the durations in 1948.

Two more unpublished index cards found among the composer's compositional sketches in Basel (worked out on "The Chief," a train Stravinsky sometimes took between New York and Los Angeles) reveal further revisions. These undated documents were probably completed in May 1947 since the composer was returning in late April from meetings with Balanchine and Kirstein in New York. The first card includes a brief description of the Pas d'action in French, and a second card indicates a further rethinking of the same section, reading "Song of Orpheus—Furies—Eurydice—Orfeo's eyes are blinded when he looks back." On this second card, the composer also adds the timing, "two minutes." Other marked durations include: "Pas de Deux 4′, Bacchantae 2½–3, and Apothéose 1½–2."

In perhaps the most often retold tale in the annals of the Stravinsky-Balanchine collaborations, Tallchief reports that when Eurydice died in the Pas de deux the composer asked, "'Maria! How long it will take you to die?' Nicky [Magallanes] was standing there, so I put my head on his shoulder and began to fall to the floor, as the choreography demanded, and hands reached out from where the silk curtain would be to drag me back to Hades. Stravinsky began snapping his fingers—snap, snap, snap, snap—I think it was four counts. 'That is enough,' he decided. 'Now you are dead.' And he put those counts into the score."[45]

There are various accounts of the incident, each more embroidered than the next. Nonetheless, it is clear that Stravinsky either had not decided on the pacing completely or was flexible enough to alter his original idea. Tallchief's memory of four counts ("snap, snap, snap, snap") seems accurate as evinced by one measure of silence equaling four beats, one measure before Rehearsal 121— "Orpheus tears the bandage from his eyes. Eurydice falls dead." The Basel sketches reveal that Stravinsky originally wrote "G.P." in the silent measure (meaning "grand pause") but later removed it, and simply counted the beats exactly. Tallchief also recalls that Balanchine and Stravinsky worked "side by side in the rehearsal studio. Ordinarily, when George was choreographing, Stravinsky kept his distance. But this time was different. He was always making suggestions, and was exacting about what he wanted." Nor was Tallchief the only dancer with whom the composer worked. As Balanchine biographer Bernard Taper remembers, "Stravinsky spent some hours with Tanaquil Le Clercq and the other Bacchantes, helping Balanchine make the dancers understand and be comfortable with the complex rhythms" (fig. 8.6).[46] Stravinsky also often rehearsed the score in Balanchine and Tallchief's New York apartment, continuing to revise passages as the choreographic plan emerged. And as usual, he involved himself totally in every aspect of the production, even attending Jean Rosenthal's lighting rehearsals the day of the premiere.

Before Stravinsky arrived in New York to work with the dancers, Balanchine began choreographing from the composer's summary sketches, which arrived section by section as Stravinsky completed them. Tallchief remembers that her husband "would sit down at the piano and play each note over and over, picturing in his mind the movements he wanted and the patterns he'd create. I'd never seen him so absorbed." Ann Hutchinson, who prepared the Labanota-

8.6 Tanaquil Le Clercq as the Leader of the Bacchantes and Nicholas Magallanes as Orpheus in the Ballet Society Production of *Orpheus* (Choreography by George Balanchine © The New York City Ballet. Jerome Robbins Dance Division, The New York Public Library for the Performing Arts, Astor, Lenox and Tilden Foundations.)

tion score on the spot as Balanchine choreographed each section, recalls that he began the first rehearsal with the Furies, that is, a passage that begins well into the ballet. "At the very start Balanchine arranged the dancers in sleeping attitudes here and there on the stage. . . . I watched how Balanchine held his own body while demonstrating the slithering, menacing steps to be performed by the troupe."[47]

The preliminary compositional sketches for *Orpheus* are difficult to assemble chronologically—certainly more so than in either *Apollo* or *Jeu de Cartes*. Nonetheless, they reveal the same compositional methodology. In the Air de danse, for example, Stravinsky first composed material that eventually stands at Rehearsal 23 (more than seventy measures into the ballet), then returned to compose music toward this juncture. Frequently measures were added at the bottom of a sketch page in red and blue brackets, with arrows pointing toward an insertion point, suggesting that these last-minute addenda were incorporated for temporal-choreographic reasons. Moreover, most of these "new" measures are not new at all but rather literal repetitions or slight modifications of pre-existing material, thereby assuring that the organic flow of the passage would not be disrupted.

For example, the Basel sketches disclose that between Rehearsals 9 and 10 of this same Air de danse, Stravinsky extended the music by repeating a few measures he had just written after he was in the rehearsal studio. Surely this constitutes an instance where Balanchine needed a few more seconds—just as he had made similar requests in *Jeu de Cartes*. The sketches confirm that Stravinsky simply wrote the same measures at the bottom of the page (where there was room) and noted in red pencil to insert these at the needed juncture.

As apparent in the rough sketches of the composer's earlier ballets, each passage in *Orpheus* is meticulously calibrated. Sometimes Stravinsky brackets durations for two separate compositional sketches, just as he bracketed several precompositional durations, seen in figure 8.2. Certainly the precision of these markings relate primarily to choreographic needs, but perhaps not exclusively. On the reverse side of one compositional sketch sheet Stravinsky marks, "5 sides: I—3' 57", II—3' 46", III—4' 10", IV—4' 08", V—3' 27"." These five divisions correspond to the five Arabic numerals written in the original scenario draft, as seen in figure 8.2. Eager to market the score as a phonograph recording from the start, the composer was well aware of how much music would fit on one side of a commercial long-playing record, even as he sketched ideas and assembled individual sections of the ballet.

The composer certainly understood the central role the harp would play in representing Orpheus's lyre. Is there a more supple moment in all of Stravinsky's music than the motionlessly descending harp melody of the ballet's opening passage? It is a marvel of stasis, capturing not only the music's eternalness but also the ancient power of the myth it seeks to evoke. But an early sketch marks the initial entrance of the harp not in the first measure of the ballet but in the third. In the ballet's closing scene too, Stravinsky rethought his original employment of the harp. There the initial sketches reveal a much thicker, more embellished harp solo (two measures before Rehearsal 146), but ultimately the composer thinned the line. It is Stravinsky's explanation of the harp's use in the epilogue too—now employed as a poignant memory of Orpheus's past—that Nicolas Nabokov so wonderfully captured in his famous "Christmas with Stravinsky" essay:

Then, coming to a passage in the Epilogue where a harp solo interrupts the slow progress of the fugue, he would stop and say, "here, you see, I cut off the fugue with a pair of scissors." . . . "I introduced this short harp phrase, like two bars of an accompaniment. Then the horns go on with their fugue as if nothing had happened. I repeat it at regular intervals, here and here again. . . . You can eliminate these harp-solo interruptions, paste the parts of the fugue together, and it will be one whole piece." I asked him why he introduced the harp solo. "What was the point of cutting up the fugue this way?"

He smiled maliciously, as if he were letting me in on one of his private secrets. "But did you hear?" He turned the pages to the middle of the score. "It is a reminder of this—the Song of Orpheus." And he added thoughtfully: "Here in the Epilogue it sounds like a kind of . . . compulsion, like something unable to stop . . . Orpheus is dead, the song is gone, but the accompaniment goes on.[48]

The composer copiously marked the published score from which he often conducted *Orpheus*. He corrected errors, noted durations at the end of each section, adjusted tempi and changed metronomic markings (perhaps to accommodate the dancers?), added notes to several instrumental parts, and suggested clearer dynamics to help highlight certain musical ideas. He added corrections in red pencil to an already compiled errata list. Some of these emendations were incorporated into subsequent printings of the published score, but others were not. Most of these changes were performance-tested, resulting from the composer's making immediate adjustments in matters of orchestral balance and tempo, probably beginning with the very first rehearsal.

At Rehearsal 3, for instance, Stravinsky circles the cello line, suggesting that it must sound clearly amid the ethereal five-voice string counterpoint that concludes the opening scene. Crescendi and decrescendi are added at several points —subtleties to be sure, but in a fragile work whose fabric is built upon nuance, such shadings are critical. At Rehearsal 31, a bassoon trill should be extended; three measures after Rehearsal 137, the composer altered several pitches, for the horns and trumpets, but the changes have never made it into print; and a few measures later, at Rehearsal 139, the prominent timpani figure should be repeated for two more measures, yet the original published full score does not include Stravinsky's handwritten addendum. Accents are added (for the violins at Rehearsal 99), pauses inserted (between the second and third measures of Rehearsal 84), and numerous other refinements are made that still go unrealized in contemporary performances.

Regarding tempo, in the coda following Eurydice's death, the printed score marks *a tempo* over the last two measures of the passage following a *poco a poco rall* in the previous measure; but Stravinsky crosses out the tempo resumption, wanting the music to continue fading of its own accord through the final cadence.[49] Contemporary dance critics are often quick to point out that the Balanchine ballets we see today are not what the choreographer intended, for they have lost something as they pass through other dancers and directors. But the same can be said for the music. How much of *Orpheus* as we hear it today is as Stravinsky intended it to be heard fifty years ago, since the scores in many cases remain inaccurate?

With the much-anticipated premiere of *Orpheus,* Morton Baum, chairman of the executive committee of the City Center of Music and Drama, invited Ballet Society to become City Center's resident ballet company, thus joining the New York City Opera and City Center Orchestra. Under Fiorello La Guardia's mayoral aegis, City Center rescued the young struggling company almost by a quirk of fate, allowing it to become the New York City Ballet. Fifteen years after their casual lunch meeting in London, Kirstein and Balanchine had finally realized their dream.[50] Even John Martin conceded that although *Orpheus* "will never be anything like a popular favorite . . . it is a notable work, nonetheless, with great distinction and a rich beauty for those who can find it."[51]

Some were unable to find such vibrancy. Walter Terry complained in a 23 February review for the *Herald Tribune* that there wasn't much dancing, and that Noguchi's "surrealistic vision of a heroic tale" contributed to what Terry saw as a "disappointing affair." In a May 1948 review for *Musical America* Robert Sabin concurred, objecting that "Noguchi smothered the legend in an all-too-ingenious setting and in costumes and props full of symbolic meaning. . . . He has overlooked the stage and the underworld looked like nothing so much as a mixture of spaghetti and huge frankfurters waving from wings." And while Sabin considered Stravinsky's score a "masterpiece," he not only found Balanchine's choreography "confused and unconvincing" but grumbled about the "very little actual dancing"—easily the most common reproof of the now, regrettably, too seldom performed ballet.

At the root of the ballet's criticism was Balanchine's decision to let the dance play only one of many contributing roles to the production, along with the dramatic sets, costumes, the message of the myth, and the serenity of the music. It is true that *Orpheus* is not so much a ballet as a combination of what some see as a hybrid of modern dance and theater.[52] Balanchine knew exactly when to get out of the way of the music, to paraphrase his well-known maxim. As he and Mason summarized *Orpheus* in *101 Stories of the Great Ballets,* "The ballet tells this story and its aftermath as simply as possible with its music, its dramatic action, and its dancing." By 1948 harangues against Balanchine were nearly obligatory.

Perhaps he was too much of a musician for his own good. Anticipating the protests *Orpheus* would probably bring, Kirstein preempted the criticism in a piercing article released in December 1947. "Critics seem to assume that Balanchine actually wishes he were a musician. It is true that few choreographers share Balanchine's intense musical preoccupation. However, to claim that he is musical as if it were an accusation of a one-track mind is like saying that a painter draws too well, or that his single interest is in paint texture alone, color alone or formal composition alone."[53]

For Kirstein and Stravinsky both, Balanchine's misperceived weakness only augmented the tranquil power of *Orpheus*. It was Balanchine's courage, his sensitivity to artistic interaction, his willingness to risk understatement as part of a theatrical, rather than narrowly choreographic, creative expression, and his consummate sense of balance that made the ballet a unified whole. Stravinsky too had again, as usual, placed himself at risk. *Orpheus* was a dignified, gracious work, far away from the bombastic, hard-driving Russian scores critics still longed to hear. Anything short of them would be a disappointment, even a betrayal. But no matter, both the composer and choreographer were of one mind, and in its calm confidence, the score made a powerful expressive statement.

On 29 April 1948, the day following the premiere, Kirstein wrote to Stravinsky, thanking him for the ballet and expressing his gratitude for allowing Ballet Society to work with "the greatest artist of their epoch."[54] More portentously, he wasted no time in explicitly reasserting his own vision of a Greek trilogy: "*Apollo* gave me confidence in the line of the academic classic dance, and on it our school has been founded. To me *Orpheus* is the second act of a great lyric-drama. Which leads me on the day after the second act, to ask you to write a third act."

Chapter 9 *Agon:* Recapturing the Past and Confronting the Future

Agon is a suite of dances. The score lasts twenty minutes, and never becomes louder than chamber music. Onstage the dancers are twelve at most, generally fewer. The ballet has the form of a small entertainment, and its subject—first, an assembling of contestants, then the contest itself, then a dispersal—corresponds to the three parts into which the score is divided.

The subject is shown in terms of a series of dances, not in terms of a mimed drama. . . . The "basic gesture" of *Agon* has a frank, fast thrust like the action of Olympic athletes, and it also has a loose-fingered goofy reach like the grace of our local teenagers.
—*Edwin Denby, "Three Sides of* Agon*," 1959*

Lincoln Kirstein's vision of a Greek trilogy all but evaporated during the interregnum separating Ballet Society's 1948 *Orpheus* from *Agon*'s 1957 New York City Ballet premiere. He would never receive the third act of his once hoped-for "great lyric-drama." Although at least nominally Greek, *Agon* hardly represents a dramaturgical culmination of what had begun nearly thirty years earlier with *Apollo*. In almost every imaginable way—musically, theatrically, choreographically, even spiritually—*Agon,* the last of Stravinsky and Balanchine's epoch-making full-length ballets, stands a world apart from *Orpheus* and *Apollo*. And while Denby's memorable description captures the Olympian spirit of one of this century's most ingenious ballets, the collaborative genius behind the work came at a slow, hard-earned price. Both in historical context and artistic conception, *Agon* remains an absorbingly complex, resistant work. Only by uncoiling its convoluted gestation—a protracted incubation that transformed the lives of both of its creators—can we begin to untangle its many intricate riddles.[1]

Following Morton Baum's invitation to join City Center, Balanchine's first order of business was to establish a solid footing for the city's new resident ballet. Kirstein promised Baum a first-rate company within three years, and Balanchine worked tirelessly to fulfill the pledge. Initially, the upstart company was a part-time endeavor—a financially shaky one, at that. The first season lasted less than a month. Balanchine spent the autumn of 1948 toiling in a familiar field, choreographing several productions for the other municipal arts resident, the New York City Opera: *Carmen, Don Giovanni, Le Nozze di Figaro, La Traviata, Aïda*—a well-worn list of war-horses. He also continued his Broadway freelancing, preparing dances to Frank Loesser's score for the 1948 musical *Where's Charley?* featuring Ray Bolger, one of Balanchine's many fans from the ranks of Hollywood and Broadway dancers.

The New York City Ballet presented its first full program on 11 October 1948. Since the repertoire was a familiar one—*Concerto Barocco, Orpheus,* and *Symphony in C*—the production costs were relatively low, which was an important consideration. Balanchine himself conducted the Bizet score to rave reviews. Kirstein had always considered him an "elegant . . . *chef d'orchestre,*" as he once wrote to Stravinsky. Having attended a 1948 performance of *Theme and Variations* conducted by Balanchine at the Metropolitan Opera, the composer heartily agreed. Given his other duties, Balanchine did not often take the podium in the years ahead. Nonetheless, many orchestral musicians playing under his baton report that he was a first-rate conductor. Tamara Geva remembered in a 1983 Los Angeles memorial radio broadcast that her former husband always wanted to be a conductor, professionally, but his health was too poor, and conducting took too much out of him—much more than dancing, he claimed.

Balanchine worked wherever he felt his presence might benefit his young company dancers. A year after *Orpheus,* he prepared choreography featuring Tanaquil Le Clercq for an early CBS network telecast of *Cinderella* (to the music of several symphonic excerpts from Tchaikovsky's early symphonies). Television was burgeoning, bringing "culture" to the public, especially through the image-based forms of opera and classical ballet. Because it afforded a hitherto unimagined visibility, which might help establish his troupe, and despite his outspoken reservations about the medium, Balanchine was willing to go along. All the while the company continued taking shape. In 1949 Jerome Robbins came aboard as both a dancer and associate artistic director. That same year Sol Hurok suggested that Balanchine build a new production of Stravinsky's perennially popular *Firebird* around Maria Tallchief. It would mark another major turn in City Ballet's young history.

Originally prepared for Ballet Theatre's 1945 production, Marc Chagall's sets and costumes could be reused. While he admired Chagall's designs, Stravinsky had been unhappy with Bolm's choreography, in which Alicia Markova danced the leading role. The composer was delighted to have Balanchine choreograph his streamlined 1949 score; and he was especially delighted with Tallchief, whose dancing he much admired.[2] Unsurprisingly, the composer actively involved himself in reshaping the ballet, working closely with Balanchine, as the choreographer remembered, and conducting the premiere. The Sacher Stiftung retains a telegram from Eugene Berman sent to Stravinsky in Hollywood the day after the 27 November 1949 premiere: "Balanchine's new *Firebird* marvelous, wonderful, and deeply moving choreography. Maria absolutely magnificent. A real triumph which may change the whole destiny of Ballet Society."

Berman was prescient: the company's fortunes changed almost immediately. Extra performances were scheduled. Even the normally taciturn Balanchine was pleased with some of the magical effects he had conjured. The press was unanimous in its praise, the audience enraptured. As Tallchief remembered from her stage vantage: "A firestorm of applause erupted in the City Center, and the audience was on its feet clapping, stomping, and shouting. We just stood there dumbfounded. People were screaming, 'Bravo!' shouting themselves hoarse. It was pandemonium. The theater had turned itself into a football stadium, and the audience was in a frenzy." The production provided just the kind of blockbuster City Ballet needed to be accepted as the metropolitan cultural institution Baum wanted. A year later, the New York City Ballet undertook a six-week summer season in England, its first tour abroad. Balanchine's repertoire featured the recently triumphant *Firebird* as well as *Orpheus*.[3]

Although the British audiences were courteously approving, *Firebird* fared poorly in the eyes of Fokine's many loyalists. They considered Balanchine's tampering with the untouchable masterpiece tantamount to sacrilege. As he had done in the 1930s, Kirstein spoke out in Balanchine's defense. Not only did he respond bluntly to the British press, but he made it a point to keep Stravinsky apprised of the tour's tribulations. A 23 August 1950 letter grumbled that although the audience itself considered the performance of *Firebird* an "overwhelming triumph" the ballet was "—excuse me, as Pavlik would say—peed on in every part of the intellectual press."[4] He further charged that the Covent Garden management went out of its way to be obstinate. The company had been promised that royalty would be in attendance, but the management had reneged.

Kirstein's letter, perhaps the lengthiest ever written to Stravinsky, fulminates with a litany of allegations implying sabotage of the tour. His indictment was necessarily harsh, he explained to the composer: "All I am attempting to describe to you, and this long letter is important for you to digest, since it will be the background of our future work together[,] is that what we did, *we did on our own* [underlined by Stravinsky in his copy of the letter]."[5] Stravinsky sympathized with Kirstein's assessment, in a letter of 25 August congratulating him and Balanchine on their success "despite all traps laid in your path by the old London press idiots and the new British chauvinists." In a 22 September letter Kirstein informed Stravinsky that by performing *Orpheus* and *Firebird* in the British provinces, and especially in the cities of Manchester and Liverpool, the company had lost revenue and was returning to New York "bankrupt." Consequently, Balanchine would restage two existing works: "We have décor and costumes for *Baiser* and *Jeux de Cartes*. Balanchine will do both at once, revising *Jeux de cartes* entirely."[6]

As Kirstein promised, *Le Baiser de la Fée* was given in the fall of 1950 with Tallchief as the Fairy and Le Clercq as the Bride. *The Card Game*, as *Jeu de Cartes* was now billed, followed a few months later, in early 1951. And in November, Balanchine mounted the now retitled *Apollo, Leader of the Muses* with a phenomenal cast that included André Eglevsky as the young god, Tallchief as Terpsichore, Diana Adams as Calliope, and Le Clercq as Polyhymnia. Stravinsky was pleased to see his neoclassic ballets gaining an appreciative audience in New York, thanks mainly to Balanchine and his well-trained dancers. While other companies in America and abroad occasionally presented Stravinsky's old St. Petersburg ballets, the New York City Ballet quickly became synonymous with definitive interpretations of the composer's newer works.

Balanchine and his company had won Stravinsky's imprimatur. And while the composer was constantly approached about commissions, his acceptance of a new project hinged increasingly on Balanchine's interest and availability. In

1952 he was asked to provide an hour's music for a film script entitled "A Fable of Fortune" (about an English window washer who becomes a millionaire in America). Agnes de Mille was suggested, along with Helen Hayes, who would narrate the new work, described as a pantomime and ballet. But in unpublished correspondence, the composer immediately asked his publisher to contact Balanchine about collaboration. If Balanchine would not do it, neither would he.[7]

Following *Orpheus,* Balanchine's productivity spread widely in all directions: choreographing for ballet, opera, Broadway, and television, touring the company, remounting productions, and staging new ones—in addition to running a school and a company. Stravinsky continued touring and recording, but with the exception of his *Mass,* which he completed in 1948, the years 1948–51 were devoted to his opera *The Rake's Progress.* The composer was completely focused, for the challenge of writing an English-libretto opera was formidable. At two and a half hours in length, it would be the most ambitious compositional undertaking of his life, and he did not allow other commissions to compete. Kirstein's invitation to complete the trilogy of Greek ballets could not have come at a more inopportune time. Balanchine and Kirstein had known of Stravinsky's plans for *Rake' Progress* even before *Orpheus* was first presented. Kirstein's letters to the composer mention the opera as early as October 1947, that is, even before the librettist, W. H. Auden, and Stravinsky met in Hollywood for their initial round of discussions.

Even as he asked Stravinsky for the "third act" in his 29 April 1948 letter, Kirstein knew to qualify his request: "I know that you are working on *The Rake's Progress,* and that it will take three years, but would you consider, after that, doing another piece, which can be a third act, which would perhaps show the maturity of Apollo?" Kirstein saw the new ballet as a silver anniversary commemoration of *Apollo.* In a 16 February 1951 letter, Kirstein also proposed in specific terms an American staging of *The Rake's Progress* in New York following its premiere in Venice, going on to suggest that Balanchine direct the stage production.

Balanchine would do just that, although not immediately after the 11 September 1951 Venetian premiere conducted by Stravinsky. The first American performance was given at the Metropolitan Opera on 14 February 1953. Balanchine assumed responsibility for overhauling the problematic stage direction. Characteristically, he saw his role as being a conduit through which Stravinsky's music would be channeled. It was a particularly critical role too, for the composer was dismayed by the original Venetian staging. He now entrusted Balanchine with redesigning the action. Chester Kallman, Auden's co-librettist, suggested drastic changes for the American premiere, including cuts and re-orderings of certain scenes. Stravinsky responded to Kallman's 27 January 1952 letter a few days later: "If the original staging of 3 scenes per act is to be observed . . . Balanchine must know it once and for all before anyone in order to make . . . plans adequately now."

Other unpublished letters to Rudolf Bing of the Met reveal that Balanchine played a decisive role in choosing other key production personnel, especially the set designer, Horace Armistead. Eugene Berman, who had wanted the position, was seriously considered, but Balanchine disapproved; and despite Berman's vociferously voiced protests to Stravinsky, the composer sided with Balanchine. He also asked Bing to employ Mme Karinska for the costumes, but Bing informed Balanchine that it was too late ("I have already made a contract with Mme Pons who has started on the costumes").[8]

We can only assume that Balanchine must have grinned a little when he returned to the Metropolitan Opera House. No longer consigned to the menial position endured during the 1930s, while jingoistic critics disparaged him, now he would shape a major American premiere. Still, despite Balanchine's respected reputation in the New York dance world, Stravinsky's choice of a choreographer-turned director raised eyebrows. Balanchine heard the rustling and addressed the matter head-on:

> It may seem odd to many people that a choreographer of ballets has been entrusted with the stage direction of an opera which has, in fact, no dance movement at all in it. But in this opera I think of myself entirely as Stravinsky's messenger. . . . My job as a messenger is to bring, as movingly as I can, the music for voice from stage to audience. Here, I have never been a choreographer, as some opera directors in the recent past have attempted to be, assuming every note has its equivalent in movement—so that the result reduces the music to a sound-track, and the actions of the singers, to those of a jerky silent film. . . . *The Rake's Progress* is a most serious work. I have tried to bring to it a minimum of orderly action as clearly demanded by book and music, without decoration, delivering its message without comment of choreography.[9]

In an issue of *Opera News,* he further clarified his directorial approach: "The music must come first. If it is necessary that the singers should face front in order to be heard, they must face front. Even the scenery has been designed so that the scene changes shall not take longer than the music that has been composed for them. . . . It is not necessary for the singers to move all the time, nor to mime while they are singing. I prefer poor acting and good music to good acting and bad music."[10] Moreover, his unobtrusive approach was appreciated.

Irving Kolodin's 15 February 1953 review for the *Los Angeles Times* noted, "George Balanchine's staging did not call attention to itself, it was decidedly expert."

Nonetheless, neither the Venice premiere nor Balanchine's more musically compatible Metropolitan staging proved to be the critical success expected. Stravinsky realized this, and it bothered him. The widely publicized appearance of a major composition by the world's greatest living composer had been anticipated for three years. Much was at stake. By now Stravinsky was accustomed to braving more than his share of criticism, but this was different. *The Rake's Progress* was more than just another composition to Stravinsky: it was a personal investment that had expended him. *Rake's Progress* was a crisis of conscience, and it took its toll. It was a flashpoint as pivotal as the one confronted more than twenty years earlier in writing *Apollo*. The opera's "obsolescent neoclassic language," as critics charged, gave Stravinsky pause to rethink his future. If he were to be a part of the future—something that he very much wanted, and perhaps even needed—then at age seventy, he would once again have to change.

The history of that critical change must be chronicled in some detail, for it has everything to do with the road leading to *Agon*. Within months after *Rake's Progress*'s Italian premiere, one of the most astonishing compositional transfigurations in music history began. Following the opera's inaugural performance, Stravinsky remained in Europe for most of the fall, touring and recording. Returning to New York, he conducted *Baiser de la Fée* (called *The Fairy's Kiss*) with Balanchine's company in late November 1951, by which time plans were already under way with the choreographer for the opera's American premiere. At the beginning of 1952 he was back in Hollywood completing his *Cantata* while continuing revisions for the Met performance the next year. Then in February, momentously, Stravinsky attended several rehearsals and a performance of Arnold Schoenberg's *Septet-Suite*. About two weeks later—and apparently without much warning—the deflated composer unburdened himself one evening to his wife and Robert Craft. He had reached an impasse and feared he had nothing else to say compositionally. "For a moment he broke down and actually wept," Craft recalled. Later he admitted that Schoenberg's *Septet* had greatly impressed him.[11]

History had long since proclaimed Schoenberg and Stravinsky the two most celebrated icons of twentieth-century composition. Programmed to remain competing ideologues, they maintained an adversarial relationship, representing antipodal blocs of compositional thought. (Even though they were Hollywood neighbors, they never spoke to each other.) But with Robert Craft's arrival in the Stravinsky household in 1948, Schoenberg's death in the summer of 1951, the lukewarm reception of *Rake's Progress* a few months later, and Stravinsky's own 1952 admission of feeling adrift, the composer began exhibiting an increased, and for many of his older friends unhealthy, interest in the music of Schoenberg and his younger disciples.

Anton Webern's music was the primary attraction, and as Stravinsky's archives establish, he often studied the Viennese composer's scores, circling printing errors, tracing tone rows, marking passages of interest in red. He quickly became absorbed in the principles of serialism and dodecaphony. Since the 1920s, twelve-tone music, as it is often described, had been closely associated with the so-called Second Viennese School, a circle of composers that included Schoenberg and his gifted students Alban Berg and Webern. Now, in 1952, Stravinsky began listening to and studying their music, much of which was being heard frequently in Los Angeles, where the composer regularly attended concerts.

What immediately appealed to Stravinsky was Webern's concern with temporal pacing. He was drawn to the serial composer's music—as were many of the most prominent composers of the time including Pierre Boulez, Karlheinz Stockhausen, and Olivier Messiaen—for many reasons, not the least of which was their mutual immersion in matters of architectural symmetry. Responding to those who discounted his conversion to serialism as an unthinkable reversal, Stravinsky replied that he had always been an "interval" composer—meaning that, like Webern, he was a constructionist interested in plumbing the possibilities of the smallest compositional units. Both were economists in search of brief musical cells, or what music theorists think of as pitch sets, that could be cohesively manipulated in the cause of structural unity. Both were texturalists too, whose sense of silence, sparseness, color, and orchestration helped define and clarify the multiple layers of their intricate, contrapuntal lines.

From the start, then, there was a natural affinity, a need to write "clean" music whose orderliness was paramount. Webern was, as Stravinsky portrayed him, "the first architechnologist of our time . . . a real hero," and as will become evident, it is Webern's spirit that surges through the many structural layers of *Agon.* Stravinsky's embrace of Webern's serialism became increasingly apparent in each of half a dozen works composed between *The Rake's Progress* and the 1957 ballet. And *Agon,* slowly incubating all the while, reflects the astonishing compositional metamorphosis through which Stravinsky was passing.

The origins of this transformation are traceable to February and March 1952. During that same spring, Balanchine's company set another important benchmark. The New York City Ballet undertook the first of several grand European tours, sweeping through Barcelona, Paris, Edinburgh, Berlin, Florence, and elsewhere. Upon returning, the company added two new ballets to its repertoire: *Scotch Symphony,* to the music of Mendelssohn, created around Tallchief; and *Metamorphoses,* to a Hindemith score, for Le Clercq. Earlier in the year Balanchine's marriage to Tallchief had been annulled, and on 31 December 1951 he and Le Clercq married. It was Balanchine's fourth and final marriage. Stravinsky attended the nuptial celebration in his friend's apartment later that day. A little over a month later, Balanchine directed *The Rake's Progress.*

Stravinsky's blossoming interest in serialism during this period was shared by Balanchine. The always-curious choreographer was eager to champion the music of contemporary composers, including the less accessible music of the avant-garde. Importantly too, he was enough of a musician and dramatist to appreciate the architectural beauties of the dodecaphonic school Schoenberg had established a quarter of a century earlier, even though he may not have fully understood the myriad possibilities of the compositional techniques themselves. In her informative article "The Spelling of *Agon,*" Arlene Croce suggests that about this time Balanchine undertook his own study of "12-tone theory." Perhaps, but Craft offers a different interpretation. The choreographer had visited Schoenberg's widow, Gertrude, in 1953 while City Ballet was on tour in California. Balanchine thought that he should choreograph a Schoenberg work and was there to ask for permission.[12]

In an unpublished Balanchine file retained among his private papers, Stravinsky marked a 14 June 1954 *Herald Tribune* article by Jay S. Harrison entitled "Balanchine: He Fills Time in Space" (one of many articles about Balanchine that Stravinsky annotated). The article offers several familiar Balanchine views: "Music is something that occupies architecturally a certain portion of time. Now, in the dance, unless your body fills time, occupies time, as music does, then it means nothing. Gesture itself is meaningless." He goes on to discuss specifically his fascination with Webern's music, mentioning that it was Stravinsky who introduced it to him.

Balanchine's ballet, *Opus 34,* premiered on 19 January 1954, about the same time Stravinsky began composing *In Memoriam Dylan Thomas* (before Thomas's death in late 1953 the composer and poet had planned on doing an opera together)—an important work that evidenced the composer's growing exploration of serial techniques. Balanchine's "twelve-tone nights," as Taper refers to them, soon became a feature of each season. *Opus 34* was followed a month later by a work that could not have been more different—the first full-length production of the New York City Ballet's *Nutcracker.* Two other important (and still familiar) offerings followed in 1954, *Western Symphony* and *Ivesiana*. Balanchine continued working in various venues, creating choreography for the Kirk Browning–directed *Magic Flute,* telecast 15 January 1956 on the NBC Opera Theatre. A new ballet, *Allegro Brillante,* to Tchaikovsky's little-known Piano Concerto No. 3, premiered on 1 March 1956. In May of that year, Tanaquil Le Clercq danced in *Divertimento No. 15* (originally titled *Caracole*), to a Mozart score. Then sadly, that fall, on 31 October, tragedy struck in Copenhagen while the company was on tour: Le Clercq contracted polio and lost the use of her legs.[13]

It was a devastating blow. Le Clercq and her husband returned to New York in March 1957, and for the next several months Balanchine attended his wife full time, accompanying her to Warm Springs, Georgia, later in the year for her therapeutic treatment. Stravinsky too was concerned. He and his wife corresponded with Le Clercq, sending her gifts to occupy her recovery time. The composer retained a touching birthday note in his files from "Tanny," dated 17 June 1957 from Warm Springs, in which she thanks Stravinsky and his wife for sending two books, adding, "I have been thinking of you all week—George has talked of little else. He is so excited about seeing you both. I wish I could come and see you, and hear your music, but. . . . It is very nice here. If one has to have polio, and go through all this, this is the place to be" (ellipsis in original). The music to which Le Clercq refers is *Agon,* whose orchestral premiere Balanchine attended in California the same day as Le Clercq's note.[14] Balanchine continued caring for Le Clercq throughout the summer and fall of 1957. He was away from ballet for a full year, and rumors spread that he might never return to work. No new ballets appeared until late in the year.

But then *Square Dance,* to the music of Corelli and Vivaldi, appeared in November, followed by *Agon* in early December. It was now three years since Balanchine had followed Stravinsky's lead in exploring Schoenberg's twelve-tone style with the score for *Opus 34.* By almost every account, including Nancy Reynolds's always astute observations, the 1954 work was a "'weirdie' and no two ways about it." It was a boldly experimental work for dance, the first of its kind for Balanchine and his audience. Kirstein recalls that "some would see it as a first sketch for *Agon.*" In acquainting Balanchine with the musical vocabulary of dodecaphony and its potential for dance, it did in fact serve as a useful precursor to the Stravinsky piece, although choreographically the two works are entirely different.[15] While Balanchine familiarized himself with the Schoenberg score, Stravinsky continued probing the intricacies of Webern's music, though his interest in serialism was only one of two preoccupying interests.

During the late 1940s and early 1950s, Stravinsky had grown increasingly curious about another, seemingly unrelated, repertoire: the music of the Renaissance. The admixture of Webern's posttonal methods and those of the fifteenth and sixteenth centuries might initially appear incongruous to a non-musician. But in fact Stravinsky's dual interests constituted a perfectly reasonable commingling. Both literatures imposed strict limits, an economy of materials, and a rigorous contrapuntal discipline. Often a work's unity was so deeply embedded in its substructural layers that its interior compositional logic was penetrable only by insiders conversant with the covertly disguised techniques employed. The fundamental tenets of the compositional process in both literatures—a process of musical ratiocination venerating the beauty of order—was clear to Stravinsky, whose Cartesian instincts drew him to the precepts of Renaissance thinking.

The correlation was clear to Webern too, whose doctoral musicology dissertation had been an examination of the Flemish composer Heinrich Isaac's *Choralis Constantinus,* an exemplar of Renaissance polyphony. Indeed, Stravinsky's identification with Webern by way of Isaac is evident. In a 21 December 1952 interview for the *Herald Tribune,* Stravinsky spoke with passionate conviction of his own affinity for Isaac: "He is my hobby, my daily bread. I love him. I study him constantly. And between his musical thinking and writing and my own there is a very close connection. . . . Here is the newly published volume of his *Choralis Constantinus,* Book III. A great work. Not a home should be without it." While Stravinsky's dramatic flair often led him to hyperbole, in this case his adulation of Isaac was genuine. On 2 February 1952 Stravinsky composed the Westron Wind section of his 1952 *Cantata.* Here, notably, Renaissance verses are set extensively to imitative and canonic techniques that presage his serial music, including the multiple canons that permeate *Agon.* Moreover, it was that same February that Stravinsky experienced his crisis while listening to Schoenberg's *Septet.*

The composer's extant library includes an impressive collection of scores and scholarly books ranging over several Renaissance topics. It is hardly a leap to suggest that some of *Agon*'s deepest roots stem from the composer's immersion in these studies. He read Ernst Krenek's monograph about the Netherlandish Renaissance composer Johannes Ockeghem. He cites the *Missa l'Homme Armé* of yet another notable Flemish composer, Josquin des Prez, as a "parallel" for his own 1959 *Movements.* He owned musicologist Edward Lowinsky's landmark monograph, *Secret Chromatic Art in the Netherlands* (1946), even corresponding with the author and posing technical questions to him. Still and all, while

Stravinsky was genuinely interested in early music, he openly referred to it as "Bob's music." It is Craft's markings, not Stravinsky's, that appear on many pages of the scores and books in the composer's library retained in Basel.[16]

As early as 1949 Craft had conducted a concert at Princeton University that included music of several composers straddling the late Renaissance and early Baroque, especially Andrea Gabrieli and Heinrich Schütz, to whom Stravinsky would later refer with admiration (significantly, the composer's 1948 *Mass* was included in the same concert). Stravinsky was particularly attracted to transitional composers like Claudio Monteverdi who worked on either side of 1600—that great, though rather arbitrary historical divide marking the decline of modality and the rise of tonality. Stravinsky also heard many of the Monday Evening Concerts in Los Angeles that regularly featured a mix of early music and contemporary literature. The composer's *In Memoriam Dylan Thomas* was premiered on a 1954 program that included works of Gabrieli, Schütz, and Gesualdo.

As always, Stravinsky listened intently. The lessons learned from these two literatures seeped into his imagination, eventually coalescing and manifesting themselves in his own inimitable music. And the convergence of these two pathways leads directly to the core of *Agon*'s composite compositional design. While it was not unusual for the composer to look to the past as a way of confronting his own future, in the case of *Agon* that confrontation was especially formidable, given the diversity of models with which he was dealing. Shifting compositional course midstream, as happened during the evolution of *Agon,* invited the creation of a potentially hopeless patchwork of stylistic inconsistencies. The challenge of completing the ballet—in this regard, perhaps one of the greatest challenges of his life—was to create a musically homogeneous whole. To do so during an enormously unsettled period of his life only heightened the task. It remained for Stravinsky to filter Webern, Isaac, et al. through his own genius, to absorb, process, and ultimately fuse the divergent musical styles and compositional techniques that were shaping his path. And while all this was unfolding, it fell to Kirstein, Balanchine, and others to keep the prospect of a new ballet alive.

Between 1948 and 1957 Kirstein exchanged dozens of letters with the composer, diplomatically but persistently raising the possibility of a sequel to *Orpheus.* In addition to the 29 April 1948 letter first raising the idea of completing a trilogy, are letters of 28 October, in which Kirstein expresses his hope that Stravinsky "is thinking about the third act of *Apollo-Orpheus,*" and 28 November, where he proposes a specific idea: "I think that the story of Euripides' *Bacchae* is a wonderful thing, and Bacchus-Dionysus is in the absolute line of *Apollo—Orpheus*," to which Stravinsky responded a few days later that he was thinking about "plans for a *Third* Ballet" but that *Rake's Progress* currently consumed him.

In the summer of 1950 Kirstein informed Stravinsky that T. S. Eliot had declined to suggest a scenario for this third ballet, thinking that nothing could follow *Orpheus,* which he had just seen the City Ballet dance at Covent Garden. It may have been some of the best advice Stravinsky ever heeded. But Eliot let it be known that he was interested in collaborating with Stravinsky on a ballet based upon the two fragments of his poem "Sweeney Agonistes." In turn Kirstein passed on the proposal to Stravinsky, urging him to consider the idea but making it clear that this would be a separate enterprise completely unrelated to his own proposed trilogy.

Then on 16 February 1951 Kirstein, for the first time, formally offered the composer a $5,000 commission for the new ballet, adding, "Wystan [Auden] has suggested the Hero as Builder of Cities; Aesculapius, the doctor; or Amphion the architect?" Stravinsky answered a few days later, explaining that while he liked the idea, any discussion must be postponed. Immediately upon his return to New York from the Venetian premiere of *The Rake's Progress,* Stravinsky was again contacted by an eager—perhaps overly eager—Kirstein, on 28 November 1951. He urged the composer to meet with Balanchine before returning to Los Angeles, "about plans for *Terpsichore:* I hope we can present it a year from now. Is this too early to make plans for it? I want to ask Pavlik to redesign *Apollo* and *Orpheus,* and do the new ballet, as a consecutive three-act spectacle." Kirstein even took it upon himself to include a draft of the suggested *Terpsichore* scenario in which seven individual sections were proposed.

Whether Stravinsky and Balanchine seriously considered the outline, nothing came of the proposal, intriguing as it was. Equally fascinating is just how far Kirstein (and maybe Balanchine) had gone in specifying the action, even casting the dancers.[17] Certainly it had not developed to such an extent in the composer's mind, and since the scenario was in effect "presented" to him, it is likely that he dismissed it quickly. In fact, Kirstein's indefatigability over the years in offering the composer an ongoing menu of fairly specific ideas from which the third and final "act" could be assembled may have backfired. Despite Kirstein's good intentions (and his obvious need to make plans for upcoming seasons), Stravinsky was not about to submit to what he may have interpreted as circumscription—especially with so many other matters on his mind. The composer's letters to Kirstein and others quietly, but consistently, imply that efforts to pin him down were proving a distraction.

There is no significant correspondence during 1952, the critical year in Stravinsky's adoption of serialism. Kirstein did not write to the composer again until 26 August 1953. We must realize that until this point Stravinsky had still not indicated any formal acceptance of a commission. But with a grant from the Division of Humanities of the Rockefeller Foundation in hand, Kirstein now doubled the offer to $10,000 for a major new ballet that might run as long as forty-five minutes. Again he suggested a specific ballet trilogy, with "Apollo Architectons: builder of shelters and bridges" as the third act, all three works to be "re-designed by Pavlik Tchelitchev and presented on a single evening." On 27 August, Stravinsky accepted Kirstein's proposed fee. Writing again the next day, the composer expressed concern that if *Apollo Architectons* were viewed as a sequel to the rather solemn music of *Apollo* and *Orpheus,* he would have to write music "to overcome or counterbalance this dominating slowness." He suggested the scoring Nausicaa episode of the *Odyssey,* adding that he had been thinking about the material as an appropriate ballet theme. "I foresee it and feel it as a rather gay ballet."[18]

While it would be nice to believe that Stravinsky eagerly endorsed Kirstein's concept of a Greek triptych, the truth is he was never really sold on the idea. The notion of linked works held little interest for a composer who took each compositional challenge as a single, independent problem to be solved. Yes, in responding to Kirstein on 28 August 1953, he did offer "to compose a ballet for you to complete the *Apollo*-idea," but given other statements made out of Kirstein's earshot, it appears that the composer's willingness arose mainly from diplomacy. Stravinsky masterfully juggled commissions while making certain that he could compose what *he* wanted to compose. Shortly after telling Kirstein that he would complete the trilogy, he wrote to his publisher on 25 September, "I plan to compose my music without any blueprint for a plot. I will compose a kind of symphony to be danced."[19] Even when all three works were eventually programmed on a single ballet evening, Stravinsky insisted that *Agon* be performed second and *Orpheus* last—and thus closer in spirit to what Eliot had suggested.

Between 1948 and 1953 Stravinsky discarded each scenario Kirstein and others presented. But despite whatever reticence he may have harbored about Kirstein's forwardness, this does not nullify their importance to a composer who considered each possibility on its own merits. Eliminating ideas comprised an integral part of *Agon*'s precompositional process. But it was his interest in literary models—perhaps even more deeply than in musical ones—that almost always informed and shaped Stravinsky's thinking. The "Sweeney Agonistes" proposal (even though Eliot envisioned a balletic conception beyond Kirstein's trilogy) was no exception. Stravinsky biographer Stephen Walsh suggests that among the free exchange of ideas between Kirstein, Auden, and Stravinsky during the early 1950s, "there may have been discussion viva voce about a scenario to do with the idea of classical myth as an archetype of modern urban life, or else to do with the death of heroism in the post-war world, as in Eliot's fragmentary dialogue *Sweeney Agonistes*."[20]

Just so, the contemporization of classical dilemmas constantly fascinated the composer. *The Rake's Progress* was an opera that moralized. And soon after its completion, the composer held preliminary discussions with Dylan Thomas about a proposed opera dealing with the "re-creation of the world" following an "atomic misadventure." Even ten years later, *The Flood*—a metaphor for "the Bomb," as Stravinsky remarked—took up similar themes of temptation, good and evil, and beginning life anew. Moreover, Walsh adds that the composer's brief flirtation with setting part of the *Odyssey* as a film may owe its inception to "a reading of Eliot's Sweeney poems, where the Phaecian princess is transmogrified into the prostitute Doris." The fact is, the connection between "Sweeney Agonistes" and *Agon* is closer in spirit than history has allowed, and in tracing the roots of the ballet, we should not underestimate Eliot's influence.[21]

Unquestionably *Agon* owes its title to Eliot's poetry. Craft confirms that it was after reading Eliot's poetic fragments, as well as "the great *agon* between Aeschylus and Euripides in Aristophanes' *Frogs,* [that Stravinsky] became interested in the 'contest' concept, and it stuck."[22] The Greek definition of an *agon* encompassed many nuances, even though we are inclined to translate it simply as a contest or struggle or, as it has sometimes been defined, a combat. By the end of the fifth century, comments classicist Michael Arnush, the agon was the core of Greek comedy. It was a contest waged between the play's principals toward winning over not only the other characters involved in the dramatic action but also the members of the audience and the men sitting in judgment of the competition.

The agon stood at the center of Greek life. "From Homer on, competitions help characterize Greek behavior," observes Arnush. "Agamemnon vs. Achilles in the *Iliad,* or Priam vs. Achilles, offer two well-known examples of verbal agones, or contests. Competition (on the athletic field, in the battlefield, in public assembly) was a primary means for Greek males to demonstrate their excellence, their *arete*."[23] The term also applied to a debate among citizens in a public forum, as well as to elections in Athenian democracy.

Stravinsky was, as we know, familiar with the tragedies of Euripides and the comedies of Aristophanes. And as was his custom, he would have thoroughly familiarized himself with the concept of agon before employing it. Moreover, the notion of a contest—any contest—instinctively appealed to Stravinsky. In a compositional context, it immediately provided for the existence of a protagonist (from *agonizesthai,* "to compete") and thus some type of contrast and competing "action." The drama of physical action, specifically, was just as vital to Stravinsky as it was to Balanchine. Among the composer's childhood recollections were his ineradicable memories of peasants dancing in contests at the summer fairs he witnessed in Pechisky during the early 1890s.[24]

The Sacher Stiftung retains a typed letter from Stravinsky to Kirstein dated 8 August 1954 in which the composer left a blank to fill in the title of the new ballet. Only after the letter was finished did he fill in "AGONE" in pencil.[25] Beyond adapting his title, the composer's study of Eliot's two "agon" poems (first published in 1926–27, about the same time *Apollo* was being composed) suggests a more important influence. Originally decried as symptomatic of Jazz Age profanity and insensibility, "Sweeney Agonistes" had a quirkiness that tantalized Stravinsky. Eliot's poetic probing of Sweeney's psyche shares a common ground with the hard-edged contrasts of the ballet. Sweeney himself is lodged in a contest that both questions and celebrates the concept of difference. Eliot's vivid poetry dwells on starkly black-and-white dualities, including powerfully sensual male-and-female tensions. Sweeney is made to confront his internal demons, to reconcile the discordant claims of humanness, animalism, and spirituality. Eliot's agons were preoccupied with self-reflexivity, something Stravinsky understood as well as he understood any of antiquity's classical metaphors—and something that was especially on his mind in the early 1950s, when he once again held up a mirror to his past while contemplating his future. Coincidentally, with the pronounced failure of "Sweeney Agonistes," Eliot, like Stravinsky after *The Rake's Progress,* felt that his career as a poet was over. He admitted his youthful disillusion years later in a 1952 article appearing in the *New York Times*—shortly after Stravinsky had reached his own crisis. Being an admirer of Eliot's, surely Stravinsky read the article with considerable understanding, and perhaps reassurance.

At another level, *Agon's* music may have been formatively shaped by the temporal rhythms of Eliot's words, even if, as was typical of Stravinsky's reliance upon literary models, the influence was oblique. As we have seen, it was not the first time that the composer, an ardent student of linguistic morphology, paid heed to the flow of language, syllabication, accent, meter, and inflection; he had done the same with Boileau's alexandrines thirty years earlier. Nor was his curiosity about English prosody, including "Sweeney's" much-criticized flashy, unidiomatic speech rhythms, any less fervent. We must remember that while he was reading the linguistic twists and turns of Eliot's fragments, the composer was immersed in Auden's text for *The Rake's Progress.* Finally, in Eliot's own Aristotelian analysis, drama amounted to a "ritual consisting of a set of re- peated movements [which] is essentially a dance"—something with which Stravinsky would also have concurred.[26]

All of this was surely stirring in Stravinsky's mind as he continued mulling over Kirstein's ideas in the early 1950s. With the composer's receipt of a 31 Au- gust 1953 letter from Kirstein, everything changed. There Kirstein and Balan- chine expressed reservations about Stravinsky's earlier Nausicaa proposal. As an alternative, Balanchine, more directly than ever before, outlined his specific vi- sion. Kirstein's summary to the composer is worth reprinting since the letter is key:

> What [Balanchine] wants is a ballet-ivanich. He would like a ballet which would seem to be the enormous finale of a ballet to end all the ballets the world has ever seen, mad dancing, variations, pas d'action, pas de deux, etc., with a final terrific and devastating curtain when everyone would be exhausted. He suggested a competition before the gods; the audience are statues; the gods are tired and old; the dances re- animate them by a series of historic dances, the correct tempi of which you can quite ignore, but they are called courante, bransle, passepied, rigaudon, menuet, etc. etc. It is as if time called the tune, and the dances which began quite simply in the sixteenth century took fire in the twentieth and exploded. It would be in the form of a *suite of danses,* or variations, numbers of as great variety as you pleased.
>
> I am sending you a book which may possibly interest you along these lines. There are others like it, the Arbeau and the Rameau (no relation to the composer), and I can get them for you; but certainly you do not need them. Balanchine sees a mar- velous theatricalized cosmic space in an architectural frame, more like Palladio than baroque; your music is the drama; his dances would attempt to stage dramatic ten- sions entirely in terms of dancing, but the characters would be dressed with some ref- erence to historic styles. But you are the boss.[27]

Although all Kirstein's earlier proposals had proved unacceptable, the book he now sent made the difference. With it Stravinsky had a tangible resource— something he almost always needed—first to spark, then to guide his imagina- tion. As Balanchine later recalled, it became *Agon's* "point of departure."

Chapter 10 The Evolution of

Agon's Musical Structure

My past and present time worlds cannot be the same. I know that portions of Agon contain three times as much music for the same clock
length as some other pieces of mine. . . . We are located in time constantly in a tonal-system work, whether Josquin's *Duke Hercules Mass* or a
serially composed non-tonal-system work.
—*Igor Stravinsky*

The *Apologie de la danse* (1623) by François de Lauze constitutes the
most substantive dance treatise of the seventeenth century. When
Kirstein mailed a copy to Stravinsky, he sent the 1952 British reprint of
the book, which had been greatly supplemented by its editor, Joan
Wildeblood. The manual addressed the instruction, history, and
function of several period dances, at least "the most advantageous"
ones, as de Lauze concludes. But most important, Wildeblood offered
detailed explanations of several popular dance patterns.

Given Stravinsky's immersion in the music of the Renaissance,
Kirstein could not have sent the manual at a more propitious time.
The composer's curiosity about early music extended from the four-
teenth-century composer Guillaume de Machaut through the fif-

teenth- and early sixteenth-century works of Josquin des Prez. It even included Claudio Monteverdi, whose seventeenth-century operas and ballets (including the important 1607 opera *Orfeo,* which Stravinsky studied while composing *Orpheus)* were contemporary with de Lauze's manual. Still, even though the *Apologie* dates from the early 1620s, its spirit is more sixteenth than seventeenth century, just as *Agon's* musical roots are directly traceable to the Renaissance rather than the baroque. Indeed, the whole of *Agon's* music has a subtle but unmistakable Renaissance quality; in terms of dance, Robert Garis adds, "*Agon* is indeed a ballet in which Renaissance dance forms are brought up to the minute under great pressure."[1]

De Lauze's treatise was far more than a standard how-to dance manual: it was a lexicon of protocol, an attestation to the hallowed virtues of classicism that Balanchine, Kirstein, and Stravinsky revered. The composer surely endorsed the proprieties elucidated in Wildeblood's editorial introduction: "In an age when the manner of the Court was becoming increasingly artificial, the observance of the correct mode of behavior became a matter of supreme importance, especially for those members of society who desired to appear to have advantage in courtly circles." This call for order and deportment was terribly important to a composer whose personal code of conduct embraced carriage and deference. Equally important were the tenets of logic and reason synonymous with the courts of Louis XIII and Louis XIV (which led to the establishment of the Royal Academies of Dance, in 1661, and Music, in 1669)—tenets linked to "the artistic models of classical antiquity," yet another fundamental Stravinskyan connection.[2]

Order and proportionality were part of the French Renaissance's *belle danse,* just as they run to the core of *Agon's* tightly conceived structure. As dance master Pierre Rameau advised in his 1725 *Le Maître à Danser:* "Especially in Ball-Room dances . . . the steps should be executed with every regard for uniformity and proportion." That proportion should be numbered among the "real and natural qualities of beauty" was an old Augustinian concept in which Stravinsky firmly believed. For the Greeks, it was the principal cohesive force in all the arts. And for Descartes, the perfect proportion was two to one—a ratio visually reflected in *Agon's* eight female and four male dancers; in the many trios (two females and one male, two males and one female); and aurally in the ballet's pervasively employed short-long ♩ ♪ : ♩ rhythmic values, which are related to the short-long syllabic division of Greek prosodic meter.[3]

Balanchine remarked that it was Stravinsky "who hit upon the idea of a suite of dances based on a seventeenth-century manual of French court dances—

sarabandes, gaillards, branles—he had recently come across. We all liked the idea, especially as Kirstein and I recalled Stravinsky's other masterful treatment of polkas, and other dance forms, including ragtime rhythms." This may be a little off: Kirstein's letter first speaks of *Balanchine's,* not Stravinsky's, concept of stringing together historically fashioned dance forms, including the bransle and other named dances. Certainly, the idea was at least on Balanchine's mind before Stravinsky ever received the de Lauze. Moreover, Kirstein often spoke of Balanchine's own sense of decorum as it applied to dancing, and his appreciation for aristocratic order and courtesy. One can picture *Agon's* choreographic patterns in Kirstein's words: "How many times do we notice in the Balanchine repertory vestigial remains of court etiquette: the *reverences,* the curtsies, the formal bowed acknowledgments, which become all the more touching for their unexpected placement in an informal surround, and for the implied ironic contrast." For Balanchine, Kirstein continued, "there is still time and hope for the consideration of others, for the utility of courtesy."[4]

Balanchine's original vision of a grandiose ballet, unbounded in scope, must have mystified a composer who found precise precompositional borders imperative. Stravinsky would have nothing to do with Balanchine's fit of fancy (if, in fact, it was Balanchine's in the first place). The composer replied to Kirstein on 9 September 1953 that "the idea you and George have of doing a 'ballet to end all ballets' may prove a limitless affair," adding that "limits are precisely what I need and am looking for above all in everything I composed. The limits generate the form." More relevant—much more relevant as it turns out—Stravinsky thanked Kirstein for sending the de Lauze, adding, "I am studying it 'poco a poco.'"[5]

He did more than that: he studied it methodically, although he wouldn't admit it. In reviewing the ballet's premiere for the January 1958 *Nation,* Lester Trimble remarked, "Both Stravinsky and Balanchine have remained a little inscrutable with regard to the inspirational underpinning of their work, despite their obvious efforts to give the public a clue. It is stated in the program notes that the *Agon pieces were modeled* after examples in a French dance manual of the mid-seventeenth century. But [in] the choreography, only an occasional flicker of courtly gesture, a sudden, unexpected movement in the language of manners, give any hint of the seventeenth-century." Retaining the review, Stravinsky underlined Trimble's comment, adding in the margin: "Too little to be worth to speak about of [*sic*]—only the names, like *Bransle, Galliarde, Sarabande.*" But the composer's blasé dismissal distorts the truth, as did similar denials adamantly offered whenever he was caught "appropriating" models.[6]

An examination of Stravinsky's copy of the *Apologie,* preserved in the Sacher Stiftung, discloses the composer's across-the-board reliance upon the dance patterns outlined by de Lauze and expounded by Wildeblood. In tracing both the composer's adoption of dance titles and Balanchine's adaptation of dance patterns, a summary of *Agon's* individual divisions as printed in the published score will be useful.

I.	Pas de quatre	four males
	Double Pas de quatre	eight females
	Triple Pas de Quatre	four males and eight females
II.	Prelude	
	First Pas de trois	one male and two females
	Saraband-Step	one solo male
	Galliard	two females
	Coda	one male and two females
	Interlude	
	Second Pas de trois	two males and one female
	Bransle Simple	two males
	Bransle Gay	one solo female
	Bransle de Poitou	two males and one female
	Interlude	
	Pas de deux	one male, one female
III.	Four Duos	four males, four females
	Four Trios	four males, eight females

The many illustrations reproduced in the Wildeblood edition contributed to the shaping of both the ballet's sound and its look. At times the engravings even guided the orchestration. The second Pas de trois (Bransle Simple), scored for a trumpet duet engaged in a musical canon, took its cue from the *Apologie's* illustration entitled "A Nobleman Leading a Bransle," wherein two trumpeters perform from a balcony, as if convoking the proceedings. And the two male dancers who choreographically mirror each other along with the canonic music represent only one of many such contrapuntal exchanges in *Agon.* Musical canon constituted a standard Renaissance technique—and an almost compulsory serial procedure as well, as many of Stravinsky's earlier works from the 1950s (and Balanchine's choreographic settings) demonstrate.

Even the initial measures of the opening Pas de quatre, intoned by the famous fanfarelike announcement of the two trumpets, were surely inspired by the same illustration. As the composer's sketches for the opening reveal (and as

10.1 Sketch of opening material for *Agon* followed by the final version as it appears in the Pas de quatre (The Igor Stravinsky Collection, Paul Sacher Foundation, Basel. Also Courtesy of Boosey and Hawkes.)

we have come to expect), this opening was not composed first. Stravinsky worked at sculpting this clarion call to the dance. Compare the final, punctuated version of the ballet's opening with the rhythmic-melodic material Stravinsky first sketched (fig. 10.1).[7]

Other engravings in the manual also caught Stravinsky's eye. The "bright finger snap," as Arlene Croce describes it in her *New Yorker* essay "The Spelling of *Agon*" (12 July 1993), in the double Pas de quatre certainly owes its origins to the *Apologie* plate "Lady Snapping Her Fingers in Dancing" (fig. 10.2).

Stravinsky frequently underlined portions of the treatise, adding marginalia and highlighting particular passages. Such annotations show an assiduous composer familiarizing himself with the choreographic conventions of the French baroque a year before he and Balanchine first met to chart the ballet's course. The fact is, by the time Balanchine and Stravinsky sat down together, in August 1954, the composer already knew the de Lauze quite well, just as he knew what he pictured onstage. Long before *Agon* was conceived, Stravinsky had often spoken of his personal need to understand the fundamental tenets of dance, and which, if any, could be manipulated. In *Agon,* as in virtually every ballet he wrote, the composer was intently involved from the beginning, often envisaging specific choreographic patterns and even notating them in his compositional sketches. Suggesting that the composer did little more than tailor the music to some predetermined choreographic scheme would be gravely misconstruing the way he and Balanchine collaborated. Stravinsky was a devoted stu-

10.2 "Lady Snapping Her Fingers in Dancing," from François de Lauze, *Apologie de la danse* (1623; Geneva: Minkoff, 1977. The Igor Stravinsky Collection, Paul Sacher Foundation, Basel.)

dent of dance, and his thorough marking of the *Apologia* confirms that he did his homework.

He also studied Wildeblood's copious editorial commentary. Several passages highlighted in red divulge his particular interest in the bransle. Significantly, Wildeblood spoke of a ritualistic connection that Stravinsky also marked: "The world-wide use of this form of the dance is well known. . . . It may be of interest to record that this salient feature of pagan festivals was preserved in the clandestine rituals of the dying religion in Western Europe for many centuries." The composer also underlined a few sentences Wildeblood quotes from Margaret Murray's *The Witch-Cult in Western Europe:* "The ring dances were usually round some object, sometimes a stone, sometimes the Devil. The round-dance was . . . essentially a witch dance." Given the central importance of the bransles in *Agon,* several other relevant passages marked are worth reprinting:

> (a) The Bransle—The circle, or round dance . . . recognized to be one of the oldest forms of the group dance. (b) Bransle, with a string of dancers holding hands. (c) For Arbeau describes the clapping of hands, shaking of fingers, and so forth in certain Bransles. (d) Bransle, Brawls or Rounds. (e) A tree . . . which they erected, bedecked with ribbons and garlands. (f) Throughout the seventeenth century there is evidence that the ball was always commenced by dancing a Bransle.
>
> The Bransle—The circle, or round dance, in which the dancers form either a complete or partial circle, is generally recognized to be one of the oldest forms of the group dance. It is natural that this should be so, for it is a pattern into which a man or people will easily form if they are either dancing round some object, as in worship, or, if being joined one to another by holding hands, linking arms, or placing their arms across each other's shoulders, or backs, their dance continues to progress, either forwards, backwards, or sideways, without leaving the same dancing ground.

Stravinsky's fondness for the bransle predates Balanchine's first mention of the popular Renaissance dance in Kirstein's 31 August 1953 letter. The Allegretto movement of the composer's 1940 *Symphony in C* uses the same fundamental rhythmic pattern, ♪ ♫, that is employed in *Agon*'s Bransle Gay. Wildeblood also summarizes de Lauze's explanation of the dance; and once again Stravinsky marked the entire passage:

> In 1623, de Lauze's *Suite* consists of five *Bransles,* which he names the "*Bransle Simple,*" "*Bransle Gay,*" "*Bransle de Poitou,*" "*Bransle Double de Poitou,*" the "Fifth *Bransle,*" and lastly, the "*Gavot,*" which made the sixth dance in the *Suite.*
>
> Finally we have Mersenne's *Suite.* Though the date of his book is 1636, he had obtained the King's Privilege in 1629, six years later than the date of de Lauze's book. As the names and the order of the *Bransles* given are identical with those of de Lauze, one may conclude they were speaking of the same dances. He writes: "There are six kinds (of *Bransles*) which are danced now-a-days at the opening of a Ball, one after the other, by as many persons as wish; for the entire company, joining hands, perform with one accord a continual *Bransle,* sometimes forwards, sometimes backwards; it is done with divers movements to which are adapted various kinds of steps, according to the different airs which are used. They dance round very sedately at the beginning of the Ball, all with the same time and movements of the body. The first of which is named the "*Bransle Simple*" . . . the second is called the "*Bransle Gay*" . . . the third is named "*Bransle-à-Mener*" or "*de Poitou*" . . . the fourth

"*Bransle Double de Poitou*" . . . the fifth is called "*Bransle de Montirande,*" and the sixth is "*La Gavot.*"

The order of the *Bransles* in this *Suite* is important, for one may thereby ascertain whether the *Suite* retained a definite form[,] in *tempo* and *time,* throughout the years.

Arbeau explains that the dances in his day were divided into four kinds, as in ancient Greece. There were the "*Grave,*" the "*Gay,*" and a combination of the two, "*Grave-and-Gay.*" . . . He then places the *Bransles* in these various categories, and his explanation is that the order of the *Bransles* in the *Suite* was regulated by the persons taking part. The slower *Bransles* "*Double*" and "*Simple*" were danced sedately by the "old people," the quicker "*Bransle Gay*" by those of the next degree of dignity, the young marrieds, and the "*Bransle de Bourgoyne,*" seemingly a very quick dance, by the "youngest of all."[8]

Wildeblood's mention of Marin Mersenne, whose humanistic inquiries ranged broadly over the historical period in which Stravinsky was then interested, provides another key in tracking *Agon's* models. Stravinsky wrote on the title page of his copy of the *Apologie,* "with some musik by Marin Mersenne (1636)"—a dead giveaway of the importance of the Mersenne melodies in Wildeblood's edition. In reconstructing the period's dance patterns, Betty Bang Mather articulates what emerges as the scholar's central problem: "The lengthy descriptions by François de Lauze (1623) of the smooth and graceful steps he knew include neither timings nor music; and Mersenne's (1636) scanty explanation of the steps of his day contains music but no timings."[9] It was the combination of the two in Wildeblood's modern edition that proved most useful to Stravinsky.

A renowned French theorist, mathematician, theologian, and musician, whose sweeping interests brought him into contact with Descartes, Galileo, and Pascal, Mersenne was someone Stravinsky admired greatly. His 1,300-page *Harmonie universelle* (extracted in Wildeblood's edition) constitutes a major contemporary thesis on seventeenth-century music and instruments. Moreover, a brief but pertinent section of the third volume of his treatise addresses the complementarity of dance and music. Mersenne insisted that "the poets, musicians, and composers of dances and ballets . . . would benefit by studying the ancient Greek rhythms in order to apply them to songs and dances which they composed." Stravinsky's dependence upon the melodies Wildeblood reprints is critical; for while the temporal divisions of Mersenne's tunes are "French" on the surface, they revert to a deeper Greek wellspring. In this sense, the underlying rhythmic structure of *Agon's* courtly dances is as Greek as the mythologies upon which *Apollo* and *Orpheus* are based. Certainly Stravinsky understood the connection Mersenne stressed throughout his discourse:

The most excellent metrical feet, which have given name and birth to the rhythm of the Greeks, are practiced in the *air de Balets,* in dance songs, and in all the other actions that serve as public or private recreations, as will be proven when the [metrical] feet that follow are compared to the airs one sings or that one plays on violins, the lute, guitar, and other instruments. Now these feet can be called "[rhythmic] movements" according to the manner of speech of our musicians and composers of airs. This is why I will use this term from now on, to join theory and practice.[10]

Stravinsky's awareness of this "theory and practice" is further evinced in his marking of yet another of Mersenne's Greek admonitions that Wildeblood stressed: once a melody is chosen, "one must join it to its proper movements, which the Greeks called Rhythm"—a statement reminiscent of Eliot's "Sweeney." Mersenne openly declared his preference for bransles "since they were not restricted by the words as when composing music for songs." Consequently, the potential for rhythmic invention was greater. One by one throughout his copy of the dance manual, Stravinsky noted these passages, paying particular heed to the bransles reprinted from Mersenne's *Suite.* And, most relevant, Stravinsky marked Wildeblood's own editorial emphasis that Mersenne "writes at some length on his subject, and includes a 'Table of the movements or measured feet' of 'Twelve movements Simples.' . . . These rhythmic feet are based on the long and short syllables of Greek rhythms."

Mersenne's *Suite of Bransles* served as the model for *Agon's* famous second Pas de trois. Wildeblood supplemented her explanations with several tables graphically illustrating the very dance patterns that found their way into the composer's initial thinking and the choreographer's eventual realization. In describing one of the bransle types, for example, Wildeblood remarks, "Take the Left foot forward and outward to the side, so that it describes a semi-circle in moving, with the toe turned well out, and step on to the whole foot." Moreover, the true genesis of *Agon's* trio of bransles becomes apparent when we examine a few of the Mersenne melodies that Stravinsky bracketed in his copy of the dance manual.

The composer entered the same type of scansion notations found thirty years earlier in his *Apollo* sketchbook (and in several other works as well). These divisions reveal the ballet's fundamental rhythmic fabric. For example, Mersenne's melody No. 3 Bransle Gay, which Stravinsky marked, is directly imported into *Agon's* own Bransle Gay, where it appears as the famous castanet rhythm mimicked by the two male dancers flanking the female soloist.

Similarly, the composer segments Mersenne's Bransle à mener ou de Poitou and the Bransle double de Poitou. The fundamental patterns of these two

10.3 Mersenne's Bransle Gay as it appears with Stravinsky's markings in his personal copy of the *Apologie*, followed by the final version of *Agon*'s Bransle Gay (The Igor Stravinsky Collection, Paul Sacher Foundation, Basel. Also Courtesy of Boosey and Hawkes.)

bransles also find their converted counterparts in *Agon*. The *Apologie* holds that in the Bransle de Poitou—shortened to Bransle Double in *Agon,* although in his first sketches the composer actually used the name Bransle de Poitou—"the rhythm is counted in five beats whilst the measure is triple." As marked by Stravinsky, the Mersenne source displays the five-beat grouping that will later appear in *Agon.*

Yet beyond the obvious rhythmic replication, the composer employs melodic and even harmonic pitch materials that are unmistakably related to the Mersenne examples he carefully studied. In effect, the Mersenne melodies provided the fountainhead for *Agon*'s first Pas de trois, creating a reservoir from which Stravinsky drew many compositional ideas, not just rhythmic ones. Nor is this surprising. Stravinsky often transmuted melodic lines (most notably, folk songs in his early works) beyond the point of recognition. He would retain the essence of the original but transform it rhythmically, harmonically, contrapuntally, texturally—whatever was useful—in reconstructing the idea to meet his compositional needs. Ironically, in his encyclopedic 1588 *Orchésographie,* Thoinot Arbeau (upon whom de Lauze frequently relies) complains, "Some ignoramuses have corrupted the movements of the branle de Poitou but I will not be party to this." Yet for Stravinsky, classicist though he was, corruption was an integral part of the compositional process. As always, the composer made use of the Mersenne melodies as a catalyst to stimulate his own imaginative thinking, not as models to be considered sacrosanct.[11]

Likewise, the tune for Mersenne's Bransle Gay (fig. 10.3, top line) is replicated in the entire opening passage of *Agon's* counterpart. Stravinsky marked in red and boxed the relevant *Apologie* passage: "The second [bransle] is named 'Bransle Gay,' which is composed of four steps and in order to get the cadence better begins with the last [of these] by bending [the] knees a little so as to join both heels in rising on the toes." He actually highlights the expression "rising on the toes," once more confirming that his interests transcended the musical models he studied. The composer further marks, "One must set aside the left foot, and make the other follow it. . . . Let it go gently to the side, in sliding on the heel." That *Agon's* Bransle Gay includes patterns that reflect Stravinsky's marking of these specific passages, as we shall see, hints at the possibility that the composer discussed the *Apologie* with Balanchine when they eventually met to exchange preliminary ideas about the ballet. Moreover Stravinsky's early sketches for the dance show that he sometimes inserted specific choreographic directions directly on the page. Vera Stravinsky remembers that her husband "had little dancers posed the way he thought they should be." In a draft for the Bransle Gay, the composer writes on his sketch, "Dancer only turning her head to meet the male dancer," and marks an arrow at the exact point in the score where this gesture is to occur.[12]

Finally, *Agon's* Bransle Simple employs two males engaged in a brisk catch-as-catch-can canon, matching Stravinsky's scoring for the trumpet duet. In alluding to this specific bransle, de Lauze observes, "Young men who have an excess of agility make these divisions at their pleasure"—as good a description as any for the "agile" choreography Balanchine created. Moreover, de Lauze explains those divisions as constituting a dance having eight definable steps, also reflected in *Agon.* Musically, the Mersenne example Stravinsky studied allows six measures of double time for these same eight steps in setting the Bransle. Although eventually he deviated slightly from Mersenne's rhythmic pattern, he considered it important enough that he first copied the temporal divisions at the top of his sketch page as a preliminary guide—a procedure followed through several of *Agon's* sketches (as they were with *Apollo*). Only later did he graft his serially organized pitch materials onto these preexistent rhythmic patterns, which by that stage of the compositional process had given way to his own transformed concept of Mersenne's model.

Stravinsky marked virtually every *Apologie* passage describing the bransle; but he did not stop there. Further annotations reveal that he closely studied the history of other dance forms too. Just so, the dances of *Agon's* first Pas de trois also find their origins in de Lauze and Mersenne. Although the sarabande is not discussed in either Arbeau or de Lauze, Mersenne addresses the form in his *Harmonie universelle;* this suggests that Stravinsky's research into courtly dances was broader than many have assumed. Wildeblood's edition did include a Mersenne example of one common sarabande rhythm (there were several), and Stravinsky bases his conception of the dance in *Agon* upon that reprinted rhythmic scheme ♩ ♩ ♩ | ♩. ♩ ♩ .

Mersenne wrote, "A Sarabande is danced to the sound of the guitar and castanets—its steps are composed of tirades or glissades." Both instruments appear prominently in *Agon,* with the distinctive clacking of the castanets in the Bransle Gay and the "mandolino" in both the Galliard and the coda of the first Pas de trois (although the mandolin appears as early as measure 10 in the opening Pas de quatre). Mersenne had also written of a sarabande, "All the little bones—or knuckle bones—and little sticks of wood, or other matter, . . . are held in the fingers." The scintillating tremolos of the xylophone employed in the *Agon* version give an aural approximation of such an effect, especially the rapid figurations typical of the instruments and sounds Mersenne lists. Stravinsky's desire to bring a measure of choreographic authenticity to *Agon's* Saraband-Step is further demonstrated by several markings written directly into his compositional sketches, including, "Sarabande Step (male dancer)—Five Steps forwards and Three Steps backwards." And if any further evidence of his borrowing is needed, under the explanation of the sarabande in the *Apologie,* Stravinsky underlined, "sometimes forwards, sometimes backwards."

Agon's Galliard, choreographed for two female dancers, follows next. Arbeau's discussion in *Orchésographie* is extensive, explaining the complex dance patterns needed to complement the rhythmically intricate music. While a galliard was traditionally cast in some form of triple meter, Stravinsky's treatment was much more elaborate, employing a crosscutting metric and rhythmic scheme that purposely blurs the division of pulses. In fact, it is precisely an alternation of duple and triple divisions that marks the galliard's long history. Known to musicians as hemiola, the practice of dividing six pulses into two groups of three (♫♪ ♫♪) or three groups of two (♫ ♫ ♫) creates an aurally perceivable internal temporal division. The choreographic implications of this important musical setting surely stimulated Balanchine's thinking. As always his feel for the underlying musical structure furnished his departure point for the movement. The Galliard's multilayered rhythmic and metric framework finds its visual counterpoint in the middle section of the dance.

Arbeau's description, summarized by Wildeblood, of the galliard as a dance that contains six steps and six notes played in triple finds its analogue in Balanchine's choreography and Stravinsky's music. Here again, Stravinsky focused on the Mersenne example, also in Wildeblood, which provides the obvious architectural plan for *Agon's* Galliard. Moreover, Stravinsky widened his study, consulting additional sources as he explored the musical and choreographic components of the dance. In his earliest sketches, the composer actually notates what appear to be several samples of preexisting galliards on the manuscript page itself. Apparently they served as a handy guide while he drafted his preliminary ideas.

In *Orchésographie,* Arbeau's student Capriol remarks, "We always played a galliard called 'Romanesque' on our lutes and cithers." We know that Stravinsky was just then studying the music of several sixteenth-century lute composers, including the well-known *vihuela* player and composer Luis de Milán. He was also perusing the important galliards of the lutenist John Dowland. (Although Stravinsky once proclaimed that the lute was his favorite instrument, he clearly decided that the mandolin's more penetrating sound would cut through the ballet's instrumentation more markedly.) His acquaintance with such Renaissance music surely accounts for the unique use of a mandolin in *Agon's* Galliard. Finally, the de Lauze manual states, "From the Italians come the Gaillarde; or Romanesque," and Stravinsky writes at the top of his compositional sketches, "*Gaillarde* (Garliarde) Saltarello, Romanesca," suggesting that he was thoroughly exploring such dances. He even consulted lexicographer Paul-Emile Littré's celebrated *Dictionnaire de la langue française,* published in 1874. (Stravinsky owned the entire multivolume set, and a coffee-stained page 1816 confirms that he looked up the definition of this specific dance.) The composer copied Littré's definition on a small index card, stapling it to his compositional sketches as yet another crib to guide him.

Between 1953 and 1957, Balanchine and Stravinsky met often to discuss *Agon's* development. Balanchine claimed that it was he who decided on twelve dancers, conceding that the two-to-one ratio of eight females to four males was Stravinsky's idea. He also recalled that Stravinsky offered specific choreographic suggestions from the beginning. Once Stravinsky began composing, and even as his preliminary ideas took shape, his notations of stick figures and spatial diagrams throughout his sketches reveal a constant awareness of the work's choreographic demands. Balanchine recalled discussing the character and tempo of each dance, and as always Stravinsky's first order of business was to establish the ballet's precompositional temporal boundaries: "We discussed timing and decided that the whole ballet should last about twenty minutes. Stravinsky always breaks things down to essentials. We talked about how many minutes the first part should last, what to allow for the *pas de deux* and the other dances. We narrowed the plan as specifically as possible. To have all the time in the world means nothing to Stravinsky. 'When I know how long a piece must take, then it excites me.'"[13]

After receiving the de Lauze manual, Stravinsky informed Kirstein that the ballet would be ready "sometime in November or December 1954." But by October reality set in, and as he resumed his heavy touring, time for composition again grew scarce. The earliest rough sketches are dated December 1953 (just after the increasingly serially oriented, but not yet twelve-tone composer finished his *Three Songs From William Shakespeare*).[14] He next wrote to Kirstein in August 1954, now nearly a year after receiving the de Lauze, assuring him that completing the ballet was his priority. He informed Kirstein that he and Balanchine had already "established the whole structure" while Balanchine was in California (the New York City Ballet was performing in Los Angeles from July through mid-August). Balanchine and Stravinsky frequently met during the afternoons in the composer's Hollywood home. It was then that the architecture of *Agon* was decided. In her interview with Genevieve Oswald, Vera Stravinsky remembered hearing Balanchine and her husband talking and singing in the composer's studio, and "each time they came [out, they] were very satisfied. He [Stravinsky] would say, 'Good, we did a lot today.'"

These summer sessions yielded one of the most illuminating documents found from the Stravinsky and Balanchine collaborations. A record of their exchanges, in the form of a detailed summary chart, plots each component of *Agon's* planned action. The draft is written in Stravinsky's hand on several single leaves of paper that track his evolving ideas. At one point some leaves were cut—a part of the sheet was ripped off—and another sheet detailing revisions was substituted, as several stapled leaves reveal. This in-progress document, reproduced in a number of sources, delineates the three (not four, as many authors contend) main sections of the ballet. *Agon's* tripartite structure is represented by the three roman numerals notated by Stravinsky. The document also includes the titles of individual dances, the specific temporal durations for each section, and several stick figures drawn by Stravinsky that illustrate the various male and female configurations for each dance.[15]

As useful as this remarkable document is, it represents the end product of Stravinsky and Balanchine's summer exchanges, not the original version, as is often erroneously contended.[16] Several earlier, unpublished leaves (held in the Sacher Stiftung) reveal that the composer and choreographer often changed their minds in the normal give-and-take of discussion. Their initial ideas about the ballet's specific formal divisions, durations, dance forms, and combinations of dancers constantly changed as their concept developed. Thus the often-reproduced facsimile shows where their thought process ended as of mid-August 1954, not where it began.

Initially they conceived of a different balletic order. Several individual dances carried no durational suggestions, and those that did were often altered. What now stands as the ballet's Prelude was added later. Originally, the composer and choreographer planned a women's quartet just after the Pas de deux (Stravinsky sketched four skirted dancers in a straight line), probably to balance the ballet's opening Pas de quatre for men. Another discarded sheet exhibits a boxed area with four couples in a line ("Dance of the Four Duos," as it was originally entitled) and underneath Stravinsky wrote, "SINFONIA," a movement that was never used. Below that, he drew four groups of two females and one male each ("Dance of the Four Trios"). Farther down the sheet he sketched another boxed area with four males in a line, adding the word "EPYLOGUE" (*sic*) in the center of the box (which in effect became the final coda) and to the left and right he drew four females in each corner of the box. On the reverse side of this discarded sheet is a detailed sketch of the final scene, assigning specific positions for all twelve dancers. No durations are given for these abandoned ideas.

The titles for several of the court dances were also appended, sometimes months later. Other annotations are made in red and blue pencil, a sure tip-off (as in *Orpheus*) that these are revisions rather than first thoughts. Some of these markings may have been added after Balanchine returned to New York, and, as with the notated scenario for *Orpheus,* Stravinsky probably returned to this summary chart (fig. 10.4) as his ideas continued evolving.

By the fall of 1954 it appeared that the ballet would be ready in 1955 or early 1956—both target dates proposed by Kirstein. Then, in a 16 December 1954 letter, Stravinsky requested a lunch meeting with Balanchine and Kirstein to discuss some of the ballet's "technical problems." The luncheon led to a mutually agreed-upon postponement of the premiere until 1957. The fact is, Stravinsky

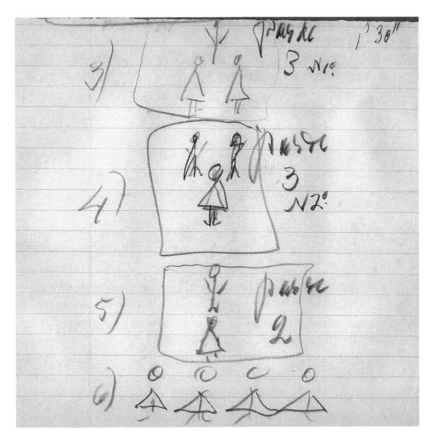

10.4 Page from an early draft of *Agon* showing Stravinsky and Balanchine's original conception for different balletic orders. The tear at the top of the sheet where Stravinsky ripped it
off is visible. (The Igor Stravinsky Collection, Paul Sacher Foundation, Basel)

wished to accept a commission from the Biennale festival in Venice. Naturally,
Balanchine and Kirstein honored Stravinsky's requested deferral.[17] Once again,
Agon was put aside. The composer resumed work in the spring of 1956, now
writing the bransles.

While awaiting the premiere of his *Canticum Sacrum* at the Biennale during
the late summer of 1956, Stravinsky continued working on the ballet. Balanchine and his company were also in Venice, and the composer and choreographer met to discuss the ballet's progress. In September, Balanchine first heard
parts of the score—perhaps through sections of the bransles just then being
composed. The next month Stravinsky suffered a stroke and Le Clercq contracted polio. The composition of *Agon* again came to a halt. On 15 March 1957,

and now back in Hollywood, Stravinsky resumed work. "Now it is my responsibility to finish the composition of *Agon,*" he wrote to Nicolas Nabokov, "but this music cannot be rushed."[18] The ballet was completed on 27 April. Balanchine arrived in California on 16 June to attend the orchestral premiere in Los Angeles the next day. The score was recorded on 18 June, and Balanchine stayed a few days to work with Stravinsky in preparation for the ballet's New York premiere that fall.

The string of interruptions plaguing *Agon's* history constantly deflected the composer's concentration. Still, the ballet was never far from his mind. In tracking the unusually large diversity of models and compositional procedures Stravinsky enlisted, the work's sketch materials prove particularly informative. As the actual workaday composing of *Agon* unfolded, Stravinsky's challenge became to find a way to meld the disparate resources and techniques employed each time he picked up, put aside, and then resumed writing. He jotted down ideas whenever he could. Unlike the evidence for the methodical, mostly sequential development of *Apollo,* there is no neatly compiled sketchbook chronicling *Agon's* day-to-day progress. Instead, there survives a mosaic of ideas, difficult to reassemble. In all, the Stiftung houses about eighty basically unordered sketch pages. The composer notated ideas on loose-leaf sheets, which are sometimes dated, sometimes not. There are countless scraps of paper (many no larger than a few inches in size) inscribed with roughly envisioned ideas of only a measure or two. Stravinsky drafted ideas on whatever paper was handy, including his wife's "La Boutique" business stationery. An assortment of index cards records everything from a short pitch series tidily charted by the composer to a subtle rhythmic change offered as an alternative to an already composed passage.

Given the serial experiments undertaken in the works immediately preceding *Agon,* it comes as no surprise that the ballet's sketches reveal a preoccupation with pitch manipulation. Stravinsky's adoption of the serialist's vocabulary, especially the technique of pitch rotation, serves as an overarching force throughout the ballet.[19] In addition, several compositional scraps (hardly qualifying even as rough sketches) demonstrate the composer's systematic and exhaustive efforts to mine the properties of a limited number of compactly constructed pitch configurations. He often sketched short motivic ideas, especially three-, four-, and six-note segments—all divisible subsets of *Agon's* numerically magical twelve.

Among the sketches is a four-by-two-inch remnant on which Stravinsky constructed one of the ballet's most fundamental four-note cells. He first notated the pitch collection abstractly (without any rhythmic character, as is typical throughout his sketches), then wrote the same series backward, constructing the retrograde version. Next he worked out the inversion of the original four pitches, creating a kind of mirror image in which an intervallic leap moves down, where it originally jumped up. Finally, Stravinsky notated the retrograde inversion in which the original series proceeds both backward and upside down. There is nothing exceptional about these commonly employed serial procedures, but the sketch confirms how meticulously Stravinsky worked through each of these operations.

Beyond matters of pitch control, Stravinsky, not surprisingly, consistently clocks individual sections of *Agon* with temporal precision. He fastidiously marks the duration of individual passages in total seconds, sometimes as often as every few measures. The chart he and Balanchine settled upon during their 1954 summer discussions served only as an initial, general guide. Once he began composing, Stravinsky started modifying the ballet's internal divisions, although he did so while constantly monitoring the music's overall flow. Throughout he was clearly aware of the ballet's temporal dimensions at every structural level as he pieced together each part of the whole.

Consider the Pas de deux, nearly six minutes in total length (when one includes the coda) and partitioned into six choreographically identifiable divisions: (1) the traditional opening adagio for both dancers (mm. 411–62); (2) the male solo variation (mm. 463–73); (3) the female solo variation (mm. 473–83); (4) a brief reprise of the solo male variation (mm. 484–94); (5) a remarkable coda for both soloists (mm. 495–511); and (6) the final quasi-stretto, providing the link to the four duos that follow (mm. 512–19). On yet another index card, Stravinsky notes the specific durations for each of six divisions as well, though these do not coordinate exactly with the six choreographic sections actually labeled in the printed score. The composer taped the card to a summary sheet that had already recorded the durations of the ballet's earlier sections (a total of 12' 15", Stravinsky carefully marked).

The index card itself (marked "Pas de deux") includes six concise comments: (1) "3 bars of 'Prelude,' 13 seconds," referring to the fact that the Pas de deux begins with material based upon the preceding Prelude, thus forging a smooth link; (2) " $\flat$ = 112, 2 minutes 40 seconds," a duration ending at measure 452; (3) "6/16 7/16 5/16 etc, 20 seconds," referring to the constantly shifting meter of measures 452–62 that brings the opening adagio to a close; (4) " $\flat$ = 126, 44 seconds," a reference to the next passage, in which the choreographic configuration of soloists is actually notated by the composer in the score ("Male

Dancer at m. 463, Female Dancer at 473, Male Dancer Refrain at m. 484"); (5) "'Coda,' ♩ = 112, 18 seconds," beginning at measure 495 (marked by Stravinsky "Both dancers" in the published score); followed by (6) "Doppio lento ♩ = 66, 28 seconds." While these internal calculations are characteristically precise, their total (marked as "4′ 03″" by Stravinsky on the card) falls more than a minute short of the actual performance length. But on the index card Stravinsky underlines the marking "28 seconds" of the doppio lento, perhaps an indication that the passage could be repeated (and perhaps resulting from Balanchine's urging?). He also later added measures 512–19 as a transition to the concluding dances, accounting for an additional 30 seconds, thus bringing the duet to its six-minute overall length.[20]

Other index cards taped onto larger sketch sheets disclose Stravinsky's many reconsiderations. One card fusses with the smallest rhythmic details. Consider the Prelude following the triple Pas de quatre. The composer notates one of the movement's basic rhythmic cells (m. 128). Originally he used the rather traditional dotted rhythm ♩. ♫ ♬ ; but he changed his mind, reversing the beginning of the figure to ♪♪. ♬ , a kind of Scotch snap, as musicians call it. Thereafter the motive's revision is retained in every subsequent appearance in the Prelude, as it is tossed imitatively through the quartet of trumpets in measures 128–30. At first glance it seems to be a minor change, but this subtle alteration tends to attract the ear because of its distinctive aural bite. Structurally, the short-long rhythmic grouping of this dyad provides a unifying function. It had first appeared in measure 10 of the Pas de quatre as an important figure. One notes its ubiquitous use in other sections too, especially in the opening of the Saraband-Step (m. 146), whose first triple-meter measure has the rhythm ♪♪. ♪♪. ♩.. Thus a subtle but important rhythmic link is forged wherein the Prelude introduces this opening dance in the first Pas de trois (it is used in several later parts of *Agon* as well, where it appears as ♪♪ or is lengthened to ♪♩).

The Saraband-Step also reveals other aspects of the composer's sketching habits. In drafting the earliest nub of an idea, sometimes he sketched only the basic contour of a line, without any specific rhythm, pitch, harmony, or texture. For example, in mapping out the beginning of the Saraband-Step, Stravinsky initially outlined what amounts to no more than a skeletal figure, doubtless based upon some of the sarabandes he was then studying. The sketch reveals that Stravinsky originally drafted four pitches that rose in one direction while overlapping five pitches that descended, both lines converging into a chord. The final version of what ultimately became measure 148 exhibits a much more embellished version, in keeping with the stylized dance's character. Now part of the original figure is assigned to the violin solo, while the two trombones fill out what was the basic descent of the lower line. The final chord of the original sketch is retained.

From the roughly envisioned preliminary shape, the composer worked through various phases in completing the details. The sketches demonstrate that he drafted four separate openings, each with a different instrumentation and all progressing toward the overall duration of 1′ 15″ that he and Balanchine stipulated (fig. 10.5). Moreover, the most identifiable sound of the dance, the xylophone, is nowhere to be found in any of these early sketches, suggesting that it was added later, perhaps to help simulate the instrumental sound recommended by Arbeau and Mersenne. As mentioned earlier, Stravinsky was aware of the dance's original choreographic structure. He marked on the sketches themselves, "Male dancer, Five Steps forward, and three steps backwards," just as in the *Apologie,* he underlined the section of the Mersenne *Suite* that specified "sometimes forward, sometimes backwards."

As usual, Stravinsky continually rethought the internal ordering of each dance's musical materials. He regularly deleted, inserted, added, and repositioned measures. Ideas that would eventually stand as the middle, climactic, or closing passage of the movement were often worked out first. Only later was the opening passage conceived, often as the last phase of the compositional process. The *Agon* sketches also show that, typically, he struggled most with transitional passages, sometimes laboring over them in multiple drafts as he created just the right link.

While many drafts are occupied with forging a cohesive pitch structure, other sketches reveal Stravinsky's reliance upon the de Lauze and Mersenne models—an overarching reliance that governs the rhythmic and metric underpinnings of both the first and the second Pas de trois. While the de Lauze dances provided a departure point, they came at the cost of a new problem; for the composer now needed to reconcile such pretonal models within a posttonal environment—Josquin's world with the world of the serialist. In the hands of a lesser composer, a collision of incongruities could easily have resulted; but Stravinsky was alert to the pitfalls of uniting these two harmonic worlds. Many sketch scraps exhibit his careful graphing of Mersenne rhythms on one side of the paper while on the other he charts pitch rotations and transpositions that were subsequently grafted onto the Mersenne scheme.

Adding to what could have easily become a hodgepodge of competing ideas and techniques, at about the midway point of the ballet the composer added one final, potentially obfuscating ingredient: a full-blown Webernesque twelve-

10.5 An early sketch for the opening of the Sarabande (m. 3), followed by Stravinsky's final version (The Igor Stravinsky Collection, Paul Sacher Foundation, Basel. Also Courtesy of Boosey and Hawkes.)

tone approach. His adoption of the technique is first manifested in the coda of the first Pas de trois. It marked a sea change—a turn of historic proportions. Actually, it is even more historic than musicians may realize since Stravinsky's sketches demonstrate that this, his first twelve-tone composition, was completed in December 1954, and thus earlier than the *Canticum Sacrum,* usually taken as his initial twelve-tone foray.

In one of the coda's first sketches (see fig. 10.6) he wrote out the row, then constructed its inversion, retrograde, and retrograde inversion—all marked clearly but without rhythmic shape. Moreover, here, as in many preliminary sketches and complete drafts, Stravinsky took the time to write in his analysis of individual rows. Using his colored pencils, he marked one form of the row in red, another in blue. He often marked each individual note in the row as the pitches wove through the orchestration. He also frequently marked which form he was employing: original, inversion, retrograde, and so on. Here, in the coda's first draft, Stravinsky immediately began sketching the music of what would become measures 198–200 as based upon this series. The top line of the sketch is the row in its original, or prime, form; while the lowest line shows the start of what will be an inversional form as it ultimately appears in the piano and trombone parts of the final score.[21] The violin solo in the middle layer is nonserial.

Stravinsky's conversion to dodecaphony was not only jolting; it was remarkably fresh and facile. He assimilated the technique deftly. From the coda to the end, with the exception of the work's final, non-twelve-tone music, which is reprised to create a cohesive closure, *Agon* becomes a dodecaphonic composition.[22] The fundamental compositional procedures of serialism and twelve-tone writing are essentially the same: a twelve-tone row, or series, is conceived and submitted to the operations of retrograde, inversion, and retrograde inversion. The composer also generates other forms of the basic twelve-tone row through rotation and transposition (that is, while the same order of notes is used, the row begins on a different pitch, thus producing a new collection). Oftentimes, Stravinsky breaks the twelve-tone row into two hexachords, exploring the various possibilities of one hexachord for half of a piece, and the second hexachord of the row for the other half.

Figure 10.7 shows an early sketch and the final score of the Bransle Simple. Stravinsky notates a hexachord in the treble clef, then in the bass clef immediately to the right he sketches the inversion. Just below the original hexachord, he works out the retrograde form. Finally, he constructs a fourth version, which amounts to a retrograde inversion beginning on the original pitch D. Below these four forms, he now sketches a rough version of what becomes the open-

a) Stravinsky's sketch for the rows

b) Author's transcribed music example of Stravinsky's sketch

10.6 Summary chart of early rows and sketches for the Coda (The Igor Stravinsky Collection, Paul Sacher Foundation, Basel. Also Courtesy of Boosey and Hawkes.)

c) Stravinsky's sketch for the first nine measures of the Coda

d) Author's transcribed music example of Stravinsky's sketch

10.6 (*continued*)

e) Final version of the section from the printed score

10.6 (*continued*)

ing of the Bransle. The composer next brackets three iterations of the hexachord. Just beneath, he also sketches a preliminary version of what will serve as
the canonic imitation ultimately assigned to the two trumpets.[23] Finally, it
should be noted that Stravinsky uses this single hexachord (with one exception)
rather than a complete twelve-tone row as the pitch material for the entire
Bransle.

Stravinsky drafted the second half of the next dance, the Bransle Gay, first
(beginning with m. 321). He dated this sketch 8 June 1956, marking at the end,
"about 50 seconds." Then, on 16 July, the composer began working out the
beginning of the dance, writing measures 310–20. A new hexachord is employed—in terms of twelve-tone theory the Bransle Gay's hexachord is the
complement to the Bransle Simple's hexachord. That is, when both are combined, a complete row constituting all twelve pitches results, and this, as we
shall see, will have choreographic consequences for Balanchine's conception of
the bransles forming this cluster.

The Bransle Double combines both hexachords, taking full advantage of the
complete twelve-tone row for the first time.[24] In that sense this final bransle is

10.7 An early sketch of the Bransle Simple, followed by the final version of the opening measures (The Igor Stravinsky Collection, Paul Sacher Foundation, Basel. Also Courtesy of Boosey and Hawkes.)

a culmination of the earlier two dances. We already know that both the rhythm and the melodic shape (though not the exact pitches) stem from the Mersenne model. As seen in figure 10.8, Stravinsky actually notated a rhythmic graph of the Mersenne bransle right onto his sketches, including the brackets he had notated in Wildeblood's edition. And while the sketch materials are cast in triple meter, Stravinsky added, "To be beaten in 3/2," which is how the score was ultimately notated. Finally, he marked at the end, "Duration = 0.44," another indication that he was continuing to keep watch of the overall temporal pacing.

For musicians, the careful structuring of the ballet's score, traceable through these few representative sketches, speaks to Stravinsky's adoption of serial and dodecaphonic techniques. Yet in a broader sense, what isn't new about the sketching process may be more important than what is. There remains a deeper unifying sense of structural coherence. It is the composer's need to fuse virtually every idea employed that may best define his fundamental creative approach. In that sense, *Agon* is not so different from a work like *Apollo,* where intra- and inter-dance connections are perhaps more obvious.

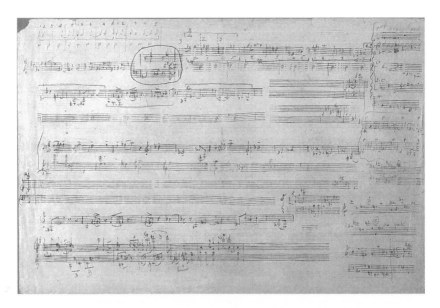

10.8 Stravinsky's sketches for the Bransle Double. Note the rhythmic graph in the upper left corner, the bracketing of measures toward the center of the top line, and the hexachordal pitch permutations down the right edge of the sketch page. (The Igor Stravinsky Collection, Paul Sacher Foundation, Basel)

The sketches may prove even more insightful for dancers. In tracking these internal operations, we can begin to discover Balanchine's coordination of the score with his choreographic techniques. He was far too wise to fall into a common trap and illustrate every pitch rotation and every retrograde inversion with a matching physical gesture. But there is no question that he understood the basic compositional principles at work. Armed with that knowledge in a way no other choreographer was capable of assimilating, he fashioned a ballet that would provide an "equivalent" (to use his word)—a parallel that is only graspable through a thorough understanding of the interior network of Stravinsky's complex score. As the composer commented, his "past and present time worlds" could not be the same.[25] To which we might add that whatever world Stravinsky inhabited, Balanchine's sensibilities allowed him to discover the perfect choreographic complement.

Chapter 11 Choreography or Carpentry? Assembling a Visual Complement to the Music of *Agon*

In order to compose dances for Agon, I have abandoned my attitude as a cook and tried to put myself in the state of mind of a carpenter. . . . I must try to find some visual equivalent which is a complement; not an illustration. Such music as Stravinsky's cannot be illustrated. *Agon* was invented for dancing, but it is hard to invent dances of a comparable density, quality, metrical insistence, variety, formal mastery or symmetrical asymmetry. Just as a cabinetmaker must select his wood for the job . . . so a ballet carpenter must find [a] dominant quality of gesture, a strain or palette of consistent movement, an active scale of flowing patterns which reveals to the eye what Stravinsky tells the sensitized ear. . . . But this ballet is not a chest of drawers. It is closer to an IBM electronic computer. It is a machine, but a machine that thinks.
—*George Balanchine, 1957*

The inviolable principles of order, discipline, symmetry, control—abstract but abiding ideas that ally Stravinsky to Ockeghem, Josquin, Mersenne, de Lauze, Arbeau, and Webern in a common protocol—can quickly be lost in the labyrinthine maze of *Agon*'s intricate pitch language. In musical terms alone, *Agon*, though written at age seventy-five, is one of the composer's freshest, most puissant works. But

although musicians may not wish to admit it, were it not for Balanchine's arresting visualization, audiences probably would not have responded to Stravinsky's score as enthusiastically as they did. "One thing is clear to me," wrote
Stravinsky and Balanchine's compatriot, the violinist Nathan Milstein, "I don't
think that anyone except for a small circle of specialists would ever have known
Stravinsky's late works if it had not been for Balanchine"; and he added, "If
contemporary audiences know *Agon,* that's thanks solely to Balanchine."[1]

Stravinsky himself doubted how well the work would be received, steering
clear of the ballet's premiere for fear the piece would fail. At home in California, he cabled Debbie Ishlon of Columbia Records in New York on 25 November: "Are you going to the premiere of AGON tomorrow? I can imagine the reaction of the listeners paying $50 a seat to [hear] my new score!" But his fears were
unfounded: *Agon* was an instant, unqualified success. The composer's son
Soulima attended the opening night performance, telegramming his father of
the ballet's astonishing success. Eugene Berman wrote on 9 December, "I am
sending you more clippings about *Agon.* As you can see for yourself, the reviews
and notices were quite extraordinary (considering the fact that most critics usually write very silly things quite beyond the point). I don't think you could ask
for greater general appreciation and elation and for more grateful joy over the
wonderful fusion of your genius with that of Balanchine."[2]

The participants in the early performances were completely entranced by the
work's energy. In another unpublished letter held by the Sacher Stiftung, Diana
Adams, who joined Arthur Mitchell in the sensuously beautiful Pas de deux,
wrote to the composer shortly after the premiere: "Just a note to tell you of our
pleasure and excitement in performing *Agon.* I wish it were on each program.
We are still not 'note-perfect' but we seize Kopeikine and the stage at every opportunity and our concentration is intense, so we improve! The audience response is tremendous, they seem to love it, and several more performances have
been added. I do hope you have seen the notices, they were marvelous. Congratulations, and thank you for our beautiful, beautiful score."

The critical praise was uncurbed. Kirstein—as perceptive as ever—spoke of
the fundamental musical-choreographic connections: "No dance work has
been more highly organized or is so dense in movement in its bare twenty minutes. Clock time has no reference to visual duration: there is more concentrated
movement in *Agon* than in most nineteenth-century ballets. . . . *Agon* was by
no means 'pure' ballet, 'about dancing only.' It was an existential metaphor for
tension and anxiety." Denby noted in his aforementioned essay that the premiere "was given an enormous ovation. . . . The balcony stood up shouting and

whistling when the choreographer took his bow. Downstairs, people came out into the lobby, their eyes bright as if the piece had been champagne. Marcel Duchamp, the painter, said he felt the way he had after the opening of *Le Sacre*. At later performances, *Agon* continued to be unreservedly applauded. Some people found the ballet set their teeth on edge. The dancers show nothing but coolness and brilliantly high spirits." Walter Terry wrote in the *Herald-Tribune*: "For sheer invention, for intensive exploitation of the human body and the designs which it can create, *Agon* is quite possibly the most brilliant ballet creation of our day." And as Clement Crisp wrote, "*Agon* is plainly a masterpiece of our time. Watching it we live more intensely, life becomes more brilliant, more electric."[3]

Agon did indeed invite viewers to live more intensely, and in that sense it was a most timely work. It erupted onto the New York ballet scene in the late autumn of 1957, hardly a month after the Soviet Union had launched Sputnik, thereby marking the dawn of the Space Age. Stravinsky and Balanchine's "futuristic" ballet, as it was quickly tagged, was bound to invite interstellar comparisons. *Agon* was "like travel in outer space," Denby wrote, pushing the envelope of the dance universe with its "jetlike extensions," "soundless whirl," and "intent stillness." Just as the Russian space shot redefined the edge of our earthly limits, Stravinsky and Balanchine's newest collaboration challenged the conception of musical-balletic time and space, producing, as A. V. Coton wrote, "a celestial marriage of music and movement." Precision was the byword. Balanchine's likening of the ballet to an electronic computer was right on the money: "It is a machine, but a machine that thinks . . . a measured construction in space, demonstrated by moving bodies." The work's computerlike temporal exactness was emblematic; its techno-precision, both musically and choreographically, matched the spirit of a new era. *Agon* was, as Denby noted, a bold new work poised on "the acute edge of risk."[4]

One of those risks was bravely asserted in the ballet's Pas de deux, which paired Arthur Mitchell with Diana Adams. In one of the most visually insinuating dances Balanchine ever conceived, this famous partnering of a black male dancer and a white female dancer appeared at a racially volatile moment in U.S. history. The very public, divisive advancement of civil rights forced the country to rethink long-crystallized attitudes. Balanchine, his dancers attest, was acutely aware of the inevitable controversy; but rather than shrink away, he exploited it fully. Melissa Hayden remembered, "The first time you saw Diana Adams and Arthur Mitchell doing the pas de deux it was really awesome to see a black hand touch a white skin. That's where we were coming from in the fifties."[5]

11.1 Arthur Mitchell and Suzanne Farrell in the Pas de deux from *Agon,* from a 1967 production by the New York City Ballet (Photograph by Martha Swope/TimePix)

The choreographer's provocative coupling of Mitchell and Adams, however, should not be misconstrued: Balanchine had no desire to use dance as a public soapbox for defiant political statements. Rather, he had always delighted in creating jarring visual impacts. More than anyone, he realized that such a stark contrast would viscerally intensify the visual polarity that *Agon* often sought (fig. 11.1). It was just one further aspect of the "contest" that went to *Agon*'s core. Whatever racial implications others would read into the pairing of Mitchell and Adams did not seem to concern him one way or another. As Mitchell himself recalled, "There was a definite use of the skin tones in terms of Diana being so pale and me being so dark, so that even the placing of the hands or the arms provided a color structure integrated into the choreographic one."[6] More than any perceived racial overtones, Balanchine worried about the audience's reaction to the choreographic challenges the dance summoned. Marian Horosko joined Balanchine in the wings as the Pas de deux was performed that first night:

> He was standing there watching and then the audience began to laugh, titter, and I thought, "well, they just don't understand or they think it's strange or something." (You know, Arthur's hand coming out in strange places. Mr. B. had a little perverse sense of humor sometimes. He was naughty in a pixie-ish way. That was one part of

him and the other sense of humor was a sexy sensuality. That was the combination I think that Arthur and Diana brought to that particular movement and the audience caught it and laughed. I think, because it was slightly embarrassing and they didn't understand it.) I took a quick look at him, because I was startled by that and I think I caught him the only moment he was ever off guard. And the look of hurt in his face was really quite pronounced and there were almost tears in his eyes.[7]

Indeed, some of the images portrayed in the Pas de deux were exceedingly suggestive, summoning another level of risk. The female was allowed, as no woman had been before, to participate in explicitly shaping the sexuality of the action. No longer does she demurely play the manipulated, submissive respondent. To a far greater degree than the women of *Apollo* and *Orpheus, Agon's* eight women symbolize a new level of empowerment. In terms of both gender and sexuality, not only does the ballet "celebrate strong, independent women and present triangular partnerships dispassionately," as Sally Banes suggests in *Dancing Women,* but it offers a "modernist" view of love.[8] It bids us pause to question both the virtues and the limitations of cultural traditions, just as Mitchell and Adams's integrative dance forces us to question too-often engrafted biases.

Whatever political and gender connotations we care to assign, Balanchine's approach to the ballet, as always, began with his study of the score. It is doubtful that even he, outstanding musician that he was, could have fully understood either the complexity of Stravinsky's rhythmic transformation of the Mersenne models or the composer's manipulation of pitch collections. How could he? So deeply encoded was Stravinsky's intricately woven web of diverse materials that today's music analysts continue to argue about how to untangle it. But there is no question that the choreographer was keenly aware of the work's cryptography. He worked especially hard to decipher its many conundrums; for only by solving them could he, as the musician-choreographer he was, conceive of a synchronous visual complement.

Balanchine heard the rhythmic implications of *Agon's* many musical canons and visualized them inventively, not just imitatively. He recognized that the basic serial procedures of pitch inversion and retrograde could find a choreographic correlation in the many mirror images permeating the ballet. And most important, he understood that *Agon's* "differentness" demanded a new approach—an approach, he wrote, that would produce a "visual equivalent which is a complement; not an illustration." Moreover, he realized, as do serial and twelve-tone composers, that divisions of the whole were more important than the whole itself, that subsets, not sets, furnished the bonding agent that would tie together *Agon*'s multiplex sources and models. It mattered little to him that Stravinsky's symmetrical ordering of musical cells and transmutative rhythms was inaudible at the music's surface. It was the substructure that counted, especially when it came to expressing choreographically the musical form of a dance.

Balanchine's efforts to master the complex score are well documented. Not only was he in Los Angeles for *Agon*'s 17 June 1957 orchestral premiere, but he also attended at least one rehearsal. He obtained a copy of the orchestra taping Stravinsky had made just after the premiere. Acquainting himself with Stravinsky's orchestration was especially crucial. The use of harp, mandolin, and castanets, as well as the chamberlike reduced orchestra of the middle third of the work, was intimately tied to Balanchine's choreographic concept. It comes as no surprise, for example, that choirs of instruments were associated with gender depictions. The trumpets of the ballet's opening fanfare and Bransle Simple that accompany the males, and the harp and flutes of the Galliard that attend the females are obvious matches, particularly given the composer's explicit references to the many instrumental associations outlined by Arbeau, Mersenne, and de Lauze.

Stravinsky sent the piano reduction of the ballet to Balanchine in April 1957, so the choreographer was already familiar with the score by the time he heard the orchestral premiere. A copy of this informatively annotated document, held in the Sacher archives, reveals Stravinsky's own scrupulously labeled analysis of *Agon*'s serial structure and twelve-tone rows. Thus Balanchine would have been aware of the music's inner workings, at least partially, even before he heard it, through the composer's notated structural analysis. The score is annotated too, possibly by Balanchine himself. Several particularly thorny contrapuntal and rhythmically complex passages are marked to clarify the composer's intent for the dancers. And whether the markings are Balanchine's or not, it is clear that such matters were on his mind while the ballet unfolded and took choreographic form in the rehearsal studio. We know that Balanchine would constantly consult the piano score, darting back and forth from the dancers to the piano in an effort to match what he was seeing with what he was hearing. Sometimes he did more than that.

Melissa Hayden recalls how excited the company was that Balanchine was once again choreographing a new Stravinsky work. She remembers her exhilaration in watching Adams and Mitchell work through the evolution of their duet. Balanchine himself, Hayden remarked, often sat at the piano playing the score. In the Bransle Gay, for instance, he demonstrated to the dancers the different layers of rhythmic activity that Stravinsky had built into the music. He clapped out individual lines, constantly counted the beats of a pattern, marked the accents, described the Spanish flavor of the rhythms, and played various melodic ideas at the piano. He choreographed the first part of the dance without the piano, but the second section was worked out with the piano, in about thirty minutes. Finally, Hayden recalls that she was asked to dance the same bransle a bit faster than he first conceived the tempo, about $\downarrow = 60$. But ultimately Stravinsky wanted it even faster, "jazzier," she recalled, with a tempo of $\downarrow = 72$.[9]

The music's newness—and more to the point, its utterly foreign style—challenged the twelve dancers in unprecedented ways. Simply "counting" the piece posed a considerable task, as Lawrence Sherr learned in an interview with dancer Barbara Walczak: "The challenge was in the patterns—getting past other people on time without hitting somebody and still being on the counts. It was very difficult." Several of the original dancers told of Balanchine piecing *Agon* together in isolated sections. He sometimes sent the cast to different parts of the rehearsal studio so that he could work on different parts of the ballet simultaneously. Consequently, "the dancers were not aware of the overall choreographic design, even after the piece was completed," Walczak reported. Diana Adams spoke of *Agon*'s many musical and choreographic hurdles, including some pedestrian traffic jams: "We used to have hilarious rehearsals in the first part of *Agon* because we were in three groups and at the end of one section when we cross and go to a different position we were always getting there on a different count."[10]

From the start, the composer involved himself in shaping the choreography's fundamental design, as his annotated sketches and frequent meetings with Balanchine demonstrate. Still, his suggestions furnished only a general outline; the details were left to his trusted friend to realize back in the Manhattan studio. Stravinsky did not see any of the ballet until 10 November 1957, a few weeks before the premiere. Even then he was reluctant to attend the rehearsal to which Balanchine, through his close associate Lucia Davidova, invited him. Balanchine was somewhat on edge, working with such a new Stravinsky style. He confided to Davidova that he was worried about the validity of his concept. "I don't even know whether I'm on the right path or not. Would you do me a favor?"—he beckoned Davidova—"Bring him to rehearsal so that I can know his reaction."[11] After some initial hesitation, Stravinsky, who was about to return to Los Angeles, agreed to attend. Roy Tobias, remembered for his dancing in the bransles, recounted his memory to Richard Buckle: "Balanchine was so happy when Stravinsky came downstairs. Everyone was 'at attention.' Stravinsky went to the piano, took off his coat and scarf and said, 'George, to work! To work!' Hitherto, in the opening pas de quatre the four boys had faced the audience. The composer suggested that they should turn their backs. This was agreed. In Melissa's variation [the Bransle Gay, central section of the second Pas de trois] Balanchine made me beat on the stair rail with a stick to represent the castanets. While we were working on the Bransle double . . . [Balanchine] made the boys enter together rather than in canon. During the pas de deux, Kopeikine, at the piano, said, 'I'm terribly sorry. There are parts of this music I don't understand.' Stravinsky said, 'It's perfectly all right. I don't understand them either!'"[12]

Those in attendance reported that Stravinsky was ecstatic about Balanchine's conception. He frequently nodded his approval, conducted passages, complimented the dancers, consulted with Kopeikine, and listened intently to the choreographer's directions and comments. Of the several suggestions he himself offered, none would have been more important than turning the four males away from the audience as the ballet begins, though in fact this was not a new idea: the original chart that he and Balanchine had constructed years earlier specifically directs the men to face toward the back of the stage. According to Bernard Taper, also an observer that day, Stravinsky changed not only Balanchine's beginning but also the ending, including how the males positioned their arms during their closing movements. There also seems to have been discussion about tempi, particularly Balanchine's suggestions to slow down certain sections (the Bransle Gay notwithstanding), with which Stravinsky generally agreed.[13]

Dance historians and critics have offered a profusion of choreographic interpretations for the ballet. The fact that *Agon* is more plotless than any earlier Stravinsky-Balanchine collaboration seems to have roused the most imaginative hypotheses. Robert Garis advances the notion that Balanchine's Pas de deux was at least partially autobiographical. A central influence may have been the choreographer's "work with Le Clercq in physical therapy," he submits. Garis does not suggest that the duet is some mimicry of therapy, but rather, "in both cases the man and woman seem required by some urgent necessity to move quietly, cautiously, with all the skill and courage they can muster, and in a mood of held-breath crisis." Croce submits that *Agon* paints a vibrant portrait of New York City: "The blare and heat in the music, the crazy timing, the disconcerting eruptions in the choreography . . . match the hectic behavior of city streets." Stephanie Jordan's exacting (sometimes measure by measure) dissection of the ballet's compositional and choreographic intersections is less lyrical but surely closer to what Stravinsky and Balanchine had on their minds as they coolly constructed the ballet with the nuts and bolts of their respective crafts.[14]

Several commercial videos of various sections of the ballet are available, including *The Balanchine Celebration: Part Two,* which offers a complete performance of *Agon*'s middle section. Here I address the first Pas de trois and the three bransles of the second Pas de trois since these constitute the de Lauze archetypes Stravinsky studied.[15] The videotape begins with the Prelude, wherein the dancing structurally reflects the music's clearly delineated halves. Trumpets and timpani announce the first section (mm. 121–31) as the two females and male rush center stage with widely extended arms and legs stretching upward. The instrumental register steadily rises higher too, until the climactic trumpet sforzando in measure 131 is reached—a dramatic peak for both the orchestra and the trio of dancers. Balanchine's setting of the quickening metabolism of the music with an equally athletic choreography is eye-popping. With unison gestures throughout, the dancers create a dazzling effect that rushes right in step with the swiftly unfolding score. The incessantly driven motivic rhythms of the trumpet, timpani, and tom-toms provide the foundation for a dynamic contrapuntal exchange between the woodwinds and the strings. Collectively they form one energetic layer of the structure, while the unified visual image of the dancers furnishes another, independent layer of activity that enhances but does not overwhelm the Prelude's overall message. The second half of the Prelude features woodwinds (mm. 136–45) in a dramatically slowed meno mosso section. Whereas the brassy opening section was frenetic, here a mood of stasis prevails. There is a stately Renaissance feel to the dotted rhythms and embellished figures of the flutes and bassoons. The music now proceeds calmly, deliberately, with the processional pace of a regal overture. The two females stand to the side of the male in a mirrored arabesque. It is a gesture reminiscent of the tranquil, unhurried decorum of *Apollo.* The courtly bow performed by all three ushers in the de Lauze dances of the first Pas de trois, as the women depart and the man prepares for the ballet's first solo variation.

The Saraband-Step retains many of the characteristics normally associated with its sixteenth-century model, though it is nigh impossible to detect any historical connection upon first viewing. As Denby remarked, a resemblance to anything remotely familiar is difficult to fathom: "The boy, left alone, begins to walk a Sarabande, elaborately coiled and circumspect. It recalls court dance as much as a cubist still life recalls a pipe or guitar. The boy's timing looks like that of a New York Latin in a leather jacket. And the cool lift of his wrong-way round steps and rhythms gives the nonsense so apt a turn people begin to giggle."[16] It may indeed appear cubist, but the distortion is purposeful; whatever our first impression, Stravinsky and Balanchine's tightly organized setting makes complete structural sense on its own terms.

In keeping with the binary nature of the original form, the dance is divided equally into eight-measure halves (with a two-measure codetta). Its triple meter and rhythmic accents are also consistent with historical models. In both the *A* and *B* halves of the dance, the xylophone part is rhythmically identical, although such substructural connections are not obvious on the surface. But it is precisely these inaudible links that bring compositional coherence to the work at the deeper, foundational level of the music. The notated triple meter is unarticulated, making it difficult to perceive any recurring pattern. Likewise, Balanchine avoids recurrent strong beats too, choosing instead to add a separate layer of dance that seems to contravene Stravinsky's compositional divisions, disguised as they often are. It appears that Balanchine took his cue from Stravinsky's own choreographic notes, which were entered, it will be recalled, into both his copy of the de Lauze manual and his compositional sketches. A series of glissades, as well as the continual cutting back and forth, and up- and downstage ("sometimes forwards, sometimes backwards," as Stravinsky underlined in the manual), are evident throughout the dance, although the viewer who is unaware of the de Lauze model would have no reason to make the historical connection.

The Saraband-Step's one unambiguously established internal formal division arrives at the end of the *A* section, at measure 153. Although the *B* section constitutes a variation of *A* (transposed, in keeping with the tradition of the stylized dance), because the music will now be at least somewhat familiar, Balanchine enlivens the male solo with more flourishes. But it is his pacing of the choreographic gestures that is significant. As Jordan observes, it is only in this *B* section that the "male soloist performs a jumping and turning step combination in four counts. . . . This is performed four times against three bars of $\frac{3}{4}$."[17] A contrapuntal dialogue of dance and music results—a dialogue reminding one of many other wonderfully asymmetrical overlays, in works as early as *Apollo.*

Stravinsky never hesitated to explain to Balanchine the structural divisions of his music (there are several published and unpublished film clips, for example, in which the choreographer attentively listens to the composer's explications). This seemed especially the case in instances where such divisions might otherwise go unnoticed. For instance, the Saraband-Step's two-measure codetta (mm. 162–63) constitutes a reprise of the dance's opening. Historically, such closing links were typical of binary dance forms (and their musical counter-parts)—further evidence of the composer's reliance upon the Mersenne models that Wildeblood discussed. Just as Stravinsky restates the sarabande's initial compositional flourish now in the form of a cadential gesture, so too does Balanchine. The male dancer's opening movements, aristocratically devised by the choreographer in such a way that the male presents himself proudly to the audience, are now repeated as a courtly close, including "five steps forward" (as Stravinsky marked in his copy of the de Lauze) and a final bow. In effect, the edges of the dance—the beginning, ending, and the one interior cadence—are clearly fixed, whereas the internal material is allowed to proceed along separate but congruent musical-choreographic planes.

Whereas the sarabande is binary, the Galliard is cast in a ternary form ($A =$ mm. 164–70, $B =$ mm. 171–78, $A =$ mm. 179–84). Once again each musical division is choreographically demarcated, this time by the two female dancers, who proceed for the most part in mirrored gestures. The detail of those gestures, submits Jordan, are related to orchestral and spatial planes. We can do no better than to refer to her perceptive analysis:

> In the first section, the dance accents are usually at a high level—*entrechats* and *relevés*—and they connect with the syncopated flute and string lines. In the central section, the dancers emphasize a descending three-note pattern in the piano line, again with *relevés* (bars 171–172). Then, the dance accent goes down to low level with *pliés,* marking the two-beat grouping of the music (in bars of $\frac{6}{4}$). Here, the mandoline and harp writing seems to emerge more strongly. Rhythmically, the Gailliarde is intriguing. It demonstrates that, although the dance steps can be neutral in accent, the music invites the viewer (and perhaps the dancer) into perceiving an accent that is in some way complementary to, or harmonious with, itself.[18]

Although these spatial levels are indeed important, both choreographically and orchestrally, they should not be separated from the movement's pervasive use of canon. Jordan is correct in noting the congruence between the two dancers and the outer limits of the orchestral range Stravinsky employs—for example, the flutes and lower strings in the A section. But in this instance the dancers/strings, working together, serve an accompanimental function. It is the interior layer of the music that is central. The harp and mandolin solos proceed in strict canon—a canon that, as usual, is not easily heard unless one is made aware of it. Nor was it particularly important to Stravinsky that the canon be heard. As in so many other instances, it served its function as a sub-structural means of organizing his musical materials—similar, in fact, to the wonderful (but for the most inaudible) canon employed nearly thirty years earlier in *Apollo*'s Pas d'action.

Jordan further points out that these two solo instruments "emerge more strongly" in the *B* section, a function perhaps of their registral placement. But still the canon continues, though now the mandolin takes the lead, whereas in the *A* section the harp set the tune. This middle section, as indicated in the score, carries repeat signs, and in the repetition Balanchine, following his custom of setting new choreography to already-heard music, alters the dancers' movements, including three hand claps by the women to help stress the prevailing musical pulse. The final *A* section (mm. 179–84) includes a musical complement to Balanchine's mirrored females, for example in the mirrored flutes of measures 179–80. More extensively, the canon between the mandolin and harp proceeds; but this time the mandolin takes over the melody that the harp sounded in the original *A* section, and the harp now plays the role of the follower. It is a slight textural modification, yet such orchestral reapportionment was not lost on Balanchine, whose own choreographic variations were just as subtle. Likewise, Balanchine was keenly aware of the need to continue physical movement during longer note values in the music. Stravinsky ends the Galliard's last measure with a sustained final harmony, eschewing any other musical activity in this multilayered, texturally variegated dance. Balanchine reciprocates: the two dancers assume a stationary, mirrored pose. With graceful hand movements, they gesticulate each of the final chord's interior pulses.[19]

Inasmuch as the coda of the first Pas de trois marks Stravinsky's fateful turn to twelve-tone writing, an equally memorable dance was needed to match the moment. Descriptions of Balanchine's choreography run the gamut. Don McDonagh suggests, "The man is no longer the faintly creaky aristocrat, but a bold young male with two slinky and competitive women on his hands." Banes is more analytic: "The three dancers again do identical steps, now in canon rather than unison, and as in the Sarabande, they mix and match jazz and ballet steps. They do a soft-shoe, a Susie-Q, and hip thrusts; they do attitudes, grands battements, and pirouettes."[20] Jordan pursues the coordination of music and dance, especially the cross meters created in the canonic passages by the dancers and orchestra. Ultimately, however, the coda's structure cannot be fully understood without tracking Stravinsky's row segmentations and Balanchine's parallel choreographic divisions. Here, perhaps more than in any other individual dance in

Agon, Balanchine's visual realization of the musical structure, instinctive or otherwise, is paramount.

Whereas the Saraband-Step was divided into two sections (*A-B*) and the Galliard into three (*A-B-A*) the coda offers yet a third formal design (*A-A'-B*)—an opening statement (*A* = mm. 185–210) followed by a slight variation (*A'* = mm. 211–33) and a contrasting closing section (*B* = mm. 234–53). As he so often does in the ballet, Stravinsky uses specific instrumental colors to signal important structural junctures. Throughout the $\frac{6}{8}$ meter, the fundamental beat remains clear—the clearest to this point in the ballet. It is as though Stravinsky wanted to provide a consistently regular pulse as a counterweight to his initiatory use of a twelve-tone row, whose pitch vocabulary was apt to perplex both the dancers and the audience.

In the coda's *A* section, for instance, he snakes his first twelve-tone row statement through a harp and cello solo. At the same time the trumpets sustain and the mandolin strums an open-fifth harmony that has nothing to do with the row. We get the impression that the composer is holding onto the tonal world of the tonic-dominant "c-g" pitches in the trumpets and mandolin, while simultaneously abandoning it with the two dodecaphonically conceived solo lines (mm. 185–90). Balanchine surely sensed the musical momentousness of these opening measures. The two females stand to the side of the male but then immediately engage in their own canon as he comes to the foreground, then retreats, as though announcing the inauguration of an important event and alerting the audience. His welcoming front-kick gesture (frequently used by *Agon's* males to declare a new musical idea) ends just as the first iteration of the row ends.

The composer disassembles the next row statement texturally (mm. 191–98—the row illustrated in figure 10.6), punctuating individual notes between the piano and the two bass trombone parts. The percussive sound of the piano and the edginess of the trombones effectively isolate the progressively unwinding statement of the row. At the same time, the double-stops of a solo violin engage in a succession of tonal, non-twelve-tone-like intervallic sixths. The dodecaphonic world, expressed by piano and brass, is texturally partitioned from the tonally oriented world of the solo violin, although both proceed together throughout the passage. Balanchine responds to the music's textural division with a completely new choreographic design. Just as the row begins in the piano (m. 191) the male dancer is pressed into solo action, while the two females perform as a separate unit, producing a male-female duality analogous to the score's dodecaphonic-tonal dichotomy. Indeed, virtually every time Stravinsky introduces one of the eight row statements used in this *A* section (including transpositional, inversional, and retrograde transformations), Balanchine marks the juncture with a new pattern.

Choreographic articulations occur in the other two sections of the coda as well. The reprise of the *A* division begins in measure 211 with the statement of the original twelve-tone row in the piano and trombones—just as it had in the beginning (there are six complete row statements in this section, ending in measure 233). Because the music is essentially the same, Balanchine creates a different design, combining the man and two women in new configurations. Finally, the *B* section introduces another statement of the original row, this time for the violin solo, trumpet, and mandolin (mm. 234–41), while at the same time the three flutes combine in two more versions of the same row in its inverted and retrograde forms. Balanchine's dancers, who now participate in a new canon, echo the increased activity. Perhaps most dramatic, when Stravinsky introduces another row statement in measure 242 (there are seven separate statements in this final *B* section), he does so with a textural spatiality that is close in spirit to Webern. The music is now pointillistic, with notes seemingly splattered (but in reality carefully positioned) across the orchestral register. Special effects such as fluttertonguing trumpets are employed. The violin soloist performs sul ponticello (a trill is played at the instrument's bridge, creating a glassy effect). Other vaporous-sounding bleeps join a parade of instrumental devices, including pizzicati, glissandi, con sordino (a muted bass trombone, for example). All of these add to the singular sound of the passage. It is a new universe for Stravinsky, and he bolts into it with great imagination.

Using his own carpentry analogy, we can say that Balanchine skillfully met the challenge by building equally new visual images. Here for the first time all three dancers converge. There is nothing remotely classical about their special-effect gestures, which include jutting movements starting at the top of their torsos and moving from shoulders to arms to legs. Sometimes they collapse upon themselves, touch shoulders, stand abruptly erect, and generally engage in angular motions that are as spatially widespread and unanticipated as the music's pointillistic style. When Stravinsky resumes a more linearly oriented row statement in measure 244, the cello and violin soloists present separate inversional and retrograde row statements. And finally, as the last musical gesture unfolds with sustained chords beginning in measure 249, an even more complex retrograde-inversional statement of the row unfolds. To match the intricacy of these final row presentations, Balanchine choreographically marks the passage as another structural pivot. The two females each do two pirouettes in succession—the most classical of gestures—to form a revolving line. The male attends both of them as they rotate through his support; and as the coda concludes, there is yet another courtly bow.

The music of the Prelude returns (now retitled Interlude) and is danced in canon by two males and a female. The Bransle Simple—a straightforward three-part design (A = mm. 278–87, B = mm. 288–97, A' = mm. 298–309)—opens the second Pas de trois. As illustrated in Chapter 10, Stravinsky's marking of Mersenne's bransle model makes evident his conscious adaptation of the same Long-Short-Short (L-S-S) accent patterns explained by both Mersenne and de Lauze in Wildeblood's edition. While the congruence is not immediately obvious, music theorist Mark Richardson convincingly argues that Stravinsky based his own setting upon Mersenne's fundamental eight-step dance pattern (L-S-S-L-L-L-S-S), expanding each individual accentual component to a phrase length. The architecture of Stravinsky's tripartite dance, therefore, arises from an alternation of L-S phrases directly analogous to Mersenne's original pattern.[21]

Choreographically, the two males replicate the musical canon of the dueling trumpets throughout the A section, with one important difference. Stravinsky's canon unfolds at the time interval of a half-note while Balanchine's dancers chase at the distance of a quarter-note—in effect, twice as fast. A contest of aural and visual layers ensues (parallel perhaps to what Banes sees as the two competing males, who "ball up their hands into fists and thrust out their chests as they jump in adversarial poses"), each proceeding along its own time line, though always in perfect temporal harmony. Moreover, the various segmentations of the fundamental hexachordal pitch collection that Stravinsky uses throughout (complete with retrogrades and inversions) is often articulated by Balanchine. For example, in measures 283–84, at the peak of the canon's melodic line, the composer employs the first retrograde transmutation of his six-note set. It is at that precise juncture that the dancers engage in the "three turning hops" to which Jordan alludes—a defining moment in the progression of the choreographic line.[22] Indeed, throughout all three formal divisions of the dance, Stravinsky's hexachordal segmentations are paralleled by the dancers' choreographic enunciations.

Texturally, the B section is quite different. Its fragmentary phrases, now vertically constructed as opposed to the earlier canon's horizontal line, are tossed between instruments. The dancers abandon the close drill of the canon and engage in a long mirrored passage over the entire ten-measure central section. The return of *A* is restored with one important textural variation: the canon is now accompanied by two solo lines, the harp and bass clarinet. The choreography, however, remains the same until the cadential chord, where the two men hook arms pointing upward in opposite directions.

The female soloist's Bransle Gay is also cast as a tripartite design (*A* = mm. 310–20, *B* = mm. 321–31, *A* = mm. 332–35), with the two men now standing at the rear and miming the sound of the clacking castanets. Melissa Hayden, who danced the premiere, remembered, "Never have I felt more totally on my own on stage. There was no story, no melody, no mood to the music to guide me. I was there alone with sharp shifting rhythms, isolated notes, and sharp angular movements."[23] Indeed, the constantly shifting meter and angularity of the soloist's gestures that Balanchine fashioned complements Stravinsky's compositional design. The dialogue of music and dance is as tightly interlaced here as it is anywhere in the Stravinsky-Balanchine repertoire.

The castanets' underlying $\frac{3}{8}$ rhythmic pulse once more finds its origins in the Mersenne model Stravinsky studied. The *S-S-L-L* pattern is a direct borrowing, characteristic of this brand of bransle. The fact that Stravinsky constantly shifts his notated meter between $\frac{7}{16}$ and $\frac{5}{16}$ (as divisions of twelve—divisions that Balanchine emphasized to Hayden when they rehearsed the dance) does nothing to compromise the powerful $\frac{3}{8}$ pull of the ostinato; it only adds another layer of potentially interesting choreographic and musical opportunities to be explored.

It is Stravinsky's control of pitch materials—again using one basic hexachordal collection (the complement to the hexachord used in the Bransle Simple, it may be remembered)—that unifies the dance. As with *Agon*'s earlier dances, the composer texturally divides interior divisions of the tripartite structure. The *B* section, for example (recall that this central division was actually written first), stands alone, with its contrapuntal layering between solo flutes and clarinets. On four occasions the composer also uses a measure of solo castanets as formal markers: to introduce the dance, to separate the two phrases of the *A* section, to divide that entire section from the *B* section, and finally to close the dance. In the first two instances, the female soloist dances "through" the ostinato with an independent gesture, while she replicates the rhythm with her arm movements in measure 320 (dividing *A* from *B*) and again in the final bar.

Banes writes of the diverse patterns the female soloist dances, including "rising up and down on a single pointe with the other leg extended; doing a double *développé* while remaining on pointe; making half-turns to do an arabesque in profile first in one direction, then the other; alternating pirouettes with arabesques—all completely unsupported."[24] But what must be added is that the initiation of virtually every one of these choreographic patterns coincides with Stravinsky's hexachordal divisions. At the beginning of the *B* section, for example, Stravinsky assigns two retrograde-inversion statements of the prime hexachord to the first flute (mm. 321–25). These two short statements find their choreographic correlation in the series of four gliding movements the female soloist undertakes. She ends her motion just as the second iteration of the hexachord drops off; and as a new hexachordal statement begins in the clarinet, so too a new choreographic pattern emerges.

Mersenne's Bransle de Poitou served as the rhythmic and metric model for the Bransle Double of *Agon*. While the opening violins play a clearly articulated triple meter emphasizing each strong beat, the trumpet and tenor trombone engage in a duet comprised of duple divisions. The pattern of grouping three pulses against two is consistent with the Mersenne original, and it will be recalled that Stravinsky actually graphed the three by two rhythmic division onto his sketch page. His textural setting aids in the delineation of these two interacting layers of string and brass sounds. Clearly, Balanchine understood the crosscutting meter; accordingly, he matched the textural differentiation choreographically. As the dance begins, the female is tossed between the two males, just as the aural ambiguity as to where the beat really is seems to be tossed between the strings and brass. She also performs a series of jouncing splits supported by the two males, again creating the analogy of splitting the texture and meter into two competing levels. As for pitch, a complete twelve-tone row is now employed for the first time in the second Pas de trois, combining the two hexachords of the previous two bransles.

The form of this final bransle is more expansive than the earlier two dances. Essentially it is the same tripartite statement-contrast-reprise, but here extended to form an *A-A'-B-A* plus coda. The opening *A* (mm. 336–43) is immediately repeated, but with the important orchestral addition of the lower strings, thus amounting to a kind of *A'* (mm. 344–51). The *B* section (mm. 352–64) begins with intermitting piano chords that introduce a more vertical sound in contrast to the earlier contrapuntal layers. The notated meter also shifts from triple to an unambiguous duple. The reprise of *A* (mm. 365–86) includes a substantial coda beginning in measure 373—strong enough to stand as a separate structural division and be treated by Balanchine as an individual section.

As with the earlier bransles, Balanchine's choreography defines the Bransle Double's major and internal subdivisions. Just as the woman and men helped to distinguish the crosscutting meter of the opening *A* section by dancing in canon, the *A'* division is spatially shaped by the three dancers. They now move out of what was a vertical alignment facing the audience to a horizontal deployment across the front of the stage, the woman center. They dance in unison, the clearest indication, since the change in the score is difficult to distinguish (though obviously Balanchine was able to), that a new structural division has begun. It is only toward the end of the *A'* section that the three dancers resume their original vertical plane, with the woman in front of the two men.

She now assumes the role of a soloist. As Banes comments, "As she continues to dance downstage, the men strike poses behind her, forming an ornamental moving sunburst pattern that recalls both the Double Pas de Quatre and *Apollo*. In a witty gender reversal, the men seem to take on a feminine decorative function, while the woman does the masculine 'hard work,' which includes the lunges with arms pushing through that were earlier marked as a male movement."[25] Once again, Banes's observations can be linked to the score. For this important gender reversal occurs precisely at the start of the *B* section. It alerts us to the change in texture (both musically and choreographically) but also calls attention to the appearance of a new twelve-tone row statement, whose materials will then be transformed throughout this *B* section.

The final *A* section (again in triple meter) is marked by the dancers' return to unison movements, just as Stravinsky returns to his opening material. Compositionally, the coda commencing in measure 373 comprises a series of interwoven twelve-tone transformations—transposed primes, retrogrades, inversions, and retrograde-inversions combined. It represents the most elaborate intersection of row forms to this point in the ballet. Shifting again to duple meter, the steady half-note motion establishes a clarity of pulse while signaling an important change. The music now moves more slowly, deliberately. The choreographic movement shifts to a slower pace too, as the three dancers join hands at the exact moment the coda begins. Just as the complex interweaving of the twelve-tone row transformations begins, the trio engages in a series of arm movements that have the dancers crossing underneath one another while positioned in a stationary pose. The final leap of the woman from the arms of one male to the other provides a choreographic accent (reminiscent of her being tossed from male to male in the opening), just as Stravinsky halts the musical motion with a single pizzicato chord on the last beat.[26]

I have focused on those dances directly related to both the de Lauze and Mersenne models. Yet *Agon*'s famous Pas de deux—"the pas de deux to end them all," as Croce rightly proclaims in "The Spelling of *Agon*"—must at least be mentioned. Deservedly, it is the subject of several illuminating analyses, particularly those of Sally Banes and Stephanie Jordan. Representing a new plateau in the Balanchine repertory, it is at once intriguing and unorthodox in its choreographic structure. Yet despite its innovation, like virtually everything Stravinsky and Balanchine undertook its roots are classical, as is its traditional design, beginning with a formal entrance, followed by a supported adagio for the male and female, individual male and female variations, and finally a return partnering in the form of a coda. As discussed earlier, Stravinsky carefully calibrated each of these sections abstractly before composing the music. Temporal pacing, as ever, was uppermost in his mind. But how did the choreographer and composer articulate these important internal divisions? A few representative passages are offered.

The music of the opening Prelude once again ushers in the dancers. As in the second Pas de trois, it is retitled Interlude here. The music is recapitulated, with one important and often overlooked orchestral detail: the first seven measures (mm. 387–93) now include a brilliant, unmuted trumpet duet marked "tremolo," thus providing a fanfarelike reveille for the male and female principals. The brassy sound cuts through the by-now familiar music, signaling that something important—or more to the point, something completely different—is about to happen. This opening passage begins in measure 387 and ends in measure 396, with the same intensifying sound and rising lines heard in the first two iterations of the Prelude/Interlude. The entire section covers thirteen seconds (as precisely marked in Stravinsky's sketches), and the added trumpets cadence after eight seconds (m. 393), that is, in a 2:1 temporal relation over the entire passage.

Balanchine casts this dynamic choreographic entrance in accordance with the same proportional division. The couple begin the Interlude side by side facing the stage. As the trumpet-enhanced passage opens, they twirl canonically, the woman leading the way with the male following in pursuit. Their series of pirouettes, continually moving to their right, stop at the precise moment the new trumpet sections ends (m. 393), whereupon the woman abruptly reverses her direction, moving back to her left with a series of kicks, as the male continues to follow canonically. Finally, at measure 396, where the passage cadences, the male and female join. "He catches her," describes Banes, "as she turns, pitches forward, and strikes a high back attitude that angles around his torso," in perhaps one of the most famous visual images associated with the ballet.[27]

Stravinsky employs a twelve-tone row in the adagio that follows. But it is used only as a resource, for compositionally he is almost exclusively committed to segmenting the pitch material into smaller, symmetrical divisions. Jordan remarks that there is a new musical structure at work here: "no longer a series of jaggedly contrasting motoric formal cells, but a number of fragile short gestures—some bounded by rests, or passages of a gradual piling up of sound."[28] Exactly so, and once again Webern's influence is unmistakable. The basic pitch cell employed throughout all the individual sections of the Pas de deux consists of a symmetrically constructed tetrachord: the first two notes of the cell divided by a half-step, then an intervening interval of a whole step, and finally the final two pitches divided by a half-step. It is one of Webern's (and now Stravinsky's) favorite four-note patterns.[29]

Yet this tetrachordal cell is deployed so that the pitches are almost always spatially split widely, beginning with the first measure, and once more creating a notably pointillistic, Webernesque texture. The pitch contours are in effect stretched in the same sense that Balanchine stretches the choreographic gestures, as with the female's constant extensions of arms and legs, lunging in every direction. Yet the two dancers are always in contact as the male continues furnishing support. Moreover, the choreographic symmetry of their gestures, often mirroring each other, replicates the symmetrical structuring of Stravinsky's pitch materials. Balanchine continues to articulate major intersections in the score. For example, measure 427 marks the first point of musical repose, where violins, violas, cellos, and basses participate in a long, sustained cadence—a cadence that descends through the strings using the same tetrachordal, symmetrical set that forms the adagio's pitch basis. It is at this moment that the female is elevated for the first time, legs and arms stretched to the limit, supported by the male, who gently and gradually lowers her back to the floor. Likewise, the sustained sound of the strings also progressively dissipates at the same temporal juncture. The entire section is repeated, but now with completely new choreography exuding the provocative "sexual acrobatics" discussed by Banes.

The brief, ten-measure male variation beginning in measure 463 and marked by a series of grands battements is again underscored musically by the same split intervals. Here again a canonic treatment at the temporal distance of one measure prevails, now set for piano and three horns in stark contrast to the earlier string writing. The solo male's leaps and hand gestures support the suddenly brighter music. Since the male soloist alone cannot project a two-line canon, Balanchine fashions an independent counterpoint with the piano and horn trio. The dancer is not in sync with the music; rather, he moves at a slower, deliberate pace, in effect adding one more plane to the texture. Combined, we now hear and see three intersecting layers of music and choreography.

The female initiates her eleven-bar solo at measure 473, with a duet of doubling flutes supported by the strings. Stravinsky employs three- and four-note segmentations for the flute's melodic material, largely based upon the same tetrachordal material first seen in the adagio but now in a very un-Webernesque way. The notes are mostly contiguous without any of the dramatic pitch splitting previously employed. The musical underpinnings performed by the string section provide an underlying ostinato for the female, who now eschews her own earlier splits and contortions. Balance is stressed as she takes center stage, engaging in the most classically oriented gestures seen to this point in the Pas de deux. The movement presents Balanchine's response to the classically composed music of the Pas de deux, with its clearly delineated melodic motives and just as clearly defined accompanimental chordal structure. Both musically and choreographically, these brief eleven measures provide a respite before the male's refrain recommences at the "l'istesso tempo" of measure 484, wherein the canon of the horns and piano returns.

The coda, beginning in measure 495, now combines strings and brass, offering the most assertive music yet. More aggressive than ever, the male grabs the woman, pulling her to him as they begin a series of linked movements, each one temporarily starting and stopping wherever Stravinsky segments the pitch material and marks a pause (either by a fermata or rest). The doppio lento at measure 514 marks a critical juncture, a return to the adagio mood of the duet, and again marking a resumption of the more pointillistic texture. Moreover, for the first time since the first Pas de trois the mandolin returns—a stunning moment of synthesis as the ballet's earlier Renaissance world is now finally and convincingly fused with its "Space Age" complement. Perhaps for the first time in the entire composition, the ballet's seemingly disparate styles make sense. And with this amalgamation, the two soloists renew all the suggestive, sensual tensions of Balanchine's choreography. Finally, the spent couple, physically and emotionally exhausted, collapse into each other's arms. And just as the Bransle Double concluded with a string pizzicato, snapping the music's last moment, here too the cello's final, punctuating pluck draws this most ingeniously conceived Pas de deux to a sudden close.

In dealing with the complexity of *Agon,* a myriad of approaches must be enlisted. The historical models Stravinsky first consulted and then employed as a springboard cannot be dismissed as quickly as the composer would have us do. Especially for a ballet whose gestation was so slow, the initial period of incubation was particularly key. In which direction would Stravinsky's imagination have led him without Kirstein, Eliot, and Mersenne? Likewise, Balanchine's choreographic setting is intimately tied to the composer's study of the de Lauze manual, even if only as a starting point for his own creative thinking. Nor can one hope to understand the structural network that Stravinsky assembled without addressing the composer's new approach to pitch collections, as analytically demanding as this sometimes proves to be. That Balanchine so beautifully visualized *Agon*'s multiple layers, clarifying its many sophisticated serial and dodecaphonic segmentations with musically illustrative dancing, signifies his truly extraordinary understanding of Stravinsky's score.

Ultimately, however, *Agon* is not only or even chiefly about pitch but rather about the temporal flow of rhythm. It concerns symmetry—or more precisely, as Balanchine observed, "symmetrical asymmetry." And perhaps best defined, the ballet is about "architectonics," to use the composer's own term. *Agon* is the musical-choreographic exemplification of how the beauty of architecture grows in splendor the more it is regulated and even restricted by the discipline of classical templates—templates that the composer had embraced long before he sat down to write the first note. As always, Stravinsky, the indefatigable classicist, turned to the past, to models that would provide the structural foundation he needed to construct his "futuristic" creation. In his *Autobiography* the composer quoted Verdi: "Let us return to old times, then we will progress."

Balanchine was, of course, Stravinsky's most sympathetic collaborator. Perhaps more than any of the composer's many collaborators, he understood—and more to the point actually "saw"—what the composer wanted to say. Together, they created, or perhaps Balanchine would have preferred "erected," what the choreographer referred to as "the most perfect" ballet. *Agon* is justly hailed as a masterpiece of abstraction, of stark, powerful contrasts producing a cohesive, wondrous musical-balletic unity. That the power of this innovative work owes its genesis to sources as distant as the Renaissance is befitting. For in the estimate of both Balanchine and Stravinsky, the pathway to the future could never be separated from the achievements of the past.

Chapter 12 Television,

The Flood, and Beyond

Seldom have so many anticipated so much and received so little. It has been estimated that some seven million viewers saw *Noah and the Flood,* Igor Stravinsky's first work for television. The same ratings reveal that at least one million had dropped out by the time the hour program was over. . . . From its pompous beginnings to its tiresome and witless conclusion, *Noah and the Flood* was a bitter disappointment.
—*Emily Coleman,* Dance Magazine, *January 1963*

With *Agon'*s stunning success, the Stravinsky-Balanchine partnership appeared poised for more triumphs. Yet during the early 1960s, one publicly aired stumble occurred. The 14 June 1962 CBS premiere of *The Flood* (or *Noah and the Flood,* as it was first advertised) was telecast as a network special on Breck Shampoo's *Golden Showcase.* History has never known quite what to do with the piece, stigmatizing it as artistically muddled and ambivalent. Albert Goldberg of the *Los Angeles Times* panned the production as an "inglorious flop—an all-time dud." Was the harsh criticism that quickly spread across the country's newspapers really fair? Was the medium itself—that "vast wasteland" as Kennedy-appointed Federal Communications Commission chair

Newton Minow described the industry that same year—solely culpable for the televised failure? Or was the commercially motivated network guilty of skimping on what might have been a much richer artistic experience? Finally, how much of the "blame" was Balanchine's, since his participation in this curious "dance-drama" (as Stravinsky described the work) was at best an uneager favor to an old friend? From the start, the choreographer feared for the production.

The twenty-three-minute work was produced by Robert Graff of Sextant and directed by Kirk Browning, both experienced veterans during those still relatively experimental years of early television. Stravinsky scored the biblical tale for orchestra and chorus. Balanchine choreographed two sections for his New York City Ballet. The cast included Laurence Harvey as the Narrator, Sebastian Cabot as Noah, Elsa Lanchester as Mrs. Noah, and Robert Robinson as Satan. Two actors were used to portray the Voice of God, John Reardon and Robert Oliver. There are six large sections including a Prelude, the Building of the Ark (choreographed), the Catalogue of the Animals (Paul Tripp read the part of the Caller), the Comedy, the Flood (choreographed), and the Covenant of the Rainbow.

Laurence Harvey delivered the broadcast's opening commentary—more homily than introduction—posed against an empty black backdrop. He spoke of flood myths, of Zeus purging the earth of its transgressions, of Noah's unquestioned faith that God was cleansing a sinful world and in the renewal of life. The somber-looking Harvey spoke forebodingly about "the Bomb" and the fragile times in which we lived. These were familiar auguries sounded repeatedly in consciousness-raising movies like *On the Beach, Fail-Safe,* and *Dr. Strangelove.* If *Agon* captured the promising dawn of the Space Age and our increasing awareness of the universe, then the expansive range of ICBM warheads in the early 1960s reminded us that this same universe could be demolished in an eye's blink. To the builders of more than 100,000 bomb shelters in the 1950s, the world had become a tinderbox.

Stravinsky's newest work was intended to emphasize this gravity, to resonate with a public that worried about somebody pushing "the button." Like many of the composer's earlier works, *The Flood* moralized about the future by revisiting the past. Harvey explained all this, adding that we should consider ourselves lucky that Stravinsky had chosen television as his medium. The actor then faded to black, from which emerged a solemn Stravinsky himself, telling us that he was happy to present "a very dear subject for audiences who can surely appreciate the drama. I don't want to speak you more, I want to play you more," and with that the first, and last, televised performance of *The Flood* began.[1]

Television's early effort to bedazzle the audience with visual trickery—angels tumbling from the heavens, silhouetted male and female hands simulating the procreative act, figurines of Noah's menagerie (which actually belonged to Balanchine), malformed aliens as conceived in the pre-Spielberg era, dancers emerging from a huge rippling blanket representing the flood itself—smacked of contrivance. The production was sliced into short segments interrupted by shampoo commercials that completely fractured its flow. As the performance itself ended, the camera zoomed in on a coldly glowering Stravinsky. Then the elocutionary Harvey reappeared, reminding us that every epoch produces great men like Stravinsky, whose "works have changed the musical ears of the world."

To fill out the hour broadcast (since the work itself consumed less than half the airtime), the composer was shown discussing what he anticipated would be the problems the public would have in accepting his newest creation (performed on the eve of his eightieth birthday). There are also shots of him rehearsing the orchestra (in Los Angeles, where the work was prerecorded) and of Balanchine demonstrating some ballet sequences for his dancers (in New York, where the choreography was filmed).

The Flood cannot be decontextualized from the astounding phenomenon of American television—the most powerful cultural symbol of the electronic age. During the early 1950s, the golden age of a Hollywood now under siege from the censure of "the Hollywood Ten" faded as television's star rose. Ticket sales for films plummeted at a rate of ten million a week. In 1946 there were an estimated sixty-five hundred television sets in the United States. By 1948 there were more than a million, and by 1950 four million. Sixty percent of all television sets were sold on credit to middle- and low-income families in 1950 alone. The ubiquitous "tube" was about to change the fabric of American life; and it provoked an inevitable clash between classical art and American populism. This was a volatile time, when creative license was incriminated by a widely diverse media audience wanting not so much to be uplifted as to be entertained by one sitcom after another. Television was no more than "chewing gum for the eyes," as the always-acerbic Frank Lloyd Wright remarked.

Whatever its purpose, television was hypnotically successful. But if an artistic program were to survive, it would have to be attuned to demographics, to the appeal of commercials, and ultimately to sponsorship. Besides ballet, opera was a likely candidate to win at least a small share of the public market. The spectacle might appeal to visually oriented viewers. Composer Gian Carlo Menotti became an overnight hit with the unparalleled success of the 1949 *Amahl and the Night Visitors.*[2] This especially commissioned work set the standard for what televised opera aspired to be. Surely this is what the sponsors had in mind when Stravinsky was approached. But the teary-eyed sentimentalism of *Amahl* annoyed Stravinsky. Nor was he particularly enamored of the telegenic Leonard Bernstein's popular *Young People's Concerts,* broadcast in the late 1950s and early 1960s.

A media blitz over-billed *The Flood* as no less than a major historic event, a cultural milestone. The *Congressional Record* praised shampoo baron John Breck (who actually delivered the opening remarks for the televised performance) for his vision and the endeavor's "cultural high-mindedness." The names Stravinsky and Balanchine carried weight, and television wagered that Americans, whether or not they had ever heard anything beyond *The Firebird* or *The Nutcracker,* would recognize the production's significance. Forty-six million homes, nearly 88 percent of American households, now owned a "magic carpet." Television burst forth as the new demagogue. If Walter Cronkite said a thing was so . . . then it was so. And if Stravinsky and Balanchine's new work was important enough to be beamed into their living rooms on a Saturday night, viewers had better watch it.

Balanchine's reservations about television were on record; but the composer's feelings vacillated. "A televised concert is a great bore," Stravinsky confided to the choreographer during an interview for *Saturday Review* the week the work aired. "Yes, of course you can see the timpani and the trombone and the oboe person by person as they play, but what is the interest of that?" Yet two weeks later in a follow-up article, the composer remarked, "I feel that television is the greatest medium for a new musical form, and if I decide to write another opera myself, I know that it will be for the electronic glass tube. . . . the one 'specific' of the medium that guided me in my conception of *The Flood* [was that] visualization can be instantaneous."[3]

Still, given his equivocation (as well as Balanchine's hesitance), why did the composer involve himself in a project over which he would have little control? Perhaps he was motivated by the prospect of having his music more widely circulated than he could ever have imagined. Perhaps he felt that such programming would bring him the same notoriety it won for Pablo Casals or Bernstein. Moreover, while ridiculing the "idiot box" as a venue for dolts, trusted literary friends like Aldous Huxley and Christopher Isherwood were thinking of exploiting its high exposure. Isherwood's diary entry of March 1960, for instance, reveals that he was considering doing a televised film for Lincoln Kirstein's *Sleeping Beauty.* And more relevantly, his diary notes "Bob Craft's idea that I should narrate something for a Stravinsky composition—in 1962!" which became *The Flood,* although Isherwood never was involved.[4]

From the outset, Stravinsky discussed the project with obvious trepidation. It would not be an opera or a ballet, "perhaps not a theater piece at all," he stressed in April 1961 to his publisher. He constantly scuttled the assumption that his new piece would be operatic, preempting any comparison with Menotti. The composer would only confirm that it would be a work expressly for television, and that Balanchine would stage some ballet fragments. Choreography was envisioned from the start. Balanchine was involved in a variety of television shows during the 1950s, and his frequent interchanges with Stravinsky sensitized the composer to the potential pitfalls of the new medium. Certainly, Balanchine was far more conversant than the composer with television's potential as well as its limitations. After all, Balanchine was hardly a newcomer to television.

Even in the medium's infancy in the late 1940s, Balanchine was creating dance sequences for CBC Television in Montreal.[5] He had arranged a made-for-television version of *Cinderella* (with Tanaquil Le Clercq as Cinderella) that was first broadcast on 25 April 1949 on CBS's pioneering dance program *Through the Crystal Ball.* A decade before *The Flood,* his *One, Yuletide Square* was broadcast on Christmas Day 1952 on NBC, again featuring his wife Le Clercq in what was an abridged version of *Coppélia.* For the popular *Kate Smith Hour* on NBC, the choreographer presented yet another made-for-television ballet, *The Countess Becomes the Maid* (1953), based on excerpts from *Die Fledermaus.* And on Christmas Night 1958, Balanchine himself played Drosselmeyer in a widely viewed and highly praised hour-and-a-half version of *The Nutcracker* for CBS.

Perhaps his most ambitious televised achievement was *The Magic Flute,* expressly prepared for television and based on an adaptation by W. H. Auden. Balanchine was completely responsible for the stage direction. First telecast on 15 January 1956 on the popular *NBC Opera Theater,* the cast featured a young Leontyne Price; the choreographer also prepared dance sequences for the Queen of the Night's Three Ladies. And finally, Balanchine's dancers became near-regulars on *The Bell Telephone Hour* beginning in 1959 and lasting nearly a decade. Abbreviated passages of everything from *Apollo*'s Pas de deux (with Jacques d'Amboise and Melissa Hayden) to *Square Dance* (presented in both 1966 and 1968 on the NBC program) were presented in prime time.

For all television's limitations, Balanchine realized that the far-reaching lens of the camera could not be ignored. In addition to presenting several ballet excerpts on commercial networks, he participated in the Ford Foundation–sponsored NET project *USA: Dance.* In 1965 dancers of the New York City Ballet joined him in a documentary that included a discussion of *Agon.* As Brian Rose describes the program: "The show opened with a stone-faced Balanchine, surrounded by his prize performers, as they intently watched a tape of the pas de deux from his ballet *Agon.* With a camera circling around them, the dancers were heard, in simple, quiet comments, discussing choreography and the joys of dancing for 'Mr. Balanchine.' . . . The program was quite successful in making the audience feel like they were getting an insider's view of City Ballet performance style and group dynamics."[6]

But Balanchine found it an unhappy experience, electing not to participate directly in another American network program until the *Dance in America* series more than a decade later. Ever since Maria Gambarelli had first appeared on television in New York on 26 May 1931 (confining her movements to a five-foot-square space so that she would fit on the small screen), choreographers were chary of the medium's ability to capture unhampered dance movement. Now Edward Villella's athletic soaring across the T.V. screen was big business, reaching all corners of the country.

When Villella was invited to dance on *Omnibus* in a 1958 program conceived by Gene Kelly ("Dancing Is a Man's Game"), Balanchine objected. As Villella recalls, the choreographer felt that "quality, development of an idea, the investigation of how a dance could be adapted to the medium, were not given a high priority."[7] Balanchine complained that regardless of the artistic efforts devoted to such productions, regardless of what was agreed to, the program itself never quite jelled. The medium impeded dance, inevitably leaving viewers with a distorted impression. If music placed a "corset on the dance," as Balanchine liked to say, then television put manacles on it. He always felt obliged to preface any of his televised choreography with a stern caveat: "What you're going to see is really going to be pretty awful." The screen image did an injustice to the beauty of dance and his dancers, he complained.[8]

Nor did his feelings change over the next several years, even though he relented, reluctantly one guesses, and agreed to work with Stravinsky on their first joint project since *Agon.* During the taping of *The Flood* Balanchine carefully studied the television monitor, making adjustments as needed. Then too, it was largely within the context of commercially successful dance programs that *The Flood* was advertised. Thus expectations for a significant choreographic component were high. So while Stravinsky was busy refuting assumptions that *The Flood* was operatic, Balanchine was busily countering the notion that it was a ballet:

> This is a miracle play more than a masque. As I see it, it's a church play or a choreographed oratorio. Most importantly it's *not* a ballet. *The Flood* could have been produced with actors speaking, or with singers and actors, or it could have been an opera. Our version is a *musical* composite. It's all done in gesture by dancers and objects. The most important thing about it is that it's Stravinsky. It's his work. His music is not accompaniment for the dance. Actually it's about Stravinsky himself, as a composer. And we are not trying to interfere with his music. The most important thing for me is for his music to be heard.

Balanchine's frank comments were offered to Arthur Todd during the taping of the choreography. As Todd reported, "Quite naturally [Balanchine] envisaged the movement only to enhance and enliven the score, but never to illustrate it." Todd, who witnessed the process unfolding, spoke of Balanchine always having the camera in mind and by extension, of his concern for the viewer.[9]

Some precious clips of Balanchine actually choreographing the two ballet segments were shown as part of the original telecast's postlude. One gets the impression that Balanchine, typically, threw himself into the project—for Stravinsky's sake if for no other reason. Still, despite his enthusiasm and regardless of his personal efforts to supervise the dance segments, in the end he was as exasperated as ever with television's failure to transmit the artistic message he envisioned.

His apprehension must have spilled over into his collaboration with Stravinsky. He knew the project would be greatly hobbled by television's constraints. Regrettably, though perhaps predictably, only "a rough draft" (to use his words) of his conception was televised. "I wanted to make choreography that was not too obtrusive—which did not interfere with the music. . . . I intended to make changes and improvement—but we got into the studio, the panic took over, and then suddenly it became impossible to do what needed to be done."[10] Stravinsky originally pictured eight dancers. In fact, twenty-seven members of the New York City Ballet were ultimately employed. The company thought of their contribution as "a birthday garland for Stravinsky in gratitude for all of his great ballet scores," reported Todd.

Lincoln Kirstein was as brutally impertinent as ever in his public derision of the medium: "I've never owned a television set; the few times I've watched . . . I've been amply confirmed in my distaste." Such hubris, reminiscent of Stravinsky's earlier denunciation of film and mass culture, only widened the gulf already separating creative artists from American populism. Kirstein groused that television people "know nothing about ballet [and] nothing about any visual aspect important to a choreographer." They were only interested in achieving a commercial success and perhaps the "token prestige occasionally thrown in to sweeten a smelly pot." Vilification and overstatement abounded as each camp staked its territorial rights. And as Stravinsky's unpublished correspondence confirms, negotiations between him, his publisher, Graff, Sextant, and the network grew sharply tense. Sextant, for example, originally announced to the press that the work would be a one-hour ballet, and thus Balanchine's contribution would be substantive, but a bilious Stravinsky quickly chided Graff, replying that he had no idea whether the piece would take that form.[11]

Originally, the producer of the proposed project, Graff, suggested Auden as the librettist, but Stravinsky wanted T. S. Eliot. As we have seen, the composer's interest in the poet had been rekindled a few years earlier during *Agon*'s precompositional phase. By 1959 Eliot and the composer were discussing the idea of collaborating on an opera. Neither wanted to do a traditional opera, nor did Eliot feel confident about his abilities as a librettist. Stravinsky suggested that they develop an "alternative" kind of theatrical piece. In August, Stravinsky met with Graff at Princeton (the composer was there for a few seminars) and apparently updated the producer on his progress. He wrote to Eliot the same month, outlining the origins of what would become *The Flood.* The composer's unreleased correspondence shows that he fully expected Eliot to accept the collaboration, but as subsequent exchanges disclose, Eliot gradually retreated from the idea. By September it had become clear that Stravinsky would need to seek another partner. He turned to Robert Craft.

Craft's contribution to the work's fundamental scenario was more significant than first thought. After Stravinsky's death, Craft divulged just how central his role was.[12] The composer owned a paperback edition of *"Everyman" and Medieval Miracle Plays,* which Eliot had suggested to him, and Craft employed this as the basis for the libretto. An examination of the book (held in the Sacher Stiftung) confirms that Craft studied the text carefully, underlining certain sections that eventually became part of the scenario. The libretto drew on passages from the Chester Miracle Plays as well as the York Mystery Play cycle. In addition, an unpublished transcript in the Stiftung records a lengthy exchange between Craft and Graff in New York during the spring of 1960. Craft outlines everything from the specifics of the scenario to the style of the music that would be written, suggesting that the work would be contemporized to address the day's issues. He also assured Graff that the work would be conceived with television in mind.

Balanchine joined Stravinsky in California, and between 14 and 16 March 1962 they assembled the final scenario. The work was recorded and videotaped at the CBS studios in Hollywood two weeks later. Craft conducted the orchestra for the sound recording (although the televised program did nothing to dissuade the audience from the belief that Stravinsky himself was at the podium). The videotaping of the dance segments took place in New York over a two-day (and night) period two months later, in early June. As Todd reported, "The choreographer's deep involvement was obvious, whether in studio rehearsal or during the taping with director Kirk Browning. Camera angles, placement and timing were all planned in sympathetic collaboration between choreographer and director."[13]

On 15 April, Stravinsky and Balanchine sent a jointly composed cable to Graff: "We are now absolutely clear in our minds that nothing should be changed, cut, or repeated and that the work should be heard exactly as it now stands." They reassured the still very much in the dark producer that the work would take twenty-five minutes, but this would be achieved only "by lengthening of pauses . . . not by the repetition of unrepeatable music." Whereas Stravinsky had previously argued that the work was not a ballet piece, now he backpedaled, saying, "We have worked out a choreographic visualization . . . and your earlier publicity releases about *The Flood* calling it a Stravinsky-Balanchine ballet are now more precise than we at that time thought."[14]

Several compositional sketches confirm how late the decisions were made. Measures were added, deleted, shifted, repeated. Some passages were even taped into the score at the last moment, especially in the dance sequences. Typically, the composer carefully timed every fragment. Durations marked as precisely as "seventeen seconds" are common. The sketches also establish that the music was not completed until 14 March, the afternoon Balanchine arrived to begin blocking the stage action. The performance script is heavily marked with suggestions for revising the wording of sentences, advice on textual enunciation, and specific inflections in delivering lines. The actual pacing of the narration and the entrances and exits of the characters were all carefully regulated to ensure that the program would run neither over nor under the allotted broadcast slot. Craft seems to have been the guiding force in all these technical issues, and Stravinsky seems to have listened to him.

The composer and choreographer continued assuring Graff that the work would be twenty-five minutes long; yet the matter remained unresolved after

Stravinsky and Balanchine concluded their March meetings. In an unpublished letter of 2 April, Graff informed the composer that he must now lengthen the work—or, more to the point, that Craft would have to. Specifically, Graff wanted a dance work that would last more than thirty minutes. This must have unnerved Stravinsky and Balanchine, both of whom had been growing more tentative about the production's chances of succeeding. The composer was particularly concerned with the script for the introduction, as well as the choice of the narrator ("I would like to see what your writer has done by way of introduction to the show and I would like to see Arutunian's sketches. The success of the show will depend to a great extend [*sic*] *on the narrator,*" Stravinsky underlined).[15] His wariness intensified as he wrote to his friend Rolf Liebermann in late March: "I hope *The Flood* will not be *A Flop.*"

The production was videotaped, and the commitment to televise was made. The tape was not viewed until two days before the telecast. Reactions such as "pandemonium," and "pushing the panic button" were heard, but it was too late to pull the program: *The Flood* aired as scheduled (fig. 12.1). Stravinsky was touring Germany as part of his eightieth birthday celebration, so he didn't see the telecast. It was just as well. He received the first report from Graff in a cable dated 19 June: "Flood played to enormous audience network. Notices generally *unfavorable.* Have no doubt work will be replayed many times. Hearty congratulations, many bravos." (Stravinsky underlined the word *unfavorable.*) As reviews from across the country came in, it became clear that Stravinsky and Balanchine's fears had been well founded.

The sponsors had gambled on the lure of Stravinsky's name, primarily, although certainly Balanchine's contribution enhanced the event's artistic significance. An enormous financial investment underwrote a publicity campaign, but the outcry following the broadcast was resoundingly negative. With one voice, "the mob" defiantly clamored that television was no place for such artistic Dada, and no place for Stravinsky's empty dialectics about impending nuclear calamity. Clive Barnes spoke of television as the "first truly democratic culture," which was entitled to govern what it would see. The "terrifying" problem, Barnes observed, was precisely what it *was* that viewers wanted to see. Had Stravinsky and Balanchine attempted to force viewers to become intellectuals? ("To make us all into intellectuals—there is the challenge of television," television executive Sylvester "Pat" Weaver once grandly declared.)

Balanchine's choreography was denounced as "restricted and dark" (certainly the lighting was horribly dim). Rouben Ter-Arutunian had gone "over-

12.1 From the CBS production of *The Flood* (Jerome Robbins
Dance Division, The New York Public Library for the
Performing Arts, Astor, Lenox and Tilden Foundations)

board in the sets, costumes and props." The overall production was little more
than "an electronics show put together to be seen in a box" and "an excess of
electronic hanky-panky," one newspaper after another charged. Jack O'Brien,
television critic of the *New York Journal-American,* complained about the
"corps de BVD . . . one huge underwear ad with all models en pointe," going
on to charge the production with "artistic larceny." The *Baltimore Sun* critic
couldn't resist the slickest of watery metaphors, writing, "Noah and the Flood
. . . was less like a deluge than a leaky faucet. It's now painfully obvious that in
television [Stravinsky] is a whale out of water."

A barrage of pre-telecast commercials led viewers to expect more dancing.
Edward Villella, Jillana, Jacques d'Amboise—all young and popular stars in
Balanchine's galaxy—were publicized as having important roles. But their
parts were so small (to say nothing of the fact that the overwhelming masks and

scenery made them unrecognizable) that they were almost entirely missed. In his *New York Times* review of 25 June, Allen Hughes wrote, "We must assume that Mr. Balanchine had no effective control over *Noah and the Flood.*"

Walter Terry for the *Herald-Tribune* critiqued the telecast from another angle. He noted that while the dancing was "incidental and beyond the obvious flaws of the patched-together hour program," Balanchine's "style" came through. He perceived a gesture similar to *Apollo* struck by Adam (d'Amboise) and Eve (Jillana), "as the two simply touch each other's extended fingertips." Terry observed the characteristically Balanchinian classical foundation of the work but noted that there were "some sharp and sudden distortions such as the choreographer has used in his *Agon.*" And in a wholly reasonable assessment, he concluded: "Choreographically, *Noah and the Flood* does not represent the most exciting and meaty of the Stravinsky and Balanchine collaborations but, during its brief course, it gives us a few very special images of movement beauty which only Balanchine can devise."[16]

Stravinsky kept more than fifty press reviews in an unpublished file marked "American critics about *The Flood* June 1962." For the composer to admit concern over what others thought of his music might allow too much exposure, and by extension, too much personal scrutiny. With a public tribunal of millions watching—and an audience forewarned that it absolutely must be edified by the relevance of the production—Stravinsky was obviously vulnerable. He had been put on the spot, especially amid the hype of the televised promises of a milestone moment.[17]

Balanchine openly voiced his general frustration with "what always happens on American television." He had hoped that given the sponsors' good sense in commissioning Stravinsky, they would "have the taste to put it on in a way that does justice, or at least not to mess it up." The problem, as Balanchine accurately perceived, was that "the producers had sold the work to the network as a one-hour package," even though the piece itself was only twenty-three minutes. The network "smothered the work by a whole goulash of other things they dumped into the package to fill it up." The choreographer complained that the package was "sickening and patronizing" in browbeating the public about the intrinsic value of "high art"—and Balanchine, certainly more than Stravinsky, understood the fine line one had to walk in dealing with the paying public.[18]

Unquestionably the padding Balanchine mentioned was distracting, but Stravinsky seems to have been aware of the show's format. To the point, television analyst Jack Gould asked, If it was all that disturbing, why did the composer agree? Stravinsky saved Gould's critical review, marking it in his unpublished papers:

> Would the composer consent to a concert appearance without a full awareness and agreement on what would occur before and after his participation? Hence the quandary. In the media in which Stravinsky and Balanchine are normally engaged, it could be assumed that *Noah and the Flood* would not see the light of day in anything like the manner in which it was offered on television. . . . If the giants of the arts in effect make the fundamental concession that television is a world apart, an irascible stepchild of creativity, can they then disassociate themselves from the consequences of their own example? . . . It would seem incumbent on major artistic figures to recognize that while expedient acquiescence may be entirely understandable, it simply cannot simultaneously be hailed as impressive artistic leadership. What television needs most desperately is the vigorous help and guidance of such persons, not their resigned compliance.[19]

Gould's exhortation could be dismissed as mere proselytizing meant to ward off the frequent accusations leveled at the medium. Even so, many musicians wondered about the meaningfulness of the production. Richard Franko Goldman, a prominent spokesperson of the day, suggested that the work signified nothing "except the ultimately vain attempt to sanctify the pretense that art can exist for itself alone, as an object, in a vacuum, not to be loved or believed, but merely to be admired or consumed." He confessed his "distress that . . . Stravinsky's genius and influence did not wish, or was unable, to make something less dismal of the production."[20]

Successful "art" programs of the day, such as *The Voice of Firestone,* showcasing opera divas or beautiful ballerinas in the elegant white tutu tradition of *Swan Lake,* were the kind of entertainment fare viewers wanted as they settled back for their weekly dose of Saturday night culture. These were what American television audiences had come to expect in the 1950s and early 1960s. Television Land wanted something coddling, something to verify comfortably packaged ideas about art, and that is surely what the sponsors expected Stravinsky and Balanchine to provide. The television audience was unprepared to deal with a canting miracle play set to music in a still unfamiliar—and to most, "unmelodic"—compositional style. The production came across as nothing more than a garish mishmash. "What did they expect," asked Stravinsky, "sea chanties?"[21] That is precisely what they expected. Both the composer and choreographer were always energized by a natural contrariness. They delighted in flouting convention. How could the producers of *The Flood* not have known this?

Did they really expect the kind of sugary pabulum Menotti had served up in the emotionally sappy *Amahl?*

In the end, *The Flood* drowned in its own homiletics. Did the production, as Arthur Todd suggested in his essay's subtitle, "set music and dance on TV back a decade"? The unbridgeable abyss separating the artist of range and imagination from the reality of American television was horrendously misjudged by everybody involved, even though the musical score itself is as cohesive and imaginative as the composer's other serial works of the period.

What *The New Grove Dictionary of American Music* calls "possibly the most spectacular failure among television opera performances" (though of course it was not an opera) surely hurt Stravinsky. The composer has often been portrayed as a craggy, unflappable iconoclast, immune to public ridicule. But he was not. At age eighty, surely he was injured personally—and very publicly, through the far-reaching lens of the television camera. It is unlikely that his own premonition of a flop was swallowed as easily as he and others would have us believe.

Balanchine had less at stake. Besides, he was more capable of tossing the criticism aside as trifling and moving on. As always, he remained loyal to the composer, defending *The Flood* as an important and powerful composition and even restaging it (with the help of Jacques d'Amboise) on 11 June as part of the 1982 Stravinsky Festival at Lincoln Center.[22] Ter-Arutunian's sets and costumes were retained (although there were a few changes), and John Houseman now took the important role of the narrator. Adam Lüders and Nina Fedorova were Adam and Eve, and Francisco Moncion played Noah. Using the original CBS videotape as a guide, the choreography was essentially the same as the 1962 telecast, although some of the music was cut. Whereas Balanchine's figurines were photographed as part of the original filming, now students of the School of American Ballet, carrying huge cardboard representations of the Ark's animals, paraded across stage. The reception was mixed. Some felt that the restaging was more effective than the original telecast, confined as it was to television's "small screen," but others still considered the work to be ineffectively staged, and as one critic suggested, in need of "computer graphics to achieve a density equivalent to the music."[23] While both Stravinsky and Balanchine welcomed and indeed flourished in confined boundaries, in this one instance, both the restrictions imposed and the inability of the creators to control the final production may have created too tight a stranglehold. The work has yet to enter the repertoire.

The Flood was one of more than a dozen serial works that Stravinsky completed after *Agon.* From the late 1950s through 1966, the date of his last major opus, the composer did not write another new ballet. Instead, he produced an impressive string of choral and instrumental works, among them *Threni* (1958), *Movements* (1959), *Abraham and Isaac* (1963), *Variations* (1964), and the extraordinarily powerful *Requiem Canticles* (1966). There were a few brief works as well, especially the less-than-a-minute-long *Fanfare for a New Theatre* (1964), written for two trumpets and dedicated to Balanchine and Kirstein on the occasion of the opening of the New York State Theater at Lincoln Center.

The new venue was to be inaugurated with performances of *Agon* and *Movements.* Publicly, Kirstein declared, "We had commissioned no novelty to serve as an appropriate launching of the occasion, but Stravinsky sent us a delightful surprise—a twelve-tone fractured fanfare with trumpets sounding from the top balcony." But in fact, Kirstein was the behind-the-scenes angel here; for it was he who quietly commissioned the "surprise." He approached Craft, not Stravinsky, successfully hoping that Craft could convince the composer to write a new piece to open the festivities. Stravinsky composed the vignette on the afternoon of 23 March. Even here, in the briefest of works, the exacting composer took time to sketch materials and carefully construct the serial structure of the work, which was played opening night, 24 April. A jointly composed Balanchine-Kirstein cable of 26 April reported to Stravinsky that "your trumpet Fanfare . . . was absolutely wonderful, and brilliant beginning to our first public performance. . . . Only thing lacking to make the evening a total success was your absence [*sic*]. Looking forward to seeing you soon. Love. Lincoln and George."[24]

Between *Agon* and *The Flood,* Balanchine continued creating a wide array of stylistically varied ballets. The popular *Stars and Stripes,* with Sousa tunes adapted by Hershy Kay, appeared only a month after *Agon.* From the spring of 1959 came the serially structured *Episodes,* based upon Webern's orchestral music, and jointly assembled with Martha Graham.[25] In early 1960 he redid *Theme and Variations* for Violette Verdy and Edward Villella. Later that same year came *The Figure in the Carpet, Donizetti Variations,* and the beautiful *Liebeslieder Walzer,* to the music of Johannes Brahms, this latter work created at the request of Balanchine's old advocate Morton Baum. The work was popular enough to be televised the next year over the *L'Heure du concert* series on the CBC in Montreal (with which Balanchine worked often).

Although *The Flood* was officially the last work on which Balanchine and Stravinsky collaborated, the choreographer remained on the lookout for preexisting, nonballetic Stravinsky scores. One such work was prepared and premiered in 1960 between *Donizetti Variations* and *Liebeslieder Walzer.* During that spring, Stravinsky completed his *Monumentum pro Gesualdo di Venosa ad CD Annum,* consisting of three Renaissance madrigals rewritten for instruments and commemorating the 400th anniversary of Gesualdo's birth. Balanchine produced the ballet that same fall (with the simpler title *Monumentum pro Gesualdo*), with Diana Adams and Conrad Ludlow, and twelve additional paired dancers.

Exactly when the idea of choreographing the short instrumental collection first entered Balanchine's mind cannot be determined. Richard Buckle suggests that the eager choreographer immediately "seized upon the score," but Robert Craft claims it was he who had to convince Balanchine to take on the project.[26] Each of these three brief instrumental madrigals is choreographed separately, and the entire ballet lasts only about seven minutes. Years earlier, Stravinsky had begun listening to the music of Gesualdo—alternately hailed or disputed as one of the more adventuresome (and to some ears, outlandishly dissonant) of the chromatically progressive late Renaissance composers. But Stravinsky's instrumental recomposing of the three madrigals here is not nearly so extensive as his modification of Renaissance models in the earlier *Agon.* Here everything is closer to the original, more in the composing style of the reconstituted *Pulcinella* of 1920. To be sure, *Monumentum* is unmistakably Stravinskyan, just as the choreography is clearly Balanchinian, but both men had in mind more of an homage than a broadly transformed composition.

As Clive Barnes wrote in the 25 October *New York Times:* "Just as Stravinsky complied with the music's Renaissance flavor in his adaptation, so Balanchine, while not actually quoting from old dances, has managed with the sketch of a flourish, the hint of a gesture, to convey an impression that, while completely modern, offers, if only in its formal poses, the recollections of a civilization long past." The emphasis is more on a quiet and orderly musical and choreographic statement, in keeping with the courtly manner of the Renaissance. While the dance was originally made on Adams, Suzanne Farrell, who took on many of Adams's ballets, soon became associated with it. Farrell fondly remembers how generous Adams was in helping to teach her the work during the mid-1960s, attending early rehearsals as it was assembled and advising her on the style and manner Balanchine had in mind. In September 2001, as part of the George Balanchine Foundation's "Interpreters Archive," Farrell was filmed teaching excerpts from *Movements for Piano and Orchestra* and *Monumentum pro Gesualdo.* The video is forthcoming. Nancy Reynolds, the foundation's director of research, and dance writer Joan Acocella of the *New Yorker* interviewed Farrell. The video records Farrell coaching two dancers from the Suzanne Farrell Ballet, Runqaio Du and Jennifer Fournier.[27]

Balanchine's *Ragtime (I)* appeared a month later. Using Stravinsky's 1918 *Ragtime* (written for eleven instruments, including winds, brass, percussion, and the Hungarian cimbalom—an instrument that had captured the composer's interest), the four-and-a-half-minute score was choreographed for Diana Adams and Bill Carter. This brief duet was part of a larger, jointly choreographed ballet entitled *Jazz Concert,* a quartet of short twentieth-century scores that included another Stravinsky composition, the 1946 *Ebony Concerto,* originally written for Woody Herman, here prepared not by Balanchine but by John Taras.[28] Stravinsky's flirtations with American jazz around the time of the First World War had produced several ragtime scores, including the splendid trio of popular period dances (Tango, Waltz, and Ragtime) danced by the Princess in *L'Histoire du soldat* (1918). The composer's *Piano-Rag-Music* followed in 1919 (later choreographed by Todd Bolender for the 1972 Stravinsky Festival).

Balanchine recalled that he first set *Ragtime* in his pre-Diaghilev days, possibly as early as 1922, as one of several divertissements choreographed before he left Russia. And even though Stravinsky always intended the work as a concert piece, Balanchine was not the only choreographer who was unable to resist the contagious cabaret sound of the music as a prime candidate for dancing. Also in 1922, for example, Léonide Massine and Lydia Lopokova had prepared and performed a duet to the imaginative score at Covent Garden. Balanchine's 1960 setting did not generate much enthusiasm, and it was quickly tossed aside as nothing more than an amusing but innocuous triviality. Still, the choreographer found the music and dance possibilities engaging enough to prepare a completely new version of the score, *Ragtime (II),* produced as part of a July 1966 music festival of Stravinsky's music ("A Festival of Stravinsky: His Heritage and His Legacy") at Lincoln Center's Philharmonic Hall. In addition to a performance of *L'Histoire du Soldat* (with Aaron Copland as the Narrator, Elliott Carter as the Soldier, and John Cage as the Devil) and other important works, Lukas Foss had asked Balanchine to choreograph a few Stravinsky works that could be presented on the apron in front of the orchestra.[29]

Suzanne Farrell and Arthur Mitchell, already up in Saratoga Springs for City Ballet's annual summer residence, returned to New York for the performance. The work was given again six months later, in early 1967 across the plaza on the larger stage of the State Theater. But the critics still dismissed it. As Doris Hering wrote for *Dance Magazine:*"There are exaggerated extensions; little circling promenades, one foot flat, the other on pointe or half toe; there are finger-snappings and hands circling at the wrist. But a trifle is a trifle. And jazz is Balanchine's one choreographic weak spot."[30]

That Balanchine thought enough of the work to set it twice is not surprising. Historically it is a more important work than one might at first think, for it summarizes Stravinsky's treatment, or stylization, of ragtime as he understood it at a time when the form was all the rage, attracting not only his attention but that of other European composers as well. The composer recalls studying "a whole pile of this music" because it captivated him with its "freshness, and the novel rhythm which so distinctly revealed its Negro origin," and allowed him to create "a composite portrait of this new dance music."[31] The energy of the music—music suffused with Joplinesque syncopations—was part of the overall rhythmic fabric of the composer's work that always enchanted Balanchine.

With 1961 came Balanchine's *Raymonda Variations,* and in early 1962 the important full-length two-act ballet, *A Midsummer Night's Dream.* The hapless television premiere of *The Flood* followed on 14 June, although both Stravinsky and Balanchine had traveled to Hamburg for the composer's 18 June birthday, where the octogenarian's celebration culminated in a New York City Ballet performance of his three "Greek" ballets.[32] Balanchine's next ballet, *Bugaku,* with a commissioned score by Toshiro Mayuzumi and created for Allegra Kent and Edward Villella, premiered in the spring of 1963.

A month later, on 9 April, one of Balanchine's most innovative ballets made on a Stravinsky score originally intended for concert was given. *Movements for Piano and Orchestra,* begun in 1958 and finished at the end of July 1959, is a terse, densely compacted nine-minute work employing a prominent, but still chamberlike *concertante* piano part. As Stravinsky himself pointed out, the five-movement opus was the most intricately conceived serial composition he had undertaken to date. Indeed, the compositional distance covered since *Agon* less than two years earlier is staggering. Balanchine's newest ballet eventually came to be performed in tandem with *Monumentum* (with only a brief curtain in between)—a felicitous coupling for many reasons, including the juxtaposition of Stravinsky's own dual interests in the literature of the Renaissance and the Webernesque *Movements.*[33]

While *Movements* was not as much of a genuine collaboration as *Agon,* there is little question that Balanchine discussed the score with the composer. Several German and Canadian television directors and filmmakers, for instance, were following Stravinsky around at the time, recording his every move for their documentaries. They often capture Balanchine in conversation with the composer, asking questions about how a work is put together; and Stravinsky in turn offers explanations to a nodding Balanchine about pulses, rhythms, and structural relations. They jointly conduct a score silently, each stressing the beats. Stravinsky attended a rehearsal of *Movements* (part of which was also recorded on film) only a few days before Suzanne Farrell, Jacques d'Amboise, and an ensemble of six women premiered the work on 9 April at the City Center of Music and Drama. Gordon Boelzner, Balanchine's erstwhile rehearsal pianist, performed the important piano obbligato, and his own recollections of the event are useful in understanding the choreographer's treatment of the complex score—complex not only serially but rhythmically as well.[34]

Reporting on the rehearsal in *Themes and Episodes,* Stravinsky recalled that he was amazed that the dancers' knowledge of the music was so thorough that they could count precisely without the music being played. He described the ballet as a double concerto in which the male and female soloists are "identified" with the piano solo that filters through all five concise movements, while the corps de ballet represents the varied timbres of the colorful orchestration. Moreover, it was *Movements* that prompted the composer to speak more glowingly of Balanchine's illuminative powers than ever before:

> Balanchine's visualization of the *Movements* exposed relationships of which I had not been aware in the same way. Seeing it, therefore, was like touring a building for which I had drawn the plans but never completely explored the result. He began by identifying familiar appendages of my musical style, of which I myself became conscious only through his eyes. And as I watched him fastening on the tiniest repeated rhythmic figure, I knew that he had joined the score to my other music faster than it could ever get there by way of the concert hall. Beyond that, he discovered the lyricism of the piece; his dramatic point is a love parable—in which ballet is it not?— and his coda has a suggestion of the ending of *Apollo.*[35]

This is easily one of the most magnanimous assessments of a fellow artist that Stravinsky ever offered. But how much could Balanchine have really enlightened the composer about the work's deep-seated serial organization? Certainly, Stravinsky was thoroughly familiar with the network of interiorly complex structural relations—relations that were far more interrelated even than in a work like *Agon.* More likely, Balanchine's visualization simply but elegantly revealed for the composer the beauties of the "building's" architecture. It is here particularly that choreographic analyses—too often underestimated by musicians—are capable of addressing structural parallels and deeper relations invisible to the composer or listener who may be too close to the score to hear. Moreover, musico-choreographic analyses may lead us to a recognition of how the elements of music and dance interact—and those interactions are easily missed unless both sides of the music-dance equation are pursued. Still, Garis is right on the money in suggesting that "perhaps not until he saw Balanchine's choreography for *Movements* did Stravinsky come not so much to *understand* the piece he had just composed as at last to *like* it."[36] The two views are, of course, perfectly compatible. Finally, Stravinsky was no fool: what he understood indubitably was that *Movements,* far more even than *Agon,* would have remained one of many impenetrably obscure twelve-tone essays had Balanchine not staged it so magnificently.

Despite the terseness of Stravinsky's music, the same fundamental compositional principles of tension, release, and architectural balance are apparent. In essence, Balanchine treats the score no differently from earlier Stravinsky works, tonal or serial. Texture, instrumentation, the division between the pianist and orchestra—all these were used to help define the music's structure choreographically. But we are so overwhelmed by the way in which we must reconceive these elements that only a person like Balanchine would have the courage to undertake the project and modify his own notions about dancing— or in this case, a minimum of dancing.

The six women of the corps are paired most notably in two trios and dominate the sculpturelike poses of the four interludes separating the five brief movements. As the London *Times* reported, *Movements* seemed to be a work unfolding in suspended animation: "Its appeal is at once musical and spatial and its dancers seem like a mobile caught in the breath of the music."[37] Very little motion is expended in the dancers' occupation of stationary space, just as the brief interludes (which Stravinsky added as an afterthought to the score) help distinguish the material of the piano soloist and orchestral ensemble. In fundamental ways the small corps of women functions similarly to the corps in *Agon* and even sections of *Apollo,* that is, they are more than supportive in defining the music's multileveled layers.

As for the two soloists, *Movements* will always be associated with d'Amboise; but it was the brilliant introduction of Suzanne Farrell, during the company's final year at the City Center, that in some ways would change City Ballet and, just as significantly, Balanchine himself. Of all his muses, perhaps no ballerina had such an enrapturing influence on him and the company. Farrell joined the company in 1962 and in the eyes of many of the dancers soon became Balanchine's obsession. Adding to her allure, her relationship with the choreographer remained shrouded in a certain mystery, even when center stage shone its bright light on her, as it did for many years.

At the last moment Farrell was called upon to replace Diana Adams (who had been the first to point out the young dancer to Balanchine). Adams's pregnancy prevented her from dancing the premiere of *Movements.* As they often-told story goes, Farrell was dragged off to Adams's apartment, where the dancer, now consigned to a couch by her physician, taught the complex choreography to the eager, wanting-to-please Farrell within a few hours. Balanchine, naturally, was reluctant to entrust such an important Stravinsky ballet to a young and untried seventeen-year-old. Even though the premiere was scheduled, he seemed ready to cancel; but John Taras and Jacques d'Amboise prevailed in convincing him that the gifted, quick-learning Farrell was up to the task.

Farrell addressed this historic turning point in her autobiography *Holding On to the Air.* She remembers that d'Amboise took over, rehearsing their intricately intertwined solo parts as well as the ensemble. When she learned the choreography at Adams's apartment, there was no music; she rehearsed with Boelzner the next day; then a day later Balanchine watched her work through the ballet with d'Amboise. As she recalls that fateful rehearsal, Balanchine must have observed a choreography that wasn't quite what he had originally conceived for Adams's body; but evidently what he saw pleased him: "Rehearsals with him were immediately scheduled with the six corps girls. He began altering, fixing and changing things to fit, although he remained as quiet and calm as usual."[38] She also recalls that on 7 April, just two days before the first performance (the premiere was part of an all-Stravinsky program that included *Apollo* and *Orpheus*), she rehearsed the work for a group of visitors that included not only Lincoln Kirstein but Stravinsky himself. Moreover, the rehearsal was being filmed by NDF for West German television.

Part of the filmed rehearsal was included in Tony Palmer's biopic, *Aspects of Stravinsky.* The young Farrell and d'Amboise are shown working through a section of *Movements* as Balanchine stands and moves around them in a circle, interjecting a few suggestions: "Don't shake it there," Balanchine instructs Farrell as she works through a passage with her partner. D'Amboise lifts Farrell, turning her in an inverted cartwheel while Balanchine watches closely. Farrell tests a series of precarious balances and suspensions—the kind of dynamic sculptural poses for which the ballet is known. The film catches some of the corps work as well. Everything is done slowly and deliberately so that Balanchine can judge each section clearly.[39] Balanchine is heard speaking in the background, praising Stravinsky's contribution to dance: "Everything that is now used for fifty years, it's all Stravinsky." Then the choreographer and composer are shown snacking and conversing informally in a relaxed exchange as they discuss the musical matters of pulse and accent: "You don't really need to accentuate time to be in time," Balanchine adds, to Stravinsky's approval.

Stravinsky, as with everybody else, was immediately struck by Farrell's performance of *Movements* at the rehearsal. Like Diana Adams before her, she quickly became Balanchine's primary instrument for bringing the composer's scores to the stage. Stravinsky had asked about her during the rehearsal and, so the story goes, Balanchine proudly informed the composer that she was Suzanne Farrell, "just been born." Two important works featuring Farrell followed: *Meditation* in late 1963, with Jacques d'Amboise, and then the much-discussed three-act ballet *Don Quixote,* to a score by Nicolas Nabokov, in the spring of 1965. But to say that Nabokov composed the music would be to minimize greatly Balanchine's deep involvement in the work's actual evolution.

Nabokov was in constant touch with Balanchine, and to a sizable extent the choreographer dictated the score's actual orchestration. In a 14 April 1965 letter to music director Robert Irving, Nabokov reported that Balanchine had specifically asked for three trumpets, three trombones, and church bells (even though the orchestra would have to hire additional musicians). A few days later, on 18 April (now only a month before the premiere), Balanchine wrote to Nabokov, encouraging him to compose a "'prelude' before the curtain goes up . . . about a minute long, a few slow chords, maybe. If you don't have time, we can add it later, after opening night."

The ballet would go through numerous revisions over the next thirteen years, including changes in scenery, new dances, and additional music. Writing to Barbara Horgan in 1972, Nabokov speaks to Balanchine's suggestion for several musical changes in Act 1. Writing again to Horgan in 1977, Nabokov responds to the choreographer's request for new music: "This is one of the 4 variations George wanted me to do for Act I. . . . Tell George that the finale to the classical ballet (a Waltz on the theme he knows only too well) is written, but I have not got the time to orchestrate it." Throughout the correspondence over the years it becomes abundantly clear that Balanchine had definite ideas about nearly every aspect of the ballet's musical shape and was unhesitant in asserting his ideas.[40]

Less than a year after the original 1965 production, Farrell would be featured in another Stravinsky work, *Variations,* premiered on 31 March 1966, although the

12.2 Stravinsky's short score for *Variations* (1964), which he sent to Balanchine (Harvard Theatre Collection, The Houghton Library)

score (dedicated to Aldous Huxley, who had died four months earlier) was composed as a concert piece in 1964 and first performed in Chicago in April 1965 (fig. 12.2).[41] Stravinsky's newest twelve-tone score was a set of symphonic variations, and like *Agon, Variations* was once again immediately labeled Space

Age music, meaning, one supposes, that it was inaccessible (Stravinsky himself quipped that the music was analyzed more than it was performed).

But to a far greater extent than the 1957 ballet, *Variations* was based upon manipulations of the number twelve, in terms of formal divisions (twelve-part variations) and instrumentation (twelve solo violins at one point in the score). Even though there was no direct collaboration, Balanchine again understood the structural basis of the work and accordingly organized the choreography around the "twelvness" of the music. In Balanchine's choreography, the ballet consists of three repeated iterations of the entire brief score: the first playing is choreographed for twelve women; the second iteration is for six men; and the final hearing has Farrell solo. The first section features an ensemble in countless designs that open and close like so many "lovely geometrical explosions," as Clive Barnes wrote in the *New York Times.* The second playing of the score, for six men, employs various symmetrical divisions, especially the splitting of the men into two groups that, somewhat like *Agon,* mirror each other in an attempt to show the divisions of the score. As for Farrell's concluding solo—a tour de force featuring her speed and precision—she remembers that she "slunk like an inchworm, jumped in circles, kicked on diagonals, and finally, a few worlds later, took a huge arabesque reaching to the heavens, dived to the floor, and caught myself in an acrobatic walkover before striking a classical ballet pose and running offstage."[42]

In more unreleased CBS film footage (only a brief excerpt of which is included in the Palmer documentary) Stravinsky visits the New York State Theater to watch Farrell dance a portion of *Variations.* He and his wife get out of their limousine, and Vera says, "Now we will see what we will see," to which a glinting Stravinsky replies, "Now we will see the girls." He is led backstage, where Balanchine and Farrell join him. Composer and choreographer converse while Farrell stands demurely with her eyes cast down, not saying a word. "I find that music is more useful than statements," Stravinsky offers; Balanchine agrees, adding, "A statement is a cliché because it lasts longer and everybody repeats it and they don't know what it means."

Stravinsky thanks Balanchine for choreographing *Variations* so wonderfully: "To say that I was very happy with what you did with my music is not enough." He then approaches Farrell, formally shakes her hand with his familiar courtly bow, and says, "I thank you for what you do, for your dancing." Farrell, as timid as she was in the NDR filming of *Apollo,* replies almost inaudibly, "I enjoy dancing," then quickly turns away with an obvious gesture of relief at having survived the moment. One sympathizes with the young dancer, understandably nervous in the presence of the great composer. The film then cuts to Stravinsky seated onstage watching Balanchine work with Farrell, clearly all arranged for the camera's benefit. He poses her in various positions for Stravinsky to observe. Choreographer and composer walk offstage together, speaking in Russian, leaving the young ballerina to trail along, unsure where she should be or what she should be doing.

Farrell next appeared, again with d'Amboise, in the final, gypsy Rondo alla Zingarese movement of Balanchine's *Brahms-Schoenberg Quartet,* staged less than a month after *Variations.* That summer she danced a newly choreographed solo to Stravinsky's 1944 *Elégie* for solo viola as part of the Stravinsky Festival at Philharmonic Hall. (She repeated it in Saratoga a few weeks later, along with *Ragtime (II).*) Another new work, *Jewels,* in which Farrell and d'Amboise were featured, premiered in the spring of 1967. The now celebrated couple danced the final *Diamonds* section to the music of Tchaikovsky. The first section, *Emeralds,* was set to music of Fauré.

But *Rubies,* the central section of this plotless, full-length ballet of three unrelated acts, was based on another old, brilliantly orchestrated Stravinsky score, the 1929 *Capriccio* for piano and orchestra. The composer had originally written the twenty-minute concerto for himself at a time when he was touring as a pianist. Gordon Boelzner now played the demanding solo part.[43] Stravinsky took up the piece immediately after finishing *Le Baiser de la Fée,* and the dance-like quality of that Tchaikovskyan score is evident in sections of the *Capriccio.* But more than anything it is the colorful orchestration and frenetic textural "speed" of the yet-to-be composed *Jeu de Cartes* that pours out. In many ways, the third and last movement of *Capriccio* is an obvious sketch study for that 1937 ballet.

Balanchine surely understood the danceability of Stravinsky's 1929 piano work; and he catches Stravinsky's neoclassic adaptation of the jazz with which the composer was so enamored during that period. Nor can there be any doubt that Balanchine would have been familiar with the score since the composer regularly performed it throughout Europe during the late 1920s and early 1930s. In his *Autobiography,* Stravinsky remembered that the work was based on the true definition of a capriccio as given by Praetorius: a fantasy with a freely organized form allowing flights of imagination without a rigorous architectural scheme. "This form enabled me to develop my music by the juxtaposition of episodes of various kinds which follow one another and by their very nature give the piece that aspect of caprice from which it takes its name."[44] Villella, for whom the work was created, remembers that Stravinsky's free-swinging score (especially the last movement, wherein the piano and orchestra chase that runs throughout is matched by Villella's virtuosic running around the stage pursued by the other male dancers) was one of Balanchine's favorites.

Villella's memories of his close interaction with Balanchine on the work are illuminating for an understanding of how Balanchine worked to meld many disparate models as fundamental material on which to base his choreography:

> I felt Mr. B used everything he knew about me in the pieces, and his intimacy with my technique gave me security. . . . He was fond of horses, adored the Lippizaners of Vienna [even learning to ride one during the 1966 Saratoga season]. And the company had recently been spending time in Saratoga, during the racing season. The track atmosphere was one of the many elements he was integrating into *Rubies;* horse racing seemed to be behind all our prancing. . . . There were other influences . . . Degas, Astaire, the world of jazz and show dancing, the brashness and confidence of Broadway nightclubs. Balanchine choreographed a tango into the pas de deux. He even worked cakewalk movements into some of the steps. This kind of layering is a part of every Balanchine ballet and gives them an extra dimension, a subtext that he rarely took time to point out or discuss. On those rare occasions, he'd open the door a little bit and let in some light. But just a glimpse.[45]

After the box-office-pleasing *Jewels,* Balanchine would set only one other Stravinsky work while the composer, now in declining health, was still able to at least discuss matters with the choreographer. *Requiem Canticles,* written for vocal soloists, chorus, and orchestra was finished in August 1966—the last major composition Stravinsky completed. It is a thoroughly serial work based upon two twelve-tone rows and symmetrically constructed with six vocal movements. These are introduced, divided in the middle, and ended with an instrumental postlude. The text is based upon portions of the Requiem Mass. Fifteen minutes in length, it is one of Stravinsky's most moving compositions.

Balanchine presented a ballet arrangement of the score in early May 1968 as a memorial for the recently slain Martin Luther King. It was performed on the same program as the premiere of the couldn't-be-more-different *Slaughter on Tenth Avenue,* another tour de force for Arthur Mitchell and Suzanne Farrell. Kirstein organized the performance, having been a supporter of King's (he marched among the protesters in Alabama). Stravinsky was pleased with Balanchine's tribute to King, writing to the choreographer, "I am honored that my music is to be played in memory of a man of God, a man of the poor, a man of peace." Farrell and Mitchell, along with a corps de ballet, presented the work only once. With costumes by Rouben Ter-Arutunian, the dancers—or rather, processional celebrants in what amounts to a ritualized threnody—are dressed in white robes, walking barefoot, each bearing with great dignity a three-stemmed candelabrum as they move about in the dark of the stage. One woman, Farrell, during the poignant Lacrimosa section, futilely moves among the others, searching but never finding. At the end of the score Mitchell, dressed in purple robes, is raised high, representing King himself.[46]

Toward the end of Arnold Newman's collection of photographs, *Bravo Stravinsky*, there are several pictures of Stravinsky and Balanchine discussing *Requiem Canticles* together while the choreographer demonstrates some of his ideas after the two men have listened to a recording. Stravinsky was in California when Balanchine's production was given its one performance. But as the photographs demonstrate, he was still interested in having some say in the ballet. Balanchine was, as always, concerned with the look of the production, even though he realized that this would not become a repertory piece. And ever sensitive to his friend's music and opinions, he made a point of familiarizing him with the staged work as best he could. Just a few weeks after the performance, Edward Bigelow wrote to Stravinsky,

> George wanted you to see this film of *Requiem Canticles* which was done during rehearsal on the afternoon of the Second of May, on the day of the performance. You will note that there are two prints. Two cameras were used and the cameramen were instructed to shoot full stage, which you will note they did not do, but decided instead to "create"—which means the visual pictures George intended, and accomplished, are rather ruined because of our cameramen's unfortunate "creative decisions." However, looking at both prints should give a fair idea of what George did.[47]

There were to be no more collaborations based upon preexisting Stravinsky scores. The last few years of Stravinsky's life produced a few smaller works and arrangements. Still, nothing of the magnitude of the imaginative serial works of the 1960s was to come forth, and nothing that Balanchine could use in a way that would bring attention to the composer's music—the choreographer's main concern. Indeed, with a few exceptions in 1970, especially *Who Cares?* to various Gershwin tunes and *Suite No. 3* to Tchaikovsky's music, and in 1971 (*Concerto for Jazz Band and Orchestra* to a score by Rolf Liebermann), relatively few new Balanchine ballets would be made. One project especially, *PAMTGG*, proved a disaster, raising questions about the choreographer's talents and interests.[48]

Balanchine and Le Clercq divorced in February 1969. Some speculated that a despondent Balanchine would leave America for Europe. Others now took on many of the new ballets for the company, including d'Amboise, John Clifford, Richard Tanner, and especially Jerome Robbins with *Dances at a Gathering*. Of course, Balanchine remained active, with several new works during a period some have wrongly considered fallow. Still, it was not until he decided to stage the ambitiously envisioned Stravinsky Festival of 1972—notably, without his muse, Farrell, who left the company in 1969—that the world would once again witness the full, uncurbed range of his powers.

Chapter 13 After Stravinsky

Stravinsky is who is responsible for anything we are using in music . . .
everything we have in music he did first. . . . He was like Einstein—nobody
like him. He made musique dansante. There have only been three who
could do it. Delibes, Tchaikovsky, and Stravinsky. They made music for the
body to dance to. . . . We can't make time. Maybe not even space. There
are men who say there is no time, no space. But Stravinsky made time—
not big grand time—but time that works with the small parts of how our
bodies are made. . . . So we know how great Stravinsky is to us. Probably
dance would stop if we didn't have Stravinsky.
—*George Balanchine, 1972*

Igor Stravinsky died in New York on the morning of 6 April 1971, at
the age of eighty-eight. His health had been deteriorating for many
years, but his tenacity and resilience had always allowed him to rally.
Although he had attempted to compose a little and to orchestrate
some of his favorite music, it was clear that physically, at least, he
could not continue much longer. For many, the extinguishing of his
creative spirit was difficult to witness. Yet long after others abandoned
the failing composer during those final years, claiming that his decline
was too much to bear, Balanchine faithfully visited, chatted, dined,

and conversed in Russian with him, even during the week of the composer's death. To the end, the choreographer remained one of Stravinsky's most loyal, caring friends.

For well over half a century the incisive pulse of Stravinsky's music had provided Balanchine with what he once called the dancer's "floor." The music's boundless energy magnetized him. Altogether he choreographed about half of what most would consider the composer's major works. Occasionally the music so fascinated him that he took up the same score more than once, in some cases for minor refurbishing but sometimes for a complete reconstruction. Balanchine first choreographed Stravinsky's 1931 Concerto in D for violin and orchestra in 1941 as *Balustrade,* transplanting the concerto from the concert halls of Europe and the United States, where it was performed with limited success, to the New York stage.

Stravinsky may have been eager to find a new venue for his Violin Concerto since it had fared disappointingly as a concert work. Aaron Copland, who heard an early performance, wrote that despite the work's "formal perfection . . . [and] masterly orchestration," much of the material was "banal." He was left with the impression that the concerto "is essentially a mere tour de force, brilliance for its own sake, and might be pointed to as the first indication Stravinsky has given of a weakening of his powers."[1] Nor did the work ever really enter the standard concerto repertoire, much to the composer's annoyance, although it has been played (and in fact still is occasionally performed) by some of the century's finest violinists: Kyung-Wha Chung, Pamela Frank, Nathan Milstein, David Oistrakh, Arnold Steinhardt, Isaac Stern, and especially Itzhak Perlman, whose performance of the work particularly pleased the composer. But Jascha Heifetz apparently refused to play it, and to Stravinsky's irritation his friend Joseph Szigeti (with whom the composer often collaborated in piano-violin programs) did not mention the opus in his autobiography, even though he too had played it.

Thirty years after the premiere of *Balustrade,* the ballet was completely reconceived in 1972 and renamed *Violin Concerto.* "Stravinsky never wrote *Balustrade*"; Balanchine insisted, "He wrote *Violin Concerto.* The ballet should be announced as what it is. Then the musicians can come, the young people who love music and who want to hear the composition—they'll know what they're getting. They don't have to look at the ballet if it bores them, they can just listen to the music. And that's fine with me, that's wonderful."[2] In an even greater tribute, Balanchine again retitled the ballet in 1973: *Stravinsky Violin Concerto.*

As such it remains one of the New York City Ballet's most often performed, ebullient offerings.

Many feel that Balanchine was at the top of his game when choreographing concert music. He himself admitted feeling hampered by the imposition of a prefabricated scenario. Too frequently, he contended, the dance was unable to rise above a visual appurtenance since the drama of the story was expected to be illustrated in exacting choreographic detail. "A plot is a very difficult thing for the dance," he remarked. "You cannot dance a story."[3] Concert music liberated the musically astute Balanchine. It exfoliated the unneeded layers of narrative, allowing balletic movement to speak fully and singularly in behalf of the score alone. Content and structure became one. To the annoyance of his critics, as we have seen, Balanchine embraced a dictum his detractors saw as insufferable sermonizing: "You do not go to the ballet only to see, but also to hear." Although the 1941 *Balustrade* was billed as a plotless abstract ballet, nonetheless the choreographer felt encumbered by the burdensome distraction of restrictive costumes and scenery, which had "messed up the dance," as Denby then commented. Moreover, such overwhelming visual contrivances could only draw one's attention away from Stravinsky's music. Now, with his 1972 transformation of the scintillating Violin Concerto, Balanchine welcomed the occasion to create a ballet based on "nothing but pure music" and without Tchelitchev's "pussycats and birds."[4]

Violin Concerto was a benchmark—the sixty-eight-year-old choreographer's first opportunity to stage one of his old friend's works without his guidance, input, collaboration, requisite approval, even, perhaps, intervention. Indeed, it should be noted that Balanchine choreographed many of his Stravinsky ballets after the composer died, mainly as a consequence of the two important festivals of 1972 and 1982. He began rehearsing his new version of *Violin Concerto* during the autumn of 1971. But he initially thought about replenishing the ballet during the summer season in Saratoga. Nancy Goldner reports that when the company made its seasonal upstate trek, "Balanchine took with him a batch of Stravinsky recordings."[5]

Just as *Balustrade* was Balanchine's first ballet choreographed to a Stravinsky concert score (that is, not a work composed expressly as a ballet), so *Violin Concerto* now marked the first major work he would prepare in the post-Stravinsky era. After nearly fifty years of unquestioned devotion to Stravinsky, Balanchine was finally on his own. What would he do? Perhaps one sensed a sigh of relief in his precurtain remarks to the first-night audience when he jested that the recently departed Stravinsky had telephoned him from the great beyond, saying, "George, it's all yours. Do what you want." To understand what Balanchine wanted, and what he achieved, *Violin Concerto* must first be placed in the historical context of the 1972 Stravinsky Festival. The ambitious undertaking constituted the century's most prodigious musical exhibition of the composer's music—a spectacular "banquet," in the choreographer's gastronomic description.

Just before the curtain rose on the 17 June 1971 premiere of *PAMTGG*, Barbara Horgan recalls that she was taken off-guard when Balanchine suddenly unveiled to her the idea for a festival.[6] Oblivious to the backstage commotion all around him, he announced his intention matter-of-factly: this time next year, he proclaimed, there would be a Stravinsky festival. Quickly plans began taking shape. An army of choreographers, dancers, and designers worked tirelessly. Under the able leadership of Robert Irving, the orchestra learned a great deal of new music in a very short time. Vera Stravinsky and Robert Craft were consulted about repertoire. Irving joined Craft and Balanchine in finalizing what would become seven completely different programs—a staggering undertaking.

Balanchine envisaged the Stravinsky festival as a bacchanalia, not a memorial. The one-week celebration would offer a jubilant retrospective of a man whose music had literally brought about a new order in the worlds of music and ballet. As he simply and eloquently summarized his friend's legacy, "After Stravinsky we are not the same as before him." Kirstein recalled that initially a longer celebration ranging over the three-month spring season was contemplated; but Balanchine had his own idea. He "insisted on the imploded fusion of one big bang," Kirstein remembered, to commence on 18 June, which would have been the composer's ninetieth birthday.[7]

Writing in the festival's souvenir program, several of Stravinsky's closest collaborators and friends succinctly captured some of his essential qualities. In an article entitled "Craftsman, Artist, Genius," W. H. Auden remembered Stravinsky as "a paradigm of the creative artist," a man who thought of himself as a "maker" who, like Balanchine, did not wait for or depend upon inspiration. Goddard Lieberson, Vera Zorina's second husband and producer of many of Stravinsky's recordings over the years, portrayed him as "the most contemporaneous of men," continually driven to "enter new worlds" even into his eighties. This was a perpetually young, even childlike man, Lieberson firmly declared, a man unwilling to don the comfortable clothes of an elder master and churn out formulaic scores. Kirstein too wrote insightfully of Stravinsky's canon, consisting of "concreteness, stricture and structure [and] inherited objective discipline." These were not the paroxysmal musings concerning a composer romantically eulogized as an untouchable genius. Rather—and just as Stravinsky would have wanted—those who knew him best limned a more honest portrait of a hard-edged artisan always eager to tackle whatever challenge presented itself.

The festival included some of the composer's most important ballets, as well as significant nonstaged works (including the early 1908 *Fireworks* and the 1930 *Symphony of Psalms,* which solemnly closed the seventh and final program on 25 June).[8] Of the three dozen works presented during the festival, thirty were ballets. Most of these were premieres prepared by several choreographers: Todd Bolender, John Clifford, Lorca Massine, Jerome Robbins, Richard Tanner, and John Taras. But the eight newly choreographed works by Balanchine stood magisterially as the event's centerpiece. Given his everyday responsibilities supervising a huge company, let alone the logistics of mounting such a daunting, week-long production, the creation of so many new works was an extraordinary achievement. It sent a clarion signal that his energy and creative imagination, despite growing rumors to the contrary, remained undiminished. As Clive Barnes wrote about Balanchine and the company in his 2 July review for the *New York Times,* "There has never been as creative an outburst as this in the history of ballet."

As the company prepared to transport much of the festival's repertoire north to Saratoga Springs for July, Walter Terry remembered that Balanchine—uncharacteristically—had encouraged a friend to "see my *Violin Concerto.* It is very good! My other ballets? . . . Okay, but not so good." Terry himself agreed that *Violin Concerto* was unequaled in quality: "The choreographic wedding with the *Violin Concerto* is wholly new and lies in that genre of music visualization, or extension of sound rhythms and timbres into body rhythms and textures."[9] Following Saratoga, it was on to Russia in the autumn, where Balanchine boldly programmed *Violin Concerto.* He knew the work would be misunderstood, remembers Barbara Horgan, but he was adamant. The company had first toured the Soviet Union a decade earlier. And while the interim may have slightly tempered the Russian denigration of abstract ballet, much was the same. Yuri Slonimsky's September 1972 Leningrad review was to the point. In questioning Balanchine's formalist approach to dance, Slonimsky also synopsized the choreographer's visual achievement in setting the composer's music— the only standard by which Balanchine wished to be measured:

In Stravinsky's *Violin Concerto* (1931), Balanchine dons the full armor of "visible music" which, incidentally, the composer considered to be his partner's highest achievement. Balanchine consciously and wholeheartedly devotes himself and his performers to the fulfillment of this task[,] which he considers the most important. In his devotion to it he occasionally transforms people onstage into graphically outlined symbols (could this account for the dancers' black outfits?), performing every zigzag of Stravinsky's thought, irony, joke, etc. No matter how unexpected, artful and complex the combinations of sound, Balanchine immediately responds by corresponding combinations of arms, legs, torso and head. There is food for thought here—occasionally dance becomes servant to music, and the human quality to dancing. And at such times, it seems to me that the performers are like marionettes operated by an experienced puppeteer. Only in the two duets do the soloists, and in the *capriccio,* the corps de ballet, cease being the slaves of interpretation of sound, acquire flesh and blood and indulge in human emotions.[10]

Back in the United States, the ballet quickly became one of the company's most durable works. Yet beyond its popularity, *Stravinsky Violin Concerto* occupies a historically critical position in the Stravinsky-Balanchine annals for more important reasons. If nothing else, the fact that Balanchine himself recommended the ballet is remarkable. He would watch entire performances of the work from start to finish with considerable satisfaction—his "pet" ballet, it came to be known. He told Patricia McBride that it was his greatest accomplishment. Even more unexpected, when asked his opinion of the ballet, the usually closemouthed Balanchine confided to Karin von Aroldingen, one of the dancers for whom the work was created, that above all of his other works *Stravinsky Violin Concerto* was so well crafted that he felt no need to change it.[11]

The ballet is also memorable in marking a crossroads for another of its principals, Peter Martins, though he had been with the company for years. Robert Garis felt that Martins was a "major creation of the festival," having been until then only "an adequate dancer." By the time Garis saw the ballet, "the large and handsome body had at last gotten wired and Martins had become an interesting dancer, not just a beauty." As Martins wrote in his autobiography *Far from Denmark,* "*Violin Concerto* was my chance to show that I could dance 'Balanchine.' I knew that I could, and now I would prove it to him." He supposed that Balanchine conceived the choreography in terms of how he thought of Martins as a dancer. Balanchine's trust in Martins grew. "He'd come to rehearsal with the start of an idea—'Something like this, dear'—and sometimes he would say when I'd improvise around it, 'That's exactly right, that's good,' and sometimes he'd say, 'Well, could be done that way too, but . . .' Then he'd get up from his chair and show me. He made me feel as if I were collaborating with him, and in fact he considers this whole process of making ballets a true collaboration between the creator and what the body of the dancer can do—the better the body the better the collaboration."[12]

Balanchine lavished attention on *Violin Concerto,* committing more than a hundred hours of rehearsal to its preparation. It officially entered the rehearsal studio on 7 November 1971; by February 1972 the work was pronounced ready. Even so, Horgan remembers that the actual choreography was produced with undreamed-of speed and facility (as opposed to another of the festival's premieres, *Symphony in Three Movements*). The entire twenty-two-minute work was designed in only a few days. Surely the ease with which Balanchine actualized the ballet was partially a consequence of knowing the music intimately, having set it once before. And as usual, he immersed himself in every aspect of the production. These two ballets and a third, the equally impressive *Duo Concertant,* were presented in Balanchine's now-familiar leotards. The three proved to be the festival's most successful productions, and more than twenty-five years later, all remain repertoire staples. In several ways, the three form a trilogy, for compositionally all are written in the *concertante* style. Understanding the structural principles of this style runs to the heart of Balanchine's musically discerning conception of these three scores.

The root of the term *concertante* suggests that instrumental forces are working with one another "in concert." But the term carries a more specific connotation for musicians. Although historians are likely to cavil about its origins, *concertante* designates orchestral works that employ prominent solos, or compositions without orchestra in which two or more solo instruments are featured. By the end of the eighteenth century, the term was broadly viewed as describing not a work with a strictly defined formal design but rather a particular style of playing. Virtuoso display was usually stressed, and at a minimum the "concertante part" (or parts) occupied an axial role in the composition—a role akin to a concerto soloist, although it was often enfolded more integrally into the ensemble. Frequently the soloists were directly pitted against one another, or at least set apart as friendly adversaries from the separate forces of the surrounding orchestral or chamber instrumentalists. Above all, at the core of concertante compositions is a musical dichotomy expressed in terms of either a confrontation or a dialogue.

Who more than Balanchine understood the basic tenets of theater and the natural intrigue of conflict presented in a concertante struggle of pushing and pulling musical forces? As he often argued, the dynamics, ritual, and rival polarities of the male-female "dance" (both literally and figuratively) provided the only plot ballet needed. This itself was sufficient to hold an audience's attention, so why enfeeble its elemental power with unneeded, overladen story lines? Moreover, much of Stravinsky's music, by explicit title or otherwise, naturally has a concertante quality to it. There is an intrinsic textural counterpoint. And where there is counterpoint there is the potential for interplay, for conflict and conciliation, distinctiveness and dependency—a range of dualities that often unfold with endless variation, yet always within the parameters of an overarching unity. No wonder Balanchine was drawn to the dramatic opportunities such scores afforded.

As early as 1924 the young choreographer had prepared the slow movement of a Glazunov violin concerto as a pas de deux for a production in Petrograd. During the 1940s he choreographed no fewer than eight ballets based upon concertante scores, including *Balustrade, Ballet Imperial* (1941, to the music of a Tchaikovsky concerto), and quite importantly, as we shall see, *Concerto Barocco* (also 1941, using the music of Bach's Concerto in D-minor for two violins). Several concerto movements by Mozart, Saint-Saëns, Grieg, and Schumann were also choreographed. His choreography for Hindemith's *Four Temperaments,* commissioned in 1946 for Ballet Society, a resplendent concertante score for solo piano and strings, remains a masterpiece, as does the 1947 ballet *Symphonie Concertante,* based upon Mozart's score of the same name for violin and viola soloists with orchestra.[13]

Balanchine first heard the 1932 *Duo Concertant,* composed immediately after Stravinsky's 1931 Concerto in D for violin and orchestra, in France shortly after it was written. The two instruments contribute equally to the interchange, for this is not merely a violin piece accompanied by piano. And in this ballet more than in any other, Balanchine affirms the music's primacy in a stunning way. What stronger homage could he pay to Stravinsky than to have the male and female soloists stand by the piano during the opening Cantilène (the first of the five movements) listening attentively to pianist (Gordon Boelzner) and concertmaster (City Ballet's brilliant Lamar Alsop)? Kay Mazzo, who danced with Peter Martins in the premiere, recalls that after the performance Robbins asked Balanchine, "How did you have the nerve to do that—I mean they stand there for eight bars of music doing the same step. That's all they do in the beginning." And Balanchine said, "Well, that's what the music said." Mazzo also recalled her rehearsals with Martins. Balanchine commented, "I think in the first movement, Peter, you just stand and listen to the music because this dance is about music. I want the audience to listen, to really listen." Had Stravinsky lived, he surely would have cherished the moment above all others—the ultimate obei-sance from an old friend who understood the composer as well as anyone.[14]

Stravinsky's powerful *Symphony in Three Movements* dates from 1942–45. Balanchine discussed the music with the composer during a visit to Hollywood as the work was being written. He was struck by the jazzy score, which was full of life, and immediately began looking for an opportunity to stage it. In recall-ing the festival, Edward Villella referred to the ballet as "the single most com-plicated score I had ever danced to."[15] A concertante piano part figures promi-nently in the first of the three movements. An andante follows, in which a harp that is every bit as important as the keyboard played in the opening movement is now featured. Both instruments, seen as "protagonists," to use Stravinsky's own description, are highlighted in a dialogue during the closing "con moto."

Nearly twenty years before the festival, in 1953, Kirstein had asked Stravinsky whether Jerome Robbins would be permitted to create a ballet upon a series of marches—funeral march, battle march, and others—that were based upon the symphonic work, but the composer declined. And while the notion might at first have seemed too narrative to the composer, the fact is the *Symphony in Three Movements* was more programmatic than any concert music he had writ-ten. The composer even directly referred to the opus as his war symphony, de-picting in unusual pictorial detail various scenes of battle, suffering, and death. Nonetheless, Stravinsky expressed his reservations about staging the work to Kirstein: "As a symphonic composer as well as a ballet composer, I always feel uneasy at the idea of using my straight symphonic forms on the stage." Such an unequivocal proclamation is vintage Stravinsky, but not particularly accurate. Vera Stravinsky remembered that her husband, privately at least, never raised any objections to his purloined concert music being transformed into ballets. Given the right circumstances, both artistically and financially, the composer's "uneasiness" would suddenly evaporate. Besides, the *Symphony in Three Move-ments* did not begin as a "straight symphonic" form intended for the concert hall but rather as a film score. The second movement was originally planned as music for "The Apparition of the Virgin" scene for Franz Werfel's *Song of Ber-nadette,* though like so many other film scores in which Stravinsky was initially involved during the early 1940s, the project was aborted.

As with so much of the composer's music, all three scores challenge the tra-ditional way solo instruments and ensembles are supposed to interact. The *Duo Concertant* breaks free from convention. Both piano and violin are often treated percussively. And although at moments there is a wonderful lyricism (as in the closing Dithyrambe), often the two soloists contentiously go their separate ways, exhibiting a fierce show of independence. The *Symphony in Three Movements* has always resisted categorization. Is it a concerto or a symphony, Stravinsky biographer Eric Walter White once asked? Such irresolution spawned just the ambiguity Stravinsky wished to create. The composition is a hybrid of both concerto and symphony. It is content- rather than form-driven, more interested in individualizing the message than in dutifully subscribing to orthodoxy. It deliberately scumbles the lines of identifiable musical "forms," disputing the customary treatment of instruments in a way similar to that in which Balanchine often calls into question his own management of soloists and the corps.

Likewise, the composer's Concerto in D for violin and orchestra falls beyond the standard Mozartian classical concerto model. Nor does it follow the freer, more romantically engendered approaches of the well-known Mendelssohn, Tchaikovsky, and Brahms violin concerti. Stravinsky's Concerto has four rather than three movements; there is no sparkling cadenza for the soloist; the orchestral ensemble does not—as is common—intersperse a few tutti passages here and there, or serve only as background accompaniment. Soloist and orchestra often proceed on equal footing. The composer remarked that texturally his Concerto was more chamberlike than orchestral. His description could just have easily been applied to his 1924 Piano Concerto, officially and purposely titled "Concerto for Piano and Wind Instruments"—again signaling the concertante role of the keyboard soloist.

Stravinsky was never comfortable with the traditional notion of a concerto. Clearly he preferred concertante parts, with a contributory rather than prima donna nature. He worried that the concerto form would provide a platform for megalomaniacal performers, whose pyrotechnics might crush the musical message. Nor was he shy in expressing his misgivings about this potential excess. His concerns about the elusive balance necessarily struck between creator and interpreter in any performing art were no different from Balanchine's well-known wariness about the egotism of star dancers. Performers were unable to resist the temptations of virtuoso works, Stravinsky complained. Too often they pandered to public applause, often losing sight of artistic expression.

The composer's idiosyncratic approach to the violin—a temperamental instrument considered devilishly unwieldy to write for, even by composers fully conversant with its vagaries—bears directly on Balanchine's balletic transformation. The composer's close collaboration with the violinist Samuel Dushkin opens a window on his working process. The influential Dushkin connection of the early 1930s is absolutely critical for understanding the work's preballet evolution. Moreover, Stravinsky's handling of the idiom provides a correlation to Balanchine's handling of dancers—employed as visual agents of the music. Just as Balanchine encouraged Martins to help shape his role in the 1972 production (and generally welcomed collaboration from dancers he trusted), so too did Stravinsky allow Dushkin to offer important ministrations, even rewriting passages at Stravinsky's request. Without Dushkin's intercession, the sound of Stravinsky's 1931 Violin Concerto might have been as different as the look of Balanchine's 1972 *Violin Concerto* would have been without Martins, Karin von Aroldingen, or the other principals.

The Concerto was written at the suggestion of Stravinsky's publisher Willy Strecker. Dushkin recalls that initially Strecker and he bandied about the idea in Paris in 1930, hoping to entice the composer to write a work that the violinist might use on tour. Strecker then broached the topic with the composer. Knowing Stravinsky's reservations about soloists, he assured him that Dushkin was a man whose character and artistry were in keeping with the composer's own views. Still Stravinsky wavered, confessing his uneasiness in writing for an instrument he did not play. On Strecker's assurance that Dushkin was amenable to working closely alongside Stravinsky, the composer accepted. The violinist was flattered since several of the literature's most important violin concerti were written with the aid of a contemporary performer; most notably Joseph Joachim, who worked with Brahms, and Zoltán Székely, who was Bartók's collaborator. The violinist often met with Stravinsky in Paris during the winter of 1930. The composer jotted down his first idea while on tour in late November on the back of an invoice for his room at Brack's Doelen Hotel in Amsterdam. The composer completed the work at La Vironnière near Voreppe, where Dushkin, living close by in Grenoble, visited regularly.[16]

Dushkin willingly shared his knowledge of the instrument's capabilities with Stravinsky. The two men took to each other immediately; the composer saw that Dushkin was not a vacant virtuoso predisposed to inflate his ego above musical substance. He was, Stravinsky commented, "an exception in this respect among many of his fellow players." Stravinsky also offered a stereotypical portrayal of Dushkin as a Jew, who like "the great majority of leading violinists . . . possesses all those innate gifts which make representatives of that race the unquestionable masters of the violin." He had, the composer remarked, a "Jewish sound."[17]

Although the two discussed precompositional ideas during the winter of 1930–31, Stravinsky's touring commitments interrupted attempts to work regularly. Returning to Nice in March, he began consulting frequently with Dushkin. The extent of the violinist's trenchant contributions should not be under-estimated. Dushkin recounted his collaboration with the composer in his 1949 article "Working with Stravinsky," the same title, coincidentally, that Kirstein used in 1937 to describe his eavesdropping on Stravinsky and Balanchine's studio rehearsals of *Jeu de Cartes*.[18] Dushkin's observations afford a rare peek into the methodical unfolding of a major composition, and his chronicle of daily work sessions with Stravinsky reveals much about the composer's habits. Dushkin wrote of "the extraordinary neatness and order" of Stravinsky's study. He watched Stravinsky sketching out initial ideas on unlined pages, rather than prepared manuscript paper, and noticed how he worked out ideas at the piano "grunting and struggling to find the notes and chords he seems to be hearing." Stravinsky also expressed to Dushkin his belief that "first ideas are very impor-tant; they come from God." And during those dry spells when the work went poorly, he spoke to Dushkin of his faith that "ideas will come."

Most telling, Dushkin described his personal involvement in charting vari-ous technical solutions to the many questions Stravinsky raised. On one partic-ularly crucial day, Dushkin recalls that at lunch,

> Stravinsky took out a piece of paper and wrote down this chord and asked me if it could be played. I had never seen a chord with such an enormous stretch, from the "E" to the top "A," and I said, "No." Stravinsky said sadly, "Quel dommage." ("What a pity.") After I got home, I tried it, and, to my astonishment, I found that in that register, the stretch of the eleventh was relatively easy to play, and the sound fasci-nated me. I telephoned Stravinsky at once to tell him that it could be done. When the Concerto was finished, more than six months later, I understood his disappoint-ment when I first said, "No." This chord, in a different dress, begins each of the four movements. Stravinsky himself calls it his "passport" to that Concerto.[19]

"Samsky," as Stravinsky called him, stated that his role was "to advise Stra-vinsky how his ideas could best be adapted to the exigencies of the violin as a concert display instrument." The composer would show him passages he had sketched, sometimes as little as a line, sometimes larger chunks of an entire movement. Most notably, if Dushkin suggested even a relatively minor change, for example changing the textural register of a line, Stravinsky, in incorporating the revision, would also reconstruct the underlying building blocks of the pas-sage. "He behaved like an architect," Dushkin wrote, "who if asked to change a room on the third floor had to go down to the foundations to keep the propor-tions of his whole structure."[20]

The composer's own sketches bear witness to the ripples that accrued as a consequence of the slightest modification. Such emendations demonstrate the organic nature and interdependence of lines. Balanchine, perhaps more than any other choreographer, was cognizant of the need to match the visual equilibrium of a ballet with the structural layers of a musical score, and as part of that process, to refashion internal adjustments for the sake of creating coherence. Choreographically, if a soloist's role were adjusted for some reason, then the deployment of the supporting ensemble would probably also need to be rethought.

Dushkin informatively recounted Stravinsky's formulation of rhythmic patterns. Often the composer initially sketched a rhythmically straightforward version of a passage that was "somewhat symmetrical." He would then transform the passage's internal divisions, taking care to retain the same sum of "pulsations," as Dushkin described them. These subtle interior permutations personally stamped the work as Stravinskyan by virtue of their uneven and unexpected turns. Upon seeing this process constantly repeat itself as Stravinsky sketched and refined ideas, Dushkin asked the composer to define his concept of rhythm:

> In mathematics . . . there are an infinite number of ways of arriving at the number seven. It's the same with rhythm. The difference is that whereas in mathematics the *sum* is the important thing; it makes no difference if you say five and two, or two and five, six and one or one and six, and so on. With rhythm, however, the fact that they add up to seven is of secondary importance. The important thing is, is it five and two or is it two and five, because five and two is a different person from two and five.[21]

The visual implications for similar choreographic divisions are evident. As we have seen in *Apollo* and *Agon*, Balanchine defined the perimeter of a rhythmic pattern, or "sum," with clearly structured unmistakable visual cues. But within individually constructed blocks, his ordering of patterns (two and five or three and four, as Stravinsky suggested) is unceasingly imaginative, unpredictable, and often independent of its musical context.

While Stravinsky primarily relied upon Dushkin's counsel for advice on what was instrumentally possible, he also consulted his friend Paul Hindemith. A string player who was as knowledgeable about matters of instrumentation as any composer one can think of, Hindemith encouraged Stravinsky to turn his unfamiliarity with the violin to his advantage. He suggested that ignorance could prove beneficial in leading him away from "routine technique." It might "give rise to ideas which would not be suggested by the familiar movement of the fingers."[22] Evidently he was right. While the figurations found throughout the Concerto in D are frequently ungracious, they are also bold and fresh. Much of the writing goes against the grain of the violin's traditional handling—just as the composer had done in earlier string works such as his *Three Pieces for String Quartet* and *L'Histoire du Soldat.*

Boris Schwarz (the concertmaster under Stravinsky's baton for the New York premiere of *Balustrade*) correctly asserts, "Composers who do not play the violin are usually more ruthless in making technical demands. They challenge virtuosos, who in turn rise to the challenge. The term 'playable' has disappeared from the vocabulary. Did not Arnold Schoenberg recommend a six-fingered violinist for his Violin Concerto?"[23] Stravinsky was among a new breed of twentieth-century composers, Schwarz continued, whose approach to the violin emphasized "motion rather than emotion, a style intense but unsentimental, rhythmic and crisp, at times brittle." In that sense especially, the Concerto is different from the models Stravinsky is known to have studied, though in fact the composer, typically, denied consulting any of the standard violin concerti he had in his library. There was one important model, however, to which Stravinsky referred, at least obliquely: "The subtitles of my Concerto—Toccata, Aria, Capriccio—may suggest Bach, and so, in a superficial way, might the musical substance. I am very fond of the Bach Concerto for Two Violins, as the duet of the soloist with a violin from the orchestra in the last movement of my own Concerto may show."[24]

Although unsurprisingly he downplays what he sees as a negligible reliance on the Bach Concerto for two violins—just as he brushed off his reliance upon versification in *Apollo* and Renaissance dance models in *Agon*—still the *Bach Double,* as it is called, was an important starting point. Moreover the link here is quite different from the cosmetically reconstructive composing used to embellish the many baroque models found in the harlequin *Pulcinella.* Stravinsky's Violin Concerto is infused with the spirit and compositional vocabulary of Bach, beginning with shared baroque rhythmic motives. Both the opening Allegro of the Bach and the opening Toccata of the Stravinsky Concerto begin with the same identifiable, unifying idea, one that permeates both movements: ♫♫ | ♫♫. Further, figure 13.1 illustrates one of the principal motives of the third movement of the Bach Concerto (Rehearsal B, m. 21) above a similarly important motive in Stravinsky's closing Capriccio (Rehearsal 95, m. 51). While both are cut rhythmically from the same baroque cloth, Stravinsky's melodic inversion is notable. Figure 13.2 gives an example of octave displacement—another common Bachian technique—using melodic leaps so large that they create the illusion of two separate lines. Compare these opening measures of the first violin solo in the Bach Allegro with Stravinsky's similar usage at Rehearsal 68 of

Aria I. Such an implicit division of melodic lines finds choreographic equivalence in Balanchine's bifurcation of certain gestures, especially when he splits ensemble members into individual "lines."

Still, these could be seen as superficial similarities if that were the end of it. After all, such tidily chiseled baroque motives had long been part of Stravinsky's neoclassic language, as in his 1923 Octet for winds or the 1924 Concerto for piano and winds. Nor can there be any question that Stravinsky's Piano Concerto also served as a model for his Violin Concerto in both form and figuration. Many of the latter concerto's awkward passages are directly traceable to pianistic patterns that fit Stravinsky's unusually large hand. Balanchine was familiar with the Piano Concerto, even citing passages in his famous essay "The Dance Element in Stravinsky's Music" as "irresistible in the way they bring dance phrases to one's mind." It is the Stravinsky-Bach alliance, however, that runs most deeply. Manfred Bukofzer spoke of Stravinsky's revival and adoption of baroque "constructive elements."[25] It is here that the Bach-Stravinsky nexus rises above otherwise shallow comparisons. Bukofzer specifically points to Stravinsky's Violin Concerto as the embodiment of the baroque concerto "pure and simple" in both "form and style."

As for form, the opening Toccata unfolds in a series of clearly defined, separate but continuous entries and exists. This juxtapositional technique provided structurally obvious aural markers that did not escape Balanchine's attention when he was translating sound to movement. Bukofzer observes that the "rhythmic drive of the themes derives largely from the instrumental nature of the melodic invention." For instance, the violinistic *bariolage* technique manifested throughout Bach's Concerto, whereby the pitches of a critical harmony are arpeggiated, pervades the Stravinsky Concerto as well. Toward the close of the Toccata's coda (Rehearsal 47, m. 229) the composer breaks an important harmony in rapid repetition over eleven measures, thus emphasizing the final cadence by sonorously amplifying its approach and arrival.

Balanchine understood Stravinsky's affinity for Bach. The baroque "abandonment of subjectivism," as Bukofzer remarked, in favor of a deromanticized objectivity was right in line with Balanchine's own thinking. Nathan Milstein recalls that Balanchine had "a subtle sense of Bach's music" and that he was especially attracted by Bach's "mathematical basis."[26] From such a musical credo, the leap to abstraction and plotless ballets was a short one. His 1941 *Concerto Barocco* ("no sex story, no period angle, no violence," as Denby once described the "straight dancing to music") was set to the same *Bach Double*. Balanchine and his American Ballet Caravan premiered the ballet in Rio de Janeiro only six

Bach

Stravinsky

13.1 Bach, Concerto for two violins in D-minor, third movement; Stravinsky, Concerto for violin in D, fourth movement (© 2002 by permission of the publisher, Schott Musik International, Mainz)

months after *Balustrade* was first given in New York. It is a landmark. Creating these two important works in such close proximity was more than coincidental.[27]

The fundamental contrapuntal fabric of stratified musical layers evident in the *Bach Double* finds several choreographic parallels in *Concerto Barocco*. As with *Apollo,* Balanchine rejects the obvious path of mimetically visualizing the two violins that proceed throughout all three movements in almost nonstop repetition of each other. As Tim Scholl observes, "Two female soloists dance passages that suggest (but do not mirror) the fugal counterpoint of the violins. Repeatedly, the two soloists appear to oppose one another, alternating quickly between movement and stasis, kinetic potential and corporeal constraint."[28] To be accurate, it is not "fugal" counterpoint, nor is it "canonic," as others have suggested. It is simply imitative. The difference is relevant inasmuch as Balanchine understood the compositional distinction. As we have seen, he often practiced writing counterpoint, methodically completing rigorous exercises associated more with the academy than the rehearsal studio. His understanding of harmony, nonharmonic tones, species counterpoint, imitation, fugue, and canon are all evinced in those many handwritten studies now held in the Harvard Theatre Collection. Only a musician steeped in matters of harmonic function and chordal progression could recognize when dancers should be "harmonic" or "nonharmonic," and thereby fortify the tonal underpinnings of a passage or work.

The public availability of a short video clip from the first movement of *Concerto Barocco,* filmed by the CBC in Montreal in the early 1950s, allows an op-

13.2 Bach, Concerto for two violins in D-minor, first movement; Stravinsky, Concerto for violin in D, second movement (© 2002 by permission of the publisher, Schott Musik International, Mainz)

portunity to examine in some detail a key twenty-four-measure passage. The one-minute excerpt is more than enough to demonstrate Balanchine's musically enlightened treatment of Bach's score.[29] The symmetrical structures Balanchine created, and the multiple geometric permutations visible within those structures, underscore his comprehension of Bach. They also serve as a powerful harbinger for the musically informed choreographic designs that appear years later in the 1972 *Violin Concerto*—just as the *Bach Double* served as an initial model for Stravinsky.

The excerpt begins with the first solo violin appearance (m. 22), as soloist Diana Adams joins the music and moves center. Balanchine had already employed the ensemble of women to prepare for Adams's solo, just as Bach's orchestral tutti prefaced the solo violin's first entrance. By the time the violin/dancer enter, the female ensemble has split into two groups, flanking the edges of the stage and taking on the subsidiary role of an accompaniment, just as the orchestra now defers to the first violin soloist. In describing this initial solo passage, Deborah Jowitt suggests that Balanchine employed two women in portraying the two solo violins "because the virtuosic speed and sharpness of the music made him see pointework, and the way Bach mingled and separated their lines made him see equals."[30] Quite so, and for a musician it is precisely the way that Balanchine specifically "mingled and separated" the counterpoint that testifies to his musicianship.

That Adams would have joined the action at the violin's point of entry seems natural. But it is the movement that ensues during the violin's next four measures that is notable. While Adams stresses the strong beats of each successive measure—just as Bach initiates new violinistic figurations at these junctures, she does not attempt to mimic the incessant motor rhythm of the music. To do so would have been foolish, Balanchine instinctively knew, for it would have visually addled the relentless drive of the musical line as it continues in a burst of sixteenth notes. Rather, Adams's sweeping gestures (en pointe and including wonderful extensions of both arm and leg) glide horizontally left and right, each successively consuming less space until her final pirouette converges center stage just at the moment the second violin enters (m. 26). Yet Tanaquil Le Clercq, portrayed as the second violin in this duet, does not begin precisely as the violinist takes up the solo, but has already entered, dovetailing with Adams and the continuing first violin. Le Clercq then begins her opening pirouette just as the second violin plays the pick-up to measure 26. It is these compositional "corners" that are so creatively attended to by Balanchine.

Visually, Le Clercq has entered directly in front of Adams (who now stands unobtrusively motionless), just as the second violin takes over the same thematic material initially assigned to the first soloist. More important—and characteristic—Balanchine resists the natural impulse to duplicate choreographically with Le Clercq what Adams has just danced, even though the music to which Le Clercq dances is exactly the same. Or is it? For the attentive listener, the music is never really the same when reprised. The second violin soloist does indeed spin out the same theme and same rhythm note for note; but the first violin simultaneously initiates a new line, causing us to hear the second violin's repeated thematic material in an entirely new light.

Le Clercq's "line" is spatially more limited than Adams's. She moves with notable containment, not broadly and laterally as Adams had done. Rather than proceeding in the grander gestures first seen and heard as the first violin/Adams entered, now there is a more focused observance of smaller detail. Such definition now makes both visual and aural sense since we are already familiar with the musical details, having already heard the thematic material once. Moreover, such details now contribute to the contrapuntal exchange of the two violins.

The orchestra reiterates the Vivace's main theme when it reenters at measure 30 (the same rhythmic motive, ♫♫ | ♫♫, described earlier, which serves as the principal thematic material for Stravinsky's Toccata). The two solo violins continue their dialogue. Consequently, four layers of sound amass: the orchestral material is constructed upon a structural framework consisting, essentially, of its own two independent treble and bass lines. Predictably, the women of the corps rejoin the action at the orchestral point of reentry. They remain divided into two equal subgroups, one at each side of the small stage. Visually, in effect, Adams, Le Clercq, and the bifurcated ensemble represent the four separate but interlocking contrapuntal lines. But most important, the imaginative and continuous reconfiguring of this divided ensemble visually echoes Stravinsky's explanation to Dushkin of the internal variations of mathematical sums. That is, it is not the sum but the interior design of the sum in which Balanchine and Stravinsky were primarily interested.

As the combined violin solos with orchestral music of measures 30–37 unfolds—contrapuntally the most complex music seen and heard in the video clip—the women in the ensemble engage in various regroupings, sometimes evenly split, sometimes unevenly. When the two soloists are added to the equation, the resulting geometric designs (easily visible in the clip owing to the camera's high angle) are all the more wondrous. It is, as Melissa Hayden explains in her introduction to the video clip, as close as one can come to explaining Balanchine's idea of "seeing sound."

When the violin soloists reemerge on their own at measure 38 (the orchestra now recedes into a more homophonic accompaniment), Balanchine designs completely new lines for the two dancers, while the split ensemble returns to its supportive role at the sides of the stage. But now the corps does not stand in place; rather, it engages in constant but subtle movement of arms, hand, and wrists—an animated but still subsidiary way of marking the pulse. Neither heads nor torsos move—only flexible extremities. It is precisely the kind of accompanimental gesture Balanchine will use in the final Capriccio of *Violin Concerto* thirty years later. Indeed, architecturally, Balanchine's 1941 tribute to Bach through *Concerto Barocco* served as an important prequel for his 1972 Stravinsky ballet—a ballet that perhaps more than any other synthesizes the composer and choreographer's thoughts on the contrapuntal dance of sight and sound.

Chapter 14 Unity and Balance

in *Stravinsky Violin Concerto*

Stravinsky recalled Balustrade as "one of the most satisfactory visualiza-
tions of any of my works . . ." Yet a more precise bodily articulation of
Stravinsky's score than the new Violin Concerto could not be conceived.
—*Andrew Porter,* New Yorker, *9 December 1972*

Observing Balanchine choreograph part of their jointly conceived
1959 ballet, *Episodes,* Martha Graham remarked, "It was like watching
light pass through a prism. The music passes through him, and in the
same natural yet marvelous way that a prism refracts light, he refracts
music into dance." Nowhere is the refraction more evident than in
Stravinsky Violin Concerto. Dance critics applauded the 1972 ballet as a
brilliant exemplar of Balanchine's keen sense of musical visualization.
But what exactly does this mean? What is "musical visualization?" If
Balanchine truly channels Stravinsky's score through the dancers'
bodies, and his physical handling of the ensemble really represents a
new direction, then one must begin by examining the Concerto's
structure; for that is, after all, where Balanchine always began.

The listener immediately senses the iridescence of the vividly orchestrated score. The Toccata and Capriccio, with their bright pri-

mary colors of red and blue, are as radiant as any music Stravinsky composed. There is nothing subtle here: it is all circus. The two interior Arias are of a different world: serious, pensive. The sustained lines of both the solo violin and orchestra—less obviously contrapuntal than the exterior movements but equally baroque in their bounteous ornamentation—provide a stark contrast. Throughout the Concerto, the usual choirs of strings, woodwinds, brass, and timpani are available. Yet the full complement of strings—violins, violas, cellos, and basses—seldom come together as a homogeneous unit. The double basses are assigned special weight, surely a way of reinforcing the solid foundation for the solo violin. In fact, in deference to the soloist, the tutti violins are scored for a relatively small portion of the time.

In the opening Toccata, for instance, their first important appearance is reserved until Rehearsal 16—some seventy-six measures into the movement. The same sparseness applies to the woodwinds and brass. The orchestra is treated as a chamber ensemble in which selected instruments come in and out of play, join the solo violin in dialogue, then quickly withdraw. Balanchine took careful note. The counterpoint of dance and music is evident. Just as Stravinsky seldom uses the full orchestra in any sustained way, so too does Balanchine withhold the complete ensemble of twenty dancers until the last movement. The adroitly balanced score, marked by a continuous series of orchestral entries and exits, finds its counterpart in the four solo dancers and sixteen-member supporting corps, as they dash on and off stage in equally imaginative arrays. In this sense the resemblance to the choreographic groupings of *Agon* is unmistakable. In both works, multiple chamber combinations (duos, trios, and quartets of instruments and dancers) are enlisted to achieve a clean look and crystal-clear sound.

The Concerto's nearly 150 pages of sketches confirm Stravinsky's constant rethinking, refining, and reordering of ideas. His unfamiliarity with the violin, prompting Dushkin's many thoughtful revisions, no doubt added to the challenge. The sketches reveal that sometimes four or five completely worked-out versions of a few measures were notated. But given what we know about Stravinsky's compositional habits, his "scissoring and pasting" of the composition, as he once described the Concerto's evolution to Willy Strecker, comes as no surprise. Although the work was not intended as a ballet, the issue of temporal pacing was nonetheless on the composer's mind. He surrounded himself with stopwatches, carefully calibrating each section and notating timings in the sketches. His concern with what he called the Concerto's "minutage" arose here (just as in *Orpheus*) from a desire to accommodate a commercially released phonograph recording.

In writing so much music expressly for ballet, Stravinsky was acutely aware of the dancer's stamina.[1] But he does not seem to have concerned himself here (or for that matter in his earlier piano concerto) with the endurance of the musician-soloist: the violinist plays continuously, incessantly. In the closing Capriccio, for example, the soloist plays the first two hundred measures (composed almost entirely of rapid, nonstop figurations) before there is a single measure's rest. Balanchine, on the other hand, carefully balanced the temporal pace of the music with the physical limits of the dancers. The unremitting rhythmic drive of the Concerto's outer movements created a challenge that was solved by skillfully pairing the four soloists with the corps.

In other ways too, Balanchine was as practical as Stravinsky. Just as the composer bore in mind the technical considerations associated with producing a phonograph recording, compositionally adjusting the length of passages accordingly, so too did Balanchine "reconceive" (to use his description) his 1972 choreography when the ballet was subsequently filmed for a televised release. *Stravinsky Violin Concerto* was videotaped in 1977 at Opryland in Nashville as part of the *Dance in America* series produced by WNET for PBS. An earlier audiotape of the New York City Ballet Orchestra was employed in the broadcast. The choreographic modifications were partially necessitated by the smaller stage (just as Balanchine reconceived *Concerto Barocco* for the Montreal taping). But according to Karin von Aroldingen, Balanchine also made changes because he knew the camera so well. From his Hollywood days, he had become familiar with its angles and the benefits of filming dance from raised platforms. Not only did he understand its possibilities, but now he was ready to put them to use.[2]

Why the reversal in Balanchine's thinking about televised performances, especially given his outspoken displeasure over the filming of *The Flood?* For one thing, previous television directors, like their autocratic Hollywood counterparts, acted unilaterally. There was not even a pretense of artistic collaboration. With *Stravinsky Violin Concerto,* however, Balanchine's opinions were heeded. He worked closely with producer Merrill Brockway and director Emile Ardolino. By the early 1980s the turnabout was complete. Balanchine was now eager to televise his enigmatically beautiful *Robert Schumann's "Davidsbündlertänze"* ("He saw places where you can use close-ups," Brockway noted).

Brockway had directed a 1975 televised performance of *Concerto Barocco* as part of the *Dance in America* series its first year. In commenting upon the filming, Anna Kisselgoff noted the potential of crane-mounted cameras and other visual perspectives that Balanchine understood: "Anyone who has seen the ballet on stage knows that its patterns are usually seen from the front, not the side. Yet there are frequent diagonals in the ballet, and this spirit of the work is transmitted in the new diagonal created by the camera." As for *Stravinsky Violin Concerto,* Kay Mazzo told me that once they were in Nashville, Balanchine made several changes for the benefit of the camera, and he made them quickly. Mostly he changed lines to create more diagonals, she recalled; but once back in New York, he reverted to his original conception.[3] Brockway himself recounted the ballet's taping with Balanchine:

> I told Balanchine that I could promise no more than a televised representation of the staged performance, certainly not an interpretation. He listened patiently to my list of objections which centered on the limited number of people that could possibly be framed by the cameras, then said, "Let's do."
>
> The last movement . . . was densely populated; the stage teemed with moving bodies, the very thing I had been apprehensive about for screen. . . . He recognized the problem was geometric; while performance space is a rectangle, the space defined by a camera is a triangle. How were we to fit all these figures into a triangle without disproportionally diminishing the size of the dancers, not to mention the impact of Balanchine's choreography? He told me, "I fix" and swiftly directed the restaging. Many of these spacial [*sic*] changes which drew the corps closer together for the cameras were later incorporated into the stage version.[4]

Stravinsky began the opening Toccata on 24 December 1930, finishing it on 27 March 1931. Although the title was not affixed until six months later, it is well chosen. The term literally means, "to touch," a reference to its origins as a keyboard piece during the late Renaissance and baroque. By the time the loosely pieced together musical form reached the hands of Bach, it had become a virtuoso display vehicle performed at a fast tempo with rapid figurations. The correlation of the form's musical structure with Balanchine's choreography is tightly conceived. Compositionally, toccatas were parceled into distinct divisions, just as Balanchine's choreography of the first movement is divided into discrete sections. While Stravinsky's Toccata is clearly sectionalized, remnants of the more traditional sonata form typical of a concerto's first movement are also evident. There is, for example, an explicit recapitulation of the movement's first thematic material at Rehearsal 38 (m. 184). From there the opening section is repeated note for note until the coda begins at Rehearsal 47 (m. 229), whereupon the eleven-measure *bariolage* ensues, continuing until the end of the movement.[5]

As a focus, let us examine the interior musical structure of the first fourteen measures—an undanced opening passage that builds in anticipation and tension as we await the dancers' initial movement. The drama of the moment is traceable to Balanchine's understanding of the fecundity of Stravinsky's opening statement. The ultimate goal of these initial measures is the violin soloist's important entrance at Rehearsal 3, measure 15—the same critical juncture where the dancing begins. The entire passage aims for that moment.

It may be tempting to dismiss the first fourteen measures as little more than a musical introduction. But nothing was ever merely introductory for Stravinsky, just as nothing was extraneous for Balanchine. The opening passage seeds many of the compositional ideas subsequently explored. Just as Kay Mazzo's opening kick announces what follows, so too does the predanced music announce the Toccata's main thematic materials (fig. 14.1). The stillness, or perhaps better said, the silence of the dancers therefore serves two important functions. Not only does it create a growing sense of anticipation, even anxiety, for music that aches to be danced, but it also allows the ear to concentrate on the score. And concentration it demands, for Stravinsky's neoclassic skewing of his baroque-inspired model is aurally quite involved. Balanchine knew this in a way no other choreographer of Stravinsky's music did. Unless we can grasp both the spirit and the compositional techniques employed in this initial passage, the remainder of the movement makes little sense. And for Balanchine, if one could not clarify the musical sense of a work by choreographing it, then why dance it at all?

The opening passage begins in triple meter with a two-measure declaration by the solo violin supported by the lower strings alone (contrabasses and cellos). The "passport" chord of the first measure—the chord that introduces all four movements—rings vibrantly throughout all three beats. It is followed by three separate, punctuated quarter notes emphasized all the more by the composer's marking of separate down bows and accents. This series of accented chords propels the music toward the arrival of the Toccata's principal theme in measure 3. The driving force of these jabbed chords derives from a typically baroque contrapuntal convergence, created here by the descending line in the lower part of the soloist's double stops and the ascending line of the contrabass. It is meant to funnel the ear toward the unambiguous establishment of D, the Concerto's principal tonal center. The gesture is classical in its goal-oriented musical motion. Stravinsky's resourceful twisting of the passage, however, unmistakably stamps the passage as neoclassical.

For example, rather than using the pitch C♯ (the leading-tone as musicians think of it) to firmly establish the key of D, as Bach did in his D-minor double concerto, Stravinsky uses a C♮ as the highest note of the contrabass ascent (dou-

14.1 Stravinsky, Concerto for violin in D: first movement, Toccata, measures 1–14 (© 2002 by permission of the publisher, Schott Musik International, Mainz)

bled in the cello). Even for the untrained ear, something sounds askew. The C♯ seems dissonant within the context that has been established (both here and historically). Consequently it keeps us on edge, just as the composer intended; and it adds to the musical sense of suspense reflected in the expectancy of dancing. Moreover, such typically neoclassic modifications of classical models also find equivalency in Balanchine's manipulation of classical gestures.

While the rhythmic force created in the first two measures drives direction-
ally toward the principal thematic motive of measure 3, the composer interrupts the motion he has just built by inserting a rest on the first beat. The motive is delayed, arriving not on the first but on the second beat of the newly
established duple meter of measure 3. The deception is characteristically Stravinskyan: the composer creates a strong pull, or expectation, then defeats it just
at the moment where the resolution *should* have occurred. The expectation for
dancing builds all the more through letting the music speak on its own terms,
without visual competition. Finally, after the solo violinist has sounded the passport chord in the first measure and joined in the contrapuntal drive of the second, one might reasonably have anticipated that the principal motive sounded
in measure 3 would have been assigned to the soloist. But it is not. Here too the
correlation with Balanchine is important. The dancers *could* have entered at
measure 3—it would have made perfectly good musical sense—but Balanchine's appreciation for the psychology of deception (in one way at least, an important generic distinction between classical and popular music and dance)
matched Stravinsky's. After the first-beat silence of measure 3, the Toccata's
principal motive is assigned to a duet of trumpets accompanied by other woodwinds, leaving the soloist, the other strings, and the dancers still anxiously waiting.

Consider the next seven measures of this opening passage (mm. 3–9). The
meter has changed from triple to duple; but it is duple in name only, for
Stravinsky segments the notated duple divisions so that the listener is never
quite sure what to expect. While the bassoons and horns sound a clear two-beat
pattern as a background rhythm, the two trumpets, eventually joined by two
oboes, tug against the underlying pulse. Here one recalls Stravinsky's discussion
with Dushkin regarding the musician's treatment of a rhythmic sum. Since
Stravinsky specifically mentioned the number seven to Dushkin, consider how
his admonition to the violinist applies in the Toccata's opening passage, measures 3–6 (Rehearsal 1), where the trumpets intone the main theme before being joined by the oboes. Following the surprise rest that begins the duple meter
of measure 3, there are seven more quarter-note pulses articulated by the trumpets. Across these four measures, Stravinsky slices the thematic statement into
two phases, the principal motive, and a slightly altered repetition, yielding a
division of three and four quarter-note pulses: $\frac{2}{4}$ ♩♫♫ | ♩ ♩ | ♫♫ ♩ | ♩ ♩ |.
Then in measures 7–9 the incipit of the theme is sounded again, initiating a
new division in the trumpets, which is quickly taken up in imitation by the
oboes. In effect, Stravinsky has taken the principal rhythmic motive of the Toc-

cata (the same motive unifying the *Bach Double/Concerto Barocco*) and extended, modified, and truncated it—while keeping the underlying rhythmic pulse intact.

The next five measures beginning at Rehearsal 2 simultaneously conclude the introductory music and prepare the listener for the violin soloist's announcement of the theme at measure 15, Rehearsal 3. This is accomplished by a series of descending scales played by the oboes, whose rhythmic divisions also cut against the duple meter's fundamental pulse. Against this activity, the solo violin reenters at Rehearsal 2, again with multiple stops sustained for three measures before joining the descending gesture of the oboes and bassoons, which leads, finally, to the long-awaited thematic proclamation played by the soloist. The reentrance of the violin at Rehearsal 2 functions as a bridge, reconnecting the soloist to the opening sustained chords, thus forging a tripartite structure for the entire introduction. Here again Balanchine understood the concept of this multilayered preparatory gesture. The last of the three chords played by the violinist in measure 13 also marks Kay Mazzo's first dramatic kick. Now the quintet of dancers (Mazzo plus the four attendant males) springs to life, moving along with the descending violin line at the end of this section in preparation for measure 15, where the choreography—and violin solo—begin in earnest (fig. 14.2).

Compositionally, this preludelike passage is packed with information that will be developed throughout the next five and a half minutes of the Toccata. Even upon repeated hearings, the listener must work to grasp all the activity. To complicate this musical activity by piling on choreography would have overloaded our aural and visual circuitry. Would there be any chance of hearing the rhythmic shifting from triple to duple or the unexpected internal shifts of added and deleted beats? Would the statement, departure, and reentrance of the violin's sustained chords as a framework of this introduction have been heard at all if one had to deal with the more immediately attention-grabbing visual layer too? And would the careful orchestration and division of the principal thematic material appear as prominent if—as Denby complained of *Balustrade* years earlier—our perception became "annoyed" by unessential additions (unessential, at least, at this crucial moment)? Yes, there were opportunities for the dancers to enter earlier, but why risk confusion if, as Balanchine contended, the idea was to visualize the music?

Kay Mazzo remembers that Balanchine was dissatisfied with his initial conception of the Toccata's opening. He worked at it, she remarked. She also recalls that while he was working out the opening, she took ill, and when she returned,

14.2 *Stravinsky Violin Concerto,* Kay Mazzo's opening kick (1972) (Photograph by Martha Swope/TimePix)

he had redone the beginning. The contrapuntal complexity of the music's introductory statement continues throughout the movement, but now the choreography is divisible into eight clearly distinguishable sections. Balanchine stages each choreographic entrance and exit (so beautifully captured in Brockway's film) to coincide with the parade of ideas Stravinsky weaves through the movement's various sections.

The composer labored to structure each internal division. Music theorist Lynne Rogers points out that Stravinsky was particularly occupied with the stacking of contrapuntal layers pervading the music. Likewise, Balanchine's ear surely guided him in constructing what Kirstein once referred to as "spatial dynamics." He devises choreographic parallels consisting of well-defined, separate contrapuntal blocks, each with a soloist and supporting quartet of dancers. Here the Toccata's sketches are particularly instructive. Rogers demonstrates that the composer began with simple ideas and worked toward what she terms "dissociation"—that is, "a contrapuntal structure that organizes the texture into highly differentiated and harmonically independent musical layers."[6] It was an amalgam, rather than an integration of ideas, that seemed to interest the composer. And as Rogers persuasively demonstrates, Stravinsky thought carefully about which textural divisions and assignments would best clarify his intent.

Separation also seems to have been on the mind of Balanchine in creating his own dissociation of music and dance. There is an imaginative disparity here. The Toccata's eight distinct choreographic blocks do not always march in lockstep with the divisions of the musical structure. Table 14.1 summarizes the choreographic-musical correlations. Assorted combinations of male and female soloists and their accompanying quartets demarcate the eight choreographic blocks. The music's architecture, however, is sectionalized into sixteen divisions. Nor does Balanchine, as table 14.1 makes clear, simply partition the equation into an even split of two musical slices for every one choreographic division. It is this asymmetrical overlaying technique that enriches the overall aural-visual counterpoint, smoothing the intrinsic seams of the toccata form. Only at major structural points does Balanchine, without disguise, stress the division with a dramatic choreographic gesture. For example, Mazzo (in black) and the male quartet (in white T-shirts) enter as the violin plays the main theme. Martins first appears with a quartet of females (in black) at measure 107, where motivic material for the important development section of the Toccata is introduced—musically, a critical axis. Later, having just danced alone as in a choreographic cadenza, Martins is joined by his quartet of males at measure 229, whereupon the music's coda—based upon the Bachlike bariolage technique—commences.

But Balanchine's coordination of movement and sound surpasses these obvious divisions. He accents Stravinsky's structural segmentations with subtlety, especially in treating the internal dance counterpoint of the soloists and their attendant quartet within each of the eight large blocks (see music divisions 2, 4, 5, 7, 9, 12, 15, and 16 for these choreographic internal divisions). Sometimes the quartet works as a unit, sometimes it is divided into two, or three plus one; but in every instance, the ensemble contributes substantially to the action. As Deborah Jowitt rightly notes, these "little entourages . . . don't always maintain the respectful distance or the subsidiary role they might in a Petipa ballet."[7] In the first appearance of Mazzo and the four males, all five dancers go their separate ways. In measure 97, marked in the table as music division 7, Bart Cook partners one of the quartet's females, while the remaining trio performs as a unit in a straight line immediately behind the duo. Moreover, in the third choreographic division (beginning at m. 86), Cook literally pulls all four females onto the stage just as von Aroldingen exits, marking the kind of Balanchine egress

Table 14.1
Musical-Choreographic Divisions of the Toccata

Measures	Choreographic division	Choreographic groupings of soloists and ensemble	Musical division	Musical description
1–14	Introduction	No dancing	Introduction	Violin "passport" chord and announcement of main theme by winds and brass
15–34	1	One female soloist (Mazzo) and quartet of males	1	Entrance of violin soloist with same theme
35–53		Quartet divides into two groups, Mazzo at center	2	New theme for soloist in counterpoint with first theme played by flutes
54–85	2	One female soloist (von Aroldingen) and quartet of males	3	Violin soloist returns to first theme while trumpet takes over second theme just played by violinist at m. 35
		Quartet works as single unit behind soloist	4	Violin soloist sounds third new idea at key change (m. 60)
		Soloist and quartet move laterally until males exit, leaving soloist onstage for her eventual exit	5	Soloist drops out for first time; return to original key; first entrance of tutti violins, with iteration of opening theme (m. 76)
86–106	3	One male soloist (Cook) and quartet of females	6	Fourth thematic idea played by returning violin soloist
		Soloist and one female are partnered while trio of females stand toward back	7	Fifth thematic idea in winds and brass, with violin bariolage accompaniment (m. 96)
107–33	4	One male soloist (Martins) and quartet of females	8	Violin soloist with sixth thematic idea accompanied by winds and strings

Table 14.1
(*continued*)

Measures	Choreographic division	Choreographic groupings of soloists and ensemble	Musical division	Musical description
		Diagonals give way to soloist center, quartet in straight line behind	9	Violin soloist plays same material as m. 86 (m. 123)
134–59	5	One female soloist (Mazzo) and quartet of females	10	No soloist. Strings develop motive of m. 107 (four 16ths). Violin reenters at m. 157 as bridge
160–83	6	One female soloist (von Aroldingen) and quartet of females	11	Violin soloist with seventh thematic idea accompanied by winds and strings
		Soloist in center with quartet moving independently. Soloist left onstage alone, moves off during recapitulation preparation	12	Soloist plays principal motive of Introduction as preparation for recapitulation (m. 172)
184–203	7	One male soloist (Cook) and quartet of males	13	Recapitulation of m. 15 with violin soloist, same as division 1, above
204–50	8	One male soloist (Martins)	14	Recapitulation of m. 35 with violin soloist, same as division 2, above
		Solo continues while quartet of males re-enter in groups of two	15	Recapitulation of m. 54, same as division 3, above (m. 223)
		Male soloist now joined by quartet of males	16	Beginning of coda with bariolage by violin soloist until final cadence (m. 229)

that is by now so familiar. So in effect there are three levels of contrapuntal interplay: Stravinsky's independent musical counterpoint; Balanchine's soloist-ensemble counterpoint, which does not merely mimic Stravinsky's; and the combined, larger sense of aural-visual counterpoint created by the two.

The composer completed the second movement, Aria I, on 20 May 1931, originally referring to it as "Aria da capo." His original designation is important, for it makes clear the movement's *A-B-A* structure. Like the Toccata, the title is baroque in origin; and like the second movement of the *Bach Double*, Aria I is cast in the tripartite form typical of slow movements. Opening with the passport chord that announced the first movement, the thirty-eight measures of the Aria's florid *A* section in D-minor are as different as can be from the exuberantly propulsive D-major music of the Toccata. In contrast, the sixty-three measures of the *B* section (mm. 39–101)—some of the most texturally and rhythmically inventive music Stravinsky ever wrote—move beyond D-minor and are more developmental in character. The "da capo" (literally meaning "to the head," or "beginning") of the *A* section (mm. 102–27) furnishes a slightly condensed reprise.

While the opening chord is sounded, von Aroldingen (having discarded her skirt) and Bart Cook stand a few feet apart, arms and legs splayed.[8] They move laterally toward each other, converging with each of the violin's three punctuating opening chords. As the violin soloist intones the principal melodic theme, the dancers link in this, the first of two pas de deux. They continue enmeshed until the violin's melismatic theme takes up a series of descending scales—a musical crux that is sufficiently important to send both dancers to separate corners. There is no bodily contact until the next structurally defining compositional moment, where the flute (at m. 18) now repeats the original violin theme. And just as Stravinsky begins accumulating layered segments of previously introduced thematic material, sometimes overlapping or inverting ideas, so too does Balanchine now beckon his soloists to undertake a series of elaborate twists and turns under, above, and around each other. As the *A* section of the ternary movement approaches a cadence, once again the two dancers disengage until the next pivotal moment. Von Aroldingen acrobatically moves into a complete back bend on all fours—a dramatic gesture that serves as a transition to the *B* section at measure 39.

This central section comprises several subdivisions, each clearly differentiated by both composer and choreographer. At measure 68, for example, Stravinsky enlists the full orchestra to amplify materials introduced moments earlier. It is here that the two dancers recover their separate space, dancing alone for the remainder of the Aria's middle segment. This major structural division marks the first and only time that Cook assumes a more assertive role, dancing as a true soloist in an otherwise female-governed movement. At measure 77, von Aroldingen partners Cook again, now commanding the action at almost the exact golden-mean nexus of the 127-measure movement.

Another musical partition occurs ten measures later, where von Aroldingen, standing in the embrace of Cook, moves her body inwardly, legs collapsing inwardly at the knees. The two dancers stand motionless at first, as the music too is suspended while the brass and winds sustain long chords. And as the violin soloist plays an equally awkward, disjointed series of octaves and leaps, Cook and von Aroldingen visually match the jutting lines with some of the most graphically coordinated gestures of arms and legs in all Balanchine. A movement of toe, foot, knee, arm, and wrist—whatever will flex—depicts each beat of the music. As the music approaches the *B* section's cadence, it slows in its preparation, just as the dancers prepare for the coming reprise by disposing their angular contortions in favor of a more flowing ritard.

The measure 72 da capo of *A* is far from a literal reprise of the opening choreography—just as the dancing was different at the recapitulation of the Toccata. Balanchine felt no obligation to replicate the same visualization, even though Stravinsky's returning music is virtually the same, albeit slightly abridged. Von Aroldingen lifts her leg onto Cook's shoulder and turns en pointe in a complete circle. If anything, the gestures of both dancers are more economic, as if there were not as much need to illustrate the music because it has already been heard once. Stravinsky concludes with a series of rising harmonics for the violin soloist that fly upward and off into nothingness. Von Aroldingen's ending backward cartwheel and Cook's final prostration are conjoined with this fleeting final cadence, as they end in their individual spaces, just as they began.

Historically, dance critics have pointed to Aria I and Aria II as contrasting examples of Balanchine's views about the natural tensions that repel and attract males and females. "That sex rears its head in Balanchine's most cerebral Stravinsky ballets is a given," wrote Anna Kisselgoff of a 1999 performance, noting that with these two internal movements, "Balanchine created two of his most subtle studies of male-female relations."[9] In addressing these two movements in *Following Balanchine,* Robert Garis offered one of his more detailed and descriptive essays, suggesting that the melodic lines are "embroidered, perhaps tortured, by astringent ornamentation." He speaks of the music's form being "given an edge by the acidic texture." Finally, he adds that in these two middle movements, "Balanchine composed his most neurotic, twisted, screwed-up, modern, 'difficult' images of love relationships."[10]

It is a fair description, and certainly Garis has captured in words what many viewers would see as the powerful images evoked. How much Balanchine himself thought in terms of such wonderfully evocative metaphors, however, has always been a question. Would he really have summoned such emotive rhetoric in depicting these two movements? Perhaps . . . and Garis's portrayal will resonate emotionally with the casual listener or observer—indeed, in that context his description could not be more illuminating. Yet Mazzo recalls that Balanchine was all business in shaping the Arias and never resorted to emotional imagery as a way of inspiring or explaining his ideas to the dancers. It was simply, Place your leg here, Turn this way, Hold your hand that way. Balanchine, like Stravinsky, seems to have been anything but casual or emotional. A history of his exchanges with Stravinsky suggest that he did not think so much in terms of acidity as of musical dissonance (nor should one assume that the two approaches are incompatible).

Still, there is nothing to suggest that he was preoccupied not with tortured lines but rather with the strategic positioning of auxiliary notes and passing tones. He thought of appogiature, suspensions, escape tones, and the complete lexicon of dissonances expressly used by composers to intensify the music's eventual resolution. He thought like an architect committed to both function and beauty. If Balanchine were to indulge in metaphor, it is more likely that he would have described each of the two Arias as a calculated balance of arsis and thesis, breathing in and breathing out—plain and simple. He understood perfectly well the "rich Bachian-rhetoric of the basic musical form" to which Garis rightly refers; but for the musical Balanchine, ever cognizant of how dance unfolds in time, the primary occupation was with defining form and maintaining temporal balance. Balance was the very marrow of his visualization.

Just as Stravinsky created the Concerto with Dushkin's hands testing and adjusting every figuration along the way, so too did Balanchine begin with the physical attributes of his dancers. He shaped and modified his choreography around the particular strengths they could bring to the music. In fact, in both Arias, perhaps more than in any other Stravinsky piece that Balanchine undertook, the dancers are the instruments of the musical score. If as some have observed, the female appears dominant in Aria I, it is because Balanchine planned the pas de deux around Karin von Aroldingen's considerable assets as a physical, athletic dancer. Whatever stipulations Balanchine made—or perhaps because of them—Aria I seemed made to order for her. John Gruen had it right in commenting that von Aroldingen was "the perfect instrument" for Balanchine's vision. And just as important, her performance demonstrates in every measure that she was the music's willing handmaiden. As Gruen further observed, "The dancer's so-called impersonality serves as a crystal-clear vehicle for Balanchine's eye for abstract composition and movement. Von Aroldingen's work in the Stravinsky *Violin Concerto*, for example, makes clear her stunning capacity for the complex gesture, the coiling and convoluted movement. There is nothing her body cannot do, and do with austere grace and dazzling speed."[11]

It is precisely her "impersonality"—or perhaps better said, her confidently icy comportment—that perfectly matched Balanchine's visualization of Stravinsky's neoclassicism. This is particularly true in a pas de deux, where audiences are ready to ride the paroxysmal wave of every male-female sensual entwining. It is von Aroldingen's aloofness, her searing coolness, that makes the music and dance intensely poignant. She gives an unalloyed sense of equanimity, of stone-cold beauty that cuts deeper than any heart-on-the-sleeve effluence. Von Aroldingen's performance of Aria I is as close a matrimony of music and dance as one is likely to encounter.

Von Aroldingen remembers that during the fall of 1971, when Balanchine began choreographing *Violin Concerto,* the first movement he prepared was Aria I, the pas de deux in which she and Jean-Pierre Bonnefous were featured. (Bart Cook replaced Bonnefous in the 1977 video.) She told me that Balanchine viewed this second movement as the most musically complex. Musicians recognize the intricacies of a score that is the most fascinating, compositionally, of the four movements. Von Aroldingen's memory confirms that Balanchine recognized the remarkableness of the writing. She remembered that he was especially absorbed in finding just the right choreography for the beginning of the *B* section (m. 39). The Aria's contrasting central portion begins with an unusually intricate syncopation built into the three orchestral lines of the score: violin solo, the tutti violins, and the cello (fig. 14.3).

The passage's thematic and rhythmic fabric is worth detailing, for it not only provides a microcosm of Stravinsky's interest in constructing multiple levels of activity but also outlines the musical elements Balanchine would have weighed in fashioning a choreographic complement. The violin soloist plays a series of harmonics that produce an eerily glassy, unearthly sound that is among the most wondrous in all of the composer's writing. The notes themselves are based upon the opening thematic material of the *A* section, thus forging a bond with this central section. The music is notated in a straightforward $\frac{4}{4}$ meter of six

14.3 Stravinsky, Concerto in D for violin: Aria I, measures 39–44 (© 2002 by permission of the publisher, Schott Musik International, Mainz)

measures. But metrically these measures are divided into four divisions: (1) the soloist's harmonics begin on the second beat with a series of three quarter notes followed by a rest on the first beat of measure 40— ♩ ♩ ♩ | 𝄽; (2) then nine quarter notes stretching across the next two bar lines— ♩ ♩ ♩ | ♩ ♩ ♩ ♩ | ♩ ♩; (3) another quarter-note rest and three more quarter notes— 𝄽 ♩ | ♩ ♩; (4) again a quarter-note rest and a final three harmonics— 𝄽 ♩ | ♩ ♩ —before the soloist begins a downward descent of sixteenths (imitating the motive initiated by the tutti violins earlier in the measure). The result is an aural clash between triple and duple meter that confuses the ear teasingly. We feel that we are off balance, literally out of step. The tutti violins play a scalar figure (pitches D-E-F-F♯ in measure 39, for example) with accents placed on the "wrong," or weak, beats of the measure—yet another type of syncopation. The tied notes again give the impression of triple meter within duple and reinforce the metric displacement of the solo violin, particularly since these tied-over notes always occur between the articulated beats of the soloist. The cellos duplicate the tutti violins' rhythm; but rather than using a contiguous linear motive, Stravinsky displaces notes over two octaves with huge leaps so that the effect of a jagged line results.

Upon further inspection, however, we hear a larger, more slowly developing linear ascent with the bass pitches D in measure 39, E in measure 40, F♯ in measure 42, and G in measure 43 (marked in figure 14.3). The discerning listener (and certainly Balanchine, who surely studied the counterpoint) can easily hear this line since its ascent is stressed through the octave displacement and the lowest-sounding notes in the cello. It is the same basic theme as that in the tutti violins, metrically displaced here.[12] All these overlapping layers of rhythm and pitch make for a marvelous sense of imbalance that goes along with the beautiful harmonics of the soloist. It is one of the most ethereal, dreamlike passages in the literature.

Balanchine recognized how distinctive this passage was. Von Aroldingen recalls that while he usually choreographed facilely, inviting suggestions along the way, here he thought slowly and carefully about what to do. The admixture of layers Stravinsky had constructed intrigued him. Within the passage's overall sense of displacement, everything moved together in an absolutely logical unfolding. The music's interior structure made sense while the aural effect was surrealistic. Von Aroldingen remembers that she "did a back bend in a count of four. The music is counted in nine and it creates a syncopation."[13] While Balanchine clearly envisioned the added counterpoint of dance at this juncture, von Aroldingen told me that he left it to her to decide how she would get into and out of the gesture. And what a convoluted, elaborate gesture it is!

While Cook dances in classical turns in keeping with the overall strong beats of each measure of music—in effect marking the music's fundamental pulse—von Aroldingen completely bends over onto both feet and arms, rotating several times in sync with the music's metric displacement (fig. 14.4). Finally, she rises out of this exquisite contortion just as the violin harmonics end.[14] It is a spectacularly visual moment leaving little doubt about how fully Balanchine understood Stravinsky's contrapuntally structured music.

Despite the compositional riches of this first pas de deux, Aria II has always held a special fascination for most dancers and dance critics. Peter Martins ob-

14.4 *Stravinsky Violin Concerto,* Aria I, with Karin von Aroldingen and Jean-Pierre Bonnefous, 1973 (Photograph by Martha Swope/TimePix)

served that while Aria I was overtly "sexual" this second duet was subtler, more "romantic." In terms of sheer physical contrast, the Martins and Mazzo pairing triggered a startling visual impact. "Perhaps," Martins offered, "Balanchine was playing off Kay's dark delicacy and vulnerable appearance against my stolidity."[15]

Delicacy is just the right word. The distinction between von Aroldingen's forceful presence throughout Aria I and Mazzo's willing submissiveness to Martins in Aria II is palpable. The obvious dependency of the female on the male throughout this five-and-a-half-minute pas de deux has prompted pictorial prose. Don McDonagh speaks of a tenderness, intimacy, compliance, and attentiveness. During the Aria's closing moments—constituting one of the most unforgettable Balanchine images—the male soloist "softly covers her eyes with his hand to conclude their duet. She remains passively trusting in this position." Passively trusting, indeed—a description upon which Nancy Goldner elaborated in speaking of the female's "totally passive" nature: "This love scene is, indeed, an image, and he is the image-maker. . . . And the willingness with which she accedes to his manipulations suggests that she herself understands her role and knows her achievement."[16]

Balanchine had unusually specific ideas about the movement. Mazzo recalls that although the duet was difficult to learn, here—despite the choreographer's well-known willingness to adjust movement to the dancers—there was no choice but to comply; for he had conceived concrete visual complements to the score, above whatever metaphors we might choose to add. When asked to comment upon the "meaning" of the movement, Balanchine responded in a characteristically dispassionate way, underscoring his desire to highlight Stravinsky's score:

> To me, it's the music that wants you to do certain things. Dance has to look like the music. If you use music simply as an accompaniment, then you don't hear it. I occupy myself with how not to interfere with the music. And at the end of this pas de deux I made a gesture as if to say, "How do you do, Stravinsky?" That music is very Russian—reminiscent of old, nostalgic Russian folk songs—and I knew what Stravinsky meant, I understood and felt it. . . . Some people, though, see in these pas de deux only pure man-woman relationships: "The woman didn't have any guts, the man wasn't sexy enough." This isn't my business.[17]

However bloodlessly Balanchine wished to obviate the self-styled narratives that were bound to attach themselves to this poetic Aria, in this case it was Stravinsky who was apparently touched by a bittersweet image. Samuel Dushkin's wife, Louise, told filmmaker Tony Palmer that the composer held very personal feelings about the piece as he composed it. Once, while sitting with Stravinsky in the audience during one of her husband's performances of the Concerto, she saw that the composer wept. When she asked him about this uncharacteristically effusive reaction, Stravinsky confessed that he had written the aria for Catherine, his long-suffering wife. It was, he said, "the only way I could think of to apologize"—a reference to his by then decade-old, not-so-secret extramarital relationship with Vera Sudeikina.[18]

Hidden programs and metaphors aside, Aria II (composed immediately after the first Aria and in only a few weeks) is set in a loosely cast tripartite structure: *A* (mm. 1–16, but with a clearly defined *A'* in mm. 8–16), *B* (mm. 17–24), and a varied reprise of *A* (mm. 25–33). Each section is divided, essentially, into eight-measure phrases—the kind of symmetrical balance one associates with the baroque, *cantilena* melody that predominates. The spirit of Bach is also felt in the broken octaves that descend in the "walking bass" of the cello, reminiscent of that composer's own airs and arias. While the first two movements were anchored, respectively, around the major and minor sides of D, here the key center is more ambiguous (like Stravinsky's own expressed feelings of ambiguity about his wife and mistress?), fluctuating between F♯-minor and its relative A-major.

Yet the soul of the music arises from the florid bel canto violin solo line, dispelling the often-lodged criticism that Stravinsky could not write a memorable melody. Although the lush ornamentation of the line, with its constant embellishments, may seem freely composed, the structural basis of the entire Aria stems from a unifying, short descending motive. Figure 14.5 reprints the opening three measures.

The top note of the now-familiar passport chord (doubled in the winds and brass) is the pitch A, which moves by downward step to G♮ as stressed in the winds and brass, to an F♯ on the measure's fourth beat. The flute and trumpet then extend the fourth beat's melodic descent with another F♯-E-D, until these sixteenth notes resolve to a C♯, the first note of the violin solo in measure 2. The descent continues with the soloist's sustained and decorated C♯, moving to a B half-note on beats three and four (in fact, for the music analyst, a case can be made for extending the linear descent through measure 8, the end of the *A* section). Such slowly unfolding linear descents are not at all unusual for classically—or neoclassically—grounded composers like Stravinsky. Sketches for many of his works confirm that he often worked explicitly to decorate such simple scalar lines. Moreover, compositionally, the idea of a methodically evolving melodic descent has long been associated with sadness, melancholy, darkness, even death, especially in baroque music.

14.5 Stravinsky, Concerto in D for violin, Aria II, measures 1–3 (© 2002 by permission of the publisher, Schott Musik International, Mainz)

Nor can there be any question that instinctively, at least, Balanchine was aware of Stravinsky's architectural scheme—a scheme by which a simple melodic idea is spun into a sumptuous, almost improvisational melody (thus his reference to old Russian folk tunes). The correlation with the slow movement, Largo, of *Concerto Barocco,* as pointed out by Jowitt, also is appropriate: "Balanchine choreographed a profoundly tender sequence in which the man and woman never let go of each other's hands. As they slowly revolve and embrace, their linked arms become arch, barrier, support, love knot, and it is difficult to fathom what is the beginning for them and what is the end"—a pretty fair analogy to explain how Stravinsky's melody and Balanchine's choreography for Aria II similarly evolve.[19]

As the movement begins, Mazzo and Martins are to the side and back of the stage. They move center as the important, melodically descending motive begins. As Mazzo rises out of a bent position raising her head, the solo violin begins its long lament in measure 2. Mazzo drapes herself over Martins throughout the melodic descent, just as the embellishing melody is draped over the more simple descent of scalar pitches. The opening passport chord and descending motive return at measure 9—a quick reprise of the opening, as well as a transition to the central *B* section. This same measure also marks the first time that Mazzo and Martins separate as they return to the widely decussated arms and legs position seen at the movement's outset—a giant X, as it has been described.

One of the most dramatic and certainly unexpected textural changes occurs in measure 17, where Stravinsky abandons what had been a thoroughly contrapuntal dialogue between the violin soloist and the orchestra. Now the strings accompany the soloist homophonically, providing a subdued background upon which the main thematic material can continue to be spun. Here both dancers—for the only time in the piece, really—perform more classically oriented combinations, as they imitate and at times closely mirror each other. Balanchine allows the two soloists to do so here because the music is indeed accompanimental, and visually there is no need to compete with additional contrapuntal layers.[20]

Choreographically the reprise of *A* at measure 25 evokes the same opening X. But beyond this signature pose, the dancing that unfolds thereafter is not an exact reprise of the initial *A* section. Measure 28 constitutes an important transitional moment in both the music and the dance. Mazzo sinks to her knees, looking away from Martins. At measure 29 he returns to her, offering his hand, just as the final embellished violin solo begins. (It grows out of the same thematic descent discussed in figure 14.5.) From here until the final cadence, there is no dancing, as the conjoined couple stands stationary at center stage. One of the most enduring poses in all of Balanchine, it was sculpted, as usual, with a keen awareness of the music's structure.

Martins cradles Mazzo while extending his hand and gently rocking back and forth (fig. 14.6). Entwined, they bow deeply and graciously in a gesture of obeisance. "Make it look like an elephant trunk," the always disarming Balanchine is said to have instructed, "then move your hand as if you're asking for money." Even the final two gestures wherein Martins covers Mazzo's eyes as she leans back and he goes to his knees are perfectly coordinated with musically important structural points of the cadence. A formal bow to Stravinsky, as some

14.6 *Stravinsky Violin Concerto,* Aria II, with Kay Mazzo and Peter Martins, 1973 (Photo-graph by Martha Swope/TimePix)

have described it, begins in the penultimate measure, 32; Martins covers Mazzo's eyes just as the final sustained half-note is struck; he falls to his knees on the final pulse of the last measure.

Why would dance be sacrificed for pure theater at this critical cadential mo-ment? From measure 29 through the final bar (measure 33), the music is marked "flautando sino al fine" for the violin soloist—meaning it is played like a flute until the end. Violinists also interpret this as meaning played delicately with a wispy, dreamlike sound, as if from a distance. Listeners will hear that with the exception of the low, sustaining double bass, the orchestra has fallen silent. All that remains is the soloist's doleful melody and two flutes—the thinnest, most gossamer sound imaginable. It is pure chamber music, an equal partnership in which the violinist must compliantly succumb to the overall will of the music in this contrapuntal trio (though unfortunately many violin soloists tend to play too loudly here). The interaction of these coequal musical lines demands the ear's complete attention as the three instrumentalists crisscross, interwoven more closely than at any other point. There is nothing for the dancers to do but listen reflectively, swaying gently as the beauty of the music engulfs them. As with the close of *Apollo*'s Apotheosis, the choreography shows that Balanchine understood that the visual impact would be all the more intense—and in harmony with Stravinsky's musical gesture—if he accepted the grandeur of the music. It is not only the woman of Aria II who is submissive, it is Balanchine as well.

The final chord of Aria II provides a structural bridge to the last movement (composed between June and September), now again anchored in the original key of D-major. While the orchestra repeats the fundamental harmony on the downbeat of the concluding Capriccio, the violin soloist strikes the work's insignia sonority. The term *capriccio* is commonly used to describe a through-composed piece, a "fancy" falling beyond conventional statement-contrast-return musical designs. It also denotes concert etudes that demand great technical facility, as in the Paganini Capricci for solo violin. Not only is the Concerto's fourth movement rhapsodic in its procession of cheerfully tuneful melodic ideas, but it is easily the most exhilarating in its tour de force rhythmic propulsion. The soloist must play almost continually while constantly drawing from a fiddler's bag of standard tricks, demonstrating just how effective Dushkin's tutelage was in familiarizing Stravinsky with the instrument.

While the opening material is reprised at measure 108 of the Capriccio's 285 measures, the movement comprises a series of continuous episodes loosely strung together. The feeling is one of musical spontaneity, although as always Stravinsky worked at creating the impression. For the first time in the entire Concerto, the full orchestra is called upon regularly. Still, the lushness of the orchestral palette is balanced by smaller chamber combinations. Notably, the long Bachian duet for two violins extending from measure 160 to 174 seems like a page stolen from the final movement of the *Bach Double* (as Stravinsky himself suggested).

For the first time in the ballet, Balanchine employs all twenty dancers. But just as Stravinsky continues to draw on chamber pairings in alternation with the full orchestra, so too does Balanchine combine diverse arrays of soloists and their accompanying corps. This unbroken string of visual clusters complements Stravinsky's episodic music, creating the enchanting medley of images that mark this joyful gambol. The music rushes by so quickly that it is difficult for the ear—to say nothing of the eye—to follow the sequence of each coordinated event. The details of four representative, important structural junctures will illustrate the plexuslike architecture that Balanchine assembles in fusing both music and dance.

As the cascade of the violinist's opening scales flows from the passport chord, four males and four females (the women again in skirts) rush in from the wings. They quickly form two rows across the stage, the women in front. As the music's first structural division arrives at measure 8 with the announcement of a baroque-sounding violin figuration, von Aroldingen and Cook enter. They assume their soloist positions in front, waggishly waving to the eight-member ensemble—all part of the visual banter that is tossed back and forth throughout this "capricious" finale. The ten assembled dancers spring into motion in four distinct phases: first von Aroldingen, then Cook, then the line of women join, followed by the male quartet. All dance within their own confined spaces, hardly moving beyond a quadrangle. Visually each "box" is animated internally; but each of these four layers of activity moves independently, not in unison. It is an early signal of how Balanchine will deal throughout the movement with the swiftly paced motion of musical events. Rather than allow the large corps to roam freely through large spatial areas, he defines a smaller space and vitalizes the choreographic movement from within. At times there is very little dancing, but still plenty of movement.

Surely Balanchine realized that the interchange of music and dance staged within clearly defined quadrate blocks was probably his only choice, given the headlong gait of the music. The score is a coruscating bundle of speed and virtuoso violin configurations that could never be visually matched note for note without becoming overwhelming and, consequently, bewildering. Balanchine partitions divisible spatial areas that then remain anchored throughout each of Stravinsky's episodes. Within each temporal division, the choreographic collections he assembles are kaleidoscopic in their network of planes—straight lines, coordinates, diagonals, hemispheres, quadrants, octets, quartets split into duets, lateral movements, fan-shaped concentric circles—all shifting while the soloists perform independently in front of the supporting and crosscutting ensembles. This is plane geometry danced.

As we have seen in other Stravinsky-Balanchine ballets, dramatic musical junctures sometimes demand an equally dynamic visual punctuation. Measure 55 of the Capriccio marks the first moment of relief for the violin soloist in what to then has been a nonstop flurry of scales and octaves. A more relaxed motive appears, accompanied by a greatly reduced orchestra. Just as this intersection approaches, the second ensemble of eight dancers enters toward the rear of the stage while Aria II's couple, Mazzo and Martins, enter in front. Like the parting of the Red Sea, the ten dancers already on stage now open ranks, allowing the new ensemble and soloists to enter while von Aroldingen, Cook, and their entourage depart.

The reprise of measure 108 is marked by the reentrance of the von Aroldingen-Cook group. Now for the first time Balanchine stresses this critical turning point by calling all twenty dancers onstage. The soloists stand front stage with the eight males behind them and the eight females farther back, forming three collimations across the stage. (For the audience, an upper-tier aerial view is desirable since the panoramic constellations that Balanchine assembles seem right out of a Busby Berkeley film.) Arrays of two, four, eight, and sixteen dancers form and separate, all flouncing about within their own clearly defined space. Given the return to the music's rapid pace, sometimes the ensemble dancers do little more than stand almost motionless, moving only a hand or wrist or angle. This choreographic "stasis" brings to mind the Allegro from *Concerto Barocco*, where Balanchine simply marks the underlying pulse to the Bach score with subtle movements.

The final major musical division begins at measure 205 after the dramatically abrupt grand pause. The mood changes radically. The jagged music protrudes itself among hiccups of silence more typical of *The Rite of Spring*'s youthful composer. The soloist scrapes and scratches, assailing the instrument in the anti-violinistic writing style of *L'Histoire du Soldat*. In response Balanchine splits the entire cast into five quartets, the four soloists now forming their own ensemble. Marking another first, all twenty dancers join in complete unison movement the length and breadth of the stage. The choreographic fission continues as the final cadence approaches. The sixteen corps dancers again divide, now into male-female pairings that form a grand conglomeration strung across the stage. So too the four soloists, now standing in front, return to their original partners. For the only moment in the ballet, all twenty dancers are united in a final visual symmetry of ten male-female couples as the score ends. It seems the only logical resolution, made all the more satisfying because it has been withheld until the violin soloist strikes the Concerto's last chord.

It is little wonder that *Stravinsky Violin Concerto* has proven a perennial favorite. There is something for everybody: brilliant solo work for dancers and the violin soloist, wonderful ensemble passages for both the corps and orchestra, and a range of sentiments capable of stirring the audience in many different ways. It is a work to be enjoyed visually, aurally, and emotionally. Yet underneath it all, there is that ever-enduring sense of a well-planned, overarching architectural design that provided the structural hub for everything Stravinsky and Balanchine did. That the composer was no longer around to guide or endorse what Balanchine was doing to match the music choreographically made no difference whatsoever. The fundamental lessons of unity and balance had been learned long ago, and very well indeed.

Epilogue

Once a journey is designed, equipped, and put in process, a new factor enters and takes over. A trip, a safari, an exploration, is an entity, different from all other journeys. . . . We find after years of struggle that we do not take a trip; a trip takes us.
—*John Steinbeck,* Travels with Charley

Following the unparalleled achievement of the 1972 Stravinsky Festival, Balanchine continued his own journey, producing a string of new ballets. Much has been made of the fact that he did not choreograph any new Stravinsky works between the 1972 and 1982 festivals. Theories abound to explain this almost decade-long hiatus. Had he run out of scores worth choreographing? Had City Ballet's offerings become saturated by too much Stravinsky? Or could it be that he simply had had enough of his old friend's music? Whatever the speculation, Balanchine now turned his attention to other scores and other programmatic themes, including eight new works for the 1975 Ravel Festival. He also staged the splashy star-spangled production *Union Jack* as part of the 1976 U.S. Bicentennial celebration. The productivity of his late years was highlighted by some of his most poignant, autumnal works:

Vienna Waltzes (1977), *Robert Schumann's "Davidsbündlertänze"* (1980), and an entirely new production of *Mozartiana* (1981), which was one of four new ballets prepared as part of that year's Tchaikovsky Festival. These and other works have deservedly entered the repertoire of the New York City Ballet.

In 1979 Balanchine turned seventy-five. Perhaps he had slowed a bit, but for the most part he remained as creatively vigorous as Stravinsky was at the same age when he composed the youthfully exuberant *Agon*. Neither a heart attack that year nor bypass surgery soon thereafter diminished the choreographer's instinctual drive to keep making new dances, to keep "doing," as Stravinsky would have said. "Painting is just another way of keeping a diary," Picasso once remarked, and despite the frailties of his age, Balanchine kept making entries—each one more beautiful than the next.

The 10–18 June 1982 Stravinsky Centennial Celebration offered more than two dozen works prepared by various choreographers (Martins, Robbins, Taras, and others). Balanchine's contribution consisted of *Tango, Noah and the Flood, Elégie*, and lastly, *Perséphone*—the concluding work of the festival, presented on the composer's birthday. While the new festival did not have the enormous success attained ten years earlier, still it made an unmistakable statement about Balanchine's need—and ability—to say something new. Moreover, it provided one final platform for public homage to Stravinsky's accomplishments. The weeklong celebration had been in the planning stages for several years. But a few months before its scheduled opening, Balanchine's health declined seriously. He was unable to finish a fifth Stravinsky ballet in time. A few weeks after the festival's closing curtain, in early July 1982, Suzanne Farrell premiered the choreographer's final version of *Variations for Orchestra*. Ever the perfectionist, and still steadfastly swearing total allegiance to the music, Balanchine commented to Farrell, "The first time I did it I didn't have it right. Now it's exactly what the music calls for."[1]

Following the New York spring season, he made the annual trip north to Saratoga, then traveled on tour with City Ballet in the fall. But it was becoming increasing evident to him and others that physically something was acutely wrong. He grew unsteady on his feet, falling and injuring himself. After a series of incidents, he finally admitted himself to Roosevelt Hospital in November. He never recovered. Five months later, on 30 April 1983, his pulse finally gave out.

I mention "pulse" specifically, since ultimately the word may best sum up Balanchine's approach to dance and music—just as it perhaps encapsulates the dynamism reverberating throughout every page of every Stravinsky score. Indeed, across the top of a 1911 compositional sketch for the Dance of the Earth section of *The Rite of Spring*—one of the most primitively pulsating pages of music ever written—the composer wrote, "Music exists when there is rhythm, as life exists when there is a pulse."[2] If there is one thing certain about the Stravinsky and Balanchine partnership, it is that both men understood this intuitively. Balanchine once characterized the composer's music as "atomic." Every particle of every measure was electrically charged. Regardless of the slowness of the tempo, the solemnity of the mood, or the layered intricacy of his most convoluted scores, there was always an undercurrent, an inexorable beat serving as a stabilizing rudder. Stravinsky's music always pressed forward, avoiding what St. John Perse once called the menace of inertia.

From Balanchine's early days with the Ballets Russes through his 1982 restaging of the composer's *Variations for Orchestra* for Farrell, the relentless, fundamental pulse of Stravinsky's music provided the backbone for his choreographic coherence. It supplied the visual and aural ballast for the architectural order evident in their collaborations. It did so even—or perhaps especially—when it sank into the substructure, where balance must find its anchor. Even if the pulse was not immediately perceivable at the music's surface, it was there, acting as the agent of stability. Whether or not others were aware of it explicitly, Balanchine himself heard it loud and clear. As he explained in "The Dance Element in Stravinsky's Music," the absolute control of an underlying strict beat was Stravinsky's "sign of authority over time."[3] The choreographer respected that authority. His ability to hear and visualize the vitality of that pulse in every Stravinsky score became the catalyst for his many ballets. The composer realized the depth of his friend's understanding. He knew that Balanchine recognized the life-giving properties of pulse as the elegantly elemental force of musical movement.

Time's mysterious, unstoppable flow—the lifeblood of the precariously balanced marriage of music and dance—never ceased to intrigue them. It impelled them as they traveled together through a long, fruitful journey of invention. And make no mistake, it was the voyage itself, the process of embarking upon the unknowable, that they found spellbinding. For beyond the surgical precision they brought to every dimension of their work, beyond their quest for order, they both realized that even great architects must ultimately concede that control is an illusion. Today, years after their collaborative expedition has ended, no matter how many times we re-create the richness of their ballets with our own ears and eyes, we set out on our own new journey each time we see one of their ballets. What a wonderful journey their imaginations made possible— a journey for which we should be eternally thankful.

Appendix: The Stravinsky-Balanchine Ballets

This table is intended only as a quick reference. It does not include the lost settings of Stravinsky's scores that were prepared while Balanchine was still a student in Russia, nor does it list the many instances in which he revised his choreography (often several times) after the initial production. For a complete list, with full details of casting, scenery, lighting, designs, story, and other relevant information, see *Choreography by George Balanchine: A Catalogue of Works,* ed. Leslie George Katz, Nancy Lassalle, and Harvey Simmonds (New York: Viking, 1984). For another useful, easy to use guide, consult Nancy Reynolds, *Repertory in Review* (New York: Dial, 1977).

Title	Composition Date/ Ballet Premiere	Company	Comments
Le Chant du Rossignol	1917/1925	Ballets Russes	Revision of 1920 Massine production.
Apollon Musagète (*Apollo, Leader of the Muses; Apollo*)	June 1928	Ballets Russes	American premiere, April 1928, Washington, D.C., with choreography by Adolph Bolm.
Jeu de Cartes (*Card Game*)	1937	American Ballet, Metropolitan Opera	Commissioned by Lincoln Kirstein and Edward Warburg.
Le Baiser de la Fée	1928/1937	American Ballet, part of Stravinsky Festival	Original choreography by Bronislava Nijinska for Ballets Ida Rubinstein.
Balustrade	1931/1941	Original Ballet Russe	To the score of Stravinsky's Concerto in D for violin.
Ballet of the Elephants	1942	Ringling Brothers and Barnum & Bailey Circus	To the score of Stravinsky's *Circus Polka*.
Danses Concertantes	1942/1944	Ballet Russe de Monte Carlo	Originally commissioned for chamber orchestra.
Elégie	1944/1945	School of American Ballet	Originally a piece for solo viola.
Renard	1916/1947	Ballet Society	First choreographed by Bronislava Nijinska in 1922 for the Ballets Russes.
Orpheus	1948	Ballet Society	Commissioned for Ballet Society by Lincoln Kirstein.
Firebird	1910/1949	New York City Ballet	Original choreography by Michel Fokine for the Ballets Russes.
Agon	1957	New York City Ballet	Commissioned by NYCB with funds from the Rockefeller Foundation.

Title	Composition Date/ Ballet Premiere	Company	Comments
Monumentum pro Gesualdo	1960	New York City Ballet	Stravinsky originally arranged three madrigals by Gesualdo.
Ragtime (I)	1918/1960	New York City Ballet	To the composer's original score *Ragtime for Eleven Instruments.*
Noah and the Flood	1962	New York City Ballet	Written for television and telecast on CBS. Two choreographic sections by Balanchine.
Movements	1959/1963	New York City Ballet	To the composer's score *Movements for Piano and Orchestra.*
Variations	1965/1966	New York City Ballet	Original orchestral score, *Variations in Memory of Aldous Huxley.*
Rubies (from the Ballet *Jewels*)	1929/1967	New York City Ballet	Original score entitled *Capriccio* for piano and orchestra.
Requiem Canticles	1966/1968	New York City Ballet	Originally for chorus, soloists, and orchestra.
Sonata	1904/1972	New York City Ballet	Choreography for Scherzo movement of early Stravinsky piano sonata.
Symphony in Three Movements	1945/1972	New York City Ballet	Commissioned by the New York Philharmonic Orchestra.
Violin Concerto (*Stravinsky Violin Concerto*)	1931/1972	New York City Ballet	Completely rechoreographed version of *Balustrade.*
Scherzo à la Russe	1944/1972	New York City Ballet	Originally written for Paul Whiteman's band.
Duo Concertant	1932/1972	New York City Ballet	Originally written by the composer for himself and violinist Samuel Dushkin.

(continued)

Title	Composition Date/ Ballet Premiere	Company	Comments
Pulcinella	1920/1972	New York City Ballet	Choreographed jointly with Jerome Robbins. Original choreography by Léonide Massine for the Ballets Russes.
Choral Variations	1956/1972	New York City Ballet	For chorus and orchestra, based upon material by J. S. Bach.
Symphony of Psalms	1930/1972	New York City Ballet	Originally for chorus and orchestra and dedicated to the Boston Symphony Orchestra.
Tango	1940/1982	New York City Ballet	Originally a piano solo, then later arranged for various ensembles.
Perséphone	1934/1982	New York City Ballet	Choreographed jointly with John Taras and Vera Zorina. First performance by Ballets Ida Rubinstein.

A Note on Sources

I have chosen not to include a formal bibliography. The secondary literature on Stravinsky and Balanchine, especially given the enormous significance of their individual lives and accomplishments, is daunting. Rather, I have attempted to provide considerable detail on pertinent bibliographic sources in notes throughout the text. I have relied upon several primary sources, especially unpublished scores, film clips, correspondence, and other archival materials housed in various repositories, as well as upon materials and references not easily accessible to the general public. A few of the archives deserve special mention.

The Paul Sacher Stiftung in Basel, Switzerland, holds, in more than one hundred boxes which came to Basel in 1983, the vast majority of Stravinsky's correspondence, manuscripts, scores, portions of his library, unreleased films, and other archival materials. The holdings are not open to the general public, and there is no published catalogue listing specific dates of letters, the contents of the composer's library, and so on. To trace these important sources accurately, one must petition to visit the Stiftung for personal study. A useful inventory of the composer's manuscripts and sketch materials has been published; the archive also issues an annual booklet, *Mitteilungen der Paul Sacher Stiftung,* listing new acquisitions and synopses of current Stravinsky research. In references to various unpublished Stravinsky materials throughout the text, the reader can assume that the materials cited are held by the Paul Sacher Stiftung unless otherwise noted.

The George Balanchine Archive is held by the Harvard Theatre Collection, part of Harvard's Houghton Library, and includes 81 boxes of informative documents, including audio-visual materials, correspondence, books, drawings, manuscripts, contracts, programs, scores, typescripts, and other archival papers. These invaluable sources, which came to the Harvard Theatre Collection in March 1992, were a gift of Barbara Horgan and The George Balanchine Trust. I have relied extensively on many of the Theatre Collection's holdings. With proper identification, access to the Harvard Theatre Collection is permitted for scholarly study. For the sake of convenience, I have abbreviated my frequent references throughout the text: for example, Harvard Theatre Collection, George Balanchine Archive, Correspondence, Box 1/Folder 1, will appear as HTC, Correspondence, 1/1, unless otherwise noted.

The reader is often referred to materials held by the Jerome Robbins Dance Division of the New York Public Library for the Performing Arts, located at Lincoln Center. Easily the most comprehensive repository of dance materials in the world, most, but not all, of the holdings are open to the public. The extensive film archive held by the Jerome Robbins Dance Division is of particular importance to dancers and musicians. In some instances, permission to view rare film clips must be obtained in advance. The catalogue for the collection is also available in a useful and easily accessible format on the Internet (www.catnyp.nypl.org).

For readers interested in viewing videos of several Balanchine ballets, I would strongly recommend a series of tapes produced by the George Balanchine Foundation (discussed and cited at various junctures in the text). Nancy Reynolds, project director, has assembled videos of many Balanchine's dancers reconstructing lost choreography. Other tapes provide viewers with the opportunity to observe important interpretations of some of the choreographer's most memorable ballets, in which the dancers are coached by the original participants. Approximately two dozen tapes are now available; several are forthcoming. Although these videotapes are not commercially available, they may be viewed at several venues throughout the world (for example, at several major libraries and universities).

There are numerous audio recordings of the Stravinsky-Balanchine ballets. All are included in the important set of Stravinsky's complete works conducted, mostly, by the composer himself. This now-classic collection is available through SONY Classical, *Igor Stravinsky, 1882–1971: The Edition,* easily obtainable through most record distributors. Of course there is no shortage of Stravinsky recordings generally, and specific performances relevant to a particular ballet are mentioned in the text as appropriate.

Notes

Chapter 1: Commonalities and Contrasts

Epigraph: The composer's comments are excerpted from Igor Stravinsky and Robert Craft, *Memories and Commentaries* (Rpt.; Berkeley: University of California Press, 1981), 37. Balanchine's remarks originally appeared in the *Cincinnati Enquirer,* 18 June 1972.

1. *Bravo Stravinsky* (Cleveland: World, 1967). Photographs by Arnold Newman, text by Robert Craft, foreword by Francis Steegmuller. Balanchine was particularly aware of the silences punctuating Stravinsky's music. "Silence is a beat to be danced, just as all divided time in music," he once remarked to an interviewer. See Pierre Tugal, "An Interview with Balanchine," *Dancing Times* 444 (September 1947): 633–34.

2. Igor Stravinsky, *Poetics of Music* (Rpt.; Cambridge: Harvard University Press, 1975), 51; *Balanchine's Complete Stories of the Great Ballets,* ed. Francis Mason (Garden City, N.Y.: Doubleday, 1954), 532; John Steinbeck, *Journey of a Novel* (Rpt.; London: Mandarin, 1991), 106.

3. Stravinsky, *Poetics of Music,* 28. Balanchine's remarks were offered in a 1962 Canadian Broadcasting Company television documentary about Stravinsky, produced by Franz Kraemer. An index card among Balanchine's papers records one of many cryptic and roughly drafted thoughts the choreographer expressed (originally in Russian) about his concept of movement. "Move-

ment can be without music and music can exist without movement. Together they are pleasant but not indispensable. The same like tea or sugar if, to say, dance without music does not exist. Within that we definitely arrange movement in itself. On the other hand, music joining with movement acts on both senses, visual and oral [*sic*]. And if they synchronize in perfection it inevitably produces sense of staying in continuous rhythm." HTC, Correspondence, 23/28.

4. Galileo's comment is extracted from his *Il Saggiatore,* quoted in Stuart Hampshire's *The Age of Reason* (New York: Mentor, 1956), 33. Interview with Violette Verdy by Tobi Tobias, 1975. The transcript is held by the Jerome Robbins Dance Division of the New York Public Library for the Performing Arts.

5. Mikhail Druskin, *Igor Stravinsky: His Life, Works and Views,* trans. Martin Cooper (Cambridge: Cambridge University Press, 1983), 116–17.

6. Stravinsky, *Poetics of Music,* 55–56.

7. Igor Stravinsky, English synopsis of lecture originally delivered in French, 24 May 1940. Harvard University Archives, Periodical Lectures: Charles Eliot Norton.

8. Interview with Soulima Stravinsky, *Perspectives of New Music,* 10/1 (1971): 17.

9. Jonathan Cott, "Two Talks with George Balanchine," in *Portrait of Mr. B* (New York: Viking, 1984), 143. Stravinsky's statement in the 6 June 1935 issue of *Candide* is reprinted in various sources, including "Stravinsky on Art and Artists," a compilation of the composer's quotes on dance assembled by John Taras in *Dance Magazine* 55, no. 4 (April 1981): 64.

10. Lifar's comment should not be misinterpreted. His view of Stravinsky's music is closer to Balanchine's than might first be thought. Although he suggests that the composer's music "enfeebles dancing and weighs it down, and enslaves it," he quickly adds that "dancing never enhances Stravinsky's music [since it] is so beautiful in itself that it is all sufficient; it has no need of any dancing . . . and dancing only serves to distract the listener's attention." See Lifar's *Ballet: Traditional to Modern,* trans. Cyril W. Beaumont (London: Putnam, 1938), 168.

11. For specific comparisons between Balanchine's neoclassic ballets and architectural classicism, see Deborah Gans, "The Architecture of Balanchine," *Choreography and Dance* 3, no. 3 (1993): 31–47. Gans's linking of Balanchine and Le Corbusier, especially in the 1920s, has implications for watching a work such as *Apollo,* as discussed in Chapter 5.

12. Suzanne Farrell with Toni Bentley, *Holding on to the Air* (New York: Summit, 1990), 295.

13. Druskin, *Stravinsky,* 118 (also see Simon Karlinsky's discussion of preliterate Russian folklore in "Igor Stravinsky and Russian Preliterate Theater," in *Confronting Stravinsky,* ed. Jann Pasler [Berkeley: University of California Press, 1986], 3–15); Igor Stravinsky, *An Autobiography* (Rpt.; New York: Norton, 1998), 4. Stravinsky's statement about St. Petersburg is quoted by Solomon Volkov in "Stravinsky's Paradise Lost," as part of the program booklet *Stravinsky Centennial Celebration* (New York: Dubin and Dubin, 1982), 6.

14. Francis Mason, *I Remember Balanchine* (New York: Doubleday, 1991), x.

15. Richard Taruskin, *Stravinsky and the Russian Traditions,* 2 vols. (Berkeley: University of California Press, 1996), 1:536–37. Also see the author's reprint of a February 1900 letter from Rimsky to his friend, the critic Semyon Kruglikov, wherein the composer provides

a litany of reasons for why ballet had not matured, even under Petipa. Ballet was "degenerate"; it was nothing more than "miming"; the language of dance was "skimpy"; the music was written by "hacks"; scores were often performed in a "sloppy slapdash" manner. One must remember that the impressionable Stravinsky began studying with Rimsky only a few years later. No doubt his redoubtable teacher passed along several crystallized opinions.

16. This famous letter, sent on 11 July 1911 to Vladimir Rimsky-Korsakov, responded to criticisms of a recent Diaghilev production. Taruskin reprints the letter in its entirety in *Stravinsky and the Russian Traditions,* 2:972–74.

17. Theodore Stravinsky, *The Message of Igor Strawinsky,* trans. Robert Craft and Andre Marion (London: Boosey and Hawkes, 1953), 42–45.

18. In her informative study *Suki Schorer on Balanchine Technique* (New York: Knopf, 1999), Schorer remembers how aware Balanchine was of the dancer's hair, forehead, and skin color. Consulting with a beautician to see what might be done to provide more contrast, Schorer recalls that Balanchine suggested "that I make my hairline visible by darkening it with a washable light-brown dye, which he bought for me to use" (8).

19. As discussed in Chapter 3, filmmaker Tony Palmer interviewed Balanchine for a documentary about Stravinsky. Palmer's memories of the interview recall Balanchine and his need to move physically. Palmer told me that Balanchine was constantly in motion; he would not "sit still" during the interview; in fact, he refused to sit at all. He was fidgety during the entire interview, continually pacing and shifting his weight from one leg to another. Initially, Balanchine refused to be interviewed by Palmer, just as he "refused to allow himself to be filmed, taped or recorded in any way," responded Balanchine's assistant Barbara Horgan to Palmer's original inquiry. But Horgan explains that it was only later in life that Balanchine refused interviews (having done them countless times for radio and television earlier). A man of great dignity and and commanding carriage, he became increasingly self-conscious of his failing health, not wanting the camera's eye to capture for posterity his physical decline.

20. Roger Shattuck, "The Devil's Dance: Stravinsky's Corporal Imagination," in Pasler, *Confronting Stravinsky,* 84.

21. Ibid., 84.

22. George Balanchine, "How I Became a Dancer and Choreographer," in *Balanchine's Complete Stories of the Great Ballets,* 487.

23. For Balanchine's moving description of how the production affected him, see his own account in "How I Became a Dancer and Choreographer," 488–89. Also see Jonathan Cott, "Two Talks with George Balanchine," 140.

24. Andrei Melitonovich Balanchivadze was George's younger by two years. Graduating from the Tbilisi Conservatory in 1927, he studied with Mikhail Ippolitov-Ivanov, the respected composer and conductor who directed the Moscow Conservatory from 1905 to 1922. Andrei was considered a major composer in Soviet Georgia and credited with the first Georgian national ballet, *The Heart of the Mountains* (1936). Although the two brothers did not keep in close touch after Balanchine came to the United States, Balanchine's mother made sure that George was aware of Andrei's continuing compositional career. In a 1 November 1935 letter from Tbilisi to her son George, she advised him that a

copy of Andrei's piano concerto would be arriving soon, no doubt with hopes that George could secure performances in the United States. HTC, Correspondence, 6/24 (my thanks to Lynn Garafola for providing the translation of this letter). The two brothers were reunited upon Balanchine's return to Moscow in 1962 (as part of a New York City Ballet tour) after an absence of more than forty years. Even after his brother's death in 1983, Andrei remained active as a major Soviet composer, writing his Third Symphony in 1984. Slonimsky, Balanchine's friend from their childhood days, has provided by far the most important synopsis of Balanchine's youthful acquaintance with music. His remarks first appeared in *Ballet Review*, 5/3 (1975–76), and are reprinted in Mason, *I Remember Balanchine*, 19–78.

25. These cabaret performances, known as *khalturas*, were illegal, but as Geva remembered, "They were overlooked because of the hard times." See Robert Tracy with Sharon Delano, *Balanchine's Ballerinas: Conversations with the Muses* (New York: Linden, 1983), 30.

26. Author's interview with Violette Verdy, Saratoga Springs, 23 July 1990.

27. For the complete transcript, including a listing of the repertoire Balanchine was studying, see Slonimsky's article in Mason, *I Remember Balanchine*, 33.

28. Youskevitch interview in Mason, *I Remember Balanchine*, 300.

29. Nathan Milstein and Solomon Volkov, *From Russia to the West* (New York: Henry Holt, 1990), 241.

30. Balanchine's "noodling" sometimes turned to composition as well, especially Broadway-style show tunes and charming, melancholic love songs. The Harvard Theatre Collection retains several songs of this nature, incomplete as well as complete. Most of the musical ideas, though not particularly imaginative, are worked out skillfully. The lyrics, however, are less distinguished. One such tune, "The World Is Turning Fast," was published by G. Schirmer in 1982, with lyrics by tunesmith Arthur Schwartz ("Dancing in the Dark," "That's Entertainment"). According to *Ballet News* 1, no. 1 (July 1982), Schwartz heard Balanchine playing a little song on the keyboard at a party and suggested the two collaborate. What is not mentioned is that Balanchine had been working on the song for years, writing his own lyrics and entitling the song, "Love Is a Simple Thing." Moreover, several sketches confirm that he worked out the music in draft after draft. The fact is, even though Balanchine viewed composing as a kind of avocational pastime, he worked at it diligently, as with everything else he undertook.

31. Paul Mejia interview in Mason, *I Remember Balanchine*, 477.

32. Some of Balanchine's piano reductions are discussed in later chapters. In addition to those discussed, Balanchine prepared wonderfully complete reductions for Stravinsky's *Monumentum pro Gesualdo* and the *Vom Himmel Hoch Variations*. But Stravinsky was hardly the only composer for whom Balanchine reduced scores in preparing his ballets. Others include piano reductions of scores by Mozart for the ballet *Caracole*, premiered in 1952 (rechoreographed in 1956 as *Divertimento No. 15*); Tchaikovsky's Suite No. 3 used for the important 1947 ballet *Theme and Variations*; music from Verdi's opera *Don Carlos* for the 1978 ballet *Ballo Della Regina*; and several particularly informative reductions of scores by Anton Webern for the 1959 ballet *Episodes*, as discussed in Chapter 13.

33. HTC, Scores, 10/10. Balanchine neither dates nor identifies his reduction as the Stravinsky score.

34. Nonetheless, Balanchine did find Taper's fine biography useful in deflecting countless requests for interviews and providing information about a variety of issues. As the Harvard Theatre Collection archive attests, Balanchine (through Barbara Horgan) would regularly refer such inquirers to the Taper text, sometimes citing specific sections to consult. Nancy Reynolds notes that Balanchine's feeling about his place in history probably changed as he aged. She recalls that Balanchine sent a copy of her landmark study, *Repertory in Review* (New York: Dial, 1977), to Slonimsky. He wanted to familiarize his childhood friend with "an idea of his entire adult career, which due to politics [Slonimsky] had missed almost completely" (although Reynolds adds that Slonimsky may have seen a few Balanchine ballets performed in Russia when the New York City Ballet traveled there in 1962 and 1972). Reynolds also points to at least one other occasion in the late 1970s when Balanchine "appeared very interested in getting the record straight." Reynolds, whose many important interviews with and writings about Balanchine are a matter of record, kindly shared her remarks with me in a letter of 29 April 2000.

35. George Balanchine, "The Dance Element in Stravinsky's Music," has been reprinted often, as in *Stravinsky and the Theatre*, ed. Minna Lederman (New York: Da Capo, 1975), 78.

36. Balanchine to Rockefeller, 12 July 1961, HTC, Correspondence, 12/15.

37. Balanchine to Eisenhower, 1 October 1952, HTC, Correspondence, 20/8.

38. Balanchine to Mrs. John F. Kennedy, 1 August 1961. The entire, lengthy letter is held in HTC, Correspondence, 20/8. Many of the thoughts Balanchine expressed to Jacqueline Kennedy were first aired in a speech he delivered at the Woman's National Democratic Club in Washington, D.C., on 27 April as part of a program entitled "What I Would Do for the Arts if I Were President for a Day." Jacqueline Kennedy answered Balanchine's letter promptly, promising that she would do all that she could, especially in enabling children to become acquainted with the beauties of art. In 1963 Kennedy requested Suzanne Farrell to dance the Stravinsky-Balanchine *Movements* at the White House, with piano accompaniment only. Balanchine, wisely, declined, knowing Stravinsky's position on piano-reduced performances, especially for such an orchestrally rich work. See Farrell, *Holding on to the Air*, 83.

39. Lincoln Kirstein seemed more exasperated with attacks upon the choreographer than Balanchine. The above, and typically Balanchinian dismissal, was voiced to Kirstein, who in turn relayed it to Stravinsky in a 23 August 1950 letter to the composer. Stravinsky retained all Kirstein's letters, now held in the Paul Sacher Stiftung.

40. Actually, Harvard offered Balanchine an honorary doctorate several times (as did Yale), in the 1970s and as late as 1983, by which time he was too ill to accept. He did accept several honorary doctorates (University of Cincinnati, New England Conservatory, Northwestern University, Columbia University, and others), although he declined most of them, and accepted as well many other national and international awards, including the Kennedy Center Honors in 1978, presented by President Jimmy Carter. In 1983 Ronald Reagan awarded Balanchine the Presidential Medal of Freedom; although he was too ill to accept it himself, Suzanne Farrell represented the choreographer. In a letter of 13 April, President Reagan praised Balanchine as "a great ballet master [who] enriched the lives of millions of Americans" and thanked him for "outstanding contri-

butions to our society and for lifting the spirits of all who love the dance." HTC, Correspondence, 18/22.

Chapter 2: At the Crossroads

1. Lynn Garafola's *Diaghilev's Ballets Russes* (New York: Oxford University Press, 1989) provides a richly comprehensive context in its examination of Diaghilev's interactions with musicians, painters, poets, designers, and other collaborators. Other widely known biographies include Cyril Beaumont, *Bookseller at the Ballet: Memoirs, 1891 to 1929, Incorporating the Diaghilev Ballet in London* (London: Beaumont, 1975); Richard Buckle, *Diaghilev* (London: Weidenfeld and Nicolson, 1979); Arnold Haskell, *Diaghileff: His Artistic and Private Life* (London: Gollancz, 1934), written with Walter Nouvel; Boris Kochno, *Diaghilev and the Ballets Russes* (New York: Harper and Row, 1970); Serge Lifar, *Serge Diaghilev: His Life, His Work, His Legend: An Intimate Biography* (New York: Da Capo, 1976). For a more recent collection of essays, see Lynn Garafola and Nancy Van Norman Baer, eds., *The Ballets Russes and Its World* (New Haven: Yale University Press, 1999).

2. Joan Acocella, ed., *The Diary of Vaslav Nijinsky* (New York: Farrar, Straus and Giroux, 1999), 89–90. Nijinsky's comments are excerpted from the unexpurgated version, as translated by Kyril Fitzlyon.

3. See especially Kirstein's youthful description of Diaghilev in the chapter "Nijinsky and the Russian Ballet," *Flesh Is Heir: An Historical Romance* (New York: Brewer, Warren and Putnam, 1932), 189–223.

4. For a predictably kinder portrait of Diaghilev (given her unbounded allegiance to him), especially regarding his managing of the financial crises befalling the Ballets Russes, see Misia Sert, *Misia and the Muses: The Memoirs of Misia Sert* (New York: John Day, 1953) 128–29.

5. This English translation by Mercedes de Acosta first appeared in 1937. The original article was dictated to Walter Nouvel two years earlier. Nouvel then compiled the piece based upon Stravinsky's memories and his own judgment that the composer's stories could be "improved." For Acosta's 1953 translation, Stravinsky was prepared to expand the original article substantially but demanded a larger fee than the *Atlantic Monthly* was willing to offer.

6. Palmer interviewed more than fifty of Stravinsky's friends, many of them associates of Diaghilev as well. More than 90 percent of the interviews were trimmed because of the time constraints of television. This excised footage—containing some of the most revealing comments—is preserved in the Paul Sacher Stiftung in Basel. For a more complete accounting of these interviews, see my "Diaghilev and Stravinsky" in Garafola and Van Norman Baer, *Ballets Russes and Its World,* 189–215. I discuss all the Stravinsky documentaries in my *Stravinsky Inside Out* (New Haven: Yale University Press, 2001), chap. 6.

7. Richard Taruskin, *Stravinsky and the Russian Traditions,* 2 vols. (Berkeley: University of California Press, 1996), 1:536–38.

8. Tamara Karsavina, "A Recollection of Strawinsky," *Tempo* 8 (Summer 1948): 8. Moreover, in Karsavina's *Theatre Street: The Reminiscences of Tamara Karsavina* (London:

Heinemann, 1930), the celebrated dancer remembers the interactions of Fokine and Stravinsky as they worked out the score in Diaghilev's presence, turning to him to arbitrate disputes over musical matters.

9. Monteux's comments appear in Minna Lederman, ed., *Stravinsky and the Theatre* (New York: Da Capo, 1949), 128–29. Also see the interview of Errol Addison in John Drummond, *Speaking of Diaghilev* (London: Faber and Faber, 1997), 202.

10. But in conjunction with the most famous of ballets, *The Rite of Spring,* it must be mentioned that Balanchine—contrary to his often quoted public claim that the ballet was virtually undanceable—was very interested, especially in the late 1960s and early 1970s in staging the two-piano version of the 1913 ballet (my thanks to Barbara Horgan for pointing this out). Moreover Stravinsky's unedited correspondence establishes that the prospect of remounting the legendary ballet surfaced several times during the early 1950s. Both Picasso and Pavel Tchelitchev were considered as designers, and the prospect clearly intrigued Balanchine, but given the choreographer's feelings about these two artists (both their political and artistic views), the idea was not pursued.

11. *Les Sylphides* was first given under the title of *Chopiniana* in 1892, though the pieces included in the original suite, arranged by Glazunov, are not exactly the same as the Chopin selections employed by Fokine. A youthful Balanchine danced in the production, probably around 1921, during his days in the Imperial School.

12. The Nijinsky work, based on Grieg's *Lyric Pieces,* opus 71, no. 3, *Kobold,* along with a Christian Sinding piano piece that Stravinsky orchestrated entitled *Danse Siamoise,* were introduced at the Maryinsky on 20 February 1910. Stephen Walsh reports that the pieces were originally prepared for Nijinsky's appearance at "a charity ball . . . sponsored by the magazine *Satyricon.*" See Walsh, *Stravinsky, A Creative Spring: Russia and France 1882–1934* (New York: Knopf, 1999), 137. Shortly thereafter, Diaghilev enfolded both short works into the ballet *Les Orientales,* premiered in Paris on 25 June 1910, the same program on which *The Firebird* premiered.

13. Karsavina's comments are reprinted in Richard Buckle's *Diaghilev* (New York: Atheneum, 1979), 166.

14. Michael Fokine, *Memoirs of a Ballet Master,* trans. Vitale Fokine, ed. Anatole Chujoy (Boston: Little, Brown, 1961), 161.

15. Ibid., 171.

16. Many of these corrections are evident in the pages of this compositional draft, reproduced in my *Stravinsky and the Piano* (Ann Arbor: UMI Research Press, 1983). The complete draft is preserved at the Pierpont Morgan Library, New York.

17. For a detailed analysis of the evolution of Nijinsky's choreography, see Millicent Hodson, *Nijinsky's Crime Against Grace: Reconstruction Score of the Original Choreography for Le Sacre du Printemps* (Stuyvesant, N.Y.: Pendragon, 1996).

18. In his first major dance article for *Hound & Horn* (July-September 1934), entitled "The Diaghilev Period," Lincoln Kirstein misreckoned that "Markevitch, the sixteen-year-old musician, will definitely emerge from his obscurity to replace Stravinsky."

19. A letter to Walter Nouvel written on 26 August 1929 captures Stravinsky's personal sentiments. "It is difficult for me to write these lines to you as I prefer silence to a letter which expresses so inadequately what I feel. But I have summoned up courage to express

my feelings . . . feeling the sharp pain which I have in my heart as a result of the sudden disappearance of Seriozha[,] whom I loved so much." The letter is among the uncataloged materials of the Parmenia Migel Eckstrom papers in the Harvard Theatre Collection.

20. See *Christopher Isherwood Diaries,* Volume 1: *1939–1960,* ed. Katherine Bucknell (New York: Harper Collins, 1996), 763–64.

21. See John Percival's "The Movement Man," *Dance and Dancers* 30, no. 8 (August 1979): 15.

22. The review, dated 20 May, is reprinted in Yuri Slonimsky's interview, included in Francis Mason's *I Remember Balanchine* (New York: Doubleday, 1991), 74.

23. The aftermath of the October Revolution, culturally at least, was played out in various ways. Lenin's New Economic Policy of 1921–27 spanned the exact period during which Balanchine underwent a transmogrifying artistic growth spurt—one that convinced him to leave the country. But were the artistic conditions really as repressive as Balanchine implies? "This was the time of the greatest freedom and innovation in the arts," writes Sally Banes, "the formative years of the country and the culture, when debates and experiments were deemed not only possible, but important." See Banes's excellent summary in "Introduction and Context to Soviet Ballet in the 1920s," in Elizabeth Souritz, *Soviet Choreographers in the 1920s* (Durham: Duke University Press, 1990), 1–20.

24. See Elizabeth Souritz, "The Young Balanchine in Russia," *Ballet Review* 18, no. 2 (Summer 1990): 66–71, and Margaret Thompson Drewal, "Constructionist Concepts in Balanchine's Choreography," *Ballet Review* 13, no. 3 (Fall 1985): 42–48.

25. Drewal, "Constructionist Concepts in Balanchine's Choreography," 42.

26. Unpublished letter, Balanchine to Thompson R. Buchanan, 16 June 1961, HTC, Correspondence, 20/12. Balanchine's memory of hearing Lenin was recorded in his famous essay, "How I Became a Dancer and Choreographer," in his *Balanchine's Complete Stories of the Great Ballets,* ed. Francis Mason (Garden City, N.Y.: Doubleday, 1954), 492.

27. Still, Balanchine was invited to participate as a jury member in the First International Ballet Competition in Moscow in 1969. Although a politic Balanchine politely declined (claiming that he could not be there for the length of the competition), he did express an interest in attending, if for no other reason than to keep alive the possibility of taking his company back to the Soviet Union in the future: "If you find it possible to invite me not as a member of the jury, but simply as a guest I will be most grateful to you and delighted to come." HTC, Correspondence, 18/8. Letter of 6 December 1968 to Her Excellency Mrs. Yekaterina A. Furtseva, minister of culture of the USSR.

28. In a 1983 broadcast tape made for KFAC Los Angeles (as a commemoration of Balanchine's death), Dolin asserts that he had to persuade Diaghilev to audition Balanchine after Diaghilev initially refused. Moreover, Dolin recalls that Diaghilev was adamant about wanting to contract only Balanchine and Geva but that Balanchine insisted on an all-or-nothing deal. Finally, Dolin states that Diaghilev, a few years later, originally promised him, not Lifar, the role of Apollo as a way of retaining his services, although this seems unlikely. A cassette copy of the radio broadcast is retained in the Balanchine Archive of the Harvard Theatre Collection.

29. For a discussion of Misia Sert's connection to both Stravinsky and Diaghilev, see Robert Craft, "Stravinsky, Diaghilev, and Misia Sert," *Ballet Review* 6, no. 4 (1977–78): 66–77.

Stravinsky's awareness of Sert's position and the power she held over Diaghilev, as Craft reports, was such that the composer presented Sert with his sketches and score (which included his choreographic directions) of *The Rite of Spring* immediately following the historic ballet's premiere.

30. Quoted in Mason, *I Remember Balanchine,* 86. Actually, a year earlier, while still in Russia, Balanchine had choreographed the famous Chopin Funeral March as part of some ballet evening programs that he arranged. He and Danilova danced the same pas de deux then.

31. In the early 1920s Nijinska staged Stravinsky's opera buffa, *Mavra,* and his burlesque, *Renard,* in which she also danced. (It was rechoreographed by Balanchine in 1947.) Her 1923 choreography for the protracted and problematic *Les Noces* also won the composer's approval. Although Balanchine's association with opera would be a long one, as we shall see, he particularly enjoyed his rare opportunities to prepare choreography for works by Russian composers. For the Hamburg State Opera he directed and choreographed Tchaikovsky's *Eugene Onegin* in 1962 and Glinka's *Ruslan und Ludmilla* in 1969. As late as December 1974 he was contracted to choreograph the Polonaise for the Metropolitan Opera production of Mussorgsky's *Boris Godunov* (he had first choreographed the same music in 1926 for Diaghilev).

32. Drummond, *Speaking of Diaghilev,* 224–25.

33. Quoted in Dale Harris, "Balanchine on Stravinsky," *Keynote* (June 1982): 19. As the Sacher archives attest, Stravinsky also studied Verdi's operas closely, retaining and marking many of that composer's scores.

34. Lincoln Kirstein, *Thirty Years: Lincoln Kirstein's The New York City Ballet* (New York: Knopf, 1978), 9. Ida Rubinstein and Stravinsky had in fact considered a joint project as early as 1917.

35. Quoted in Solomon Volkov, *Balanchine's Tchaikovsky* (New York: Simon and Schuster, 1985), 211–12.

36. Lincoln Kirstein, "Balanchine Musagète," *Theatre Arts* (December 1947): 39.

37. Fokine, *Memoirs of a Ballet Master,* 204. For a fuller analysis of the work's impact and its association with the original 1894 Debussy score (not conceived of as a ballet), see Thomas Munro, "*The Afternoon of a Faun* and the Interrelation of the Arts," *Journal of Aesthetics and Art Criticism* 10 (1954): 95. Also see Stephanie Jordan, "Debussy, the Dance, and the *Faune,*" in *Debussy in Performance,* ed. James R. Briscoe (New Haven: Yale University Press, 1999), 119–34.

38. Herbert Farjeon, "Seen on the Stage," *Vogue,* July 11, 1928. Quoted in Garafola, *Diaghilev's Ballets Russes,* 373.

39. Robert Craft, *Stravinsky: Selected Correspondence* (New York: Knopf, 1984), 2:43n55.

40. Nicolas Nabokov, *Old Friends and New Music* (Boston: Little, Brown, 1951), 79.

41. Drummond, *Speaking of Diaghilev,* 300.

Chapter 3: An Early Encounter

1. Benois was particularly fond of the work, as his comments attest. See Alexandre Benois, *Reminiscences of the Russian Ballet,* trans. Mary Britnieva (London: Putnam's, 1941). It is

worth noting that the Benois-Diaghilev production of Rimsky-Korsakov's opera *The Golden Cockerel,* presented on 21 May 1914 (only a few days before *Le Rossignol*), also included important choreography, this time by Fokine. Richard Taruskin reprints Nikolai Minsky's review of that premiere, wherein the connection between opera and ballet are noted: "I have no doubt that this time the inspirers of the Russian Ballet have hit upon a new form of theatrical art, one that has a huge future. It is neither ballet illustrated by music nor opera flavored with ballet, but a union of two hitherto separate art forms: a union that takes place not on the stage but in the viewer's soul." See Taruskin, *Stravinsky and the Russian Traditions*, 2 vols. (Berkeley: University of California Press, 1996), 2:1071. Given the climate, it is understandable that the Benois-Stravinsky production of *Le Rossignol* would also place a higher premium on the integration of choreography.

2. In mid-November 1916, Diaghilev mailed the composer a list of twelve suggested revisions, including cuts, the rewriting of passages, newly composed accompaniments, transpositions, overlappings, and an overall curtailment of the opera's length; "otherwise the choreography will be boring." For the text of this extraordinary letter (demonstrating, if nothing else, Diaghilev's knowledge of the score), see Robert Craft, *Stravinsky: Selected Correspondence* (New York: Knopf, 1984), 2:28–29. Years later, as discussed in Chapter 13, Balanchine made similar, very specific demands of Nicolas Nabokov in preparing the ballet *Don Quixote*. Indeed, the specificity of Diaghilev's directives to Stravinsky is reminiscent of Marius Petipa's instructions to Tchaikovsky in preparing the score of *The Nutcracker:* "Soft music. 64 measures. The tree is lighted. Sparkling music. 8 measures. The children enter. Animated, joyous music. 24 measures. Moment of surprise and admiration. A few measures of tremolo. . . . Drosselmeyer enters. Awe-inspiring but comic music. A broad movement, 16 to 24 measures. The music slowly changes character. 24 measures." See George Balanchine, "Petipa's Cue Sheet," *Center: A Magazine for the Performing Arts* 1, no. 1 (February 1954): 4.

3. Stravinsky's scenario mainly excerpts quotations from Andersen's original story and was included in the published piano reduction by Edition Russe de Musique (later Boosey and Hawkes). The complete scenario is reprinted in Eric Walter White, *Stravinsky: The Composer and His Works* (Berkeley: University of California Press, 1979), 230.

4. Lynn Garafola, *Diaghilev's Ballets Russes* (New York: Oxford University Press, 1989), 79.

5. For a full account of this part of the work's history, as well as reprints of several contemporary reviews, see Stephen Walsh, *Stravinsky, A Creative Spring: Russia and France, 1882–1934* (New York: Knopf, 1999), 308–10. For the composer's comments, see Igor Stravinsky, *An Autobiography* (Rpt.; New York: Norton, 1998), 80.

6. Moreover *Le Chant,* now billed as *The Song of the Nightingale,* had made its way to American concert hall audiences. Leopold Stokowski, who served as an early advocate for Stravinsky's music in the United States, conducted the symphonic version in New York in October 1923 with considerable success.

7. See the Slonimsky interview in Francis Mason, *I Remember Balanchine* (New York: Doubleday, 1991), 76–77.

8. Quoted in Simon Volkov, *Balanchine's Tchaikovsky* (New York: Simon and Schuster, 1985), 165–66.

9. For Tchelitchev's memories see Ivan Nabokov and Elizabeth Carmichael, "An Interview

with Balanchine," *Horizon* 3, no. 2 (January 1961): 46. Geva's comments are excerpted from her interview with Mason in *I Remember Balanchine,* 15.

10. S. L. Grigoriev, *The Diaghilev Ballet: 1909–1929,* trans. and ed. Vera Bowen (New York: Dance Horizons, 1953), 203.

11. Levinson's remarks are reprinted in Garafola, *Diaghilev's Ballets Russes,* 135.

12. By far the most informative documentation of Dame Alicia's recollections is a 1995 videotape (an amazing seventy years after the premiere) filmed in London, wherein a marvelously nimble Markova re-creates several excerpts of *Le Chant* for Iohna Loots, a young South African ballerina with the Royal Ballet School. Concentrating on the Nightingale's variation and the pas de deux, Markova methodically leads Loots through every step, every arm gesture, sometimes correcting her for being too classical, recalling that while Balanchine indeed wanted the choreography to be classical, it should not be overly so. Significantly, Markova reminds the young dancer (and the camera's audience): "Certain things . . . have to go against the music and still come out together"—as pithy a description of Balanchine's approach to Stravinsky as any one will encounter. This re-markably instructive reconstruction is part of an ongoing series of indispensable video-tapes currently being compiled by the George Balanchine Foundation's "Archive of Lost Choreography" (Nancy Reynolds, director of research for the foundation and project di-rector). These videos are accessible in several major research library repositories, includ-ing the Jerome Robbins Dance Division of the New York Public Library for the Per-forming Arts, the Harvard Theatre Collection, the John F. Kennedy Center, the Music Division of the Library of Congress, and the San Francisco Performing Arts Library and Museum (to name only a few of the nearly forty venues).

13. See the interviews of Markova and Kochno in Mason's *I Remember Balanchine.*

14. Serge Lifar, *Ma Vie: From Kiev to Kiev,* trans. James Holman Mason (New York: World, 1970), 30. The American composer George Antheil recounts a similar impression on hearing Stravinsky play portions of *Les Noces* on an "electric pianola." For more on Stra-vinsky's devotion to the mechanical instrument, see Rex Lawson, "Stravinsky and the Pianola," in *Confronting Stravinsky,* ed. Jann Pasler (Berkeley: University of California Press, 1986), 284–91. Lawson has also recorded numerous pianola roles of Stravinsky's ballets on a compact disc for MusicMasters Classics (01612-67138-2), thus bringing the listener as close as possible to the music heard during Ballets Russes rehearsals.

15. See Stravinsky's open letter to Diaghilev, originally appearing in the *Times* (18 October 1921) and reprinted in Eric Walter White's biography of the composer, Appendix A, in which he praises Tchaikovsky's score—a score that "is often more profoundly Russian than music which has long since been awarded the facile label of Muscovite picturesque-ness."

16. Léonide Massine, *My Life in Ballet* (New York: St. Martin's, 1968), 147.

17. Alfred J. Barr, *Matisse, His Art and His Public* (New York: Museum of Modern Art, 1951), 103. But also see Robert C. Hansen, *Scenic Costume Design for the Ballets Russes* (Ann Ar-bor: UMI Research Press, 1985), 76–77. Hansen furnishes a useful summary of Matisse's involvement in the production, especially a description of the scenery and costumes, both of which, according to Hansen, seem to have been a little less ornate than the "elab-orate chinoiserie of Alexandre Benois' original 1914 setting." In later years Stravinsky

claimed that he was unhappy with Matisse's sets, making it clear that the painter was Diaghilev's choice, not his, and pronouncing the 1920 production a failure, largely owing to Matisse's participation. See Igor Stravinsky and Robert Craft, *Conversations with Igor Stravinsky* (Berkeley: University of California Press, 1980), 95.

18. Vernon Duke, *Passport to Paris* (Boston: Little, Brown, 1955), 199.

19. Nicolas Nabokov, *Old Friends and New Music* (Boston: Little, Brown, 1951), 86–87. But the truth is, Diaghilev's training as a musician is often underestimated. As a child he was exposed to classical repertoire during regular musical evenings at home in Perm. Moreover, not only did he hear Wagner's entire *Ring* cycle at Bayreuth, but he traveled to Ischl in Austria to meet Brahms. He studied piano, appeared in recitals, was described as a talented singer, and perhaps even more important, he composed songs (setting the poetry of Baudelaire, for example), chamber pieces, and other short works. He also worked on larger forms as well, completing both a sonata for cello and piano and the beginnings of an opera, *Boris Godunov.* The sum of these accumulated experiences may not have lifted Diaghilev to the rank of a professional musician, but it did (in his estimate at least) authorize him to render rigorous judgments on musical issues. For an excellent summary of Diaghilev's training see Israel Nesteev, "Diaghilev's Musical Education," trans. Robert Johnson, in *The Ballets Russes and Its World,* ed. Lynn Garafola and Nancy Van Norman Baer (New Haven: Yale University Press, 1999), 23–42.

20. Levinson's comments are included in Joan Acocella and Lynn Garafola, *André Levinson on Dance: Writings from Paris in the Twenties* (Hanover, N.H.: University Press of New England, 1991), 21. It is difficult to gauge Balanchine's feelings about the production. He never chose to revive the work, and for the 1972 Stravinsky Festival at Lincoln Center, John Taras, not Balanchine, choreographed *The Song of the Nightingale.* Although Balanchine allowed the other festival choreographers to choose the repertoire they wanted to set, still, one wonders why he declined to rechoreograph his first Stravinsky ballet. As Nancy Reynolds suggests, "Perhaps once was enough, for the score presents a number of problems." In essence the ballet is a "lavish costume parade," in which a "complicated story has to unfold in a limited amount of time." See Reynolds, *Repertory in Review* (New York: Dial Press, 1977), 299. By now, of course, the Matisse designs were gone, and Rouben Ter-Arutunian (who often prepared sets and costumes for the New York City Ballet) designed new scenery and costumes. Gelsey Kirkland danced the real Nightingale, and Elise Flagg the Mechanical Nightingale. Francisco Moncion was cast as the Emperor. As a retrospective, the revival was appreciated, though by 1972 critics had come to see *Le Chant* as a work whose balletic possibilities, from the start, were not particularly promising. Still, it appears that Balanchine seriously considered staging the original, full opera in 1962. A letter of 2 March 1962 from John Crosby of the Santa Fe Opera invites Balanchine to produce *Le Rossignol* during the 1962 summer season celebrating the composer's eightieth birthday. Balanchine, ultimately, did not have time to present the work. Letter from Crosby to Balanchine, HTC, Correspondence, 19/4. For a more recent discussion (and several photographs documenting the London taping of segments of *Le Chant du Rossignol* as produced by Reynolds for the "Lost Choreography Archive" of the George Balanchine Foundation) by Alicia Markova, see Nancy Reynolds, "Dame Alicia and the *Rossignol* of '95," *Ballet Review* 23, no. 4 (Winter 1995): 17–19.

21. It was also around 1925 that Balanchine became a close friend with Stravinsky's younger son. Soulima Stravinsky was much closer in age to Balanchine than his father. He was a budding young musician, and at that juncture very much a part of his father's life. They often traveled together to Paris and Monte Carlo to hear the Ballets Russes in performance and rehearsal. Soulima's skills as a pianist, developing around the time of *Le Chant,* provided a bond with Balanchine. Increasingly also, and at his father's request, Soulima was asked to sit at the piano with his father and test compositional passages in progress. He remembers that he and Balanchine spent considerable time together, sneaking into concerts, enjoying each other's company, and sharing common artistic interests. Moreover, even Soulima became caught in Diaghilev's web of machinations, sometimes being invited to lunch with Diaghilev when his father was away, during which the young man was interrogated about his father's activities and plans. For more on Soulima, see Thor E. Wood's transcript of an interview with Soulima Stravinsky, originally taped in Urbana, Illinois, in 1977, and now held by the Jerome Robbins Dance Division of the New York Public Library for the Performing Arts.

22. But as Nicolas Nabokov suggests, it was not only the composer's "religious convictions" that turned him away from ballet. Rather, ballet imposed "certain theatrical demands," obligating the composer to write "danceable" music and, to some degree at least, to submit to the "formal requirements of the choreographic art." The fact is, Stravinsky may well have declined further ballet commissions had the musically sensitive Balanchine not arrived on the scene. See Nicolas Nabokov, "Stravinsky and the Drama," in *Stravinsky in the Theatre,* ed. Minna Lederman (New York: Da Capo, 1975), 109.

23. See Denys Sutton, *André Derain* (London: Phaidon, 1959), 32.

24. And dance Balanchine did, in nearly three dozen productions during his years with Diaghilev, including several Stravinsky works: *Le Chant, Firebird, Les Noces, Petrushka,* and *Pulcinella.* For a complete listing of Balanchine's onstage participation with the Ballets Russes, see *Choreography by George Balanchine: A Catalogue of Works,* ed. Leslie George Katz, Nancy Lassalle, and Harvey Simmonds (New York: Viking, 1984), 324–27.

Chapter 4: From Delos to Paris

1. *Apollo* remains one of the most frequently staged of the major Stravinsky-Balanchine collaborations. Excerpts from the ballet are available on videotape: see, for instance, *The Balanchine Celebration, Part One,* Nonesuch VHS 40189-3. This 1993 film is part of the *Dance in America/NVC Artists* project. Two other videotaped productions deserve mention: "Stravinsky and Balanchine—Genius Has a Birthday," directed by Emile Ardolino and broadcast in 1982 as part of the PBS *Great Performances* series; and "Baryshnikov Dances Balanchine with American Ballet Theatre," directed by Thomas Grimm, first telecast on 5 February 1988 as part of the *Dance in America* series. For a comparison of these two videotaped performances, see Virginia Loring Brooks, "Apollo in Transition," *New Dance Review* 3, no. 3 (January–March 1991): 7–10.

2. Porter's remarks originally appeared in the 9 December 1972 *New Yorker* and are reprinted in Nancy Reynolds, *Repertory in Review* (New York: Dial, 1977), 47, and in Nancy Goldner, *The Stravinsky Festival of the New York City Ballet* (New York: Eakins, 1973), 222.

3. George Balanchine, "The Dance Element in Stravinsky's Music," reprinted in Minna Lederman, *Stravinsky and the Theatre* (New York: Da Capo, 1975), 81–82.

4. Guy Davenport, *Every Force Evolves a Form* (Berkeley: North Point Press, 1987), 35; "A Conversation with Igor Stravinsky," NBC television documentary, 1957.

5. For a discussion linking *Apollon Musagète* and the journal *Apollon,* see "Two Apollos" in Tim Scholl, *From Petipa to Balanchine* (London: Routledge, 1994), 79–104. Benois's *Pavillon d'Armide,* choreographed by Fokine and first staged by Diaghilev in 1909, with its classical portrayal of Versailles was surely one of many models for Stravinsky as he formulated his ideas about *Apollo.* Scholl suggests several precursors to Stravinsky and Balanchine's ballet, at least in terms of the scenario the two men constructed, including Petipa's 1871 *Two Stars* [*Dve zvezdyl*] and his 1876 *The Adventures of Pelus* [*Priklyucheniya*].

6. Igor Stravinsky, *An Autobiography* (Rpt.; New York: Norton, 1998), 135.

7. The de Schloezer commentary is reprinted in Lynn Garafola's *Diaghilev's Ballets Russes* (New York: Oxford University Press, 1989), 139–40; *Homeric Hymn to Hermes,* in Mark P. O. Morford and Robert J. Lenardon, *Classical Mythology* (White Plains, N.Y.: Longman, 1991), 221–35.

8. T. S. Eliot and Joseph Chiari, in Chiari, *Twentieth-Century French Thought: From Bergson to Lévi-Strauss* (New York: Gordian, 1975), 131–33; Jacques Maritain, "Concerning Poetic Knowledge," in his *The Situation of Poetry* (New York: Philosophical Library, 1955), 230. Soulima's memories were recorded by Thor E. Wood in 1977; the audiotape is held by the Jerome Robbins Dance Division of the New York Public Library for the Performing Arts.

9. Lincoln Kirstein, "Celebration," New York City Ballet Souvenir Booklet for the 1972 Stravinsky Festival.

10. Morford and Lenardon, *Classical Mythology,* 209.

11. For example, even the best that Diaghilev could say of Lord Berners (Gerald Hugh Tyrwhitt-Wilson) was that he was "not a bad composer." Not much is known about Balanchine's involvement in these ballets. In *The Triumph of Neptune,* for instance, the dancing was described as "straightforward," "poetical," and "graceful" without a trace of modernism (Balanchine actually danced in the production as the black character Snowball, injuring his knee in a rehearsal and hastening the end of his dancing career). Some have noted that "the ghost of *Neptune*" is apparent in the 1976 *Union Jack* for the New York City Ballet. Balanchine apparently consulted his old score of Berners's music when he was preparing his bicentennial ballet. See Edward Ricco, "The Sitwells at the Ballet," *Ballet Review* 6, no. 1 (1977–78): 80–88.

12. The inclusion of the Muses and the lyre arise from an important Homeric myth: Apollo had enlisted the nine Muses as jurors in a musical contest. Given his own celestial playing of the seven-stringed instrument, he prevailed. So enchanting was his playing that he eventually defeated Pan, thereby earning his divinity as the god of music. Stravinsky's description of the scenario appears in his *Autobiography,* 134. See also Morford and Lenardon, *Classical Mythology.*

13. Baryshnikov's comments were part of the "Baryshnikov Dances Balanchine" program for *Dance in America;* Morford and Lenardon, *Classical Mythology,* 41–42. Balanchine's remarks appear in George Balanchine and Francis Mason, *101 Stories of the Great Ballets*

(New York: Doubleday, 1989), 14. A fuller synopsis of the ballet's scenario is provided on pages 11–16.

14. American composers had been commissioned to write ballets earlier, of course, but nobody with the Old World status of Stravinsky. For a complete retracing of the American commission and premiere, see my *Stravinsky Inside Out* (New Haven: Yale University Press, 2001).

15. The composer knew Bolm (1884–1951) too, from at least 1910, when the dancer appeared in *Petrushka.* Raised in the Maryinsky tradition, Bolm was the original Chief Warrior in Fokine's *Polovtsian Dances* and frequently partnered the company's prima ballerinas. Following Diaghilev's second American tour in 1917, Bolm chose to stay. Two years later he was appointed maître de ballet of the Metropolitan Opera. For more on Bolm, see Suzanne Carbonneau, "Adolph Bolm in America," in *The Ballets Russes and Its World,* ed. Lynn Garafola and Nancy Van Norman Baer (New Haven: Yale University Press, 1999), 219–44.

16. The letter and others quoted in this chapter are among archival materials found at the Library of Congress in various uncataloged files marked "Stravinsky Old Correspondence," "Bolm Old Correspondence," and the "Coolidge Collection."

17. Arlene Croce, *Going to the Dance* (New York: Knopf, 1982), 109. In addition to the Stravinsky premiere, three other works were staged: Ravel's *Pavane,* Mondonville's comic *Arlecchinata,* and, to the music of Beethoven's *Elf Wiener Tänze,* a pastiche of loosely constructed dances presented under the title *Alt-Wien.* Bolm choreographed and danced in all four ballets.

18. In Lincoln Kirstein's *Dance: A Short History of Classic Theatrical Dancing* (1935; Princeton: Dance Horizons/Princeton Book, 1987), the author writes, "Instead of using a large *corps de ballet* as a background for soloists, Diaghileff . . . Stravinsky, and Balanchine employed only four Muses and the God (Lifar)" (317). Though four Muses never appeared in any production, Stravinsky's sketchbook does include a substantial amount of unused compositional material (about ten pages) that could suggest a lost or at least aborted variation—perhaps because Engel finally impressed upon Stravinsky the reality that there was simply not enough stage space.

19. Charles Rosen, "The Frontiers of Nonsense," in *The Frontiers of Meaning* (New York: Hill and Wang, 1994), 12–13.

20. Kirstein, *Dance,* 317.

21. For a discussion of this whiteness from a dance historian's perspective, see Robert Johnson, "White on White: The Classical Background of *Apollon Musagète,*" *Ballet Review,* 13/3 (Fall 1995). Johnson suggests that the expression itself is probably owing to Balanchine's awareness of the constructivist painter Casimir Malevich's earlier "white on white" exhibition in Russia, with which he may have been familiar—although by Balanchine's own admission, the description was Stravinsky's.

22. I wish to thank Lynne Gelber of Skidmore College for her translation of the article.

23. Nicolas Nabokov, *Old Friends and New Music* (Boston: Little, Brown, 1951), 104.

24. Serge Lifar, *Ma Vie: From Kiev to Kiev,* trans. James Holman Mason (New York: World, 1970), 56.

25. Stravinsky, *Autobiography,* 143–44. As for the Stravinsky-Craft conversation books, "who

said what" remains an unresolved issue answerable only by consulting the original manuscripts. In another of the conversation books, *Dialogues* (Berkeley: University of California Press, 1982), *Apollo* is again discussed (pp. 32–36). Here the original papers in the
Swiss archives establish that Stravinsky initially tossed off some rough thoughts about
the ballet and later corrected and approved a prepared draft. The original typescript alluded to Diaghilev's and Ansermet's intense dislike of *Apollo*, implying that their aversion prompted the famous cut in the Polyhymnia variation. None of this survives in the
published version.

26. The translation appears, among other places, in Eric Walter White's *Stravinsky: The
Composer and His Works* (Berkeley: University of California Press, 1979), 342.

27. D'Amboise, interview in Mason, *I Remember Balanchine* (New York: Doubleday, 1991),
266. Moreover, Maria Tallchief writes that Balanchine told her "frankly that Lifar had
had a lot of difficulty in *Apollo*" because the music and choreography were so challenging. "George had to stand in the wings during the performance and count so Lifar
wouldn't lose his way." See Tallchief's *Maria Tallchief: America's Prima Ballerina*, with
Larry Kaplan (New York: Henry Holt, 1997), 65.

28. Lincoln Kirstein, *Thirty Years: Lincoln Kirstein's The New York City Ballet* (New York:
Knopf, 1978), 63.

29. Danilova's interview is in Mason, *I Remember Balanchine*, 5. See Tallchief's comments in
Marie Tallchief, 64.

30. Edward Villella, *Prodigal Son* (New York: Simon and Schuster, 1992), 146.

31. Elizabeth Souritz, *Soviet Choreographers in the 1920s* (Durham: Duke University Press,
1990), 154. Goleizovsky graduated from the Imperial Ballet Academy in 1909, later
served as the premier danseur of the Bolshoi, then founded his own school in Moscow.
His charismatically expressed conviction that the expressiveness of classical ballet had
become superficial, that too many layers of edifice had segregated the dancer from the
dance, was just the kind of dissidence bound to impress the rebellious young Balanchine.
And like Balanchine, Goleizovsky was himself a fine musician (a violinist). Other similarities are evident, including Goleizovsky's ability to straddle the divide between classical ballet and more popular dance forms, choreographing everything from cabaret to the
circus. The quotation from the *New York Times Magazine* appears in Robert Johnson,
"White on White," 52.

32. De Chirico (1888–1978) was much admired by Picasso and Guillaume Apollinaire for his
classical statues and stark architecture. Diaghilev later employed him for the sets and costumes of *Le Bal*, produced in 1929 with choreography by Balanchine. Among his many
self-portraits, De Chirico included one of himself as Apollo. For Balanchine's memorable comments about Bauchant, see Nancy Reynolds, "Listening to Balanchine," in
Dance for a City: Fifty Years of the New York City Ballet, ed. Lynn Garafola and Eric Foner
(New York: Columbia University Press, 1999), 155. Also see Robert C. Hansen, *Scenic
and Costume Design for the Ballets Russes* (Ann Arbor: UMI Research Press, 1985), 113–14.
Hansen further states that the costumes were designed after those worn by the Muses in
the 1925 *Apollon* canvas. Reproductions of the curtains used for both scenes are reprinted
in Richard Hammond's article "Ballets Russes, 1928," *Modern Music*, 6/1 (November–

December 1928). Hammond comments that the "huge vase [used] in the opening scene was designed to fall apart and become a grotto for the succeeding action of the ballet."

33. Stravinsky's remarks (and we must remember that Walter Nouvel did the ghostwriting) appeared in his *Autobiography* and were later reprinted in Lederman's *Stravinsky in the Theatre* in an essay entitled "Stravinsky's Own Story," 143–66. Moreover, as Hansen reports, Bauchant's designs were simply enlargements of existing paintings, and "his contribution to the production process was minimal" (see Hansen, *Scenic and Costume Design for the Ballets Russes,* 124).

34. Quoted in Reynolds, "Listening to Balanchine," 155.

35. The interview is included in *Striking a Balance: Dancers Talk About Dancing,* rev. and ed. Barbara Newman (New York: Limelight Editions, 1992).

36. Pannain's comments, originally appearing in the periodical *Rassengno Musicale,* were later reported by Olin Downes in the *New York Times* on 29 July 1928, sec. 7, p. 5. Also see Lourié's "Stravinsky's *Apollo,*" *The Gamut* (August–September 1928): 20–21. Lourié's influence on Stravinsky during the 1920s was significant. He hailed Stravinsky as the leading exponent of neoclassicism, in opposition to Schoenberg, with his "neogothic" music. See Scott Messing, *Neoclassicism in Music* (Ann Arbor: UMI Research Press, 1988).

37. Boris Asaf'yev, trans. Richard F. French, *A Book About Stravinsky* (Ann Arbor: UMI Research Press, 1982). Stravinsky was well aware of Asaf'yev's criticism and naturally wanted nothing to do with the author, commenting that any interest in his writing was "misplaced." See the section of *Kniga o Stravinskom* beginning on page 275 for Asaf'yev's detailed comments about the ballet.

38. Levinson, like Lifar, often commented that Stravinsky's music was really too domineering for the dance. The brilliance of his colorful scores dwarfed any choreographic focus. The composer needn't visualize his music because it would then compete with the dance. "Stravinsky is sufficient unto himself and neither demands nor permits interpretation through the dance," Levinson commented in an essay entitled "Stravinsky and the Dance" for *Theatre Arts Monthly,* nearly four years before *Apollo* premiered.

Chapter 5: The Evolution of *Apollo*

1. Although one can hardly imagine the ballet without its distinctive string sound, the piano reduction reveals how Stravinsky conceived the ballet at the keyboard as it evolved. Several commercial recordings of the piano reduction exist, most notably Christopher O'Riley's for *Electra/Nonesuch, 79343–2.*

2. Igor Stravinsky and Robert Craft, *Dialogues* (Rpt. Berkeley: University of California Press, 1982), 33.

3. Julian Jaynes, *The Origin of Consciousness in the Breakdown of the Bicameral Mind* (Boston: Houghton Mifflin, 1976), 361–63. Jaynes continues, "Tacitus visited the oracle of Apollo at Claros and described how the entranced priest 'swallows a draught of water from a mysterious spring and—though ignorant generally of writing and of meters—delivers his response in set verses.'"

4. Quoted in R. Murray Schafer, *Ezra Pound and Music* (New York: New Direction, 1977).

Perhaps more than any of Stravinsky's many literary contemporaries, Ezra Pound was enamored of the cross-disciplinary use of rhythm in poetry and music, and attempted to resurrect interest in this ancient relationship in his defense of classicism. Coincidentally, it was Carl Engel who in 1931 best summarized Pound's belief: "On the whole . . . Mr. Pound's observations on rhythm are neat and sensible rather than original. He believes in an absolute rhythm. So did Heraclitus." See Engel's "Poet as Prophet," *Discords Mingled* (New York: Freeport, 1947), 172–83. Nor can it be coincidence that beyond Pound, other so-called strong-stress poets of the twentieth century, especially T. S. Eliot and W. H. Auden, were among the composer's favorite writers. Moreover, as Stravinsky himself often noted, it was never the setting of words themselves that guided him, but rather the syllables. See Auden's comments in "Craftsman, Artist, Genius," in the 1972 New York City Ballet Stravinsky Festival Souvenir Booklet.

5. Stravinsky's choice of the Apollonian myth as a ballet scenario has many precedents. The Viennese dancer and choreographer Franz Hilverding (who was a ballet master in St. Petersburg and Moscow, 1758–64) produced *Apollon et Daphné, ou Le Retour d'Apollon au Parnasse* in 1763. Jean-Georges Nouverre presented in London in 1782 *Apollon et les Muses.* Charles-Louis Didelot, who studied with Nouverre, choreographed two Apollo ballets: *Apollon et Daphné* (1802) and *Apollon et Persée* (1803). Moreover, as Tim Scholl reminds us, "The iconography of Russian ballet from the middle of the nineteenth century until the Diaghilev period is rich with depictions (and often conflations) of Apollo and *le roi soleil.* Apollo is the hero of *Dve zvedy,* the Petipa court spectacle. He appears in the apotheosis of *Sleeping Beauty* dressed as Louis XIV" (*From Petipa to Balanchine* [London: Routledge, 1994], 150–51).

6. Nor in traveling that corridor should one rule out the possible influence of the Parnassians, a nineteenth-century school of French poets who prized restraint and objective order in their poetic meter and verse forms. Stravinsky sympathized with their work. Their important anthology *Le Parnasse Contemporain* (1866–1876) reveals an underlying adulation of Greek classicism that is reflected in *Apollo.* Paul Verlaine, whose texts were the first in the French language that Stravinsky set (in 1910, just after *The Firebird*), was originally a Parnassian before turning to the newer doctrine espoused by the Symbolists.

7. Jean-Baptiste Lully (1632–87) came to court in 1652. Louis himself danced in many of the composer's ballets. Not only did the king dance Apollo, but he often appears in painting as such, for the persona of a Greek deity bolstered by divine right his title to rule. Ballet themes were regularly drawn from Greek mythology, for a belief in the power of mythical metaphor was part of one's required training at court.

8. Lincoln Kirstein, *Four Centuries of Ballet* (New York: Dover, 1984), 29. The publication is a reprint of Kirstein's original 1970 book *Movement and Metaphor.*

9. Francis Poulenc, *Mes amis et moi* (Paris: Editions la Palatine, 1963), 194–95.

10. I wish to thank Dorothy Manning of Boston, Massachusetts, for her translation of the original French.

11. Joyce often spoke of the unification of design using musical metaphors, as in his *Portrait of the Artist as a Young Man,* whence the above quote is cited.

12. George Balanchine and Francis Mason, *101 Stories of the Great Ballets* (New York: Doubleday, 1989), 14. While Balanchine may have approved the basic description, the words

themselves are no doubt Mason's, as was often the case in "Balanchine" texts of the 1950s.

13. Michael J. Reddy, "The Conduit Metaphor—A Case of Frame Conflict in Our Language About Language," in *Metaphor and Thought,* ed. Andrew Ortony (Cambridge: Cambridge University Press, 1979).

14. Calliope's importance should not be underestimated. Some stories revered her as the true leader of the nine Muses. In other accounts she and King Oeagrus were the parents of Orpheus; and in still other myths, she bore two sons to Apollo.

15. George Balanchine, "Notes on Choreography," in *The Dance Anthology,* ed. Cobbet Steinberg (New York: New American Library, 1980), 34.

16. Guy Davenport, "Ariadne's Dancing Floor," in his *Every Force Evolves a Form* (San Francisco: North Point, 1987), 59.

17. Divisions of alexandrines into three and four units (trimeter and tetrameter) were common in poetic verse. Stravinsky was intrigued by the divisibility of the number twelve not only in *Apollo* but, as we shall see, in *Agon.*

18. Stravinsky's use of metric feet as a starting point for his compositional ideas did not originate with *Apollo.* The sketches for a work as early as *Le Rossignol,* as well as *Oedipus Rex,* demonstrate that he often "measured" the meter of words in this way.

19. Balanchine and Mason, *101 Stories of the Great Ballets,* 13. As with the Variation de Calliope, Balanchine articulates the main structural points of the Variation d'Apollon's *A-B-A* form. In the first *A* section, Stravinsky's freely written violin cadenza (notated without any meter) is visualized by Apollo's rapid strumming of the lute, which he places on the ground as the *B* section (described in figure 5.5, above) begins. It is here that Apollo begins his metered "reversible iamb" dance. The return of the *A* music—again written in a more improvisatory style—is accompanied by Apollo's retrieval of the lute as the three Muses enter the stage.

20. In Stravinsky's own Columbia Symphony Orchestra recording of 29 June 1964, the four-minute Pas de deux begins about eighteen minutes into the twenty-nine-minute performance, or approximately at the .62 point of the overall duration.

21. Igor Stravinsky, *An Autobiography* (New York: Norton, 1962), 134.

22. George Balanchine, "The Dance Element in Stravinsky's Music," *Dance Anthology,* 150.

23. Apollo, along with his twin sister Artemis, was born on Delos. He initially assumed his godly powers by disguising himself as a dolphin and commandeering a ship bound for Pytho. Later he renamed the island Delphi, after the dolphin (*delphi*).

24. Paul Valéry, "Philosophy of the Dance," in *Dance Anthology,* 335.

25. Richard Buckle, *George Balanchine: Ballet Master* (New York: Random House, 1988), 45. Edward Villella confirms the story in his more recent book, *Prodigal Son* (New York: Simon and Schuster, 1992). Moreover, Barbara Horgan recalls Balanchine recounting the story for her as they passed the sign during one of the New York City Ballet's trips to London.

26. See Constant Lambert's 1936 essay "Music and Action," reprinted in *Dance Anthology,* 134.

27. The rough sketches are mixed among the early thoughts for the ballet, first drafted on 23 July. Stravinsky completely transformed this material, which he initially conceived as an accompanimental figure in a very fast tempo. The sketchbook also reveals that the canon itself was worked out before the opening of the Pas d'action.

28. Eugene Raskin, *Architecturally Speaking* (New York: Bloch, 1966), 64.

29. Jaynes, *Origin of Consciousness,* 52.

30. Stravinsky prepares for this structurally important return three measures earlier (at Rehearsal 100) by beginning a final melodic ascent in the violins and cellos. His sketchbook demonstrates that he struggled with this transition, drafting the measures early on, as was summarized in figure 5.3. This final ascent begins on the fifty-fifth beat of the piece's 89 pulses—cabalistic numbers in the Fibonacci series, and yet another instance of a golden mean ($55/89 = .617$).

31. Suki Schorer recalls that when she first danced *Apollo,* Balanchine suggested she "study the flat profile figures in the early black and red terra-cotta vases" at the Metropolitan Museum. "He mentioned that parts of the finale of the ballet were meant to look two-dimensional." See *Suki Schorer on Balanchine Technique* (New York: Knopf, 1999), 14.

32. Quoted in Dale Harris, "Balanchine: Working with Stravinsky," *Ballet Review* 10/2 (Summer 1982): 19–24.

33. In *Holding on to the Air* (New York: Summit, 1990) Farrell provides a detailed account of her relationship with Balanchine.

34. Kirstein, *Four Centuries of Ballet,* 226. Several hypotheses have been advanced to explaining Diaghilev's action. Did he make the cut, as Soulima Stravinsky suggests in his 1977 interview with Thor E. Wood (the audiotape is held by the Jerome Robbins Dance Division of the New York Public Library for the Performing Arts), because he could not stomach three sequential female solo variations, consigning Lifar to the wings for too long a period?

35. Stravinsky's admonition appears in a letter of 26 November 1935, preserved in the Sacher Stiftung. It includes a diagram indicating how the orchestra is to be seated in a semicircle. The instrumentation specified eight first and second violins each, six violas, five first and second cellos each, and five basses. This represents an orchestra nearly twice the size employed in the Washington premiere. And in an unpublished letter dated 19 July 1939 to Bernardino Molinari, conductor of the Reggia Academia di Santa Cecilia, Stravinsky again designates the exact deployment of string players. He includes another diagram, advising Molinari not to risk making the sound of the orchestra "too thick."

36. Lincoln Kirstein, *Thirty Years,* 62. The scenery was based upon Poussin's backgrounds from *Echo and Narcissus* and *The Arcadian Shepherds.*

37. See *Theatre Arts,* 21/5 (May 1937): 411, for reprints of Stewart Chaney's black and white pencil sketches of the costume designs used in the Metropolitan Opera Company production on 27–28 April 1937.

38. See John Gruen's *The Private World of Ballet* (New York: Viking, 1975), 276. For an account of Bruhn's dancing and his relationship with Balanchine, see Maria Tallchief, *Maria Tallchief: America's Prima Ballerina* (New York: Henry Holt, 1997), 292. Tallchief recalls that Bruhn had to rehearse without the Muses (one of them Tallchief herself), and was asked to perform without having partnered them, though ultimately Bruhn chose not to go through with the performance.

39. Balanchine maintained that in 1928 Stravinsky was concerned, monetarily, with the Societé des Auteurs et Compositeurs Dramatiques—an organization that paid for printed materials that would be performed. Balanchine told Gruen that Stravinsky collected

about 15 percent of each performance's receipts. "The reason [Stravinsky] divided the story into two parts was because the society considered each part a separate entity, and in that way more money could be collected." Often the choreographer was forced to defend his tampering with the by now sanctified work. Balanchine responded: "I don't have to explain why I change things. . . . They are mine. . . . I made them, and I can change them if I want to. . . . I know why I changed it, I took out all the garbage—that's why!" Quoted in John Gruen, "An Olympian *Apollo*," *Dance Magazine* 55/4 (April 1981): 85–86. Robert Garis has long contended that Balanchine eventually lost interest in Stravinsky's music, programming it less frequently after the composer died. See "Balanchine-Stravinsky: Facts and Problems," *Ballet Review*, 10/3 (Fall 1982): 9–23.

40. William Weslow interview in Francis Mason, *I Remember Balanchine* (New York: Doubleday, 1991), 321.

Chapter 6: A New Beginning

1. Lincoln Kirstein, *Flesh Is Heir: An Historical Romance* (New York: Brewer, Warren and Putnam, 1933), 220–21. Several "Ballets Russes" offshoots tried to fill the void. Many of Diaghilev's dancers and choreographers, including Danilova, Doubrovska, Balanchine, Fokine, and Nijinska, sought to carry on the tradition. See, for example, Jack Anderson, *The One and Only: The Ballet Russe de Monte Carlo* (New York: Dance Horizons, 1981); Richard Buckle, *In the Wake of Diaghilev* (New York: Holt, Rinehart and Winston, 1982); and Kathrine Sorley Walker, *De Basil's Ballets Russes* (New York: Atheneum, 1983).

2. The offer came at a price: Stravinsky's relationship with Diaghilev was irreparably ruptured. Diaghilev deemed Stravinsky's acceptance of Rubinstein's offer the coup de grâce of their already flagging relationship. He wrote to Lifar that upon seeing Rubinstein's ballet, he returned from the theater with "a fearful headache," finding the production "tiresome, lachrymose . . . drab. . . . The whole thing was still-born." And with a final barb: "Igor, my first son, has given himself up entirely to the love of God and cash." See Lifar's *Serge Diaghilev: His Life, His Work, His Legend. An Intimate Biography* (New York: Da Capo, 1976).

3. Stravinsky, *An Autobiography* (Rpt.; New York: Norton, 1998), 147. Initially the composer used Andersen's title "The Ice Maiden" as the ballet's title but changed his mind. Andersen's stories had long appealed to Stravinsky. The composer's early opera *Le Rossignol* (and subsequently the ballet *Le Chant du Rossignol*) was also based upon an Andersen fairy tale. Stravinsky based the entire ballet on several songs and piano pieces by Tchaikovsky. For a classic essay detailing Stravinsky's use of Tchaikovsky's music, see Lawrence Morton, "Stravinsky and Tchaikovsky: *Le Baiser de la Fée*," in Paul Henry Lang, ed., *Stravinsky: A New Appraisal of His Work* (New York: Norton, 1963).

4. Stravinsky's correspondence is in the Sacher Stiftung. A few days after the second letter to Païchadze, Stravinsky wrote again, this time to complain that his name was printed incorrectly in the advertisements for the premiere ("Yegor") and that Andersen should not be listed as the author since he, Stravinsky, had completely transformed the original story.

5. See Simon Volkov, *Balanchine's Tchaikovsky* (New York: Simon and Schuster, 1985), 129.

In a 1943–44 Ballet Russe de Monte Carlo program booklet that included a description of Balanchine's *Serenade,* the work's "plotless" nature is addressed. "It may well be said," the annotator wrote, "to illustrate the remark of William, the Jew, of Pesaro, when he said: 'Dancing is an action showing outwardly the spiritual movements which must agree with those measured and perfect concords of harmony which, through our hearing and with earthly joy, descend into our intellect, there to produce sweet movements which, being thus imprisoned, as it were, in defiance of nature, endeavor to escape and reveal themselves through movement.'"

6. Forty-six years later, the New York City Ballet commissioned the seventy-eight-year-old Auric to prepare a score for the ballet *Tricolore,* conceived and supervised by Balanchine. Saratogians will be interested to know that the choreographer wrote to the composer on 22 April 1976, suggesting a specific scenario dealing with the Foreign Legion, *Le music-hall* and Toulouse-Lautrec, and the Garde Républicaine. The score was originally planned for 1977, to commemorate the Battle of Saratoga (and the French-American connection), which took place in nearby Saratoga Springs "where for the last ten years we have performed annually through the month of July in a beautiful theater," wrote Balanchine. The letter is dated 21 March 1966, HTC, Correspondence, 3/3.

7. Stravinsky confirms the lamentable breakdown in a 1937 article in *L'Intransigéant.* The three works to which Lifar refers in his interview were *Le Baiser de la Fée, Pulcinella,* and *The Firebird.* Two years earlier, Rouché had been a member of a panel that rejected Stravinsky's candidacy for appointment to the prestigious French Academy—a humiliating and politically motivated rebuff that caused the composer considerable pique.

8. See Ethel Thurston's comments included in Léonie Rosentiel's *Nadia Boulanger* (New York: Norton, 1982), 312.

9. Hammond attended Diaghilev's original Paris production of *Apollon Musagète.* His review of the ballet was reprinted in *Modern Music,* 6/1 (November–December 1928): 24–28. Stravinsky knew Hammond first in Paris, then in California, during the 1940s where they became friends. For a recent essay on the dualities of Kirstein's enormous life, see Nicholas Jenkins, "The Great Impresario," *New Yorker,* April 13, 1998. Jenkins candidly addresses Kirstein's relationship with Balanchine, for "the fact remains that from the moment, in 1933, when Kirstein arranged for Balanchine to come to the United States, their lives and fates were irreducibly blended." Kirstein had actually stumbled upon Diaghilev's funeral in Venice, later describing it in his first novel, the 1932 *Flesh Is Heir.*

10. Lincoln Kirstein, "Paris, London, Balanchine 1933," in his *Mosaic* (New York: Farrar, Straus and Giroux, 1994), 226.

11. Lincoln Kirstein, *Dance: A Short History of Classic Theatrical Dancing* (Princeton: Dance Horizons, 1987), 325.

12. Lincoln Kirstein, *Thirty Years: Lincoln Kirstein's The New York City Ballet* (New York: Knopf, 1978), 8. But how could Stravinsky have "deserted" to Rubinstein when he did not accept the commission for *Le Baiser* until early 1928? For a comprehensive listing of the prolific Kirstein's earlier writings through 1977, see *Lincoln Kirstein: A First Bibliography (The Published Writings 1922–1977),* compiled by Leslie George Katz, Nancy Lassalle, and Harvey Simmonds (New York: Eakins Press Foundation, 1978). The nearly five

hundred entries attest to Kirstein's wide-ranging commentary on not only dance but also poetry, drama, architecture, sculpture, photography, film, music, history, and politics.

13. Kirstein, *Mosaic,* 243–244.

14. Ibid., 244–45. Kirstein also contends that Balanchine "swore that America had always been his dream since he had heard a jazz band as a schoolboy in Petersburg." Stravinsky, too, according to some reports, heard jazz in St. Petersburg as early as 1908. As to how enthusiastic Kirstein was before this meeting about Balanchine's ability to bring classical dance to America, there is some question among Balanchine biographers. Writing in the April 23, 1960, *New Yorker,* Bernard Taper comments, "Even before Kirstein saw what Balanchine had wrought in *Les Ballets 1933,* he knew that it was Balanchine he wanted as the instrument of his ambition. Kirstein said 'There was no question of choice, even if Fokine, Massine, or Lifar had been available to me.'" But Richard Buckle suggests that there was some early reticence, and "after three weeks in Paris [Kirstein] had not made up his mind which choreographer or performer could best preach and teach the classical ballet to Americans. By the end of the first week, he had written of Balanchine: 'He's no Fokine.'" See Buckle's *George Balanchine: Ballet Master* (New York: Random House, 1988), 65.

15. The letter is reprinted in Francis Mason, *I Remember Balanchine* (New York: Doubleday, 1991), 115–19.

16. Kirstein's letters and cables, as well as his original contract with Balanchine and his associates, are held in HTC, Correspondence, 6/21–22.

17. Balanchine immediately obtained one of the first-edition copies of Stravinsky's autobiography, *Chroniques de ma vie,* published in 1935 by Denoël et Stelle. The choreographer's well-worn, annotated copy is retained in HTC, Books, 4/17. Balanchine underlined a passage wherein Stravinsky describes his childhood loneliness. He also marked in the margin a section wherein Stravinsky writes of the "Russian Five" helping to purge music of its "old academicism." There are several words underlined and question marks placed in the margin—not unlike Stravinsky's own marginalia found throughout his own library. Perhaps most relevant, Balanchine underlined Stravinsky's discussion of counterpoint: "I was much drawn to the study of counterpoint, although that is generally considered a dry subject, useful only for pedagogical purposes. . . . The work amused me, even thrilled me, and I was never tired of it. The first contact with the science of counterpoint opened up at once a far vaster and more fertile field in the domain of musical composition than anything which harmony could offer me." See *Chronicle of My Life* (London: Victor Gollancz, 1936), 29–30, in this translation, but pages 33–34 in Balanchine's French copy.

18. Actually, *Serenade*'s premiere occurred on 10 June 1934, by invitation only at a private gathering on the estate of Felix Warburg in White Plains, New York. Warburg's son Edward became Kirstein's partner in underwriting the American Ballet. Subsequently, the work was performed in Hartford before its New York premiere in the spring of 1935.

19. Vernon Duke, *Passport to Paris* (Boston: Little, Brown, 1955), 295–96. Balanchine and Duke were close during their early years in the United States, even considering a ballet collaboration on a "Pushkinesque theme . . . 'a ballet within a ballet,' to George's imaginative scenario," though it never materialized. Duke and Balanchine did work together

on several projects during the choreographer's time on Broadway and in Hollywood. Duke had known Balanchine from the Diaghilev period, and composed the music for the 1925 Ballets Russes production of *Zéphire et Flore.* Even then the composer and Balanchine were hoping to collaborate on a proposed ballet for Diaghilev entitled *Three Seasons,* though again the work was never completed.

20. Kirstein was hardly averse to defying tradition. His editorship, beginning at age twenty, of the *Hound & Horn* during 1927–1934 marks an important benchmark in early twentieth-century literary sponsorship. This important journal (referred to by Ezra Pound as the "Bitch and Bugle") published countless essays and poetry by William Carlos Williams, e. e. cummings, Katherine Anne Porter, Marianne Moore, T. S. Eliot, Pound, and others. See Mitzi Berger Hamovitch, "Hunting for the Hound & Horn," *American Scholar* (Autumn 1982): 543–49.

21. Kirstein's comments a few years later were equally cutthroat. Writing in the 5 February 1938 *Nation,* he remarked, "In Martin's two books historical facts intended for a condemnatory resume were selected and arranged to present a case which rivals the style of the Reich's *Kulturkammer.*" See "The Critic's Lexicon," 165.

22. Lincoln Kirstein, *Three Pamphlets Collected* (New York: Dance Horizons, 1967). This collection (dedicated to Virgil Thomson, writes Kirstein, "for telling me on my twentieth [birthday] that ballet in America was not a possibility but a necessity") includes "Blast at Ballet," written in 1937.

23. In a 1938 *New York Times* article by Howard Taubman, entitled "Balanchine Out of Opera; Ballet Will Go with Him. Master of Troupe Criticizes Metropolitan's Standards," Balanchine had his say: "These people have been buying tickets to the Metropolitan for years and they have never seen the first act of any opera." He complained of his unappreciated efforts to bring authenticity to his ballets: "For my first *Aida* at the Metropolitan I went to the library and museum to study real Egyptian dances. You know the Egyptian dances were not the half-profile imitations of figures or frescoes or vases. They were mostly acrobatic. I tried to make them like the original, and they started to object. My dances the critics and dowagers did not like. They were too good."

24. Quoted in Charles Payne, *American Ballet Theatre* (New York: Knopf, 1978), 314.

25. Balanchine staged several other numbers that were dropped from the Follies without explanation. How well Balanchine and Baker knew each other in Paris is implied in Jean-Claude Baker and Chris Chase's *Josephine* (New York: Random House, 1993). "Balanchine went up the stairs. . . . Josephine appeared, naked except for three flowers glued on in strategic places." When Balanchine was asked what happened, "He smiled. 'Well,' he said, 'I think we had lunch.'"

26. Baker's performance in the Ziegfeld show drew reviews that were noisome in their open racism. The *New York Times* reported: "Josephine Baker is a St. Louis washer-woman's daughter who stepped out of a Negro burlesque show into a life of adulation and luxury in Paris. . . . In sex appeal to jaded Europeans of the jazz-loving type, a Negro wench always has a head start . . . but to Manhattan theatergoers last week she was just a slightly buck-toothed young Negro woman . . . whose dancing and singing might be topped practically anywhere outside of Paris."

27. For an important discussion of Balanchine's familiarity with and reliance upon the id-

ioms of black dance and black music, see Sally Banes, "Balanchine and Black Dance," *Choreography and Dance,* 3/3 (1993): 59–77.

28. Ray Bolger interview, in Mason, *I Remember Balanchine,* 155. Cruger's remarks were taped in a KFAC radio broadcast in Los Angeles in 1983.

29. This article, like so many others retained in the Sacher Stiftung, was thoroughly marked up by the composer.

30. Martin addressed the matter in "The Ideal of Ballet Aesthetics," first printed in *Introduction to the Dance* (New York: Norton, 1939) and later included in *The Dance Anthology,* ed. Cobbett Steinberg (New York: New American Library, 1980), 300–310. Jean Cocteau also often deprecated music as a subsidiary element of the dance. Such an attitude surely dissuaded Stravinsky from pursuing ballet projects with Cocteau, though Cocteau suggested one to the composer as early as 1914. The ballet was to be entitled *David,* but Cocteau was unable to interest Stravinsky in collaborating. For the details of Cocteau's ideas, see Glenn Watkins, *Pyramids at the Louvre* (Cambridge: Harvard University Press, 1994), 256 ff.

31. Admittedly, Downes had earned a reputation as Stravinsky's most vocal adversary, but he was no kinder to Balanchine and his young troupe. He regularly criticized the American Ballet's contributions to productions at the Met as "absurd," failing to connect to the content of the opera's scenarios. For a compilation of Downes's reviews, see *Olin Downes on Music,* ed. Irene Downes (New York: Simon and Schuster, 1957).

32. Richard Buckle, *George Balanchine: Ballet Master* (New York: Random House, 1988), 104–5, from an interview with Christensen on 6 August 1984.

33. See Anatole Chujoy, *The New York City Ballet* (New York: Knopf, 1953), 85.

34. Stravinsky had long been an admirer of the seventeenth-century French poet and satirist, whose friends numbered Boileau, Molière, and Racine. La Fontaine's timeless fables blended the kind of mirth and sardonicism that always appealed to the composer. As well, his experiments with poetic meter, as well as his affection for Plutarch, Horace, and Ovid, endeared him to Stravinsky. In a 1932 article for *Cahiers d'art* entitled "Tribute to Picasso," the composer used a few lines from La Fontaine's "The Serpent and the File" to blast the ignorance of critics: "Now this is meant for you, vapid second-rate minds, / Good-for-nothings who try to harm worth of all kinds. / Your gnashed teeth imply nothing profound. / Do you think that you could leave a toothmark / On any masterwork?" Stravinsky's complete comments are reprinted in Eric Walter White, *Stravinsky: The Composer and His Works* (Berkeley: University of California Press, 1979), 578–79. The translation of "The Serpent and the File" is taken from *The Fables of La Fontaine,* trans. Marianne Moore (New York: Viking, 1954), 113.

35. *The Fables of Jean de La Fontaine,* trans. Edward Marsh (London: William Heinemann, 1933), 83–84.

36. The exchange between Kirstein and Warburg is reported in Kirstein's *Thirty Years,* 58. The letter to Balanchine is dated 30 June 1936 and is one of a handful held at the Sacher Stiftung. Indeed, the composer's file of correspondence with Balanchine is one of the slimmest in the Swiss archives, no doubt because Balanchine was notoriously lax about responding to letters.

37. Robert Craft, *Stravinsky: Selected Correspondence,* vol. 2 (New York: Knopf, 1984), 315.

For a more complete history of the exchanges between Stravinsky, Balanchine, and others, see the chapter "Cocteau, Balanchine, and *Jeu de cartes*," pages 312–22.

38. See *Balanchine's New Complete Stories of the Great Ballets,* ed. Francis Mason (Garden City, N.Y.: Doubleday, 1968), 74–75.

39. Edward Villella, *Prodigal Son* (New York: Simon and Schuster, 1992), 136.

40. *Rudolf Nureyev,* directed by Patricia Foy, RM Associates, 1991. ISBN 0-7800-0644-5. Nureyev recounted the same story to Mason in *I Remember Balanchine,* 491. "He was working backwards, analytically, finding where the dance with the music had to climb," Nureyev recalled.

41. Violette Verdy, interview with author, July 1990.

42. Suzanne Farrell, with Toni Bentley, *Holding on to the Air* (New York: Summit, 1990), 102.

43. Lyon's comments appear in Mason, *I Remember Balanchine,* 142.

44. Warburg interview in Mason, *I Remember Balanchine,* 127.

45. Smit's comments appeared in the double issue of *Perspectives of New Music,* 9/2 and 10/1 (1971): 90–99. One cannot forget the often reproduced publicity-stunt picture of *Jeu de Cartes* in which Warburg, Stravinsky, Balanchine, William Dollar, and the four Queens of the ballet (Hortense Kahrklin, Leda Anchuitina, Ariel Lang, and Annabelle Lyon) are engaged in a poker game, with Stravinsky, naturally, smugly holding all the cards. It is reprinted in Jonathan Cott, *Portrait of Mr. B* (New York: Viking, 1984), 66, among other places.

46. This famous essay is reprinted in several anthologies, including Minna Lederman, *Stravinsky in the Theatre* (New York: Da Capo, 1975), 136–40.

47. Kirstein's comments are drawn from his *Thirty Years,* 60. In "Blast at Ballet" (the source of his remarks regarding the libretto), Kirstein adds that he found the story "undramatic and even flat." Nonetheless, "at least three Broadway revue producers wanted to whittle it down for their own shows."

48. Kirstein's comment is recorded in Lederman, *Stravinsky in the Theatre,* 139. The composer also disliked the festival costumes and décor. Sketches of the costume designs by Irene Sharaff (for *Jeu de Cartes*), Alice Halicka (*Le Baiser de la Fée*), and Stewart Cheney (*Apollon Musagète*) are reproduced in *Stravinsky in Modern Music (1924–1946),* compiled and with an Introduction by Carol J. Oja (New York: Da Capo, 1982), 158–59.

49. See Robert Garis, *Following Balanchine* (New Haven: Yale University Press, 1995), 70–71.

50. See Cott, *Portrait of Mr. B,* 142.

51. Verdy, interview with author, July 1990.

52. Virgil Thomson, "In the Theatre: High Brows Wow Local Public," reprinted in *Stravinsky in Modern Music,* 161–62.

53. In *I Remember Balanchine,* Francis Mason comments that "Carter, I believe, has a grasp of Balanchine's gifts no one else can match." The composer fondly remembered Les Ballets 1933, remarking that "I never saw anything quite as interesting as that again from Balanchine." He states that Balanchine told him that once he arrived in America, he felt obligated to produce successful ballets for Kirstein and the company. "As time went on," Carter continued, Balanchine "began to lose some of that very novel character that was striking at the beginning of his career." For a reprint of some of Carter's writings

about Balanchine, see "Balanchine and the Moderns," *Ballet Review,* 25/3 (Fall 1997): 84–90.

54. Carter interview in Mason, *I Remember Balanchine,* 165.

55. Lincoln Kirstein, *Four Centuries of Ballet* (New York: Dover, 1984), 33.

56. The translation is provided by White in *Stravinsky: The Composer and His Works,* 399.

57. See Joan Evans, "Die Rezeption der Musik Igor Strawinskys in Hitlerdeutschland," *Archiv für Musikwissenschaft,* 55/2 (1998): 91–109.

58. Denby's review, entitled "Balanchine and Stravinsky: *Poker Game* and *Baiser;* The Monte Carlo Season," first appeared in the November–December 1940 issue of *Modern Music* and is reprinted in *Dance Writings and Poetry,* ed. Robert Cornfield (New Haven: Yale University Press, 1998), 51.

Chapter 7: The War Years

1. Vernon Duke, *Passport to Paris* (Boston: Little, Brown, 1955), 388–91. Balanchine's marked copy of the play's typescript is in HTC, Typescripts, 1/1. Papers therein also attest to how much he was sought after as a Broadway choreographer. Typescripts of numerous musical comedies were sent to Balanchine for his consideration. Balanchine did choreograph *What's Up,* a musical comedy with words and music by Lerner and Loewe, in 1943. Several other typescripts and ideas were rejected. Balanchine's fondness for Tin Pan Alley songs is evinced by his collection of sheet music by Richard Rodgers, Cole Porter, George Gershwin, Vernon Duke, and especially Harold Arlen. Many scores contain Balanchine's annotations, indicating that he studied the music carefully.

2. Dunham's comments appear in Francis Mason, *I Remember Balanchine* (New York: Doubleday, 1991), 191. Stravinsky did not specifically compose *Tango* for Dunham, but he did think that the short piece might work well as a stylized dance. The piece exists in various versions, including a two-piano arrangement, a setting for piano and voice, an unpublished violin version prepared by Dushkin and Stravinsky, and an orchestral arrangement premiered by Benny Goodman.

3. Balanchine retained the original scores for both ballets, including what appear to be Duke's last-minute sketches and reworkings of certain sections, marked in pencil in the scores—perhaps at Balanchine's request to extend or modify his choreographic conception.

4. Even with the dances that were included in the water-nymph ballet, Goldwyn objected to the expensive set and the multiple camera angles upon which Balanchine insisted, although the final product did please the producer immensely. Still, Goldwyn was unusually cooperative, allowing Balanchine to import not only his dancers but also his complete retinue of rehearsal musicians, wardrobe attendants, makeup artists, and others. For a fuller account of Balanchine's Hollywood years, see Garson Kanin, "Balanchine in Hollywood," *Ballet Review,* 21/1 (Spring 1993): 45–49. Also see Vernon Duke, *Passport to Paris* (355 ff), for more on Balanchine's planned *American in Paris* ballet, which featured Zorina and was already three weeks into rehearsal when Duke arrived to work on the film. Some measure of Balanchine's conception of the *American in Paris* ballet may be gleaned from the choreographer's personal copy of the piano reduction, retained in

HTC, Scores, 8/1. Balanchine was working with Gershwin on a camera script. The score is shortened considerably, with several passages cut, repositioned, and certain measures repeated. Balanchine also makes several annotations, mostly in Russian, describing the action. He even inserts his own rehearsal numbers, marking the famous "Tempo Blues" section as a "cabaret."

5. Duke, *Passport to Paris,* 379.

6. For a summary of filmed dance, see Arlene Croce, "Dance in Film," *Cinema: A Critical Dictionary* (New York: Viking, 1980), 1:252–64. Also see Arthur Knight, "Dancing in Films," *Dance Index,* 6/8 (1947): 180–99. In *I Was An Adventuress,* for example, Knight remarks that audiences were disappointed with how little dancing Zorina did: "People who had come to see Zorina, *première ballerina,* were rewarded with six minutes of a special screen version of *Swan Lake.* . . . The dancing itself, as it turned out, was something special. . . . It [showed] a keen apprehension by George Balanchine of the difference between stage ballet and screen ballet." Balanchine even incorporated stop-motion camera work as Zorina's grand jeté "is prolonged by slow motion photography." Easily the finest survey of Balanchine's film accomplishments is Susan Roper's "Balanchine in Hollywood," *Ballet Review,* 23/4 (Winter 1995): 48–73.

7. George Balanchine, "Ballet in Films," *Dance News* (December 1944): 8. Regarding *Star-Spangled Rhythm,* for example, Balanchine procured a manuscript copy of "That Old Black Magic" (lyric by Johnny Mercer and music by one of Balanchine's favorite songwriters, Harold Arlen) long before the film went into production. His copy, preserved in HTC, Scores, 9/5, is marked up as early as 1936, suggesting that he knew the score well before he choreographed it for Zorina.

8. I discuss the failed Chaplin-Stravinsky collaboration in my *Stravinsky Inside Out* (New Haven: Yale University Press, 2001), 114–16.

9. Tamara Toumanova interview in Mason, *I Remember Balanchine,* 104. Toumanova went on to become more widely known by the general public in a few Hollywood films, especially Alfred Hitchcock's 1966 *Torn Curtain,* where she acts and—as she rarely did by this time—dances as "Francesca" in a ballet segment that takes place in the Inferno.

10. Igor Stravinsky and Robert Craft, *Conversations* (Rpt. Berkeley: University of California Press, 1980), 102. Stravinsky met Tchelitchev in 1922. He knew the artist's work with Nabokov and Diaghilev from the 1928 *Ode.* Balanchine first worked with the designer in 1933, when Tchelitchev did costumes and lighting for the Les Ballets 1933 production of *L'Errant.*

11. The Jerome Robbins Dance Division of the New York Public Library for the Performing Arts retains a watercolor of one of the female costumes, prepared by Tchelitchev and inscribed to Kirstein ("a souvenir of pink in a gray time"). Even more illuminating is the eight-minute film of excerpts from two performances and a rehearsal by the Original Ballet Russe dating from 1941 that the repository preserves. For an informative description of this brief film, see Vincent Garcia-Márquez, *The Ballets Russes* (New York: Knopf, 1990), in which the author addresses Balanchine's "interweaving of individual dancers and groups to create geometrical patterns."

12. Donald Dale Jackson, "Red, Hot & Blue," *Smithsonian,* 27/8 (November 1996): 46–57. Slonimsky's comments are reprinted in Mason, *I Remember Balanchine,* 55–56. Also see

Elizabeth Souritz, "Fedor Lopukhov: A Soviet Choreographer in the 1920s," *Dance Research Journal*, 17/2 (Fall 1985\–Spring 1986): 3–20.

13. For a good summary of several of the reviews that critiqued *Balustrade,* see Kathrine Sorley Walker, *De Basil's Ballet Russes* (New York: Atheneum, 1983), 103–5; B. H. Haggin, "Reflections on Balanchine," *Dance Magazine,* 57/7 (July 1983).

14. See Walker, *De Basil's Ballet Russes,* 103–5. Stravinsky again retained and marked several newspaper reviews.

15. Maria Tallchief recalls that early in her career, Serge Denham encouraged her to change her last name to Tallchieva. Maria Tallchief, with Larry Kaplan, *Maria Tallchief: America's Prima Ballerina* (New York: Henry Holt, 1997), 27.

16. Richard Buckle, *George Balanchine: Ballet Master* (New York: Random House, 1988), 139. Balanchine's exchange with Koussevitzky is retained in HTC, Correspondence, 20/5.

17. Stravinsky's letter came in response to an earlier note from Bender stating that Balanchine wanted to have the piano reduction of the "Elephant Ballet" as soon as it was finished, and the orchestration "no later than March 15 as [Balanchine] would like to have two weeks['] rehearsal of the orchestra." But Stravinsky would not send the score until Bender agreed to the payment schedule that the composer carefully drafted in his response. Balanchine had actually signed a contract with John Ringling North to stage several ballets for the circus that season.

18. Alicia Markova interview, Mason, *I Remember Balanchine,* 91–92.

19. De Gaulle later ordered a copy of the two-piano version. The four-minute work exists in several arrangements, including a solo piano version and a symphonic version first performed by the Boston Symphony Orchestra in 1944, with Stravinsky conducting. Stravinsky's sketches show that he worked carefully in arranging the work for strings. The respected film composer David Raksin prepared the score for the original band arrangement since Stravinsky was uncomfortable writing for band. Raksin told me that Stravinsky first invited Robert Russell Bennett to prepare the wind arrangement, but Bennett suggested Raksin. The two met often at Stravinsky's home (over vodka and Russian pastries, as Raksin recalled), going over a few pages at a time. Raksin also recalls that Stravinsky kept in touch with Balanchine as the work evolved, apprising him of its progress.

20. Unpublished letter in the Sacher Stiftung dated 22 May 1942. For a description of the rehearsals Balanchine conducted in Sarasota Springs, see Mason's interview with Constance Clausen in *I Remember Balanchine,* 223–26. Clausen danced in the Stravinsky-Balanchine work. She also indicates that Balanchine's fondness for elephants continued, since apparently he later traveled to Hollywood to discuss the possibility of "making a film musical of *Jumbo.*" In his *Passport to Paris,* Vernon Duke could not resist commenting, "Like all new music by Stravinsky, the polka featured the 'truncated line'—probably to glorify the elephants' trunks—but the animals would have none of it" (405). Several eyewitnesses recall that the confused elephants were disturbed by the pandemonium of the music.

21. Morton's remarks appear in Edwin Corle's collection of essays, *Igor Stravinsky* (New York: Duell, Sloane and Pearce, 1949), 193 ff. As for upside-down values, as late as 1950,

in a luminously propagandistic preglasnost tone, the Soviet critic V. Gorodinsky blustered that the traitorous Stravinsky had written the *Circus Polka* "in the midst of war [reflecting] a modernistic bigotry which covers up a panic fear of stormy forces dynamiting capitalist reality, the terror of the inescapable downfall of a social structure." See Nicolas Slonimsky, *Lexicon of Musical Invective* (Seattle: University of Washington Press, 1969), 204.

22. See Alfred Frankenstein, "Stravinsky in Beverly Hills," *Modern Music,* 19/3 (March–April, 1942): 172–81.

23. The exchange appeared in an interview originally published in *Intellectual Digest,* June 1972.

24. Serge Denham directed the Ballet Russe de Monte Carlo from 1938. Upon Massine's departure from the company that year, Colonel de Basil organized the Original Ballet Russe, directing the troupe from 1939–48. On 13 July 1944 Denham offered a flat fee of $2,000 for Balanchine to choreograph the Stravinsky score and *Le Bourgeois Gentilhomme.* HTC, Correspondence, 17/4.

25. Tallchief, *Maria Tallchief,* 44–45.

26. George Balanchine, "The Dance Element in Stravinsky's Music," in *The Dance Anthology,* ed. Cobbet Steinberg (New York: New American Library, 1980). The article arose from an interview with the composer conducted by Ingolf Dahl, published in a 1957 issue of *Cinema,* that was really an excuse for the still disgruntled composer to launch another tirade against the film industry.

27. Haggin's review appeared in the 29 November 1947 issue of *The Nation.*

28. John Martin, "City Center Opens Season of Ballet," *New York Times,* 11 September 1944.

29. Morton's comments are included in his essay "Incongruity and Faith." After its Philadelphia preview, an unhappy Rose suggested to Stravinsky that Robert Russell Bennett "retouch" the orchestration. (Bennett often orchestrated works for Gershwin, Cole Porter, and other Hollywood composers.) Stravinsky refused. Consequently, only a brief portion of the score was included in the New York premiere. Stravinsky never saw the show. His name was not even mentioned in many of the publicity notices touting the production. The first performance of the complete ballet had to wait until 1948, when Frederick Ashton choreographed the work for the Sadler's Wells Ballet, with Margot Fonteyn and Michael Somes.

30. Francis A. Coleman, "A Talk with Igor Stravinsky," *Dance Magazine,* 19/4 (April 1945): 30.

31. De Mille's comments were made in an interview with Vivian Perlis on 25 June 1980 and reprinted in *Copland: 1900 through 1942* (New York: St. Martin's/Marek, 1984), 357. In the 1943–44 tour booklet for the company, an opening statement makes particular mention of *Rodeo*'s "outstanding contribution to purely American ballet."

32. W. H. Auden, "Henry James and the Artist in America," *Harper's Magazine,* July 1948, 40.

33. This landmark work had its roots in the School of American Ballet and was presented at an open rehearsal in New York before the company left for South America. Originally, Eugene Berman designed the scenery and costumes, though the work is best remembered for its lack of elaborate costumes. Beginning with a 1945 performance, the dancers

dressed in white or black practice clothes, thus further emphasizing Balanchine's desire to express the purity of the music and dance without ornament.

Chapter 8: Passage to *Orpheus*

Epigraph: This and all other translations from Ovid are from Horace Gregory, *Ovid: The Metamorphoses* (New York: Viking, 1958), 274–75.

1. Martin's reviews for the *New York Times* are reprinted in Charles Payne, *American Ballet Theatre* (New York: Knopf, 1978), 109 ff.

2. Payne, *American Ballet Theatre,* 12. The actual founder of the company was Mikhail Mordkin, the Bolshoi-trained dancer who believed in the "lusty, effusive vigor of Moscow male dancing." Mordkin danced for Diaghilev's company in their first, 1909, season. In 1910 he performed at the Met in New York, partnering Pavlova, thus ushering in the prominence of Russian dancers and instructors in the United States. Chase officially ran the company beginning in 1945, but it was her patronage that endowed the enterprise. The company began in the 1920s as an outgrowth of Mordkin's company, the Mordkin Ballet.

3. Even as he served in the armed forces, Kirstein tried to keep Balanchine's enterprise alive. In a 6 March 1944 letter, he encourages Balanchine to consider merging the School of American Ballet with another well-known school in New York. "In this way we could have an independent establishment, the finest in the country, and we could accept only those we want." Kirstein suggests that Balanchine become president of the new school ("instead of me"). HTC, Correspondence, 20/30.

4. A good collection of Terry's reviews extending from 1938 through 1976, covering Chase's career, are reprinted in his *I Was There* (New York: Marcel Dekker, 1978).

5. Nicholas Remisoff, designer for the Washington, D.C., *Apollon Musagète,* was originally asked to create the décor, but Hurok dismissed him. For a discussion of Hurok and Ballet Theatre's production of *The Firebird,* see Payne, *American Ballet Theatre,* 139–40.

6. Nicolas Nabokov was also there, capturing the warmness Stravinsky and Balanchine felt for one another in his "Christmas with Stravinsky" essay, included in *Old Friends and New Music* (Boston: Little, Brown, 1951).

7. Payne, *American Ballet Theatre,* 147. Payne also reprints a letter to Chase from Ruth Page's husband, Thomas Hart Fisher, that repeats the rumor that Kirstein was biding his time until he inherited his father's fortune—which would then fund a professional company. The inheritance would also fund the construction of "a new theatre in New York City, for which [Kirstein] has already had architects' sketches prepared."

8. Surely the "gravest" obstacle to which Bernstein refers was a 1963 Ford Foundation grant awarded to Kirstein and Balanchine "to strengthen professional ballet in America." Chase's company, conspicuously, was not among the recipients. The subvention was announced among "cries of protest and of anger. . . . The internationally famous American Ballet Theater was awarded not one cent!" wrote Walter Terry in an article entitled "Ford Blows Up a Storm," *Herald Tribune,* 12 January 1964. Even more incriminatory, Terry indicted the foundation for unethically creating a plutocracy with Kirstein and Balanchine, alleging that such a sizable and exclusive grant could not be "explained away by in-

nocence alone." In fact, the Ford Foundation had contacted Balanchine as early as June 1961 and on 11 October 1963 had sent Balanchine "a rough draft of a possible letter of application . . . for the proposed grant to the ballet company." A three-page draft marked "Confidential" was enclosed, describing how the $2 million commitment over a ten-year period might be used, suggesting new productions, transportation for touring, the construction of a costume shop, and so on. Balanchine had lobbied for state-supported arts subsidies as well. Appearing before Congress in 1962 he asserted, "Congress should improve the artistic and cultural scene with legislation which would give government support to those institutions which have proved themselves worthy of the assurance of survival which a subsidy could give them." See "At Last Congress Listens," *Dance Magazine,* 36/2 (February 1962): 35.

9. Stravinsky's unpublished papers include several exchanges with Chase's company regarding the precise orchestration of *Apollo.* The composer attended several performances of Ballet Theatre's many productions in Los Angeles. In New York, Stravinsky attended a performance of *Apollo* on 30 April 1947.

10. Stravinsky retained all these communications, annotated as always, in his private papers.

11. See Lillian Moore, "American Notes: Balanchine's New American Portrait," *Dancing Times,* 436 (January 1947): 190. Actually, Balanchine and Hindemith had discussed a collaboration nearly a decade earlier, during the summer and fall of 1937. Without Kirstein or Warburg's knowledge, Balanchine commissioned the composer to write a work for the young American Ballet, with a premiere planned for 1938. Hindemith suggested that the ballet be titled "Schlaraffenland" (The Land of Milk and Honey), as papers in the Harvard Theatre Collection confirm, but he could not guarantee that the work would be completed in time for a 1938 premiere, so the idea apparently faded. Still, Balanchine remained a devotee of Hindemith's music over the next decade and the commissioning of *The Four Temperaments* was a logical outcome of their earlier discussions.

12. Todd Bolender, who danced the role of the Fox for Balanchine's production of *Renard,* reconstructed the choreography in 2001 with the Kansas City Ballet as part of a citywide Stravinsky Festival. The ever-vibrant Bolender, with the help of Kansas City Ballet Artistic Director William Whitener and Ballet Master James Jordan, resurrected a long-lost masterpiece. (The Fox was danced brilliantly by Christopher Barksdale.) As part of the George Balanchine Foundation's "Archive of Lost Choreography" project, Nancy Reynolds was there to record company rehearsals and interviews of Bolender. As with other videotapes in this series, the footage here is indispensable in preserving Bolender's thoughts about both the work itself and his relationship with Balanchine.

13. See Nancy Goldner, ed., *The Stravinsky Festival of the New York City Ballet* (New York: Eakins Press, 1973), 168.

14. Kirstein's comments originally appeared in the pamphlet "Blast at Ballet" (Rpt. New York: Dance Horizons, 1967), 32–33.

15. See Otis Stuart, "The Phoenix and the Lyre," *Ballet Review,* 21/1 (Spring 1933): 51–56. Also see Simon Volkov, *Balanchine's Tchaikovsky* (New York: Simon and Schuster, 1985), 164–65. Orpheus's "descent into darkness, the emergence into light, the loss of a beloved, the creation of an artist through suffering," as Deborah Jowitt writes in *Time and the Dancing Machine* (Berkeley: University of California Press, 1988), was also of interest

to Isadora Duncan, who danced the minuet from Gluck's *Orfeo* at London's New Gallery around 1900.

16. Balanchine's attachment to the music is confirmed by several later productions, all with changes and reconceived choreography (for example, in Hamburg in 1963 and again in Paris ten years later). The ballet *Chaconne* (again based upon the Gluck score and the Hamburgische Staatsoper production) was premiered by the New York City Ballet in January 1976. A year earlier, Balanchine had staged yet another production of *Orfeo* for Maria Tallchief's new Lyric Opera Ballet in Chicago. For critical comments by Olin Downes, see *Olin Downes on Music,* ed. Irene Downes (New York: Simon and Schuster, 1957).

17. Janine Charrat (whose first success as a choreographer came with Stravinsky's *Jeu de cartes* in 1945) and Roland Petit later danced Cocteau's play. For a description of Cocteau's staging of the danced *Orphée,* see Frank W. Ries, *The Dance Theatre of Jean Cocteau* (Ann Arbor: UMI Research Press, 1986), 108.

18. See Edward Villella, *Prodigal Son* (New York: Simon and Schuster, 1992), 279–81, and Nicholas Jenkins, "The Great Impresario," *New Yorker,* 13 April 1998: 50.

19. Chase's 8 March letter and Stravinsky's reply are retained in the composer's "Lucia Chase" file in the Sacher Stiftung. As early as May 1947, Stravinsky had planned conducting engagements for the next spring, pressuring Kirstein to settle dates. But Kirstein was besieged by financial and logistical problems, including finding an appropriate house for the performance. His correspondence reveals that he investigated producing *Orpheus* at either the Met or the Ziegfeld Theatre. (The latter lacked sufficient space in the pit for the forty-three musicians Stravinsky wanted.)

20. Lifar, temporarily dismissed from his position, was charged as a collaborationist during the Nazi occupation. A bitter division between his supporters and detractors caught Balanchine in the crossfire. In preparing for his residency in Paris, Balanchine frequently corresponded with Georges Hirsch of the Réunion des Théâtres Lyriques Nationaux. Typically, he wanted assurances that his ideas would be realized according to his and Stravinsky's wishes. He was particularly concerned that the production staff would be able to present the "special effects of water and snow needed for the presentation of *Baiser de la Fée.*" Hirsch responded that the Opera's "installation was the most modern and complete in the world." See several such exchanges of September and October 1946 in HTC, Correspondence, 17/3.

21. Maria Tallchief, *Maria Tallchief: America's Prima Ballerina* (New York: Henry Holt, 1997), 76–77.

22. Unpublished letter of 7 November 1947. Fassett broadcast *Perséphone* earlier in the year, as well as excerpts from *The Rake's Progress* a few years later.

23. An edited version of these responses appears in Vera Stravinsky and Robert Craft, *Stravinsky in Pictures and Documents* (New York: Simon and Schuster, 1978), 380–81. The original typescript, marked and edited by Craft in several places, is held in the Sacher Stiftung.

24. In a 22 July 1947 letter to the composer, Kirstein admits that he is "terrified" that Tchelitchev will misconstrue the ballet's intent and conjure up something entirely inappropriate. Tchelitchev's participation seemed so firm, however, that the early Ballet Society program booklets previewing *Orpheus* listed Tchelitchev as the designer.

25. Noguchi's best-known collaborations with Graham began in 1943 with Elizabeth Sprague Coolidge's commission of three dance pieces for the Library of Congress Chamber Music Theatre, including Copland and Graham's *Appalachian Spring*, although he had worked with Graham as early as 1935 on *Frontier.* Noguchi prepared the designs for Graham's own Greek dances in *Night Journey* and *Errand into the Maze* shortly before undertaking *Orpheus.* Graham's *Night Journey,* as Sally Banes points out, shares several commonalities with Balanchine's *Orpheus:* "Orpheus's dance of mourning in the opening section is marked by contractions—a trademark of Graham's technique—and a repeated movement of his lyre to his pelvis that emphasizes the prop's phallic symbolism, recalling the genital imagery of Graham's choreography." For other notable similarities between the two productions, see Bane's insightful essay "Sibling Rivalry," in *Dance for a City: Fifty Years of the New York City Ballet,* ed. Lynn Garafola and Eric Foner (New York: Columbia University Press, 1999), 89–92.

26. From *A Sculptor's World,* quoted in "Designs for Dance," in *The Dance Anthology,* ed. Cobbett Steinberg (New York: New American Library), 183–91.

27. Interview of Noguchi by Tobi Tobias, January–February 1979. Noguchi's comments are excerpted from the transcript of an audiotape held by the Jerome Robbins Dance Division of the New York Public Library for the Performing Arts.

28. Lincoln Kirstein, *Thirty Years: Lincoln Kirstein's The New York City Ballet* (New York: Knopf, 1978), 98.

29. See Kirstein, *Thirty Years,* 99, for his comments regarding the Petipa-Tchaikovsky collaboration. But also consult Roland John Wiley, *Tchaikovsky's Ballets* (Oxford: Clarendon Press, 1985). Wiley's illuminating introduction, "Composer and Balletmaster," provides a useful view of just how powerful Petipa's authority was, and consequently how little Tchaikovsky (by his own admission a "spectator") was involved in the overall production.

30. Balanchine's remarks were made to Jonathan Cott during the summer of 1982 and recorded in *Portrait of Mr. B* (New York: Viking, 1984), 144.

31. This final description is taken from Francis Mason and George Balanchine, *101 Stories of the Great Ballets* (New York: Doubleday, 1989), 290.

32. In "The Phoenix and the Lyre," Otis Stuart reports that "wall paintings in Roman catacombs link images of Christ the teacher with images of Orpheus among the animals that prefigure St. Francis. Among church fathers, Clemens Alexandrius characterized the cross as 'Christ's lyre.'" Whatever its mythological origins, the significance of the lyre's talismanic power and symbolism were such that it became, and remains, the logo for the New York City Ballet. For a useful summary of the Orphic legend, see Mark P. O. Morford and Robert J. Lenardon, "Orpheus and Orphism: Mystery Religions in Roman Times," in their *Classical Mythology* (New York: Longman, 1991), 331–47.

33. See Nancy Reynolds, *Repertory in Review* (New York: Dial, 1977), 87.

34. Interview of Noguchi by Tobias, January–February 1979.

35. See Ellen Graff's "*The Four Temperaments* and *Orpheus:* Models of a Modern Classical Tradition," *Ballet Review,* 13/3 (February 1985): 54–59. A. V. Coton addressed the ballet's temporal-spatial axis in a 1950 review: "The Time is eternity and the Place is everywhere that Man inhabits, in this dreadful and simple statement of the classic myth; sometimes

the movement is so simple that only the most exquisite performers can keep the shape of the incidents inside the frameworks of both the music and the stage-space." See Coton, *Writings on Dance, 1938–68,* ed. Kathrine Sorley Walker and Lilian Haddakin (London: Dance Books, 1975), 123.

36. Balanchine and Mason, *101 Stories of the Great Ballets,* 285.

37. Interview of Noguchi by Tobias. Years afterward, Balanchine asked Noguchi if he would be interested in preparing the décor of a ballet to the music of Schoenberg's student Anton Webern, but the sculptor declined. Balanchine (along with Martha Graham) first staged *Episodes* in 1959 to the complete orchestral works of Webern. An undated letter from Noguchi to Balanchine held in HTC, Correspondence, 4/6, reveals that the two thought about preparing a ballet to the music of Alban Berg, another famous Schoenberg pupil. The score was Berg's opera *Lulu*—a choice apparently made at Stravinsky's suggestion. Balanchine prepared an amazingly detailed piano reduction of a few sections (all in ink, no less; see HTC, Scores, 9/17). Not only does he mark in specific dynamics and instrumental assignments, but he also carefully notates Berg's own designations of *Hauptstimme* and *Nebenstimme,* indicating primary and subsidiary thematic ideas, which Balanchine obviously wished to take into consideration. But the ballet was never made. Noguchi informed Balanchine that he did not have time to prepare the sets for the Berg music. In the late 1970s, the prospect of reviving the ballet arose, with a scenario based upon Oscar Wilde's *Salome.* Rouben Ter-Arutunian prepared the sets. According to Barbara Horgan the ballet was even scheduled for 23 June 1977 on the same program as the premiere of *Vienna Waltzes,* but the budget did not allow it.

38. Balanchine and Mason, *101 Stories of the Great Ballets,* 287.

39. This wonderfully revealing videotape, part of the George Balanchine Foundation's "Interpreters Archive," was shot at Lincoln Center in June 1995. The eighty-two-minute documentary, entitled "Maria Tallchief Coaching Excerpts from *Firebird* and *Orpheus,*" captures Tallchief instructing Heléne Alexopoulos as she dances the variation (but includes plenty of Tallchief herself reprising the solo that was originally made on her). Nancy Reynolds and Arlene Croce interview Tallchief, providing invaluable commentary that cannot be found elsewhere.

40. For some beautiful photographs of these and other moments in *Orpheus,* see Jonathan Weinberg, "Substitute and Consolation: The Ballet Photographs of George Platt Lynes," in *Dance for a City,* 129–35. Photographs from both the 1948 and the 1951 production are included. As Weinberg points out, "Balanchine wrote that Lynes's 'secret was his sense of plasticity,' which enabled him to suggest the 'quintessential permanence of characteristic silhouette and massive form' in the choreographer's ballets."

41. Musicians will recognize the familiar "split-third" sonority (or Allen Forte's pitch-class set 3-3) that Stravinsky employs, which in its major-minor tension adds even further piquancy to this pivotal moment.

42. Interview of Noguchi by Tobias.

43. The original typescript is retained in the Sacher Stiftung. The responses, in Stravinsky's own hand, are also reprinted in Robert Craft, *A Stravinsky Scrapbook, 1940–1971* (New York: Thames and Hudson, 1983), 123.

44. Ballet Society's 1 November 1947 *Bulletin* kept its subscribers up to date on the ballet's

progress. "Igor Stravinsky has delivered to George Balanchine . . . the piano transcription and full orchestral parts of his ballet *Orpheus*. . . . Mr. Balanchine who is now engaged in making his own transcription of the score to serve him in creating and rehearsing the choreography, considers the score one of Stravinsky's greatest achievements, not only for the perfection of the formal composition which serves as the springboard for the dancing, but as an absolute musical work. The work is conceived as a classic dramatic spectacle, in the elevated style of his *Symphony of Psalms*."

45. Maria Tallchief interview in Mason, *I Remember Balanchine* (New York: Doubleday, 1991), 243. Mason and Camille Hardy conducted the interview. For a slightly different version, see Tallchief's *Maria Tallchief,* 96. There Tallchief recalls that the composer dictated five beats and wrote a fermata into the score to be counted as an extra beat: "The night of the premiere while he was conducting, Stravinsky didn't look up from the pit while I was dying. He counted five slow beats of silence and went right into Nicky's music. For him, the extended silence was eloquent."

46. Tallchief, *Maria Tallchief,* 95–96; Bernard Taper, *Balanchine: A Biography* (Berkeley: University of California Press, 1996), 224.

47. Tallchief, *Maria Tallchief,* 95; Ann Hutchinson, "The Scoring of *Orpheus:* Notes of a Dance Scribe," *Center: A Magazine of the Performing Arts,* 1/4 (June–July 1954): 13–14. A copy of Hutchinson's Labanotation score is held by HTC, Scores, 3/1, and includes many annotations relating to her description of the actual notational process.

48. Nabokov, *Old Friends and New Music,* 203–4.

49. There is a list of twenty-two corrections printed in the Boosey and Hawkes score. But the errata list itself is in error, failing to incorporate the corrections enumerated here. Even the important harp solos found throughout *Orpheus* are sometimes in question. The errata list directs the harpist to delete the *près de la table* direction (producing a muted, brittle sound) in the opening measures of the ballet and again at the reprise in the closing scene. Yet in another prominent harp solo at Rehearsal 117, while no specific direction is printed, Stravinsky marks in red the same *près de la table* textual effect. All of this confirms the unreliability of many Stravinsky works in print—a bitter irony for a composer-conductor who insisted on a faithful execution of the printed score.

50. In fact, Baum attended an *Orpheus* rehearsal and discussed the possibility of a residency with Balanchine and Kirstein in advance of the premiere. The success of the production only fortified the merger. In *American Ballet Theatre,* Charles Payne wrote, "It was for the worse in 1947 when [Chase] turned down Morton Baum's invitation for the company to become the resident ballet company of the New York City Center. She opted instead for a return to the Metropolitan Opera House and thus lost out on the opportunity of later acquiring an official residency at the New York State Theatre" (23).

51. If Martin's position had softened by the late 1940s, so too had Kirstein's. In 1952 Kirstein praised Martin, at least reservedly, on his twenty-fifth anniversary as the *New York Times* critic: "Martin cannot be bought, and not a few, in one way or another have tried to buy him. He is not a fool, and he also has learned to develop taste past prejudice or predilection. . . . However embittering may have been some of Martin's remarks over the last decade at least, there have been comparatively few occasions when a history of the dance could not have been fairly [and] accurately indicated from a collection of his first-night

notices." See "Martin of *The Times,*" *Dance News,* 20/4 (April 1952): 8. Further, in a letter of 1 March 1973, Kirstein wrote to Martin: "You were our company's earliest critic and strongest negative mentor. Without your first notices and final confidence, we would never have been as stubborn, insistent or directed as we have been." See *Dance Perspectives* 54 (Summer 1973): 8.

52. Ellen Graff, in "*The Four Temperaments* and *Orpheus,*" suggests that since Balanchine was well aware of her work, Martha Graham may have been a primary influence on him, particularly her "ritual theater" awareness of "the symbolic use of objects and the accompanying distortion of time." Maria Tallchief remarked, "George had Eurydice almost doing jazzy steps, and contractions similar to those in modern dance." See Tallchief, *Maria Tallchief,* 96. In her interview with Reynolds and Croce in the documentary "Maria Tallchief Coaching Excerpts from *Firebird* and *Orpheus,*" Tallchief again mentions that *Orpheus* is imbued with jazz idioms. "George never said Martha Graham, but he meant Martha Graham," she remarks.

53. Lincoln Kirstein, "Balanchine and the Classic Revival," *Theatre Arts* (December 1947). Nor can one forget Kirstein's witty reply in the 31 May 1948 issue of *Time* magazine, wherein immediately following the premiere, Stravinsky came onstage to take his bow with "his feet crossed in his best Position. III." But Kirstein was quick to correct this: Stravinsky, "the greatest living composer of ballets" as *Time* described him, acknowledged the audience while bowing from Fourth Position ("with weight equally divided," added Kirstein, "the forefoot is twelve inches in advance of the back").

54. This prophetic letter is reprinted in several sources, including Robert Craft, *Stravinsky: Selected Correspondence,* vol. 1 (New York: Knopf, 1982), 271.

Chapter 9: *Agon*

1. I wish to thank Columbia University Press for permitting me to reprint portions of my essay "The Making of Agon," from *Dance for a City: Fifty Years of the New York City Ballet,* ed. Lynn Garafola, with Eric Foner (New York, 1999).

2. Stravinsky followed Tallchief's career, as well as those of other Balanchine ballerinas. He retained and marked in his private files a gossipy story in the 15 October 1950 *Los Angeles Times* about what was rumored to be Balanchine and Tallchief's separation. He often exchanged letters and gifts with Balanchine's wives and other dancers, never failing to appreciate their vital contributions in the visualization of his ballets.

3. Maria Tallchief, with Larry Kaplan, *Maria Tallchief: America's Prima Ballerina* (New York: Henry Holt, 1997), 131. Tallchief provides her written remembrance of her preparation for this, including a retracing of Balanchine's creation of the choreography. Even more instructive, she coaches Hélène Alexopoulos in the Berceuse. See "Maria Tallchief Coaching Excerpts from *Firebird* and *Orpheus,*" in the George Balanchine Foundation's "Interpreters Archive" videotape. Balanchine wanted the ballerina's head pulled all the way down to the chest because it was more "Russian," Tallchief recalls. And in her interview with Nancy Reynolds (on the videotape), she reiterates that he also wanted a very "Russian character dance" to match Stravinsky's score. There was to be constant tension in the hands, pushing out, "like isometrics and swimming," she recalls Balanchine advis-

ing. She adds that the ballet's transitions (of which there are many) had to be fluid, Balanchine further stressed, especially "in between steps, like *glissade,*" so as to create continuous movement. Tallchief also confirms that Stravinsky and Balanchine were pleased with the ballet's reception, not knowing what to expect; consequently, the dancers did not even practice any bows! The ballet was revised successfully a few more times thereafter. The 1970 production was particularly important, given Jerome Robbins's choreography for the famous Infernal Dance of Kastchei. For Balanchine's comments on the 1970 revisions, see Olga Maynard, "Balanchine Talks About *The Firebird,*" *Dance Magazine* (August 1970): 43–57. Balanchine visited Chagall (whose designs served as the basis for Karinska's breathtaking costumes) in Antibes, "and he gave us more than a hundred water colors for *Firebird.*" Typical of Balanchine, he tossed off his own contribution to the stunning new production: "This is not a ballet by Balanchine with decoration by Chagall—it is a ballet in which we present Chagall's painting, and Stravinsky's music to the people." Moreover, Balanchine, more than anyone, understood the deficiencies of the work as an important dance piece: "It is beautiful music, deathless music, but *The Firebird* was never a great ballet."

4. Kirstein's unexpurgated letters to Stravinsky are retained in the Sacher Stiftung, as are the composer's unedited replies to Kirstein.

5. Kirstein's letter touched on other important matters as well, including a possible staging of *Petrushka* with a newly conceived staging by Tchelitchev. "He [Pavel Tchelitchev] has agreed formally to do it; he wants to work with you. This can be the most brilliant possible event, and we will all work like mad making something of [which] Diaghilev himself could be proud. We can count on Pavlik a hundred percent." Kirstein projected a cost of about $200,000, planning the production for February 1951. But it never took place, perhaps because Stravinsky did not approve of Tchelitchev's odd ideas, which he was aware of several months before he received Kirstein's letter.

6. This unedited letter goes on to suggest that if Balanchine's new *Nutcracker* (originally planned for a 1951 production but not staged until 1954) generated enough revenue, Kirstein would stage not only *Petrushka* in 1951, but also *Pulcinella.*

7. Unpublished letter of 9 September 1952 in the Sacher Stiftung. The script is retained in the archives as well, but it is unmarked by Stravinsky and it is doubtful whether he had much interest in undertaking the project—one of many ballets and film prospects he considered about this time. As the Balanchine archive at Harvard attests, the choreographer also continued to consider, and often reject, various ballet and film projects.

8. Stravinsky's unedited response to Kallman's letter is among Balanchine's papers in HTC, Correspondence, 19/4. Stravinsky then immediately responded to Balanchine, informing him of the "strong arguments against the tentative switching of the first scene of the Third Act to the Second Act." Further, he advises Balanchine, "You will have to find the means of making a quick change *without stopping the music* between the Auction Scene and the Churchyard Scene" (letter of 2 February 1952). In turn Balanchine, in one of his rare letters to the composer, writes on 6 February that he feels that the work "is better divided as you yourself composed it"—just one further indication of his devotion to the composer's music as originally conceived. He assures Stravinsky that he will incorporate

the change only if it can unfold on stage "very fast and smoothly." Bing's letter to Balanchine, 9 August 1952, is also in HTC, Correspondence, 19/4.

9. Balanchine's remarks appeared in an article entitled "The Met at Work—Directing a *Rake*" for a 1953 Metropolitan Opera Association Program Booklet, which Stravinsky retained in his personal files.

10. *Opera News,* 9 February 1953: 11, once again retained by Stravinsky.

11. Robert Craft, *Present Perspectives* (New York: Knopf, 1984), 252–53. Schoenberg died in July 1951, only a few months before the premiere of *The Rake's Progress.*

12. For the details of what eventually led to Balanchine's ballet *Opus 34,* based on a Schoenberg score, see Robert Craft, "On Stravinsky and Balanchine," in *Tributes: Celebrating Fifty Years of New York City Ballet* (New York: William Morrow, 1998), 56. Croce's article "The Spelling of *Agon*" appeared in the 12 July 1993 issue of the *New Yorker.* Craft's important and detailed response to Croce is given in his *The Moments of Existence* (Nashville: Vanderbilt University Press, 1996), 281–82. Kirstein contended that it was Stravinsky who introduced Balanchine to the Schoenberg score, but that seems unlikely.

13. Earlier that same month Stravinsky himself, also in Europe and conducting in Berlin, suffered a stroke, just after the New York City Ballet had left the city. By all reports Balanchine was shaken, for the immediate prognosis suggested that Stravinsky would probably not live more than six months.

14. Stravinsky retained a subsequent letter from Le Clercq written in early December in which she sends three reviews of *Agon* to his Hollywood home. Some inkling of the informality and closeness she and other dancers shared with Stravinsky are evident: "I love being home—it's a year since I've seen the apartment—of course it is difficult, but what isn't. The school gave me a t.v. set and I'm sorry to say I've become an addict. George is sitting in the living room now looking at a movie about a gorilla." (Notes from Suzanne Farrell and Diana Adams among others were also retained by the composer.)

15. Nancy Reynolds, *Repertory in Review* (New York: Dial, 1977), 152; Lincoln Kirstein, *Thirty Years: Lincoln Kirstein's the New York City Ballet* (New York: Knopf, 1978), 135.

16. Stravinsky's reference to Josquin (one of several) occurs in a conversation with Craft about Anton Webern's music. See Stravinsky and Craft, *Memories and Commentaries* (Rpt. Berkeley: University of California Press, 1981), 107. Krenek also prepared a modern edition of Claudio Monteverdi's opera *L'Incoronazione di Poppaea.* Moreover, his defense and adoption of Schoenberg's twelve-tone method was familiar to Stravinsky, who retained and studied several of his scores. That a composer of Krenek's broadly based, recondite musical abilities encompassed both music of the Renaissance and the dodecaphonic school surely provided another important model for Stravinsky during this transitional period.

17. Kirstein's original letter and scenario are preserved in the Sacher Stiftung. In this "draft" sketch, Kirstein envisioned seven sections ("Order not necessarily the one Balanchine will use") in a scene consisting of "a vast ballroom in space, between the stars. Music of the spheres." There was to be a "reception of the gods" with Apollo and Terpsichore (André Eglevsky and Maria Tallchief), Cupid (Janet Reed), Pegasus (Patricia Wilde), Prometheus (Francisco Monicon), Orpheus and Bacchante (Nicolas Magallanes and

Tanaquil Le Clercq), Venus and Mars (Diana Adams and Herbert Bliss), and Zeus (Hugh Laing). All this was to lead "up to the final dance when the previous pavane, rigaudon, menuet, waltz, tarantella, polka, develops under Jerome Robbins as Mercury, into a big jazz finale."

18. Moreover, the *Odyssey* was then on the composer's mind, for he was seriously considering a film project suggested by Michael Powell earlier in the year (twelve minutes of music for $12,000, to be ready by January 1954) dealing with the subject. Stravinsky was hoping that Dylan Thomas would provide the libretto for the film that would be "a kind of masque," remarked the composer. Similarly, a year earlier he was approached by Simon Harcourt-Smith about setting the *Odyssey* to a film script; but in both cases, as with so many other film proposals, nothing came of the project.

19. In a 30 January 1954 interview for the New Orleans *Times-Picayune,* Stravinsky remarked, "Movements of all sorts may be introduced into the dance, but on the condition that the canons of the dance and its immutable laws be respected. . . . Well, choreographers who respect these principles have become rare. I proposed to George Balanchine . . . that he give me carte blanche to do a new ballet (*Agon*) for them. . . . I told him that he had done so well in adjusting dances to symphonies that I would like to write a special symphony with the dance in mind. It is to be a dancing symphony." John Taras, "Stravinsky on Art and Artists," *Dance Magazine,* 55/4 (April 1981): 65.

20. Stephen Walsh, *The Music of Stravinsky* (Oxford: Clarendon, 1988), 228.

21. Ibid., 228. Eliot and Stravinsky met in December 1956, although they knew the other's work long before then. Eliot was acquainted with dance as early as the 1920s, and the composer frequently quoted Eliot's writings during the 1940s. Several scholars have discussed the correlation between *The Rite of Spring* and *The Waste Land.* See, for example Nancy Hargrove, "The Great Parade: Cocteau, Picasso, Satie, Massine, Diaghilev—and T. S. Eliot," *Mosaic* 31/1 (March 1998): 83–106. The composer and Eliot also discussed another possible collaboration in the late 1950s (leading eventually to *The Flood*), but Eliot withdrew. In 1962, at Eliot's suggestion, Stravinsky composed a twelve-tone anthem to Part IV of the poet's *Four Quartets,* dedicating the score to Eliot.

22. Robert Craft, *Moment of Existence,* 279.

23. My thanks to Michael Arnush, professor of classics at Skidmore College, for allowing me to reprint his explanation.

24. Igor Stravinsky and Robert Craft, *Expositions and Developments* (Rpt. Berkeley: University of California Press, 1981), 37.

25. Stravinsky also inserted an asterisk after he filled in the title. At the bottom of the page, also in a handwritten note, he writes the translation as "contest." It is likely that the title was decided, with Balanchine's approval, during the New York City Ballet's stay in Los Angeles that month. The Greek title mystified many. In April 1957, the composer received a cable from *Harper's Bazaar* in which the work was constantly referred to as "*Agony.*" Stravinsky responded with the correction, suggesting that the best description of the work was "A Ballet Suite for 12 Dancers." Balanchine was the first to caution that too much could be made by defining the ballet simply as a contest. "It is less a struggle or contest than a measured construction in space, demonstrated by moving bodies set to

certain patterns or sequences in rhythm and melody with multiple ingenuities," as he wrote for the opening night's program booklet.

26. See T. S. Eliot, "The Beating of the Drum," *The Nation and the Athenaeum,* October 1923: 11–12.

27. Kirstein's letter has been reprinted in various sources. Here again, as with all of Kirstein's correspondence, Stravinsky retained a copy (now in the Sacher Stiftung) in his private papers.

Chapter 10: The Evolution of *Agon's* Musical Structure

Epigraph: Igor Stravinsky and Robert Craft, *Conversations with Igor Stravinsky* (Rpt. Berkeley: University of California Press, 1980), 25.

1. Robert Garis, *Following Balanchine* (New Haven: Yale University Press, 1995), 82.

2. François de Lauze, *Apologie de la danse, 1623: A Treatise of Instruction and Deportment,* trans., introd. and notes Joan Wildeblood (London: F. Muller, 1952) (all quotations are taken from Stravinsky's personal copy, located in the Sacher Stiftung); Betty Bang Mather, *Dance Rhythms of the French Baroque* (Bloomington: Indiana University Press, 1987), 8.

3. Mather, *Dance Rhythms of the French Baroque,* 11 and 94.

4. George Balanchine and Francis Mason, *101 Stories of the Great Ballets* (New York: Doubleday, 1975), 2; Lincoln Kirstein, "The Position of Balanchine," *Salmagundi,* 33–34 (Spring–Summer 1976): 214.

5. As mentioned earlier, all of Kirstein's unexpurgated letters to Stravinsky are held in the Sacher Stiftung. Edited versions, including this one, appear in Robert Craft, *Stravinsky: Selected Correspondence,* vol. 1 (New York: Knopf, 1982), 287.

6. The composer's most absurd canard asserted that *Rite of Spring* did not employ preexisting folk tunes when the whole of the 1913 ballet grows out of one familiar tune after another. See Richard Taruskin's by now classic debunking article, "Russian Folk Melodies in *The Rite of Spring," Journal of the American Musicological Society* 33 (1980): 501–43.

7. Not only would Stravinsky draw the ballet's critical opening measures from this initial, relatively formless line by pruning its shape considerably, he would later link the passage cohesively to the Pas de quatre closing passage by using the latter part of the sketch's melodic material. Compare, for example, the sketch with mm. 46–60, wherein the identical rhythmic figuration is employed.

8. Kirstein offers a similar account of the bransle's history, suggesting that the dance was "linked to the satyr-dance of 'Sikinnis.' They were also know as 'Brawls'; thus our word for rough-house." He also categorizes specific bransles, as did Wildeblood. The *Bransle gais* was danced by the "young marrieds," and the Burgundy Bransles were danced by "youths and maidens . . . from side to side in double-time, like the others, only faster." Lincoln Kirstein, *Dance: A Short History of Classic Theatrical Dancing* (Princeton: Dance Horizons Princeton Book, 1987), 159. All of chapter 9, "The Ballet Comique and the Ballet de Cour" (pp. 148–67), proves instructive in understanding the courtly backdrop of *Agon's* first and second Pas de trois. Finally, the grouping of bransles into a suite (consisting of four, five, or more dances) was a common occurrence as early as the sixteenth century.

9. Mather, *Dance Rhythms of the French Baroque,* 93.

10. Excerpted from Mersenne's *Harmonie universelle, contenant la théorie et la pratique de la musique* (1636). The translation by Roger E. Chapman is included in Mather, *Dance Rhythms of the French Baroque,* 37.

11. Poitou was a province in France. The Bransle de Poitou eventually led to the establishment of the minuet as the most popular dance in the court of Louis XIV. Supposedly Stravinsky did not know Thoinot Arbeau's *Orchésographie* while writing *Agon,* though Kirstein called it to the composer's attention in his 31 August letter. Still both de Lauze and Mersenne were thoroughly familiar with Arbeau's cornerstone work and their reliance is reflected in the *Apologie.* Even Mersenne's Bransle de Poitou melody, as reprinted in the copy Stravinsky studied, draws its melodic shape from the notated ligature included in *Orchésographie.*

12. The sketch is reprinted in Vera Stravinsky and Robert Craft, *Stravinsky in Pictures and Documents* (New York: Simon and Schuster, 1978), 429. Vera Stravinsky's comments were made in an interview to Genevieve Oswald in an audiotape recorded on 14 June 1976 held by the Jerome Robbins Dance Division of the New York Public Library for the Performing Arts.

13. Balanchine's description appears in Balanchine and Francis Mason, *101 Stories of the Great Ballets* (New York: Doubleday, 1989), 3.

14. For the most thorough discussion of Stravinsky's sketches for *Agon* and other works from this period, see Susannah Tucker, "Stravinsky and His Sketches: The Composing of *Agon* and Other Serial Works of the 1950s," Ph.D. diss., Oxford University, 1992.

15. Of the numerous descriptions of this amazing document, Irene Alm's, in "Stravinsky, Balanchine, and *Agon:* An Analysis Based on the Collaborative Process," *Journal of Musicology* 7/2 (Spring 1989): 254–69, is the most complete. Alm includes a facsimile of the document (housed in the Sacher Stiftung) as well as her own transcription of Stravinsky's annotations. The document was originally included as a centerfold in the New York City Ballet's 1982 Stravinsky Centennial program. A more recent, beautiful reproduction is included in *Tributes: Celebrating Fifty Years of New York City Ballet,* ed. Christopher Ramsey (New York: William Morrow, 1998), 57.

16. For example, Stravinsky made notes on the lower part of one sheet, then, dissatisfied, ripped it from the original page (the tear marks match), wrote a new version, and stapled it to the original. One need only consult the discarded section to trace his and Balanchine's earlier thoughts. Another discarded portion of a page was torn from the bottom of the page that Alm and others have reproduced in facsimile.

17. Stravinsky had been in touch with Alessandro Piovesan, director of the Biennale di Venzia, much earlier. He wrote to Piovesan a month before he requested his meeting with Kirstein and Balanchine suggesting that if Venice wanted a work before his ballet was completed, the festival would have to make him an ironclad offer immediately: "I will not decide anything until I receive the commission and to be frank commission and contract will have to be forthcoming before I complete my ballet" (unpublished letter of 5 November 1954, Sacher Stiftung). At the time, the composer indicated to Piovesan that *Agon* would premiere in 1955. Eventually, Stravinsky did accept a commission for what

would become the *Canticum Sacrum,* premiered in September 1956 in Venice, necessitating a further delay in the completion of *Agon.*

18. See Lawrence Sherr, "The Genesis of *Agon:* Stravinsky, Balanchine, and the New York City Ballet," D.M.A. diss., University of Illinois, 1988. The music that could not be "rushed" was that for the Pas de deux, the Four Duos, and the Four Trios.

19. Pitch rotation, briefly stated, amounts to switching the precise placement of an individual note in a series each time that it appears, thus generating different orderings of the original motive. But the reordering is rigorous. For example, in a four-note series, the pitches "c-d-g-a" say, the first transformation would be "d-g-a-c," the second reordering "a-c-d-g," and so on, each pitch shifting one position in each subsequent rotation.

20. Performance times vary. Stravinsky's original 18 June 1957 recording with the Los Angeles Festival Symphony Orchestra (which Balanchine heard) is just under twenty-four minutes, as is the more recent 1996 recording of the ballet by Michael Tilson Thomas and the London Symphony Orchestra (BMG Classics, CD 09026-68865-2).

21. Once Stravinsky had worked out this passage, he returned to the beginning of the piece and wrote music based upon this inversion. Musicians will also notice that the row is octatonic, that is, a symmetrical scale that alternates whole steps and half steps, with the exception of the last two notes. Indeed, most of the materials for *Agon* are based upon such familiar Stravinskyan symmetrical sets.

22. Balanchine recapitulates the same choreography at the end of the ballet to match Stravinsky's returning music. Often, but not always, Balanchine fashioned new choreography or at least a modification of earlier choreography for recurring music. Here, however, the need to bring closure to the ballet is especially important, given all the internal stylistic diversity, a factor the choreographer no doubt took into consideration—especially since the returning music might not have been recognized as such with its foreign sound. The returning dance was surely intended to help clarify the connection.

23. Music analysts will note that the composer uses the I-9 form of the hexachord as the middle iteration, and that both overlap and rotation are employed in linking the hexachord's three appearances. Stravinsky uses other forms of the hexachord, as well as transpositions, throughout the remainder of the Bransle, often assigning a specific hexachord to a specific orchestral color. For example, the trombones in measures 284–86 sound the inversional form of the original hexachord. Stravinsky took the time in his sketches to mark all the forms.

24. Stravinsky marked them "1st hexachord and 2nd hexachord" in his score and added other analytic annotations as well; for example, he labeled one form "I.O. transposed," indicating that he had taken the original pitches and inverted and transposed them to a new pitch level.

25. Stravinsky and Craft, *Conversations with Igor Stravinsky,* 25.

Chapter 11: Choreography or Carpentry?

Epigraph: George Balanchine, "A Word from George Balanchine," *New York City Ballet Playbill,* 25 November 1957.

1. Nathan Milstein and Solomon Volkov, *From Russia to the West* (New York: Henry Holt, 1990), 129, 243. In his memoir, Milstein includes two pertinent chapters: "Stravinsky and His Interpreters" and "My Friend George Balanchine," both offering a personal glimpse into their relationships that is not found elsewhere.

2. Leon Barzin conducted the New York performances—one of the few major premieres that the composer did not conduct himself. Stravinsky's telegram to Ishlon refers to *Agon's* preview performance on 27 November for the March of Dimes benefit, as a tribute to Le Clercq. In a letter written ten days earlier, Balanchine told Elsa Maxwell that he and Stravinsky were giving the gold Sibelius medal (which the composer had received) to the Polio Foundation. "The whole purpose of my giving it to the Polio Foundation was raising additional money, as the medal is worth $700 in gold. My thought was of auctioning it at the ball after the *Agon* performance." HTC, Correspondence, 12/15. There may have been other reasons, perhaps dealing with funding, why the composer did not attend either the preview or official premiere. He had been upset with Kirstein for several months. In a note to his attorney on 17 August, the composer wrote, "As for Lincoln, I am very disappointed and even not a little humiliated that the Stravinsky Festival has dwindled to nothing. I do not even have a concrete proposition or a date for my ballet [*Agon*]. And it appears from Lincoln's last letter that he has canceled the St. Thomas church concert without some [*sic*] much as advising me first. . . . I do not blame Lincoln for not being able to find the money, but for his very peculiar actions to ourselfs [*sic*] who are his old and dear friends." And a few weeks later from Venice, Stravinsky again wrote to his attorney: "I have the bitter impression that *Agon* will not be performed in the City Center this season. Now even Balanchine keeps silent. May I ask you to let me know what is there going on?" When Stravinsky returned from Europe in late October, surely he was eager to get back to Los Angeles and continue working on his new composition, *Threni*. Still, it is probable that the composer would have remained in New York long enough to attend the premiere had there not been some misunderstanding with Kirstein. In a letter written the day after the opening night performance, a friend wrote to Stravinsky, "Even Lincoln Kirstein appeared quite repentful at the performance because I overheard several people ask why you weren't there and he became very uncomfortable in attempting to explain it away. . . . You and Balanchine would have been hoisted up to the crowd's shoulders like football heroes if you had been there." All these letters and cables are held by the Sacher Stiftung.

3. Kirstein's comments are especially worth consulting since he goes on to discuss Renato Poggioli's *Theory of the Avant-Garde (1962–68)* regarding "Agonism" and "Futurism." See Kirstein, *Four Centuries of Ballet* (New York: Dover, 1984), 242–43. (This is a reprint of the author's *Movement and Metaphor,* originally published in 1970 by Praeger.) For Terry's and Crisp's reviews see Nancy Reynolds, *Repertory in Review* (New York: Dial, 1977), 182 ff.

4. Denby's remarks are from "Three Sides of *Agon*." A. V. Coton's review of the ballet is reprinted in *Writings on Dance, 1938–68* (London: Dance Books, 1975), 126. Balanchine's reference to *Agon* as a thinking machine was first mentioned in "A Note from George Balanchine," included in the opening night program booklet. Stravinsky retained a copy in his archives.

5. See Hayden's interview in Francis Mason, *I Remember Balanchine* (New York: Doubleday, 1991), 359.

6. Balanchine was always sensitive to colors and contrasts. When he agreed to choreograph sections of Samuel Goldwyn's 1952 film *Hans Christian Andersen,* starring the red-haired Moira Shearer, he wrote to Goldwyn that the right male partner had to be found in terms of skin color. In responding to one suggestion the producer offered, Balanchine replied, "It seems to me that his coloring is not suited to Moira's, as he is rather pale, and in technicolor, will not stand out sufficiently against Moira's red hair." HTC, letter of 24 July 1951, Correspondence, 19/7. See Mason, *I Remember Balanchine,* for Mitchell's remarks (395). If the duet caused a stir in the United States during those racially strained times, the Soviet press criticized it even more intensely in 1962 during City Ballet's first tour of the Soviet Union. As Kirstein recalls in his *Thirty Years: Lincoln Kirstein's the New York City Ballet* (New York: Knopf, 1978), 171, "In the Muscovite press . . . Balanchine's expression of Stravinsky's mutations of Mersenne and de Lauze's Renaissance dances was interpreted as a Negro slave's submission to the tyranny of an ardent white mistress."

7. See Horosko's interview in Lawrence Sherr, "The Genesis of *Agon:* Stravinsky, Balanchine, and the New York City Ballet," D.M.A. diss., University of Illinois, 1988, pp. 86–87. Sherr's thesis is particularly useful because his interviews of several dancers do not appear elsewhere.

8. Sally Banes, *Dancing Women: Female Bodies on Stage* (London: Routledge, 1998), 195.

9. Hayden's memories were recounted for a 1983 KFAC Los Angeles radio interview, broadcast as a memorial shortly after Balanchine's death. For a recent description of *Agon* from one who attended several rehearsals of the 1957 premiere, see Nancy Goldner, "*Agon* as Icon," *Dance Now* 10/2 (Summer 2001). Goldner recalls that at one rehearsal, "Balanchine and Stravinsky spent more time adjusting a metronome than anything else. And at the other one, Stravinsky watched their mathematical delicacy unfold with a smile on his face" (31).

10. See Sherr, "Genesis of *Agon,*" 71, for Walczak's remarks. For Adams's comments, see Robert Tracy with Sharon Delano, *Balanchine's Ballerinas: Conversations with the Muses* (New York: Linden Press/Simon and Schuster, 1983), 123–24.

11. Davidova, in Mason, *I Remember Balanchine,* 134.

12. Quoted in Richard Buckle, *George Balanchine: Ballet Master* (New York: Random House, 1988), 212–13.

13. Bernard Taper, *Balanchine: A Biography* (Berkeley: University of California Press, 1996), 264–71. Not only does Taper include several of Martha Swope's now classic photos of the Stravinsky-Balanchine working session, but his accompanying commentary is also pertinent.

14. Robert Garis, *Following Balanchine* (New Haven: Yale University Press, 1995), 118; Arlene Croce, "The Spelling of *Agon,*" *New Yorker,* 12 July 1993: 84; Stephanie Jordan, "*Agon:* A Musical/Choreographic Analysis," *Dance Research Journal,* 25/2 (Fall 1993): 1–12. Also see Jordan's more recent, insightful discussion of the ballet in *Moving Music* (London: Dance Books, 2000), 151–67.

15. *The Balanchine Celebration, Part Two* videotape was taken from the *Dance in America* se-

ries, Nonesuch 40190-3. The performance was taped in 1993. The dancers include: first Pas de trois, Peter Boal, Zippora Karz, Kathleen Tracey; second Pas de trois, Albert Evans, Arch Higgens, Wendy Whelan; Pas de deux, Darcey Bussell and Lindsay Fischer. A certain caution must be noted: there are several other videotapes (both commercial and in various repositories) incorporating choreographic interpretations that differ, sometimes in minor but at times in more substantive ways. Those interested in viewing an alternative performance should see *Peter Martins: A Dancer,* a 1979 taping available through the Kultur Profile Series, no. 1118, in which Martins and Suzanne Farrell dance *Agon*'s Pas de deux, also discussed here.

16. Denby, "Three Sides of *Agon*," 266. Todd Bolender, who first danced the Saraband-Step, remarked in a spring 2001 interview with me that Balanchine intentionally took everything and purposely angled it.

17. Jordan, "*Agon,*" 8. For an important study of other such choreomusical analyses, see Robynn Stillwell, "Stravinsky and Balanchine: A Musico-Choreographic Analysis of *Agon,*" Ph.D. diss., University of Michigan, 1994.

18. Jordan, "*Agon,*" 9.

19. The dancers' hand gestures define each of the individual beats in this 9/4 measure. It should be noted, however, that these articulated hand movements changed over the years. I wish to thank Stephanie Jordan for calling this to my attention.

20. Don McDonagh, *George Balanchine* (Boston: Twayne, 1983), 125; Banes, *Dancing Women,* 200.

21. See Mark Richardson's Ph.D. dissertation, "Igor Stravinsky's *Agon* (1953–57): Pitch-Related Processes in the Serial Movements and Rhythm in the Named Dance Movements Described in De Lauze's *Apologie de la danse* (1623)," Florida State University, 1996. Richardson's study is easily the finest, most comprehensive attempt to deal with the composer's integration of pitch and rhythm. Throughout, the author puts forth cogent arguments to explain Stravinsky's sometimes nearly impenetrable transformation of Mersenne's models. In the Bransle Simple, Richardson suggests that each *L-S* component is lengthened by Stravinsky to represent longer phrase periods. For example, the first *L* of Mersenne equals the nine measures of Stravinsky's *A* section (mm. 279–87), the next two *SS* sections of Mersenne equal the *B* section of Stravinsky's setting (mm. 288–92 and mm. 293–97), etc. See pp. 199–201.

22. Banes, *Dancing Women,* 201; Jordan, "*Agon,*" 3.

23. Quoted in Sherr, "Genesis of *Agon,*" 71.

24. Banes, *Dancing Women,* 201.

25. Ibid., 202.

26. For an excellent discussion (including several photographs) tracing the choreographic changes in the ballet over its forty-plus year history, see Leigh Witchel, "Four Decades of *Agon,*" *Ballet Review,* 25/3 (Fall 1997): 53–78.

27. Banes, *Dancing Women,* 203.

28. Jordan, "*Agon,*" 9.

29. For musicians, the pitches, when ordered, are 0,1,3,4, or Forte's 4-3, a symmetrical, octatonic recurring segmentation.

Chapter 12: Television, *The Flood,* and Beyond

1. The telecast was never released commercially; however the thirty-five-millimeter black-and-white film is preserved in several libraries, including the Jerome Robbins Dance Division of the New York Public Library for the Performing Arts. For a more detailed study of the work's historical context, see my *Stravinsky Inside Out* (New Haven: Yale University Press, 2001).

2. In 1953 Balanchine choreographed the opera's Shepherds' Dance for a production in Florence, conducted by Leopold Stokowski.

3. The first interview, with Robert Lewis Shayon, was given in *Saturday Review,* 16 June 1962. The second was published two weeks later in the 30 June issue.

4. *Christopher Isherwood, Diaries, Volume 1 (1939–1960),* ed. Katherine Bucknell (London: Harper-Collins, 1996), 847.

5. Through the 1960s Balanchine made no secret of his preference for Canadian rather than American televising of ballet. He found the cameramen more sensitive to angles that would highlight the dancer's movement and more willing to stay with a sequence until Balanchine was satisfied. He also expressed his preference for filmed ballet for television rather than live performances, albeit Canadian productions were for the most part live presentations.

6. Brian Rose, *Television and the Performing Arts* (New York: Greenwood, 1986), 38–39.

7. See Edward Villella with Larry Kaplan, *Prodigal Son* (New York: Simon and Schuster, 1992), in which Villella speaks in some detail about his interactions with the medium. In a 1979 interview with Balanchine, Don McDonagh remembers that the choreographer often turned down opportunities to present his company on *The Ed Sullivan Hour* and other nationally known programs. "He didn't like the way that the camera made the dancers' noses and feet long and their legs short," wrote McDonagh in his biography *George Balanchine* (Boston: Twayne, 1983), 118.

8. George Balanchine and Bernard Taper, "Television and Ballet," in *The Eighth Art: Twenty-Three Views of Television Today* (New York: Holt, Rinehart and Winston, 1962), 118. The choreographer almost always turned down persistent requests from cinematographers and later videographers to film his ballets either in rehearsal or in performance (except for the wonderful collection of films held by the Jerome Robbins Dance Division of the New York Public Library for the Performing Arts, and even there permission is required to view these treasured films for educational rather than commercial purposes). He did allow Peter Martins and Suzanne Farrell to dance the Tchaikovsky *Pas de Deux* for Twentieth-Century Fox's 1976 film *The Turning Point,* waiving his own fee and asking instead for a donation to the School of American Ballet.

9. See Arthur Todd, "What Went Wrong," in *Dance Magazine* 36 (August 1962). This informative article includes Martha Swopes's wonderful photographs shot during the taping. Todd sent his article to Stravinsky on 20 August, reporting to Stravinsky that he spent seventeen hours in the CBS Studio observing Balanchine choreographing the various passages.

10. Balanchine and Taper, 120–21.

11. See Lincoln Kirstein, *Thirty Years: Lincoln Kirstein's the New York City Ballet* (New York: Knopf, 1978), 277. The composer's publisher, Boosey and Hawkes, was unaware that Stravinsky was already in the process of negotiating a television contract. In a 5 July 1960 letter, Ernst Roth of Boosey and Hawkes wrote to the composer: "I was profoundly shocked [with] the terms of an agreement you intend to make with some people called Sextant who are entirely unknown to me. . . . I implore you not to sell your youngest child into slavery." The unpublished letter is held in the Sacher archives.

12. See Robert Craft, *Present Perspectives* (New York: Knopf, 1984), 240. Craft notes that Stravinsky "pasted several pages of my notes to him" into the manuscript of *The Flood* dealing with "technical questions as well as musical symbolisms."

13. Todd, "What Went Wrong," 40. By the time Balanchine met with Stravinsky, the composer had already developed his own ideas about staging. In his *Chronicle of a Friendship* (Nashville: Vanderbilt, 1994), 287, Craft reports that two months before the composer and choreographer sat down to make their final decisions, Stravinsky spoke with Auden about the ballet, reporting his vision of how the flood should be shot: "I do not want waves, or any back and forth movement. I have an idea instead for a single dancer turning this way and that and bobbing like a piece of wood, always in the same place." As for the sound recording, Leonard Bernstein taped a few excerpts in New York. Stravinsky had telegraphed Bernstein in early April, "Would you lunch with me before or after the screening [on May 5]? Another great favor I have to ask is could you please record three snippets John McClure [of Columbia Broadcasting] has from *The Flood.*"

14. The complete, unedited version of this important letter is held in the Sacher Stiftung.

15. Unpublished letter to Graff, 21 February 1962. The sketches, by Rouben Ter-Arutunian, are also in the Sacher Stiftung. Todd records Ter-Arutunian's comments about his designs in "What Went Wrong": "This work is a positive statement of spirituality." "I used masks for Noah and his family . . . because he was to be a spectacular Noah and not the way an actor or dancer would portray him."

16. Walter Terry's 15 June 1962 review of *The Flood* for the *Herald-Tribune* is reprinted in Mark Wentik, ed., *I Was There* (New York: Marcel Dekker, 1978), 417–18.

17. The severity of the composer's bruises became apparent in a 24 June telegram that he wired to the New York *Herald-Tribune,* which printed it. The composer was retaliating for a damaging review by the paper's critic, Paul Henry Lang—a longtime Stravinsky nemesis. Among several unjust swipes, Lang criticized "the junior high school quality" of the work's prologue. Stravinsky responded (with Craft's help, one suspects) that Lang's review was "entirely stupid and suppurating with gratuitous malice. The only blight on my eightieth birthday is the realization my age will probably keep me from celebrating the funeral of your senile music columnist."

18. Balanchine's comments originally appeared in Balanchine and Taper, "Television and Ballet," and are reprinted in Bernard Taper, *Balanchine: A Biography* (Berkeley: University of California Press, 1996), 246.

19. Jack Gould, "Noah Submerged—Program Shows a Lack of Cooperation Between TV and Leaders in Arts" (review of *The Flood*), *New York Times,* 24 June 1962.

20. Richard Franko Goldman, "Current Chronicle," *Musical Quarterly,* 48 (October 1962), 516.

21. Igor Stravinsky, *Themes and Conclusions* (Rpt. Berkeley: University of California Press, 1972), 106.

22. The 1982 restaging was made possible through a gift from the Gerald and May Ellen Ritter Memorial Fund. On 7 June 1982, Balanchine wrote to the foundation, "I have for sometime wanted to stage this work for the New York City Ballet, not being completely satisfied that this wonderful score was presented well by CBS-TV production in 1962." HTC, Correspondence, 14/3.

23. Don Daniels, "Stravinsky III," *Ballet Review*, 10/3 (Fall 1982), 46. To some extent Daniels's suggestion was realized in a bizarre filming of the work, adapted in 1985. Designed and directed by Jaap Drupsteen and produced by NOS-TV and the Stiftung Muzt in Amsterdam, the videotape is now commercially distributed through NVC Arts International. This Dutch production, with a psychedelic, computer-generated light show animating the work in vivid graphic images, actually employs the original 1962 "soundtrack" of the Columbia Symphony Orchestra and Chorus.

24. See Kirstein, *Thirty Years*, 184, for his statement about the *Fanfare*. His copy of the telegram to Stravinsky is held in HTC, Correspondence, 20/9.

25. For a description of this odd marriage of Balanchine's and Graham's choreographic approaches—or rather "confrontation," as the author puts it—see Roger Copeland, "Backlash Against Balanchine," *Choreography and Dance*, 3/3 (1993): 3–5. Balanchine not only prepared a piano reduction of Webern's Symphony, Opus 21, as part of *Episodes*, but he also prepared a short score in which he plotted the choreography right on the music score itself—quite unusual for him, but very informative. He uses, for example, "J = Jonathan Watts" and "V = Violette Verdy" to mark their entrances. Moreover, he includes such notations as "boys walking turns," "walking back [and] forth," as well as specific positions and gestures that he incorporates—promenade, arabesque, entrechats, and so on.

26. Richard Buckle, *George Balanchine* (New York: Random House, 1988), 229. Craft reports that Balanchine consulted him as early as May 1960, only a month or so after the composition was completed: "Balanchine comes to my room at the Gladstone and I go over the *Monumentum* with him, convincing him to choreograph it." *Chronicle of a Friendship*, 3 May entry, 219.

27. Suzanne Farrell, with Toni Bentley, *Holding On to the Air* (New York: Summit, 1990), 103.

28. The other two works were Darius Milhaud's *Creation of the World*, prepared by Todd Bolender, and Francis Poulenc's *Les Biches*, choreographed by Francisco Moncion.

29. Stravinsky encouraged Balanchine to participate in the tribute, as revealed in an unpublished 31 January 1966 handwritten letter held in the Harvard Theatre Collection. "Dear George, I'm sending you Lukas' letter to me which speaks for itself. Let me add only that I also would be very pleased if this big effort built around me and my work would involve you also." The note was sent to Balanchine three days after Stravinsky received Foss's 28 January letter in which Foss relates that Balanchine is indeed eager to create a ballet "for one or two dancers (Susan [*sic*] Farrell) to one of your chamber works." Foss suggested specific compositions that Stravinsky might like to have choreographed, though Balanchine had his own ideas. See HTC, Correspondence, 4/2.

30. Doris Hering, "Let's Talk About Ballet," *Dance Magazine*, 41/3 (March 1967): 57. Marcia

Marks's September 1966 review for the same journal (pp. 32–34) was also unkind, both finding faults with Balanchine's matching of movement to Stravinsky's "low-keyed lament" *Elégie* and taking Farrell to task in *Ragtime* for falling back on "some Govrinesque habits she's been displaying of late." For a pictorial comparison of the two versions of the dance (the 1960 performance with Diana Adams and Bill Carter danced in front of the riverboat drop with Karinska's velvet costumes, and the 1967 staging with Suzanne Farrell and Arthur Mitchell), see Nancy Reynolds, *Repertory in Review* (New York: Dial, 1977), 211 and 247.

31. Igor Stravinsky, *An Autobiography* (Rpt. New York: Norton, 1998), 78.

32. Stravinsky's friend the writer Stephen Spender reported that in a conversation with Balanchine during the Hamburg stay, the choreographer mentioned that Stravinsky's conducting of certain sections of the *Agon* performance were becoming difficult to follow because the composer was aging. "It's a matter of his arm," Balanchine commented. "He begins quite right. The mind knows. But the muscles do not quite function. So he begins to get slow. It is a question of sickness, the muscles of the right side. But if one understands one can adjust oneself." Quoted in John Goldsmith, ed., *Stephen Spender: Journals, 1939–1983* (New York: Random House, 1986), 238.

33. Stravinsky composed both works at about the same time. For an insight into Stravinsky's "recomposition" of the Gesualdo madrigals in conjunction with *Movements,* see Glenn Watkins, "The Canon and Stravinsky's Late Style," in *Confronting Stravinsky,* ed. Jann Pasler (Berkeley: University of California Press, 1986), especially pp. 234–35. *Movements* premiered on 10 January 1960 in New York with Stravinsky conducting. On the same program, notably, Craft conducted several Renaissance compositions, including some of Gesualdo's music. Both *Monumentum* and *Movements* were programmed together on orchestral programs before Balanchine coupled the two ballets.

34. See Arlene Croce and George Dorris, "An Interview with Gordon Boelzner," *Ballet Review,* 3/4 (1970): 57. As Boelzner observed, "Stravinsky was writing shorthand rhythmic phrases; that is, they're not what you'd call scannable, really, to the ear. But they could be made scannable without the dreariness of following a score because Balanchine can visually clarify the meter."

35. Igor Stravinsky, *Themes and Conclusions* (Rpt. Berkeley: University of California Press, 1982), 34. But alas, whether Stravinsky himself really formulated this statement must be questioned. Musicologists have come to question the validity of Stravinsky's statements in the last few "conversation" books. Stravinsky himself admitted that by the time *Themes and Conclusions* was compiled, he had lost interest in the series of books he and Craft had undertaken years earlier.

36. Robert Garis, *Following Balanchine* (New Haven: Yale University Press, 1995), 158.

37. As reprinted in Reynolds, *Repertory in Review,* 220. See Reynolds for several important reviews of the work, including one by Allen Hughes, whose enthusiasm bubbled over: "Only prudence keeps me from saying outright that I think it as nearly perfect a work of dance art as I have ever seen."

38. Farrell, *Holding On to the Air,* 78

39. For those who might be slightly puzzled by the filmed segment included in the Palmer

clip, it should be noted that while *Movements* is shown being rehearsed, it is the music of Stravinsky's *Variations* that is being played.

40. Copies of the exchanges between Nabokov and Balanchine are found in HTC, Correspondence, 4/7. According to other materials found among these letters, Francis Mason recalls that Nabokov and Balanchine were interested in making a ballet on the Don Quixote theme since the late 1940s.

41. The short score—meaning the first complete version of the 1964 work in Stravinsky's own hand before being orchestrated—is held in HTC, Scores, 9/16. In the catalogue that accompanied the Balanchine materials acquired by the Harvard Theatre Collection, the manuscript is mistakenly described as Balanchine's own piano reduction; but there is no question that this is the original Stravinsky manuscript. The composer had sent a tape recording of the composition to Balanchine, who wished to use the work for a ballet. It is likely that he also sent along this manuscript so that the choreographer could follow the score and study the work at the piano.

42. In some unreleased film footage shot by CBS in Chicago at the April 1965 premiere, the composer is shown in his hotel room and asked to discuss how he composed his newest work. He obliges by displaying the sketchbook for his "precompositional ideas" (his term), which include various serial rows and charts that he plotted before he actually started to write. Yet in almost the same breath, he declares that his first idea for the work was absolutely not a premeditatively constructed row but rather a pure melody, which he only later discovered, almost coincidentally, had twelve different notes. He makes it clear that he was not controlled abstractly by dodecaphonic matrices: "The melody was first, then came the charts." He flips through several pages of the sketchbook for the camera, commenting as he goes, and making certain that viewers realize they are watching the actual creation of the work right before their eyes. Also see Farrell, *Holding On to the Air*, 150.

43. *Rubies* was first danced by Patricia McBride, Edward Villella, Patricia Neary, and a cast of eight women and four men. So popular was the ballet in showcasing the talents of his dancers that several casts danced the work, including Gelsey Kirkland, Paul Mejia, Karin von Aroldingen, and Mikhail Baryshnikov, who danced the male solo during the late 1970s. *Rubies* was telecast several times in subsequent years on both NBC and the PBS *Dance in America* series. In February 1979 Baryshnikov and Heather Watts danced the pas de deux at the White House for a performance entitled "An Afternoon with Mikhail Baryshnikov" sponsored by President and Mrs. Jimmy Carter (Balanchine did not attend).

44. For the most perceptive description of the choreography, see Clive Barnes's 14 April 1967 review in the *New York Times*, parts of which are reprinted in Reynolds, *Repertory in Review*, 248. And for a brief but informative musical-choreographic analysis, see Stephanie Jordan, "Music Puts a Time Corset on the Dance," *Dance Chronicle* 16/3 (1993): 313–16. See also Stravinsky, *Autobiography*, 159. The composer played the work often, and by 1931, only two years after its premiere, more than twenty performances had been given. A few years later the composer introduced his son Soulima to the public as the soloist, while Stravinsky himself conducted. In his 1977 interview with Thor E. Wood (the au-

diotape is held by the Jerome Robbins Dance Division of the New York Public Library for the Performing Arts), Soulima claimed that the compositional ideas for the *Capriccio* are attributable to Soulima's constant practicing in 1928 of Carl Maria von Weber's 1821 *Konzertstücke*—a piece with pianistic idioms conspicuously similar to Stravinsky's piano work.

45. Edward Villella, *Prodigal Son* (New York: Simon and Schuster, 1992), 191–92.

46. With choreography by Jerome Robbins, the work was presented again as the closing work of the 1972 Stravinsky Festival. Reynolds reports that King's death, an inspiration for many, was the catalyst that first started Mitchell thinking about establishing what became the first black classical ballet company, in Harlem—which of course continues successfully today as the Dance Theatre of Harlem. Stravinsky, ill but quarrelsome as ever, read the 3 May review in which the statement appears: "The company's principal conductor, Robert Irving, implacable as he continued with his task of molding *this difficult Stravinsky score*" (underlined by Stravinsky). In the copy of the review he retained in his unpublished papers, the composer added, "not more than any of my new scores!"

47. Unpublished note to Stravinsky, Paul Sacher Stiftung, 14 May 1968, from Edward Bigelow.

48. Earlier, in 1964, a story was released suggesting that Balanchine was arranging a new ballet to fourteen "new" songs of Gershwin. As Balanchine wrote to Ira Gershwin, who suggested the idea, on 4 March of that year, he was indeed considering such a project but "it is impossible to make a hurried arrangement of the music, because the 14 songs are short and there must be some logic as to the musical form of the piece as a whole. . . . As you know, I have always been interested in doing a ballet to George's music . . . [but] . . . I feel it would be wrong to present his music incorrectly, and I really do not think these songs will lend themselves to a cohesive arrangement, because they are so individual and fragmentary. So I have decided not to use the music for a ballet." Ira Gershwin responded on 13 March, expressing his understanding of Balanchine's decision, though explaining that a "cohesive ballet" was not what he had in mind. "What I had in mind . . . was a group of short choreographic vignettes of New York. I'd make notes of a dozen-or-so tentative titles such as 'On the Staten Island Ferry,' 'Coney Island Carousel,' 'Standees at the Met,' 'New Show at the Guggenheim,' etc." HTC, Correspondence, 3/4.

Chapter 13: After Stravinsky

Epigraph: Remarks offered by Balanchine on the opening evening (6 March) of the 1972 Stravinsky Festival, reprinted in Nancy Goldner, *The Stravinsky Festival of the New York City Ballet* (New York: Eakins, 1973), 13–15.

1. Aaron Copland, "Stravinsky and Hindemith Premieres," *Modern Music* 9/2 (January–February 1932): 85–86.

2. Quoted in Bernard Taper, *Balanchine: A Biography* (Berkeley: University of California Press, 1996), 321.

3. Interview with Louis Botto, "Balanchine: Work in Progress," *Intellectual Digest* (June 1972), reprinted in *Dance as a Theatre Art,* ed. Selma J. Cohen (New York: Harper and Row, 1974), 188.

4. Ibid., 188.

5. Goldner, *Stravinsky Festival,* 229. Goldner's compilation of interviews, photographs, and complete tracing of the festival's history offers an indispensable record.

6. Ms. Horgan kindly shared this with me in a telephone conversation of 28 February 2000. *PAMTGG* was perhaps Balanchine's most maligned undertaking. Ironically, it unfolded onstage as Balanchine was already laying plans for the Stravinsky Festival, one of his greatest achievements. Moreover, it did so on 17 June, Stravinsky's birthday (although after 1900 the composer celebrated his birthday on 18 June, the date on which the Stravinsky Festival began a year later).

7. Lincoln Kirstein, *Thirty Years: Lincoln Kirstein's the New York City Ballet* (New York: Knopf, 1978), 214. "Our ambition," Kirstein continued, "was to display a panoply of Stravinsky's representative scores, some without staging; from first to last recognizing his entire range in one compact, monumental week."

8. The festival opened with an impromptu performance of a recently discovered scherzo from Stravinsky's long-lost 1903–4 Piano Sonata in F-sharp minor—so it was announced. But the attendees were actually listening to a completely different piece. The Balanchine Archive (HTC, Correspondence, 4/2) includes a glossy photo of the music that was performed that first evening, marked "New York City Ballet Stravinsky Festival June 18–25, 1972, Scherzo from the Lost Sonata." But in fact this is not the scherzo from the F-sharp minor sonata but rather an independent scherzo written even earlier, in 1902, which had also been recently discovered. This earlier, much less ambitious effort, is Stravinsky's first complete, extant piano piece, possibly written as an audition piece for a place in Rimsky-Korsakov's composition class.

9. Walter Terry, "Stravinsky's Ballets Revisited," originally appearing in the *Saturday Review,* 19 August 1972, and reprinted in *I Was There* (New York: Marcel Dekker, 1978), 607. Also see his 15 July article, "Balanchine's Ballet Tribute to Stravinsky," for a general summary of the Stravinsky Festival, also reprinted in *I Was There,* 605–6.

10. Slonimsky's review for the *Evening Gazette* is reprinted in Kirstein, *Thirty Years,* 223–24. During the 1962 tour *Agon,* predictably, evoked similar charges of impersonality. Soviet choreographer Rostislav Zakharov then described that ballet as "nearer to mathematics than to art. . . . This work being addressed to the brain says nothing to our heart." For a review of the 1962 performances in Russia, see Natalia Roslavleva, "A Lively Controversy on New York City Ballet Soviet Season," *Dancing Times,* 53/628 (January 1963): 229.

11. Francis Mason recorded the comments of McBride and Von Aroldingen in *I Remember Balanchine* (New York: Doubleday, 1991), 448 and 500, respectively.

12. Robert Garis, *Following Balanchine* (New Haven: Yale University Press, 1995), 209; Peter Martins, with Robert Cornfield, *Far from Denmark* (Boston: Little, Brown, 1982), 61.

13. Even before the 1972 festival, Balanchine choreographed two Stravinsky concertante scores during the 1960s: *Movements for Piano and Orchestra,* and *Rubies,* to the andante rapsodico movement of the 1929 *Capriccio* for piano and orchestra. So it is not surprising that Balanchine (who said he would prepare whatever scores the festival's choreographers passed over) felt comfortable in taking on three major concertante works.

14. See Francis Mason's interview of Mazzo in *I Remember Balanchine,* 526. Mary Ellen Moylan recalled that her first onstage appearance in New York was with Nicholas Magal-

lanes in Balanchine's 1942 *Pas de Trois for Piano and Two Dancers,* performed as part of a benefit for the Russian War Relief. "Theodore Chanler was the composer," remembered Moylan, "and he played the piano on stage. His presence was an integral part of the ballet, he made the pas de trois." *I Remember Balanchine,* 217.

15. Edward Villella, *Prodigal Son* (New York: Simon and Schuster, 1992), 236. Villella provides a useful description of Balanchine's preparation of the ballet on pages 236–38.

16. American composer Blair Fairchild, who had known Stravinsky for years (and who helped in the collection of funds for Stravinsky during the composer's Swiss exile), formally commissioned the work through Strecker the same month. Fairchild, who introduced Dushkin to Strecker in 1913, had adopted the young Russian-born violinist and provided his education in Paris with Fritz Kreisler and in New York with Leopold Auer. Stravinsky, Dushkin, and the Lamoureux Orchestra first recorded the concerto on 28–29 October 1935 in Paris, at the Salle Pleyel. The composer reviewed several test pressings, indicating which takes he wanted to use before the final version was issued on the Polydor label. This historic performance was rereleased in 1997 on compact disc (WHL 037), *Stravinsky Conducts Stravinsky,* by Biddulph Recordings, London.

17. Stravinsky, *An Autobiography* (Rpt. New York: Norton, 1998), 166. The reference to Dushkin as a gifted Jewish violinist was deleted from *Erinnerungen,* the German translation of Stravinsky's autobiography, first released in 1937. As late as 1983, a reprinting of the German publication omitted Stravinsky's praise of Dushkin. As Joan Evans writes, the statement was originally "pruned to avoid offending the 'Nazi Reader.'" See Evans, "Some Remarks on the Publication and Reception of Stravinsky's *Erinnerungen,*" in *Mitteilungen der Paul Sacher Stiftung,* No. 9, März 1996 (Basel: Schwabe, 1996), 21.

18. The essay appears in Edwin Corle, ed., *Igor Stravinsky* (New York: Duell, Sloan and Pearce, 1949), 179–92.

19. Ibid., 182.

20. Ibid., 186.

21. Ibid., 185.

22. Igor Stravinsky, *An Autobiography* (Rpt. New York: Norton, 1998), 168.

23. Boris Schwarz, "Stravinsky, Dushkin, and the Violin," in *Confronting Stravinsky,* ed. Jann Pasler (Berkeley: University of California Press, 1986), 302.

24. Igor Stravinsky and Robert Craft, *Dialogues* (Berkeley: University of California Press, 1982), 47. But Stravinsky arrived at the titles of the four-movement work rather late, as was often his custom. Only a month before the work premiered he wrote to Strecker that he had come to realize that he should entitle each of the Concerto's movements: "I also realized at this late date that each movement of the Concerto should have a title so that the audience has an idea of the character, especially since the tempi are only metronomic indications." See the composer's letter to Strecker of 15 September 1931 in Robert Craft, *Stravinsky Selected Correspondence,* Volume 3 (New York: Knopf, 1985), 228.

25. George Balanchine, "The Dance Element in Stravinsky's Music," reprinted in *Stravinsky and the Theatre,* ed. Minna Lederman (New York: Da Capo, 1975); Manfred Bukofzer, "The Neo-Baroque," *Modern Music* 23/3 (March–April 1945): 152–56. The article is reprinted in *Stravinsky in Modern Music,* ed. Carol J. Oja (New York: Da Capo, 1982), 79–83.

26. Nathan Milstein and Solomon Volkov, *From Russia to the West: The Musical Memoirs and Reminiscences of Nathan Milstein* (New York: Henry Holt, 1990), 256. Milstein further remarks that it was he who suggested that Balanchine choreograph the Bach Concerto.

27. As noted in the Balanchine catalogue, *Concerto Barocco* "was begun as a School of American Ballet exercise in stagecraft. When it entered the repertory of the Ballet Russe de Monte Carlo in 1945 the dancers were dressed in practice clothes, probably the first appearance of what has come to be regarded as the ballet uniform pioneered by Balanchine." *Choreography by George Balanchine: A Catalogue of Works,* ed. Leslie George Katz, Nancy LaSalle, and Harvey Simmonds (New York: Viking, 1984), 150. Also see Nancy Selleck, "*Barocco* Turns 50," *Ballet Review* 19/1 (Spring 1991): 89–97.

28. Tim Scholl, *From Petipa to Balanchine* (London: Routledge, 1994), 122. David Michael Levin offered a similar observation: "The patterns of the dancers in their larger groupings often translate abstract musical space into an aesthetically equivalent corporeal stage-space. Chords, for example, and counterpoint, inversions, and discrete melodic phrases, as well as figures of musical time, or rhythm, have their unique counterparts in both the floor-plane and the frontal spatializations of the dance groupings." See Levin's article, "Balanchine's Formalism," in *Salmagundi* 33–34 (Spring–Summer 1976): 216–36.

29. The ballet was included in the CBC program *L'Heure du concert.* The excerpt discussed here is included in Anne Belle's film *Dancing for Mr. B: Six Balanchine Ballerinas* (The Balanchine Library, Nonesuch VHS 40187-3). This telecast version included only six, rather than the usual eight, women as the supporting ensemble to the two female soloists (Diana Adams and Tanaquil Le Clercq). The reduction is understandable given the spatial restrictions of the stage. That Balanchine made the adjustment so easily, without any compromise to the overall choreographic structure, only confirms his flexibility in dealing with whatever hand he was dealt. But there are also films of the standard female octet setting, and, in fact, the symmetries displayed are the same. For a more recent discussion of the original 1941 choreography, see the George Balanchine Foundation "Interpreters Archive" 1997 video, "*Concerto Barocco*" with Marie-Jeanne (who danced in the premiere) coaching excerpts. John Taras and Suki Schorer also contribute to the choreographic reconstruction. Stephanie Jordan and Nancy Reynolds lead an interview in which Marie-Jeanne and Taras recall that originally the tempi were much faster and that Balanchine particularly liked the "jazzy" style of Bach, often breaking the metrically regular four counts of each measure into different choreographic combinations.

30. Deborah Jowitt, *Time and the Dancing Image* (Berkeley: University of California Press, 1988), 258.

Chapter 14: Unity and Balance in *Stravinsky Violin Concerto*

1. As was Balanchine, of course. As unpublished correspondence in the Harvard Theatre Collection shows, he refused to permit his company to dance in Mexico City because the altitude was above 3,000 feet and thus would be too much of a strain.

2. The filming was directed by Merrill Brockway and the videotape is available as part of The Balanchine Library (Nonesuch VHS 40178-3). I use this tape in discussing the bal-

let here. Peter Martins, Karin von Aroldingen, and Kay Mazzo reprise their roles; but in place of Jean-Pierre Bonnefous, who danced the premiere, Bart Cook performs. The *Dance in America* series, begun in 1975 and funded by the National Endowment for the Arts, was intended "to take existing choreographic works and translate them into television." See Herbert M. Simpson, "WNET TV's Dance in America," *Dance Magazine* (January 1977): 45. Karin von Aroldingen's comments here and elsewhere in the chapter were shared with me during a telephone interview of 15 March 1999.

3. The performance to which Kisselgoff refers was by the Pennsylvania Ballet. The televised performance also included such special effects as superimposition of soloists over the ensemble. See Kisselgoff's review, "How Dance Conquered the TV Screen," *New York Times,* 30 May 1976, sec. 2, p. 1. Kay Mazzo's remarks, here and later in the chapter, were shared with me during a telephone interview of 27 January 1999.

4. Brockway's liner notes are included with the videotape of *Stravinsky Violin Concerto.* Balanchine made several changes for other televised versions of his ballets, including *The Four Temperaments* and selections from *Jewels.* For a summary of Balanchine's mixed history with televised dance, see Brian G. Rose, *Television and the Performing Arts: A Handbook and Reference Guide to American Cultural Programming* (New York: Greenwood, 1986). Chapter 2, "Dance on Television," pp. 21–90, includes a useful bibliography.

5. Although some music analysts have contended that the use of such an explicit recapitulation was unusual for Stravinsky, the composer employed the technique in several works during the 1920s. Especially noteworthy is the first movement of the piano concerto, which not only includes a recapitulation, but also employs the same kind of pre-recapitulative material and even a similar *bariolage* coda as heard in the Violin Concerto's Toccata.

6. Lynne Rogers, "Stravinsky's Break with Contrapuntal Tradition: A Sketch Study," *Journal of Musicology,* 13/4 (Fall 1995): 476–507. Rogers details the music of Rehearsal 32–36, which she sees as the most contrapuntally intricate. It occurs at approximately the two-thirds point of the movement, she adds—just as with other Stravinsky passages earlier discussed in *Apollo* and *Agon.*

7. Deborah Jowitt, *Time and the Dancing Image* (Berkeley: University of California Press, 1988), 257.

8. It should be noted, however, that some differences exist between the televised version of the ballet and live performances, though essentially the choreography is the same.

9. Anna Kisselgoff, "New York City Ballet: A Modernism Rerun, in Leotards," *New York Times,* 7 January 1999. The performance of *Stravinsky Violin Concerto* was part of City Ballet's fiftieth anniversary celebration of the Stravinsky-Balanchine repertory.

10. Robert Garis, *Following Balanchine* (New Haven: Yale University Press, 1995), 210–11. The author further suggests that the ballet "seemed to express a new attitude toward difficult relationships," referring specifically to Balanchine's attachment to and loss of Suzanne Farrell during this period.

11. John Gruen, *The Private World of Ballet* (New York: Viking, 1975), 345.

12. Sketches confirm that Stravinsky had this larger line in mind for many of his works. Often he would first draft a continuous line of pitches, then in subsequent, more-developed sketches, displace them by dropping one an octave lower, thus creating what musicians term a compound line.

13. See Francis Mason's interview with von Aroldingen in *I Remember Balanchine* (New York: Doubleday, 1991), 501. One suspects that by "syncopation" von Aroldingen means a sense of interaction between the backbends, unfolding in an evenly measured meter, and the music, which proceeds in a different, but equally evenly measured meter.

14. Von Aroldingen also mentioned that Balanchine choreographed Aria I first, then Aria II, then the Capriccio, and finally the first movement, Toccata. She also recalled that he would always bring his metronome to rehearsal and check the tempi carefully.

15. Peter Martins, *Far from Denmark* (Boston: Little, Brown, 1982), 61. But Mazzo told me that Balanchine asked her with whom she wanted to be partnered, both in *Stravinsky Violin Concerto* and *Duo Concertant* (where again she danced with Martins).

16. Don McDonagh, *George Balanchine* (Boston: Twayne, 1983), 165; Goldner, *Stravinsky Festival*, 80. This is hardly the first instance in a Balanchine ballet where the male becomes the dominant image-maker while the compliant female is "totally passive." Charges of misogyny were bound to dog a man who asserted that it was woman's business to accept her role, though one must dig a bit deeper to understand the full meaning of Balanchine's statement. Ann Daly suggested that Balanchine's "glorified Woman" must be questioned "in an age of backlash against feminism, when women's efforts toward progressive social change are losing ground to blithe conservatism [and] 'glorification' smacks of regressive politics." See Daly's "The Balanchine Woman: Of Hummingbirds and Channel Swimmers," *Drama Review*, 31, no.1/T-113 (Spring 1987): 8–21. But in response to what some see as an oversimplification of a thorny issue, see Sally Banes, *Dancing Women: Female Bodies on Stage* (London: Routledge, 1998), especially her response to Daly on pages 209–10, where Banes enlists several examples in suggesting that "one can never say with confidence that [Balanchine] has a singular, univocal view of a stereotyped, one-dimensional Woman." Also see Stephanie Jordan and Helen Thomas, "Dance and Gender," *Dance Research* 12/2 (Autumn 1994): 3–14.

17. See Jonathan Cott's interview with Balanchine in *Portrait of Mr. B* (New York: Viking, 1984), 135 and 138.

18. Palmer interviewed Louise Dushkin for his biopic, *Aspects of Stravinsky,* although none of the interview was used. The filmmaker shared the story with me during an interview in Zurich during the winter of 1991.

19. Jowitt, *Time and the Dancing Image,* 258–59.

20. Stravinsky's sketches reveal that this entire middle section was a last-minute addition. Thanks to Lynne Rogers for pointing this out. Actually, the composer did not contemplate redesigning the movement until one version was completely finished, as a letter to Strecker confirms. Why the composer changed his mind and undertook such a major compositional interpolation remains a question, though the length of the final version is closer in keeping with the duration needed for one side of a phonograph record—a practical consideration known to have been on Stravinsky's mind.

Epilogue

1. Balanchine's initial choreography of the composer's 1965 *Variations,* first danced by Farrell and an ensemble in 1966, was restaged for Farrell alone and intended to be part of the

1982 festival. Twenty-five works were presented for the Stravinsky Centennial Celebration, including several ballets. Balanchine prepared two new and two costaged productions. For a complete listing of the programs, see *Choreography by George Balanchine: A Catalogue of Works,* ed. Leslie George Katz, Nancy Lassalle, and Harvey Simmonds (New York: Viking, 1984), 316–18. For a summary of the 1982 festival, see Don Daniels, "Stravinsky III," *Ballet Review* 10/3 (Fall 1982): 37–46. For Balanchine's comment to Farrell, see Bernard Taper, *Balanchine: A Biography* (Berkeley: University of California Press, 1996), 384.

2. Stravinsky boxed the exordium on the top of the sketch page. See Robert Craft's comments in Appendix 1, *Igor Stravinsky, The Rite of Spring, Sketches 1911–13* (London: Boosey and Hawkes, 1969), 12.

3. The article is reprinted in *Stravinsky and the Theatre,* ed. Minna Lederman (New York: Da Capo, 1975), 75.

Credits

Except as expressly provided below, the copyrights in all of the Balanchine choreographies either quoted in this book or depicted in photographs included in this book are owned by The George Balanchine Trust. These choreographies include: *Le Chant du Rossignol, Apollo, Jeu de Cartes, Le Baiser de la Fée, Balustrade, Circus Polka, Danses Concertantes, Renard, Firebird* (1949), *Agon, Monumentum pro Gesualdo, Elégie, Ragtime, The Flood, Movements, Variations, Rubies, Requiem Canticles, Symphony in Three Movements, Stravinsky Violin Concerto, Scherzo à la Russe, Choral Variations, Symphony of Psalms, Tango,* and *Perséphone.* I am grateful for the cooperation of the Trust in permitting me to quote from and to depict those works. I also wish to thank Kay Mazzo for permission to include *Duo Concertant;* the New York City Ballet for permission to include *Orpheus;* and the Jerome Robbins Estate for permission to include *Pulcinella.*

The examples of music theory exercises with markings in Russian, the waltz "Ashfield Nights," the manuscript "Love Is a Simple Thing," and the piano transcription of the first movement of Stravinsky's "Three Pieces for String Quartet" are all by Mr. Balanchine and are copyright ©The George Balanchine Trust. I also wish to express my gratitude to Boosey and Hawkes, Inc., and Schott Musik International, for permission to reprint music examples by Igor Stravinsky.

Although none of the uses of "Balanchine" in this book is intended to constitute a trademark use, Balanchine™ is a registered trademark of The George Balanchine Trust.

Photographic reproductions of ballets and music manuscripts are included courtesy of the Harvard Theatre Collection of the Houghton Library, Harvard University; the Igor Stravinsky Collection of the Paul Sacher Foundation in Basel, Switzerland; Martha Swope/ TimePix; the New York City Ballet for photographs of *Orpheus;* and the Jerome Robbins Dance Division, The New York Public Library for the Performing Arts.

Index

Page numbers in italics indicate illustrations.